Course	Annual Editions: Multicultural Education, 17/e
Course Number	**Edited by** **Nancy Gallavan**

http://create.mheducation.com

ISBN-10: 1308058314   ISBN-13: 9781308058313

Contents

Credits

Preface

The seventeenth edition of *Annual Editions: Multicultural Education* offers you an array of articles to assist and inspire teacher candidates, classroom teachers, school administrators, along with teacher and leadership educators, to become aware of the presence and power of cultural diversity in ourselves, among one another, across society, and in our schools. Awareness happens both by chance and by choice: some people seem to be more naturally attuned to the world around them; other people tend to become aware through both unintentional and intentional events that awaken them. Through guidance and support, educators in all capacities benefit from opportunities to increase their awareness by broadening the scope of their consciousness and deepening the extent of their understanding. Ultimately, from awareness, educators are equipped and empowered to advance the teaching, learning, and schooling in developmentally appropriate ways to advocate for social justice.

This text is divided into eight units, extending the rigorous reflections and critical conversations of awareness. Awareness of others starts with recognizing the biases in people's words, actions, and interactions. Concentrating on the people around us stimulates us to realize that biases and prejudices not only exist, they are manifested in behaviors that stereotype and marginalize people. Frequently, becoming aware of others reveals that the individuals we love and honor--our families, friends, and authority figures—are the ones who may knowingly or unknowingly perpetuate beliefs that demonstrate respect for all people. Included are articles that provide insights for improving your beliefs, thoughts, words, actions, and interactions with other people with various approaches for understanding critical pedagogy and activities to increase your funds of knowledge.

Awareness of self builds upon previously established concepts, and you are given guidelines to recognize ways that biases and prejudices influence your beliefs and teaching. Articles related to issues of race and privilege as a person and a teacher reinforce the importance for adopting a philosophy of education that embraces diversity personally, professionally, and pedagogically, i.e., visible and viable in the teaching, learning, and schooling. Guidelines are presented for understanding self, others, school, and society from the perspectives of underrepresented populations with concepts and practices furthering selfhood and solidarity.

Discussions of others and self are connected to teacher preparation. You will be given multicultural teaching competencies to strengthen teachers in all grade levels and all content subject areas. Too often, teachers may unrealistically assign cultural diversity to classrooms and schools with large numbers of students from unrepresented populations. Likewise, the topics and issues related to cultural diversity may be presumed to be academic expectations limited to social studies or literature courses. Conversely, multicultural teaching competencies must be featured into all grade levels and all content subject areas both in content and practices. All students (and teachers) are on traveling their individual journeys for becoming multicultural persons. The presence and power of consonance, counterpoint, dissonance, and resonance should be recognized and reconciled with culturally responsive pedagogy, as provided in this unit.

You will see an intensified awareness on learners—the individuals coming to school with eager expectations to be with friends, acquire new information, and prepare for their futures for learning, earning, living, and giving. All students must be ready for college, career, and citizenship in a world that currently does not exist. Just as teachers of yesterday primed their students for today, today's teachers are responsible for launching their learners into tomorrow. Today's students will become tomorrow's teachers, parents, leaders, explorers, etc. All students deserve the same topics, tools, techniques, and treatment so each one is well-informed, capable, and excited to become an active member in our interdependent global society. Articles are showcased that relate to U.S. migrants through history and today in the contexts of their challenges and the responsibilities of educators; the disproportionate number of underrepresented students labeled special education and the types of services they receive in many classrooms; the inequalities in education that students in rural settings receive; student resistance stemming related to culture and cultural competence; and the roles and responsibilities of English language learner (ELL) facilitators.

Many teacher candidates and classroom teachers consider their teaching the most important concern; however, all educators are strongly encouraged to reflect first upon their thoughts, beliefs, words, actions, and interactions associated with awareness in others, self, teacher preparation, and learners that influence their teaching. This text was organized thoughtfully to fulfill the purposes of transforming educators as they enter the classroom and begin their teaching careers. You will find articles to help clarify the multiple even ambiguous meanings of social justice and to apply concepts and practices for teaching social justice in the classroom. Articles describe a democratic framework, especially related to the impact of legislature during the terms of Presidents Johnson, Reagan, and G.W. Bush. The articles will lead discussions regarding the tensions that exist between high-stakes accountability in schools with culturally competent pedagogy in teacher education programs, and detail various projects that help teachers connect literacy and culture in their school communities.

Awareness in classrooms is examined. You may not consider the environment as an essential element in communicating with your learners; however, learners of all ages and at all stages are more likely to attend class, engage in activities, contribute to conversations, and complete assignments when the environment is welcoming, safe, and learner-centered. Articles are included that explain the disparity found in early childhood classrooms between the racial/cultural backgrounds of students and teachers; describe strategies for increasing awareness, knowledge, skills, and dispositions to recognize biases and use responsive pedagogy; and guide teachers to draw strength from literature to empower students to learn about themselves, others, society, and systems that will help them through life. Articles also present ideas for teachers and learners to understand ways to establish pluralistic perspectives and relate to the "Other;" to connect the goals of cultural competence found in university teacher preparation courses with clinical field placements; and to discuss Banks' curriculum transformation in combination with Wiggins and McTighe's backward design to enhance cultural competence in the classroom.

Teacher self-efficacy embodies the teacher's belief to be successful in meeting the learning needs and wants of all students to increase achievement. While learned from external experiences and self-perception, efficacy changes from beliefs to abilities. Teacher candidates and novice teachers in particular, gain the most from teacher education courses that incorporate multicultural education that is honest, natural, authentic, and holistic. Articles are presented that discuss the many challenges in schools for teaching purposive activities and explain the processes for negotiating tensions in teaching for equity. Readers investigate ways to differentiate uncommon teaching from commonsense practices and to relate democracy and democratic pedagogy to effective classrooms. The articles also detail White identity and its influence on teacher self-efficacy and the ability to understand TWA (talking with attitude) and its relationship to voice and choice.

Agency advances efficacy into ownership with the recognition and acceptance of the responsibilities to increase student achievement, enhance self-efficacy, and improve school programs and services. These articles guide and support educators in their multicultural education journeys to understand the presence, power, and importance of parents and families to support their children's learning. The articles provide strategies to recognize the importance of communication between homes and schools in ways that are useful for both groups and to discuss the value of knowing students' cultural backgrounds and sharing various selections of children's literature that relevant to their cultures and interests. Readers learn to explain proficiencies that teachers must demonstrate for connecting their students with various genres of children's literature.

Techniques to describe the effectiveness of differentiated multicultural instruction and to relate differentiated multicultural instruction to knowledge construction, content integration, and prejudice reduction are included too.

Each unit begins with Learning Outcomes to establish a specific context, guide the learning expectations, and pique the reader's interest. All articles conclude with Critical Thinking questions to encourage discussions stimulating reflection, application, and extension generating more questions and discussion both inside and outside the classroom. Each unit also includes a list of Internet resources to further explore article multicultural topics and issues. Plus, you are invited to go to www.mhhe.com/createcentral on the Annual Editions: Multicultural Education Website/Online Learning Center to find an additional article I have written in honor of Dr. Martin Luther King's 1963 speech applying Dr. King's Six Principles of Nonviolence and Six Steps of Nonviolence to today's classrooms. This may be easier to comprehend and accomplish by using the Gallavan Journey to Cultural Competence (JtCC) Model, designed to extend the Gallavan Cultural Competence Compass (2010).

This edition of Annual *Editions: Multicultural Education has been crafted carefully to guide and support all educators in all capacities in the personal growth, professional development, and pedagogical expertise and efficacy.* I want to heartily thank the team of editors at McGraw-Hill for their continuous guidance and gracious support to maintain the outstanding quality we have come to expect from this outstanding publication. I have used *Annual Editions: Multicultural Education* for many years with my undergraduate and graduate teacher candidates as well as my master and doctorate candidates. Each year, the volume of articles surpasses my expectations for a well-organized and meaningful collection of research and practice that I can use with my students and to teach to my students. I am pleased with the submitted articles and encourage readers to submit more articles for future volumes.

Nancy P. Gallavan, PhD
Editor

Academic Advisory Board

Members of the Academic Advisory Board are instrumental in the final selection of articles for the *Annual Editions* series. Their review of the articles for content, level, and appropriateness provides critical direction to the editor(s) and staff. We think that you will find their careful consideration reflected in this book.

Julia Ballenger
Texas Wesleyan University

Julie Bao
Shippensburg University

Lilia Bejec
Aurora University

Correlation Guide

The *Annual Editions* series provides students with convenient, inexpensive access to current, carefully selected articles from the public press. **Annual Editions: Multicultural Education, 17/e** is an easy-to-use reader that presents articles on important topics such as *diversity, religion, poverty,* and many more. For more information on *Annual Editions* and other *McGraw-Hill Contemporary Learning Series* titles, visit www.mhhe.com/cls.

This convenient guide matches the units in **Annual Editions: Multicultural Education, 17/e** with the corresponding chapters in our two best-selling McGraw-Hill Multicultural Education textbooks by Cushner et al. and Kottak/Kozaitis.

Annual Editions: Multicultural Education, 17/e	Human Diversity in Education: An Integrative Approach, 7/e by Cushner et al.	On Being Different: Diversity and Multiculturalism in the North American Mainstream, 4/e by Kottak/Kozaitis
Unit: Awareness of Others	**Chapter 1:** Education in a Changing Society **Chapter 3:** Culture and the Culture-Learning Process **Chapter 9:** Religious Pluralism in Secular Classrooms	**Chapter 1:** Introduction **Chapter 2:** Culture **Chapter 3:** Globalization and Identity **Chapter 7:** Race: Its Biological Dimensions **Chapter 8:** Race: Its Social Construction
Unit: Awareness of Self	**Chapter 4:** Classrooms and Schools as Cultural Crossroads **Chapter 6:** Creating Classrooms That Address Race and Ethnicity	
Unit: Awareness of Teacher Preparation	**Chapter 6:** Creating Classrooms That Address Race and Ethnicity **Chapter 13:** Improving Schools for All Children: The Role of Social Class and Social Status in Teaching and Learning	**Chapter 16:** Families
Unit: Awareness of Learners	**Chapter 3:** Culture and the Culture-Learning Process **Chapter 6:** Creating Classrooms That Address Race and Ethnicity **Chapter 8:** Developing Learning Communities: Language and Learning Style	**Chapter 4:** The Multicultural Society **Chapter 5:** Ethnicity **Chapter 15:** Linguistic Diversity
Unit: Awareness of Teaching	**Chapter 8:** Developing Learning Communities: Language and Learning Style	**Chapter 15:** Linguistic Diversity
Unit: Awareness of Classrooms	**Chapter 1:** Education in a Changing Society **Chapter 6:** Creating Classrooms That Address Race and Ethnicity	**Chapter 6:** Religion
Unit: Awareness of Efficacy	**Chapter 4:** Classrooms and Schools as Cultural Crossroads	**Chapter 2:** Culture
Unit: Awareness of Agency	**Chapter 13:** Improving Schools for All Children: The Role of Social Class and Social Status in Teaching and Learning	**Chapter 4:** The Multicultural Way

Topic Guide

This topic guide suggests how the selections in this book relate to the subjects covered in your course.

All the articles that relate to each topic are listed below the bold-faced term.

Unit 1

UNIT

Prepared by: Nancy P. Gallavan, *University of Central Arkansas*

Awareness of Others

Multicultural education begins with the awareness of other people. Consider the word "multicultural" as meaning "many different traditions, customs, beliefs, characteristics, and norms shared by a group of people and exhibited by an individual person." Every one of us possesses various cultural characteristics, holds membership in assorted diverse groups, and travels a life-long path seeking self-identity.

In our quest for self-identity, we define ourselves based on our knowledge and beliefs about other people whether or not our knowledge and beliefs about other people are accurate and/or acceptable. We tend to identify ourselves as possessing specific qualities that we perceive to be similar to or different from the qualities possessed by other people. As we compare and contrast ourselves, we tend to align ourselves with groups and individuals who share our cultural characteristics related to background, environment, setting, situation, interactions, and perspectives.

Clearly, no one exists in a vacuum; we live among many other people we know and people we don't know who shape our understanding of and appreciation for the stories encompassing the past, present, and future. Our individual selection and collection of knowledge and beliefs form the stories or the cultures that we tend to honor, adopt, and repeat.

The intersection of our stories with other people's stories establishes context. Context refers to the interrelated conditions in which people, places, and things exist or occur including background, environment, setting, situation, interactions, and perspectives. By chance and by choice, these conditions are passed along to us through birth and socialization. As we grow and develop, we begin to recognize our individual stories or cultures, other people's stories or cultures, and the various conditions that mold our identities, stories, and cultures.

Our knowledge and beliefs of other people and their cultures are established by our families and friends as well as various other people who influence our lives including authority figures such as teachers. Our sense of culture is transmitted to us socially both formally and informally throughout our lives. Shaped by patterns conveyed explicitly and implicitly, culture tends to be passed along from generation to generation. Consequently, individuals establish beliefs that may translate into the notion that their way is the only way or the right way generating a bias toward other people. At this basic stage of awareness, people tend to ignore, marginalize, even resist, the existence of cultural differences and avoid conversations and, thus, controversies associated with cultural differences.

As people increase their awareness of other people, they may begin to recognize other ways or cultures but still consider their ways, their cultures, to be the preferred or best ways. At this stage of awareness, cultural differences are viewed as sources of problems, and people disregard and discount the importance of other cultures. Advancing to more tolerance, but not reaching whole-hearted acceptance of people unlike them, at the next stage of cultural awareness people realize that cultural differences attribute to both problems and solutions. People are willing to become more constructive by building upon cultural diversity and cultural competence to mediate situations and to promote understanding. Finally, the optimal stage of cultural awareness empowers people from different cultures to collaborate to overcome obstacles and establish a community that uses culture to produce common ground or shared beliefs.

In this unit, the array of articles provides information and guidance to support your awareness of others. Your journey may start with some resistance or misunderstanding as you progress toward consideration, tolerance, and acceptance. You are strongly encouraged to read, reflect, self-assess, and interact with other people traveling the same path toward cultural competence with multicultural education professional development.

Article　　　Prepared by: Nancy P. Gallavan, *University of Central Arkansas*

Understanding Unconscious Bias and Unintentional Racism

Acknowledging our possible biases and working together openly is essential for developing community in our schools.

JEAN MOULE

Learning Outcomes

After reading this article, you will be able to:

- Internalize the importance of becoming aware of biases.

- Improve your beliefs, thoughts, words, actions, and interactions with other people.

In the blink of an eye, unconscious bias was visible to me, an African American. A man saw my face as I walked into the store and unconsciously checked his wallet. On the street, a woman catches my eye a half block away and moves her purse from the handle of her baby's stroller to her side as she arranges the baby's blanket. In the airport, a man signals to his wife to move her purse so it is not over the back of her chair, which is adjacent to the one I am moving toward. What is happening in these instances? Were these actions general safety precautions? If so, why did the sight only of my brown face, not the others who moved among these individuals, elicit these actions?

I believe these are examples of "blink of the eye" racism. Such unconscious biases lead to unintentional racism: racism that is usually invisible even *and especially* to those who perpetrate it. Yet, most people do not want to be considered racist or capable of racist acts because the spoken and unspoken norm is that "good people do not discriminate or in any way participate in racism" (Dovidio and Gaertner 2005, p. 2).

Such unconscious biases affect all of our relationships, whether they are fleeting relationships in airports or longer term relationships between teachers and students, teachers and parents, teachers and other educators. Understanding our own biases is a first step toward improving the interactions that we have with all people and is essential if we hope to build deep community within our schools.

Biases are rooted in stereotypes and prejudices. A stereotype is a simplistic image or distorted truth about a person or group based on a prejudgment of habits, traits, abilities, or expectations (Weinstein and Mellen 1997). Ethnic and racial stereotypes are learned as part of normal socialization and are consistent among many populations and across time. An excellent illustration of this phenomenon is a recent exchange that repeated Clark's classic 1954 doll study. In a video, completed by a 17-year-old film student and disseminated through the media, a young black child clearly reflects society's prejudice: The child describes the black doll as looking "bad" and the white doll as "nice" (Edney 2006). Children internalize our society's biases and prejudices, as have all of us; they are just a little less able to hide it. I am reminded of the story of a 4-year-old in an affluent suburb who remarked to her mother upon seeing a young Latina while in line at the grocery store, "Look, mommy, a baby maid."

And when we receive evidence that confronts our deeply held and usually unrecognized biases, the human brain usually finds ways to return to stereotypes. The human brain uses a mechanism called "re-fencing" when confronted with evidence contrary to the stereotype. Allport coined the term: "When a fact cannot fit into a mental field, the exception is acknowledged, but the field is hastily fenced in again and not allowed to remain dangerously open" (Allport 1954, p. 23). This is illustrated by such statements as "some of my best friends are black." That statement, while used to deny bias, has within it the seeds of a defense of negative feelings toward blacks. The context of the statement usually means that "my best friend" is an exception to stereotypes and, therefore, that other blacks would *not* be my friends. Thompson (2003) refers to this as *absolution* through a connected relationship (i.e., I am absolved from racism because my best friend is black). Dovidio and Gaertner describe this inability to connect stated beliefs and unconscious bias as *aversive racism*, "the inherent contradiction that exists when the denial of personal prejudice co-exists with underlying unconscious negative feelings and beliefs" (2005, p. 2).

Uncovering Biases

Because people are more likely to act out of unconscious or hidden bias, knowing that you have a bias for or against a group may cause you to compensate and more carefully consider your possible responses or actions. Acknowledging biases often opens doors for learning and allows people to consciously work for harmony in classrooms and communities (Polite and Saenger 2003). How do we find a key to unlock this door to the mind? The Implicit Association Test (IAT) has helped millions of people—those who accept the often startling results—reveal their unconscious biases to themselves (https://implicit.harvard.edu/implicit/).

Anthony Greenwald and Mahzarin Banaji developed the test in the mid-1990s because "it is well known that people don't always 'speak their minds,' and it is suspected that people don't always 'know their minds' " (Greenwald, McGhee, and Schwartz 1998). The IAT "presents a method that convincingly demonstrates the divergences of our conscious thoughts and our unconscious biases," according to the Harvard website on Project Implicit.

Strangely enough, the first evidence of this unconscious bias came from insects and flowers. Greenwald made a list of 25 insect names and 25 flower names and found that it was far easier to place the flowers in groups with pleasant words and insects in groups with unpleasant words than the reverse. It was just difficult to "hold a mental association of insects with words such as 'dream,' 'candy,' and 'heaven,' and flowers with words such as 'evil,' 'poison' and 'devil' " (Vedantam 2005, p. 3).

Greenwald then took the next step and used stereotypically white-sounding names, such as Adam and Emily, and black-sounding names, such as Jamal and Lakisha, and grouped them with pleasant and unpleasant words. According to Vedantam, Greenwald himself was surprised: "I had as much trouble pairing African-American names with pleasant words as I did insect names with pleasant words" (Vedantam 2005, p. 3). His collaborator, Banaji, was even more self-reflective, "'I was deeply embarrassed,' she recalls. 'I was humbled in a way that few experiences in my life have humbled me' " (p. 3).

This unconscious pairing has direct real-world consequences. Unconscious bias allows people who consciously said they wanted qualified minority employees to then unconsciously rate résumés with black-sounding names as less qualified. With other factors held constant, white-sounding names at the top of résumés triggered 50% more callbacks than African-American names. Human resources managers were stunned by the results. Explicit bias can occur not only without the intent to discriminate, but despite explicit desires to recruit minorities (Bertrand and Mullainathan 2004).

In *See No Bias,* Vedantam (2005) shares the disappointment and surprise that two recent test takers experienced when they found that their results on the Implicit Association Test did not mesh with their perceived views of themselves. To the dismay of these individuals, the test results were also in conflict with their life and career goals. Vedantam describes in detail a woman, an activist, taking a recent version of the test:

The woman brought up a test on her computer from a Harvard University website. It was really very simple: All it asked her to do was distinguish between a series of black and white faces. When she saw a black face, she was to hit a key on the left; when she saw a white face, she was to hit a key on the right. Next, she was asked to distinguish between a series of positive and negative words. Words such as "glorious" and "wonderful" required a left key, words such as "nasty" and "awful" required a right key. The test remained simple when two categories were combined: The activist hit the left key if she saw either a white face or a positive word, and hit the right key if she saw either a black face or a negative word.

Then the groupings were reversed. The woman's index fingers hovered over her keyboard. The test now required her to group black faces with positive words, and white faces with negative words. She leaned forward intently. She made no mistakes, but it took her longer to correctly sort the words and images.

Her result appeared on the screen, and the activist became very silent. The test found she had a bias for whites over blacks.

"It surprises me I have any preferences at all," she said. "By the work I do, by my education, my background. I'm progressive, and I think I have no bias. Being a minority myself, I don't feel I should or would have biases."

"I'm surprised," the woman said. She bit her lip. "And disappointed." (p. 2)

Such reactions should not really be a surprise according to the writings of many white anti-racist activists, including Tim Wise, who acknowledge residual racism still inside them. Wise notes how unconscious bias relegates the role of whiteness or race "to a nonfactor in the minds of whites" (2005, p. 18). When the role of whiteness or race becomes clear to a person, such as the activist described above, surprise and disappointment are likely results.

In many situations, from either the dominant or the oppressed, simple unconscious associations may drastically change outcomes. An example is Steele and Aaronson's (1995) work on *stereotype threat,* in which the performance of African-American students in a testing situation was cut in half by asking them to identify their race at the start of the test. This simple act unconsciously reminded students of the stereotypes connected with their race. Moreover, when asked at the end of the test, the students who were primed to remember their race were unable to identify the reminder as a factor in their poorer test score (Steele 1997).

In ambiguous situations, people's minds may also *reconstruct* a situation in order to conform to their stereotypes. An example is a study of people who harbor negative attitudes about African Americans: In a quickly seen image in which a white man with a weapon chases a black man, some people reverse the race of the perpetrator of the violence in order to make it conform with their preconceived notions (Diller and Moule 2005). Such unconscious biases have a role in determining the length of jail sentences (Vedantam 2005) and the fact that, regardless of explicit racial prejudices, police officers are more likely to shoot an unarmed black target than an unarmed white target (Correll et al. 2002).

Regarding violence, it is important to remember that we are programmed to quickly discern who is enemy and who is friend, for in the past—and certainly in many places in the world today—the ability to quickly identify friend or foe may be a matter of life or death (Begley 2004).

While I started this piece with evidence of people who responded to their gut reactions to my brown skin in surprising nonverbal ways, many of the same people would be quite gracious if given another second or two. Recent research shows that while most people have an instant activity in the "fight or flight" amygdala part of their brains upon encountering an *unexpected* person or situation, that first reaction is often consciously overridden in a nanosecond by many people in order to overcome built-in biases and respond as their better, undiscriminating selves. This ability to overcome embedded biases is particularly important when we consider that, "although many white Americans consider themselves unbiased, when unconscious stereotypes are measured, some 90% implicitly link blacks with negative traits (evil, failure)" (Begley 2004, p. 1).

I pick up subtle clues, either consciously or unconsciously, as to who is a good, open contact for me versus someone who may have difficulty engaging with me easily based on race.

Changing Attitudes

Do we have the ability to change our attitudes and behaviors? Gladwell explains the two levels of consciousness in a manner that gives us hope. He says that in many situations, we are able to direct our behavior using our conscious attitudes—what we choose to believe or our stated values—rather than our "racial attitude on an *unconscious* level—the immediate, automatic associations that tumble out before we've even had time to think" (2005, p. 84). He continues, "We don't deliberately choose our unconscious attitudes . . . we may not even be aware of them" (p. 85). Because our unconscious attitudes may be completely incompatible with our stated values, we must know just what those unconscious attitudes are, for they are, as Gladwell states, a powerful predictor of how we may act in some spontaneous situations.

Gladwell describes the type of circumstances where blacks and whites will both engage and disengage around climate and personal relation issues:

Table 1   Biased and Unbiased White Individuals' Time to Complete Paired Task

White Member of Pair	Time to Complete Task with a Black Person
Unbiased in word and behavior	4 minutes
Biased in word and behavior	5 minutes
Unbiased by self-report, behavior shows bias	6 minutes

If you have a strongly pro-white pattern of associations . . . there is evidence that that will affect the way you behave in the presence of a black person. . . . In all likelihood, you won't be aware that you are behaving any differently than you would around a white person. But chances are you'll lean forward a little less, turn away slightly from him or her, close your body a bit, be a bit less expressive, maintain less eye contact, stand a little farther away, smile a lot less, hesitate and stumble over your words a bit more, laugh at jokes a bit less. Does that matter? Of course it does. (pp. 85–86)

Gladwell goes on to describe the possible repercussions of these unconscious biases at a job interview. The same factors may affect behaviors in parent-teacher conferences or affect student outcomes in classrooms.

Another study describes matching whites with blacks for the completion of a task (Dovidio and Gaertner 2005). Whites were first divided into two groups: those who expressed egalitarian views and those who expressed their biases openly. These individuals were then observed to see if their actions, such as those described by Gladwell, showed unconscious biases. Each white person then engaged in a problem-solving task with a black person. The time it took to complete the joint task was recorded (see Table 1).

Two important points bear emphasis here. First, the African-American individuals, either consciously or unconsciously, were aware of the behavior that showed bias. In this study, "blacks' impressions of whites were related mainly to whites' unconscious attitudes . . . the uncomfortable and discriminatory behavior associated with aversive racism is very obvious to blacks, even while whites either don't recognize it or consider it hidden" (Dovidio and Gaertner 2005, pp. 3–4). I know that as an African American, when I enter a room of white people, I pick up subtle clues, either consciously or unconsciously, as to who is a good, open contact for me versus someone who may have difficulty engaging with me easily based on my race.

Second, white individuals who said they were unbiased, yet showed nonverbal biased behavior, reported their impressions of their behavior related to their *publicly expressed* attitudes and were likely to maintain their stated level of biases when questioned. Therefore, they are likely to blame *the victim*, the black individual, for their slowness in completing the task (and incidentally, possibly reinforce their stereotypes). Sleeter

When Race Becomes an Issue

Dovidio and Gaertner Offer Some Suggestions for Action:

- When a person of color brings up race as an issue—listen deeply!
- If the person indicates that he or she is offended, don't be defensive.
- Do not begin talking quickly.
- Do not explain why they are misinterpreting the situation.
- Do not begin crying. (These are some of the most infuriating responses people of color encounter when they challenge a situation that feels wrong.)
- If you hear about something third-hand, don't get angry. Remember that it is almost never completely safe for a person of color to challenge a dominant perception.

Source: Dovidio, Jack F., and Sam L. Gaertner. "Color Blind or Just Plain Blind." *Nonprofit Quarterly* (Winter 2005): 5.

contends, "We cling to filters that screen out what people of color try to tell us because we fear losing material and psychological advantages that we enjoy" (1994, p. 6).

We are far better off to acknowledge our possible biases and to try to work together openly with that knowledge.

It is important to note that the *well-intentioned* are still racist:

Because aversive racists may not be aware of their unconscious negative attitudes and only discriminate against blacks when they can justify their behavior on the basis of some factor other than race, they will commonly deny any intentional wrongdoing when confronted with evidence of their biases. Indeed, they do not discriminate intentionally. (Dovidio and Gaertner 2005, p. 5)

For example, if white individuals who are self-deceived about their own biases were sitting in a position to influence a promotion decision, they might not support the advancement of a "difficult" black individual and would select another factor as a reason for their action, rather than see or acknowledge their own conflicted perceptions.

This study on task completion strongly suggests that we are far better off to acknowledge our possible biases and to try to work together openly with that knowledge. If we mask our true attitudes, sometimes invisible to our own selves, we will continue to work slowly or unproductively. Consider the white individuals whose conflict over their true or hidden selves and their outward statements made a simple

task both time-consuming and psychologically difficult for both the black individuals and themselves (Dovidio and Gaertner 2005).

Unintentional racism is not always determined by whether an individual possesses prejudiced beliefs or attitudes, and it can take many different forms. These forms include the unconscious gestures mentioned before or "the dominant norms and standards."

Because many people believe these norms and standards are culturally neutral and universally right, true, and good, they do not understand how these norms and standards oppress others. They are not even aware of this possibility—and, in this sense, such racism is unintentional. (Applebaum 1997, p. 409)

Hard Work of Honesty

Unpacking our levels of consciousness and intent requires hard work. First, there needs to be unswerving, unnerving, scrupulous honesty. Individuals need to become less focused on feeling very tolerant and good about themselves and more focused on examining their own biases. One must realize and accept that the foundation and continuation of a bias may have, at its root, personal and group gain.

I recall sharing with my graduate and undergraduate students that true equity will be reached when 40% of all service people . . . meaning hotel housekeepers, groundskeepers, etc., are white men. The loss from 80% of the managerial jobs in this country to 40%, their proportion of the population, would be an actual loss in the number of jobs currently *allotted* to them based on race and gender. That is, they would not have the jobs they may perceive as expected and modeled as their right in the workplace. Can we all embrace such a future? Delpit maintains, "Liberal educators believe themselves to be operating with good intentions, but these good intentions are only conscious delusions about their unconscious true motives" (Delpit 1988, p. 285). I am not quite that cynical. I believe in change, slow as it may be.

Individuals need to become less focused on feeling very tolerant and good about themselves and more focused on examining their own biases.

Finally, Teaching Tolerance, a group dedicated to reducing prejudice, improving intergroup relations, and supporting equitable school experiences for our nation's children, says, "We would like to believe that when a person has a conscious commitment to change, the very act of discovering one's hidden biases can propel one to act to correct for it. It may not be possible to avoid the automatic stereotype or prejudice, but it is certainly possible to consciously rectify it" (2001, p. 4). Otherwise, we are all at the mercy of a blink of the eye.

References

Allport, Gordon. *The Nature of Prejudice*. Cambridge, Mass.: Addison-Wesley, 1954.

Applebaum, Barbara. "Good, Liberal Intentions Are Not Enough: Racism, Intentions, and Moral Responsibility." *Journal of Moral Education* 26 (December 1997): 409–421.

Begley, Sharon. "Racism Studies Find Rational Part of Brain Can Override Prejudice." *Wall Street Journal,* November 19, 2004, p. B1.

Bertrand, Marianne, and Sendhil Mullainathan. "Are Emily and Greg More Employable Than Lakisha and Jamal?" *American Economic Review* 94 (2004): 991–1013.

Correll, Joshua, Bernadette Park, Charles. M. Judd, and Bernd Wittenbrink. "The Police Officer's Dilemma: Using Ethnicity to Disambiguate Potentially Threatening Individuals." *Journal of Personality and Social Psychology* 83 (December 2002): 1314–1329.

Delpit, Lisa. "The Silenced Dialogue: Power and Pedagogy in Educating Other People's Children." *Harvard Educational Review* 58 (August 1988): 280–298.

Diller, Jerry V., and Jean Moule. *Cultural Competence: A Primer for Educators*. Belmont, Calif.: Wadsworth, 2004

Dovidio, Jack F., and Sam L. Gaertner. "Color Blind or Just Plain Blind." *Nonprofit Quarterly* (Winter 2005).

Edney, Hazel Trice. "New 'Doll Test' Produces Ugly Results." *Portland Medium,* August 18, 2006, pp. 1, 7.

Gladwell, Malcolm. *Blink: The Power of Thinking Without Thinking*. New York: Little, Brown, 2005.

Greenwald, Anthony, Debbie E. McGhee, and Jordan L. K. Schwartz. "Measuring Individual Differences in Implicit Cognition: The Implicit Association Test." *Journal of Personality and Social Psychology* 74 (June 1998): 1464–1480.

Harvard University. "Project Implicit." 2007. https://implicit.harvard.edu/implicit.

Polite, Lillian, and Elizabeth B. Saenger. "A Pernicious Silence: Confronting Race in the Elementary Classroom." *Phi Delta Kappan* 85 (December 2003): 274–278.

Sleeter, Christine E. "White Racism." *Multicultural Education* 1 (Summer 1994): 1, 5–8.

Steele, Claude. "A Threat in the Air: How Stereotypes Shape Intellectual Identity and Performance." *American Psychologist* 52 (June 1997): 613–629.

Steele, Claude M., and Joshua Aaronson. "Stereotype Threat and Intellectual Test Performance of African Americans." *Journal of Personality and Social Psychology* 69 (November 1995): 797–811.

Teaching Tolerance. "Hidden Bias: A Primer." 2001. www.tolerance.org/hidden_bias/tutorials/04.html.

Thompson, Audrey. "Tiffany, Friend of People of Color: White Investments in Antiracism." *International Journal of Qualitative Studies in Education* 16 (January 2003): 7–29.

Vedantam, Shankar. "See No Bias." *Washington Post,* January 23, 2005, p. 3. www.vedantam.com/bias01-2005.html.

Weinstein, Gerald, and Donna Mellen, "Anti-Semitism Curriculum Design." In *Teaching for Diversity and Social Justice,* ed. Maurine Adams, Lee Anne Bell, and Pat Griffin. New York: Routledge, 1997.

Wise, Tim. *White Like Me: Reflections on Race from a Privileged Son*. Brooklyn, N.Y.: Soft Skull, 2005.

Critical Thinking

1. What biases, stereotypes, prejudices, and racism have you observed or experienced in schools?

2. What did you discover about yourself by taking the Implicit Association Test (IAT)?

3. What changes can you make to be more aware of your own beliefs, thoughts, words, actions, and interactions that contribute to biases, stereotypes, prejudices, and racism?

4. What teaching strategies and learning experiences can you incorporate into your repertoire to help your students be less biased?

Create Central

www.mhhe.com/createcentral

Internet References

AAS Committee on the Status of Women
http://www.aas.org/cswa/unconsciousbias.html

Teaching Tolerance
http://www.tolerance.org/supplement/test-yourself-hidden-bias

---

JEAN MOULE is an associate professor at Oregon State University, Corvallis, Oregon, and president of the Oregon Chapter of the National Association for Multicultural Education. She is co-author of the book, *Cultural Competence: A Primer for Educators (Wadsworth, 2004)*, and writes the "Ask Nana" column for Skipping Stones, a multicultural magazine for children.

From *Phi Delta Kappan*, by Jean Moule, January 2009, pp. 321–326. Reprinted with permission of Phi Delta Kappa International, www.pdkintl.org, 2009. All rights reserved.

Article   Prepared by: Nancy P. Gallavan, *University of Central Arkansas*

Becoming Citizens of the World

**The future is here. It's multiethnic, multicultural, and multilingual.
But are students ready for it?**

VIVIEN STEWART

Learning Outcomes

After reading this article, you will be able to:

• Expand understanding from an international global
perspective.

• Recognize the challenges facing the world's future.

T he world into which today's high school students will
graduate is fundamentally different from the one in
which many of us grew up. We're increasingly living
in a globalized society that has a whole new set of challenges.
Four trends have brought us here.

The first trend is economic. The globalization of economies
and the rise of Asia are central facts of the early 21st century.
Since 1990, 3 billion people in China, India, and the former
Soviet Union have moved from closed economies into a global
one. The economies of China, India, and Japan, which represented 18 percent of the world's gross domestic product (GDP)
in 2004, are expected to represent 50 percent of the world's
GDP within 30 years (Wilson, 2005). One in five U.S. jobs is
now tied to international trade, a proportion that will continue
to increase (U.S. Census Bureau, 2004). Moreover, most U.S.
companies expect the majority of their growth to be in overseas
markets, which means they will increasingly require a workforce with international competence. According to the Committee for Economic Development (2006),

> To compete successfully in the global marketplace, both
> U.S.-based multinational corporations as well as small
> businesses increasingly need employees with knowledge
> of foreign languages and cultures to market products to
> customers around the globe and to work effectively with
> foreign employees and partners in other countries.

Science and technology are changing the world and represent a second trend. In *The World Is Flat,* Thomas Friedman
(2005) describes how the "wiring of the world" and the digiti-
zation of production since 1998 are making it possible for people to do increasing amounts of work anywhere and anytime.

Global production teams are becoming commonplace in business. In addition, scientific research, a key driver of innovation,
will increasingly be conducted by international teams as other
countries ramp up their scientific capacity.

The third trend involves health and security matters. Every
major issue that people face—from environmental degrada-
tion and global warming, to pandemic diseases, to energy and
water shortages, to terrorism and weapons proliferation—
has an international dimension. Solving these problems will
require international cooperation among governments, professional organizations, and corporations. Also, as the line
between domestic and international affairs blurs, U.S. citizens
will increasingly vote and act on issues—such as alternative
energy sources or security measures linked to terrorism—that
require a greater knowledge of the world. In response to this
need, a 2006 report from the National Association of State
Boards of Education recommends infusing classroom instruction with a strong global perspective and incorporating discussions of current local, national, and international issues and
events.

The fourth trend is changing demographics. Globalization
has accelerated international migration. New immigrants from
such regions as Asia and Central and South America are generating a diversity in U.S. communities that mirrors the diversity
of the world. Knowledge of other cultures will help students
understand and respect classmates from different countries and
will promote effective leadership abroad.

In short, U.S. high school graduates will

• Sell to the world.

• Buy from the world.

• Work for international companies.

• Manage employees from other cultures and countries.

• Collaborate with people all over the world in joint
ventures.

• Compete with people on the other side of the world for
jobs and markets.

• Tackle global problems, such as AIDS, avian flu,
pollution, and disaster recovery (Center for International
Understanding, 2005).

However, U.S. schools are not adequately preparing students for these challenges. Surveys conducted by the Asia Society (2002) and National Geographic-Roper (2002) indicated that, compared with students in nine other industrialized countries, U.S. students lack knowledge of world geography, history, and current events. And shockingly few U.S. students learn languages that large numbers of people speak, such as Chinese (1.3 billion speakers) and Arabic (246 million speakers).

Many countries in Europe and Asia are preparing their students for the global age by raising their levels of education attainment; emphasizing international knowledge, skills, and language acquisition; and fostering respect for other cultures. The United States must create its own education response to globalization, which should include raising standards, increasing high school and college graduation rates, and modernizing and internationalizing the curriculum.

What Global Competence Looks Like

The new skill set that students will need goes well beyond the United States' current focus on the basics and on math, science, and technology. These skills are necessary, of course, but to be successful global citizens, workers, and leaders, students will need to be knowledgeable about the world, be able to communicate in languages other than English, and be informed and active citizens.

World Knowledge

Teaching about the rest of the world in U.S. schools has often focused on the superficial: food, fun, and festivals. Today, we need deeper knowledge, such as understanding significant global trends in science and technology, how regions and cultures have developed and how they interconnect, and how international trade and the global economy work. For example, students might consider how increasing the supply of fresh water or changing forms of energy use in one country could have major effects on another country.

In a world in which knowledge is changing rapidly and technology is providing access to vast amounts of information, our challenge is not merely to give students more facts about geography, customs, or particular conflicts. Rather, our challenge is to hone students' critical-thinking skills and to familiarize students with key concepts that they can apply to new situations. In this way, they can make sense of the explosion of information from different sources around the world and put factual information into perspective and context. Only then can this information become meaningful.

Teaching students about the world is not a subject in itself, separate from other content areas, but should be an integral part of *all* subjects taught. We need to open global gateways and inspire students to explore beyond their national borders. Programs like iLEARN and Global Learning and Observations to Benefit the Environment (GLOBE) make it possible for students to work collaboratively with peers in other countries.

School-to-school partnerships enable both real and virtual exchanges.

U.S. students are global teenagers, similar in many ways to their technology-enabled peers around the world. Adding an international dimension to subjects and encouraging students to reach out to peers in other countries are powerful ways to make the curriculum relevant and engaging to today's youth.

Language Skills

Only about one-half of U.S. high school students study a foreign language. The majority never go beyond the introductory level, and 70 percent study Spanish (Draper & Hicks, 2002). This results in a serious lack of capacity in such languages as Arabic and Chinese, both of which are crucial to the prosperity and security of the United States.

The United States should do as other industrialized countries in Europe and Asia do—start offering foreign languages in the elementary grades, where research has shown that language learning is most effective (Pufahl, Rhodes, & Christian, 2001), and continue the emphasis in secondary school to create pipelines of proficient language speakers. U.S. students need opportunities to learn a broader range of languages, as in Australia, where 25 percent of students now learn an Asian language (Asia Society, 2002). Heritage communities in the United States—communities in which a non-English language is spoken at home, such as Spanish or Navajo—provide rich sources of teachers, students, and cultural experiences (National Language Conference, 2005). Specific practices, such as immersion experiences, can greatly enhance language proficiency.

As the line between domestic and international affairs blurs, U.S. citizens will increasingly vote and act on issues that require a greater knowledge of the world.

The growing interest in learning Chinese, as shown by the fact that 2,400 U.S. high schools expressed interest in offering the new advanced placement course in Mandarin, suggests that parents and teachers are realizing the importance of communication skills in a multilingual, multicultural world (see www .AskAsia.org/Chinese). Even if graduates don't use a second language at work, quite possibly they will work in cross-cultural teams and environments.

Civic Values

U.S. students need to extend traditional American values into the global arena. These include a concern for human rights and respect for cultures that differ from the United States. By learning to understand other perspectives, students can develop critical-thinking skills and enhance their creativity.

Students should focus on becoming active and engaged citizens in both their local and global environments. Schools can promote civic engagement by weaving discussions of current events throughout the school day and through participatory forms of education, such as Model UN or the Capitol Forum on America's Future, in which high school students voice their opinions on current international issues. Schools should use technology to connect students directly to peers in other parts of the world and promote service learning projects on issues that students can address at both the local and international levels, such as alleviating hunger, providing education support to students in poverty, and improving the environment.

What Schools Can Do

Across the United States, many schools already define their mission as producing students who are prepared for work, citizenship, and leadership in the global era. These schools have found that internationalizing the curriculum creates a more exciting environment for students and teachers alike (Bell-Rose & Desai, 2005). Several approaches have proven successful.

Have a large vision of what you want to achieve, but start slowly, one course or grade level at a time.

Introducing an international studies requirement for graduation. More than a decade ago, the school board of Evanston Township, Illinois, introduced an international studies requirement for graduation and asked the high school's teachers to develop the necessary courses. Now, every sophomore in this diverse Chicago suburb must complete the one-year international studies requirement. Students choose from a series of in-depth humanities courses on the history, literature, and art of Asia, Africa, Latin America, and the Middle East. Simulations and participatory projects are central to instruction, and partnerships with local universities ensure that teachers have ongoing professional development in international affairs.

Creating an elementary school immersion program. After surveying parents and local businesses about the future needs of the community—they cited skills in English, Spanish, and Japanese as important—Seattle public schools created the John Stanford International School, a public elementary bilingual immersion school. Students spend half the day studying math, science, culture, and literacy in either Japanese or Spanish; they spend the other half of the day learning reading, writing, and social studies in English. The school also offers English as a second language courses for immigrant students and after-school courses for their parents. As a result of the school's success, the city of Seattle has recently decided to open 10 more internationally oriented schools.

Developing international schools-within-schools. The Eugene International High School is a school-within-a-school on four high school campuses in Eugene, Oregon. The school is open to all interested students. The four-year sequence of courses centers thematically on culture, history, and the political, economic, and belief systems of different world regions, such as Asia, Africa, the Middle East, and Latin America. The school also emphasizes independent research courses to give students the tools to address global issues. An extended essay and a community-service requirement in 11th and 12th grade both have an international focus. For example, one student wrote a 4,000-word research essay on hydrogen cars and their place in the world economy. Students volunteer at such places as Centro Latino Americano, University of Oregon International Education and Exchange, and Holt International Children's Services. Finally, students have the option of pursuing the International Baccalaureate.

Teaching crucial language skills to prepare for the global economy. With strong support from Mayor Richard M. Daley, whose goal is to make Chicago a hub for international trade, the city has created the largest Chinese-language program in the United States. Twenty public schools teach Mandarin, from an all-black school on the West Side to a nearly all-Hispanic school on the South Side to more diverse schools throughout the city. For many of these students, Chinese is their third language after English and Spanish. The program resulted from partnerships among political, business, school, and community leaders and the Chinese Ministry of Education, which provides Chinese teachers and organizes a summer cultural program for Chicago educators in China.

Redesigning urban secondary schools with an international focus. Using the International High School of the Americas in San Antonio, Texas, and the Metropolitan Learning Center in Hartford, Connecticut, as anchor schools, the Asia Society has created a network of small, internationally themed secondary schools across the United States (see www.international studiesschools.org/). The mission of each school is to prepare low-income students for college and to promote their knowledge of world regions and international issues. Each public or charter school incorporates international content across the curriculum, offers both Asian and European languages, provides international exchange opportunities, and provides links to international organizations and community-service opportunities. To date, 10 schools have opened in New York City; Los Angeles; Charlotte, North Carolina; Denver, Colorado; and Houston, Texas. Additional schools are slated to open in other locations, such as Mathis and Austin, Texas, and Philadelphia, Pennsylvania.

Using student-faculty exchanges to promote curriculum change. Two public high schools in Newton, Massachusetts—Newton North and Newton South—run an exchange program with the Jingshan School in Beijing, China. Created by two teachers in 1979, the exchange enables U.S. and Chinese teachers and students to spend time in one another's schools every year. The program has served as a catalyst for districtwide curriculum change, bringing the study of Asian cultures into various academic disciplines, from social studies to science, and adding Chinese to the district's broad array of language options. The leaders of this exchange now help schools around the United States develop exchange programs with China as a way to internationalize their curriculums.

Using a K–12 foreign language sequence to promote excellence. The Glastonbury School District in Connecticut has long promoted language study, beginning with a K–8 language requirement. Ninety-three percent of students study at least one foreign language, and 30 percent study more than one. The foreign language curriculum is thematic and interdisciplinary, integrating both foreign language and world history standards. All high school students take a one-semester history course on a non-Western geographic/cultural region and a civics/current issues course that includes international content. The school district's reputation for languages and international studies is a major draw for families moving to the area.

These and other pioneering schools offer models that all schools can replicate. What are the lessons learned? Have a large vision of what you want to achieve, but start slowly, one course or grade level at a time. Involve parents as well as business and community leaders in planning and supporting international education and world languages. Focus on professional development for teachers, including partnerships with local colleges, so teachers can broaden and deepen their international knowledge. Include a focus on mastery of languages, including nontraditional languages, and start at the lowest grade levels possible. Use international exchanges, both real and virtual, to enable students to gain firsthand knowledge of the culture they are studying. If it is unfeasible for students to travel, try technology-based alternatives, such as classroom-to-classroom linkages, global science projects, and videoconferences (Sachar, 2004).

What Policymakers Can Do

Recognizing that future economic development and jobs in their states will be linked to success in the global economy, many states are developing innovations to promote international knowledge and skills. Nineteen states have been working together through the Asia Society's States Network on International Education in the Schools. States have developed commissions (North Carolina, Vermont); statewide summits (Delaware, Indiana, Massachusetts, Washington); and reports to assess the status of international education in their state

Wisconsin). They are revising standards (Delaware, Idaho) or high school graduation requirements (New Mexico, Virginia) to incorporate international content. Some states are offering professional development (Oklahoma); initiating new language programs (Connecticut, Delaware, Illinois, Minnesota, Wisconsin, Wyoming); engaging in school exchanges with China (Connecticut, Massachusetts); adding crucial foreign language courses to their virtual high schools (Kentucky); and adding an international dimension to science, technology, engineering, and math (STEM) schools (Ohio, Texas). Finally, some (Arizona, Massachusetts, North Carolina, Washington)

have introduced state legislation to provide additional funds to incorporate a global dimension into their schools (see http://Internationaled.org/states).

> **Many states recognize that future economic development and jobs in their states will be linked to success in the global economy.**

In 2006, the National Governors Association held a session on International Education at its annual meeting. In addition, the Council of Chief State School Officers recently adopted a new policy statement on global education (2007). These state efforts are a good start, but the United States has yet to make international knowledge and skills a policy priority on the federal level and develop the systems and supports necessary to get high-quality international content into U.S. classrooms.

States need to pursue four policy goals to make this happen. They should

- Redesign high schools and create new graduation requirements to motivate higher achievement and promote important international knowledge and key skills.
- Expand teacher training to deliver rigorous study in world history and cultures, economics, world regions, and global challenges.
- Develop world language pipelines from primary school to college that focus on crucial languages, such as Chinese, and that address the acute shortage of language teachers.
- Use technology in innovative ways to expand the availability of international courses and ensure that every school in the United States has an ongoing virtual link to schools in other countries.

For almost 50 years, the U.S. government has played a crucial role in fostering foreign languages and international education in *higher* education. We need to extend this commitment to K–12 education and make it an urgent priority. By doing so, we ____ ___ts' international knowledge and skills and ___ __ ___e edge and security of the United

_conomics of Knowledge: Why Edu-
_e's Success*, Andreas Schleicher from
the Organisation for Economic Cooperation and Development wrote,

> The world is indifferent to tradition and past reputations, unforgiving of frailty and ignorant of custom or practice. Success will go to those individuals and countries which are swift to adapt, slow to complain, and open to change.

Part of the great strength of the United States is its adaptability. U.S. schools adapted to the agrarian age, then to the industrial age. It's time to open to change once more and adapt to the global age.

References

Asia Society. (2002). *States institute on international education in the schools: Institute report, November 20–22, 2002.* New York: Author.

Bell-Rose, S., & Desai, V. N. (2005). *Educating leaders for a global society.* New York: Goldman Sachs Foundation.

Center for International Understanding. (2005). *North Carolina in the world: A plan to increase student knowledge and skills about the world.* Raleigh, NC: Author.

Committee for Economic Development. (2006). *Education for global leadership: The importance of international studies and foreign language education for U.S. economic and national security.* Washington, DC: Author. Available: www.ced.org/docs/report/report_foreignlanguages.pdf

Council of Chief State School Officers. (2007). *Global education policy statement.* Washington, DC: Author. Available: www.ccsso.org/projects/International_Education/Global_Education_Policy_Statement/

Draper, J. B., & Hicks, J. H. (2002). *Foreign language enrollments in secondary schools, fall 2000.* Washington, DC: American Council on the Teaching of Foreign Languages. Available: http://actfl.org/files/public/Enroll2000.pdf

Friedman, T. L. (2005). *The world is flat: A brief history of the twenty-first century.* New York: Farrar, Straus, and Giroux.

National Association of State Boards of Education. (2006). *Citizens for the 21st century: Revitalizing the civic mission of schools.* Alexandria, VA: Author. Available: www.nasbe.org/publications/Civic_Ed/civic_ed.html

National Geographic-Roper. (2002). *2002 global geographic literacy survey.* Washington, DC: Author.

National Language Conference. (2005). *A call to action for national foreign language capabilities.* Washington, DC: Author. Available: www.nlconference.org/docs/White_Paper.pdf

Pufahl, I., Rhodes, N. C., & Christian, N. (2001). *What we can learn from foreign language teaching in other countries.* Washington, DC: Center for Applied Linguistics.

Sachar, E. (2004). *Schools for the global age: Promising practices in international education.* New York: Asia Society.

Schleicher, A. (2006). *The economics of knowledge: Why education is key for Europe's success.* Brussels: Lisbon Council. Available: www.oecd.org/dataoecd/43/11/36278531.pdf

U.S. Census Bureau. (2004). Table 2. In *Exports from manufacturing establishments: 2001* (p. 8). Washington, DC: U.S. Department of Commerce.

Wilson, W. T. (2005). *The dawn of the India century: Why India is poised to challenge China and the United States for global economic hegemony in the 21st century.* Chicago: Keystone India. Available: www.keystone-india.com/pdfs/The%20India%20Century.pdf

Critical Thinking

1. How do the world's economies impact societies and education?

2. How is health related to education?

3. Why should U.S. students become more educated about the world?

4. What are some of the challenges of living in a globalized society?

Create Central

www.mhhe.com/createcentral

Internet References

U.S. Census Bureau
http://www.census.gov/

United States Citizenship and Immigration Services
www.uscis.gov/portal/site/uscis

VIVIEN STEWART is Vice President, Education, at the Asia Society, 725 Park Ave., New York, New York, 10021; vstewart@asiasoc.org.

Article   Prepared by: Nancy P. Gallavan, *University of Central Arkansas*

Welcome to America: Now Speak English

BRIDGET A. BUNTEN

Learning Outcomes

After reading this article, you will be able to:

- Articulate your beliefs and strategies for teaching English Language Learners (ELL).

- State one goal for meeting the needs of ELL to increase student achievement.

Introduction

As the students in my undergraduate methods class, which focuses on the teaching of writing, prepared for their presentations at the end of a recent fall semester, I sat in the small audience and caught a glimpse of the words on the front of one student's t-shirt. Shaking my head in disbelief, I concluded that it was part of his costume and had to reveal something about the character that he was portraying. Once the performance began, I saw the t-shirt clearly, which confirmed my initial belief; it said: *Welcome to America, now speak English.* During the performance, I realized that this t-shirt was not part of his costume.

As a former bilingual and ESL teacher for both adult immigrants and children of immigrants, I cringe whenever I see this exact t-shirt hanging on carts in the mall or on tables at a county fair. I also feel disheartened by the idea that some members of our society consider bilingualism and multilingualism to be a threat and believe that our national security and unity could be strengthened by demanding that speakers of other languages only speak English.

Now, a student whom I had spent a semester teaching in my language arts and writing methods course was sending a message loud and clear, which I felt contradicted not only the cultural and linguistic sensitivity that I tried to teach my preservice teachers, but also some of his own comments in his written assignments regarding working with English language learners (ELLs) in the writing classroom.

After the performance, which was a final project for another course in their teacher education program, I left the building wondering what to do. Should I address him about the conflict I see between the message on his shirt and the teaching philosophy that he is in the process of developing? What would I say? Should I say anything at all? What did I hope to accomplish by bringing it up with him? I struggled with these questions and

my own confusion about the incident for a few days. Finally, I decided to bring my reaction to his attention in hopes that he would reflect on the message his shirt sends and what it reveals to others about his beliefs and values. In an email to him, I wrote the following:

> There is something I wanted to mention to you because I've been thinking about it for a few days now. I was a bit shocked and confused when I read the writing on the black shirt that you wore the day of your performance (Welcome to America, now speak English). You mentioned being sensitive to English language learners in your teaching philosophy, your reading responses, and class discussions, so I was wondering if you see a contradiction between the message that is sent by the words on your shirt and what you have said about ELLs. (Personal communication, 12/13/07)

He responded to my email on the same day with the following message:

> Thank you for your response and I didn't even think before putting on that T-shirt . . . I do realize how it might offend people and I am sorry if it offended you and it is not how I feel about English language learners. I do see the contradiction in it and I would not treat any of my students differently because they are not native English language speakers . . . I am sorry. (Personal communication, 12/13/07)

I suppose that I expected to feel better about this after writing to him and receiving his response, but I felt bewildered by the exchange and struggled with my own desire to somehow "fix" the situation. To me, it appeared as though he viewed my email as a scolding and failed to explain why he owns such a shirt or when he would consider it a good choice to wear it. He also did not say that he would get rid of the shirt, but rather framed the situation as an offense to me, thus placing my reaction at the center of the issue.

While reflecting on the semester as a whole, I considered the various readings and classroom discussions that had focused on the literacy development of ELLs and the inequalities that can exist in schools about their language use. I found my undergraduate students to be very honest in expressing their concerns and anxieties surrounding the teaching of writing to a child who is learning English. Many of them had completed a writing analysis assignment using writing samples from ELLs and provided fair, caring, and sensitive assessments of the child's abilities, followed by insightful and well-informed instructional recommendations. So, how was it that being involved in a constant dialogue about providing linguistically and culturally appropriate writing instruction to ELLs had not made this student think twice when he chose to wear that shirt?

I continued to struggle with this issue as a new semester began in January, and I wondered if and how I should change class readings, discussions, and assignments. Then, one morning during class, I was passing out writing samples from a 5th and 6th grade classroom in which we would be working on a reading and writing project throughout the semester. There were six native Russian speakers in the classroom we were going to visit. Thinking it might help me to deepen my understanding of the preservice teachers' learning processes, I decided to investigate the experience of the six preservice teachers who volunteered to work with these ELLs. For this project, the preservice teachers would meet with their students to conduct one-on-one interviews about their reading and writing, hold conferences with them, and share their own writing as well.

Being a former elementary school teacher in both bilingual and sheltered English programs, I am personally and professionally invested in the education of ELLs. As a teacher educator at a large public university in the northeast, I am challenged to engage my students in readings, discussions, and experiences that energize their thinking and understanding about teaching reading and writing to the culturally and linguistically diverse children who will sit in their future classrooms. I believe that the opportunity that these six preservice teachers had to work on their project with ELLs was a chance to expose them directly to the rewards and challenges that lie ahead of them.

Thus, in this article I investigate the following questions: (1) How did preservice teachers describe their experience of working directly with an ELL? (2) To what extent did a direct experience with an ELL affect preservice teachers' thinking? (3) What can the preservice teachers' discussion contribute to our understanding of how students are influenced by discourses and what that influence means? Answering these questions will offer us insight into the evolving perspectives of preservice teachers and how they negotiate the challenges of addressing the needs of ELLs.

ELLs Speak through Their Numbers

The students that sit in public school classrooms represent the astonishing increase in our nation's cultural and linguistic diversity. The PK-12 ELL population grew by 57.17% from the 1995-1996 school year to the 2005-2006 school year as compared to a 3.66% growth in the overall PK-12 population. During the 2005-2006 school year in particular, ELLs represented 10.3% of the total PK-12 enrollment (National Clearinghouse for English Language Acquisition [NCELA], 2007a). In that same decade, the states that saw the highest percentage growth rates of ELLs in the nation were South Carolina (688.2%), Arkansas (361.3%), Indiana (349.7%), North Carolina (346.2%), and Tennessee (296.0%) (NCELA, 2007b).

However, in spite of these growing numbers, there are only four states that have specific ELL coursework or certification requirements for all teachers. The teacher certification standards for all teachers in 17 states contain reference to the special needs of ELLs and another eight states refer to "language" as an example of diversity. There are 15 states that do not require all teachers to have expertise or training in working with ELLs (NCELA, 2008). Both the student demographics and the limited state requirements for preservice teachers of ELLs clearly demonstrate that more attention needs to be placed on the successful preparation of teachers in order to provide them with the knowledge, skills, and experience required to meet the needs of our nation's children.

Teacher Education and ELLs

In response to these changing demographics and the struggles of schools and teachers to respond to them, researchers have sought out the voices of preservice teachers, current teachers, and teacher educators as a preliminary step to proposing a course of action. My review of the literature reveals four main areas that researchers address for working with preservice teachers in relation to ELL issues.

The first area focused on the necessity to consider and learn from the experiences and concerns of current ELL educators. Valuable insight can be gained from these educators as they share the challenges they faced, the solutions they devised, and the negotiations they made regarding ELLs, individual beliefs, school context and language policy. As a result, modifications in course offerings that reflect teachers' experiences and concerns are a necessary and proactive stance on the part of teacher education programs (Batt, 2008; Isenbarger & Willis, 2006; Varghese & Stritikus, 2005).

The second area further supplements the first through the work of Costa, et al. (2005) who argue that change in teacher education programs begins with the involvement of faculty. During a faculty institute on ELLs (held in Massachusetts), faculty members identified the following aspects that preservice teachers need to develop in order to be effective teachers of ELLs: "(a) deeper respect for the culture of ELLs and their families, (b) the ability to question their own assumptions, and (c) the ability to discuss issues of identity, privilege, and ethnocentricity" (Costa, et al., 2005, p. 109).

A third area in the literature addresses the importance of opportunities for preservice teachers to investigate their personal views and experiences with diversity by sharing their feelings about minorities, ELLs, and exposure to different races and cultures (Lee & Dallman, 2008). The beliefs and practical knowledge of the preservice teachers highlight the importance of teacher education programs to consider "various diversity issues from multiple perspectives...constructing knowledge and practical teaching of diversity...considering personal experience with diversity in teacher preparation...[and having] field experiences with culturally diverse children" (Lee & Dallman, pp. 42-43). The above contributions demonstrate the necessity of including the ideas and perspectives of teachers, preservice teachers, and teacher educators while considering how to respond to the increasing diversity in the public schools.

A fourth area in the literature identifies the need for significant changes in teacher education programs due to an apparent mismatch between the cultural and linguistic background of the majority of teachers and their students. In the United States, the teaching force is relatively homogenous with a predominance of *European/American* teachers and preservice teachers (Commins & Miramontes, 2006; Costa et al., 2005; Giambo & Szecsi, 2005/06; Grant & Gillette, 2006; Zygmunt- Fillwalk & Clark, 2007) while the diversity of the student population is growing at an alarming rate.

Commins and Miramontes (2006) assert that preservice teachers need to be prepared to work with students that traverse this wide range of cultural and linguistic diversity. In order to do so successfully, teacher education programs need to incorporate coursework and field experiences that integrate the application of knowledge and skills that are effective when working with ELLs (Commins & Miramontes, 2006; Giambo & Szecsi, 2005/06; Lucas, et al., 2008; Varghese & Stritikus, 2005).

Finally, constant reflection and reexamination of one's own cultural beliefs and assumptions about people of different races, cultures, and languages is an integral part of the courses and field experiences that are being developed. For example, language shock classes (Washburn, 2008) and immersion experiences (Zygmunt-Fillwalk & Clark, 2007; Zygmunt-Fillwalk & Leitze, 2006) allow preservice teachers to develop empathy for ELLs, learn strategies for teaching ELLs, and construct a new reality for teaching in a multicultural classroom. Within these contexts, the preservice teachers modify their educational philosophies in light of their new experiences, but this change does not occur neatly overnight or even in the confines of one semester. Zygmunt-Fillwalk and Clark (2007) assert that "becoming multicultural thus emerges as a recursive process rather than a destination. A cyclical process emerges as individuals encounter, reflect, de-construct, and re-create worldviews. With novel experiences, individuals begin the process anew" (p. 292).

With these concerns in mind, I constructed opportunities for preservice teachers to work with ELLs while giving them a chance to reflect and interpret their experiences. I investigated their discussions about those experiences and identify how it contributes to our understanding of their development as preservice teachers. Foucault (1978) and Bakhtin (1981) inform my understandings of discourse, which helps me to interpret my students' expressions in relation to ELLs.

Two Ways of Thinking about Discourse

The work of Foucault (1978) and Bakhtin (1981) provide me with a theoretical lens through which I can view the discursive

practices of preservice teachers as they combine with social relationships and lived experiences to formulate pedagogy. According to Foucault (1978), discourses are social constructions that display a "*tactical polyvalence*" with different power capabilities and functions depending on the context in which they are taken up (p. 100). Certain discourses, therefore, may be more powerful for some people than for others by both shaping and consequentially being shaped by individuals in their contexts.

For example, my student's t-shirt would be well received in some places; thus in some communities it would make him more popular with the powerful while also making the discourse it promotes more powerful. In this way, individuals can use discourses strategically and intentionally, and people can use multiple discourses to defend, support, and/or protect arguments or beliefs. For Foucault (1978), this use of varying discourses is a complex and often unstable process that involves a deliberate employment of diverse discursive elements. During this employment, it is enlightening to see how a discourse can function as enabling, limiting, or opening up possibilities to explore further. An individual thus uses discourse in various ways to position oneself in relation to a particular occurrence, experience, or issue.

Within a particular teaching and learning context, discourses are thus capable of positioning the teacher and the students in relation to one another through the arrangement, categorization, and mapping of their behaviors as *appropriate* or *inappropriate* within different situations (Luke, 1992). Therefore, the actions and minds of the teacher and the students are being shaped by the varying discourses that are evident both in and out of the classroom. As Luke (1992) asserts, I also believe that it is crucial for us to consider how the use of discourses have tangible and political consequences for students and teachers.

What I found to be significant in understanding my research is Foucault's assertion that, "there can exist different and even contradictory discourses within the same strategy" (1978, p. 102). This acknowledgement has opened the door for me to examine the possible contradictions among a preservice teacher's use of varying discourses and those that were presented in our course readings and discussions. In this light, discourse can be seen as "a hindrance, a stumbling-block, a point of resistance and a starting point" (p. 101) employed by a preservice teacher who is currently in between the multiple ways of being a college student, a future teacher, and a member of a particular family and community.

Interwoven throughout their contributions are references to their own lives and experiences in school, which clearly play a large role in determining which discourses they engage in and how. It is through this lens that I will investigate the discourses that are evident in their discussion, and how they position themselves and others, define limits, and articulate possibilities.

Bakhtin adds to Foucault's notion of discourse through his focus on the struggle and relationship between authoritative discourse and internally persuasive discourse. According to Bakhtin (1981), the act of becoming (in this case becoming a teacher) is a process of "assimilating the words of others" with our own and thus the discourses other's use in an attempt to make sense of our own experiences (p. 341). Involved in this process is *heteroglossia,* which is the occurrence of two or more contradicting voices (or discourses) at any given time in an individual's particular context. Our world is inherently *heteroglossic* due to the often-conflicting coexistence of different discourses (Bakhtin, 1981).

This *heteroglossic* process of meshing and partial reformation of others' discourses plays a significant role "in an individual's ideological becoming" (Bakhtin, 1981, p. 342). Therefore, we take up the discourses of others and use them as a basis for our own interactions with people in particular contexts, thus influencing our behaviors, actions, and words. While taking up a discourse, we use it strategically to perform various functions, which may result in the positioning of people in particular categories, similar to how Foucault (1978) argued that discourses are employed.

Bakhtin (1981) discusses the antagonistic relationship that is evident between authoritative discourse and internally persuasive discourse, which exist simultaneously and can to a certain extent determine one's ideological becoming. An authoritative discourse represents the "received and static knowledge" of others that functions as a particular way of thinking in a variety of social contexts, and is often based on a line of thinking that comes from a theoretical deduction as opposed to actual experience (Britzman, 2003, p. 42).

Therefore, an authoritative discourse could represent particular assumptions that one possesses about ELLs, their parents, or what is involved in learning English prior to having direct contact with ELLs or their real-life experiences. In addition, the alternative discourses that I present through class readings and discussions about ELLs can also be seen as authoritative discourses for the preservice teachers because they are the words, ideas, and beliefs of others, which they have not taken on as their own yet.

> **The extent to which an authoritative discourse aids in determining our perceptions of the world is related to the rigor with which we examine these categories and refuse to view them as displaying the natural order or truth about something or someone.**

Similar to Foucault's view of discourse as capable of arranging and mapping our words and behaviors, an authoritative discourse also creates "normative categories that organize and disorganize our perceptions," which can result in a competition between these normativities (Britzman, 2003, p. 42). The extent to which an authoritative discourse aids in determining our perceptions of the world is related to the rigor with which we examine these categories and refuse to view them as displaying the natural order or truth about something or someone.

In contention with authoritative discourse is internally persuasive discourse, which acknowledges the existence of contradictory social practices that are often "in opposition to socially sanctioned views and normative meanings" (Britzman, 2003, p. 42). An internally persuasive discourse is an "everyday discourse" that reflects what one thinks for her- or himself and has the potential to change and evolve while interacting with others (Ball, 2006, pp. 66–67). One's own words, thoughts, ideas, and beliefs are present in an internally persuasive discourse and may not have its authority acknowledged by others. For Bakhtin (1981), an individual often experiences an inner struggle between the authoritative and internally persuasive discourses that takes place at a "zone of contact" where these discourses both partially belong to the individual while partially belonging to the other (p. 345).

Therefore, the "internally persuasive discourse is a discourse of becoming" as we struggle to take what we already know and decide to expand it, abandon it, or keep it (Britzman, 2003, p. 42). The "zone of contact" resembles Foucault's (1978) assertion that one individual can simultaneously be employing the strategic use of different and often contradictory discourses in a process of "trying things on" to see how they fit (or don't fit) with one's actions, behaviors, and beliefs.

In many ways, the internally persuasive discourses of the preservice teachers mirrored the authoritative discourses of the dominant culture that they brought to the university, which are at odds with the academic and research discourses of ELLs that were presented in class. In the process of becoming a teacher, and in this case, a teacher who works with ELLs, both authoritative and internally persuasive discourses are evident and are often conflicting. Both Foucault and Bakhtin provide a framework within which to consider the point of conflict, or "contact zone," where authoritative and internally persuasive discourses collide, as capable of providing valuable pieces of information or insight into one's experience and use of particular discourses.

Methods of Data Collection and Analysis

The preservice teachers (five European-Americans and one Asian-American) were juniors in their early twenties majoring in elementary education, and were enrolled in my writing and language arts methods course at a large, public university located in what is otherwise a rural area. They were partnered with ELLs who were native Russian speakers with varying degrees of time spent in the U.S. school system. The Russian speakers attend a local charter school (grades 5-8) that is organized around project-based learning and the incorporation of technology throughout the curriculum, where the student–teacher relationship is more collaborative than authoritarian. The preservice teachers worked with the ELLs on two separate occasions for a total of three hours.

In order for the preservice teachers to share their experiences working with ELLs, I conducted a 60-minute semistructured focus group interview (Glesne, 2006; Morgan, 1997) with five out of the six preservice teachers. One was unable to participate due to scheduling conflicts. The interview was audio-recorded in order to accurately capture the responses of the interviewees and the interview was fully transcribed. The interview guide is included in Appendix A. All the data were scrutinized through content analysis to look for patterns and themes. First I used open coding to identify salient themes among the participants' comments. Upon further analysis, I began to see strands that for me represented different discourses used by at least three out of the five participants.

Drawing from both Foucault's and Bakhtin's notions of discourse, I identified authoritative and internally persuasive discourses that the preservice teachers used to talk about their experience with ELLs. In particular, I identified potential "contact zones" marked by the recognition of a change in thinking or introduction of new ideas. It is at these sites where their internally persuasive discourses were developing and either contradicted or aligned with previously held authoritative discourses.

Findings: Discourses in Three Contact Zones

In reviewing the transcript from the focus group interview with the preservice teachers, there were a variety of discourses and potential zones of contact that emerged. However, for the sake of this project, I decided to focus on three contact zones in particular because each was taken up by at least two (if not more) of the five participants in the interview and there was also evidence of the development of internally persuasive discourses that conflicted with alternative authoritative discourses.

The first, and most predominant, authoritative discourse that was evident in the transcript was the belief that *the proper classroom setting is similar to one's own experiences in school as a student.* Nearly all five of the preservice teachers made comments that compared their own school experiences to that of the school where the ELLs attended, such as:

> When I was in school it was very regimented, our subjects were divided. I thought it was really interesting, seeing all of the projects they did. I liked how everything . . . it seems like they had a lot of freedom to really look at things they were interested in. (Student 1's thoughts about the students' integrated projects)

> I thought it was really weird that they had two different grades in one classroom (Student 2, expressing her opinion about the multi-age 5th/6th grade classroom that the ELLs were in)

> Most of the kids at her elementary school are just coming in for the first time . . . So when I walked into this classroom that's what I was expecting. (Student 3, comparing her mother's ESL students to the native Russian speaking ELLs who had been in the country for years)

> I thought it was really laid back just the way that the kids talked to their teacher and the teacher talked back to them. I thought it was really interesting

> because usually in school it's not so much like talking to an equal I felt. But I think the kids definitely love their teachers a lot and love the school a lot. There's a lot of school pride, so I think that that's something that is good. (Student 4)

Sharing one's own prior experiences in schools and as a student is a way to connect to the current situation. Perhaps for these preservice teachers, this authoritative discourse presents a context that is familiar, comfortable, and unthreatening to them because it is what they knew to be true when they were in school and had previously taken up this discourse unquestioningly.

Three of the above contact zones show where the preservice teachers are beginning to consider internally persuasive discourses that were in direct conflict with the "proper classroom" under the authoritative discourse. As a result of their experience in the school and interacting with the students, the formation of an alternative internally persuasive discourse was evident in Student 1's positive thoughts about students' projects and individual freedom, Student 3's realization that some ELLs are not new arrivals to the country, and Eve's conclusion that the more informal relationship between the teachers and students was beneficial.

The second authoritative discourse that was evident in the discussion had to do with the time that the ELLs had been living in the U.S. and reinforced the idea that *learning English was contingent upon how much time one spends in an English speaking environment.* The child's environments were identified as being in school (English), at home (mostly Russian), or in an English speaking country (the U.S.). Most of the preservice teachers' comments revealed this discourse and expressed their surprise at the apparent slow rate of English acquisition of the native speaking Russian students, thus blaming their academic struggled on their native language. Some of their comments included:

> Then I learned that he grew up here his whole life, so for a 5th/6th grader I felt that he should have been a little more advanced than that because he has been in English schools since he was young. But then after meeting him, I learned that his parents only speak Russian at home and they don't read any English at all. (Student 5)

> So at first I was a little confused because he was also born here . . . but then I realized his parents speak primarily Russian so I guess it made more sense to me once I met him. (Student 1)

> My kid was born in Russia and then he moved here when he was one, so that really surprised me that he had been here for that long. (Student 4)

> I thought he wasn't going to be able to speak very well English and he spoke it perfectly and he told me that he basically lived in America his whole life. So, I was really confused as to why his writing was so bad. (Student 2)

As evidenced by the above comments, the preservice teachers placed a higher value on the *quantity* of time that the ELLs spend in English speaking environments as opposed to the *quality* of instruction or interactions in English. However, one of the preservice teachers in particular began to explore other factors that would influence how one learns a language, other than the amount of time spent in situations where that language is predominantly used. Student 4 reflected on her own assumptions and mentioned the possible influence of prior school experiences and a student's intrinsic motivation as key factors affecting language acquisition, as shown below:

> But I think that the fact that they've been here for so long really surprised me. It made me wonder about what their experience was like at school before [here] because I don't know if English as a Second Language or their being Russian was embraced or instead maybe they felt ashamed of it. So I'm not really sure about their background, but I think they've been in school for so long so it made me wonder why are they behind, or what I think is behind, in their writing? . . . At an early age I feel like if they've been in U.S. public schools for so long that their writing would have progressed further, but I guess their motivation is a lot.

In response to these statements, both Students 3 and 5 then agreed that they were interested in knowing about the other elementary schools that the ELLs had attended and that knowing about their prior experiences in schools could provide them with valuable insight into the language proficiency of the students they worked with. For these three preservice teachers, Student 4's comment created a contact zone for the other participants to engage in, which allowed the internally persuasive discourse of time in an English-speaking environment not being a predetermining factor of the successful acquisition of the English language began to formulate.

By working so intimately with one ELL, the pre-service teachers have begun to reformulate the authoritative discourse regarding oral proficiency and writing ability.

The third and final authoritative discourse that was evident in the focus group discussion was the conviction that *an ELL is someone whose oral proficiency in English is lacking and whose writing ability should match her/his oral proficiency.* Overall, the preservice teachers expressed surprise upon meeting their students, having read their writing pieces prior, because they felt as though their students' oral proficiency was too advanced to produce written work with "so many errors." The following comments display the preservice teachers' use of this discourse:

> I mean his writing was just so bad. When I first got him I thought he wasn't going to be able to speak

> very well English and he spoke it perfectly . . . so, I was really confused as to why his writing was so bad. (Student 2)

> She just had so many ideas and none of them were making sense because none of them were connected. But when I met with her in person, I didn't even know that she was an ESL student, she spoke perfectly and I was just shocked that her writing was just not complete. (Student 3)

> I was also shocked that he spoke perfect English, like perfectly. I was thinking about if his English speaking would be as poor as his writing and it wasn't, he doesn't even have the accent, I would have never know that he was Russian. (Student 2)

These are just a few samples of the comments that the preservice teachers made with regards to their reactions at the discrepancy that existed between the oral proficiency and writing ability of the ELLs that they worked with. Within this contact zone an opening is created where the preservice teachers acknowledge an experience that challenged a discourse and forced them to search around for another explanation.

Perhaps a new explanation will emerge that comes from our class readings, from our class discussions, or from another origin completely and will result in an internally persuasive discourse. As the conversation continued, they started to uncover the differences between social language and academic language as well as the differences between oral skills and literacy skills. The quotes below show evidence of this internally persuasive discourse that marked a change in their thinking:

> But she had this amazing story that she didn't even write down . . . she didn't want to write, it's like a chore, a task for her. Even though she's interested in her story, she's really not interested in writing it down. (Student 3's student orally told her an elaborate story that she struggled to write down on paper)

> Making sure that the questions I'm asking that he understands what I'm talking about, that might be the most challenging. (Student 1, in response to the fourth interview question)

> Well I did reword a lot and I asked him as much as I . . . "Do you understand what I'm saying? Do you know what I mean?" (Student 2, when asked what she could do if she felt as though her student didn't understand her)

> But I think the language thing was also difficult because he knew what he wanted to say. It was sort of like he knew what he wanted to say but he didn't really know how to make the right transitions and to show what he was thinking in his mind to like, be on the paper. (Student 4)

By working so intimately with one ELL, the pre-service teachers have begun to reformulate the authoritative discourse regarding oral proficiency and writing ability. At this point, they begin to search for a new way of understanding their experience in order to help explain what they see happening with the ELLs, which may be influenced by our class, our relationship, or any multitude of other facts.

Clearly they started to realize that the ELLs' oral proficiency differed when talking about themselves and their interests versus talking about their writing in an academic way. In addition, the preservice teachers recognized that there are differences that can exist between one's oral skills in English and one's literacy skills in English.

Discussion, Reflections, and Concluding Thoughts

Within the contact zones described above, there were four different categories of conflict that emerged. First and foremost, there was the conflict that existed between the authoritative and the internally persuasive discourses that were used, as evidenced by my discussion above.

A second type of intrapersonal conflict that existed was the potential for tension to materialize between discourses that were used by the same person. At this critical stage of becoming a teacher, these preservice teachers show evidence of working in a zone of contact and attempting to identify and appropriate their own internally persuasive discourses.

The third type of conflict was interpersonal in nature because it existed between the views of two or more of the participants. There were moments when one of the participants was visibly bothered by the comments of another, but chose not to challenge each other in this potential site for friction. Perhaps this was due to the context of the focus group interview and would be better addressed in a classroom situation or activity.

However, Student 4 in particular shared thoughts that revealed both sensitivity and compassion toward her student's situation in response to other, less empathetic comments (usually by Student 2). As a teacher educator, I need to realize that each opportunity is only one piece of their infinite development as teachers and be thankful that an initial experience with ELLs has sparked them to think and respond to ELLs in a slightly different way.

Lastly, and of great interest to me as a teacher educator, was the fourth category of conflict that existed between some of the discourses that the preservice teachers used during the interview and those that were prevalent in the readings and discussions we had in class. Forcing them to take up my perspective about ELL education would equate to moving them from one authoritative discourse to another.

While I realize the discourses about ELLs that were presented by me through course readings and discussions can be viewed as authoritative by the preservice teachers, I ironically felt disappointed that they had not embraced them completely and unquestioningly. Therefore, I am forced to consider, why do I feel this way and what is the consequence? I must take

caution against labeling certain discourses as "bad" (ones I deem to be insensitive toward ELL issues) and others as "good" (discourses I consider to display empathy and sensitivity towards ELLs).

I realized that, as with the student's shirt, simply introducing new authoritative discourses does not ensure that objectionable internally persuasive discourses will be integrated or transformed in any way, which is supported by Foucault's (1978) assertion that one person holds conflicting discourses simultaneously. There are no guarantees as to what, how, or why my students take up particular discourses (specifically with regards to teaching ELLs) and not others or how what is presented in class or in the readings contends with their own internally persuasive or authoritative discourses. Additionally, I cannot be certain that they will take these into consideration during their future teaching and learning experiences.

I conducted this inquiry with the preservice teachers who worked with the ELLs because I desire to reach a better understanding of how my undergraduate students were engaging with the possibility of teaching culturally and linguistically diverse students in their future classrooms. To a certain extent I would like to think that our class readings and discussions along with this experience has provided those six preservice teachers with a deeper understanding of and sensitivity toward the lives and learning processes of ELLs.

However, this experience comes with no guarantees as to how my interactions with them impact the current perspective and future teaching practices of the six preservice teachers. This inability to be certain is particularly evidenced by the excerpts from the interview that show changing perspectives and the development of internally persuasive discourses by the preservice teachers.

In fact, the process of ideologically becoming a teacher involves competing discourses that *require struggle and uncertainty,* which are part of the conditions of Bakhtin's (1981) *heteroglossic* world. At this point, I can appreciate the fact that I provided students with a personal connection to a student who is both succeeding and struggling with learning English and finding a place in the American school system, which I can only hope will lead to an increased sense of empathy and compassion for ELLs.

In moving forward as a teacher educator and advocate for ELLs, I have identified three implications from this research that may lead to a richer understanding of my teaching, of my students' process of becoming, and of the realities that ELLs experience. First of all, I find that it would be beneficial to think about ways in which I can encourage preservice teachers to conduct an inquiry into their conflicting discourses. How can I provide them with opportunities that engage them in an interrogation of what these discourses are saying about themselves, ELLs, their teachers, their families, and learning English? An initial step will consist of encouraging preservice teachers not only to name these discourses, but also to point out the conflicts among them and within themselves.

Secondly, as their instructor I can reflect on what readings, discussions, and projects I can develop in order to assist the preservice teachers as they struggle within the discourse of becoming (teachers) in an attempt to make their thinking visible and open to interrogation. This would take place in the contact zones that are created in my classroom and other spaces where they are contemplating and applying new theories to their practice in an attempt to internalize discourses and make them their own (Bakhtin, 1981).

A third implication encourages me to discover ways in which I can continue to challenge and encourage them to move past the potential attractiveness of authoritative discourses while allowing them to take up and form their own internally persuasive discourses. While I recognize the challenge of going against the normative ways of being and thinking in the world, I hope that through their process of becoming they are able to formulate discourses that speak to their passions, concerns, and desires, as opposed to those of others. Success for my students and myself cannot lie in particular discourses being taken up wholeheartedly and unquestioningly, but rather with the introduction and engagement of alternative ideas as well as experiences that provide preservice teachers with opportunities for reflection and self-interpretation.

As Zygmunt-Fillwalk and Clark (2007) pointed out:

> *Becoming multicultural thus emerges as a recursive process rather than a destination. A cyclical process emerges as individuals encounter, reflect, de-construct, and re-create worldviews. With novel experiences, individuals begin the process anew. (p. 292)*

For the student with the t-shirt, this might happen through direct, authentic ELLs in a classroom that is followed up with opportunities to reflect and interpret his experiences. I do not wish to move preservice teachers from one authoritative discourse to another over the course of a semester, but rather to stimulate their thinking in a way that fights stagnancy and allows for the appearance of ideas that were previously absent so that they can develop internally persuasive discourses that serve their own intentions, purposes, and teaching.

Acknowledgment

This research and article would not have been possible without the intellectual guidance of my previous professors from the Pennsylvania State University, Dr. Gail Boldt and Dr. Patrick Shannon. I am also thankful to the teachers and students of the charter school who so willingly collaborated with our language and literacy program.

Appendix

During the focus group interview, the following questions were asked:
1. What are some of your first impressions about the school that we are visiting?
2. When you first received your ELL's writing sample, what did you think about the writing and the student?
3. After meeting and spending time with your student, what surprised you about working with an ELL?
4. While working with your student, what was the most challenging part?
5. Is there anything else that you would like to add that you have not had the chance to share yet? Do you have any final thoughts, comments, or questions?

References

Bakhtin, M. M. (1981). Discourse in the novel. In M. Holquist (Ed.), *The dialogic imagination* (pp. 259–422). Austin, TX: University of Texas Press.

Ball, A. F. (2006). *Multicultural strategies for education and social change: Carriers of the torch in the United States and South Africa.* New York: Teachers College Press.

Batt, E. G. (2008). Teachers' perceptions of ELL education: Potential solutions to overcome the greatest challenges. *Multicultural Education, 15,* 39–43.

Britzman, D. (2003). *Practice makes practice: A critical study of learning to teach.* Albany, NY: State University of New York Press.

Commins, N. L., & Miramontes, O. B. (2006). Addressing linguistic diversity from the outset. *Journal of Teacher Education, 57,* 240–246.

Costa, J., McPhail, G., Smith, J., & Brisk, M. E. (2005). Faculty first: The challenge of infusing the teacher education curriculum with scholarship on English language learners. *Journal of Teacher Education, 56,* 104–118.

Foucault, M. (1978). *The history of sexuality: An introduction (volume 1).* New York: Vintage Books.

Giambo, D., & Szecsi, T. (2005/06). Opening up to the issues: Preparing preservice teachers to work effectively with English language learners. *Childhood Education, 82,* 107–110.

Glesne, C. (2006). *Becoming qualitative researchers: An introduction* (3rd ed.). Boston: Pearson Education.

Grant, C. A., & Gillette, M. (2006). A candid talk to teacher educators about effectively preparing teachers who can teach everyone's children. *Journal of Teacher Education, 57,* 292–299.

Isenbarger, L., & Willis, A. I. (2006). An intersection of theory and practice: Accepting the language a child brings into the classroom. *Language Arts, 84,* 125–135.

Lee, S., & Dallman, M. E. (2008). Engaging in a reflective examination about diversity: Interviews with three preservice teachers. *Multicultural Education, 15,* 36–44.

Lucas, T., Villegas, A. M., & Freedson-Gonzalez, M. (2008). Linguistically responsive teacher education: Preparing classroom teachers to teach English language learners. *Journal of Teacher Education, 59,* 361–373.

Luke, A. (1992). The body literate: Discourse and inscription in early literacy training. *Linguistics and Education, 4,* 107–129.

Morgan, D. (1997). *Focus groups as qualitative research,* 2nd ed. Newbury Park, CA: Sage.

NCELA [National Clearinghouse for English Language Acquisition & Language Instruction Educational Programs]. (2007a). *The growing number of limited English proficient students: 2005–2006 Poster.* Retrieved February 25, 2009, from http://www.ncela.gwu.edu/stats/2_nation.htm

NCELA [National Clearinghouse for English Language Acquisition & Language Instruction Educational Programs]. (2007b). *What are the five states that have experienced the greatest growth in their ELL population in the last decade?* Retrieved February 25, 2009, from http://www.ncela.gwu.edu/expert/fastfaq/8.html

NCELA [National Clearinghouse for English Language Acquisition & Language Instruction Educational Programs]. (2008). *Educating English language learners: Building teacher capacity.* Retrieved February 25, 2009, from http://www.ncela.gwu.edu/practice/mainstream_teachers.htm

Varghese, M. M., & Stritikus, T. (2005). *"Nadie me dijó* (Nobody told me)": Language policy negotiation and implications for teacher education. *Journal of Teacher Education, 56,* 73–87.

Washburn, G. N. (2008). Alone, confused, and frustrated: Developing empathy and strategies for working with English language learners. *The Clearing House, 81,* 247–250.

Zygmunt-Fillwalk, E., & Clark, P. (2007). Becoming multicultural: Raising awareness and supporting change in teacher education. *Childhood Education, 83,* 288–293.

Zygmunt-Fillwalk, E. M., & Leitze, A. (2006). Promising practices in preservice teacher preparation: The Ball State University urban semester. *Childhood Education, 82,* 283–288.

Critical Thinking

1. What are your beliefs about teaching ELL students?
2. How do your beliefs contribute to or deter from your effectiveness?
3. What steps can you take to change your beliefs and practices?
4. How will changing your beliefs and practices benefit your effectiveness?

Create Central

www.mhhe.com/createcentral

Internet References

EdWeek
www.edweek.org/topics/englishlanguagelearners/

United States Department of Education, Office of English Language Acquisition
www.ed.gov/about/offices/list/oela/index.html

Bridget A. Bunten is an assistant professor of education and coordinator of elementary education at Washington College, Chestertown, Maryland.

Bunten. Bridget. From *Multicultural Education,* Summer 2010, pp. 2–9. Copyright © 2010 by Caddo Gap Press. Reprinted by permission.

Article   Prepared by: Nancy P. Gallavan, *University of Central Arkansas*

"What Are You?" Biracial Children in the Classroom

TRACI P. BAXLEY

Learning Outcomes

After reading this article, you will be able to:

- Explain race relations in the United States and how "color blindness" impacts everyone.

- Detail biracial identity and the practices that support biracial students.

Over the last 30 years, biracial individuals have become one of the fastest growing populations in the United States. Despite this rapid growth, these citizens are only slowly beginning to be acknowledged among monoracial groups and in academia ("New Way," 2001; Root, 1996; Wardle, 2007). Because biracial identities "potentially disrupt the white/ 'of color' dichotomy, and thus call into question the assumptions on which racial inequality is based," society has a difficult time acknowledging this section of the population (Dutro, Kazemi, & Balf 2005, p. 98).

Biracial heritage can mean mixed parentage of any kind. This can include, but is not limited to, African American, white, Latino, Asian, and Native American. "Biracial," "interracial," "multiracial," and "mixed-race" are used interchangeably and are often self-prescribed by individuals and their families (McClain, 2004; Root, 1996; Wardle, 1992). As this group increases in the general population, teachers are beginning to see more of these children in their classrooms. How are biracial children different from monoracial children? How do biracial children challenge us to think differently about racial identity and curricular issues in our classrooms?

Historical Glance at Biracial Children

Biracial children and their families are often marginalized by members of monoracial heritage, and specifically by leaders of minority communities (Root, 1996; Wardle, 2006). According to Brunsma (2005), biracial people have always been an issue for U.S. society, because they go against the structure of American's racial order and white privilege preservation.

Many white slave owners and enslaved black women produced light-skinned offspring, known as "mulattoes," who sometimes looked more like the fathers than their mothers. Having a biracial heritage was not a choice at the time and these children were categorized not by their appearance, but rather by the "one drop rule," meaning if one had *any* known African ancestry, one was considered black both legally and socially (Tatum, 1997). The "one drop rule" was established by the U.S. Census Bureau. Before the 1920s, the Census count categorized "mulatto" and "pure Negro." Between the 1920s and 1960s, the previous categories were dropped and replaced with "black," as defined by the "one drop rule."

In 1967, a Supreme Court ruling in the case of *Loving v. Virginia* overturned the remaining laws prohibiting interracial marriages (FindLaw, 2007). The ruling not only helped remove the legal taboo, it may have increased acceptance of, and therefore the number of, interracial marriages in the United States.

Not until the 2000 Census, however, were Americans given the opportunity to identify themselves as multiracial (Census-Scope, n.d.; "New Way," 2001). About 2.4 percent of Americans (equal to about 6.8 million people) were able to validate all of their heritages. The four most commonly reported interracial categories were white and some other race—white and American Indian, white and Asian, and white and black. From the multiracial community's perspective, this was a giant step in the right direction. However, many minority groups, including the National Association for the Advancement of Colored People and the National Asian Pacific American Legal Consortium, were not in favor of this new Census category because of the possibility of jeopardizing federal funds, civil rights laws, and voting rights issues ("New Way," 2001). Selecting more than one race can affect the number of people who previously checked one of the single minority boxes.

Biracial Identity

Experts recognize that biracial identity development is different from that of white and minority children (Tatum, 1997; Wardle, 1992). Multiple factors should be considered when racial identity is developing, including individual personalities and phenotype, familial relationships and racial identities, and geographical locations and local communities (Root, 1996; Tatum, 1997). Root (1996) recognizes five possible options for biracial identity: 1) accept the racial identity given by society; 2) identify with the minority race; 3) identify as white, if the individual physical features allow; 4) identify as "biracial" (no individual race identified); and 5) identify with more than one race. Root (1996) states that any of these choices can be positive if the individual makes that choice and if that individual doesn't feel compromised or marginalized by his/her choice.

Earlier studies concluded that biracial children were confused about their identity due to their lack of ability to connect completely to either of their heritages (Brandell, 1988; Gibbs, 1987; Herring, 1992). More recently, researchers believe that unresolved identity issues remain for biracial children because their unique heritages are not acknowledged by schools or society in general (Tatum, 1997; Wardle, 1992). In spite of this resistance from society, biracial citizens have demonstrated a sense of achievement, positive self-awareness, and emotional well-being (Tatum, 1997; Tizard & Phoenix, 1995).

Wardle (2007), when analyzing current child development textbooks, found that only two of 12 books addressed multiracial children at all. Wardle also addressed the absence of biracial people in many multicultural education books that focus solely on monoracial and monoethnic groups of people. Wardle suggests that biracial children are not included within the diversity construct of academia because multicultural and diversity experts view America as a "salad bowl" with separate racial/ethnic contributions, view diversity from a narrow-minded American viewpoint, and rely on one critical theory—the ownership of power—that requires each race/ethnic group to be completely separate in a hierarchically oppressed system.

Classroom Practices to Support Biracial Children

The 2000 Census revealed that approximately 4 percent of all children under 18 in the United States are multiracial, and that there are 1.6 million interracial married couples (Census-Scope, n.d.). This cannot be ignored when it comes to classroom practices. Teachers who say they treat everyone in the class "the same" need to re-evaluate the idea of equity, ensuring that *every* student is afforded opportunities for academic excellence, and begin to acknowledge their own misconceptions and discomforts when addressing racial issues and identity in their classrooms. This includes investigating their personal stance regarding biracial children (Wardle, 1992). When conducting a self-analysis, a teacher might ask such questions as: How do I feel about interracial marriages? What preconceived notions do I have about biracial people? What have my experiences been with biracial people? Do these experiences impact my perceptions about biracial people? If so, what can I do about it? (Harris, 2002; Tatum, 1997). Biracial parents often feel as if "at best, teachers do not know how to support their children's healthy identity development in the classroom and, at worst,

force them to identify with their parent of color, or parent of lowest status" (Wardle & Cruz-Janzen, 2004, p. 13).

In 2002, Harris found that school personnel who were actively engaged in cultural diversity and awareness programs held more accurate perceptions of biracial children. Ignoring students' racial identities and being "color blind" is actually a disservice, not only to biracial students, but also to all students. Biracial individuals may begin their schooling having embraced their double heritage and possessing positive self-images; however, their monoracial classmates may not understand them, and, even worse, may have preconceived notions regarding race. Biracial children who appear to "look black" may be taunted by monoracial black students for being light-skinned and having curly hair. Similarly, a biracial child who appears to be more "white" may receive negative comments from peers when her black parent enters the classroom. Living in a racially and culturally conscious society dictates that the classroom climate should deal fairly with racially charged issues and enable students to work toward positive solutions.

The parents of biracial children hold various views regarding their children's identity. Therefore, it is imperative that teachers communicate with these parents and ask them what racial designation they feel most appropriately conveys their child's heritage. More and more parents are teaching their children to embrace the term "biracial" in order to identify with both heritages (Tatum, 1997). Teachers can develop appropriate activities for their curriculum by listening to parents' suggestions regarding ways to increase awareness of biracial children.

The growth in the number of biracial students in classrooms requires educators to examine their instructional practices and evaluate any adjustments in order to acknowledge and accommodate this population. According to Wardle and Cruz-Janzen (2004), biracial students are "totally invisible in the schools' curriculum: no stories, pictures, articles and reports, books or textbook items that reflect their unique family experiences" (p. 13). Biracial students present a distinctive challenge to educators partly because of prevailing stereotypes that surround their identity. One stereotype is that biracial children must *choose* to identify with one racial heritage only, usually that of a minority heritage (Harris, 2002; Wardle, 2006). Although this practice may have held sway in the past, thereby causing feelings of guilt over the rejection of the other parent, the last 30 years have given biracial children more choices. Biracial youth are proud of their heritages and are becoming more proactive in speaking out against the racism and opposition around them. Organizations, such as the Association of Multi-Ethnic Americans (AMEA), have sprung up as resources to support multiracial families while educating people from monoracial backgrounds. Teachers who want to address issues regarding biracial students can find a wealth of information from these organizations.

Another stereotype is that biracial students do not want to talk about their racial identity or that they have racial identity issues (Harris, 2002; Tatum, 1997; Wardle, 2006). While some may find it difficult to discuss these issues, educators need to make certain that their questions are sincere and nonjudgmental (Harris, 2002). Many families of biracial children are proactive in communicating to their children who they are and teaching them to have pride in their background (Wardle & Cruz-Janzen, 2004). Teachers need to include an extensive array of approaches and practices in their instruction in order to encourage peers to acknowledge and accept biracial children, as well as to support biracial children in developing positive identities. In addition, teachers should model appropriate ways to engage in discussions focused on people's similarities and differences.

We must move beyond what Banks (2003) calls the "heroes and holidays" approach to teaching multicultural education, in which only surface level concepts are being taught but the mainstream curriculum remains the same. According to Wardle and Cruz-Janzen (2004), this approach "marginalizes and trivializes" non-mainstream white cultures (p. 40). Instead, teachers need to encourage students to shift to Banks' (2003) social action approach. This approach is more comprehensive and means that students must engage in problem-solving and critical thinking activities that require them to *evaluate* and *take action* on social issues.

Balf's 4th- and 5th-grade class was assigned a critical literacy culture project in which three biracial students were able to reveal both parts of their heritage and discuss it with their peers (Dutro, Kazemi, & Balf 2005). Most classmates were not aware of the students' backgrounds. From this assignment, subsequent whole-group discussions became necessary in order for the biracial students to articulate how they felt, both positively and negatively, about being biracial. Ultimately, these discussions became insightful for the researchers, the teacher, and the other students. More important, it changed the way the monoracial students viewed the biracial students in the class.

Biracial students should see themselves in the curriculum through famous biracial or multiracial historical individuals, such as George Washington Carver, Frederick Douglass, W. E. B. Du Bois, as well as more contemporary ones, such as Bob Marley, Tiger Woods, Colin Powell, Halle Berry, Derek Jeter, Alicia Keys, and Barack Obama. Also, inviting members from the local community into schools to reinforce the presence of biracial role models not only validates racial identity for biracial students, but also helps white and other minority children recognize the growing number of biracial and multiracial people around them. Having real role models is crucial to students' overall success and positive racial identity (Wardle & Cruz-Janzen, 2004).

Finally, teachers should supply their classroom libraries with picture books, adolescent novels, and reference books that focus on biracial children. This requires effort on the teachers' part, due to many schools' and libraries' lack of resources about biracial children. The following list of resources may be helpful in supporting teachers as they incorporate culturally responsive practices in their classrooms.

Reference Books

Dalmage, H. M. (2000). *Tripping on the color line: Black-white multiracial families in a racially divided world.* New Brunswick, NJ: Rutgers University Press.

Gaskins, P. F. (1999). *What are you?: Voices of mixed-race young people.* New York: Henry Holt & Company.

Nissel, A. (2006). *Mixed: My life in black & white.* New York: Random House Publishing Group.

Rockquemore, K. (2005). *Raising biracial children.* New York: AltaMira Press.

Wright, M. A. (1998). *I'm chocolate, you're vanilla: Raising healthy black and biracial children in a race-conscious world.* San Francisco: Jossey-Bass.

Picture Books

Ada, A. F. *I love Saturdays y Domingos.* New York: Atheneum.

Adoff, A. (1973). *Black is brown is tan.* New York: Harper.

Adoff, A. (1991). *Hard to be six.* New York: Lothrop.

Cheng, A. (2000). *Grandfather counts.* New York: Lee & Low.

Cisneros, S. (1994). *Hairs/Pelitos.* New York: Knopf.

Cole, H., & Vogl, N. (2005). *Am I a color too?* Bellevue, WA: Illumination Arts Publishing Company.

Davol, M. W. (1993). *Black, white, just right.* Morton Grove, IL: Albert Whitman & Company.

Edmonds, L. (2004). *An African princess.* Cambridge, MA: Candlewick Press.

Friedman, I. (1984). *How my parents learned to eat.* New York: Houghton.

Hoffman, M. (1990). *Nancy no-size.* New York: Mammoth.

Igus, T., & Sisnett, A. (1996). *Two Mrs. Gibsons.* New York: Little Book Press.

Johnson, A. (1996). *The aunt in our house.* New York: Orchard Books.

Katz, K. (1999). *The color of us.* New York: Henry Holt & Company.

Lamperti, N. (2000). *Brown like me.* Norwich, VT: New Victoria Publisher.

Little, O. M. (1996). *Yoshiko and the foreigner.* New York: Farrar Straus & Giroux.

Mills, C. (1992). *A visit to Amy-Claire.* New York: Macmillan.

Monk, I. (1998). *Hope.* New York: Carolrhoda Books.

Rattigan, J. K. (1993). *Dumpling soup.* New York: Little, Brown Books.

Ringgold, F. (1996). *Bonjour, Lonnie.* New York: Hyperion.

Spohn, D. (1991). *Winter wood.* New York: Lothrop.

Straight, S. (1995). *Bear E. Bear.* New York: Hyperion.

Wing, N. (1999). *Jalapeno bagels.* New York: Atheneum.

Wyeth, D. S. (1996). *Ginger brown: Too many houses.* New York: Random House.

Adolescent Books

Curry, J. (2005). *Black canary.* New York: Simon & Schuster Children's Publishing Division.

Forrester, S. (1999). *Dust from old bones.* New York: HarperCollins.

Meyer, C. (2007). *Jubilee journey.* New York: Harcourt.

Nash, R. D. (1995). *Coping as a biracial/ biethnic teen.* New York: The Rosen Publishing Group.

Viglucci, C. P. (1996). *Sun dance at turtle rock.* Rochester, NY: Stone Pine Books.

Woodson, J. (2003). *The house you pass on the way.* New York: Puffin Books.

Wyeth, D. S. (1995). *The world of daughter McGuire.* New York: Yearling Books.

References

Banks, J. A. (2003). *Teaching strategies for ethnic studies* (7th ed.). New York: Pearson Education Group.

Brandell, J. R. (1988). Treatment of the biracial child: Theoretical and clinical issues. *Journal of Multicultural Counseling and Development, 16,* 176–187.

Brunsma, D. L. (2005). Interracial families and the racial identification of mixed-raced children: Evidence from the early childhood longitudinal study. *Social Forces, 84*(2), 1131–1157.

CensusScope. (n.d.). Retrieved September 29, 2007, from www.censusscope.org/us/chart_multi.html

Dutro, E., Kazemi, E., & Balf, R. (2005). The aftermath of "you're only half": Multiracial identities in the literacy classroom. *Language Arts, 83*(2), 96–106.

FindLaw. (2007). *The fortieth anniversary of Loving v. Virginia: The personal and cultural legacy of the case that ended legal prohibitions on interracial marriage.* Retrieved September 27, 2007, from http://communities.justicetalking.org/blogs/findlaw/archive/2007/05/29/the-fortieth-anniversary-of-loving-v-virginia-the-personal-and-cultural-legacy-of-the-case-that-ended-legal-prohibitions-on-interracial-marriage-part-one-in-a-two-part-series.aspx

Gibbs, J. T. (1987). Identity and marginality: Issues in the treatment of biracial adolescents. *American Journal of Orthopsychiatry, 57,* 265–278.

Harris, H. (2002). School counselors' perceptions of biracial children: Pilot study. *Professional School Counseling Online.* Retrieved October 6, 2007, from http://findarticles.com/p/articles/mi_m0KOC/is_2_6/ai_96194762

Herring, P. D. (1992). Biracial children: An increasing concern for elementary and middle school counselors. *Elementary School Guidance and Counseling, 27,* 123–130.

Lanier, S. (2000). *Jefferson's children: The story of one American family.* New York: Random House Books for Young Readers.

McClain, C. S. (2004). Black by choice: Identity preferences of Americans of black/white parentage. *The Black Scholar, 34*(2), 43–54.

New way to measure America. (2001). Retrieved September 8, 2007, from www.tolerance.org/news/article_print.jsp?id=140

Root, M. (1996). A bill of rights for racially mixed people. In M. Root (Ed.), *The multiracial experience: Racial borders as the new frontier.* Thousand Oaks, CA: Sage.

Tatum, B. D. (1997). *"Why are all the black kids sitting together in the cafeteria?" And other conversations about race.* New York: Basic Books.

Tizard, B., & Phoenix, A. (1995). The identity of mixed parentage adolescents. *Journal of Child Psychology and Psychiatry, 36,* 1399–1410.

Wardle, F. (1992). Supporting the biracial children in the school setting. *Education & Treatment of Children, 15*(2), 163.

Wardle, F. (2006). *Myths and realities.* Retrieved September 13, 2007, from http://csbchome.org

Wardle, F. (2007). *Why diversity experts hate the multiracial movement.* Retrieved September 13, 2007, from http://csbchome.org

Wardle, F., & Cruz-Janzen, M. I. (2004). *Meeting the needs of multiethnic and multiracial children in schools.* New York: Pearson Education.

Critical Thinking

1. What is biracial identity?
2. How do current classroom practices help and hinder biracial students?
3. What transformational practices help all students?
4. Why do you need to address biracial identities specifically?

Create Central

www.mhhe.com/createcentral

Internet References

Association of Multi-Ethnic Americans (AMEA)
www.ameasite.org
Center for the Study of Biracial Children
www.csbc.cncfamily.com/

TRACI P. BAXLEY is Assistant Professor of Literacy, Department of Teaching and Learning, Florida Atlantic University, Boca Raton.

Author Note—Traci P. Baxley is the mother of four biracial children.

From *Childhood Education,* June 2008, pp. 230–234. Copyright © 2008 by the Association for Childhood Education International. Reprinted by permission of Traci P. Baxley and the Association for Childhood Education International, 17904 Georgia Avenue, Suite 215, Olney, MD 20832.

Article   Prepared by: Nancy P. Gallavan, *University of Central Arkansas*

The Possibilities and Challenges of Developing Teachers' Social Justice Beliefs

ALTHIER LAZAR

Learning Outcomes

After reading this article, you will be able to.

- Increase awareness of your attitudes toward students' test scores and their cultural backgrounds.

- Examine the balance between concern for job security and for educational equity and social justice.

The majority of teachers educated today come from mainstream backgrounds, and their dominant status relative to growing numbers of students from nondominant cultural communities leaves them susceptible to underestimating these students' literacy abilities. This is because many hold naive and uncomplicated views about schooling, race, and literacy (Lazar, 2007). They often subscribe to the meritocratic view that achievement depends solely on one's merits and work habits (Castro, 2010) and tend to blame students and their caregivers for "failing" at school rather than recognizing "the system of failure embedded in institutional practices that disfavors and disenfranchises minority groups" (p. 207).

It is possible to challenge deficit perspectives through teacher education programs that infuse social justice goals (Villegas & Lucas, 2002). Examining inequalities, engaging in personal reflections of self and others, and participating in action research within schools and communities have helped teachers develop understandings about student capacity and their own responsibility for teaching (Zeichner, 2009). Programs have also focused on developing teachers' understandings about relationships between race, class, culture, literacy, and language (Ball, 2009; Lazar, 2007) and developing understandings about students' cultural capital and building on students' existing knowledge through culturally responsive teaching (Gutierrez & Lee, 2009; González, Moll, & Amanti; 2004; Ladson-Billings, 2009). It is especially important that teacher education occur in the context of inquiry communities and focus on developing intellectual, political, and critical stances (Cochran-Smith, 2004).

While social justice goals are considered vital to promoting social activism among teachers, they are threatened by the current political climate that focuses on the evaluation of teachers on the basis of students' standardized test scores (Zeichner, 2009).

Teachers are not encouraged to advocate for students and challenge programs and policies that undermine student achievement; rather, they are criticized for failing to raise test scores. In such a climate, social justice education takes a back seat to professional development programs that focus on test preparation and skill development. While social justice teaching is a fundamental goal of many teacher education programs, it is still not a core value across all programs (Zeichner, 2009). Without compelling research that shows the significance of social justice goals in teacher preparation, there is little hope that they will be universally prioritized in these programs.

Teacher educators need to evaluate how their programs prepare teachers to serve students from nondominant cultural communities. Toward this goal, I will explore the impact of a course called "Sociology of Literacy" on teachers' social justice beliefs, and particularly, their views toward the capacities of students.

Method

Participants and Course

Set in an urban-based university in the mid-Atlantic region of the U.S., 41 teachers participated in the Sociology of Literacy course. I compared the responses of this group to 46 teachers who did not take the course. Ninety-five percent of the teachers in both groups were white, five percent were African American, and almost all considered themselves middle class. All but three were women. The majority were novice teachers with less than five years of teaching experience.

The Sociology of Literacy course involved reading and responding to research on the following topics: the complexity of culture, issues related to social inequality, institutional racism, poverty, white privilege and racial identity, language variation and identity, emergent bilingualism, cultural capital, and culturally responsive instruction. Teachers wrote reflectively about these topics and shared their insights in small and whole group discussions.

Teachers also participated in the ABC Model of Cultural Understanding and Communication (Ruggiano-Schmidt & Finkbeiner, 2006). This involved writing an autobiography that includes information about family, beliefs, values, traditions, racial/ethnic identity, and their ways of being privileged or subordinated based on race, class, gender, or other affiliations. Teachers wrote about their access to school-valued literacy practices and mainstream language communities. Teachers also wrote a biography of someone culturally different from themselves after interviewing this person about key life events, similar to those addressed in their own autobiographies. They also addressed topics related to culture, power, or privilege, based on their level of comfort in discussing these issues with interviewees. For the cross-cultural analysis, teachers compared their autobiographies to the biographies and generated a list of similarities and differences between themselves and the person they interviewed.

Data Sources & Analysis
Surveys

Both teacher groups were asked to respond to twelve statements on the survey, *Learning to Teach for Social Justice – Beliefs (LTSJ-B)* (Enterline, Cochran-Smith, Ludlow, Mitescu, 2008; see Appendix). This instrument is designed to measure key beliefs associated with social justice. These include: 1) high expectations and rich learning opportunities for all pupils; 2) an asset-based perspective on the cultural, linguistic and experiential resources pupils and families bring to school; 3) the importance of critical thinking in a democratic society; 4) the role of teachers as advocates and agents for change; 5) challenges to the notion of a meritocratic society; 6) teaching as an activity that is related to teachers' deep underlying assumptions and beliefs about race, class, gender, disability, and culture; and 7) the idea that issues related to culture, equity, and race ought to be part of what is visible in all aspects of the curriculum.

Participants were asked to indicate their level of agreement with each of the survey statements using a Likert scale (1=strongly disagree, 2=disagree, 3=uncertain, 4=agree, 5=strongly agree). Seven of the 12 items (3, 5, 6, 9 10, 11, 12) are negatively worded such that low scores (1 or 2) on these items are associated with a stronger social justice orientation. These were reversed scored (e.g.: negatively worded statement receiving a score of "1" was changed to a "5") and consequently the statement was reversed in my analysis (e.g.: Statement #10, "it's not their job to change society" was changed to "it is their job to change society"). This allowed for consistency in scoring as all high (4 or 5) scores were aligned with a social justice orientation.

Means for each item were calculated and compared using independent sample t-tests. The central question of the study is the degree to which the Sociology of Literacy course could challenge teachers' deficit attitudes toward students from non-dominant communities. For this, I focus the analysis on those items and responses that relate to teachers' understanding of student capacity. These include the negatively worded Items 6: *It's reasonable for teachers to have lower classroom expectations for students who don't speak English as their first language* and 9: *Economically disadvantaged students have more to gain in schools because they bring less into the classroom.*

Written Statements

Teachers were asked to write in response to the following statement: *Please describe how you would approach teaching students in urban high poverty communities.* Thirty-six "Course" teachers and 33 "non-course" teachers chose to participate. Teachers were given 20 minutes to write a response. These papers were read and open-coded for themes and patterns (Charmaz, 2006). Statements were coded as either an "assertion" or "assumption." Assertions were either recommendations for instruction (28 codes) or statements about urban school conditions (11 codes), or the impact on teachers (1 code). Assumptions were generalizations about students' homes/caregivers (7 codes) or students (10 codes). All of the codes were displayed with the identification numbers of the teachers who wrote them. Percentages of statements from course and non-course teachers were calculated. The most salient differences between the two groups are reported, as well as central trends among the items, especially as they relate to teachers' beliefs about student capacity.

Analysis involved examining consistencies within and between data sets. Based on general trends across these sets, I generated assertions about the course impact, and lack of impact, on teachers' understandings.

Findings
Surveys

Course teachers scored higher on all 12 LTSJ-B survey items, and significantly higher on four of the twelve items than teachers who did not take the course. Findings from the survey show that the course had a significant impact on teachers' understandings about the need to examine one's own attitudes and beliefs about race, class, gender, disabilities, and sexual orientation (Item 1; Course: 4.82, No Course: 4.29; p < 01). There were also significant differences between three of the negatively worded items: 1) *For the most part, covering multicultural topics is only relevant to certain subject areas such as social studies and literature* (Item 3, Course: 4.46, No Course: 2.65; p < .001), 2) *Economically disadvantaged students have more to gain in schools because they bring less into the classroom* (Item 9, Course: 4.34, No Course: 3.61; p < 01), and 3) *Although teachers have to appreciate diversity; it's not their job to change society* (Item 10, Course: 4.02 , No Course: 3.45; p < .05). Based on these four items, the course helped teachers recognize the importance of: 1) examining one's own attitudes toward several dimensions of cultural diversity, 2) addressing multicultural topics not just in social studies and literature, but throughout the curriculum, 3) recognizing that economically disadvantaged students bring something of value (presumably knowledge or understandings) to the classroom, and 4) that teachers' role is to not only appreciate diversity, but to also change societal views to be more accepting of diversity.

The finding that course teachers recognized student capacity, based on their higher rates of disagreement to Item 9 (*Economically disadvantaged students have more to gain in schools because they bring less into the classroom*), was not matched by their responses to a similar Item, #6 (*It's reasonable for teachers to have lower classroom expectations for students who don't speak English as their first language*). While course teachers disagreed with Item 6 at a higher rate than non-course teachers (more consistent with a social justice orientation), the difference was not significant.

Table 1 Teachers' Assertions about Capacity of Students in Urban High Poverty Communities

"Teachers should/must . . ."	Non-Course Teachers N = 33	Course Teachers N = 36
Treat each student as a valuable resource.	3	36
Recognize students' "funds of knowledge."	0	19
Build on students' prior knowledge.	0	14
Learn about students' communities.	0	14
Recognize students' home literacies.	0	11
Validate students' home language.	0	11

Course teachers' significantly higher rates of disagreement with statement #10 (*Although teachers have to appreciate diversity; it's not their job to change society*), reflected their tendency to identify as change agents. Yet there was no significant difference between the two groups in their response to other statements that related to teacher advocacy. Both groups tended to agree with statement #7: *Part of the responsibilities of the teacher is to challenge school arrangements that maintain societal inequities* (Course=4.21; No Course=4.15). One explanation is that statement #7 may have been interpreted as more reasonable than #10 because it includes the qualifying phrase "part of the responsibilities of the teacher." In other words, "challenging school arrangements" could be *one of many* teaching responsibilities and therefore it is plausible that even those who do not have strong social justice views would agree with this. Yet there was no significant difference between the groups in response to statement #12: *Realistically, the job of a teacher is to prepare students for the lives they are likely to lead.* Both groups tended to be fairly uncertain about this statement (Course=2.82; No-Course=2.76). Those who felt that teachers could change the life trajectories of students would disagree with this statement.

Written Comments

There were some consistencies between survey responses and teachers' written comments in the area of recognizing student capacity. An analysis of the two teacher groups' written comments shows very distinct patterns of response to the prompt: *Please describe how you would approach teaching students in urban high poverty communities.* Table 1 indicates that statements written by course teachers were more focused on recognizing student capacity than those who did not take the course. Course teachers wrote much more consistently about teachers' need to know students and value their knowledge:

More than a third of the course teachers indicated that teachers should recognize students as valuable resources in the classroom, and almost one-fifth stated specifically that students' funds of knowledge should be recognized. Course teachers who included either type of statement account for 55.5% of the group. Further 66.6% (24 out of 36) of teachers who participated in the course included at least one or more of these statements in their written response. None of the non-course teachers recognized urban students' knowledge as valuable. The trend of course teachers recognizing students' capacity is matched by their relative absence of negative commentary about students and their caregivers. Table 2 shows that none of these teachers made negative comments about students or their caregivers:

Table 2 shows that nearly a quarter of those who did not take the course indicated that caregivers did not care about their children's education. Additionally, several teachers in this group wrote certain kinds of statements about students that were not shared by course teachers. These include: 1) students could not put as much effort into school because of outside responsibilities, 2) students must be employed to help pay the bills, 3) students do not develop at a normal rate, 3) low literacy abilities exist at home, and 4) students have few highly educated role models.

These tables reflect salient differences between the teacher groups in the area of recognizing student capacity. About two-thirds of course teachers acknowledged student capacity in some form, where only one of the non-course teachers did. Additionally two of the teachers who did not take the course indicated that students brought little to no prior knowledge to school. Written statements indicate that teachers who did not participate in the course tended not to acknowledge students' intellectual or academic capacities.

Table 2 Teachers' Assertions about Students and Their Caregivers

I feel that . . .	Non-Course Teachers N = 33	Course Teachers N = 36
Caregivers do not care about their children's education.	24	0
Students do not care about their education.	6	0
Students come to school with little/no prior knowledge.	6	0

Consistencies/Inconsistencies across Data Sets

Two-thirds of the course teachers recognized student capacity in their written statements and this finding matched these teachers' higher level of disagreement that economically disadvantaged students brought less to the classroom. Additionally, none of the course teachers commented negatively about students or their caregivers, as did some non-course teachers. While not a significant difference between the two groups, more course teachers disagreed with statement 6: *"It is reasonable to have lower expectations for students who do not speak English as their first language."* Consistent with this finding, about one-tenth of course teachers recognized the worth of students' home language in their written comments yet none of the non-course teachers discussed the value of students' home language.

Findings were inconclusive about the impact of the course on strengthening teachers' sense of activism. More course teachers felt it was the teachers' job to change society to appreciate diversity, but none wrote about this. There were no significant differences between the two groups regarding teachers' responsibility to challenge school arrangements that maintain societal inequities or the idea that the job of teachers is to prepare students for the lives they are likely to lead. No teacher from either group provided written commentary related to these items, as most focused on how they would serve students instructionally.

Significance/Implications

Teachers who took the Sociology of Literacy course conveyed beliefs that were more consistent with social justice goals than those who did not take the course. Findings also showed that differences between course and non-course teachers were robust in some areas, such as acknowledging students' capacity, although not as in the area of valuing students' linguistic capital or articulating understandings about the institutional and societal structures that advantage or disadvantage particular communities.

A generally acknowledged tenet in this body of research is that one course will not produce teachers who fully appreciate and own social justice perspectives. It is necessary, however, to define the possibilities and limitations of individual courses so that they may be improved. Having teachers complete the ABC project with emergent bilingual students might improve teachers' recognition of students' cultural and linguistic capital. More specific explorations of how students' native language bolsters their acquisition of English would be necessary for raising teachers' expectations of emergent bilinguals (Garcia & Kleifgen, 2010). The findings also inform a more explicit focus on the roles of teachers as activists. This calls for course experiences that go beyond reflecting on inequalities, to actually being in the company of teachers who are involved in activist-oriented work in schools.

Conclusion

Findings from this study affirm that the Sociology of Literacy course made a difference in helping teachers acquire a social justice orientation, especially in the areas of valuing culturally responsive teaching practices and seeing students' capacities. These align with two of the dimensions of social justice teaching discussed by Cochran-Smith (2010): promoting equity in learning opportunities and outcomes for students and respecting the knowledge traditions of students from all cultural groups. The course might make an even greater difference if it was fortified by internship experiences with more expert teachers who see students' capacity and work as student advocates and activists in their schools. I believe these components would contribute to the value of the course for helping teachers acquire the social justice orientation they need to serve students in nondominant communities.

References

Ball, A. F. (2009). Toward a theory of generative change in culturally and linguistically complex classrooms. *American Educational Research Journal, 46*(1), 45–72.

Castro, A. J. (2010). Themes in the research on preservice teachers' views of cultural diversity: Implications for researching millennial preservice teachers. *Educational Researcher, 39*(3), 198–210.

Charmaz, K. (2006). *Constructing grounded theory: A practical guide through qualitative analysis.* Thousand Oaks, CA: Sage Publications.

Cochran-Smith, M. (2004). *Walking the Road: Race, Diversity and Social Justice in Teacher Education.* New York: Teachers College Press.

Cochran-Smith, M. (2010) Toward a theory of teacher education for social justice. In M. Fullan, A. Hargreaves, D. Hopkins, & A. Lieberman (Eds.), *The International Handbook of Educational Change* (2nd ed.): pp. 445–467

Enterline, S., Cochran-Smith, M., Ludlow, L. H., Mitescu, E. (2008). Learning to teach for social justice: Measuring change in the beliefs of teacher candidates. *The New Educator, 4*, 267–290.

González, N., Moll, L., & Amanti, C. (Eds.). (2004). *Funds of knowledge: Theorizing practices in households, communities, and classrooms.* Mahwah, NJ: Lawrence Erlbaum Associates.

Gutierrez, K. & Lee, C. D. (2009). Robust informal learning environments for youth from nondominant groups: Implications for literacy learning in formal schooling. In L. Morrow, R. Rueda, and D. Lapp (Eds.), *Handbook of research on literacy and diversity* (pp. 216–232). New York, NY: Guilford Press.

Ladson-Billings, G. (2009). *The Dreamkeepers* (2nd ed.). San Francisco, CA: Jossey-Bass.

Lazar, A. M. (2007). It's not just about teaching kids to read: Helping preservice teachers acquire a mindset for teaching children in urban communities. *Journal of Literacy Research, 39*(4), 411–443.

Ruggiano-Schmidt, P. & Finkbeiner, C. (eds.). (2006). *The ABC's of Cultural Understanding and Communication: National and International Adaptations.* Greenwich, CT: Information Age Publishing.

Villegas, A. M. & Lucas, T. (2002). Preparing culturally responsive teachers: Rethinking the curriculum. *Journal of Teacher Education, 53*(1), 20–32.

Zeichner, K. (2009). *Teacher education and the struggle for social justice.* New York: Routledge.

Appendix

The *Learning to Teach for Social Justice*—Beliefs Scale (Enterline, Cochran-Smith, Ludlow, Mitescu, 2008)

Directions: Respond to the statements below using the following Likert categories: Strongly Disagree = 1, Disagree=2, Uncertain=3, Agree=4, Strongly Agree=5

1	An important part of learning to be a teacher is examining one's own attitudes and beliefs about race, class, gender, disabilities, and sexual orientation.
2	Issues related to racism and inequity should be openly discussed in the classroom.
3R*;	For the most part, covering multicultural topics is only relevant to certain subjects areas, such as social studies and literature.
4	Good teaching incorporates diverse cultures and experiences into classroom lessons and discussions.
5R*	The most important goal in working with immigrant children and English language learners is that they assimilate into American society.
6R*	It's reasonable for teachers to have lower classroom expectations for students who don't speak English as their first language.
7	Part of the responsibilities of the teacher is to challenge school arrangements that maintain societal inequities.
8	Teachers should teach students to think critically about government positions and actions.
9R*	Economically disadvantaged students have more to gain in schools because they bring less into the classroom.
10R*	Although teachers have to appreciate diversity, it's not their job to change society.
11R*	Whether students succeed in school depends primarily on how hard they work.
12R*	Realistically, the job of a teacher is to prepare students for the lives they are likely to lead.

*R: Statements are reverse scored.

Critical Thinking

1. What are your beliefs about educational equity and social justice in schools and classrooms?
2. What are your experiences with teaching students from culturally nondominant communities?
3. Why is teaching all students important for the country?
4. Why is teaching all students important for you?

Create Central

www.mhhe.com/createcentral

Internet References

Critical Pedagogy - WinkWorld
www.joanwink.com/cp3/cp3_pgs123-129.php

Freire Project
www.freireproject.org

Lazar, Althier. From *Online Yearbook of Urban Learning, Teaching and Research*, vol. 8, 2012, pp. 33–41. Copyright © 2012 by Althier M. Lazar. Reprinted by permission by the author.

Unit 2

UNIT

Prepared by: Nancy P. Gallavan, *University of Central Arkansas*

Awareness of Self

Humans function through four domains of learning: cognitive, affective, psychomotor, and psychosocial. Cognitive functions entail mental intelligence and thinking; affective functions encompass emotional beliefs and feelings. Psychomotor functions involve physical movements and actions; and psychosocial functions include social communications and interactions. All four domains of learning rely upon the five senses (sight, sound, smell, taste, and touch) to inform our repertoire of knowledge, to guide our decision-making skills, to awaken our consciousness of dispositions, and to strengthen our wisdom of expression.

Increasing one's awareness of self begins by concentrating on each domain of learning both as an individual function and as integrated functions combined with the functions from the other three domains. By logically and reasonably considering one's thoughts, feelings, actions, and interactions, people become attuned to their individual routines and rhythms. However, the processes are complex and challenging in our attempts to maintain objectivity.

Thus, identifying and applying the information we collect through our senses is far more difficult and problematic than we may realize. Frequently, we see and hear the sights and sounds that we may have been conditioned to see and hear or that we want to see and hear. Beginning with infancy, each of us receives information through our senses that establishes our understanding of the world around us that continues to expand as we age and grow. We learn techniques to gain new information that we develop individually and by imitating other people, people who may or may not be appropriate role models. These techniques are accompanied by a range of thoughts, feelings, words, and interactions that each of us creates and acquires consciously and unconsciously. In our desire to be accepted by family and friends, we cultivate a persona that may or may not be clear to us or constructive for us, particularly as educators.

Together with the people around us, awareness is enlightened through the images we actually or choose to see and the words we actually or choose to hear on three levels through attention, realization, and extension. The outermost level of awareness is the surface or external appearance. This level of awareness includes everything that is noticed and gains our attention in our vicinity happening in the immediate time and near future. We begin by identifying the stimulus, categorizing it with similar stimuli, assign meaningful connections that explain the stimulus to us right away, and determine issues of safety, usefulness, and relationship. Yet at this level of awareness, our attention is framed by the messages we have received throughout our lives and tend to honor, adopt, and repeat.

Through the four domains of learning, we form initial thoughts, feelings, actions, and interactions and then determine the application and appropriateness of our realizations. We rely upon the past patterns we have learned coupled with the recognition of probable, possible, and improbable outcomes. Comprehension is advanced as we start to adjust our thoughts and feelings to make sense of the situation. At this level of awareness, we begin to negotiate from the accepted approaches and repeated routines with a different level of awareness that opens new challenging concepts and more professional practices. During our negotiations, we manifest a range of reactions and responses as we reconcile the level of awareness that we have experienced with the level of awareness being introduced awakening consciousness.

Only by sharing our thoughts, beliefs, and interactions with other people and listening to them, can we embark on the reciprocity or exchange of sensations accompanying deeper levels of awareness. We move below the surface level of attention, negotiate the intermediary level of realization, enter the deep level of extension, and through extension, strengthen our wisdom.

Article   Prepared by: Nancy P. Gallavan, *University of Central Arkansas*

'I Don't Think I'm Biased'

PAT CLARK AND EVA M. ZYGMUNT-FILLWALK

Learning Outcomes

After reading this article, you will be able to:

- Recognize ways that biases, stereotypes, and prejudices influence your teaching.

- Discuss issues of race and privilege.

Multicultural understanding and proficiency have never been more important to teachers than they are right now. Never before have we had so many young children entering schools populated by teachers who reflect neither their race, nor their language tradition, nor the communities from which they come. This growth in culturally diverse classrooms has unfortunately coincided with an "achievement gap" of historical proportions.

In our work as teacher educators over the years, we have carefully watched and listened as pre-service and practicing teachers struggled with their own understandings of diversity — and consciousness of their own racial, ethnic and class identities and how these identities affect their teaching. While white students are often confronting these identities seriously for the first time when they reach our classroom, this is work that all teachers need to do in order to reach their students effectively.

With few exceptions, the process of becoming competent in multicultural discourse is advanced by an initial event or "encounter" that challenges individuals to reconsider their beliefs and attitudes. The encounter, according to Gay, is "an experience or event that shatters a person's current feelings. . . It may be real or vicarious, personal or social, verbal or visual." The design and provision of such encounters is a decisive component of our diversity work.

While some of the most powerful encounter experiences involve immersion in a different culture, these experiences are not always available or accessible. Because of this, we have worked to identify encounter experiences that can occur within the walls of university classrooms or schools—and have found that many of these encounters can elicit similar outcomes.

The Teaching Diverse Students Initiative (TDSi), now available at www.tolerance.org/tdsi, includes a number of resources to help create an encounter experience. The section on "Understanding the Influence of Race" includes tools to help teachers examine their own biases and think critically about what "race" really means.

Another encounter experience that we use can be found at the website for the Public Broadcasting Service television series "Race: the Power of an Illusion." The "Sorting People" exercise asks participants to categorize individuals into racial/ethnic groups based solely on their visual appearance. Participants' error scores ease the transition into a dialogue about race as a social construct. The website provides support materials and other experiences to help students further explore this content.

We have also used more traditional means to provide opportunities for teachers to examine beliefs, attitudes and biases. One of the most powerful readings for our predominantly white, female students is Peggy McIntosh's 1999 article, *White Privilege: Unpacking the Invisible Knapsack.* Most of these students are unaware of the privileges they receive just by being born white in the United States and are startled to read this article. We often accompany it with another article, *White Privilege in Schools,* by Ruth Anne Olson (1999). These two articles examine racism on a systemic level and challenge students to consider the perpetuation of injustice on a larger, more daunting scale.

The experiences presented above encourage reflection in novel ways. We have found that individuals exhibit a range of responses when confronted with the potential of personal bias, and that these responses present important scaffolding opportunities for teacher educators. In the following sections, typical responses are detailed, along with strategies to facilitate processing and further engagement.

Dismissal

"None of this is true; the author obviously has a political agenda."

When individuals are presented with information or experiences that challenge their beliefs, one possible response is to reject the source. Taking the stance that "it's simply not true" can end the conversation quickly. This can be a convenient strategy to avoid the potentially painful process of reflecting on hidden bias.

One of the least effective strategies we have found in addressing this response is trying to convince the individual of the accuracy of the source. Approaching bias in a "hard sell" fashion is rarely palatable, and resistance will likely increase.

By allowing individuals time to explore a variety of information on bias and listen as peers discuss the issues, we can provide a cooling-off period. Afterward, individuals may be more inclined to consider the potential of personal bias. We can then employ many of the strategies listed below.

Disbelief

> *"I don't think that I can really be biased. I grew up in a diverse neighborhood, and I have a lot of friends who are African American." or "I didn't grow up privileged. My family didn't have a lot of money, and we worked for everything we got."*

An equally common response is the disbelief that individuals experience when they encounter information that is incompatible with how they perceive their beliefs and practices. Teachers view themselves as "good" and "fair" people, and they are skeptical about being biased. They are typically eager to cling to the comfort of their perceived neutrality on such issues, which again can provide a roadblock to productive dialogue and reflection.

To address this response, we encourage teachers to consider how they were socialized as children. Many are quick to report that individuals in their family had racist attitudes, which they actively reject, but which may have played a part in the associations that are part of their subconscious. At this point, we share excerpts from films such as *Mickey Mouse Monopoly* (Sun, 2001), which examines how the "other" is portrayed in Disney films. In addition, we show the short documentary *A Girl Like Me* (Davis, 2006), where young African American girls recount their issues with race, and repeat the historic experiment asking children to choose the doll they want for a friend. As teachers watch young African American children consistently select the white doll, their eyes are opened to considering how such associations develop for children at a very young age. These experiences elicit rich dialogue about how associations may develop under our radar and, when unchallenged, potentially become ingrained.

Acceptance

> *"It makes sense to me that I am biased, because I am white and I grew up only around white people." or "I do think I have received privileges because of being white, but that is how things are. There's nothing I can do about it."*

When teachers read articles about white privilege, we find that many accept bias and privilege as realities in their lives. While individuals express regret, they indicate that they are not surprised, having relatively little exposure to diversity as a child, and working in a homogenous, majority setting. This line of reasoning rationalizes their bias and sense of privilege. They see bias and privilege as societal issues, rather than personal ones, and this allows them to avoid taking responsibility for their attitudes and biases.

The teachers with whom we work accept the societal factors that have contributed to bias but don't see their inaction as contributing to the problem. At this point, we use readings from Tatum's (2003) book, which provides the example of the moving sidewalk at the airport as analogous to racism in America. Her metaphor—of standing still while the walkway moves forward—shows how failure to challenge prevalent systems can unintentionally perpetuate injustice. This visual illustration effectively resonates with teachers as they consider their prior acceptance as problematic.

Discomfort

> *"Much of this is surprising to me as well as embarrassing. I am mortified by the fact that I have taken issues of privilege for granted that people of color struggle with on a daily basis." or "I have always been proud of being color blind and treating people fairly ... now I'm wondering if I was being unfair."*

Discomfort is another common reaction to becoming aware of bias. Teachers are frequently distressed by what this might mean for their life and work. In this case, we usually reassure teachers that the first step to addressing their biases is to acknowledge them. We note that everyone has hidden biases, but that these are most dangerous when they are unrecognized. One of the resources that we refer to is the movie, *Crash*, which shows the devastating effects of overt and hidden bias.

Discomfort can manifest itself in other ways as well. Some teachers with whom we work frequently hold great pride in their pronouncement of being actively "color bind" when it comes to their students. They view this as an expression of their lack of bias, and it can be difficult to readjust this thinking. A powerful reading that we provide at this point is *I Don't Think of You as Black*, a series of written correspondences between Naomi Tutu and her friend, Rose Bator. This reading helps teachers recognize the impact that race has in all our lives, but particularly for people of color in the United States.

When teachers express discomfort, we encourage them to explore ways to take action to combat stereotyping and discrimination. We suggest examining materials in classrooms for racism and sexism, addressing and eliminating racist language, and examining school policies and practices that discriminate against particular groups of students. We encourage teachers to incorporate diversity into their classrooms in authentic ways in order to combat societal bias. Derman Sparks, Ramsey and Edwards provide teachers with some concrete strategies to begin to address such issues, even in environments where little diversity exists.

Disclosure

> *"Everything I am experiencing shows me that I have strong preference for African American individuals. I interpret this as a distrust of white people, which is unfortunately true."*

A less common response is when individuals actually disclose a conscious bias. This differs from the *acceptance* response, where an acknowledgment of a hidden bias is recognized. This response is characterized by an open admission of prejudice— a step beyond acceptance. This confession requires a great deal of honesty and courage and can be disquieting to divulge.

Although there is the potential for this response to elicit alarm, our experiences indicate a level of self-awareness that differentiates these respondents from others. Individuals who disclose personal bias frequently express how hard they work to intentionally focus on others' abilities, without regard to race. Their consciousness of prejudice guides their active attention to guard against a translation of attitude to practice. They generally recognize the historical and contemporary roots of their prejudice, and they frequently articulate anger toward a society that perpetuates racism.

We find it critical to actively support teachers who have made this proclamation. The consequences of slavery and colonialism are decidedly visible in our society, and individuals' experiences with racism are real and must be validated. As individuals confront the realities of racism, their awareness is critical in making conscious decisions about themselves, others and their role in affecting change.

Conclusion

As teacher educators, we continue to challenge ourselves to provide varied opportunities for teachers as they engage in the exploration of education for social justice. This work is not achieved without challenge. As we present pre-service and practicing teachers with new ideology and experience, we also must acknowledge ourselves as cultural beings continuously encountering and interpreting ideas and interactions. This process of continuous mindfulness and self-examination seats us as co-learners, with each discourse providing opportunity for illumination.

We find it important to remind ourselves, and the teachers with whom we work, that the process of addressing personal bias isn't about reaching a destination. According to B.J. Cahill and E.M. Adams, "No one ever arrives; they just bring more of themselves through each time." As we open our heads and hearts to new understandings through the invitation of persistent experience and inquiry, we embrace the journey.

Critical Thinking

1. How were you socialized with and about different cultures as a child?

2. How were you taught with and about different cultures in school?

3. How were you taught with and about different cultures in your teacher preparation program?

4. Why is it essential for teachers and candidates like you to examine your attitudes about race and privilege?

Create Central

www.mhhe.com/createcentral

Internet References

Center for Social Justice
http://csj.georgetown.edu
Urban Education Institute
http://uei.uchicago.edu

Dr. **Pat Clark** is an Associate Professor of Early Childhood Education in the Department of Elementary Education at Ball State University in Muncie, IN. Pat teaches undergraduate and graduate courses in diversity and early childhood education.

Dr. **Eva Zygmunt** is an associate professor of early childhood education in the Department of Elementary Education at Ball State University. Eva teaches courses at the undergraduate and graduate levels in multicultural education, family and community relations, and creativity.

Article   Prepared by: Nancy P. Gallavan, *University of Central Arkansas*

Cultivating an Understanding of Privilege among Teacher Candidates

JUDITH S. KAUFMAN AND S. MAXWELL HINES

Learning Outcomes

After reading this article, you will be able to:

- Experience the 2003 PBS documentary, *Race: The Power of an Illusion.*

- Apply the data found on the Institute of Government and Public Affairs to better understand the current status in the United States.

The development of Long Island has been long and storied. Although mostly rural farmland prior to World War II, returning GIs and New York City dwellers fleeing the rising cost of living as well as ethnic changes in the urban landscape migrated to Long Island in droves. The two counties that comprise Long Island, Nassau and Suffolk, were settled as a hodgepodge of little hamlets whose legacy has remained in the suburbia that it is today. In 1930, the population of Long Island was approximately 450,000 people, of whom 97% described themselves as White (Singer & Hines, 2001). In 2008, the population of Long Island had swelled to over 2.86 million people, of whom 81% described themselves as White (U.S. Census Bureau, 2008). These numbers suggest that Long Island communities have experienced a significant amount of integration but that could not be farther from the truth. The influx of people of color into Long Island in the late twentieth century was fraught with legal wrangling over redistricting of county and township legislative bodies, the pattern of property tax assessment, real estate and banking practices, and inequities in school funding based on local resources (Singer & Hines, 2001). Even under the scrutiny of the courts, Nassau and Suffolk county legislators and business interests have resisted change to the suburban political, economic and social environment they have created. During the last decade, Long Island communities consistently rank within the top five most segregated areas in the United States (Frey & Meyers, 2005).

This segregation is further indicated by the 126 separate school districts that operate within a two-county radius. According to census projections, with an influx of new Asian and Latino families, in the next decades Long Island will become even more ethnically diverse (Holmes, 1996; Evans, & Moritsugu, 1999, Long Island Index, 2008). It is also predicted that the 21st century will see a sharp decline in the number of ethnic minority teachers while the number of ethnic minority students will steadily increase (AACTE, 1999, Villegas & Davis, 2008). This eventuality necessitates that teacher preparation programs prepare teachers and teacher candidates to teach students who very likely have had a very different life experience than that of their teachers. Gay (2002) contends that the failure to prepare teachers to be culturally responsive to all students results in cross-cultural misunderstanding of behavioral norms. Such teachers also experience difficulty in constructing curriculum and instruction that is congruent with students' life experiences (Irvine, 2001; Ladson-Billings, 1995), and are often unable to bridge home–school differences (Gay, 1993; Goodwin, 2000). The consequences are the continued reproduction of underachievement, academic failure, and significantly lower high school graduation rates (Cochran-Smith, 2003; Rao, 2005; Sleeter, 2008).

The teacher candidates studied in this program are enrolled in a teacher preparation program that emphasizes social justice in its mission statement, weaves issues of diversity and social justice throughout its curricula, and provides out-of-class opportunities for developing diversity sensitive dispositions (Hines, Murphy, Penzone, Singer, & Stacki, 2003). Despite this though, we know that many of our White teacher education students lack consciousness with regard to their own "racial positioning" (Bell, 2002) in a society stratified by race. Our students grew up on segregated Long Island, and though they may be convinced of the need for culturally responsive teaching, it will be nearly impossible for them to move beyond a holidays and heroes approach to multicultural education if they cannot come to grips with their own privilege. Episode 3, 'The House We Live In,' from the Public Broadcasting System's documentary, Race: The Power of an Illusion (Adelmman, 2003), seemed perfect for challenging our White students to think more deeply about their own privilege. It details the history of two local communities, one Black and one White, each situated within two miles of the University and very familiar to our students. The White community benefited from federal policies that guaranteed loans to returning White GIs after WWII. The Black community, a formerly White community that became integrated after the 1964 civil rights legislation was passed, was devastated by block busting that depressed the value of real estate. The comparison between the two communities highlights how differences in accumulated wealth are directly attributed to the value of one's home. These differences in turn stem from racist federal housing policies, such as redlining, which denied federal loan guarantees to any community with a significant population of people of color. Not only does this film recount the history of the development of the concept of race in the United States, it details how societal institutions constructed the concept of Whiteness and how the privilege associated with Whiteness is compounded over generations institutionally. The presentation of facts is both arresting and riveting and challenges viewers to examine the truth about one's ability to pull oneself up by the bootstraps. We thought the film would be even more powerful and challenging for our students because it directly addresses the communities they grew up in and the differences in wealth between those communities.

Research in learning and cognition has established what is by now a truism, that ideas, concepts, and skills that are linked to and build on a learner's knowledge and experience are learned far more effectively than isolated concepts and ideas (Bransford, Brown, & Cocking, 1999). Community is directly implicated in this idea of connection, such that when a learner sees the relevance of an idea or understands that the idea has a legitimate connection to their community, the learning is seamless. In this sense, learning does not occur in a vacuum, rather effective learning occurs as individuals participate in contexts rich with connections to what they know and to their communities. (Lave & Wenger, 1991; Rogoff, 2003).

This idea has found its way into the research literature on the impact of multicultural education curricula on teacher candidates. Sleeter (2001) did an extensive review of this work and one of the more prominent findings is that "coursework may be most successful when it builds on life experience" (218). In one of the studies she cites (Guillaume, Zuniga-Hill, & Yee, 1998), the experiences referred to were multicultural life experiences. Garmon (2004) reaches a similar conclusion in a case study of Leslie P., a 22 year-old White woman. This study extended conclusions from an earlier study (Garmon, 1998) where he found that students who were open to new ideas, self-aware and self-reflective were positively influenced by multicultural courses. Students who did not display those characteristics appeared to be unchanged. In the case of Leslie P., Garmon found what he called dispositional and experiential factors in Leslie's history that would account for her "positive multicultural development." He confirmed his earlier findings of openness and self-awareness/self-reflectiveness, and a third factor of commitment to social justice. The experiential factors were intercultural experiences, support group experiences, and her educational experiences. We would argue with Garmon's separation of disposition from experience because dispositions can come out of experience. Leslie refers to experiences in her upbringing that led to her openness. Causey, Thomas and Armento (2000), in a three-year follow-up found that one White teacher maintained a commitment to social justice and diversity, while a second White teacher's concern for equity dissipated. The authors speculate that the former teacher's "disposition for thoughtfulness and reflection" (p. 43) might account for her continued commitment to diversity in her teaching.

Pohan (1996) administered personal and professional belief scales (Pohan, 1994) to 492 education students from four universities across the United States and found that those who had more cross-cultural experiences tended to have more favorable beliefs about learners from different ethnic groups. Smith, Moallem, and Sherrill (1997), analyzed students' autobiographical narratives and found that those who reported they were taught discrimination growing up, but "changed their beliefs toward greater equality" (p. 54) attributed those changes to four factors; exposure to individuals from different cultures, travel, education and personal experiences with discrimination. Similarly, Smith (2000) speculates, based on a case study of two student teachers that prior experience with diversity may account for effective multicultural teaching.

Haberman (1988, 1995) has long argued that we should only recruit and select those teacher candidates who have the experiences and dispositions that will enable them to succeed in culturally diverse schools. He identified seven attributes in successful teachers and developed an interview based on those attributes. He was able to predict who would succeed based on the results of his interview (Haberman, 1988).

Returning to the idea that we learn more effectively by building on our experience or knowledge and findings from the multicultural literature, it would appear that prior experience needs to be almost isomorphic to the demands of a new learning context, i.e., your prior experience must prepare you for multicultural awareness and sensitivity for you to effectively learn from current experiences and coursework focused on multiculturalism. From a learning theory perspective, those are the optimal conditions for transfer of knowledge to a new context. But what if the prior experience or knowledge is local and very familiar, but rarely considered in critical ways? What happens when you subject the familiar to critical analysis? In this study, we have tweaked the idea of building on what you know because we have essentially asked our students to make the familiar strange. Episode 3 of *Race: The Power of an Illusion . . .* challenges viewers to interrogate what they know and potentially build on and alter their knowledge base.

Methods

One hundred and thirty-three teacher candidates from three graduate sections of adolescent development, one graduate section of reflective classroom analysis, and two undergraduate sections of reflective classroom analysis viewed Episode 3, 'The House We Live In,' from the Public Broadcasting System's documentary, *Race: The Power of an Illusion* (California Newsreel, 2003).

After viewing the local history segment, the teacher candidates were asked to 'free write' their impressions anonymously, without any additional prompting. The results of those 'free writes' were analyzed qualitatively using an iterative method for reducing the data (Huberman & Miles, 1994). Initial patterns or themes focused on emotional responses to the film, such as moved, interested and informed. These categories proved too unwieldy and difficult to validate. Ultimately, the data reduced neatly to four categories; students who personally identified with the film by relating their own experiences growing up in segregated communities in the area, students who responded to the film's prominent illustration of institutional racism but did not relate personal experiences, students who wrote general responses to racism, but did not include any response to institutional racism, and three student responses that we categorized as non-responses. We did not find substantive differences between the undergraduate and the graduate responses. The graduate students were a bit more sophisticated in their responses and a bit more articulate, but overall there were no differences.

Results: Personal Identification

Fifty-two students or 39% personally identified with aspects of the documentary in their free writes. Some were not surprised by what they saw and related similar experiences of segregation and racism in the communities they grew up in on Long Island. Others were aware of the segregation, but the film gave them an understanding of how government policies laid the groundwork for the segregation they grew up with. A few students responded to their privilege and how they benefited from racist housing practices.

Some of the students were not surprised by what they saw in the film, because as one said, "I am living it." Another student who grew up in Levittown said, "Sometimes I want to hide it for fear of seeming a bigot." Others reflected on the all-White neighborhoods they grew up in and the racism of their parents. Some described how their parents moved out of a neighborhood because Blacks were moving in. Another student observed that "living in the Uniondale area [a segregated community on Long Island] for the last 8 years has taught me more about racial division than I ever would have learned had I stayed in rural Maryland."

Many more of the students remarked on a new awareness and reflected on what they understood about growing up on Long Island. The film explained the how and why of segregation and how the government engineered that segregation. The film also explained the stereotypes they grew up with. A student recalled a friend saying to her, "I can't believe the Westbury jewelry store robber was White." Another said, "I began to think to myself all the stereotypes that me and my friends have about the different neighborhoods . . . this is something that comes out of a segregated Long Island." Others expressed that they now understood why there is such a divide between Roosevelt and Levittown. A student who acknowledged in her free write she was Black said, "I knew that racism still existed, but I never realized how pronounced it really was." She was especially surprised at the enormous amount of racism left over from the 50's on Long Island and felt that racism " . . . is only now really making sense to me." A student who described working in Roosevelt for years observed that he had a new perspective and understanding on why the community has suffered.

A few of the students related the film to their school placements in communities of color. They described having to deal with their own feelings about being placed in areas that their friends and families labeled as "bad" or "dangerous." Another student thought he understood why some "minority students think 'what's the point?' in doing well in school since they can't advance anyway, which is so unfortunate."

In a slightly different way of personally identifying, a student was prompted to think about his relationship with a friend who is "half Jewish and half Chinese." The student noted that, "he always took the conservative side when they discussed America's stance toward minorities." The video opened his eyes and so "Nat and I have to have a long conversation when he returns from Taiwan."

Many of the free writes included reference to remarks made by a Levittown resident who observed, "we had the golden chance after World War II, and we flubbed it. Because, uh, here, here we had a GI Bill, that was, uh, uh, supposed to, you know—that was available to everybody; but in a way they didn't make it available to everybody and, uh, and that was a golden opportunity in this country, and we missed it. We really missed it." (from Race: The Power of an Illusion). The student posed the question "what if they didn't segregate Levittown?" and wondered if Long Island could have been an entirely different place. Other students expressed feelings of helplessness and thought that little could ever change on Long Island.

Unearned wealth as a result of government policies and subsidies is a focal point in this segment of the documentary, but interestingly, only 11 students responded directly and referenced their Whiteness and middle class status. One student wrote, "Personally, just being a White male has put me at such an advantage in so many ways." Another said, "[It is] almost embarrassing to think of how much opportunity has been and still is available to me because of my skin color." Yet another student said, "I have always heard of the privilege of growing up in America as a White (usually male). I was never (or I never took the time to really consider what that meant." One student who denied his/her privilege said, "Part of me saw the truth" but I still believe that we make our own choices."

Results: Institutional Racism

Fifty-three students (40%) responded directly to the ideas concerning institutional racism in the documentary. None of these students personally identified with the film, but their responses were very similar to those of the students above. They responded with shock, dismay and outrage. Some expressed hope that things would improve, and some expressed a sense of hopelessness. A few of the students were very familiar with the ideas in the film ("This is not new, but the material never loses its acid."), and many admitted to learning about much of it for the first time. Some reflected on the extent of their naiveté after viewing the film. Similar to one response in the previous category, a student expressed a meritocratic view and disagreed with "blaming the country for these problems . . . everyone has choices."

Several of the free writes focused on race as a construct. A student paraphrased an idea in the film that "physical differences don't make race, rather it is the laws and practices that affect chances and opportunities based on those differences." Many students were shocked by Supreme Court rulings in the 1920s that based citizenship on race and classification as "White."

Another group of comments focused on Levittown and general issues of housing and discrimination. Again, though, none of the students related their comments to their own experiences. One student expressed disbelief about Levittown. Another said, "I can't believe that . . . that this one aspect of life (buying a home) drastically altered our society and views on race." Another student expressed her lack of knowledge concerning the housing issue and said, "I knew that minorities occupied lower social strata, but never knew why. Commenting on the Whiteness and sterility of Levittown, a student observed, "It is easy to ignore the true raw facts when it comes to inequality. When people surround themselves with people of the same race and economic standing, it indeed creates a false sense of reality." Some of the students were unaware of the link between property worth and racial division. Another was surprised that discrimination was legal into the 1960s.

Some general reactions to the government's role in reproducing inequality included the idea that "the government played a big part in creating the poverty they claim they want to resolve . . . they extended racism instead of combating these attitudes." A student wrote, "We were all created equal and the government does not have the right to deny that fact or discourage that idea to anyone." Power relations are expressed in the following: " . . . even in a post civil rights America, economic policy becomes a covert avenue to uphold "the safeguarding" of White America from minorities." Other students reiterated the ideas in the film concerning unearned wealth.

Some of the students expressed dismay. One wrote, [It's] exhausting to learn about the struggles of minorities . . . seems like almost nothing they can do . . . my idealistic view of the world is shattered." Another student said, "What saddens me is that Blacks have been a part of this country since its birth and White immigrants were accepted long before Blacks will ever be . . . this movie is shocking and painful." One student observed, "Economic segregation evolved out of racism, which then evolved into a basis for racism. . . . Is it too late? Can we reverse the process?" Other students did not think progress could be made. One observed that racism is hidden and seems more pernicious. "If they don't see it happening, how are they supposed to know what to fix? It is one of those things that has to hit you over the head to take note of it." Once again students focused on the Levittown resident who observed in the film that the government had "missed the boat" in effectively excluding Black soldiers from using the G.I. bill to buy housing. Several students thought inequality and racism would be "a thing of the past," if the government had not "missed the boat."

Many students linked their comments on the film to teaching, and expressed hope that they can impact the views of their students on race. Referring to poor students of color, comments were focused on helping students "realize that school is the key to having a better life," and on making sure that "as a teacher that students are treated fairly."

Parallel to the first category above on personal identification, eight students in this category referenced White privilege in their free writes. One student observed, "Opportunities afforded to Whites are still in full force." Another discussed subsidies for White homeowners and divestment for Black homeowners. A student wrote that the film put things into perspective and wondered, "What does it mean to be White?" Another observed, "even if a White person is not racist, they were still receiving the benefits of racism." Begging the question on whether the film stimulated guilt, a student wrote, "The film doesn't make me feel bad about being White, because if I had the choice I would change suburbia to be integrated, and I know I have done my best to make things better, even though it may only effect a small amount of people." Finally, a student wrote, "Through oppression of non-White races, we have in a sense made them become what we ignorantly thought they were."

General Response to the Film

In this category of responses, 24 students or 18% of the sample did not personally identify with the film or include any response to institutionalized racism in their free writes. The comments either generally addressed the idea of racism and or they referred to racism on an individual level. One student wrote, "[I am] extremely agitated by the ignorance of the general attitude of White people towards all other races." Another student said, "We as a society need to work on ourselves and each other." More general comments included, "Neighborhoods are still segregated, prejudice and racism still exist." A student thought we should be able to learn from cultural differences, but "the prejudice of our forefathers has been carried through the generations." One student expressed shame that "we have not made much of a dent on equality in society." Another was disturbed by the film, but still felt we have come a long way."

Responses related to teaching were focused on teachers really needing to understand the concept of race. A student wrote about how important it is to understand their students' backgrounds. Others wrote about inspiring the next generation to move past racism and they underlined the importance of multiculturalism in the classroom.

Three students, or 2% of the sample, were bored by the film, did not understand the film as is evident in their comment "in the suburbs, especially, there is much less of a segregation issue," and finally, critiqued the film because it did not account for suburbs that "are not segregated."

Discussion

When we teach about issues of race in our methods and theory classes, we often find that White students resist talking about race, particularly with students of color; they believe that the country is increasingly less racist, and they deny benefiting from the impact of racism, but recognize that it impacts other people's lives. Additionally, when asked to consider why children of color experience disadvantage in schools, they resort to deficit thinking and locate the problem in language and cultural mismatches. They neither consider nor appear to understand how the larger system is implicated and reproduces inequality. Their power and privilege remains invisible (McIntosh, 1989). However, after viewing this film almost 80% of our students came away with an understanding of racism at an institutional level and half of those were able to relate personal experiences relevant to institutional racism. Additionally, 14% of the students directly addressed their own privilege.

Unsurprisingly, students expressed surprise, naiveté, and disbelief in their responses; we did not reach all the students. Some held on to their meritocratic views and thus denying their own privilege observed that "everyone has choices." A few others, also avoiding discussion of their privilege, distanced themselves from the film; "seems like almost nothing they can do" and expressing the idea that if racism is hidden, "how are they supposed to know how to fix it?" And, as noted above, three students provided what we called non-responses to the film. What we did find surprising was that so few of the students responded to the film's focus that was unearned wealth as a result of government policy and subsidy and made the rather obvious connection to their own experiences growing up in Long Island. It is quite possible that students focused on other aspects of the film. The first 26 minutes of this 55-minute episode are devoted to the history of the concept of race and how it played out in the wave of immigration spanning the end of the 19th and beginning of the 20th centuries. It also captures how race played out in the courts, culminating in the 1922 Supreme Court decisions declaring that Mongolians are not White and South Asians are not Caucasian and thus cannot become U.S. citizens. The remaining 29 minutes are devoted to tracking the idea of unearned wealth through home ownership. It is quite possible that the film made the familiar too strange and because the concepts were so new, students were unable to accommodate the ideas despite the fact that they were contextualized "in their own backyards." It is also possible that they lost track of the dense detail in the film that tracks the notion of unearned wealth from the new deal legislation spawning FHA, redlining, the GI Bill, the 1964 Civil Rights Act, and blockbusting. Additionally, some of the students focused their free-writes on the first half of the film and thus found the discussion of unearned wealth less compelling. Finally, it may have been just too difficult for the students to grapple with compelling evidence that they have personally benefited from institutional racism. Much of this emerged in our later class discussions of the film and much of our speculation suggests directions and activities for further class work. For example, students might be engaged in researching home ownership in their own families and the transfer or not of wealth from generation to generation.

It is quite possible that the preparation of White teachers will become even more challenging in the wake of Barack Obama's election as the 44th president of the United States. Belief in a post-racial America may prevail. Views among White preservice teachers, that racism is no longer a problem, that we do not need to interrogate race or learn how to talk about racism, may become even more entrenched. In this context, we think *Race: The Power of an Illusion*, may take on even more value for its currency. The film is not a panacea, but if utilized as a pedagogical tool in what Sleeter (2008) calls a "coherently-planned teacher education program that explicitly addresses issues and concerns of White preservice teachers" (p. 572), we believe it can help White students move beyond their interpersonal notions of racism to an understanding of institutional racism.

With regard to our own students, we are unsure how long an understanding of institutional racism will stay with them, but at least temporarily they have moved to a new place. We attribute this shift in thinking to learning about institutional racism in the context of their own communities. This last assumption requires further study, perhaps a comparison with students who did not grow up on Long Island.

With regard to implications, this film can be shown to students who grew up in any suburban tract across the U.S. subsidized by the G.I. Bill. So, for example, if a teacher educator was preparing teachers in Peoria, he or she would need to do a bit of research (or engage students in this research) on the suburbs in and around Peoria to contextualize the ideas in the film.

References

Adelman, L. (2003). Race: The power of an illusion [DVD]. (Available from California Newsreel, 500 Third Street, Suite 505, San Francisco, CA 94107).

American Association of Colleges for Teacher Education. (1999). Teacher education pipeline IV: Schools, colleges, and departments of education enrollments by race, ethnicity, and gender. Washington, DC: ERIC Document Reproduction Service ED 432571.

Bell, L.A. (2002). Sincere fictions: The pedagogical challenges of preparing White teachers for multicultural classrooms. *Equity and Excellence*, 35(3):236–244.

Bransford, J.D., Brown, A.L., & Cocking, R.R. Eds. (1999). *How people learn: Brain, mind, experience, and school*. Washington, DC: National Academy Press.

Causey, V.E., Thomas, C.D., & Armento, B.J. (2000). Cultural diversity is basically a foreign term to me: The challenges of diversity for preservice teacher education. *Teaching and Teacher Education*, 16:33–45.

Cochran-Smith, M. (2003). The multiple meanings of multicultural teacher education. *Teacher Education Quarterly*, 30(2):7–26.

Evans, M. & Moritsugu, K. (1999, January 3). Long Island: Our future: The faces of tomorrow. *Newsday*, H16.

Frey, W.H. & Meyers, D. (2005, April). *Racial segregation in U. S. metropolitan areas and cities 1990–2000: Patterns, trends and explanations*. Report 05-579, Population Studies Center, University of Michigan Center for Social Research, Ann Arbor, Michigan.

Garmon, M.A. (1998, April). *Preservice teachers' learning about diversity: The influence of their existing racial attitudes and beliefs*. Paper presented at the Annual Meeting of the Mid-Western Educational Research Association, Chicago.

———. (2004). Changing preservice teachers' attitudes/beliefs about diversity: What are the critical factors. *Journal of Teacher Education*, 55(3):201–213.

Gay, G. (1993). Building cultural bridges. *Education & Urban Society*, 25(3):285–299.

———. (2002). Culturally responsive teaching in special education for ethnically diverse students: Setting the stage. *Qualitative Studies in Education*, 15(6):613–629.

Goodwin, A.L. (2000). Teachers as multicultural agents in schools. In R. Carter (Ed.), *Addressing cultural issues in organizations: Beyond the corporate context*, pp. 104–114. Thousand Oaks, CA: Sage.

Guillaume, A., Zuniga-Hill, C., & Yee, I. (1998). What difference does preparation make? In M.E. Dilworth (Ed.), *Being responsive to cultural differences*, pp. 143–159. Thousand Oaks, CA: Corwin Press.

Haberman, M. (1988). Proposals for recruiting minority teachers: Promising practices and attractive detours. *Journal of Teacher Education*, 39(4):38–44.

_____. (1995). Star teachers of children in poverty. West Lafayette, IN: Kappa Delta Pi.

Hines, S.M., Murphy, M.O., Penzone, M., Singer, A.J., & Stacki, S.L. (2003). New teachers' network: A university-based support system for educators in urban and suburban "ethnic minority" school districts. *Equity and Excellence in Education*, 76(4):300–307.

Holmes, S. (1996, March 14). Census sees a profound ethnic shift in U.S. *The New York Times*, A8.

Huberman, A.M. & Miles, M.B. (1994). Data management and analysis methods. In N.K. Denzin & Y.S. Lincoln (Eds.), *Handbook of qualitative research*, pp. 428–444. Thousand Oaks, CA: Sage.

Irvine, J.J. (2001). *Caring competent teachers in complex classrooms*. The Charles W. Hunt Memorial Lecture for AACTE. Dallas, Texas.

Ladson-Billings, G. (1995). Toward a theory of culturally relevant pedagogy. *American Educational Research Journal*, 32:465–491.

Lave, J. & Wenger, E. (1993). *Situated learning: Legitimate peripheral participation*. Cambridge: Cambridge University Press.

Long Island Index. (2009). Retrieved May 25, 2009 from, http://www.longislandindex.org/fileadmin/pdf/2009_Index_Files/LIINDEX_2009.pdf

McIntosh, P. (1989). White privilege: Unpacking the invisible knapsack. *Peace and Freedom*, (July/August), 10–12.

Pohan, C.A. (1994). Measuring educators' beliefs about diversity in personal and professional contexts. *American Educational Research Journal*, 38(1): 159–182.

Pohan, C.A. (1996). Preservice teachers' beliefs about diversity: Uncovering factors leading to multicultural responsiveness. *Equity and Excellence in Education*, 29(3):62–69.

Rao, S. (2005). Effective multicultural teacher education programs: Methodological and conceptual issues. *Education*, 126(2):279–291.

Rogoff, B. (2003). *The cultural nature of human development*. New York, NY: Oxford University Press.

Singer, A.J. & Hines, S.M. (2001) *Troubled past, contentious present, problematic future: Race and Long Island schools since World War II*. Hempstead, NY: Long Island Suburban Studies Conference Proceedings, Hofstra University.

Sleeter, C. (2001). Preparing teachers for culturally diverse schools: Research and the overwhelming presence of Whiteness. *Journal of Teacher Education*, 52,:94–106.

_____. (2008). Preparing White teachers for diverse students. In M. Cochran-Smith, S. Feiman-Nemser, D.J. McIntyre, & K.E. Demers (Eds.), *Handbook of research on teacher education:*

Enduring questions in changing contexts, pp. 559–582. New York: Routledge/Taylor & Francis.

Smith, R.W. (2000). The influence of teacher background on the inclusion of multicultural education: A case study of two contrasts. *The Urban Review*, 32(2):155–176.

Smith, R., Moallem, M., & Sherrill, D. (1997). How preservice teachers think about cultural diversity: A closer look at factors which influence their beliefs towards equality. *Educational Foundations*, 11(2):41–61.

Villegas, A.M. & Davis, D.E. (2008). Preparing teachers of color to confront ethnic racial disparities in educational outcomes. In M. Cochran-Smith, S. Feiman-Nemser, & D.J. McIntyre (Eds.), *Handbook of research on teacher education: Enduring questions in changing contexts*, pp. 583–605. NJ:Routledge.

U. S. Census Bureau. (2008). http://factfinder.census.gov/servlet/SAFFPopulation?_event=Search&_name=nassau+county&_state=04000US36&_county=nassau+county&_cityTown=nassau+county&_zip=&_sse=on&_lang=en&pctxt=fph

U.S. Census Bureau. (2008). http://factfinder.census.gov/servlet/SAFFPopulation?_event=Search&_name=suffolk+county&_state=04000US36&_county=suffolk+county&_cityTown=suffolk+county&_zip=&_sse=on&_lang=en&pctxt=fph Accessed June 17, 2009.

Critical Thinking

1. What is your personal attitude about race and privilege in society?

2. What is your professional attitude about race and privilege in schools?

3. What attitudes are the same and/or different?

4. What are your goals for enhancing your attitudes about race and privilege?

Create Central

www.mhhe.com/createcentral

Internet References

Institute of Government and Public Affairs
http://igpa.uillinois.edu/programs/racial-attitudes/brief

Public Broadcasting Service; Race: The Power of an Illusion
www.pbs.org/race/000_General/000_00-Home.htm

JUDITH S. KAUFMAN is Associate Professor in the Department of Curriculum and Teaching at Hofstra University, Long Island, New York. Her scholarly work is in the areas of cognition, human development, and teacher education.

S. MAXWELL HINES is Professor in the Department of Education at Winston-Salem State University in Winston-Salem, North Carolina. Her scholarly work includes multicultural education, the intersection of ethnicity, class, gender, and exceptionality in science teaching and learning.

Article Prepared by: Nancy P. Gallavan, *University of Central Arkansas*

A Case Study of Seven Preservice Teachers' Emerging Philosophy about Multicultural Education

Margaret M. Ferrara, Patricia J. Larke and Jemimah Lea

Learning Outcomes

After reading this article, you will be able to:

- Reflect on ways your philosophy of education continuously evolves throughout your professional development.
- Discuss the various influences that could potentially alter your preconceptions about teaching.

A Case Study of Seven Preservice Teachers' Emerging Philosophy about Multicultural Education

Students enter a teacher education program with a set of preconceptions about teaching formed from their own personal experiences that are often a reflection of the values and practices of a dominant culture (Nieto, 2009; Nieto & Bode, 2007). In today's school environments, these preconceptions may not "fit" because classrooms are and continue to become more diverse (Cho & DeCastro-Ambrosetti, 2006; Davidman & Davidman, 2000). It seems then that educators who come from non-diverse experiences and who have been trained in "the traditional programs" are not prepared to teach in environments of diversity (Grossman, 2003; Author, 1992). Higgins and Moule (2009) note that many of these preservice teachers are being prepared to teach in classrooms that are not part of their personal histories. Van Hook (2002) states that preparing student teachers to meet the challenges of school diversity warrants the development of multicultural education courses and the fusing of multicultural education ideologies in all student teacher course work. Multicultural education brings to the forefront the worth of diversity. Multicultural education cements the foundation stones of a philosophy of education that, in turn, sets the parameters within which the value of diversity thrives

(Banks & Banks, 2009; Grant, 2009; Sleeter & Grant, 1994; Pang, 2005). Likewise, if preservice teachers are ignorant of their biases, the likelihood of them offering an equitable learning environment within their classrooms is low (Alderman, 1999; Parsons, 2005).

A growing body of literature suggests that a strong association between personal life experiences, values, and one's own teaching style is important in enhancing the awareness of diversity issues to preservice teachers (Sleeter, 2001; Gay, 2000). When the aforementioned philosophical perspectives are implemented effectively in student teacher course work, it is probable that cultural sensitivity levels rise to reflect positive attitudes, beliefs, and behaviors toward culturally and economically diverse students (Hernandez, 2000; Ladson-Billings, 2009; Author, 1990). As student teachers develop cultural sensitivity and gain knowledge about human diversity, it is likely that these educators will apply cultural awareness information to ensure that diverse learners are academically successful (Banks & Banks, 2009). Thus, the purpose of this study is to describe how seven future educators developed their philosophy of multicultural education during their teaching education preparation and student teaching experience, More specifically, the study (1) examines preservice teachers' educational philosophical statements on the importance of multicultural education at three benchmarks during their preservice education program, and (2) describes characteristics of preservice teachers' conceptualizations of multicultural education during their preservice multicultural course and their student teaching experience with diverse learners.

Conceptual Framework

Cultural pluralism, a term coined by Horace Kallen 1924, provided the impetus for promoting acceptance and respect for human diversity in the educational system (cited in Golnick

& Chinn, 2008). This theory has three basic principles:(a) people do not choose their ancestry; (b) each ethnic group's culture has something positive to share with the American culture; and, (c) the idea of democracy and equality carries an implicit assumption that although there are differences, people should be viewed as equal (Cushner, McClelland, & Safford, 1992). The ideologies of multicultural education have been formed from this theory. Multicultural education is viewed as a philosophy, that is, a way of thinking; and as a process, that is, a way of doing. Multicultural education (a) augments the pedagogical knowledge base and sharpens a teacher's effectiveness in facilitating the achievement of all the students regardless of their racial-ethnic identity language ability their socioeconomic status, and (b) modifies a teacher's attitudes, values, and beliefs concerning students of color and poverty. According to Mills (1983), multicultural is defined as: a philosophy and a process by which schools demonstrate—in staffing patterns, curriculum, instructional practices and school—community relations acceptance and respect for human diversity as a means of providing all children an equitable quality education in preparation for living in a culturally pluralistic society. It means that an education system must be cognizant of more than the skin colors, backgrounds and religious beliefs of people (Kyles & Olafson, 2008; Alderman, 1999).

The Study

The subjects in this study were seven European American preservice teachers with similar educational preparatory backgrounds from a large university in the Southwest. The sample includes one male and six females who followed the current teacher education program requirements at the university, and received their multicultural education course from the same professor in the same course section during the spring semester. The students were assigned to an elementary school with grades 2–4, or middle school with grades 5–8 in a small urban community with a diverse population that included 30% African Americans, 30% Hispanics, 30% European Americans and 10% Asian and Native Americans.

Assessment of the change in preservice teacher's philosophy of education was taken three times during the teacher preparation experience. Data were obtained from philosophical statements from each of the subjects before each entered the teacher education program. The students responded to the question prompt: "Why do you want to become a teacher?" A second benchmark statement was taken during the time the students were enrolled in a multicultural education course. Each student was administered a Minority Mentorship Project Questionnaire at the beginning and at the end of the intensive five-week course in multicultural education (Author, 1990).

Additional data taken from preservice teachers' written assignments during their multicultural education course and from the thematic units and supporting lesson plans during their student teaching experiences were analyzed for key domains and further sorted into categorical units (Lincoln & Guba, 1985; Lincoln, 2003). Preservice teachers' reflective

logs and supervisor observations during the student teaching experience, as well as pre-and post-interviews with cooperating teachers and building administrators, were also analyzed for descriptive features.

Discussion

Ironically, preservice teachers began their teacher education program from a relatively similar philosophical stance. The preservice teachers were assigned to schools that reflected a high degree of diversity. Emerging changes in the philosophy of education of each preservice teacher became more apparent during their multicultural education course and were reflected in their journal writing during this time. The most significant changes, however, were noted in their journals written during their student teaching experiences. Through these expressed changes in their perceptions of education, one can draw inferences from the teachers in their elementary or middle school teaching assignments.

The following sections contain summaries of some of the major themes that emerged over time as preservice teachers evolved into student teachers and eventually into degreed undergraduates in elementary education. Each preservice/ student teacher/undergraduate teacher is designated by a capital letter to maintain anonymity. The major common themes addressed in this paper are the initial philosophy of education statement; reactions, and sensitivity levels during the multicultural education course; categories related to diversity during the student teaching experience; and the philosophy of education and multicultural education after undergraduate graduation.

The Initial Philosophy of Education
Teacher A

Teacher A attended a small, rural school, was involved in the academic decathlon, vocational programs, 4-H, and highly active in sports. His previous experience with children began with a pre-employment childcare program he took in high school. He enjoyed the first course so much that he decided to take the second year of the course. In college, Teacher A continued to work in a KIDS KLUB in the after school program as a staff person and eventually, as a supervisor at an elementary school site. "Since I was in high school I've known I wanted to be a teacher." Teacher A continues on his student teaching application . . . "I want to become a teacher because I love kids . . . . working with them and watching them learn and grow." He continues that teaching is difficult and frustrating but that he believes that he will be one of those "special teachers" who gives students the tools to build on their natural love of learning.

He requested a science education position with older elementary students. Teacher A was assigned to a seventh grade physical science classroom in an upper middle school. The first day in his journal, Teacher A revealed that he was getting nervous about being a student teacher. The classes that he "loved" had been successful at making people feel relaxed and comfortable around me. I enjoy making them laugh and talk about themselves. I think this is especially important when you work with children." When he first heard about his student teaching assignment, he expressed concern. After he visited the school site, he reported that he was excited about the experience.

Teacher B

Teacher B, on the other hand, wanted to be a teacher because she had several relatives in the teaching profession and they had encouraged her to become a teacher. Her first experience teaching had been in a Vacation Bible School. Since that time, she had taught flag routine to other students in high school. From these experiences, she felt that teaching was a profession where a person has the "opportunity to really make a difference in the lives of others."

Like Teacher A, Teacher B came from a small, rural setting. Her area of academic specialization was mathematics and she had requested lower elementary grades. She had graduated as valedictorian of her class, voted the ideal student, and most versatile in her class. She was assigned to a third-grade, lower-tracked classroom.

Teacher C

When Teacher C entered the teacher education program, she saw the classroom as a place to find challenges, experiences, and opportunities for success in teaching children. She considered herself motivated to meet these challenges. Teaching, she felt, would be an interesting and rewarding experience, one where it would be possible to learn from making mistakes. As a teacher, she anticipated that she would take pride that "her job will help shape the future of our world and our nation by shaping children's learning and giving students the knowledge and skills they would need to become competent, successful adults . . . to make a difference in their lives."

Teacher C requested a lower elementary placement in reading and language arts. She was placed in a seventh grade reading classroom for students with remedial or enrichment needs in reading. In high school she was voted the "wittiest" and felt that this was a special quality to be an effective teacher. I made inferences from their summative essays on the values of education especially in a multicultural setting and the role of the teacher in diverse learning environments.

Teacher D

Teacher D had a similar background to the other student teachers in the study. She graduated second in her class, served as class president for four years, was active in sports, and won several academic scholarships. She also requested a lower elementary classroom with a specialization in reading, Unlike Teacher B, she was assigned to a high tracked fourth grade classroom.

Teacher D also felt that she had much to contribute to the knowledge base of a student. "Children have so much to learn and I want to contribute to their knowledge." Moreover, she writes, "I enjoy watching children learn and being a part of the complex profession called teaching." Before she entered the

teacher education program, Teacher D, like the other preservice teachers, had little teaching experience. She had taught in a Bible School and tutored in an advanced middle school science program.

Teacher E

Teacher E began her reason for becoming a teacher with a common phrase . . . "Coming from a family of relatives in the teaching field, I learned early how important a teaching career was from each one of them . . . my family puts a great deal of work into their job . . . their stories, concerns, and pride . . . told me it was all worth their while." Teacher E further wrote that she always enjoyed children. She had experience helping her younger brother with schoolwork. She writes, "He has learning problems and I enjoyed the challenge of motivating him and helping him read." She concluded that teaching was a job she would enjoy doing and something in which she would be successful. Teacher E moved from a large city when she was in high school to a small rural area when her father lost his job. She had worked during high school in after-school clerical positions in the school district. During her preservice course work she continued to work part-time as a clerk in the university bookstore. She quit her job halfway though her student teaching experience. She requested a primary classroom with a specialization in reading. Her placement was in a remedial third grade classroom.

Teacher F

Teacher F entered the teacher education program because teaching "excited her" and she wanted to help children learn. Before she entered the teacher education program, Teacher F had experienced several "wonderful" teachers whom she felt made an "incredible" difference in her life. She felt that even though teaching would not be easy, she would welcome the challenge. She hoped to use several instructional approaches like "whole language experience" and "holistic thinking" in her classroom. She adds, "I want to see how theory looks when it is put into practice."

Teacher F had previous experience working with younger children. She worked in a Bible school, helped in a preschool program and cared for children since she was in seventh grade. During college, she worked as a waitress part-time in a popular restaurant but continued to do volunteer work in an after school preschool program. She had requested a lower elementary classroom with a specialization in language arts. She was assigned the highest tracked second-grade classroom in the district.

Teacher G

Teacher G stated before she entered the professional program that she would not teach school. She planned on attending graduate school after she completed her bachelor's degree in order to pursue a degree in speech pathology. She chose elementary education because she felt it would be a beneficial experience for her future career. She adds, "I truly love children and always have . . . I enjoy my education classes and am happy in my major."

Like the other student teachers, Teacher G attended high school in a small, rural setting. In school, she had been active in cheerleading, class leadership roles, and the National Honor Society. Her working experiences included clerical work at a law office and the campus library. She felt she had little experience with children. "My teaching experience has only been through the nursery at church." Even though she requested a lower elementary classroom with a specialization in reading, she was placed in a sixth grade lower level tracked classroom.

Overall, it appears that prior to beginning their student teaching experience, none of the teachers had extensive experience teaching, especially working with students of diversity. Their understanding of being an educator was developed from personal models, especially family members who generally had positive teaching experiences All of the teachers gained most of their "know-how" of the classroom and how it operates from their won experiences in small, rural classrooms. While it is uncertain if the teachers had been in tracked programs, it seems that all of them were in the top ten percent of their class academically. It also appears that each of these teachers, as they began their professional program in education, perceive themselves in a contributory role. In other words, they believed that the role of the educator is to provide knowledge to students so they could be successful in the future. The seven teachers also felt that they enjoyed working with children and were anticipating working with them in a teaching–learning environment.

Reactions and Sensitivity During the Multicultural Education Course

The seven students were enrolled in a daily, five-week course along with 14 other preservice teachers. Data collected during this time demonstrated that each of the teachers demonstrated differing degrees of sensitivity development during the course. However, the sensitivity instrument used in the study failed to demonstrate a significant change in sensitivity during their course work. A more revealing source during this time was their journal entries where there were references made to the multicultural education course. Teacher A made one entry about the course. "I feel that I will be learning a lot from the multicultural education class." After this journal entry, Teacher A made no more mention of the multicultural education course. Teacher B referred to the course because she became interested in multicultural literature. She developed a multicultural social studies unit and as part of the process, she sought out books about Japan and Japanese Americans.

The activity made her "more excited" about getting into a classroom where she could share all the books she found with her class. Teacher C did not mention the multicultural course in her journal. She appeared to be more concerned that she had been assigned to do her student teaching in seventh grade reading. She felt that people "made faces" when she told them what grade she was assigned. She also wrote about her concern for effective discipline but concluded, "I'll do fine . . . it will be nice to be out of this hectic school setting and into the classroom."

Teachers D and F probably spent the most time writing in their journals about their multicultural education experiences. Teacher D wrote how she gave an oral report on a holiday called the Carnival and felt that she learned from others in the class about different international holidays. She felt that celebrating international holidays would be great to do in her classroom when she became a teacher. She added, "Kids should become familiar with various cultures and their traditions." The following day, Teacher D had a test in another class. She felt she learned a lot of information that she knew she would forget right after the test. She writes, "I hope that in my future classroom, I will not require my class to have to memorize a lot of facts for a test . . . I want learning to be more fun!" A movie that Teacher D saw the following weekend also impacted her philosophy of multicultural education. She found that the movie seemed to say that existence on earth is minute compared to the larger scheme of life. She disagreed with the movie, and countered that each person needs to make the best of his/her life and do what can be done to make life enjoyable. The movie also brought up issues that Teacher D had not experienced, like the poverty state of low-income of Blacks in L.A. She writes, "A lot of bad things go on out there that I've never had to deal with . . . It feels good to keep up with what is going on because the children in our classes will all have different experiences. We need to try to relate to each one of them."

Teacher E did not appreciate the timing and the placement of the multicultural education course. She began her student teaching semester with two emotional states—fatigue and excitement. She found that course work during this time was "frustrating." Too much material was being crammed into five weeks." She felt that if teachers continued at this pace, she would be "sooo, burnt out." She added, "I'm already tired of hearing multicultural this and that. It's not that I don't think it's important but—four hours a day, five days a week for five weeks is a little much."

Teacher F and G, on the other hand, had high praise. Each preservice teacher's first entries into the journal were highly positive about her multicultural education course. Teacher F found the course interesting because even though she felt she knew the information, it was important for the preservice teachers to be reminded about multicultural education. In her next entry, she describes several multicultural literature books she bought for her future classroom. She found the teacher to be "a highly informative, dynamic person." She found that although she enjoyed "all the time we have with her," she was surprised to discover that many of the students did not agree with the multicultural education teacher. Teacher F concluded, "It proves that I as a teacher may not be able to get through to every student. Sometimes, my opinion will clash with others because my teaching style may conflict with others' learning styles."

Teacher G found the multicultural education enjoyable. She felt that the class got into many interesting classroom discussions about school in general and why some students get a better education than others. She added, "We also have had some classes dealing with prejudice in the class and with parents. She found it interesting to listen to other class members' perspectives on this "touchy" subject. By the end of the course, however, teacher G grew impatient and like teacher E, felt that she had enough schoolwork and was ready to put practical knowledge into action. She added, "We are not exposed to classrooms sufficiently. I never observed a classroom until last semester . . . that is crazy." Preservice teachers, she wrote, are taught how to write units and lesson plans. The real lessons however, she felt should be learned and practiced in the classroom.

In summary, the preservice teachers had mixed feelings about the multicultural education course. Some of the negative reactions might be credited to the time it was scheduled in the preservice student coursework. For some of the preservice teachers, it was impractical to plan in an artificial situation when the realistic situation was less than five weeks away. It also seemed "same-old" knowledge for some of the preservice teachers who had been exposed to multicultural concepts in another college course. Teacher F might have effectively summed up the feeling of many preservice teachers during their five-week multicultural course in a journal entry: "What we (preservice teachers)need is an 'eye-ful' of classroom experiences, not an 'ear-ful' of information on methods and theories."

Emerging Categories Related to Diversity during Student Teaching Experience
First Reactions to the Diverse Learner

None of the preservice teachers had previous experience with students of diversity. The first impressions of the diverse classroom were captured in some of the journal entries. The descriptions suggest that the preservice teachers as a whole were unfamiliar with the appearance, actions, and processing of the students. Sometimes, their apprehensions were reflected in how they perceived students as global learners. Other times, student teachers focused in more on specific characteristics.

Teachers A, C, and F reflected the concerns of inexperienced teachers who look at diverse learners from a global perspective. Teacher A felt that he was not prepared to work in a middle school based on his limited observation experience. Moreover, he was nervous about student teaching because the sixth grade that he observed was "different" from the other elementary program he observed, and teachers were telling him that his upcoming middle school experience would be a challenge. To become better prepared, he found a sixth grader down the street from his home and played basketball with him. After this, Teacher A found more confidence working with middle school students by becoming involved in a Big-Brother program at a local middle school. When he visited the school site and met his cooperating teacher and students, Teacher A felt he became more confident with middle school students. He found there was a wide range of intellectual abilities ranging from "some whiz kids to some very low students."

In like manner, Teacher C, who also taught seventh graders, looked at her students from a teacher–learner perspective.

She found that her cooperating teacher considered students from two perspectives as positive individuals and different learners. Seasoned teachers thought she was "crazy" because she enjoyed the students. She felt that one of her challenges was adapting to learning styles and individual abilities. Teacher F found on her first visit to the school that the class "seemed diverse and exciting." During her student teaching experience, she made several entries into the journal, which reflected her concern for adjusting the instructional pace of the lesson and bringing in a diversity of art materials, multicultural literature, and speakers from the community. Overall, these teachers did not single out students in their classes by their race, ethnicity, socioeconomic level, or intellectual ability.

The other female preservice teachers, on the other hand, brought out these student characteristics in their journal writing. Teacher B found the fifth grade classroom where she would be working as "very diverse." She adds, "The class was pretty much equally divided between African Americans, Whites, and Hispanics." Her cooperating teacher told her the class was the "lowest and most immature" group she had in 20 years of teaching. She added that if Teacher B could teach "these children," she could teach almost anywhere. During her student teaching experience, Teacher B found two African American boys and one African American girl as constant discipline problems. She referred to a small, quiet Hispanic male as her favorite student. The African American students had "bad home lives," "cried easily," and were constantly in trouble.

Teacher D wrote a research paper during the five-week course work on African American children's behaviors in the classroom and concluded that African American children are still being discriminated against in the classroom. She wrote in her journal, "This (situation) has to change." The second week of student teaching, Teacher D wrote about a "multicultural experience." "I had an African American child come up to me and tell me someone called him the [']f'] word. Since I didn't hear this when it happened, there was nothing I could do. I really felt sorry for the student, though." In another classroom incident, one of her fourth grade students told other students in the class that the new girl in the class had been raped. What Teacher D found out was that the story was true and, she did not react to the incident any further. Her next sentence in the journal, . . . "I have a school loan meeting tonight . . . I need to find resources to go to graduate school."

Teacher E found the students "adorable" and added in her journal entry, "they look to be lower SES." In further describing the students, Teacher E found that the second graders in the class were unconcerned about their appearance. "Most of them had ratted windblown hair and all seemed to accept each other." She compared the students to others with whom she had worked in a higher socioeconomic elementary site, a place where "it was obvious that their parents were 'professionals' and the students were a little more spoiled and self-centered." In a follow-up phone call to the school, her cooperating teacher told Teacher E that one of the students had guessed what the student teacher would look like. It seems that when the cooperating teacher told the class they would have a student teacher, one of the students asked if the new teacher would be White or

Black. Another student said, "I'll bet she's White." The teacher reports that when she saw Teacher E, she realized she was right and made sure to remind the cooperating teacher about her accurate prediction. Teacher E concluded the journal entry wondering if the girl was disappointed.

Teacher G received her first "shock" about her students during an introductory phone conversation with her cooperating teacher. It seems that one of the fifth graders brought a condom to school and showed it to her friends. Teacher G was shocked that a fifth grader would have a condom. The student, when brought to the principal's office, explained that the condom belonged to her older (fourteen-year-old) sister. Teacher F adds, "What is happening in our society when fourteen-year-olds are having sex?" She concludes, "That's why I could never teach junior high school."

When Teacher G visited the classroom the first time, a "little Black girl" greeted her at the school building door and showed her to the classroom. Teacher G described the child as "a mess . . . one of her front teeth is cracked in half . . . so prissy and definitely a strong influence in the room." She added, "I hope I can handle her." She described two "little Black boys" as "shy" and slower than the rest of the students. She felt after the visit that the students overall were all lower middle class to poor. Demographically speaking, the classroom was 50% White, 30% Black, and 20% Hispanic. During her student teaching experience, Teacher G found that she was having trouble with the two "shy" Black boys. A "Mexican" boy, a student who just moved to the United States from Mexico during the year, was not a problem. "He just sits there and does nothing . . . except in the afternoon when he goes to ESL." She found that she just wanted to reach out and help him but she felt helpless not knowing his language.

Behavior Management

The common concern for all the student teachers was effective behavior management. During their student teaching experience, the teachers worked in classrooms that used a modified assertive discipline-type program. For some students, this was a minimal concern. Teacher A, for example, found that by the second week, his most difficult class had developed a collaborative spirit. They sang "Friends in Low Places" together at the end of the class period. For the other students, especially the females, the behavior management program seemed difficult to learn and largely inconsistent. Some of the teachers linked misbehavior with students of diversity. The other teachers were more concerned with misbehavior and effective behavior management techniques for the classroom rather than focusing on a particular student.

Teacher B, for example, found that she had three students in particular, all Black students, who had consistent behavior problems. One of the students, Fred, refused to do his work and repeatedly was sent to the office. The other two students got their names on the board because they shouted out in class, talked to other students during instruction, and called other students names. Teacher B also felt that the most disruptive student modeled negative behaviors for other students. For example, when one male student tried to look up a female student's dress,

Teacher B felt that the student was being affected by Fred's behavior. The cooperating teacher used assertive discipline technique, monitoring negative behavior by placing straight pins by the student's name when the student did not follow a direction. When this did not work, the student teacher tried to use another tracking device, two school buses. All the students' names were placed on the "good" school bus. If the student did not follow the rules, he or she was moved to the "bad" school bus. That meant the student did not get to play on the playground that day. If the student followed the rules for the following day, the student could move back to the "good" bus. At the end of the week, all the students on the "good" school bus got popcorn. The first week, the bus idea worked. After that, the same three Black students stayed on the "bad" bus all week. Gradually, it got more "crowded" on the "bad" bus with names of other students. Fred eventually was suspended from school several times. The other Black boy's mother came to school and demanded to see the "real" teacher. After the conference, the mother decided to go to the school board with her complaint. The Black girl was sent to the office several times; eventually, she became very quiet and withdrawn in the classroom.

During the final week of student teaching, Teacher B was confronted with a problem she had never anticipated. One of the students was acting very quiet and, after the students began their group work, she burst into tears. She became highly upset and when she calmed down a little, she told Teacher B that someone came into her room during the night and touched her where he wasn't suppose to. Teacher B took the student to the office to see the counselor (who was not there), and waited until the girl talked to the female assistant principal. The assistant principal contacted someone from child protective services who promised to go home with the girl that afternoon. By the next day, Teacher B found out that the man was a friend of her father's who had been released from prison that week after serving time for molesting children. Teacher B writes that the student seemed better the rest of the day but that "as for me, I was pretty shook up . . . I don't remember being prepared for this situation in my classes . . . I just went by instinct and what little I've heard about dealing with these problems."

Teacher B and the cooperating teacher continued to explore ways to control their students' behaviors. The cooperating teacher contacted parents and got permission to paddle the students. These techniques seemed to settle the students down. By the middle of the following month, the students had settled into a more consistent routine of good behavior. One day the students were able to get all the squares filled in and earned 15 minutes of recess. By the afternoon, however, things returned to normal, that is, too many names on the board, Teacher B writes about this frustration, "I try to stay positive and think that different ideas will work, but so far they only seem to work for a few hours and then the behavior goes back being unacceptable . . . 17 names on the board . . . I'm running out of ideas." Even though Teacher B never felt she found the behavior management plan that worked, she felt in reflection she tried several techniques that worked for a time effectively.

Teacher C wrote in her journal that discipline would be one of her biggest challenges, but she did not "blame" any particular student for the problem. Rather, she credited the misbehavior to adolescent development. "Nature is having its way with the students right now so people should not judge the students so harshly." However, she was also realistic that behavior problems would exist. She added, "Serious problems need to be handled swiftly and surely." By the end of the second week, Teacher C exclaimed in her journal, "I still like my kids!" She found that although she used different behavior management techniques than her cooperating teacher, she found the students responded positively. The most serious problem that Teacher C felt existed was with the class scheduled the last period of the day. Once in her journal, she described them as a "nightmare," a time when she felt "helpless" unless she worked directly with them. Even though she felt frustrated by the class, she also felt she was doing an "okay" job working with them. Another time when seventh period acted out again, she wrote, "I really don't dislike the kids, but I just can't understand why they refuse to cooperate with me." She looked to herself for the solution to their behavior. "I need to get a good grip on several strategies for dealing with them on days like today,"

During her full teaching responsibilities, Teacher C felt that while everything went well, the "discipline was messy" and she did not feel "on" at times. Their behavior escalated later that week and she writes, "I knew the day would be coming. I had no idea how bad it would be." She writes that the problems started in sixth period when she sent her first student ever to the office. Until that time, she had always handled all the discipline problems in the class. When she tried to give a full class period lecture, students continued their "ugly" behavior. When she felt she could no longer tolerate their behavior, she had them put their heads on their desks for 5 minutes. The next day, the students behaved, the class discussion was interesting, and in two of the classes, "students asked higher order questions." From these experiences, Teacher C concludes in her last entry in the journal, "I have really had a positive experience in student teaching and a great experience working with diverse learners. I now have confidence I can handle the challenges I will face in my classroom."

Teacher D also had a global view about behavior management and classroom behavior. After a fairly uneventful start to student teaching, she confronted her first behavior problem. Toward the end of the second week, she writes in the journal about a problem she had with a student classified as hyperactive. The student wrote that she hated Teacher D on a piece of paper. The child was sent to the time-out area in the room for five minutes. When the child returned from the area, she hit two girls with a stick. The cooperating teacher called the student's mother to get permission to paddle the student. When the mother refused permission, the student was assigned two-week cafeteria clean-up duty as punishment. Teacher D credited the next series of behavior problems with the proximity to spring break. During this time, Teacher D treated misbehavior lightly. "It is close to the break and they (the class) are hyper . . . kids are getting worse . . . had discipline problems today but understandable . . . Hurrah for spring break." She also seemed to enjoy students' excuses for their behavior. One student was absent for four days. When she returned, she announced to the class that

she had her appendix taken out the previous day. Another student challenged this statement by telling the student she also had her appendix out and was out of school for two weeks. The returning student countered this statement by saying, "Well, I have to go back today so they (the doctors) can finish."

Teacher D reflected more concern for her teacher's behavior than that of her students. When two students were not paying attention during a lesson, she reported their behavior to her cooperating teacher. However, Teacher D adds, "I don't think she (the cooperating teacher) will do anything about it." For the most part, however, Teacher D remained enthusiastic about the students and maintained a positive outlook on their behavior. "I thoroughly enjoyed today," Teacher D writes in one of her last journal entries. She adds, "I tried a new discipline procedure . . . instead of using the board to record the names of students being bad, I wrote down students' names for being good." By the end of the day, she was able to write every student's name in the class on the board.

Teacher E began her student teaching experience in a stressed condition. She writes, "Today wasn't so good. I left with a real headache. The kids were bad." It seems that when she took the students to the bathroom, one of the students spent 5 minutes in the boy's bathroom. When she went into the bathroom and asked the students to hurry up, he told her did not need to rush because she did not know his real name. Another student told her she could not do anything anyway because she was not a "real" teacher.

Even though Teacher E's cooperating teacher "took care of the misbehaving students, Teacher E was concerned about the incident. She felt her cooperating teacher did not have an effective behavior management system. The cooperating teacher was new to the district and even though she was a veteran elementary teacher, most of her experience had been in a small, rural Midwestern school. She reported to Teacher E that she had not experienced discipline problems like this previously.

Of all the student teachers, Teacher E was the most focused on the behavior management program in the classroom. By the third week, she questioned the worth and effectiveness of the behavior management program in place in the classroom. The students did not seem to respond to rewards and punishment. They had a substitute teacher and acted up all day. By the end of the day, Teacher E wrote, "I'm just so glad the day is over. I don't want to think about or talk about student teaching again until Sunday night."

After this two-day break, Teacher E hypothesized that she needed to relax more and learn more from her time in the classroom. This change in attitude may have helped make a difference in students' behaviors the following days. Teacher E reports the students were calm and cooperative. The next time she confronted student misbehavior, she felt angry and upset with the students but deduced, "I am learning—that's good and I will figure out how to handle these boys without driving myself insane." The more Teacher E focused on the positive, the less she perceived behavior problems. The first few entries in her journal after spring break reflect Teacher E's more positive outlook on her students' behavior. She found that it was easier to ignore a student's negative behavior and to consider students as "kids'" not "robots" and for some of them, she adds, "School is not where they choose to be." By the end of her student teaching experience, Teacher E found that she would be sad to finish her student teaching experience. At first, she writes, "I didn't sit back, enjoy the kids, and enjoy myself I am so glad I have this last week off from teaching so I can really enjoy them." She concludes, "they aren't' really bad—they're just kids."

Teacher F entered student teaching highly enthusiastic about the two units she had previously prepared. She found that the students "tested" her initially and she had to write some of their names on the board. Information from her journal entries and supervising teacher reports during this time, however, appear to suggest that she was unhappy with the district and classroom program. She did not enjoy following the highly structured math program and basal reading series. Even though she felt that the students needed the basics," the programs did not foster a deeper understanding of concepts. She found her teacher to be an effective disciplinarian but highly traditional. Teacher F hoped to use journals in the classroom, have students work in cooperative groups, and write their own books.

Teacher F writes little about student misbehavior. Even though one of the students brought bullets to school, chewed them, and passed them around the classroom, she did not seem to be alarmed in her journal entry. The student was sent to the office and the bullets were confiscated from him. During this time, Teacher F appeared to be more concerned with personal problems—her car breakdowns, her boyfriend break-up, and her sister's admissions to a psychiatric unit. Personal problems appear to have affected her teaching performance. Her formative evaluation report during this time from her supervising teacher and cooperating teacher reflect concern that Teacher E was unprepared for the lesson, delivered a fragmented lesson, and used minimal reinforcement.

As Teacher F worked through her personal problems, she appeared to become more concerned about the behavior management program in the classroom. She set the students into cooperative groups and developed a behavior management program for each group. In the plan, groups would receive points for correct behavior. The teacher would ignore negative behavior. At the end of the week, the groups that have the fewest marks will eat lunch in the classroom with Teacher F and the cooperating teacher. Even though Teacher F never adopted the behavior management program of the classroom entirely, she found that this modified plan was an effective compromise.

Initially, Teacher G found her cooperating teacher "all together" and "nice." After the first week of student teaching, Teacher G was not pleased with the behavior management program in the classroom. She felt that the behavior problems in the class existed because the cooperating teacher had "no" behavior management program. Three students in particular, two Black boys and a Hispanic boy, took advantage of this situation. She also felt un-stimulated by the classroom. "The class, I hate to say, is very boring," she writes. She felt she had too many high expectations from her education classes at college, a place where the settings are ideal. In contrast, in the classroom the teacher uses basal readers in every subject and "everything seems lifeless and mundane . . . no higher order thinking going on."

Teacher G adds, "The teacher uses assertive discipline which I don't like and yet, she does not seem to have control over some of the students, especially the Black boys." Teacher G felt she would not have the same problem because the boys "loved" her.

By the fourth week, Teacher G was having trouble getting the two Black boys (who loved her) to complete their work, stay in their seat, and stop shouting out. She sent them out into the hall, talked to them sternly, and finally, sent them to the office. She writes of her frustration, "Even when I spoke to them firmly in the teachers' lounge, they did not take me seriously. They laughed and talked back." She recounts, "I just wanted to hit all three of them I really don't think they respect me or are scared."

A month into student teaching, Teacher G taught her first lesson—in health. She felt that the lesson went "fine." Students in the classroom, however, continued to misbehave. Teacher G found typically inappropriate behaviors consisted of shout-outs, laughing, shouting, silly remarks, put-down comments, and poor listening. She concluded that she needed to be explicit before she started a lesson, to tell the students "only speak when I call on you." She reports that she felt disappointed that the students were old and mature enough to know this and grew to realize that they did not.

Several times in the journal entries Teacher G wrote that she felt the problem lay with the cooperating teacher. Basically, she felt her cooperating teacher ignored Teacher G's comments and concerns about the classroom. As the behavior problems in the classroom continued, the cooperating teacher told Teacher G to handle them herself. When she felt she "had reached the limit," Teacher G took a student to the principal's office and the principal called his mother. The student, one of the Black boys, told her, "it's ok, call my mother. She wants to talk with you, too." The next week, Teacher G's cooperating teacher disappointed her again. It seems that her cooperating teacher was flirting with another teacher during lunch. She felt that the behavior was plain embarrassing and the individuals were not acting like professionals. During the incident, Teacher G reports she "kept a smile on her face . . . like a good little student teacher."

As time passed in her student teaching experience, the toll of behavior problems and her unhappiness with her classroom placement seemed to be the main message of her journal writing. "The days seem to be getting better . . . I have resorted to becoming a witch." Teacher G found that in order to be an effective teacher, she needed to act this way. However, she felt that it was important to be "extra friendly" in the halls or on the way to lunch. She was excited about her upcoming units on Japan and Mexico. However, she concludes the journal with thoughts for the future, "I am glad we only have six more weeks. I'm ready to go on . . . although I will really miss [the university] and [her sorority]. She also writes, I HATE TEACHING 6TH GRADE AND I'LL NEVER TEACH THIS GRADE AGAIN.

Teacher G ends the journal with . . . "I'm ready for this to be over. I'm sorry, but it's the truth." In her last entry as a student teacher, Teacher G reflects back that she would miss "my" class. She felt that some of the students who had given her the most trouble really did like her. She felt that she had not given the experience a 100% effort and that probably the burnout of school affected how well she did in student teaching. She also felt that she walked into a situation where there had been no established discipline or classroom management. She added that it was difficult to get the situation in order during the short time she was there . . . or as she stated, "I felt like I was beating a dead horse."

Collectively, the student teachers found that their perceptions affected the degree to which they experienced discipline problems. The teachers who looked at discipline in a more global perspective seemed to experience less frequent and less severe discipline problems. Teachers who perceived their placement as inappropriate, attributed discipline problems to external conditions -the cooperating teacher, the ineffective discipline plan imposed by the district. As the teachers looked to internal conditions like "becoming more relaxed with the students," they did not focus as much on a particular student's or the class's behavior problem.

The Philosophy of Education and Multicultural Education after Graduation

A month after the student teachers graduated from school, they were contacted by mail and asked to write their reactions to several open-ended questions: "How do you perceive the role of a teacher . . . of a student in the educational learning process?" "What instructional strategies and curricula materials did you find effective with the diverse learner?" "How important is multicultural education in today's classroom? today's school? today's world?" "What additional insights about teaching have you gained from your student teaching experience?" Most of the students answered the questions by the middle of July. Teacher A and C completed the questions after the second letter was sent.

One reason Teacher A offered for his late response was his "whirlwind" experience with job interviewing. Within a week after he finished student teaching, Teacher A had received four offers for a teaching position. He accepted a middle school position in a setting similar to his student teaching setting. In his philosophical statement about education, Teacher A reports that he found that teaching was a challenge because students were different day-by-day.

These differences made the classroom unpredictable and even with a strong behavior management program, the most effective way he found to make learning meaningful was to work with students in cooperative groups. Even though he had not worked with middle school students previous to his experience, Teacher A found that this setting was highly rewarding and challenging. Teacher A also felt that while multicultural education as a formal course is important, it is more essential for preservice teachers to gain real life experiences in order to be effective with diverse populations. His final words continued

to reflect his positive philosophy about teaching: "I am excited about beginning my teaching in the fall and intend to use the summer to get ready for the challenges that I will face in my classroom."

In a follow-up letter, Teacher B reported that she intended to begin teaching at a junior high school in a small town by her home. Her philosophy of education, however, reflected a growth in her perception of education. She writes "With the current emphasis on the ability of Americans to compete in a global economy and the necessity to deal with many social problems in this country, education is more important than ever." She continues that in a diverse society of learners, in a society where values are no longer being taught in the home, it is the role of education to provide for these challenges and encourage students to set high goals. Teacher B adds that it is the role of teachers to teach real-life skills that are relevant to students' daily lives. It is also important that instructional materials should be used that relate to the experiences that students have had, but also allow students to learn about new ways of life. It is only through gaining respect for their own and other cultures that students will be better able to be successful members of the emerging global village. She adds that it is important that teachers accommodate different learning styles but that these differences need to be accepted but not over-emphasized.

Teacher B also suggests that teachers of today play a stronger role for students. "In the nontraditional family, she adds, "the teacher has more influence on the lives of children than their own parents. In these situations, teachers should act as positive role models and teach students to respect the opinions and feelings of others. Students need to be encouraged to participate in their community and to be contributing members of society." She concludes that "teachers have a unique opportunity to make the lives of our students more productive and rewarding." Reflecting on her experiences during student teaching, Teacher B writes, "I learned that no college classroom experience is as valuable as actually being in the school. During our course work, I feel we need to have more instruction about classroom management and gaining control of a classroom. I certainly did not feel prepared to do this during my student teaching experience."

Teacher C was given a position two months later as a seventh grade-reading teacher in a predominately Hispanic school district. She writes, "I could not have hand-picked this job better . . . only 60 different students . . . I am nervous and very excited." She continues, "I see my role as a teacher to do more than relay information." She adds that a teacher needs to motivate, facilitate, attract the students toward learning, and monitor the learning that takes place. Also, she adds, "a teacher must work with each learner as needed for specific skills and theories. Everything that a teacher does, she continues, needs to be centered on the student. The student is a sponge in the process, taking in new information and it is the teacher's role to ensure that each student has an adventure in the discovery process of learning."

Teacher C perceived multicultural education as "the state of education everywhere today." "It makes sense to address multicultural education," she concludes, "because we live in a multicultural world. It should not be a question of what we include; we need to integrate multicultural education as a natural component of education."

In her follow-up letter, Teacher D writes that she had begun graduate school and was looking for a job in an elementary school by the university. In her philosophy of education statement, Teacher D continued to look at learning through the eyes of the learner." She adds that if students do not enjoy school, they will have limited learning. She continues, "Children should be able to relate what they learn to real life, and it is the job of the teacher to help motivate children to learn." She writes in her next paragraph that "each child is an individual learner, and a teacher needs to use various approaches in teaching like cooperative learning, peer tutoring, student-centered activities and manipulative to ensure that all students learn." "Some of the students," she continues, "develop at different rates and operate in the classroom at different levels. It is the role of the teacher to act as a 'guide,' to keep students moving in their learning and to explore learning on their own."

On the aspect of multicultural education, Teacher D writes, "Multicultural education should be brought into the classroom." She adds that even though the United States is a pluralistic society, schools don't reflect this. She found that diverse students should not feel like outsiders and teachers need to "attend to their needs too . . . to help them feel successful." She concludes, "Multicultural education benefits all children . . . we can learn a lot through exploring the various cultures of the world."

In follow-up correspondence, Teacher E reported that she had found a position in a small rural elementary school similar to the one in which she had worked. Reflecting back on her time at the university student teaching practicum, Teacher E felt that she had made significant growth and change in her philosophy of education. She writes, "I believe that students learn from many different viewpoints. Furthermore, they don't act like each other. The problem sometimes is that teachers expect students to act differently and that is all right." She adds, "multicultural education is important so that students can recognize that each one of them is different from another and that each one shares some similarities with others."

Teacher F completed her student teaching assignment quietly. The last week, she visited other classrooms and talked with teachers about their techniques. She also spent a day going through her cooperating teacher's files. Most of her notes are effective in an upper elementary grade (i.e.,3rd -5th grade). Teacher F, ironically, became a seventh grade reading teacher at a moderately diverse middle school. Just before she received her position, Teacher F writes, "As a teacher, I feel that I need to address the students' basic needs before I begin to tech them. Once the child's sense of belonging, love, and worth is intact, it is possible to develop mutual respect between the teacher and child. The teacher at this point becomes the guide of the classroom." She adds that the teacher shifts roles -sometimes leads and sometimes watches in an attempt to have students take control of their own learning process. The students also have a role -to take control of their own learning. To do this,

students need to work individually, in pairs, or in groups to reach educational goals.

Furthermore, Teacher F perceives multicultural education as exceedingly important. She felt that just having the knowledge of groups and cultural differences is not enough. "We, as teachers, must learn and teach others the way to accept differences. Sometimes, it is productive to show differences and sometimes, it is not effective. The knowledge of attributes and deficits should be used as a base to improve, not a crutch to explain why something did not work."

In a follow-up letter, Teacher G reflected that the role of the teacher was to act as a facilitator of learning, acting as a guide in the learning process. She added, "Teachers must not dictate, but rather initiate and allow students to manage their learning as much as is practical." Students, she felt, need to be active participants in the ideas, goals, curricula, and activities. The student, also, she adds, must feel like an important player in the classrooms. Multicultural education, she concludes, is of utmost importance in today's classroom. "I feel the classroom is the one place, besides the home, where racial tension and prejudice can be 'nipped at the bud.' We, as teacher, are with these young people the majority of the day, how influential we must and can be." It is important for students to study other cultures. They are learning about their friends. For example, she found that in the unit she taught about Mexico, about 30% of the class was Hispanic and the teacher felt that the Hispanic students especially enjoyed the unit and felt a sense of pride. She concludes, 'The diverse learner must be identified and the curricula should be personally meaningful in order for all to be given the best education."

Discussion and Implications

One of the noteworthy issues brought out in this paper is that the most impactful course for each teacher was student teaching. It appears from the data gathered in this case study that coursework previous to this time did not seriously impact any of these teachers' philosophy of the issues of diversity as they appear in the context of the classroom. Teacher F appears to have emerged from the course with the highest course in sensitivity. However, the realities of the classroom and her personal problems affected her overall performance in student teaching and possibly limited her ability to apply the processes and knowledge she learned in the multicultural education course.

Another strong message that comes from this study is that typically, teachers perceive multicultural education as a quality that is important in the lives of their students. They, however, remained distanced from thinking of themselves as multicultural students. Each of these teachers affirmed that multicultural education is an important aspect of education. Students need to respect the differences of others and appreciate what each other brings to the classroom. However, as McLaren (1989) has pointed out in his work, educators persist in thinking of themselves in benevolent relationships. Each of these teachers to some degree continued to perceive of himself or herself as one who acting as an "expert" in multicultural education would help those who presumably lack these resources.

What was missed or perhaps perceived but not spoken of in this study is that the individuals needed to have opportunities to continue reflective processes and sensitivity of self-awareness. It seems that once these teachers left the course, completed student teaching, they began to lose sight of how they impacted their students' perceptions through their own perceptions and modeling. While their responses to the questions appear to be "text-book correct," they missed the key ingredient in multicultural learning: "Who am I?" followed by "Who are we?"

Also, it is interesting to note that the student teachers shared a series of common concerns—student teaching grade placement and behavior management. It is more interesting to note that each student teacher's perspective of the situation impacted how the issue was handled. The more objective or global the student teacher became about the situation, the easier the student teacher handled the situation. When Teacher D looked at student teaching as a learning experience rather than a time to "try out all the wonderful ideas in her unit," the more relaxed and energized she became. As she reports, the more she "enjoyed her students."

In like manner, student teachers who looked at their actions in the classroom rather than focusing on the actions of others, who were able to ask themselves, "What else can I try?," felt enthusiastic at the end of their student teaching assignment. Teacher B who continued studies in graduate school and Teacher E who entered advanced coursework in speech pathology remained the most distant from their involvement in the classroom. The other teachers, especially Teachers A and C began to search within themselves for alternative strategies from the first week. When they left their student teaching assignments, their students, unlike the other student teacher classrooms, gave them going away parties. While these are not strong cases, it might suggest that a stronger emphasis on reflectivity skills during preservice teaching empowers a student teacher. As McLaren (2003) suggests, students who develop a high degree of reflectivity are able to "critically appropriate knowledge existing outside their immediate experience in order to broaden their understanding of themselves, the world, and the possibilities for transforming the taken-for granted assumptions about the way we live" (p.186).

What are the implications for future teacher education programs that hope to instill a richer sense of multicultural awareness through self-perceptions? One possibility is to make the lessons of this case study explicit. For example, each of the "stories" in this case could be written as a scenario and preservice teachers could analyze the situations in light of a multicultural education course. Another possibility is to continue this line of research and develop more effective checkpoints where preservice teachers and inservice teachers could conduct a more thorough self-analysis of their perceptions. In this study, the checkpoints were data points. It would also be interesting to have these times also serve as reflection points about some common issues. Finally, the student teachers in this study came from a similar background: a small, rural, homogeneous high school. It would be interesting to see if there was a difference if the sample came from a large inner city school setting with high diversity.

References

Alderman, M. K. (1999). *Motivation for achievement: Possibilities for teaching and learning.* Mahwah, NJ: Lawrence Erlbaum.

Banks, C., & Banks, J. (Eds.). (2009). *Multicultural education: Issues and perspectives* (6th ed.). New York City, NY: John Wiley & Sons.

Banks, J,. & Banks, C. (Eds.). (2004). *The handbook of research on multicultural education* (2nd ed.). San Francisco, CA: Jossey-Bass.

Bennett, C. (2006). *Comprehensive multicultural education: Theory and practice.* Boston, MA: Allyn and Bacon.

Cho, G., & DeCastro-Ambrosetti, D. (2006). Is ignorance bliss? Preservice teachers' attitudes toward multicultural education. *The High School Journal, 89*(2), 24–28.

Davidman, L., & Davidman, P. (2000). *Teaching with a multicultural perspective: A practical guide.* White Plains, NY: Longman.

Delpit, L., & Dowdy, J. (2002). *The skin that we speak: Thoughts on language and culture in the classroom.* New York City, NY: The New Press.

Delpit, L. (2006). *Other people's children: Cultural conflict in the classroom.* New York City, NY: New Press.

Garcia, E. E. (1999). *Student cultural diversity: Understanding and meeting the challenge.* Boston, MA: Houghton Mifflin.

Gay, G. (2000). *Culturally responsive teaching.* New York City, NY: Teachers College Press.

Giroux, H. A. (1981). Toward a new sociology of curriculum. In H. A. Giroux, A. N. Penna, & W. F. Pinar (Eds.), *Curriculum and instruction* (pp. 106). Berkeley, CA: McCutchan Publishing Corporation.

Gollnick, D. & Chinn, P. (2008). *Multicultural education in a pluralistic society* (6th ed.). Upper Saddle River, NJ: Merrill.

Grant, C. (2009). *Teach! Change! Empower!: Solutions for closing the achievement gaps.* Thousand Oaks, CA: Corwin.

Grossman, H. (2003). *Classroom behavior management for diverse and inclusive schools.* Lanham, MD: Rowman & Littlefield.

Guba, E., & Lincoln, Y. (1989). *Fourth generation evaluation.* Newbury Park, CA: Sage.

Hernandez, H. (2000). *Multicultural education: A teacher's guide to content and process.* Columbus, OH: Merrill Publishing.

Higgins, K., & Moule, J. (2009). "No more Mr. nice guy": Preservice teachers' conflict with classroom management in a predominantly African American urban elementary school. *Multicultural Perspectives, 11*(3), 132–138.

Kyles, C., & Olafson, L. (2008). Uncovering preservice teachers' beliefs about diversity through reflective writing. *Urban Education, 43*(5), 500–518.

Ladson-Billings, G. (2009). *The dreamkeepers: Successful teachers of African American children.* San Francisco, CA: Jossey-Bass.

Author. (1992). Effective multicultural teachers: Meeting the challenges of diverse classrooms. *Equity & Excellence, 25,* 133–138.

Author. (1990). The minority mentorship project: Changing attitudes of preservice teachers for diverse classrooms. *Action in Teacher Education, 12,* 5–11.

Lincoln, Y. S., & Guba, E. G. (1985). *Naturalistic inquiry.* Newbury Park, CA: Sage Publications.

Lincoln, Y. (2003). *Turning points in qualitative research: Tying knots in the handkerchief.* Walnut Creek, CA: AltaMira Press.

Lyotard, J. F. (1984). *The postmodern condition: A report on knowledge.* Minneapolis, MN: University of Minneapolis Press.

Mills, J. (1983). Multicultural education: Where do we go from here? *Journal of Social and Behavioral Sciences, 29*(2), 43–51.

Nieto, S. (2009). Language, culture, and teaching: Critical perspectives for a new century. New York City, NY: Routledge.

Nieto, S., & Bode, P (2007). *Affirming diversity: The sociopolitical context of multicultural education* (5th ed.). Boston, MA: Allyn & Bacon.

Pang, V. O. (2005). *Multicultural education: A caring-centered reflective approach* (2nd ed.). New York City, NY: McGraw-Hill.

Parsons, E. (2005). From caring as a relation to culturally relevant caring: A White teacher's bridge to Black students. *Equity & Excellence in Education, 38,* 25–34.

Posner, G. J. (1998). Models of curriculum planning. In L. E. Beyer & M. K. Apple (Eds.), *The curriculum: Problems, politics, and possibilities.* Albany, NY: SUNY Press.

Ramirez, M., & Castaneda. (1974). *Cultural democracy, bicognitive development and education.* New York City, NY: Academic Press.

Rodriguez, F. (1999) *Affirming equity: A framework for teachers and schools* (3rd ed.). Dubuque, IA: Kendall/Hunt Publishing Company.

Sleeter, C. E., & Grant, C. A. (2009). *Making choices for multicultural education: Five approaches to race, class and gender* (6th ed.). Hoboken, NJ: John Wiley & Sons.

Swartz, E. (2009). Diversity: Gatekeeping knowledge and maintaining inequalities. *Review of Educational Research, 79*(2) 1044–1083.

Van Hook, C. (2002). Preservice teachers' perceived barriers to the implementation of a multicultural curriculum. *Journal of Instructional Psychology, 29*(4), 254–264.

Villegas, A. M., & Lucas, T. (2002). *Educating culturally responsive teachers: A coherent approach.* Albany, NY: SUNY Press.

Critical Thinking

1. What was your philosophy of education when you entered your teacher preparation program?
2. What was your philosophy of education when you began your internship/student teaching?
3. How did your philosophy of education change by the time you began your first teaching position?
4. Why is it important to reflect upon your philosophy of education as you mature in your professional growth and development?

Create Central

www.mhhe.com/createcentral

Internet References

Awesome Library for Teachers
www.awesomelibrary.org/teacher.html

Education World
www.education-world.com

MARGARET M. FERRARA, PhD is an Associate Professor and Department Head in the Department of Curriculum, Teaching, and Learning at the University of Nevada Reno in Reno, NV. **PATRICIA J. LARKE, EdD** is a Professor in the Department of Teaching, Learning, and Culture in the College of Education and Human Development at Texas A&M University in College Station, Texas. **JEMIMAH LEA** is a Graduate Student in the Department of Teaching, Learning, and Culture at Texas A&M University in College Station, Texas.

Ferrara, Margaret M.; Larke, Patricia J.; Lea, Jemimah. From *National Forum of Multicultural Issues Journal,* vol. 7, no. 1, June 2010, pp. 1–22. Copyright © 2010 by National Forum Journals. Reprinted by permission.

Article   Prepared by: Nancy P. Gallavan, *University of Central Arkansas*

Unheard Voices of Minority Teacher Candidates in a Teacher Education Program

TUNDE SZECSI AND CAROLYN SPILLMAN

Learning Outcomes

After reading this article, you will be able to:

- Understand teaching, learning, and schooling from the perspectives of underrepresented populations.
- Discuss the importance of financial, academic, and social support for minority teacher candidates.

Introduction

Giving voice to those who are representative of the minority teachers of the future can and will provide an important response to the growing concerns over the disproportionate balance of cultures between students and teachers in schools across the country (Bennett et al., 2006). In reality, the number of students with diverse cultural backgrounds in the P-12 schools is rapidly growing, while the number of minority teachers is not.

Currently, for example, 8% of elementary teachers and 7% of secondary teachers are Hispanic (NCES, 2010). Yet between 1988 and 2008 the Hispanic public school student population increased from 11% to 22% and African-American students increased from 6.8% to 7.5% (NCES, 2010). According to a report by the National Center for Education Statistics (2007), by the year 2020 the minorities are predicted to represent 39 percent of the total U.S. population, which will constitute a 6% increase over 15 years.

Emerging concerns question not only the degree of underrepresentation of minority teachers, but also its cause. As we move toward a view of celebrating assets from all cultures, instead of lamenting deficits, it becomes clear that with increased numbers of minority teachers the schools will have a richer multicultural knowledge base (Dee & Henkin, 2002), stronger role models (Bennett et al. 2006; Zirkel, 2002), more shared experiences between teachers and students (Mayes & Cutri, 2004), and greater numbers of insider experiences that help build bridges between cultures (Villegas & Davis, 2007).

The benefits of supporting minority teachers are abundant. Examination of the factors that may either hinder or support the transformation into teaching of this population is clearly warranted.

Historical Hinderances

Historically, assumptions regarding the low numbers of culturally diverse teachers include such factors as low pay (Gursky, 2002), difficulties with standardized tests (Bennett, et al. 2006), negative school experiences, lack of support in college, and lack of academic/emotional preparation (Gordon, 2005). These factors are hindrances that are presumed to play a significant role in one's choice to enter the teaching profession or not.

Efforts to recruit and retain minority teachers have proven more successful when they are begun early in the post-secondary school experience. Flores, Clark, Claeys, and Villarreal (2007) report that ethnic minority students often begin their studies in community colleges and transfer to four year institutions. Even with concentrated support programs focused on Latino students, graduation rates of the total student population are reported in one study to be only 8.8% (Flores et al. 2007). Teacher attrition and mobility rates when compared with ethnic indicators show that among White Non-Hispanic teachers, 8% left the profession in 2008–2009 while 9% of African-American teachers left and 5.6% of Hispanic teachers left the field (NCES, 2010).

Therefore, teacher education programs that encourage minorities to choose teaching as a career and promote a support system for recruitment, retention, and development of culturally diverse teachers are crucial. Although there are several research studies on recruiting, preparing, and retaining teachers of culturally diverse backgrounds (Flores et al., 2007; Villegas & Davis, 2007), there have been a limited number that explore minority teacher candidates' perception about the practices and support systems in teacher education programs (Clark & Flores, 2007; Nieto, 2006).

Now is a critical juncture for looking deeply at issues of recruiting and retention. Schools need teachers who can relate to their students, understand their backgrounds and their cultures, and build bridges to relationships and curriculum. A culturally responsive environment is expected in all classrooms and from all teachers, but minority teachers who have shared experiences with the students, both positive and negative, can bring a higher level of relevance to the classroom.

The purpose of the study reported here was to gain an in-depth understanding of minority teacher candidates' perceptions about the process of becoming teachers with a special focus on factors that support or hinder their transformation into the teaching profession. Through in-depth interviews with and observations of three minority teacher candidates, this study offers insights into their motivation to become teachers, perceptions of their strengths and weaknesses as teachers, and the reviews support they received and challenges they faced in the teacher education program.

Methodology
Setting

This study was conducted in an undergraduate elementary education program at a predominantly White university located in the southern United States. The university serves five neighboring counties, some of which are rural. By race and ethnicity, the teacher candidates at the university are as follows: 3.3% are African American, 1.8% are Asian, 9.4% are Hispanic, 80% are White, and 5% are not identified. According to the university's mission and guiding principles, which emphasize social justice and diversity, the teacher education program has implemented a plan of action for recruiting and retaining teacher candidates from diverse backgrounds.

Participants

Teacher candidates who identified themselves with minority backgrounds were contacted with a request for participation in the study. To represent a variety of cultural backgrounds and diverse statuses (junior, senior), three female teacher candidates majoring in elementary education out of six volunteers were selected. No male students were identified.

Heidi (all names are pseudonyms), a 21-year-old Haitian-American junior involved in a part-time internship, was born in the U.S. However, she lived in Haiti for three years during her early adolescence. She had intermediate proficiencies in Haitian-Creole. She was a first generation college student, although her sisters and brothers-in-law had graduated from college. Her academic excellence qualified her for participation in the Honors program.

Esmeralda, a 22-year-old Dominican-American junior also in a part-time internship, was born in the U.S., but soon her family moved back to the Dominican Republic and lived there until she was eight. She is bilingual, fluent in Spanish both orally and in writing. She lived with her boyfriend and young child. Her parents had very limited education, while her sister was also a college student.

Aashia, a 22-year-old Asian-American senior in her final internship, was born in the Philippines but grew up in Guam and moved to the U.S. at 16. At that time she started to learn English, and also maintained her native language, Tagalog. Her parents are college graduates.

At the time of this study, all participants had successfully completed at least three semesters in the teacher education program. During the ten-month period of this study all participated in either part-time or full time internships and took college courses.

Data Collection and Analysis

After the participants signed a consent form, the researcher conducted an open-ended, structured interview of approximately 90 minutes with each of the three students. Subsequently, during the next ten months, the researcher completed participant observations in university and internship classrooms as well as in extracurricular activities. Observation notes were taken. The total time of the observations with the three participants was approximately 20 hours. Finally, the researcher conducted a follow-up structured interview for 60 minutes with each participant. The researcher tape-recorded and transcribed all interviews, and analyzed all interview transcripts and observation notes in accordance with grounded theory methodology (Strauss & Corbin, 1998). Coding was used to identify the distinguishing themes related to the teacher candidates' perceptions.

Results and Discussion

The analysis revealed that all participants experienced some hesitation about the teaching profession in discussions with their families. However, various life experiences had guided them into teaching, and during these years they received diverse support in their socio-cultural context. The challenges and occasional biases made them aware of needed support systems and of their role as teachers. In this section, the results are embedded in narratives about the factors that strengthened or moderated their journey of becoming a teacher.

Theme #1

Although the teaching profession was not their primary choice, various life experiences lead them into this profession.

No participants in this study selected teaching as their first career choice, mainly because their families considered other professions—physician, psychologist, and accountant—to be more prestigious and better paying. Heidi, who first considered pediatric medicine, recalled "my father discouraged it; he did not want me to go into teaching; he didn't understand how I could go from wanting to become a doctor to becoming a teacher." Although with reservation, her brother supported her; "he's encouraged me, but he thinks that eventually I should go into becoming a principal or assistant principal and not just stick with teaching." His viewpoint clearly implied the perceived low prestige of teachers versus administrators.

Aashia's parents also held culturally determined expectations about her career; "my first choice was nursing, or anything in the medical field because my parents placed so much emphasis on math and science and said, 'in our culture, the Asian culture, either a math major or a science major or somewhere in between.'"

Similarly a lack of acceptance surfaced from Esmeralda's parents as she stated:

> When I did say that I wanted to become a
> teacher, I didn't get the best reaction; they
> were like "oh, ok, but why?" and I said "this
> is what I want to do." They knew that I
> was going to go to college for four years
> and they kind of wanted me to make more
> than the "average Joe."

In spite the families' perception of teaching as a profession with low prestige, the three participants decided to become teachers. They had an encounter with an influential teacher and/or a positive educational experience that guided their decision to override their family's reservation about teaching. For example, Heidi recalled former teachers as role models:

> I had really good teachers, especially in
> elementary school, who really made me
> want to learn and made me enjoy school
> in itself so I want to do that for someone
> else. I want to motivate them; I think
> it would be nice for students to have a
> young teacher or a teacher of color to
> show them that you don't have to go into
> the entertainment industry or ... into the
> professional world ... the athletic world in
> order to be successful.

Esmeralda's decision was influenced by an outstanding college course and confirmed with other people's experiences:

> I took the Intro to Education and I loved
> it. At that time I was working at Ralph
> Lauren Polo and I was talking to my
> manager about my desire to be a teacher.
> I was thinking about the money and about
> what my parents had told me ... and I
> remember my manager was like "look
> there's one thing I am going to tell you
> is never spend your life chasing money; I

> went to school to be a business man, I'm
> working here and that's all I do is chase
> money." I think the point is when I said "I
> am just going to be a teacher; I don't care
> what anybody else says, I am just going
> to be a teacher."

Although their career choices were first heavily challenged, ultimately all three families accepted the participants' decisions and offered various forms of strong support during the years of teacher education studies.

These three minority teacher candidates recognized their options and discussed the impact of their parents' advice on a career choice. Although they ultimately convinced themselves to go into teaching, a serious concern remains with the overall image of teachers that is perpetuated in many minority families, reflecting a lack of respect for the teaching profession (Gordon, 2000). This lack of respect has evolved through the negative experiences of many minorities as students and is remembered by them when making career choices or when guiding their own children toward careers (Gordon, 2000). For many African-American students, making money and gaining occupational stability are important factors in career selection (Wilder, 1999).

When minorities choose teaching, they often do so as a way to "give back" to the community. Ramirez (2009) explored reasons for minorities choosing the teaching field and found that due to low pay, they considered the positions almost like volunteer jobs. Disturbing is the fact that many in Ramirez's study equated good pay with high respect and felt that without respect, it was hard for one to make a desired impact. Even so, many of those interviewed planned to teach in their own communities when possible. Very similar to the three teacher candidates in our study, Ramirez found that family members directly told them not to teach for fear that they could not provide for their future families.

The interviews with the three teacher candidates suggest that teachers and coworkers were influential factors in the decision to become teachers. Having educators in the family, having a bond with a teacher, and having previous teaching experiences have also been found to play a role in deciding to become a teacher (Chamness & Hidehiro, 2005). It is apparent that intrinsic factors overshadowed the extrinsic factors in the decision making of these participants.

Theme #2

Although they want to be a role model for all children, they perceive themselves as a great fit with culturally diverse children due to shared experiences.

Without exception, the participants recollected incidents of prejudice and bias that they had experienced during their schooling. They believed these painful experiences made them more sensitive and compassionate toward children at risk; however, they firmly stated that their goal was to be a role model for all children regardless of their backgrounds.

Describing her encounters with stereotypes, for example, Aashia recalled her very first days in this country when a teacher commented that Aashia "was supposed to wear a grass skirt and coconut bras" considering her arriving from Guam. At a parent meeting during her internship, some parents failed to hide their hesitation about her, which she interpreted as a reaction to her being Asian and having an accent. Regardless of these aching incidents she felt that her cultural capital had strengthened the bond between her and the minority students. She noted:

During my internships, I have been the

only Asian teacher. I feel like I gain more

connection with my students who are

minority because they understand what

I am going through; saying certain words

incorrect—it's because of my accent, but I

do serve as a role model to all of them.

In addition, the participants demonstrated awareness of their knowledge about culturally diverse parents' expectations and experiences, and sought to utilize it to better serve their students. For example, Heidi discussed her unique skills for easing Haitian parents who feel intimidated to make contact with the teacher due to their lack of English proficiencies and familiarity with the school system. She expressed:

I really feel like I can help those parents;

you know, make them feel more comfortable;

show them that there is someone

who is similar to them, teaching their

students. You know we do have something

in common. They can reach out to me

and I will reach out to them. I am here

for them.

Esmeralda also encountered biases. For example, in a store she was conversing in Spanish and another customer said "Speak English; we're in America." Often her college classmates too commented on her improper pronunciation, which made her uncomfortable and cautious about her language. Despite these humiliating incidents, she considered her Hispanic background an asset. To support this notion, she commented on her reaction to the cooperating teacher's inappropriate interaction with a child from an Asian background:

I told the teacher "let me work with her"

... I know that she [the child] can be a

little bit of concerning ... but I can help

her and I [can] work with her, ... because

at one point I was her and I was labeled

and I did get screamed at for not saying

something the correct way ... So I understand

because I was her.

Ultimately, she visualized herself as a teacher in a diverse classroom in which she wanted to "let them [children] know that it's okay to be themselves," and in a school where the principal will recognize minority teachers as assets. She noted, "Hopefully they [principals] will value [minority teachers] and say 'you know what; we need people like you because we have a lot of minority students.'" Although with high hopes in terms of being appreciated, she and Aashia felt that minority teacher candidates needed to work twice as hard as majority teacher candidates to prove their teacher competencies.

In spite of experiencing painful prejudices, these teacher candidates recognized the strengths that they bring to a classroom. Instead of harboring ill feelings, they were looking at the advantages of being a minority teacher. Gursky notes that "Many students will complete their K-12 school without having been taught by a single teacher of color" (2002, p. 11). How sad when children are deprived of role models from their own culture. It is through seeing adults who look like they do, who are in positions of leadership that plant the seed for what they can do in their lives.

Further, Bennett et al. (2006) suggests that the lack of teachers of color may have an impact on low high school completion rates among African-Americans, Native Americans, and Latinos. A goal is to have more role models with varied ethnic backgrounds, so students will be able to see appropriate teacher roles. The divide between teachers' and students' backgrounds leaves students without support for bridging cultures and curriculum (Souto-Manning & Dice, 2007).

These three teacher candidates expressed clear self-identities. They knew who they were and they recognized their potential value to all of their students, but especially to minority students. As they have each indicated, they are the face of their minority students and share the experiences of being a minority, including all of the unjust experiences such as prejudice and low expectations. These future teachers understand themselves and the role that culture has played in their own development; therefore, they will be more likely to recognize and honor cultural differences among the students they will teach (Nieto, 2006).

Theme #3

An extensive support system in the teacher candidates' socio-cultural contexts facilitated their experiences in the teacher education program.

All three participants cherished the variety and quality of courses in the teacher preparation curriculum, and felt prepared for the profession due to the various forms of support available from their families, schools, and community. They all appreciated the financial support that they had received due in part to their minority backgrounds and academic excellence. They believed that only with these funds were they able to pursue a college degree.

When describing their academic experiences in the program, they valued the mandatory courses on culture, language, and diversity-related issues. However Heidi also called attention to the gap between the theoretical and pragmatic approaches to diversity at this predominantly White university, and noted, ". . . look, we talk about diversity a lot in the teacher education program but then if there is no diversity among us, how much are we actually learning about it?"

Furthermore, they enjoyed and benefited from cooperative learning experiences in college courses, and acknowledged that they usually worked with other minority students in groups. Esmeralda and Aashia stated that working with other minority students was their comfort zone in the university classes:

> In the beginning I was very intimidated
>
> because I did sit in a classroom and I was
>
> like the only Hispanic student. Then I
>
> met Maria and Isabel from the Dominican
>
> Republic and from that time on we would
>
> take every single class together, mostly
>
> because, I guess you could say, it was a
>
> comfort. Ummm, a little "blanky."

Furthermore, the participants found the internship experiences beneficial and well-supported. They all acknowledged that the internship experiences opened their eyes to the difference between their ideals about teaching and reality. For example, Heidi expressed disappointment about the scripted curriculum, ability grouping, and external rewards that she found commonly used.

Regarding support, Esmeralda and Aashia appreciated that their mentors were minority teachers; on the other hand Heidi did not indicate the need for a mentor who would share her cultural background. These interviews support the use of case studies; teacher educators must get to know their students because each one is different.

In terms of college life, Esmeralda highlighted the importance of student clubs, specifically Hispanic organizations that allowed her to make friends with other Hispanic students. However, not all of them found the minority student clubs supportive. Heidi, who is Haitian-American, was disappointed with a person in the African-American club who once commented about her "She's one of my students but she does not want to be." Heidi emotionally added,

> I didn't say anything to her, I just walked
>
> away. But even right now that kind of
>
> ignorance just really upsets me that
>
> people still think that just because we're
>
> the same skin color I automatically have
>
> to do everything that you do; and if I don't
>
> do that then that means that I am not really

> African American or I am not really
>
> proud of my culture or I am not proud of
>
> my race.

In addition to the support from the university, the three participants had received support from their families and friends which facilitated their journey of becoming teachers. With no exceptions, they believed that their parents' high expectations in terms of hard work and success made them diligent and self-reliant students. As Aashia noted "I've always been taught that hard work really does come a long way, especially with my parents who grew up in a third world country." She also commented on how her family background engendered her strong self-reliance skills:

> After 5th grade I couldn't depend on my
>
> parents because they didn't really understand
>
> the English language and certain
>
> content areas. So I was basically saying
>
> "Okay, gotta teach myself this" or "I can't
>
> get this wrong" or "I can't be confused"
>
> because if I asked my parents they would
>
> not know.

Furthermore, Heidi passionately discussed how the expectations of many people around her had intensified her determination which resulted in success:

> I am deeply afraid of failure, and I don't
>
> want to fail when it comes to teaching. I
>
> am not fully paying for school by myself,
>
> but at the same time I don't want anyone's
>
> hard earned money to waste. Because of all
>
> those people who paved the way and look
>
> up to me I feel like I have no choice but to
>
> succeed. I can't let all those people down.

These three teacher candidates were candid in their discussion of their academic experiences, including the strong values received from family, financial support, and their own self determination. They noticed that there was not much diversity among their peers on campus and minority role models were sparse. Two of them, particularly, migrated toward the few minorities in their program for group work. All three of these teacher candidates are from cultures considered to value collectivism, which means that they prefer collaborative group work (Tileston & Darling, 2008).

Teacher education programs wisely will offer opportunities for collectivist experiences that may help alleviate feelings of isolation and give support to stressful situations. It is not unusual for ethnic minority students to feel the stress of academic competition, along with additional pressures that could produce negative outcomes (Irizarry, 2007). Not only do they need role models and opportunities to work with others who share similar value systems, but they need to be recognized by and acknowledged for the way they "participate, see, and are in the world" (Dilliard, 1994, p. 9).

In addition, these teacher candidates were positive about their relationships with their mentors during internships. Their in-school experiences were pleasant, with the only conflicts revealing a disconnect between their philosophical stance on curriculum and pedagogy and what they actually found in the classrooms. This disconnect is not unique to minority teachers, but it is clear that such a mismatch between what teaching is about and what potential candidates perceive as the role of teachers is a hindrance to entering the profession (Hoodles, 2004).

Theme #4

Additional support is needed to meet all challenges; however no preferential treatment is expected.

Although the three participants were successful students in the teacher education program, they struggled with challenges for which additional support was needed. For example, in terms of course work, Esmeralda and Aashia found writing, grammar, and class presentations difficult, especially when occasionally they had received disturbing comments on their accent and their incorrect usage of the English language from other peers.

For these participants, the most challenging program requirements were the state required certification exams; however for different reasons. Aashia and Esmeralda commented on the lack of proper test preparation and remediation after failing the tests. They would expect more effective and extensive academic support specifically targeting the reading and writing competencies. Repeatedly they referred to their second language learner backgrounds as a possible barrier.

In addition, Aashia shared her frustration about her limited knowledge in certain subject areas which forced her to retake the subject area test numerous times. Though she suggested no significant role of her minority background in this issue, she pointed to the need for effective preparation and guidance in subject areas in general. On the other hand, Heidi experienced difficulties with exam schedules. Her religion prohibited her from taking an exam on Saturdays, and a staff member's misleading information about the Saturday exam days made her panic: "What am I going to do with the conflict between my religion and what I want to pursue as my career?" Afterwards, she found an alternative date to take her exam, and she commented: "She [program secretary] just didn't know what was going on and she didn't try to help out."

When further discussing the possible support system at the university, Heidi also mentioned the need for social events:

The College of Education should have

more social things so that the students

could get together and learn from each

other. My best friend who went to another

school; they had a lot of round table discussions

and picnics and Bar-B-Ques. If we

wanted to do something on the weekend,

there just isn't a lot of social stuff that the

College of Education does.

Although they felt that extra support would enrich their experience of becoming a teacher, they made clear that no preferential treatment was needed or appreciated. Esmeralda elaborated on this from her perspective:

I don't want to be treated differently because

I am Hispanic; I think that would

bring more reasons for teachers and other

students to be like "well she's Hispanic so

we've got to be a little more careful; she's

in this program." And I guess because

there is such a low number of minority

students, I just wouldn't want to stand

out like that.

These teacher candidates were positive regarding their road toward completion of the teacher education program in spite of recognizing some problems along the way. They were also adamant that they wanted to be treated like everyone else with no special benefits, but they wanted to be able to access appropriate kinds of support. They felt that they had worked hard, had earned their status at this point in time, and did not want to be dependent on special treatment. They wanted to be supported for the strengths that they bring to the programs and, subsequently, to the schools where they will teach.

It is clear, however, that they did not escape the challenges of state licensure exams and other teacher certification tests. Even with the disadvantages of entering a different culture and coming from a different language background, they were able to meet the expectations through much hard work and study to complete the requirements. That is not true for many prospective minority candidates as the Praxis exam, required in most states, shows great disparity in passing rates for White teachers at 82% versus 46% for African Americans (Gursky, 2002). Not only did these teachers navigate the exam hurdles, but they successfully met and conquered many issues of miscommunication along the way.

Implications and Conclusions

This study has explored minority teacher candidates' perceptions of becoming teachers. Their experiences align in many ways with those experiences reported in the research literature. We find that minority candidates are indeed making decisions to enter the teaching profession. This is welcome news, since this study also showed that the teaching profession is not viewed as attractive and prestigious to the minority students' families; therefore those families initially discouraged their children's interest in becoming teachers.

However, these participants had a special calling, an intrinsic motivation and/or a significant friend, coworker, or teacher who made them confident about pursuing their dream (Chamness et.al. 2005; Gordon, 2005). Therefore, outreach programs and support provided early, often through mentors as role models in high school, plus special guidance during general education courses all appear to have had the potential to attract and retain these particular minority teacher candidates.

Both in college and internship classrooms, these participants appreciated and valued collaborative efforts with peers, professors, and mentors (Souto-Manning & Dice, 2004). Consequently, incorporating collaborative projects in university teacher education courses might support the collectivist value of many cultures and should therefore be encouraged. Special consideration should be given to creating support and learning groups; specifically, professors should give freedom and flexibility for teacher candidates in selecting group members to ensure smooth group interaction and optimal learning.

Three types of support—academic, financial, and social—were found to be important for these minority teacher candidates. Specifically, high quality assistance in academic endeavors appears to be needed, with a focus on individualized needs such as test preparation and completion of course assignments. Furthermore, much needed social support was not institutionalized in the teacher education program in this study.

However, we believe these assistance programs should not be organized as a result of affirmative action, but rather to accommodate individual needs. In addition, appropriate social support such as student groups and out-of-class social activities would be essential to create and maintain a feeling of belonging, especially in an institution which has a low percentage of minority students. However, no expectations regarding participation should be imposed on minority teacher candidates.

The teacher candidates in the study, to some extent, were already aware of their cultural capital, which they found beneficial when interacting with minority students and parents (Souto-Manning & Dice, 2004). It appears important to further reinforce minority teacher candidates' consciousness of the unique value of their competencies resulting from their bilingualism and biculturalism. Environments both at the university and in internship classrooms that appreciate multiculturalism and multilingualism should be nurtured and sustained.

These teacher candidates expect to be strong teachers for all students—not just for minorities. They have participated in a teacher preparation program that has promoted culturally relevant pedagogy for all classrooms (Edwards & Kuhlman, 2007; Richards, Brown & Forde, 2007) and for all teachers. They are the ones who through their own backgrounds carry the funds of knowledge from various cultures (Moll & Gonzales, 2004) and can thus be the bridge to shared experiences, relationships, and relevant curriculum for their future students and for other teachers.

To further increase and retain such minority teachers more must be done to ensure that potential candidates are given every opportunity to choose teaching as a career and to be supported in ways that will allow them to grow and not feel patronized or expected to be dependent on special treatment. This is the challenge to be addressed by all teacher education programs.

References

Assaf, L., Garza, R., & Battle, J. (2010). Multicultural teacher education: Examining the perceptions, practices, and coherence in one teacher preparation program. Teacher Education Quarterly, 37(2), 115–135.

Bennett, C., McWhorter, L., & Kuykendall, J. (2006). Will I ever teach? Latino and African-American students' perspectives on PRAXIS I. American Educational Research Journal, 43(3), 531–575.

Chamness, M., & Hidehiro, E. (2005). Journey to becoming a teacher: The experiences of students of color. Multicultural Education, 25(1). 2–9.

Clark, E., & Flores, B. (2001). Who am I? The social construction of ethnic identity and self-perceptions in Latino preservice teachers. The Urban Review, 33(2).

Dee, J., & Henkin, A. (2002). Assessing dispositions toward cultural diversity among preservice teachers. Urban Education, 37(1), 22–40.

Edwards, S., & Kuhlman, W. (2007). Culturally responsive teaching: Do we walk our talk? Multicultural Education, 14(4), 45–49.

Flores, B., Clark, E., Claeys, L., & Villarreal, A. (2007). Academy for teacher excellence: Recruiting, preparing, and retaining Latino teachers through learning communities. Teacher Education Quarterly, 34(4), 53–69.

Gordon, J. A. (2000). The color of teaching. New York: Rutledge Falmer.

Gordon, J. A. (2005). In search of educators of color. Leadership, 35(2). 30–35.

Gursky, D. (2002). Recruiting minority teachers. American Teacher, 86(5). 11–12.

Hoodless, P. (2004). Are you just helping? The perceptions and experiences of minority ethnic trainees on a one-year primary initial teacher training course. Research in Education, 72, 32–46.

Irizarry, J. (2007). "Home-growing" teachers of color: Lessons learned from a town-gown partnership. Teacher Education Quarterly, 34(4), 87–102.

Mayer, A. P., & Tucker, S. K. (2010) Cultivating students of color: Strategies for ensuring high academic achievement in middle and secondary schools. Journal of School Leadership, 20(4), 470–90.

Mayes, C., & Cutri, R. (2004). First year Latino teacher. Multicultural Education, 12(1), 2–9.

Moll, L., & Gonzales, N. (2004). Engaging life: A funds of knowledge approach to multicultural education. In Banks, J. & McGee Banks, C., Handbook of research on multicultural education (2nd Ed.). New York: John Wiley & Sons.

Nieto, J. (2006). The cultural plunge: Cultural immersion as a means of promoting self-awareness and cultural sensitivity among student teachers. Teacher Education Quarterly, 33(1), 75–84.

National Center for Educational Statistics. (2010). The condition of education. Retrieved February 3, 2011 from http://nces.ed.gov/pubs2010/2010353.pdf.

National Center for Educational Statistics. (2007). Status and trends in the education of racial and ethnic minorities (2007). Retrieved February 3, 2011 from http://nces.ed.gov/pubs2007/minoritytrends/ind_1_1.asp.

National Center for Educational Statistics. (2010). Teacher attrition and mobility: Results from the 2008–2009 teacher follow up survey. Retrieved February 3 from http://nces.ed.gov/pubs2010/2010353.pdf.

Ramirez, A. (2009). Ethnic minorities and teaching: An examination of the low numbers in the teaching profession. Multicultural Education, 16(4), 19–24.

Richards, H., Brown, A., & Forde, T. (2007). Addressing diversity in schools: Culturally responsive pedagogy. Teaching Exceptional Children, 39(3), 64–68.

Souto-Manning, M., & Dice, J. (2004). Reflective teaching in the early years: A case study for mentoring diverse educators. Early Childhood Education Journal, 34(6). 425–429.

Strauss, A., & Corbin, J. (1998). Basics of qualitative research techniques and procedures for developing grounded theory (2nd edition). London, UK: Sage.

Tileston, D., & Darling, S. (2008). Why culture counts: Teaching children of poverty. Bloomington, IN: Solution Tree.

Villegas, A., & Davis, D. (2007). Approaches to diversifying the teaching force: Attending to issues of recruitment, preparation, and retention. Teacher Education Quarterly, 34(4), 137–147.

Wilder, M. (1999). Reexamining the African-American teacher shortage: Building a new professional image of teaching for the twenty-first century. Equity and Excellence in Education, 32(3), 77–82.

Zirkel, S. (2002). "Is there a place for me?": Role models and academic identity among White students and students of color. Teachers College Record, 104, 357–376.

Critical Thinking

1. What are your experiences with teachers from underrepresented populations?
2. What are your beliefs and thoughts about preferential treatment for teachers, candidates, and students from underrepresented populations?
3. Why is it important to increase the number of teachers and candidates from underrepresented populations?
4. How can you contribute to increasing the number of teachers and candidates from underrepresented populations?

Create Central

www.mhhe.com/createcentral

Internet References

Center for Multicultural Education
http://education.washington.edu/cme
National Education Association
www.nea.org/home/29031.htm

Tunde Szecsi is an associate professor in the College of Education at Florida Gulf Coast University, Fort Myers, Florida and **Carolyn Spillman** is a professor in residence with the Lastinger Center for Learning of the College of Education at the University of Florida, Gainesville, Florida.

Szecsi, Tunde;Spillman, Carolyn. From Multicultural Education. vol. 5. Winter 2012. pp. 24–29. Copyright © 2012 by Caddo Gap Press. Reprinted by permission.

Article   Prepared by: Nancy P. Gallavan, *University of Central Arkansas*

Rediscovering Good Teaching: Exploring Selfhood and Solidarity in Urban Contexts

TIMOTHY MAHONEY

Learning Outcomes

After reading this article, you will be able to:

- Increase awareness of your attitudes toward students' test scores and their cultural backgrounds.

- Examine the balance between concern for job security and for educational equity and social justice.

This paper began in early 2002 when new federal educational policy suggested, and eventually demanded, a particular definition of a good teacher. This policy, which began as *No Child Left Behind* (2002) and is now known as *Race to the Top* (Department of Education, 2009), employs a conception of good teaching that involves standardizing both the content good teachers were expected to know and the methods good teachers were expected to use to communicate this content. As a result of this policy, school districts and individual schools have adopted regulatory practices that enforce particular pedagogical models across all grade levels and narrow curriculum to focus on preparation for high stakes tests (Crocco & Costigan, 2007; Hill, 2007; Cawelti, 2006). Within the policies, there's no clear definition of what counts as a "qualified teacher," an "effective teacher," or a "good teacher" for any school, let alone an urban school, beyond passage of standardized content tests. This paper will not propose a definition of a good teacher either, but instead will try to extend the conception of good teaching to include a number of qualities that seem absent from any conception of qualified, effective, or good teaching available in the literature.

In a charitable sense, *No Child Left Behind* and *Race to the Top* have shed important light on the lack of educational opportunities in urban schools. However, the mandated teaching practices and narrowed curriculum have had a disproportional effect on the educational experiences in urban schools, and have resulted in some of the questionable teaching practices and administrative policies described so vividly in Jonathan Kozol's *Shame of the Nation* (2005) and illustrated in documentaries such as *Hard Times at Douglass High: A No Child Left Behind Report Card* (2008) Further, mandated pedagogies and narrowed content do not seem to be a pathway toward better teaching in urban classrooms, as any improvements in learning or teaching practices gained in the years since 2002 are suspicious (Forum for Education and Democracy, 2009; Meier & Wood, 2004).

This lack of progress begs the question, "What is an effective pathway to good teaching, and good teaching in urban schools in particular?" Existing research (see Darling-Hammond & Bransford, 2005; Cochrane-Smith & Zeichner, 2005 for many examples) has generated many frameworks and lists of the qualities of good teachers and the practices good teachers employ. However, although these lists of qualities and practices may describe good teaching in a general sense, they do not explain why teachers who possess them do not necessarily become effective teachers.

This paper will propose two potential solutions to this problem. First, one reason that descriptions of effective teaching in general fall short is that they fail to incorporate *teacher selfhood* (Palmer, 1998) in the conceptions. This failure results in teacher certification programs, school administrators, and teachers themselves overemphasizing the wrong things, such as content and teaching methods, in the preparation for and supervision of classroom practice. Secondly, a possible reason that teachers with all the requisite skills fail to teach effectively in urban schools is their inability to achieve a sense of *solidarity* (Rorty, 1989) with their students. Instead of enabling teachers to know their students in deep and meaningful ways, teachers are taught surface tricks and techniques to know students which maintain the separation between teacher and student, disabling real communication and connection. Using the Philadelphia Urban Seminar as the context, this paper will illustrate how 17 beginning teachers came to understand how they could become good teachers through the exploration and rediscovery of selfhood and solidarity.

Conceptual Framework: Selfhood and Solidarity

In *The Courage to Teach* (1998), Palmer proposes a rich, yet seemingly simple, way to connect the qualities of good teaching to the practice of good teachers. He asserts that knowledge and skills alone do not make teachers effective. What does is the way knowledge and skills are put to use in relation to each teacher's personal identity *as* a teacher. As he writes, "good teaching cannot be reduced to technique; good teaching comes from the identity and integrity of the teacher." (p. 10). This identity and integrity, what Palmer calls *teacher selfhood,* goes beyond classroom management skills, knowledge of child development, and sensitivity to diverse students. Teacher selfhood is a deeper commitment to deconstruct and reconstruct initial images of how teachers work in classrooms to escape the orthodoxy of standardized methods of instruction, scripted curriculum, and rigid adherence to external mandates that can inhibit their development, particularly in urban schools. As Palmer writes, "as we learn more about who we are, we can learn techniques that reveal rather than conceal the personhood from which good teaching comes." (p. 24).

The philosophical framework of solidarity (Rorty, 1989) puts this personhood to work. Rorty writes that solidarity "is not about clearing away prejudice or burrowing into repressed anger or fear, but rather as a goal to be achieved through imagination—the ability to see unfamiliar people as fellow travelers–it is not only discovered through reflection, but is created by increasing our sensitivity to their circumstances . . . " (1989, xvi). The concept of solidarity provides a framework for understanding students where the distinctions between "us" (the teachers) and "them" (the students) become less clearly defined. This move toward solidarity is particularly important in urban schools and with urban students, as the myriad of bias, stereotype, and real obstacles to successful educational experiences often conflict with the well-intentioned efforts of teachers striving to become effective in urban settings (Steinberg & Kincheloe, 2007).

The Philadelphia Urban Seminar

The Philadelphia Urban Seminar (the Seminar) is a two-week residential course focused on urban teaching in Philadelphia. The Seminar combines 10 full days of field experience in Philadelphia public schools, professional development meetings, daily seminar meetings focused on processing the experiences in urban schools, and service projects in the neighborhoods surrounding the placement schools.

Subjects

This project focuses on 17 teacher certification students, all of whom, self-selected to participate in the Seminar in 2008. They were all traditional undergraduate students in the teacher certification program at a university in Pennsylvania. All subjects were white, and all came from suburban or rural communities. Although they all had one field experience in urban schools, none of them had any consistent contact with the kinds of schools or students they would encounter in Philadelphia before the Seminar began.

Data

Data for this paper are taken from a larger longitudinal project describing the development of this group of teacher candidates through their certification programs and into their first years of teaching. This paper focuses on transcriptions of three Seminar meetings, although the analytical framework includes transcriptions of all ten Seminar meetings as well as interviews, reflective coursework, and field notes from classroom observations. Data were continually analyzed using the constant comparative method pioneered by Glaser and Strauss (1967). All names in this paper are pseudonyms.

Findings and Discussion

Seminar meetings centered on equipping students to unpack their daily experiences in urban classrooms through reflective discussion. The meetings juxtaposed field experiences with structured reflection as explicitly as possible, and often involved community members, experienced urban teachers, and urban students in the conversations. During the first Seminar meeting, directly after their first day in classrooms, a lengthy discussion occurred surrounding the physical space of the schools.

Most teacher candidates, although they had read books about inner-city schools and done a previous field experience in urban settings, were generally shocked by their first encounter with Philadelphia schools. Three teacher candidates began the discussion with these comments:

Tara: I was really shocked that there were 29 students and only one teacher occupying a space that might fit 15 kids comfortably. That really threw all my thoughts about teacher to student ratio and optimized learning environments out the window in about 15 seconds. There are just too many kids with really extreme level differences. If the room was a little bigger there may have been the possibility of working in small groups, but there just wasn't room—to really make the learning effective and organized.

Heather: Yeah, there are 32 kids in my room, and you can't even walk around the room without bumping into desks, and some kids don't even have desks. They sit on the windowsills with low tables piled with the teacher's stuff. It's really hard to imagine how anyone could learn in there.

Kristen: I think the thing that affected me the most was the whole respect for space thing. When I went down to the cafeteria my teacher pointed out this black shriveled-up thing in the rafters, it looked sort of like a tennis ball, and it turned out that it was an orange somebody threw up there three years ago, and I was thinking, "You have got to be kidding me." If we are setting this example that the school doesn't need to be respected, then that sends the message that education doesn't need to be respected either. There were classrooms that looked like they came straight out of *The Wire,* that show on HBO? I thought that was TV, but apparently not. Like how can people function in trash and mess? Like dirty? (Personal communication, May 12, 2008).

These teacher candidates represented the dispositions of all subjects in beginning the experience thinking of the space of the classroom in the same way they thought of themselves—through a lens of normativity. They compared what a "normal" school or classroom should look like, based on whatever ideas they had about what a classroom should be, and ascribed "less than" qualities to these classrooms that didn't look "normal" or work normally.

This represented a real difficulty in encouraging beginning teachers to develop a complete sense of teacher selfhood. Liston & Zeichner (1996) write that since many beginning teachers come from homogeneous communities, in essence they are "prisoners of their own experience," as they have had little contact with people and children of different background from their own. So, though these prospective teachers began the Seminar with a positive outlook, their lack of experience with diverse students prevented them from seeing the school and the children clearly, with compassion and understanding (p. 68).

A central focus of the Seminar is interrupting the "missionary mindset" (Mahoney, 2008), the idea that good teachers need to *save* the students and that the students *needed saving* from their circumstances. By seeing the positive dimensions of urban neighborhoods, through structured reflection and conversations, service projects, and contact with community leaders, all 17 of the student teachers began to see the hope and promise their students lived within, as well as the poverty and despair. As their eyes opened to the positive dimensions of urban communities, they realized that urban students needed great teachers that recognized the valuable resources that surrounded the schools, not people to rescue them from these resources. The shift from saving students to teaching students represented a major milestone on their path to finding their selfhood in the Seminar, and a first step on their path toward a fuller sense of solidarity with their students. This shift is also deemed essential for effective urban teachers (Stairs, Donnell & Dunn, 2012; Steinberg & Kincheloe, 2007) and one that is entirely neglected in many teacher certification programs, in professional induction programs for new teachers, and in professional development for practicing teachers.

At the start of a Seminar meeting at the end of the first week, this interaction took place:

Ellen: I can't stop thinking about what I saw on the way to school this morning: A mother in a nightdress and slippers sending her kids to school from the porch. The kids were really cute in their uniforms and backpacks and they seemed to have so much energy, but what struck me is that I would have seen a completely different scene two days ago. I would have seen a beat-up house in a beat up neighborhood and an overweight woman in pajamas who can't walk her own kids to school through a really scary neighborhood because she can barely get out of bed. Today, I saw a family trying to start their day.

Karey: You know, I don't think I ever realized how uncomfortable I felt being so surrounded by students, only students of color. You know, because I am. Today, at about noon, boy, it hit me, and I don't even know what happened, but things clicked, and maybe what happened is that I stopped looking at color and started looking at what we have in common.

Then, I started talking to them the way they talked to me, like I started saying, "y'all are nasty." and stuff like that. I know. Its ridiculous, and I don't even know that I have been saying that, you know, but this morning the kids were sniffing their armpits. They are in sixth grade. And I was like, "What are you doing?" and they were like, "Well, we are just sniffing our armpits." And I said "y'all are nasty!" and I walked away. And I was like, "I just said 'y'all are nasty!' What am I doing?" (Personal communication, May 16, 2008)

As they started to question the normalization of communities, schools, and students and reject the missionary mindset, these teacher candidates began to articulate how they were growing to understand urban students in the short duration of the Seminar. After nine days in school, this interaction took place during a Seminar meeting in response to a question about how teachers can truly know their students:

Susan: I totally agree, I think our relationships with the kids are the first thing we want to think about, but I was thinking about how hard I found that to be here. How much I had to work on finding ways to relate.

Amanda: OK, so Susan, I mean our question really is how can we relate to these kids, that we are dealing with here, but really anywhere, and I am not sure that there is an answer, because we don't know, and we can't know, what these kids are going through, because we are not them. What we can do is show them that, yes, we do not understand what they are going through, but that doesn't take away from our ability to sit and listen to them. And it's hard to talk about, but just giving them the option to come to you as someone they can confide in, that goes a long way. And maybe we can't relate to the bigger things they have going on, but some of the smaller things, that's maybe a place we can reach them, find commonalities.

Michelle: Yeah. I'm obviously not black. I'm not in sixth Grade. I'm not in foster care. I don't live in inner city Philadelphia. But I think where we find common ground is that every day for the past two weeks I have been looking into the eyes of someone who I don't know how he is going to react, and I think he is looking at me the same way. That is where the common ground is, in saying that I don't know if I can trust this person, I don't know who this person is, but I am going to risk it, and I think that is enough of a commonality to build off for us, to begin trusting each other.

Valerie: This morning two boys were arguing over who had darker skin. I decided to ask them to compare my arm to theirs, and I could see them working through the idea of who cared about lighter or darker. I think I really made them think about the color issue because they never talked about it the rest of the day. I just think that since we talked so freely about race with each other, I felt liberated to talk about it with my kids, and because I was so open, it worked. I felt like I had a major victory for myself and those boys. (Personal communication, May 22, 2008).

The movement these students show toward understanding their students is stronger than empathy or sensitivity, as there is still a demarcation between self and other in those dispositions. Taking solidarity seriously as a way to understand students goes deeper. Rorty (1989) writes that our sense of solidarity is strongest when we think of those with whom solidarity is expressed as one of us, where *us* is defined as something smaller and more local than "the human race." In this way, the teacher candidates' desire to work with city kids was deepened to go beyond some vague obligation to work with less fortunate kids, or altruistic notions of helping kids who did not have the same advantages they had. Those ideas persist in placing the person at the center and the other at the margin. Through the reflection of the Seminar, notions of altruism and the conception that "we" are there to save "them" began to disappear as their sense of teacher selfhood expanded. Henry (1966) called the intellectual work required to imagine teaching in such a way "the assertion of self" and identified such work as a key component in developing alternative practices in an environment that emphasizes standardization over creativity and innovation. This is not to suggest that teachers should focus exclusively on self-knowledge if they want to become good teachers in urban schools, but the assertion of self may be the essential component that binds all the other characteristics of good teaching together. Without this binding, there is no structure to hold all the qualities of good teachers together and integrate them into more than a checklist or a list of attributes. They can only become qualities teachers practice through the assertion of self.

Conclusion

Despite the possibility of illuminating the nexus of teacher and students through a concept like solidarity, Margolis (2007) rightly cautions teachers to reject the idealism that they can somehow dismiss existing relations of power and privilege and find some commonalities with their students as equals. For these students to "understand" life in poverty, growing up in urban neighborhoods, or childhood for a person of color is ridiculous.

However, Rorty (1989) writes that one way to come to terms with what he calls the "slogan" that might define the work of good teachers, that people should try to help other people succeed, is to expand as far as possible our sense of "us"—to actively seek common ground with others. While this is not something that only teachers should do, it is a movement that is essential for good teaching. This is because if the call for good and effective teaching—in many ways the slogan "No Child Left Behind" is one of them, can be understood and acted upon, then thinking about our students through solidarity provides a new vocabulary for reweaving notions of good teaching to accommodate the new discoveries of commonality, equality and worth.

That might be the most critical part of this project, and what most definitions of good teaching neglect. A teacher, school administrator, or policy maker can not simply decide to leave no child behind any more than a teacher can say "I am a good teacher" and thus become one. Teaching in a way that every student can learn is an idea that has to be created through the interaction and understanding of the teacher and the students. It cannot be forced upon teachers and students in the hope that they will

eventually come to accept it. Until policy makers, administrators and teachers realize that leaving no child behind or winning the race to the top involves recognizing that the students can succeed before we implement policies that will require them to succeed, there is little hope for large scale improvement of urban schools.

Further, until teacher candidates are allowed to explore their selfhood and engage in field experiences that involve an explicit focus on building solidarity through recognizing the positive resources surrounding diverse schools, it seems likely that the missionary mentality will persist in the way they frame teaching in urban schools, and there is even less hope that they will be prepared to be great teachers in urban schools through their certification programs.

References

Cawelti, G. (2006). The side effects of NCLB. *Educational Leadership, 64*(3), 64–68.

Cochran-Smith, M. & Zeichner, K. M. (Eds.) (2005). *Studying teacher education: The report of the AREA panel on research and teacher education.* Mahwah, NJ: Lawrence Erlbaum.

Crocco, M. S., & Costigan, A. T. (2007). The narrowing of curriculum and pedagogy in the age of accountability: Urban educators speak out. *Urban Education, 42*(6), 512–535.

Darling-Hammond, L. & Bransford, J. (Eds.). (2005). *Preparing teachers for a changing world: What teachers should learn and be able to do.* New York: Jossey-Bass.

Department of Education: Overview Information; Race to the Top Fund; Application for New Awards for Fiscal Year (FY) 2010, 74 Fed. Reg. 59863 (2009).

The Forum for Education and Democracy. (2009, December). Beyond standardized tests: Investing in a culture of learning. Retrieved from The Forum for Education and Democracy: http://forumforeducation.org/sites/default/files/u48/Learning_Brief_1209_v1.pdf

Glaser, B. G. & Strauss, A. L. (1967). *The discovery of grounded theory: Strategies for qualitative research.* Chicago, IL: Aldine.

Henry, J. (1966). Vulnerability and education. *Teachers College Record, 68,* 135–145.

Hill, J. (2007). What is urban education in an age of standardization and scripted learning? In S. Steinberg & J. Kincheloe (Eds.), *19 urban questions: Teaching in the city* (pp. 119–127). New York: Peter Lang.

Kozol, J. (2005). *The shame of the nation: The restoration of apartheid schooling in America.* New York, NY: Crown Publishers.

Liston, D. P. & Zeichner, K. M. (1996). *Culture and Teaching.* Mahwah, NJ: Lawrence Erlbaum.

Mahoney, T. (2008). Pushing the comfort zone: Pre-service teachers, inner-city schools, and anti-racist pedagogy. In J. Bao, L. Vold & M. Tidwell (Eds.), *Preparing urban teachers collaboratively in Philadelphia: Practices, research and reflections* (pp. 54–68). El Cajon, CA: National Social Science Press.

Margolis, F. (2007). A relational ethic of solidarity? *Philosophy of Education Archive,* 62–72.

Meier, D., & Wood, G. H. (Eds.) (2004). *Many children left behind: How the No Child Left Behind Act is damaging our children and our schools.* Boston: Beacon Press.

No Child Left Behind Act (2002). (Public Law 107–110) U.S. Department of Education. Retrieved March 16, 2012 from: www2.ed.gov/policy/elsec/leg/esea02/107–110.pdf

Palmer, P. J. (1998). *The courage to teach: Exploring the inner landscape of a teacher's life*. San Francisco, CA: Jossey-Bass.

Raymond, A. (Producer), & Raymond, S. (Producer) (2008). *Hard times at Douglass High: A No Child Left Behind report card* [DVD]. Available from http://www.hbo.com

Rorty, R. (1989). *Contingency, irony and solidarity*. Cambridge, MA: Cambridge University Press.

Stairs, A. J., Donnell, K. A., & Dunn, A. H. (Eds.) (2012). *Urban teaching in America: Theory, research and practice in K-12 classrooms*. Los Angeles, CA: Sage.

Steinberg, S. R., & Kincheloe, J. L. (2007). *19 urban questions: Teaching in the city*. New York, NY: Lang.

Critical Thinking

1. What does teacher selfhood mean to you?

2. Why is teacher selfhood important for all teacher candidates and classroom teachers to understand and incorporate into their practices?

3. What does teacher solidarity mean to you?

4. Why is teacher solidarity important for all teacher candidates and classroom teachers to understand and incorporate into their practices?

Create Central

www.mhhe.com/createcentral

Internet References

Critical Pedagogy - WinkWorld
www.joanwink.com/cp3/cp3_pgs123-129.php

Freire Project
www.freireproject.org

Tim Mahoney is Assistant Professor of Educational Foundations at Millersville University.

Mahoney, Timothy. From *Journal of Urban Learning, Teaching, and Research*, vol. 8, 2012, pp. 53–60. Copyright © 2012 by Timothy Mahoney. Used with permission by the author.

Unit 3

UNIT

Prepared by: Nancy P. Gallavan, *University of Central Arkansas*

Awareness of Teacher Preparation

Through the years, teacher preparation programs have modified their labeling of and emphasis on multicultural education; today teacher education uses the term *cultural diversity* or, more appropriately, *cultural competence*. Decades ago, teacher education programs started to include topics and issues in selected courses, i.e., foundations, although most programs either ignored or resisted all teaching, learning, and schooling associated with multicultural education, cultural diversity, and cultural competence. Over time, teacher education programs began to offer one credit-hour courses that slowly expanded to become three credit-hour courses.

National accreditation standards advanced the discussion by publishing expectations that cultural diversity should be evident in all courses through natural integration of content and that culturally diverse teaching experiences should be featured during field placements. College of education began crafting proficiencies they could apply across their programs. Although some teacher educators continue to ignore and/or resist the presence and power of cultural competence for contemporary teacher candidates, most teacher educators are advocates of cultural competence in their course content, their program outcomes, their university faculty, their clinical field experience mentors and cooperative teachers, and all their educational partners.

Concomitantly, teacher education conversations about cultural competence that may have once danced around topics and issues of race, now openly and objectively delve into race as well as all other topics and issues of cultural competence. Addressing democratic principles, educational equity, and social justice are essential for all educators in order to optimize the educational enterprise in the 21st century.

Teacher candidates, classroom teachers, school administrators, and teacher educators must be equipped and empowered with the knowledge, skills, dispositions, and advocacy to emphasize cultural competence in all aspects of teaching, learning, and schooling. Educators must possess content knowledge that features many different people who from the past, present, or future contribute to, are users of, and benefit from the concepts and practices associated with every specific academic discipline. No longer can limited examples be illustrated in textbooks, displayed on bulletin boards, or celebrated for a particular week or month in isolation and out of curricular context.

Likewise, educators must possess pedagogical knowledge that enables them to teach culturally enriched content to all learners in ways focused on cultural competence. Educators of all ages and at all stages need to conduct self-assessments of their teaching styles and attitudes. These self-assessments could include knowledge about one's own cultural backgrounds, beliefs, behaviors, and bridges to the future and the backgrounds, beliefs, behaviors, and bridges of other people, especially other people in their immediate communities. Teacher candidates must be taught and experience various types of teaching methods, i.e., direct instruction, experiential, constructive, cooperative, and so forth; supplemented with various kinds of resources and materials; aligned with various forms of assessments, i.e., selected answers, constructed responses, spoken communications, demonstrated performances, and combinations of these forms that feature interactive classroom learning environments that allow all learners to express and exchange their own cultural competence while understanding and respecting cultural competence in other people, society, and institutional systems.

Many of today's teacher candidates appear to be more comfortable interacting with people unlike themselves; however, they need the tools and techniques for individualizing the learning so every student is provided fair and equitable information, access, opportunities, and equipment to maximize their potential, express their creativity, and make powerful connections with their peers, their learning, and their living. In their university coursework and their clinical field experiences, teacher candidates must be prepared for the teaching, learning, and schooling that matters.

Article   Prepared by: Nancy P. Gallavan, *University of Central Arkansas*

What Influence the Development of Multicultural Teaching Competencies?

EUNSOOK HONG, PORTER TROUTMAN, STEPHANIE HARTZELL AND CARLI KYLES

Learning Outcomes

After reading this article, you will be able to:

• Discuss multicultural teaching competencies.

• Explain the importance of becoming a multicultural person.

A widening gap of sociocultural factors between the teaching force and student population in the United States has been indicated in various census data. Although nearly half of elementary and secondary student populations are ethnic minorities, the teaching population is predominantly White, female, middle class, and monolingual (Gollnick & Chinn, 2002; Zumwalt & Craig, 2005). The nearly monocultural characteristics of preservice teachers being prepared to teach the massive numbers of multicultural K-12 students makes the case for the necessity of adequate preparation of educators to meet the needs of diverse learners (Bennett, 2003). Teachers' knowledge, awareness, and attitudes towards students, especially those who are ethnically and culturally different from their own, influence teaching and student learning (Jackson, 1995; Ladson-Billings, 1994; Sleeter, 2001). The demographic disparity between K-12 students and preservice teachers underscores the responsibility of teacher educators to ensure that preservice teachers are well prepared to teach in various sociocultural contexts in today's public schools.

Research findings indicate that preservice teachers have negative beliefs and low expectations of success for minority students even after they have taken some coursework in multicultural education (Garmon, 1998; Scott, 1995). Numerous multicultural education scholars have observed that preservice teachers lack the knowledge, skills, and dispositions required to work with minority and low-income students (Gay, 2000; Ukpokodu, 2007). When preservice teachers were asked about their preference for student-teaching placement, most gave a socially acceptable response initially, but changed their answers later, indicating a preference for working in a suburban school with the majority of White students (Terrill & Mark, 2000). Sleeter (2001) concluded that White preservice teachers bring very little cross-cultural knowledge, experience, and

understanding to teaching, possess stereotypical beliefs about urban students, and have little knowledge of racism, discrimination, and structural aspects of inequality.

Without adequate knowledge of social constructs such as race, class, and gender, and how these social constructs award power and privilege to some and how others experience alienation and oppression, preservice teachers are at a disadvantage to understand the importance of multicultural education in their classroom. Gay (2001) contends that preservice teachers must know about the richness, complexity, and vitality of American cultural diversity, the cultural experiences, values, characteristics, and learning styles of different ethnic students, and develop concrete skills relative to curriculum design, instructional strategies, and interaction abilities.

Underachievement of ethnic minority groups and students in urban schools in general is pervasive (Morrier, Irving, Dandy, Dmitriyev, & Ukeje, 2007; Tidwell & Thompson, 2008). To tackle this difficulty, teachers need to understand cultural dynamics in schools and classrooms to be effective manager and teachers. Preservice teachers need to be aware of the subtle but powerful forms of cultural discrimination and how the cultural undertone affects class dynamics and ultimately, students' cognitive and affective learning (Tidwell & Thompson, 2008).

To address these issues, teacher education programs have included multicultural education for preservice teachers that provides continuous development from program entry to exit. However, some scholars of multicultural education argue that teacher education programs need to be examined to improve multicultural education in teacher education. Valentin (2006) contends that programs in colleges of education need to be examined to assess the effectiveness of multicultural education, suggesting infusion of diversity topics throughout all education courses and programs. Similar assertions were made for urban teacher preparation, stressing the importance of infusing multicultural approaches into all aspects of teacher preparation programs (Tidwell & Thompson, 2008) or calling for approaches beyond the isolated-course approach, allowing long-term exposure that provides continuous development of multicultural knowledge and skills throughout teacher-education programs (Ngai, 2004).

There are, however, a few approaches that have been evidenced as effective for helping preservice teachers acquire multicultural teaching competency (e.g., Hasslen & Bacharach, 2007). Reyes and Bishop (2005) found an effective instructional approach to surmount the challenges inherent in preparing teachers at an institution with predominantly White students in teacher education. They report the development of a partnership between a teacher preparation program and an urban after-school program in a neighboring state to provide preservice teachers with an environment where they can experience working with students of diverse backgrounds. Taylor and Sobel (2003) in their multicultural course and fieldwork experiences found that preservice teachers value guided exposure to "real-world" cross-cultural interaction, observations of theory-practice applications in course work, and interactions with the clinical teachers.

Although efforts to improve multicultural education within teacher education programs have been made to some extent, research investigating other, non-teacher-education factors that affect preservice teachers' multicultural awareness and competencies is rare. The current study examined whether the length of college experience, as a proxy to having more chances to meet with people of diverse backgrounds, predicts their perceived multicultural awareness and competency. We also examined whether personal experiences with racial diversity make a difference in their multicultural competency by directly asking preservice teachers of their experiences and relating them to their perceived competency. To our knowledge, no study examined whether volunteer experience in programs involving people from the inner city would help preservice teachers become more aware and competent in multicultural education. We examined whether White preservice teachers in fact perceive themselves as lacking in multicultural competency as compared to non-White preservice teachers. We also examined a teacher-education related variable to determine whether taking multicultural courses has any relationship with multicultural teaching competency.

In summary, the current study examined the relationship of multicultural experiences with multicultural teaching competencies. Several proxy variables that represent differing levels of multicultural experiences were examined in this study. Specifically, we predicted that there would be differences in perceived multicultural teaching competencies of preservice teachers of different (a) class standing, (b) race, (c) multicultural courses, (d) experience with inner-city program volunteer experience, and (e) personal experience with racial diversity.

To assess preservice teachers' perceived multicultural teaching competency, an instrument was developed. The instrument measures multicultural competencies in knowledge, skills, and dispositions that preservice teachers should acquire as they move through a teacher education program. To our knowledge, no studies have been conducted using knowledge, skills, and dispositions domains of self-perceived multicultural teaching competencies. However, based on related studies reviewed above, we predicted significant group differences in most of these variables. As an example, those who volunteered to get involved in an inner-city program might have accumulated more skills and acquired desirable dispositions in multicultural awareness and competencies, although volunteer experiences might have been less influential on the acquisition of formal knowledge regarding diversity and multicultural education.

Method

Participants

Preservice teachers at a college of education in a large southwestern urban university in the U.S. were the sample. Participants ($N = 184$) included 145 females and 38 males (1 unspecified), 77% of these students were 25 or younger, and varied class standings with 2% freshmen, 26% sophomore, 34% junior, 24% senior, 2% licensure, 3% graduate students, and 9% unspecified. The majority of participants were European Americans representing 58%, followed by 12% bi- or multi-racial Americans, 11% Hispanic Americans, 8% African Americans, 6% Asian Americans, and 5% other races.

Participants were asked whether they have taken multicultural courses and if so, how many. There were 60% of students who have taken a course(s), 38% not taken, and 2% unspecified, with most of students having taken only one course (79%). Twenty-five percent of the participants reported having had volunteer experiences in inner-city programs, 65% no experience, and 11% unspecified. When participants were asked their personal experiences with racial diversity, 2% reported very limited experience, 29% limited, 53% extensive, and 16% very extensive, with 1% unspecified. Most participants (96%) perceived student body at the university as consisting of multiple racial groups.

Instrument

Development background

Self Assessment Questionnaire: Multicultural Teaching Competencies (SAQ: MTC) was used to collect preservice teachers' perceived multicultural teaching competencies. Items for this questionnaire were developed based on the general guidelines of the *National Council for the Accreditation of Teacher Education* (NCATE) standards that emphasizes the competency development in three domains—knowledge, skills, and dispositions. The *NCATE Standard 4*, Diversity (2006, 2008), requires teacher education programs to design, implement, and evaluate curriculum and experiences for candidates to acquire and apply the knowledge, skills, and dispositions necessary to help all students learn. To accomplish this objective, teacher education programs are to help preservice teachers understand the importance of diversity in teaching and learning via clearly articulated proficiencies. In addition, the importance of assessments of preservice teachers' competencies and the use of assessment data to provide feedback to candidates for improving their knowledge, skills, and disposition are underscored. These criteria were adopted as the foundation for item development. Also consulted in the deliberation of item development were existing literatures and instruments on multicultural education (e.g., Bennett, 2001; Brown & Kysilka, 2002; Gay, 2001; LeBrec, 1993; Pohan & Aguilar, 2001).

Questionnaire items

Each questionnaire item represented competence in one of the three domains. In the *knowledge* domain, items were grouped under three categories: (a) general knowledge on diversity (e.g., "I know U.S. historical events and issues related to race, class, and gender"); (b) effects of diversity on learning and teaching ("I understand how culture and language influence learning and teaching"); and (c) instructional implications of diversity ("I know various teaching techniques and strategies for students with diverse backgrounds"). In the *skills* domain, items for two categories were developed: (a) multicultural teaching techniques/strategies ("I can structure the classroom environment to meet the needs of culturally diverse students"); and (b) multicultural awareness in classroom teaching and community relationship ("I can bring multiple perspectives into the classroom when discussing various subject matters"). In the *dispositions* domain, items were grouped under three categories: (a) beliefs and values of teaching in multicultural environment ("I have high expectations for students with diverse backgrounds as well as others"); (b) experiences with diversity ("I have a wide variety of work experiences with diverse students"); and (c) awareness of cultural biases ("I take the initiative to dispel prejudices, stereotypes, and misconceptions among people").

The original questionnaire included 24 items in knowledge, 27 items in skills, and 29 items in dispositions. A four-point scale was selected over a five-point scale to prevent respondents from choosing the middle point as an easy way out for unwillingness to devote effort: 1 = Not at all; 2 = Somewhat; 3 = Moderately so; 4 = Very much so. A complete list of items will be available upon request.

Initial validation

This questionnaire was subjected to empirical validation; we provide a brief report on internal consistency and factor analysis. Cronbach's alpha was estimated for each of the knowledge, skills, and dispositions domains of the *SAQ: MTC* on the data collected from preservice teachers. Alpha coefficients were .87, .95, and .83, respectively. All item discrimination indices were acceptable.

We subjected participants' self-ratings to exploratory factor analysis to determine whether the hypothesized structure in each domain underlies the *SAQ: MTC* scores. The factor structure of the knowledge domain was largely well defined, with the three extracted factors corresponding to the hypothesized factors and most items of extracted factors loading on the hypothesized three categories of the questionnaire. However, some items related more closely to other factors that were not originally hypothesized to relate to and some items crossloaded on two factors. Except for a minor revision on one item and removal of two items, the rest of the items remained for future validation studies with different samples.

All skills' items define one factor, *Multicultural teaching technique and strategies*. The hypothesized three-category structure of the Dispositions domain was empirically represented with a four-factor structure. The first factor, as defined empirically, describes an important aspect of dispositions in

multicultural education (*beliefs, values, and commitment in diversity*). Items in the second extracted factor (*valuation on cultural biases*) measure participants' opinion and attitude about cultural biases, mostly as an observer of these issues in society. The category, experiences with diversity, was divided into two empirical factors: *experiences (learning) with diversity and experiences (working/living) with diversity*. One item was dropped from the questionnaire.

Procedure

Data collection

Instructors who were teaching various teacher education courses (e.g., Introduction to Elementary/Secondary Education, Educational Psychology, Tests and Measurements) were contacted for their assistance in data collection. In each participating class, the *SAQ: MTC* was distributed to all students, along with two copies of a consent form and demographic information sheet. The purpose of the study and general data collection procedure were described by the researcher. Students who volunteered to participate in the study completed the demographic sheet and questionnaire and turned them in with the signed consent form. Students kept the other copy of the consent form. Students who did not wish to participate kept the materials for their information.

Data analysis

We examined whether factor scores within each domain discriminate various groups. Factor scores were computed based on the items that loaded on specific factors with loadings larger than .30. For the items loading on more than one factor, we selected the factor with a larger loading in the computation of the factor score.

As indicated earlier, the five grouping variables were class standing, race, multicultural courses, inner-city program volunteer experience, and personal experience with racial diversity. Gender difference was not examined due to a large disparity in the sample sizes (145 females vs. 38 males).

Multivariate analyses of variance (MANOVAs) were performed using Wilks' Lambda criterion, followed by univariate analyses of variance (ANOVAs) for three Knowledge scores and four Disposition scores. Analyses of variance were conducted for the one Skills score. Because the development of multicultural competencies may be influenced by many life factors over which one may not have much control over (e.g., race), we set a liberal probability level ($\alpha = .10$) to test the statistical significance for multivariate tests. Due to multiple testing at the univariate level, conservative probability levels were used for Knowledge scores (.033) and for Disposition scores (.025). Post hoc multiple comparison tests were performed with Bonferroni adjustments for probability levels. The assumption of the homogeneity of variance and covariance matrices on multivariate analysis was met in all cases. For univariate analysis, the homogeneity of variance assumption was met except for two cases. Those two instances are explained in the relevant sections below.

Results

Findings are provided for each group variable in the order of class standing, race, multicultural course, inner-city volunteer program, and personal experience with racial diversity.

(1) Class standing: Freshmen/Sophomore versus Junior versus Senior. Due to having a small size for freshmen in this study, we combined freshmen and sophomores (proximity in class standing) and compared it with juniors and seniors. In the knowledge domain, the ratings of the three levels of class standing were significantly different on the combined knowledge score, $F(6, 308) = 1.95, p = .07, =\eta_p^2 = .04$, indicating a small effect size. Follow-up univariate ANOVAs indicated that only F3 (the 3rd empirical factor) scores (*instructional implications of diversity*) were statistically significant, $F(2, 156) = 4.66, p = .01, \eta^2 = .06$ (medium effect size), with seniors ($M = 3.57, SD = .38$) scoring higher than freshmen/sophomores ($M = 3.34, <SD = .45$), $<p = .02$, and juniors, $p = .03$. The differences between freshmen/sophomores and juniors were not statistically significant.

A significant group difference was also found in the skills domain, $F(2, 155) = 6.92, p = .001, \eta^2 = .08$, again with seniors ($M = 3.62, <SD = .37$) scoring higher than freshmen/sophomores ($M = 3.36, <SD = .42$), $p = .005$, and juniors, $p = .005$. The difference between freshmen/sophomores and juniors was not significant.

The group difference was significant on the combined disposition score, $F(8, 302) = 3.01, p = .003, \eta^2 = .07$. Follow-up univariate ANOVAs indicated that only the scores of F2 (*valuation of cultural biases*) and F3 (*learning experiences with diversity*) were significantly different, $p = .001; \eta^2 = .09$ and $p = .006, \eta^2 = .07$ respectively. Seniors ($M = 2.85, SD = .83$) scored higher on F2 than freshmen/sophomores ($M = 2.36, SD = .61$), $p = .003$, and juniors ($M = 2.33, SD = .68$), $p = .001$. On F3, however, a significant difference was found only between seniors ($M = 3.49, SD = .53$) and juniors ($M = 3.12, <SD = .55$), $<p = .004$. Although F4 (*working/living experiences with diversity*) was significant at .01 level, the assumption of homogeneity of variances on this variable was not met; furthermore, the largest variance was aligned with the smallest sample size, requiring an even more conservative probability level for significance testing.

(2) Race differences: White versus Non-White. The only statistically significant difference found in multivariate analysis was dispositions scores, $F(4, 176) = 3.55, <p = .008, \eta^2 = .08$. Except for F4 scores (*working/living experiences with diversity*), White preservice teachers scored higher than non-White peers. However, none of the univariate ANOVA was statistically significant.

(3) Multicultural courses: Taken versus Not-taken. The two groups were significantly different only in the multivariate analysis of knowledge scores, $F(3, 177) = 3.43, p = .018, \eta^2 = .06$. Students who took multicultural courses scored a little higher on F1 scores (*instructional implications of diversity*) ($M = 3.47; SD = .42$) than those who did not ($M = 3.34; SD = .41$), $p = .036$, but the difference was not statistically significant at 033. Skills and dispositions scores were very similar between the two groups.

(4) Inner-city program volunteer: Volunteers versus Non-volunteers. Significant differences were found in skills and dispositions scores between those who had volunteered to help in an inner-city program(s) and those who had not, $F(1, 161) = 4.87, p = .029, \eta^2 = .03$, in skills; $F(4, 157) = 2.64, p = .036, \eta^2 = .06$, in dispositions. Follow-up ANOVAs for dispositions indicated that F3 (*learning experiences with diversity*), $p = .003, \eta^2 = .06$, and F4 (*working/living experiences with diversity*), $p = .011, \eta^2 = .04$, showed statistically significant group differences. The effect sizes were small. For these univariate analyses, the homogeneity of error variances assumption was not met. However, the group sample sizes and variance sizes were congruent, indicating the significance level was rather conservative. Knowledge scores did not differ between the two groups.

(5) Personal experience with racial diversity: Limited versus Extensive versus Very extensive. The extent of personal experience with racial diversity was categorized into three groups. Group differences were statistically and practically significant in all three domains. The combined knowledge score (multivariate) was significantly different among the three groups, $F(6, 354) = 7.18, p < .0005, \eta_p^2 = .11$. Univariate ANOVAs indicated that group differences in F2 (*effects of diversity on learning and teaching*), $F(2, 179) = 9.00, p < .0005, \eta^2 = .09$, and in F3 (*instructional implications of diversity*) were statistically significant, $F(2, 179) = 11.73, p < .0005, \eta^2 = .12$. In general, preservice teachers with more experience scored higher in the knowledge domain than those with less experience. However, preservice teachers' *general knowledge on diversity* was not related to personal experiences with racial diversity, likely because most items in this category regarded factual information (e.g., know historical events; know history and culture; know U.S. founding documents). In F2, significant differences were found between limited and very extensive, $p < .0005$, and between extensive and very extensive, $p = .005$. The same pattern was observed in F3 with $p < .0005$ and $p = .001$, respectively.

A significant group difference was also found in skills scores, $F(2, 178) = 4.50, p = .012, \eta^2 = .05$. Post hoc tests indicated that the scores were statistically significantly different only between the groups with limited and very extensive experiences, $p = .01$.

In dispositions, the group difference was significant on the combined dispositions score, $F(8, 348) = 4.47, p < .0005, \eta_p^2 = .09$. Univariate ANOVAs indicated that group differences in scores of F1 (*beliefs, values, and commitment in diversity*), $p = .006, \eta^2 = .06$, and F3 (*learning experiences with diversity*), $p = .010, \eta^2 = .05$, as well as F4 (*working/living experiences with diversity*), $p < .0005, \eta^2 = .13$, were statistically significant, with moderate effect sizes. As expected, preservice teachers with more experience rated higher than less experienced peers. In F1, the groups with limited and very extensive, $p = .007$, and those with extensive and very extensive experience were significantly different, $p = .016$. In F3, only limited and very extensive groups were significant different, $p = .017$. In F4, significant differences were found between limited and extensive, $p = .001$, and between limited and very extensive, $p < .0005$.

Discussion

The *NCATE Standards* on diversity underscore the importance of assessment of preservice teachers' multicultural teaching competencies and of the use of assessment data to provide feedback on their ability to work with all students. As the U.S. became more racially and culturally diverse, the importance of teacher preparation for multicultural awareness and competencies have been emphasized by numerous scholars in multicultural education (e.g., Bingham, 2009; Sleeter, 2001; Valentin, 2006). Understanding factors that might have impacts on preservice teachers' multicultural teaching competencies is important as multicultural competencies may take various experiences to acquire beyond what teacher education programs provide.

In general, findings support the importance of various personal experiences in acquiring multicultural teaching competencies. Group differences were demonstrated in multicultural teaching competencies self-reported by preservice teachers. Seniors perceived that they had higher multicultural teaching competencies than freshmen/sophomores and juniors in knowledge, skills, and dispositions, although not all subscale scores were statistically significantly different. Consistently, juniors were not different from freshmen/sophomore students. This might indicate that awareness of multicultural competencies becomes more prominent later in their college experiences. Upper class preservice teachers are exposed to more teacher education-related courses where multicultural issues in classrooms are more frequently discussed than in other university general-education core requirements (e.g., life and physical sciences). In addition, seniors in teacher education have field experiences in elementary or secondary schools as part of their teacher training experiences. Other general-education cores include experiences in courses that meet multicultural/international requirements. The higher the class standing, the more chances students would have experienced multiculturalism. Having higher-education experience where students from various cultural backgrounds including international students may be beneficial for preservice students, as similarly reported in the Jayakumar's study (2008). Although Jayakumar's study regards higher education in general, the author concludes that postsecondary institutions provide lasting benefits to White students; that is, exposure to racially diverse student body during college have positive impacts on postcollege cross-cultural workforce competencies.

Race differences were not found in the knowledge and skills domains. Interestingly, more White preservice teachers self-rated higher in disposition items than non-White peers, except for one factor (*working/living experiences with diversity*). Due to the non-White group having been composed of various races for the study (limited sample sizes), how each minority group of preservice teachers would differ among each other and from White preservice teachers could not be tested. The racial composition of the current sample reflected that of teacher education programs in general, with the majority of preservice teachers being White females (Zumwalt & Craig, 2005). White preservice teachers in this study perceived that they were aware of cultural biases, had more learning experiences with diversity, and had positive beliefs and values of teaching in multicultural environment more so than non-White peers, although they reported that they had less working/living experiences with diversity. This contradiction might speak to the notion of social desirability or aversive racism as a factor for White preservice teachers' higher self-ratings on disposition items. On the other hand, the findings might reflect what they indeed perceive. Whether perceived and actual multicultural competencies are consistent should be examined using additional assessments such as observations. Studies comparing racial subgroups as well as studies using qualitative research approaches might provide in-depth understandings of this phenomenon.

The no-differences in multicultural knowledge, skills, and dispositions between preservice teachers who have taken stand-alone multicultural education courses and those who have not are of concern. Previous studies also indicated that preservice teachers' beliefs about minority students did not change even after they had taken some multicultural courses (e.g., Scott, 1995). Preservice teachers in Bingham's study (2009) reported that although their field-based experiences influenced their preparation to teach diverse children, they observed a disconnect between the teacher education curricula and field-based experiences (Bingham, 2009). As reviewed earlier, some researchers of multicultural education contend that multicultural curricular transformation needs to take place in teacher education (Ambe, 2006). Ngai (2004) contends that newer approaches beyond the common isolated-courses on multicultural or diversity courses should be attempted in teacher education programs, and other scholars (Morrier et al., 2007; Tidwell & Thompson, 2008; Valentin, 2006) suggest education reform in multicultural education may be needed to prepare effectively preservice teachers for increasing diversity in the school.

Volunteering in inner-city programs had some relationship with multicultural teaching competencies, especially in skills and disposition domains, but not in knowledge, possibly due to experiential learning that volunteer activities provide. Similarly, the more personal experience preservice teachers have with racial diversity, the higher scores in all three domains, although not all subscale scores demonstrated significant differences.

An advantage of using the current instrument for assessing preservice teachers' multicultural teaching competencies is apparent in the finding of the difference demonstrated between freshmen/sophomores and seniors. With the adoption of this or similar instrument as one of the tools for assessing the development of multicultural competencies from program entry to program exit, preservice teachers will have additional opportunities to self-assess their development of multicultural awareness and competencies. In addition, with multiple opportunities to assess their own multicultural competencies, preservice teachers will be able to understand their levels of competencies and put forth efforts to gain the necessary knowledge, skills, and dispositions for becoming a multicultural educator. This process will also help preservice teachers realize that becoming a multicultural educator is not acquired inherently, intuitively, or through one or two multicultural courses and that they must be developed consciously, deliberately, and repeatedly (Gay, 2001).

Limitations and future research.

The current study comes with the common problems that all studies that rely on self-report face. Although the research purpose was explained and anonymity was assured to participants, it is possible that participants' self-assessment did not represent their multicultural teaching competencies as teacher educators would have rated. This questionnaire offers one approach to assessing preservice teachers' multicultural teaching competences. If this questionnaire is to be used for the outcome measure of preservice teachers' competencies, it should be used in conjunction with other measures such as observations, logs, interviews, portfolio, and/or other behavior manifestations.

Studies to determine whether differences in multicultural competencies can be found between undergraduate and graduate standings and between preservice and inservice teachers are warranted as findings can shed light on the effect of education and of teaching practice. Moreover, various samples from different areas of the country (e.g., rural versus urban versus suburban) should be utilized to further understand multicultural education in practice. We analyzed cross-sectional data in this study. Longitudinal studies would provide researchers with opportunities for gathering multiple assessments to determine the developmental trajectory of multicultural competencies.

Conclusions

Many countries are faced with changing demographics and diversity issues in schools and society in general. Cultural diversity in schools demands teacher preparation for multicultural teaching competencies. Teacher education programs should address the need for adequate training of prospective teachers with proper curriculum and assessment tools, so preservice teachers are prepared with proper knowledge, skills, and dispositions for teaching diverse students.

The current findings indicated that personal experiences in diversity in general are important predictors of preservice teachers' perceived multicultural teaching competencies. Nieto (1996) contends that to become a multicultural teacher, one first needs to become a multicultural person. However, although multicultural education has been a significant part of teacher education programs, many educators call for reform in multicultural education (e.g., Morrier et al., 2007; Tidwell & Thompson, 2008). Providing "real-world" personal experiences during teacher education programs (Reyes & Bishop, 2005) might be one way to increase multicultural competencies to deliver effective and culturally responsive pedagogy for all learners, but creative solutions should be sought to provide effective experiences for prospective teachers.

Finally, the type of instrument used in this study can be a useful tool for assessing perceived multicultural teaching competencies. Providing multiple opportunities for preservice teachers to assess their own multicultural teaching competencies in knowledge, skills, and dispositions would help them become more reflective of their competency development. Especially with the number of minority students growing rapidly, it is imperative that teachers be equipped with multicultural teaching competencies to help themselves become effective educators for all learners.

References

Ambe, E. B. (2006). Fostering multicultural appreciation in preservice teachers through multicultural curricular transformation. *Teaching and Teacher Education: An International Journal of Research and Studies, 22,* 690–699.

Bennett, C. (2001). Genres of research in multicultural education. *Review of Research in Education, 71,* 171–217.

Bennett, C. (2003). *Comprehensive multicultural education: Theory and practice* (4th ed.). Boston, MA: Allyn & Bacon.

Bingham, T. (2009). Teaching for diversity: Preservice teachers' beliefs and ways to enhance teacher preparation program. *Journal of Multiculturalism in Education.* retrieved October 9, 2009, from http://multicultural journal.com/issues/#bingham.

Brown, S. C., & Kysilka, M. (2002). *Applying multicultural and global concepts in the classroom and beyond.* Boston, MA: Allyn & Bacon.

Garmon, M. A. (1998, October). *Preservice teachers' learning about diversity: The influence of their existing racial attitudes and beliefs.* Paper presented at the Annual Meeting of the Midwestern Educational Research Association, Chicago, IL. (ERIC Document Reproduction Service No. ED 452 161)

Gay, G. (2000). *Culturally responsive teaching: Theory, research and practice.* New York: Teachers College Press.

Gay, G. (2001). *Multicultural preparation and teacher effectiveness in desegregated schools. Theory Into Practice. 17,* 149–156.

Gollnick, D. & Chinn, P. (2002). *Multicultural education in a pluralistic society* (6th ed.). New York: Macmillian.

Hasslen, R., & Bacharach, N. (2007). Nurturing multicultural competence in an early childhood graduate teacher licensure program. *Action in Teacher Education, 29,* 32–41.

Jackson, S. (1995). Autobiography: Pivot points for engaging lives in multicultural contexts. In J. Larkin & C. Sleeter (Eds.), *Developing multicultural teacher education curricula* (pp. 31–44). New York: State University of New York Press.

Jayakumar, U. M. (2008). Can higher education meet the needs of an increasingly diverse and global society? Campus diversity and cross-cultural workforce competencies. *Harvard Education Review, 78,* 615–651.

Ladson-Billings, G. (1994). What we can learn from multicultural education research. *Educational Leadership, 51*(8), 22–26.

LeBrec, S. (1993). *How to Respond to Your Culturally Diverse Student Population.* Alexandria, VA: Association for Supervision and Curriculum Development.

Morrier, M. J., Irving, M. A., Dandy, E., Dmitriyev, G., & Ukeje, I. C. (2007). Teaching and learning within and across cultures: Educator Requirements across the United States. *Multicultural Education, 14*(3), 32–49.

Ngai, P. B. (2004). A reinforcing curriculum and program reform proposal for 21st centry teacher education: Vital first steps for advancing K-12 multicultural education. *Equity and Excellence in Education, 37,* 321–331.

Nieto, S. (2000). Placing equity front and center. *Journal of Teacher Education, 51,* 180–187.

Pohan, C., & Aguilar, T. (2001). Measuring educators' beliefs about diversity in personal and professional contexts. *American Educational Research Journal, 38,* 159–182.

Reyes, C., & Bishop, P. A. (2005). Meeting in the middle: Preparing teachers on predominantly White campuses for diverse classrooms. *Teacher Education and Practice, 18,* 137–156.

Scott, R. M. (1995). Helping teacher education students develop positive attitudes toward ethnic minorities. *Equity and Excellence in Education, 28,* 69–73.

Sleeter, C. E. (2001). Preparing teachers for culturally diverse schools: Research and the overwhelming presence of whiteness. *Journal of Teacher Education, 52,* 94–106.

Talyor, S. V., & Sobel, D. M. (2003). Rich contexts to emphasize social justice in teacher education: Curriculum and pedagogy in professional development schools. *Equity & Excellence in Education, 36,* 249–258.

Terrill, M., & Mark, D. L. H. (2000). Preservice teachers' expectations for schools with children of color and second-language learners. *Journal of Teacher Education, 51,* 149–155.

Tidwell, M., & Thompson, C. (2008). Infusing multicultural principles in urban teacher preparation. *Childhood Education, 85*(2), 85–90.

Ukpokodu, N. (2007). Breaking through preservice teachers' defensive dispositions in a multicultural education course: A reflective practice. *Multicultural Education, 9*(3) 25–33.

Valentin, S. (2006). Addressing diversity in teacher education programs. *Education, 127*(2), 196–202.

Zumwalt, K., & Craig, E. (2005). Teacher's characteristics: Research on the demographic profile. In M. Cochran-Smith & K. M. Zeichner (Eds.), *Studying teacher education: The report of the AERA panel on research and teacher education* (pp.111–156). Mahwah, NJ: Erlbaum.

Critical Thinking

1. What are the critical factors that influenced teacher candidates' perceived multicultural teaching competencies?
2. Why is personal experience with racial diversity important for teacher candidates?
3. What role does the teacher candidate's race play in developing multicultural teaching competencies?
4. How are you becoming a multicultural person?

Create Central

www.mhhe.com/createcentral

Internet References

United States Citizenship and Immigration Services
www.uscis.gov/portal/site/uscis

United States Department of Health and Human Services
www.hhs.gov/specificpopulations

Hong, Eunsook;Troutman, Porter;Hartzell, Stephanie;Kyles, Carli. From *Multicultural Teaching Competencies,* vol. 24, 2010, pp. 1–24. Copyright © 2010 by West Texas A&M University. Reprinted by permission.

Article   Prepared by: Nancy P. Gallavan, *University of Central Arkansas*

Productive Dissonance:

A Musical-analytical Exploration of Teacher Educator Perceptions in a Multicultural Education Program

LYNN VIOLET CLARK

Learning Outcomes

After reading this article, you will be able to:

• Identify the presence of consonance, counterpoint, dissonance, and resonance in cultural competence.

• Discuss the perceptions you have about teaching in a culturally diverse society.

Dissonance is an essential element in almost any musical work; it is present when two notes that do not seem to fit together push toward a resolution. While "dissonance" comes out of a Western musical tradition and what is labeled "dissonant" varies depending on cultural context, the idea of using conflicting notes to develop a musical idea is a universal construct. Although dissonance can be destructive, turning music into noise, it is more often productive, resulting in a tension that moves the music forward. The purpose of this study is to explore, using a musical metaphor, some of the tensions inherent in a large-scale multicultural teacher education program. In particular it examines how the needs of the program to create a cohesive curriculum and the needs of the instructors to develop an individual approach may generate a "productive dissonance" that has the power to transform the program.

Multicultural Teacher Education Programs

By its very nature, a multicultural teacher education program must embrace multiple perspectives and discourses (Gay, 2010). Drawing on the collective research in the field, Christine Bennett (2010) outlines four broad principles of multicultural education that should be addressed with all pre-service teachers: a theory of cultural pluralism; ideals of social justice; affirmations of culture; and visions of educational equity and excellence. James Banks (1994) posits that multicultural teacher education should illuminate how cultural assumptions and biases shape the way in which we process information. Geneva Gay (2000) explains

that we must move beyond cultural categories to see the interrelationship between cultures while maintaining a critical perspective to "deconstruct and reconstruct common ethnic and gender typecasting" (p. 143). Christine Sleeter (2004) argues that the "ideals of social justice" are not enough; multicultural teacher education should help students "name and actively challenge forms of injustice, not just recognize and celebrate differences" (p. 123). Gloria Ladson-Billings (1991) reminds us that pre-service teachers must develop a willingness to explore and discuss their own feelings about the issues and attitudes related to multicultural education. What emerges is a multicultural teacher education program that includes a nuanced approach to cultural and cognitive pluralism, a complex and critical perspective, powerful strategies for reflection and dialogue, and an insistent call to action.

Although stand-alone multicultural education classes are an essential element of most teacher education programs, there is little evidence that these classes can fundamentally change the attitudes and beliefs of mainstream preservice teachers (Cochran-Smith, 2003; Gay & Howard, 2000; Larkin & Sleeter, 1995). Advocates of multicultural teacher education often criticize stand-alone classes because they believe an isolated course "trivializes and marginalizes multicultural education and does little to prepare beginning teachers to move beyond traditional approaches to teaching culturally diverse students" (Larkin & Sleeter, 1995, p. ix). Current trends in teacher education show an increase in an infused approach to multicultural teacher education that replaces distinct courses dedicated to diversity with multicultural experiences or themes woven throughout all teacher education coursework (Irvine, 2003; Potts et al., 2008).

Geneva Gay (1997) calls for an integrated approach to multicultural teacher education that combines the two approaches for "a dual presence in the program offerings" (p. 160). She suggests that themes of cultural and ethnic diversity be included in all foundational courses as well as providing distinct courses in the theory and practice of multicultural education. She argues that multicultural teacher education has become a political issue and asks, "If knowledge and diversity is not an integral part of a professional preparation program, how and when are teachers supposed to learn the knowledge and skills they need to teach diverse students?" To Gay (2005), the implications are clear:

"The ones who are least valued can be easily overlooked without the reformers seeing any contradictions in their visions and action proposals" (p. 223).

To help frame curricular reform, Christine Bennett (2010) suggests six goals of comprehensive multicultural curriculum.

These six goals are interrelated and draw on the following core values of multicultural education: a responsibility to the world community, respect for the earth, acceptance and appreciation of cultural diversity, respect for human dignity and universal human rights. In addition, the goals and values work on different levels. Whereas the six curricular goals might be more explicit in the curriculum, present in the organization and content of the course, the values would more often be implicit in the approach of the instructor and the structure of the class. Finally, these goals are a framework, not a mandate, for curricular reform. The model does not suggest that each goal carry the same weight but that the goals serve as a guide for course development. Bennett suggests that "ideally teams of teachers within a school . . . college or university would collaborate on the sequencing and articulation of multicultural perspectives in curriculum objectives, strategies, and materials" (Bennett, 2010, p. 34).

Method

This study examines a multicultural teacher education program in a large Midwestern university, which follows the hybrid model suggested by Geneva Gay and was originally designed using the six goals of Bennett (2010). Currently, the program weaves the themes of cultural and ethnic diversity through all methods classes as well as provides a mandatory stand-alone course for all undergraduate pre-service teachers during their sophomore or junior year. Nine sections of the course are offered at both the elementary and secondary levels each semester. Two faculty and seven graduate students teach different sections of the 3-unit course. The faculty and graduate students also participate in a biweekly seminar that provides pedagogical and theoretical support. Although all graduate students participate in a lengthy interview and screening process by faculty and peers, once selected to teach the course, they are given complete autonomy. The result is a diverse and personal approach to course content and classroom strategies. The purpose of this study is to explore that diversity in approach through interviews and analysis of course syllabi to uncover the unique "melody" of each faculty member and graduate student (hereafter referred to jointly as instructors) and how it relates to current research. The data were also analyzed collectively to determine the *consonance,* or harmony, within the program; the counterpoint, or contrast, of distinct but compatible approaches; the *dissonance* of conflicting approaches; and the *resonance,* or reverberation, of certain approaches to shift the tone and structure of the program as a whole.

Data Collection

In an effort to explore the unique approach, or melody, of each instructor, I developed an interview protocol with lead and follow-up questions based on my three research questions:

1. What curricular and instructional approaches to multicultural education are instructors currently using?
2. How do these different approaches relate to current research in the field of multicultural education?
3. How do these approaches relate to the cultural perspectives and teaching experiences of the instructors?

I conducted face-to-face interviews with all instructors teaching the elementary and the secondary multicultural education courses (N = 9). First, I interviewed the seven graduate students (4 male and 3 female). All seven graduate students were doctoral candidates; two of them were international students from Hong Kong and Korea respectively and one self-identified as Latino. I interviewed the two faculty members (female) who self-identified as White and American Indian. In addition to teaching course sections, the faculty members also co-directed the bi-weekly seminar that supported the graduate students. I received syllabi from all nine instructors for content analysis.

Interviews were tape-recorded, took place in an informal setting, and ranged from 30 minutes to one hour. I used a semi-structured protocol that allowed participants to direct the interview, and I used the course syllabi as a prompt for dialogue.

Data Analysis

Transcribed Interviews were sent to participants for member check, and in some cases, they were returned with clarifications. The approved transcriptions were entered into qualitative software for analysis (Hyperresearch). These data were then analyzed using both *a priori* and emergent coding schemes at the descriptive, interpretive, and pattern level (Miles & Huberman, 1994). *A priori* codes reflected the current research in multicultural education, in particular the conceptual framework of Christine Bennett (2010), while the emergent codes arose from those themes that resonated with multiple participants. In addition, I examined instructors' descriptions of students' receptiveness and resistance to the content and how these perceived reactions might relate to the instructional approach and power relations. I triangulated my analysis of individual interview data with a similar analysis of each instructor's course syllabus. Working with a second reader, I refined my coding scheme at the pattern level (Lincoln & Guba, 1985).

Because the context of the interview was one of lengthy talk, I also used an arts-based research approach that examined the structure as well as the tone of the talk (Carspecken, 1996). I used a musical-analytical approach because music provides another "language" with which to describe, interpret, and ultimately understand different approaches to teaching and curriculum (Barone & Eisner, 1997). In an effort to perceive the combined music of the program, I examined the data collectively as if the participants were discrete musical passages within a shared composition. In particular, I documented instances of counterpoint (harmonizing but discrete melodies), consonance (groups of harmonious tones in a chord), and dissonance (lack of harmony that seeks to be resolved) between and within participant interviews. Finally, I looked for areas of resonance (complementary tunings: all strings vibrate when only one of the strings is struck) that were program wide.

Areas of Consonance, Counterpoint, Dissonance, and Resonance

As noted earlier, I used the Bennett's (2010) Six Goals of Multicultural Curriculum as an analytical frame. Although every instructor addressed all six goals in one way or another, the time, importance, duration, and dynamic placed on each goal were different for each instructor. What emerged were themes related to each goal that were emphasized by all instructors (consonance), themes that were unique to each instructor but supported a cohesive philosophy or theory (counterpoint), and themes that seemed to be in conflict with each other (dissonance). Finally, the analytical frame provided a referent to track those trends that suggested future areas of growth within the program (resonance).

Consonance

Consonance is when two or more musical notes sound good together; it is considered the opposite of dissonance. As noted earlier, musical ideas like consonance and dissonance differ according to culture, but in general, consonance is when a chord, interval, or harmony seems stable and free from musical tension. For example, there is common agreement amongst instructors that the course is merely one step in a succession of steps that begin before the class period and will continue beyond these "four walls." All instructors felt that the course serves as a prompt to activate modes of understanding, confront assumptions and misconceptions and "wake up" the students to the cultural and socio-political forces that shape their existence.

There was also universal agreement that the nature of the predominantly Midwestern student population was a strong determinant in course organization and focus: "If we taught somewhere else, we would construct our course very differently." The instructors see their students as homogeneous, middle to upper middle class, White, and traditional with a limited perspective: "So many of the students come from small towns, where there is not a lot of diversity that they see—everyone looked like me and went to the same church." Additionally, instructors felt that the students were generally blind to issues of privilege and power: "They don't recognize the privilege of where they are—for the most part they are white middle class students." Furthermore, instructors felt that the classes provided few direct experiences of diversity because of the homogeneity of the student population: "I have taught 100 students—four black students, and two openly gay and about ten Jewish students—other than that [the class] is white, middle class or higher, predominantly Christian, and heterosexual."

This cultural homogeneity is also tied to the primary misconception of most students—this class is not about them. One instructor summed up the experiences and frustrations of the group: "On the first day of class, I have them write a paragraph about their culture. The white kids can't do it: 'I guess I am kind of a mutt.' They will define 'culture' as ethnic roots, but they can't make the connection between family, language, and living. They think that they don't have a culture."

Several instructors also noted that their students felt the class was redundant ("I have already had a class in diversity—like you can have a class and you are done") or inconsequential ("I am going back to my small little town and there is one black family, so I don't have to worry about it"). One instructor noted the students also had misconceptions about the course approach: "They think that it is all going to be self-reflections, that if they just talk about their feelings they will be fine." A few instructors also mentioned that students had misconceptions about meritocracy and the "protestant work ethic" as just constructs.

Instructors were given a lot of autonomy in course design and were encouraged to draw on their unique cultural perspectives. "We have a lot of flexibility to design the course," noted one instructor, "I bring a lot of my own strengths." All instructors used broad definitions of culture that went beyond race and ethnicity to include sexuality, socio-economic status, gender, exceptionalities, language, and religion. All focused on the interactions between those categories and how they related to current and historical issues. The themes of power and privilege run through every course syllabus, as do the related themes of normality and diversity.

In addition, there seems to be a concerted effort to use an inquiry approach to learning: ". . . although the course is about the body of work of authors, there is an attempt to teach depth of inquiry as teachers—not just content and strategies." This emphasis on "teachers as researchers and intellectuals" was present in all but one of the interviews, and then it was a conscious omission: "In the class we don't do the theory; theory doesn't apply. I remember being an undergraduate; I could care less about theory."

Another area of consonance is the focus on dialogue. In several cases, course assignments centered on students' development of dialogic skills. Whether the dialogue took place in person or online, there was a focus on informed speech that went beyond opinion: ". . . people don't talk about these issues. They want to talk, but the discussion is uninformed. They talk about their feelings, but they don't have a lot of information." In some courses there was more of an emphasis on the development of discussion strategies and student-to-student interactions, with references to how these would prepare students for future interactions with colleagues and the community, while in other courses there seemed to be more emphasis on the development of the individual voice and inner dialogue. However, all instructors recognized that dialogue should work on two levels—an inner dialogue and an outer dialogue. "They must have dual consciousness; they must always have two levels. They have to make sense of 'that' [gesture out there] and 'this' [gesture into self]," noted one instructor. "At the end of the course I say, 'We learned about a whole lot of other people, but the person you have really learned about it you.' Whereas these areas of consonance created a rich harmonic structure that served as a framework for the program, there also seemed to be independent melodies that moved within that harmonic frame.

Counterpoint

Counterpoint is when there are simultaneous melodic lines in a piece of music. These melodic lines work within a common harmonic structure, but they rise and fall independently—each creating a unique melody. For example, instructors organized their courses in distinct ways. Several of the instructors took a conceptual approach, constructing their courses around the idea of pluralism as a democratic mandate and how that related to different issues and themes within multicultural education. Other instructors divided their syllabi into cultural categories and focused on the complexity within and interaction between these categories. Still other instructors immersed their students in real-world examples and experiences. These same instructors also organized their class by cultural category but then critically examined these categories through case study examples and direct experiences in an effort to confront students with the issues related to each cultural category.

In an effort to deepen the dialogue, instructors took different approaches to diffuse traditional teacher/student power relations. Whereas some teachers systematically removed themselves from the dialogue through a series of guest speakers, others remained in the conversation but created a safe space for dialogue where the students would not just "tell me what I want to hear." Instructors drew on their own cultural "funds" to shape the power dynamic in their classroom. Some instructors shared their perspectives as a prompt for discussion, some presented stereotypical images or materials to engage students, and some said they "sit back and let it happen. I will write down a note to say [something], and it will get said [by a student]." Many tried to make the process transparent: "I am a learner. I may be seen in a position of power, but at the same time I am learning . . . even though I construct the class."

Instructors also shared their unique cultural identity with their students and used it as a resource to prompt dialogue and inquiry. Several of the instructors have lived overseas or are bilingual. Some identified strongly with their gender or sexuality, while others drew on their ethnic backgrounds. In particular, one instructor, who is fair-skinned with red hair and a Hispanic name, uses the common misconceptions about his/her cultural heritage to make students aware of their assumptions:

> I am Hispanic but from Galicia [Spain] and it is a heavily Celtic area. So I always have to explain and rationalize. I dealt with all of the assumptions—do I speak Spanish? The first day [of class] I write on the board: What do you think I look like? What language do I speak? We want to put people in unique categories, but people don't always fit in these categories.

Each instructor also focused on developing different aspects of their students' awareness of cultural diversity through related materials and activities. One instructor used film to "push them to see the diversity around them." Another instructor focused on classroom dialogue to create a "strong voice," while another tried to engage his/her students in "direct experience." One instructor focused on the inner-dialogue and "social consciousness," while another focused on "teaching in action." Finally, one instructor sought to engage the hearts of his/her students by beginning and ending class with the statement: ". . . the work we do here is about loving and teaching all children." What emerges from these diverse foci is an image of a human being—made up of an eye, a mouth, a hand, a heart, a mind engaged in reflection, and a body ready for action. This in turn highlights an interesting aspect of counterpoint. Even when notes seem to be moving together as chords (e.g., all lines have the same rhythm) the individual musical lines may still be considered counterpoint. By listening to the inner voices within a chord, one can hear how the rich bass line serves as a countermelody to the expressive soprano line and the alto and tenor are singing a duet.

Dissonance

In contrast to the first two musical categories, dissonance describes those notes that sound harsh or unpleasant when played at the same time; whereas counterpoint may have contrasting voices within a common harmonic structure, dissonant notes often operate outside that shared structure. Because dissonance is considered unstable, it creates a musical tension that has the power to expand the harmonic structure by pulling the listener toward a resolution that may lie outside of the existing structure. How and when dissonance is used frequently provides insight into a particular musical style or tradition. In the Western musical tradition, dissonance is often used to develop and extend musical themes. In the study, instructor perceptions of student receptiveness to the course content and activities were often dissonant. While there was an overall recognition that "they don't want to read," some instructors seemed more receptive to the limitations of their students ("They are unskilled undergraduate students. I try to be really sensitive about this"), while others felt that they must "protect our teacher-in-training's future students" by using guest speakers and provocative activities to "shock" teacher candidates into awareness.

Moreover, the instructor's perception of students' positive or negative response seemed to be linked to the overall tonality of the interview. In other words, if instructors were positive about their students' ability to grasp the course content and expand their perspective, the interview was generally upbeat, or in a major key, whereas those instructors who were less positive about their students' misconceptions and limitations often spoke in a melancholic or minor key. This is not to say that there were not minor chords within major keys or that "minor" should be viewed pejoratively, rather that these minor moments served to illuminate areas for further exploration. For example, some instructors were discouraged with the state of the multicultural education field in general and a shift away from social justice themes in many teacher education programs. Others were frustrated by the demographic and socio-political context of the course (e.g., Midwestern university, politically conservative state, mostly White population) and the lack of diversity in the classroom. Finally, several were upset about the institutional constraints that provided only one course that focused on multicultural issues in the teacher education program.

In one interview that was more minor in mode, the idea that the students perceived the course as having less value than other courses emerged: "There is not another course like this—where you have to rationalize why you teach the course." Although this was not part of the original interview protocol, as the topic was explored in subsequent interviews, it became clear that this was an issue for other instructors: "Students perceive this class as of less value." When asked how s/he dealt with student perceptions, the instructor explained how s/he had students look for teaching jobs, "All of the jobs were located in cities . . . I said, 'You tell me how this class is not important.'" Other instructors appealed to the patriotism of their students ("pluralism as a democratic mandate . . . I use it like a mantra"). These instructors maintain that there is a core of knowledge that is essential to becoming, "active agents in a pluralistic, multicultural society."

Perhaps the most striking dissonance in instructional approach was how instructors addressed power relations in the classroom. Whether they perceived themselves as the primary motivator ("I consider myself progressive and a very animated teacher . . . I teach very outspoken"), or as the mediator of power ("Ten out of the fifteen classes, I am outside of the classroom . . . removing myself . . . giving the power to the person leading the group. I am tired of being in that position"), some instructors sought to maintain traditional student/teacher power relations. At the other end of the continuum were instructors that divested themselves of power by giving it to their students: "I really want to give power to them. I do not want to be a powerful figure in my classroom." This de-centered approach mirrors the approach taken by the course administrator during the biweekly seminar that supports the instructors: "There weren't clear lines between who was a professor and who was a doctoral student . . . We were each able to contribute to each other's knowledge."

Resonance
Whereas the first three categories describe the different ways in which notes were interrelated within a musical work, resonance describes the phenomenon in which harmonically related strings will vibrate when only one is struck. As noted earlier, the bi-weekly seminar is a chance for the seven instructors and two professors to share their resources and challenges from the classroom. Two of the newer instructors noted that the seminar was a "fund for activities," while the more experienced instructors valued the pedagogical support. What is evident in those interviews that referenced this seminar as a source of support was that it was a safe and rich space in which to "tune" their craft: "I think the meetings are more supportive of ourselves than they are necessarily telling us what to do. At the beginning [of the semester] we talked more about pedagogical support (here is a great activity or tip), now it is more support of who we are." A critical component seems to be the modeling of the program advisor: "When she talks about teaching, she describes what she does. She will respond in a certain way. She will show me ways to protect the student." "The "tuning" that

takes place during these seminars not only contributes to the individual development of each instructor's melody, but to the collective music of the multicultural education program.

One example of resonance amongst instructors is a growing value placed on an international perspective. Most of the instructors made a point of including an international perspective within their course content and activities or expressed an intention to do so: "In the future I will bring in more international readings." The focus may be due in part to the inclusion of two international graduate students as fellow instructors but also may be a result of the personal philosophy of the course advisor; she values the funds of knowledge that international students bring to undergraduate teacher candidates. One noninternational instructor summed up, and seconded, her philosophy, "I applaud [our advisor's] focus on having international students teach the class. They are not valued; they are marginalized as graduate students. [Our advisor] recognizes that they can bring something to the discussion that WASPS can't." In an effort to promote understanding, the advisor also includes an activity in her syllabus that has students interview an international graduate student over the length of the course. She noted that this activity not only gave international graduate students opportunities to work on their English, but often changed the perspectives of her non-international students: "There are not as many opportunities for students to have empathetic relationship with their instructors; they don't think that if they just work on listening, they will get it. Before when they were in these classes [taught by international students], they felt incensed. Now, they are advocates for the [International Associate Instructors]."

Productive Dissonance
While it is tempting to focus on the rich contrapuntal composition of the program presented in the findings, it is the areas of dissonance that provide the greatest insight. Using the six goals of multicultural curriculum as a heuristic, these data suggest that although all six goals are explicit in all nine of the instructors' syllabi and referenced in their interviews, the core values, chief among them "acceptance and appreciation of cultural diversity" and "respect for human dignity," seem to be integrated into the class structure of only some of the instructors. In her article, "Acting on Beliefs in Teacher Education for Cultural Diversity," Geneva Gay (2010) argues that multicultural education programs must affect the underlying value assumptions of both instructors and students. She cites Cuban (1988) in arguing that programs must make second order changes to effectively address current multicultural issues. Like Banks' (2005) transformative curriculum, second order changes work at the structural level to impact all dimensions of classroom practice.

For example, while every instructor proclaimed a respect for multiple perspectives (Goal 1) and eschewed the deficit model, some instructors also recognized the core value that their teacher candidates had diverse and valuable cultural perspectives: "I have never met a student that just really didn't want to be a good teacher—didn't care. For the most part my students seem to be really passionate about teaching." As noted earlier, some instructors seemed more receptive to their students' perspectives and consciously created a space for diverse voices in the classroom. Several instructors began their classes with assignments or activities that asked students to explore their cultural identity and how it was shaped by and impacted other cultures (Goal 2: cultural consciousness). In some classrooms instructors deliberately divested themselves of their power so that they could listen for those voices that might be perceived as dissonant (Goal 3: intercultural competence): "It is their classroom . . . not mine. So I am in there as a colleague and not an instructor. If I give them my power, they give my power back."

Although there was an overt emphasis in each syllabus on recognizing White privilege and combating racism (Goal 4: combat racism), some instructors took care to address their students' resistance to the topic of racism (core value respect for human dignity). When asked to discuss students' misconceptions, instructors' responses echoed the work of Beverly Tatum (1992). Students thought race was a taboo topic ("She thought it would be racist to say that the woman was white"), they thought that the USA was a just society regarding racial issues ("At the beginning of the class a lot of students say that we have no racial problems [in the USA]"), and they denied any personal prejudice ("They believe that they are not racist"). Although some instructors chose to meet these areas of resistance through whole class instruction and teacher-led discussions, others engaged their students individually and privately, probing students' misconceptions through personal email correspondence, extensive comments in papers, and activities that allowed students to construct their own meaning.

As noted earlier, some instructors addressed global issues more than others; however, the inclusion of two international instructors clearly communicates the value placed on an international perspective by the course advisor. Because of their active participation in the bi-weekly seminar, these voices have the potential to resonate beyond the explicit content (Goal 5: Awareness of global dynamics) to produce an internalization of the core value "responsibility to a world community" by those instructors who value the biweekly seminar.

All instructors addressed issues of social justice and the call to social action in their syllabi; however, their instructional approaches lay along a continuum with those that favored a more passive approach at one end ("They don't need to go out and protest, but they need to be informed") and those that favored a more active approach at the other ("I would have them write a letter about a diversity issue in school"). While most instructors interviewed would have agreed with Christine Sleeter (2004) that the ideals of social justice are not enough, several instructors felt that "time was a barrier" to meeting this goal (Goal 6: Build Social Action Skills). One instructor suggested that the course have two sessions, one in the classroom and one in the field. Another invited students to continue the conversations begun in class beyond the term: "That is the hard part of this class—there is no way to follow up with the students who want to engage in this level of thinking and teaching. The invitation remains open with me, but not enough come back." Although all instructors recognized the limitations of

their stand-alone class, there is the shared expectation that students will be different, if not transformed, at the end of the course: "My fundamental belief is when they get out of this course, ignorance is no longer an excuse."

As noted earlier, dissonance is most pronounced in those core values that relate to diverse student responses to the program content and student/teacher power relations. Because dissonance is in itself relational (e.g., one note can only be dissonant in relation to another note), it is not surprising that it is in the relationships—between students and instructors and students and new ideas—that one perceives the most dissonance in the program. However, it is the response to dissonance that determines whether that dissonance is productive or destructive to the program overall.

To refine the musical metaphor, these findings suggest that it is not the consonance or dissonance of individual voices, but rather the overall musical form, or program structure, which should be examined. In Western musical tradition, dissonance is viewed very differently depending on the time period. In classical musical forms, dissonant notes must be first prepared and then resolved, or begin and end in consonance; however, modern, or 20th century, music has become increasingly accepting of dissonance that is both unprepared and unresolved. These new musical forms allow for dissonance that is both part of and apart from the harmonic structure of the piece. In this way, dissonance ceases to be an either/or binary that is constrained by the consonant sounds, or norms, of the group. Instead, dissonance has the potential to produce a new musical structure, or form that is liberated from the driving need to resolve all differences.

What this means to multicultural education is that dissonance, if it is viewed as productive, can possibly transform a program at the structural level. This has implications for research in student resistance to multicultural education courses (Brown, 2004) and issues of student voice within the classroom (Delpit, 1988; Ladson-Billings, 1991). Furthermore, the bi-weekly seminar, which seems to offer a safe and shared space where dissonance can exist unresolved, has implications for practice in large-scale multicultural education programs.

References

Banks, J., & Banks, C. (2005). *Multicultural education: Issues and perspectives.* Hoboken, NJ: Wiley Jossey Bass Education.

Banks, J. (1994). An introduction to multicultural education. Needham Heights, MA: Allyn & Bacon.

Barone, T., & Eisner, E. W. (1997). Art-based educational research. In R. M. Jaeger (Ed.), *Complementary methods for research in education* (pp. 73–94). Washington, D. C.: American Educational Research Association.

Bennett, C. (2010). *Comprehensive multicultural education: Theory and practice* (7th ed.). Boston: Allyn and Bacon.

Brown, E. (2004). What precipitates change in cultural diversity awareness during a multicultural course: The message or the method? *Journal of Teacher Education, 55*(4), 325–340.

Carspecken, P. (1996). *Critical ethnography in educational research.* New York: Routledge.

Cochran-Smith, M. (2003). The multiple meanings of multicultural teacher education: A conceptual framework. *Teacher Education Quarterly, 30*(2), 7–26.

Cuban, L. (1998) How schools change reforms: Redefining reform success and failure. *Teachers College Record. 99*(3), 453–477.

Delpit, L. D. (1988), The silenced dialogue: Power and pedagogy in educating other people's children, *Harvard Educational Review, 58*(3), 280–298.

Gay, G. (1997). Multicultural infusion in teacher education: Foundations and applications. In A. M. M. K. Kitano (Ed.), *Multicultural course transformation in higher education: A broader truth.* Boston: Allyn & Bacon.

Gay, G. (2000). *Culturally responsive teaching: Theory, research, and practice.* New York: Teachers College Press.

Gay, G. (2005). Politics of multicultural teacher education. *Journal of Teacher Education, 56*(3), 221–228.

Gay, G. (2010). Acting on beliefs in teacher education for cultural diversity. *Journal of Teacher Education, 61*(1–2), 143–152.

Gay, G., & Howard, T. (2000). Multicultural teacher education for the 21st century. *Teacher Educator, 36*(1), 1–16.

Irvine, J. J. (2003). *Educating teachers for diversity: Seeing with a cultural eye.* New York: Teachers College Press.

Ladson-Billings, G. (1991). Preparing teachers for diverse student populations: A critical race theory perspective. *Review of Research in Education, 24*(1), 211–247.

Larkin, J. S., & Sleeter C. E. (1995). *Developing multicultural teacher education curricula.* Albany: State University of New York Press.

Lincoln, Y. S. & Guba, E. G. (1985) *Naturalistic inquiry.* Beverly Hills, CA: Sage.

Potts, A., Triplett, C., & Rose, D. (2008). An infused approach to multicultural education in a pre-service teacher program: perspectives of teacher educators. *International Journal of Multicultural Education, 10*(1). Retrieved March 5, 2010 from http://ijme-journal.org/index.php/ijme/article/view/39/145

Miles, M. A., & Huberman A. M. (1994) *Qualitative data analysis: An expanded sourcebook.* Thousand Oaks, CA: Sage.

Sleeter, C. (2004). Critical multicultural curriculum and the standards movement. *English Teaching: Practice and Critique, 3*(2) 122–138.

Tatum, B. D. (1992). Talking about race, learning about racism: The application of racial identity development theory in the classroom. *Harvard Educational Review, 62*(1), 1–24.

Critical Thinking

1. What elements associated with cultural competence in your teacher preparation program demonstrate consonance for you and why?

2. What elements associated with cultural competence in your teacher preparation program demonstrate counterpoint for you and why?

3. What elements associated with cultural competence in your teacher preparation program demonstrate dissonance for you and why?

4. What elements associated with cultural competence in your teacher preparation program demonstrate resonance for you and why?

Create Central

www.mhhe.com/createcentral

Internet Reference

United States Department of Justice
   www.usdoj.gov/
United States Equal Employment Opportunity Commission
   www.eeoc.gov/types/race.html

LYNN VIOLET CLARK is an Assistant Professor in the College of Education at the University of Louisiana at Monroe.

Article   Prepared by: Nancy P. Gallavan, *University of Central Arkansas*

Discarding the Deficit Model

Ambiguity and subjectivity contribute to the disproportionate placement of minorities in special education.

BETH HARRY AND JANETTE KLINGNER

Learning Outcomes

After reading this article, you will be able to:

- Increase awareness of cultural diverse special education students and special services

- Examine resources dedicated to improving the teaching, learning, and schooling of all students.

Many authors in this issue of *Educational Leadership* describe students as having "learning needs" and "learning challenges." How we wish this language truly reflected the common approach to students who have difficulty mastering the information and skills that schools value! Many students have special learning needs, and many experience challenges learning school material. But does this mean they have *disabilities?* Can we help students without undermining their self-confidence and stigmatizing them with a label? Does it matter whether we use the word *disability* instead of *need* and *challenge?*

Language in itself is not the problem. What *is* problematic is the belief system that this language represents. The provision of special education services under U.S. law—the Education for All Handicapped Children Act in 1975 and the Individuals with Disabilities Education Improvement Act in 2004—ensured that schools could no longer turn away students on the basis of perceived developmental, sensory, physical, or cognitive limitations. However, the downside of the law is that it has historically relied on identifying a disability thought to exist within a child. The main criterion for eligibility for special education services, then, has been *proof of intrinsic deficit.* There are two problems with this focus: First, defining and identifying high-incidence disabilities are ambiguous and subjective processes. Second, the focus on disability has become so intertwined with the historical devaluing of minorities in the United States that these two deficit lenses now deeply influence the special education placement process.

We recently completed a three-year study that throws some light on the issue (Harry & Klingner, 2006). We looked at the special education placement process for black and Hispanic students in a large urban school district in a southeastern U.S. state. The 12 elementary schools involved represented a range of ethnicities, socioeconomic statuses, and rates of special education placement. On the basis of data we gathered from classroom observations, school-based conferences, interviews with school personnel and family members, and examination of student documents (such as individualized education programs, behavioral referrals, and evaluation reports), we found that several conditions seriously marred the placement process. These included lack of adequate classroom instruction prior to the student's referral, inconsistencies in policy implementation, and arbitrary referrals and assessment decisions. It was also clear that students in poor neighborhoods were at risk of receiving poor schooling, which increased their risk of failing and of being placed in special education.

Minorities in Special Ed

The disproportionate placement of some minority groups in special education continues to be a central problem in the field. As noted in a report by the National Research Council (2002), the categories with the highest incidence of disproportionate minority-group placement are also those categories whose criteria are based on clinical judgment: Educable Mental Retardation, Emotional/Behavioral Disorders, and Learning Disability. The categories whose criteria are based on biologically verifiable conditions—such as deafness or visual impairment—do not show disproportionality by ethnicity.

Across the United States, African American students are represented in the category of Educable Mental Retardation at twice the rate of their white peers; in the category of Emotional/Behavioral Disorders, they are represented at one and one-half times the rate of their white peers. In some states, Native American and Hispanic students are overrepresented in the Learning Disability category (National Research Council, 2002).

The roots of this problem lie deep in U.S. history. Looking at how the mandate for school integration intertwined with special education, Ferri and Connor (2006) analyzed public documents and newspaper articles dating from *Brown v. Board of Education* in 1954 to the inception of the Education for All Handicapped Children Act in 1975. The authors show how African American students entering public schools through forced integration were subject to low expectations and intense efforts to keep them separate from the white mainstream. As the provision of services for students with disabilities became a legal mandate, clear patterns of overrepresentation of Mexican American and African American students in special education programs emerged. Plagued by ambiguous definitions and subjectivity in clinical judgments, these categories often have more to do with administrative, curricular, and instructional decisions than with students' inherent abilities.

Dilemmas of LD and EMR

The label of Learning Disability (LD) used to be assigned mainly to white and middle-class students. African American students—and in some states, Hispanic and Native American students—were more likely to be disproportionately assigned to the more severe category of Educable Mental Retardation (EMR). More than two decades ago, various scholars offered thoughtful analyses of these patterns. Sleeter (1986) argued that the Learning Disability category came into being to create a space for students from predominantly white and middle-class homes who were not living up to family and community expectations. She noted that the other side of this coin was that students with learning difficulties who were from low-income homes were more likely to end up in the Educable Mental Retardation category.

In a careful examination of how the construction of the Learning Disability category affected African American students, Collins and Camblin (1983) argued that the definition of *learning disability* and the means of identifying it guaranteed this pattern. First, the requirement for a discrepancy between IQ score and academic achievement was designed to indicate that the student was unexpectedly achieving below his or her measured potential. This requirement was intended to ensure that the learning difficulty was the result of a specific, not generalized, learning disability. In other words, the student was capable of higher achievement, as evidenced by his or her IQ score, but some specific disability seemed to be holding him or her back.

But how do we measure cognitive potential? Through IQ tests. It is widely acknowledged that IQ tests are really "tests of general achievement, reflecting broad, culturally rooted ways of thinking and problem solving" (Donovan & Cross, 2002, p. 284). It is not surprising, therefore, that if we measure intelligence this way, then groups with inadequate exposure to the skills and knowledge required to do well on these tests will score lower than their mainstream counterparts. Thus, as Collins and Camblin pointed out, African American students' lower scores on IQ tests make it more unlikely that their scores will reflect the "discrepancy" required for admittance into the Learning Disability category.

Collins and Camblin's second argument focused on the "exclusionary clause" of the Learning Disability definition.

In addition to ensuring that the student does not have some other intrinsic limitation, such as mental retardation or sensory impairments, the exclusionary clause requires that school personnel establish that the source of the problem inheres in the student, not in his or her environment or experience. Consequently, African American students living in poor socioeconomic circumstances were less likely to receive the Learning Disability label because their environments tended to exclude them from this category.

This brings us to the paradoxical impact of the Learning Disability category on minority students. On the one hand, the underrepresentation of poor and minority students in this category—also known as a pattern of false negatives—is a problem if it means that students fall between the cracks and do not receive appropriate instruction. Further, there are benefits associated with the Learning Disability label. For example, students in this category can receive accommodations on secondary and college-level testing, which many middle-class white families continue to take advantage of.

On the other hand, the number of minorities represented in this category has begun to increase. We might now face the possibility of overrepresentation of minorities—or false positives—in the Learning Disability group. Some researchers have argued that many students currently in the category should actually qualify for Educable Mental Retardation (MacMillan, Gresham, & Bocian, 1998). Moreover, our research showed that some psychologists use the Learning Disability label to protect a student from the more stigmatizing and isolating label of Emotional/Behavioral Disorders (Harry & Klingner, 2006).

The real problem is the arbitrariness and stigmatizing effects of the entire process. Students shouldn't need a false disability label to receive appropriate support. They also shouldn't acquire that label because they had inappropriate or inadequate opportunities to learn. And they shouldn't end up in programs that don't offer the truly specialized instruction they need.

Students shouldn't need a false disability label to receive appropriate support.

Dilemmas of EBD

The use of the Emotional/Behavioral Disorders (EBD) label grew by 500 percent between 1974 and 1998, from just over 1 percent in 1974 to just over 5 percent in 1998 (National Research Council, 2002). This category is plagued by as much ambiguity as the Learning Disability category is. To qualify for the EBD label, a student must display inappropriate behaviors to a "marked degree" and for a "length of time." These criteria depend on subjective judgment.

Also, decisions about what evaluation instruments to use vary widely across states (Hosp & Reschly, 2002). Some states use projective tests, which are well known for their inherent subjectivity. Students respond to stimuli, such as pictures or sentences, and then a psychologist interprets their responses as a projection of their feelings. Other states rely on checklists, which are equally subjective. Our research revealed that different teachers using the same instrument rated the same student very differently. For example, using a behavioral checklist to rate a 2nd grade African American boy, one teacher checked four items relating to poor self-concept as occurring "excessively" (more than 50 percent of the time), whereas another teacher checked those same items as occurring "seldom" (1–10 percent of the time).

One teacher in the study commented, "They're not disturbed. They're just a pain in the neck!" As many scholars have observed, it's often difficult to tell whether the behavior is mostly troubling to school personnel or whether it reflects a troubled child.

Two Distorting Lenses

The intertwining of race and perceptions of disability are so deeply embedded in our way of thinking that many people are not even aware of how one concept influences the other. Let's consider how this works in light of the study we conducted.

The Disability Deficit Lens

Many teachers in the study saw disability as a simple fact. One teacher noted, "These children have disabilities, just like some children have blue eyes." When a student experiences continued difficulty mastering academic skills, all too often the first question someone asks is, "Does this student have a disability?" The Learning Disability label requires that we exclude potential environmental reasons for the student's difficulties. But barring obvious developmental limitations, how can we separate a student from his or her social and cultural experience?

Let's consider some environmental experiences that could interfere with a student's learning. Most often, the experiences cited as exclusionary include poverty, detrimental home and community environments, or lack of opportunity to learn. In and of itself, poverty does not cause learning difficulties. Most children from poor homes have effectively mastered the usual developmental childhood tasks of motor and language skills, and they have learned the values and social practices of their homes and neighborhoods. But they often haven't learned particular forms of the language or the ways in which schools use that language to the extent that their middle-income peers have.

For example, in a study of African American preschoolers' language development, Brice-Heath (1983) demonstrated how their social environments prepared students for an imaginative form of storytelling but not for answering the testlike, factual questions prevalent in schools. Moreover, the students' vocabularies may not be as extensive or as sophisticated as those of children growing up in middle-class homes. Students may also not have had extensive experience handling printed materials or listening to stories told in the linear fashion so common to many children's books. Their lack of experience in some of these areas can make children seem unprepared for academic learning.

Absence from school as well as poor instruction in the early years can also be sources of a student's low achievement. Our research found that school personnel were always ready to blame the students' home contexts but seldom examined the school context. Even when students were referred for special education evaluation, members of the placement teams seldom asked whether poor classroom climate or instruction contributed to the students' difficulties or whether peer pressures could be the source of their withdrawal or acting out.

> **School personnel were always ready to blame the students' home contexts but seldom examined the school context.**

The Social/Cultural Deficit Lens

When a habit of looking for intrinsic deficit intertwines with a habit of interpreting cultural and racial difference as a deficit, the deck is powerfully loaded against poor students of color. Speaking about her African American 1st graders, one teacher in the study pointed out that "they don't know how to walk, talk, or sit in a chair. It's cultural!" Comments like this really don't refer to whether the students can or cannot do these things. Instead, they show that the manner in which the students do these things is unacceptable to the teacher. The teacher's focus on deficiencies predisposed her to see the students as limited by their culture and, ultimately, to refer almost one-half of her class of normally developing children for evaluation for special education.

If it is evident that students' early home and community experiences have not prepared them well for schooling, what do schools do? Do the schools then provide the students with adequate and appropriate opportunities to learn? Does instruction begin where the students are? Does it move at a pace that enables them to become accustomed to the new norms and expectations? Are the students made to feel that the school values the knowledge they bring from their homes and communities? Do teachers build on these "funds of knowledge" (Moll, 1990), or do they see only deficits in the students?

Variation, Not Pathology

Beyond the fact that these processes affect minorities unduly, the steady and dramatic increase in the use of disability labels in our schools is a cause for serious concern. The figures are startling. According to the National Research Council (2002), the risk of *any* student (averaged across ethnic groups) being identified as having Specific Learning Disabilities has increased from 1.21 percent in 1974 to 6.02 percent in 1998.

The truth is that the law's provision of disability categories for students who have learning and behavioral difficulties has become a way for schools to dodge their responsibility to provide high-quality general education. The deficit model is based on the normative development of students whose homes and communities have prepared them for schooling long before they enter school. Children who come to school without that preparation, and without the continuing home support of family members who can reinforce the goals of schooling, face expectations that they have not had the opportunity to fulfill. All too quickly the students become candidates for suspected "disability." Further, the special education programs into which they are placed are disproportionately of low quality in terms of curriculum, instruction, and ratio of students to teachers.

So why can't we see students' difficulties as "human variation rather than pathology" (Reid & Valle, 2004, p. 473)? Some encouraging trends are under way. The recent reauthorization of the Individuals with Disabilities Education Act allows for a change in the discrepancy model. The law now recommends tiered interventions by which schools can screen students early for signs of difficulty and provide more intensive and individualized instruction in needed areas without applying a special education label. The recent reauthorization enables schools to spend 15 percent of their special education funds on early intervention services.

The three-tiered Response to Intervention (RTI) model is currently receiving great attention in the field (Klingner & Edwards, 2006). The first tier involves quality instruction and ongoing monitoring within the general education classroom. In the second tier, schools provide intensive intervention support for students who have not met expected benchmarks. In the final tier, students who do not respond to second-tier interventions are evaluated for possible placement in special education.

The RTI model holds promise for preventing academic failure. It also provides support for culturally and linguistically diverse students before they underachieve. Educators are becoming increasingly aware that they need to apply the model in culturally responsive ways (see Klingner & Edwards, 2006). This might mean considering whether suggested instructional interventions have proven effective with *all* students, including English language learners. Also, educators should avoid a one-size-fits-all approach because culturally diverse students or English language learners may require different tier-one or tier-two interventions.

The law also calls for increased and specific efforts to include parents in all phases of the placement process. Schools must ensure that parents understand the proceedings of individualized education program (IEP) meetings and provide an interpreter if necessary. They also must notify parents early on about meetings to help ensure attendance and provide parents with a copy of the IEP.

These changes in the law signal a need for revising the concept of "disability" as the single criterion for eligibility for specialized and intensive services. We need a new vision of special education—one that reserves the notion of disability for students with clear-cut diagnoses of biological or psychological limitations and uses the categorization only for the purpose of delivering intensive, specialized services in the least restrictive education environment possible. Students who have no clear-cut diagnoses but who struggle to master school-based tasks should be eligible for specialized services according to explicit criteria based on level of achievement. The Response to Intervention model monitors the progress of all students so that teachers can provide extra support—within the general education context—to those students who are not making adequate progress.

Rather than devoting extensive resources to finding out whether students "have" disabilities, we should devote those resources to assessing students' exact instructional needs using models like Response to Intervention. Schools will need to provide this instruction through collaboration between general and special education personnel to ensure that all students continue to have full access to the general curriculum. As Lisa Delpit (2006) noted, let's stop looking for disabilities and just "teach the children what they need to know" (p. 3).

References

Brice-Heath, S. (1983). *Ways with words: Language, life, and work in communities and classrooms.* Cambridge, UK: Cambridge University Press.

Collins, R., & Camblin, L. D. (1983). The politics and science of learning disability classification: Implications for black children. *Contemporary Education, 54*(2), 113–118.

Delpit, L. (2006). Foreword. In B. Harry & J. K. Klingner, *Why are so many minority students in special education? Understanding race and disability in schools.* New York: Teachers College Press.

Donovan, S., & Cross, C. (2002). *Minority students in special and gifted education.* Washington, DC: National Academies Press.

Ferri, B. A., & Connor, D. J. (2006). *Reading resistance: Discourses of exclusion in desegregation and inclusion debates.* New York: Peter Lang.

Harry, B., & Klingner, J. K. (2006). *Why are so many minority students in special education? Understanding race and disability in schools.* New York: Teachers College Press.

Hosp, J. L., & Reschly, D. J. (2002). Regional differences in school psychology practice. *School Psychology Review, 31*, 11–29.

Klingner, J. K., & Edwards, P. (2006). Cultural considerations with response-to-intervention models. *Reading Research Quarterly, 41*, 108–117.

MacMillan, D. L., Gresham, F. M., & Bocian, K. M. (1998). Discrepancy between definitions of learning disabilities and school practices: An empirical investigation. *Journal of Learning Disabilities, 31*, 314–326.

Moll, L. C. (Ed.). (1990). *Vygotsky and education: Instructional implications and applications of socio-historical psychology.* Cambridge, UK: Cambridge University Press.

National Research Council. (2002). *Minority students in special and gifted education.* Washington, DC: National Academies Press.

Reid, K., & Valle, J. W. (2004). The discursive practice of learning disability: Implications for instruction and parent–school relations. *Journal of Learning Disabilities, 37*(6), 466–481.

Sleeter, C. (1986). Learning disabilities: The social construction of a special education category. *Exceptional Children, 53*, 46–54.

Critical Thinking

1. What is the Deficit Model?
2. How do teachers identify students needing assistance?
3. What can teachers do to support their students needing assistance?
4. Why are more resources necessary to expand curriculum and communities?

Create Central

www.mhhe.com/createcentral

Internet References

National Association of Special Education Teachers (NASET)
http://www.naset.org/

Unlocking the Classroom on the Deficit Model
http://unlockingtheclassroom.blogspot.com/2008/06/saying-no-to-deficit-theory-culture-of.html

BETH HARRY is Professor in the Department of Teaching and Learning at the University of Miami, Florida; 305–284–5363; bebeharry@aol.com. **JANETTE KLINGNER** is Associate Professor in Bilingual Special Education in the Division for Educational Equity and Cultural Diversity at the University of Colorado, Boulder; 303–492–0773; jkklingner@aol.com.

From *Educational Leadership*, February, 2007, pp. 16–21. Copyright © 2007 by ASCD. Reprinted by permission. The Association for Supervision and Curriculum Development is a worldwide community of educators advocating sound policies and sharing best practices to achieve the success of each learner. To learn more, visit ASCD at www.ascd.org

Article   Prepared by: Nancy P. Gallavan, *University of Central Arkansas*

Approaches to Diversifying the Teaching Force
Attending to Issues of Recruitment, Preparation, and Retention

ANA MARÍA VILLEGAS AND DANNÉ E. DAVIS

Learning Outcomes

After reading this article, you will be able to:

- Examine the shortage of teachers of color and the effects on all students.

- Understand the challenges associated with increasing the number of teachers of color.

The widening cultural chasm between teachers and students in elementary and secondary schools is a serious problem in American education demanding concerted action. As the works in this special issue of *Teacher Education Quarterly* make clear, the shortage of teachers of color has real consequences for all students, but especially for students of color. Despite the urgency, programs of teacher education are not giving this matter the attention it deserves. In this context of relative inattentiveness to the need for teachers of color, it is encouraging to read a collection of articles that feature a variety of carefully designed and well documented approaches to diversify the teaching force. Our goal in this commentary is to place the approaches described in this issue within the broader discussion of recruiting, preparing, and retaining prospective teachers of color.

Bringing People of Color into Teaching

Programs of teacher education have historically played a passive role in student recruitment. It has generally been assumed that the market need for teachers will automatically draw students into teacher education. The passage of the Civil Rights Act of 1964 inadvertently challenged this approach to recruitment, however. Prior to the enactment of this legislation, teaching was one of the few careers available to women and people of color. As a result, programs of teacher education—whether at Predominantly White Institutions (PWIs) or Historically Black Colleges and Universities (HBCUs)—had a captive pool of talented people from which to draw students. As professional opportunities opened up in this country for women and racial/ethnic minorities, undergraduates from these groups began to defect in large numbers from education to other fields such as business, engineering, and the health professions (Carter & Wilson, 1992; Urban, 2000). The declining popularity of teaching, coupled with increased demand for teachers over the past fifteen years, has pushed programs of teacher education to take on a more active and thoughtful role in recruiting students. Below we discuss the major approaches used during this time to bring candidates of color into teaching, weaving throughout our discussion the approaches described in this issue. Such approaches are distinguished primarily by the population targeted for recruitment, as we explain below.

Enrolled Undergraduates with Undeclared Majors

Teacher education programs seeking to diversify their enrollments often recruit undergraduates of color at their institutions with undeclared majors. An advantage of this approach is that potential recruits are on campus already and generally eager to give direction to their professional futures. Unfortunately, because the number of students of color who matriculate directly at four-year colleges is limited, programs of teacher education must compete aggressively with other fields on campus for this small population. To promote interest in teaching, recruitment efforts are crafted to help identified students understand the valuable contributions that educators make to society, the many opportunities available to someone with a teaching credential, and the type of preparation and support the teacher education program is ready to provide.

This recruitment approach is exemplified by the teacher preparation program Wong, Murai, Avila, White, Baker, Arellano, and Echandia describe in this issue. Although the

Multilingual/Multicultural Teacher Preparation Center (M/M Center) at California State University, Sacramento, was designed as a fifth-year credential program, the recruitment of potential students begins as early as their freshman year in college. The Freshman Seminar, sections of which are taught by M/M Center faculty, exposes students to the merit of a teaching career. Faculty from the M/M Center also offer an undergraduate minor in Multicultural Education (into which the pre-requisites to the teacher credential program are built) and teach capstone courses for Social Science majors with an interest in teaching. These contacts enable program faculty to effectively nurture the young people's interest in a teaching career and to help them begin to envision themselves as the type of social justice teacher the program aims to prepare.

Once admitted to the program, participants receive support services designed to help them navigate the intricacies of the higher education bureaucracy, such as connecting student to sources of financial aid, providing assistance with their application to the teacher education program, tracking their progress through the program to ensure the timely completion of requirements, and creating a built-in network of peer support through the use of cohort groups. Beyond recruitment and support services, students benefit from exposure to a coherent, race- and language-conscious curriculum that is thoughtfully designed to prepare teachers to create learning opportunities for poor students from diverse racial and ethnic backgrounds and to advocate on their behalf. In fact, one of the more important contributions of this article to the literature is the attention it gives to the content of the preparation participants receive in the program to enable them to act as agents of change in schools. In so doing, the authors move the discussion about the diversification of the teaching force beyond the customary focus on issues of recruitment and support services needed.

Targeting students of color already admitted into four-year colleges/universities for recruitment is an approach best suited for institutions that serve large numbers of racially and ethnically diverse students, such as HBCUs and Hispanic Serving Institutions (HSIs). Because the overwhelming majority of teacher education programs in this country are housed in PWIs, settings with consistently low enrollments of students of color, this recruitment approach alone—while helpful—is not likely to alter the overall racial/ethnic composition of the U.S. teaching force in any appreciable way. To significantly increase the representation of people of color in teaching, the pool of potential candidates must be expanded beyond those who are already enrolled in four-year colleges/universities. It is not surprising, then, that most efforts to diversify the ranks of teachers recruit non-traditional candidates—pre-college students who might not otherwise go to college, community college students, paraprofessionals in elementary and secondary schools, and people of color who already hold a bachelor's degree and are open to making a career switch. The literature shows that such recruitment approaches are tailored to the targeted population and provide recruits with the necessary support to experience success, as we describe below.

Pre-College Students

One way of expanding the pool of potential teachers of color is to identify likely candidates prior to their senior year in high school, even as early as the middle grades, and involving them in intervention programs that aim both to cultivate the students' interest in teaching and to facilitate their admission to college. Project FUTURE, described in this issue by Stevens, Agnello, Ramirez, Marbley, and Hamman, is illustrative of the early recruitment approach. This Texas Tech University initiative targets students enrolled in sixth grade through senior year in high school and involves them in an array of activities over the years to strengthen their resolve to go on to college and to promote their teaching self-efficacy. As Stevens et al. detail, Project FUTURE advances these two goals by bringing students on campus frequently to give them a window into college life, involving them in exercises that allow them to better understand the relationship between having a college degree and earning potential, providing information about financial aid for college as well as the college application process, offering workshops that focus on the development of test-taking strategies, engaging students in teaching simulations to give them practice with instructional strategies, and exposing them to different teaching styles and having them reflect on those experiences. As described by the authors, this initiative builds on the collaboration of members from the university community, the school districts in which the participants are enrolled, and the broader communities in which those schools are located. Other types of activities used in early recruitment efforts, as reported in the literature, include Future Educators Clubs, introductory teacher education courses that offer college credit to high school juniors and seniors, inspirational speakers who give students information about the teaching profession and encourage them to become part of it, summer programs that provide students intensive teaching experiences in addition to academic support, and work study programs in which upper high school students of color tutor younger children in community programs (Zapata, 1998).

While teacher cadet programs, such as Project FUTURE, have the potential to bolster the pool of racial/ethnic minorities for teaching, they are long-term efforts that take minimally five to eight years to produce results, and typically much longer. Equally important, while such programs have been shown to increase the number of racially and ethnically diverse college entrants, they do not necessarily guarantee that college recruits will actually seek admission into teacher education or that those who are admitted continue in this field through graduation (Clewell et al., 2000).

Community College Students

Community college students represent another important, yet largely untapped pool of prospective teachers of color (Hudson, Foster, Irvine, Holmes, & Villegas, 2002). After all, the overwhelming majority of people of color who pursue a post-secondary education first enroll in community colleges. Since teachers must earn a bachelor's degree before they can be certified, students who start at community colleges must transfer to four-year colleges or universities to become teachers. Sadly, the transfer rate from two- to four-year institutions is disappointingly low (Nettles & Millet, 2004). As discussed in the literature, part of the problem is the lack of clear articulation agreements between the partnering institutions that establish which community college credits will be accepted at the four-year institution. As a result, community college students often lose credits upon transfer. The difficulty of the transfer process is confounded further by a general lack of support services to facilitate the students' successful integration into the teacher education program at the four-year institution once the transfer occurs.

The Teacher Academy Learning Community at the University of Texas, San Antonio—featured in the Busto Flores, Riojas Clark, Claeys, and Villarreal article—typifies initiatives that focus recruitment efforts on the community college student population. This program was designed primarily to meet the needs of students transferring into teacher education from San Antonio College, the largest two-year college in the geographic area serving a largely Latino population. (The University of Texas component of the program is also open to incoming freshmen and students with undeclared majors at the institution.) The article focuses on the support structures put in place to facilitate the integration into the university system of transfer students pursuing teacher education. A key element of the support structure is a collaborative network of student service offices at the partner institutions through which transfer students are identified for program participation. Support begins with careful advisement of students at the community college to ensure they take the appropriate courses prior to their transfer into teacher education at the University of Texas. Upon transfer, students are involved in a Summer Bridge Institute that gives them an orientation to university life and exposes them to other activities intended to strengthen the academic and problem-solving skills they will need to succeed at the university.

Once on campus, participants receive a variety of supports including monitoring of their progress through the teacher education program; referrals for assistance with time management, study skills, and tutoring when such needs are identified; counseling with personal issues that present a threat to their persistence in college; activities that guide them through an exploration of their professional dispositions; and mentoring and coaching on professional matters both throughout the teacher education program and during their initial year of teaching. These support services not only smooth the transfer process to the university, but also enhance the capacity of the teacher education program at the University of Texas, San Antonio, to produce teachers of color who will persist in the profession. Particularly noteworthy in this initiative is the mentoring and coaching support graduates of the teacher education program receive during their initial year of teaching, a time in which teachers are most vulnerable to attrition. There is little in the literature about the mentoring of new teachers of color.

Residents of Communities of Color

Partnerships between teacher education programs at colleges and universities and various types of organizations/agencies in communities of color have been established with the goal of increasing the supply of certified teachers of color for schools in those communities. This "grow your own" recruitment approach builds on the belief that people of color who live in the community are particularly well suited to teach children from that community. These individuals are said to bring to teaching personal insight into the lives of the students and a commitment to improving the young people's academic performance. Indeed, there is much evidence in the literature to support these claims (Villegas & Davis, in press). Most of this work has focused on paraprofessionals in schools. Programs of teacher education that recruit paraprofessionals work closely with the school districts that employ them. As part of these "career ladder" initiatives, paraprofessionals continue their salaried positions while enrolling in courses each semester toward the completion of requirements for teaching certification, and usually a bachelor's degree as well. Such programs, which typically take a minimum of three years to produce teachers, offer a variety of support services to enable participants to make it through graduation and obtain their certification (Villegas & Clewell, 1998).

The Pathways Program at Armstrong Atlantic State University (AASU), described by Lau, Dandy, and Hoffman, is a good example of a career ladder program for paraprofessionals. In this initiative, AASU collaborates with the Savannah-Chatham County Public School District (SCCPS) to select participants for the program. The selection process gives attention to a variety of indicators of ability and future success as teachers, including exemplary track records as paraprofessionals in schools and commitment to teaching in high need school environments. Because one of the goals of the program is for completers to be hired as teachers in the partner district, recommendations from SCCPS teachers and administrators carry special weight in selection decisions. To address the needs of paraprofessionals—many of whom bring academic lags resulting from inequitable schooling, have children to support, and shoulder major financial responsibilities for their households—the program offers various services. These include tight monitoring of participants' academic progress, tutorials and other academic supports for those experiencing difficulties in courses, a system of peer support promoted by the use of cohort groups, test-taking preparation for certification exams, and financial assistance in the form of tuition scholarships and textbook vouchers. Among the many salient features of this nationally recognized program, two stand out. One is the creative arrangement that the partnering school district and institution of higher education have worked out to secure release time with pay for paraprofessionals to attend classes at the university, thereby shortening the time they would otherwise need to complete the required coursework. The second is the successful restructuring of the student teaching experience so that participants can complete this certification requirement without having to lose salary and benefits during this time.

Two other initiatives featured in this issue—the Hopi Teacher for Hopi Schools (HTHS) program described by White, Bedonie, De Groat, Lockhard, and Honanie, and Project TEACH described by Irizarry—also use the grow your own recruitment approach. But instead of limiting recruitment efforts to paraprofessionals, these two programs targeted adults in the community with an interest in teaching, including paraprofessionals. This broader reach was possible because the partnership involved formal relationships with the community beyond the local schools. A community-based organization committed to creating pathways into higher education for community residents was a key collaborator in Project TEACH, helping to identify potential participants and securing funding to cover the cost of tuition for some of them. Similarly, the HTHS program was planned and implemented with direct input from representatives of the Hopi Nation. Given the sense of program ownership on the part of the communities involved, the strong critique of the university curriculum evident in both articles is not surprising. In the university/tribal collaboration, for example, the program was pushed to make the coursework for participants more inclusive by adding elements of "red pedagogy" to the curriculum. In Project TEACH, participants were offered "supplemental" professional development activities to compensate for the relative lack of attention given to issues of diversity and social justice in the teacher education courses they took.

Readers of the Irizarry article, in particular, walk away with a clearer understanding of the difficulties involved in respectfully integrating into existing programs of teacher education people from historically oppressed groups who are committed to returning to their communities to work toward changing the many inequities built into the everyday fabric of schools. For this to happen, programs of teacher education need to attend to issues of recruitment and provide support services to see the recruits through graduation. But equally important, if not more so, programs must be willing to rethink the curriculum in fundamental ways. As Irizarry astutely explains, recruiting people of color into teacher education, while "failing to prepare them to promote educational equity does little to alter a system of education characterized by significant disparities in opportunity and achievement. Solely focusing on the representation of teachers of color in university or K-12 classrooms is tokenism and not transformative. Representation, while important, is not enough." Unfortunately, most of the literature on diversifying the teaching force continues to focus on representation, without giving sufficient attention to the type of preparation new recruits of color need to serve as agents of change in schools. We were pleased to see that the Wong et al. article in this issue dealt squarely with this topic.

Holders of Bachelor's Degrees

People of color who already hold bachelor's degrees in fields other than education comprise another important pool from which to draw new teachers. In fact, schools with severe teacher shortages, overwhelmingly urban schools, routinely fill vacant positions with candidates from this pool, either by issuing them provisional certificates or bringing them into teaching through an alternative route program. The latter option generally allows recruits to take on instructional positions in subject areas with teacher shortages, contingent on their successful completion of a program that provides some preparation in pedagogy and an internship experience in classrooms. The provisional certificate approach allows individuals without preparation in pedagogy to work as teachers for a period of time, usually three to six years, during which they are expected to complete the

requirements for certification. While these two pathways into teaching receive a fair amount of criticism in the literature, they are nevertheless used widely to fill vacancies in urban schools. In fact, without them, teacher shortages in those settings would be even more severe than they currently are. Clearly, traditional programs of teacher education must work harder to produce more teachers for urban schools, regardless of their race/ethnicity. In addition, they need to assume some responsibility for ensuring that those who enter teaching in urban schools with provisional certification or through alternative routes have the preparation they need to teach students successfully. Project 29, highlighted in the Sakash and Chou article, is an example of such an effort.

The goal of Project 29, a collaborative initiative involving the University of Illinois at Chicago and the Chicago Public Schools (CPS), was to enable provisionally certified bilingual (Latino) teachers in the partner district to secure their standard teaching credentials while receiving in-class support to speed their development of pedagogical skills for teaching English language learners (ELLs). Several elements of the program contribute to its documented success over the past 13 years. To begin with, participants are carefully selected based on attributes that program staff have found predictive of future success as teachers, such as parenting experience, involvement in activism and leadership activities, and perseverance in overcoming problems, in addition to having an acceptable grade point average. Participants receive an individualized plan of study after a careful review of their transcripts. They meet regularly throughout the program in small "advisory" groups for peer support on academic, professional, and personal issues of concern to them. The curriculum focuses on assisting the Scholars, as participants are called, to see connections between what they learn at the university and what they experience daily as teachers of ELLs in urban schools.

Ongoing observations of the Scholars' performance in their classrooms by university field instructors serve two critically important functions in the program. They provide participants support and guidance for improving their pedagogical skills and enable the faculty to continuously modify the content of the education courses to address the specific difficulties Scholars are experiencing in their teaching. The redesigned "student teaching" experience—which calls for participants to complete inquiry projects in their own classrooms and to conduct a project on issues related to the education of ELLs jointly with a general education monolingual teacher from the school—provides a more authentic learning experience for this population of teacher candidates than the traditional student teaching. This curricular modification also allows participants to complete the "student teaching" requirement without experiencing an interruption in salary and benefits. In brief, the article by Sakash and Chou shows how a teacher education program committed to improving the conditions of urban schools can do so.

It is interesting to note that the majority of people of color entering teaching over the past 15 years did so either as provisionally certified teachers or through some form of alternate route (Allen, 2003). This is explained, at least in part, by the challenges involved in getting candidates of color from non-traditional teacher pools into and through traditional teacher education programs. We suspect, however, that another explanation is the blasé attitude toward diversifying the ranks of teachers that prevails in many programs of teacher education. Even when publicly claiming to be committed to that goal, little energy is actually devoted to making this happen.

Looking across the Approaches

From reading this collection of articles, several conclusions can be drawn about how best to diversify the teaching force, all of which are consistent with the existing literature on this topic. Collectively, these works suggest that to increase the proportions of teachers of color will require more than luring college-bound students of color away from financially profitable fields into teacher education. A true expansion will necessitate developing the potential of others who might not otherwise go on to four-year colleges. A comprehensive recruitment approach, one that targets different pools of potential talent—pre-college students, community college students, and others who serve children and families within the community in addition to college students with undeclared majors—is needed. The article by Landis and colleagues, in this issue, underscores this conclusion.

Another lesson learned is that programs of teacher education seeking to diversify the teaching force must collaborate with different organizations/agencies to successfully recruit candidates from diverse racial and ethic backgrounds. To recruit from the pre-college student population calls for the involvement of the school districts in which those students are enrolled. Partnerships with school districts are also needed to recruit employed paraprofessionals. Clear articulation agreements that spell out which community college courses will be accepted by the partnering four-year college are essential to tap the large pool of students of color in two-year colleges. Collaborations with organizations based in communities of color—including churches, civic organizations, and various types of service agencies—are also helpful in identifying potential recruits with an interest in teaching and a commitment to return to their communities as teachers. (For a detailed explanation of the central features of such partnerships, see Clewell & Villegas, 2001.)

To successfully recruit teacher candidates of color from non-traditional pools, tuition assistance is essential. Several articles in this collection emphasize this point. Without financial incentives, few candidates from non-traditional teacher pools can afford to complete an undergraduate program of study. To address this need, teacher education programs could secure scholarships through grants from private foundations and/or government agencies. Forgiveness loans that are erased after graduates have taught in schools for a specified period of time are similarly helpful. The recent difficulty finding funding sources for this purpose presents a major obstacle to diversifying the teaching force, as the authors of several articles in this issue rightly point out.

From the works published in this issue of *Teacher Education Quarterly* we also learn that teacher education programs must work diligently to retain students of color from non-traditional pools through graduation and certification. As the authors

explain, this involves offering a comprehensive network of academic and social support services, including orientation to the college/university, a strong advisement and monitoring system, prompt referrals to academic support services for students experiencing difficulties with their coursework, workshops designed to help participants develop test-taking skills, and the use of structured groups or cohorts to promote peer-support.

Looking Ahead

Upon reflecting on the literature, it is clear to us that we already know much about how to recruit people of color into teacher education and how to support them through graduation and certification. We know relatively little, however, about how to adequately prepare prospective teachers of color and how to facilitate their successful transition into the profession. Part of the rationale for increasing the diversity of the teaching force is that people of color bring to teaching knowledge about the lives of students of color and insider experiences that enable them to relate well to students of color and to build the necessary bridges to learning for them. However, unless teacher candidates of color are appropriately prepared to draw on this unique knowledge and insight to shape their pedagogy, the yield of those resources will be limited at best. Similarly, unless teacher candidates of color are appropriately prepared to act as change agents, their commitment to making schools more equitable and just for students of color is not likely to produce the desired results. Unfortunately, there is little in the literature that speaks directly to these two important topics.

We have argued elsewhere that the addition of large numbers of teachers of color represents our best chance to make schools in this country more democratic and just (Villegas & Davis, in press). But to maximize the benefits that could be derived from having a diverse teaching force, programs of teacher education must go beyond issues of recruitment and retention and attend to the preparation candidates of color need for the task. That is the immediate challenge ahead for those who are truly committed to diversifying the ranks of teachers.

References

Allen, M. B. (April 2003). *Eight questions on teacher preparation: What does the research say?* Denver, CO: Education Commisison of the States.

Carter, D. J., & Wilson, R. (1992). *Minorities in higher education: Tenth annual report.* Washington, DC: American Council on Education.

Clewell, B. C., Darke, K., Davis-Googe, T., Forcier, L., & Manes, S. (2000). *Literature review on teacher recruitment programs.* Washington, DC: The Urban Institute.

Clewell, B. C., & Villegas, A. M. (2001). *Ahead of the class: A handbook for preparing new teachers from new sources: Design lessons from the DeWitt-Reader's Digest Fund's Pathways to Teaching Career Initiative.* Washington, DC: Urban Institute. http://www.urban.org/url.cfm?ID=310041.

Hudson, M., Foster, E., Irvine, J. J., Holmes, B., & Villegas, A. M. (2002). *Tapping potential: Community college students and America's teacher recruitment challenge.* Belmont, MA: Recruiting New Teachers.

Nettles, M., & Millett, C. M. (2004). *Student access in community college* (Issue Paper). Washington, DC: American Association of Community Colleges.

Urban, W. J. (2000). *Gender, race, and the National Education Association: Professionalism and its limitations.* New York: Routledge-Falmer.

Villegas, A. M., & Clewell, B. C. (1998). Increasing teacher diversity by tapping the paraprofessional pool. *Theory Into Practice, 37*(2), 121–130.

Villegas, A. M., & Davis, D. (In press). Preparing teachers of color to confront racial/ethnic disparities in educational outcomes. In M. Cochran-Smith, S. Feiman-Nemser, & J. McIntyre (Eds.), *Handbook of research on teacher education: Enduring issues in changing contexts* (3rd ed.). Mahwah, NJ: Lawrence Erlbaum.

Zapata, J. (1998). Early identification and recruitment of Hispanic teacher candidates. *Journal of Teacher Education, 39,* 19–23.

Critical Thinking

1. What are the unfortunate consequences for all students with a shortage of teachers of color?

2. How can teachers of color be recruited?

3. What specific steps must be taken to support teachers of color?

4. Why is having teachers of color essential for all students?

Create Central

www.mhhe.com/createcentral

Internet References

AISNE Guide to Hiring and Retaining Teachers of Color
www.aisne.org/services_resources/AISNE%20Guide%20to%20Hiring%20 and%20Retaining%20Teachers%20of%20Color%20(2:02)%20By%20 Michael%20Brosnan.pdf

Diverse Issues in Higher Education
http://diverseeducation.com/article/53254/

ANA MARÍA VILLEGAS is a professor of curriculum and teaching and **DANNÉ E. DAVIS** is an assistant professor of early childhood, elementary education, and literacy education, both with the College of Education at Montclair State University, Montclair, New Jersey.

Unit 4

UNIT

Prepared by: Nancy P. Gallavan, *University of Central Arkansas*

Awareness of Learners

Throughout their careers, most teachers are traveling on lifelong quests to understand their learners and to increase their students' achievement in learning. Associated with these goals are the needs to enhance one's self efficacy in teaching and to improve the curriculum, instruction, assessments, and management related to schooling. The Gallavan Journey to Cultural Competence Model illustrates the stages necessary for fulfilling the quest. Teachers must become aware of cultural competence in concept, in practice, as a personal characteristic strongly influencing the teaching, and as a personal characteristic strongly influencing the learning.

Similar to the last line of Lincoln's Gettysburg Address, cultural competence should be considered about the people, by the people, for the people, and of the people. That means, cultural competence is about all people, their cultures, cultural characteristics, beliefs, traditions, customs, etc., and the ways they interact both within their cultural communities as well as between and among cultural communities. Simply stated: the content of cultural competence encompasses all the stories about all the people. Learners bring their own content; they want to know their own stories and the stories of all other people, society, and systems around them from the past, through the present, and into the future. Too often, school curriculum does not include all people's stories.

Cultural competence is by the people. We must ensure that our own stories are recorded and preserved. Each of us needs to be encouraged to write our individual stories, investigate our stories for accuracy, and share our stories again within our own communities as well as between and among other communities. We cannot allow other people to write our stories without our permission and guidance. Although school curriculum is limited, teachers must engage students with instructional strategies that empower students to express and exchange their own stories.

The purpose of cultural competence is for the people to be informed about the world so we live richer more fulfilling lives. All people benefit by investigating their own stories and by hearing or experiencing other people's stories. Through literature (read silently, read aloud, told, viewed, acted, etc.), art, dance, travel, and many other experiential forms of learning, people are invited into the cultures of other people from which we draw valuable inferences and make vital connections.

Cultural competence is of the people. Every one of us is grounded on a cultural foundation based on our backgrounds, beliefs, and behaviors that guide and support our bridges into the future. In order for each person to become all that he or she can be, then each of us must understand and respect the cultural foundations of all other people. To accomplish this goal, it is important to realize the knowledge, skills, dispositions, and communications that you possess and you do not possess at this time. As teachers and students, it is imperative to admit that we don't know everything, that we may not be skilled with cross-cultural interactions, our assumptions may not make sense, and that our communication skills are not adequate.

Accept that there are similarities and differences among all people and in ways that we may or may not anticipate or expect. Stay alert and increase awareness without making snappy judgments and inaccurate evaluations. Try to understand other people by viewing the world from their perspectives. Developing empathy allows us to treat other people as we want to be treated.

Learn to listen, ask questions, and stay neutral about topics, issues, insights, and opinions. As we mature and feel better prepared to tackle the complex, challenging, uncertain, and ambiguous aspects of learning and living, we may inadvertently offend other people. Perhaps the human need to control more or all aspects of our lives limits our abilities to stay open and grow. Change is difficult, especially for ourselves.

Find a cultural comrade, someone with whom you have established trust. Ask your cultural comrade to give you honest feedback about your body language, facial expressions, word choices, activity selections, and so forth. Each of us usually is the last to realize when we are being biased or prejudicial, especially when we are focused on advancing cultural competence. Then celebrate accomplishments.

Article   Prepared by: Nancy P. Gallavan, *University of Central Arkansas*

Immigrant Students and the Obstacles to Achievement

Today's immigrants bring needed skills and attitudes to the United States. It's about time we helped them work for the American Dream.

TAMIKO STRATTON, VALERIE OOKA PANG, MARCELINA MADUEÑO, CYNTHIA D. PARK, MIRIAM ATLAS, CINDY PAGE, AND JENNIFER OLIGER

Learning Outcomes

After reading this article, you will be able to:

* Describe the history and contributions of U.S. immigrants through history and today.

* Identify the challenges that immigrants face and the responsibilities educators should fulfill.

The graduates await their opportunity to cross the stage and receive their diplomas. The auditorium is filled with families from many cultures. This urban high school is home to an array of immigrants from Mexico to Somalia, Vietnam to Peru. The ceremony is conducted in English, Spanish, Arabic, Vietnamese, and Cambodian. The hope of the American dream can be seen shining on the faces of the high school graduates.

Renee sits in the front row wearing a white cap and gown with gold cords draped around her shoulders, signifying graduation with highest honors. Her family sits proudly in the audience, awaiting her turn to walk across the stage. This is Renee's first step from adolescence to adulthood, and she's worked toward this opportunity since immigrating to this country seven years earlier. It has taken time, stacks of paperwork, and sacrifice to bring the family together for this momentous occasion. Her family came member by member over 15 years through legal channels. The most recent addition is her father, a former auto dealer in Peru who is now starting over as a dishwasher in a downtown hotel. Virtually all of Renee's adolescence was spent anxiously hoping for his arrival and helping her mother with the paperwork so her father could emigrate.

Now graduation day is here, and attending college is not just a pipe dream for Renee. She has been accepted to several top universities. It's a great accomplishment—one made of sacrifice and hard work during a lifetime of making difficult choices. Now she is struggling over yet another tough decision—to stay in the city and attend a local university as her parents wish, or to go to a highly competitive university, leaving just when her dream of a reunited family has finally been realized.

Mohamed also is dressed in white, but he is sitting on the stage. He is translating the greeting for other Somalis in the audience. Mohamed has a green card because he is a refugee from Somalia. His family fled across the border to a refugee camp in Kenya, then waited 10 years to emigrate to the United States. They originally lived in Mogadishu but had to flee on foot. Despite this difficult existence, Mohamed always dreamed of an education. Life in the United States has not always been easy for his parents. In the evenings and after school, Mohamed worked at a local theme park to help his family financially. Mohamed's parents are proud of his achievements; he is graduating with honors even though he worked throughout high school.

Brenda sits with the rest of her class. She reflects on her years in public school and feels a sense of pride and accomplishment. Her mother, a Mexican immigrant who never made it past 2nd grade, waits to hear her daughter's name; her father is not here because he had to work. Brenda earned a 3.3 grade point average and already received credit for college-level Spanish by passing the Advanced Placement test. Although her parents always encouraged her to do her best, once she hit high school, she was largely on her own to fail or succeed. Despite being in the United States for over 20 years, neither parent speaks much English. Her family owns a local taco shop, and Brenda and her older brother worked there since middle school. As the eldest female of five siblings, Brenda learned to negotiate for her parents—she filled out all of the school registration forms every fall for her family, helped her siblings with their homework, and translated for her parents when necessary.

Like the other students in the front row, Maria is graduating with honors. Maria is the Associated Student Body Vice President and has been instrumental in planning the class graduation celebration. However, for her, this day is bittersweet. Today marks the end of Maria's educational opportunities in America. Maria is undocumented. Her mother, a single parent, migrated to the United States from Mexico when Maria was a toddler. Many years ago her mother was admitted into the United States with a visa, and she found a job at a fast-food restaurant and never left. Her employment allowed the family to survive. Maria, now an accomplished high school student, wishes to become a nurse. In order to pursue her career goals, she has to make a decision. Her mother has found a young man who has agreed to marry Maria so she can pursue a path to citizenship and her dreams. Maria considered joining the armed forces, but her mother needs her help with her younger sisters, so marriage seems to be the best option. Although Maria can't discuss her predicament without tearing up, she knows that this is what she must do to remain in this country.

The students described above are composites of actual students, but examples of hardworking immigrant students and their families can be found in every state. Many young immigrants are negotiating their place in society. They believe in the American Dream and struggle with issues of poverty, language, cultural assimilation, and the desire to further their education.

In 2000, about 11% of the more than 300 million people in the United States were immigrants. In addition, each year roughly one million people immigrate to the United States, with researchers estimating that an additional 500,000 people enter the country illegally (Haskins 2007). About 20% of the youths in the United States are immigrants themselves or children of immigrants, and about 75% of children of immigrants are native-born (Suárez-Orozco and Suárez-Orozco 2001).

The United States was built on the toil and intellect of many immigrants throughout its history. Today, many undocumented immigrants make important contributions to U.S. production. For example, California State Senator Gilbert Cedillo has indicated that 90% of agricultural work, 30% of service industries, and 20% of construction labor are carried out by undocumented immigrants (Cedillo 2008).

Critics of immigration often claim that immigrants contribute to unemployment among native-born citizens and lower the wages for blue-collar jobs. However, the Hispanic Pew Center found that there is no significant correlation between immigration and unemployment rates in 10 critical states with high immigration rates (Kochhar 2006). Furthermore, the Council of Economic Advisors discovered that immigrants contributed positively to the U.S. economy with a greater innovation per capita rate than native-born workers. Immigrants also provide important skills, though their labor is less costly. In addition, immigrants add to our national tax revenue, replacing retirees' contributions to social security and Medicare at a time when the U.S. workforce is aging (Kochhar 2006). As countries become increasingly tied to one another in the global economy, the skills immigrant children bring to the workforce, such as speaking more than one language and possessing a

To learn more about the views of children of immigrants, view the documentary *30 Days: Immigration*. A member of the Minuteman organization lives with a Mexican-American family for 30 days. Two of the younger children in the family are U.S. born, and the other family members are undocumented immigrants.

See the program at www.hulu.com/watch/56908/30-days-immigration #s-p3-so-i0.

multicultural perspective, are increasingly valuable (Cornelius 2005; Erisman and Looney 2007).

Social Contributions

Immigrant families bring a wealth of traditional values, such as a strong work ethic, the strength of family and community ties, and a belief in education. An ethnographic study by Marjorie Orellana (2001) documents the contributions that immigrant children bring to the United States. For example, Orellana found that students are family- and community-oriented and often volunteer in classrooms, schools, and local libraries, assisting teachers and librarians and tutoring younger children.

Immigrant students' strong sense of family provides a solid foundation for citizenship education. For example, one of the children in a Southern California school, Monica, who came to the United States in 2nd grade with no literacy skills in her primary language and no knowledge of English, has been a trailblazer for her three younger siblings. Because of her mother's strong belief in the value of education, she enrolled her daughter in every before- and after-school program available, volunteered in Monica's classrooms, developed relationships with

Intelligent, hardworking, bilingual students in our nation's classrooms contribute greatly to the economic and political health of the country. At the same time, these students pay a high cost. Undocumented elementary students suffer the consequences of limited medical care, poverty, and the potential loss of their primary caregivers to deportation. Undocumented high school students feel lost, confused, depressed, and even angry when they find out that they cannot secure a driver's license or apply for financial aid for college because, though they may have lived in the United States since childhood, they are not citizens.

The Development, Relief, and Education for Alien Minors (DREAM) Act, which is pending in Congress, would provide the opportunity to earn conditional permanent residency for undocumented immigrant students who graduate from a U.S. high school, are of good moral character, arrived in the United States as children, and have been in the country continuously for at least five years before the bill's enactment, The students would obtain temporary residency for a six-year period.

To learn more about the DREAM Act, visit http://thomas.loc.gov/cgi-bin/bdquery/z?d108:SN01545:@@@L&summ2=m.

teachers at the school, and finally sought assistance from one of the teachers to transfer Monica to a higher performing middle school outside their neighborhood. The younger siblings are reaping the benefits of this family's dedication and resourcefulness. The youngest daughter, a 1st grader, possesses a sophisticated command of the English language and is already reading and writing significantly higher than grade level.

Immigrant students make important contributions in school. For example, Maria took on many leadership positions including being voted Associated Student Body Vice President. She developed important communication and organizational skills. Her school was extremely diverse with students representing a range of cultures from Vietnam, Korea, Somalia, Mexico, and the United States. Sometimes, Maria acted as a cultural broker. She was aware of the importance of building bridges between students in order to create an inclusive school. Even with a grade point average of 3.5, Maria conducted many meetings and planned such school events as dances, an international festival, and homecoming.

In her ethnographic study, Orellana found that immigrant children like Maria play an integral role in running households by caring for younger siblings and helping them with homework, making appointments for family members, preparing meals, and helping with household chores. These contributions help form the strong work ethic and family values that are critical to the immigrant family's survival and are a positive model for other students. Some children also work alongside their parents, thereby contributing to the family income by doing piecework, helping clean offices, and working in restaurants. Due to their new mastery of English, they commonly serve as interpreters for their parents, teachers, and even other children.

The work children do at home and in the community can bolster their chances for academic and professional success. A study by Gándara (1994) found that two-thirds of a sample of 50 high-achieving Chicano professionals said that it was their duties at home as children and taking part in the work of their parents that led to their self-reliance and work ethic.

Although many immigrant parents are thought to be uninvolved or uninterested in the education of their children, they are present in large numbers in classrooms where their home languages are recognized and on school governance committees when translation is offered (Pang 2009). In some schools, Chinese-American and Latino parents who do not feel confident in their English skills volunteer by putting up classroom bulletin boards, cutting material for student projects, and copying materials for teachers. In fact, immigrant parents who volunteer regularly often find substitutes for themselves if they miss their day of school service (Pang 2009). In addition, research by Lopez (2001) shows that when schools try to meet the needs of their diverse immigrant families, parents demonstrate a profound interest in being involved in their children's education.

Immigrant parents have sacrificed much so they can offer their children a better chance at an education and a future, and they often feel indebted to teachers and the education system at large. For example, in 2008 when so many dedicated teachers faced layoffs because of cuts to California's education budget, many immigrant parents and their children organized rallies, marched side by side with their teachers, and wrote letters of outrage and support to school boards in both their native languages and English. Immigrant children from many families are active citizens making their voices heard in efforts to advocate for effective schools.

College and the American Dream

As members of the Class of 2009 cross the stage to receive their diplomas, bursts of cheers erupt from various families in the audience. Every young adult who shakes hands with the principal has fulfilled a dream; the beaming faces reflect the pride and sense of accomplishment that each graduate feels. In this moment, there is only happiness and celebration. But soon, decisions will have to be made.

Renee has waited 15 years to have her entire family together, yet she also believes it is important for her future to attend the best university she can. "When I came, I had all these beliefs from my parents, but I now have the values that I have learned in American schools also." In the end, Renee's choice combines the best of both worlds; she is somewhere in the middle. She now lives in a dormitory at a highly respected university, close enough to travel home on the weekends to enjoy family dinners.

Mohamed has opted for the path of least resistance and is attending the state university 40 miles from his home. His major is criminal justice, and he is a member of the class of 2012. He was honored with an AVID scholarship, which covers most of his tuition and books. Still, he wonders how his life might have been different if he had followed his heart instead of his faith and went to the University of California Berkeley.

Brenda took on the task of negotiating through the college application process on her own, as this was uncharted territory in her family. She applied only to the local state university and community college. She didn't know about other options and relied on a friend in school to help her when she got stuck on her application. In the fall, she attended City College and is working on transferring to a four-year university. She will major in criminal justice. She has cousins who are successful in the Border Patrol and encourage her to get her bachelor's degree and then join as well. She knows her command of English and Spanish is an asset in this or similar careers.

Maria has decided to get married. In spite of several college acceptances, Maria will be attending a community college because she can't afford even state college tuition. By the time she's ready to transfer, she expects to be a legal resident of the United States. However, she will need to put her personal career goal on hold in order to support a family.

Teachers see the amazing potential of immigrant students on a daily basis. They are gifted young people who contribute to and are part of our school communities. The vibrancy of a democracy demands a diverse, young population. Young immigrants bring new ideas and valuable linguistic and cultural competencies that enrich our democracy. They also bring important multiple perspectives and cultural expertise that are needed more than ever as the United States works collaboratively to gain the respect of other nations and provide strong leadership around the globe (Friedman 2008).

The President and Congress must support immigration reform that addresses the needs of young immigrants. There are thousands of these young people graduating from high school every year, and they believe in the American Dream. These youths have the vision that this country needs.

References

Cedillo, Gilbert. "Foreword." In *Underground Undergrads: UCLA Undocumented Immigrant Students Speak Out*. Los Angeles, Calif.: UCLA Center for Labor Research and Education, 2008.

Cornelius, Wayne A. "Controlling 'Unwanted' Immigration: Lessons from the United States, 1993-2004." *Journal of Ethnic and Migration Studies* 31, no. 4 (2005): 775–794.

Erisman, Wendy, and Shannon Looney. *Opening the Door to the American Dream: Increasing Higher Education Access and Success for Immigrants*. Washington, D.C.: Institute for Higher Education Policy, 2007: www.eric.ed.gov/ERICDocs/data/ericdocs2sql/content_storage_01/0000019b/80/29/86/3f.pdf.

Friedman, Thomas L. "Finishing Our Work," *New York Times*, November 5, 2008. www.nytimes.com/2008/11/05/opinion/05friedman.html?em.

Gándara, Patricia. "Choosing Higher Education: Educationally Ambitious Chicanos and the Path to Social Mobility." *Education Policy Analysis* 8, no. 2 (1994). http://epaa.asu.edu/epaa/v2n8.html.

Haskins, Ron, "Immigration: Wages, Education, and Mobility Washington, D.C.: Brookings Institution, 2007. www.brookings.edu/~/media/Files/rc/reports/2007/07useconomics_haskins/07useconomics_haskins.pdf.

Kochhar, Rakesh. "Foreign-Born Workforce and Employment of Native Born." Washington, D.C.: Pew Hispanic Center, 2006. pewhispanic.org/reports/report.php?ReportID=69.

Lopez, Gerardo R. "The Value of Hard Work: Lessons on Parent Involvement from an (Im)migrant Household." *Harvard Educational Review* 71 (Fall 2001): 416–437. www.eric.ed.gov/ERICDocs/data/ericdocs2sql/content_storage_01/0000019b/80/29/86/3f.pdf.

Orellana, Marjorie Faulstich. "The Work Kids Do: Mexican and Central American Immigrants," *Harvard Educational Review* 71 (2001): 366–389.

Pang, Valerie Ooka. "A Model for Achievement: Characteristics of a High Achieving, Low-Income, Majority Asian American School." Paper presented at the annual meeting of the American Educational Research Association, School Improvement Special Interest Group, San Diego, California, April 13-17, 2009.

Suárez-Orozco, Carola, and Marcelo M. Suárez-Orozco. *Children of Immigration*. Cambridge, Mass.: Harvard University Press, 2001.

Critical Thinking

1. What are your experiences with immigrant students?
2. What are your experiences with immigrant families?
3. Why is it important for educators to understand, accept, and offer assistance to immigrant students and their families?
4. How will you teach immigrant students in ways that are like and unlike teaching other students?

Create Central

www.mhhe.com/createcentral

Internet References

The Chronicle of Higher Education
 chronicle.com/article/Obama-Embraces-Reform-Plan/136899/
Immigration Policy Center
 www.immigrationpolicy.org/just-facts/dream-act

TAMIKO STRATTON is a high school teacher in the San Diego City Schools. **VALERIE OOKA PANG** is a professor at San Diego State University. **MARCELINA MADUEÑO** is a high school teacher in the Oceanside School District. **CYNTHIA D. PARK** is a professor at San Diego State University. **MIRIAM ATLAS** is an elementary teacher in the San Diego City Schools, where **CINDY PAGE** is a high school teacher and **JENNIFER OLIGER** is an elementary teacher.

Article   Prepared by: Nancy P. Gallavan, *University of Central Arkansas*

Status of the Dream: A Study of Dr. King in Little Rock and Memphis Classrooms

ANGELA WEBSTER-SMITH

Learning Outcomes

After reading this article, you will be able to:

- Relate the events of 50 years in the past to today.

- Understand the influences of Dr. Martin Luther King, Jr.'s legacy.

Introduction

The author was present for what would become the last speech of Dr. Martin Luther King, Jr., (MLK) when she was an elementary school student in Memphis, Tennessee, in 1968. Being present for such a historical event was life-altering in shaping her views on equity with reference to what is known as *the American dream* (Webster-Smith, in press). Today, as a professor of leadership studies who helps to prepare and develop school leaders, she continues to see the significance of this watershed moment in history as it relates to what is believed to be the new American civil right: education. Dr. King's influence extends far beyond U.S. borders and offers a model for peace around the world.

Over 40 years after his death in 1968, the author investigated a total of 50 elementary school teachers in Little Rock, Arkansas, and in Memphis, Tennessee, regarding the life and legacy of Dr. King in contemporary classrooms. Selecting populations of teachers from these venues was important because both cities attracted national attention and fashioned defining moments during the Civil Rights era. The Little Rock crisis involved high school students known as the Little Rock Nine who were initially prevented from entering a racially segregated Little Rock Central High School, whereas the Memphis emergency concerned the Sanitation Strike of 1968 that culminated with Dr. King's death. Because the investigator was born, reared, and lived in the greater Memphis area for many years but currently lives in the greater Little Rock area, often she has wondered about the contemporary effects of Dr. King's legacy on

instruction in schools in areas where civil rights battles were fought publicly.

This paper acquaints the reader with how the MLK dream is operationalized in the personal and professional lives of a small sample of modern-day teachers. Specifically, this paper speaks to the ways in which elementary school teachers are honoring a piece of American history in their classrooms and will offer implications for teacher education.

Literature Review

The National Council for the Social Studies (NCSS, 2010) defines social studies as an integrated study of the social sciences and humanities to promote civic competence in K-12 and college/university settings. Its framework consists of 10 themes including culture, change, people, places, environment, institutions, power, authority, governance, society, global connections, civic ideals, and practices. In alignment with these precepts, elementary school teachers must routinely help their students understand the relevance and significance that everyday citizens have on the symbols, icons, and traditions of American history. The teachers must chronicle the events, protocols, laws, and the basic structures of American life, how those procedures came to be and how such systems affect contemporary living.

Teachers must be able to give credence to Americans who take risks to secure the liberties that are enjoyed in this land of the free. When honoring the nation's heroes, teachers should include individuals from a diverse group of populations. Furthermore, teachers of social studies have the responsibility of engaging students in the processes of critical thinking, ethical decision making, and social participation because these tenets are necessary for democratic living (Ligon, 2005). Principles of the democratic ideal should be taught in ways that allow students to become more conscious of civic life and to see themselves as actors in history (Ayers, Kumashiro, Meiners, Quinn, & Stovall, 2010). Critical reflection and critical discourse are especially important in classrooms where minority students are taught as these instructional methods engage the learner in the process of intellectual border-crossing in that the students can move beyond the borders that have been constructed throughout the course of history through political (power, privilege, and policy) and social contexts (norms, culture, and ethos) (Ingram & Waters, 2007).

Additionally, ideals that educators have for themselves and for their students should include those that pertain to the character and courage that strengthen democracy, equity, and social justice in classrooms and throughout the school (Gallavan, 2011). Freire (1970) purported that education is a practice of freedom and necessary to experience the fullness of humanity; without education, people do not make their own way. They merely become what history makes for them. So, in order to ensure consistent and widespread implementation of teaching democracy, it is important that teachers become comfortable, confident, and competent in designing and presenting lessons to and about a multicultural America and a multicultural world.

Standards for the National Council for Accreditation of Teacher Education (2008) compels colleges and universities to ensure that teacher candidates as well as leadership candidates demonstrate their abilities to apply proficiencies related to diversity and to develop classrooms that value diversity. Therefore, institutions of higher education must offer experiences that help candidates confront issues of diversity and inclusiveness that affect teaching effectiveness and improve student learning. Such experiences would afford candidates opportunities to practice the integration of multiple perspectives in their disciplines and to connect curriculum and instruction to their students' experiences and cultures. These informed practices include knowing how to explain, in developmentally appropriate contexts, the effects of cultural and historical events on general and minority populations for the success of all students and the good will of the nation (Banks, 2007; Davis, 2009; Gay, 2000; Grant & Sleeter, 2007; Irvine, 2007).

Multicultural education is a broad concept that calls for school wide transformation for an empowering, inclusive, and equitable school culture and social structure. It also promotes a leadership team that works with teachers from all disciplines to understand and prepare for their highly interrelated roles (Banks, 2007). While developing students' consciousness and building democratic participation are building blocks in multicultural education (Grant & Sleeter, 2007), curriculum and instruction are crucial components. To that end, teachers must discern the confluence of culture and academic achievement on their roles as effective teachers (Banks, 2007; Davis, 2009; Gay, 2000; Grant & Sleeter, 2007; Irvine, 2007).

For all intents and purposes, teachers should be able to employ culturally responsive pedagogy (Gay, 2000) with consistency and confidence. Of the key elements of multicultural education is the consideration of various approaches and perspectives with an appreciation of how such interpretations are based upon beliefs and social identity (Davis, 2009). Banks (2007) recommends the transformative approach to multicultural education. In this approach, the overall framework of the curriculum is structured such that concepts, issues, and themes are considered from a variety of perspectives. Accepting knowledge as a social construction, teachers present diverse understandings, explanations, and interpretations of the same event.

When used by teachers, the social construction practice helps students understand how the knowledge that is constructed is influenced by the ethnic, racial, and social-class backgrounds of the people constructing that knowledge. In view of the growing diversity in America's schools, this study captures a snapshot of how a small group of teachers integrates the NCSS social studies frameworks that offer a concept map, the NCATE diversity standards that guide best practice and prevailing multicultural education principles that offer practical applications for teaching.

Conceptual Framework

This study was conducted specifically to explore the vitality of Dr. King's dream in contemporary classrooms. Of the many possible approaches for framing these phenomena, the author chose to use integrated lines of investigation to construct and to contextualize this study with respect to its place and connection to key, related standards for teaching. The conceptual framework also honors the influence of phenomenology and phenomenology of practice (van Manen, 2007) as it affords teachers a means of considering what they believe and how that translates into how they act in everyday situations.

Phenomenological research gives credence to individuals and how they make sense of their lived experiences. Through this approach, individuals are also given conceptual space to address the significance of events, time, self, and others as they are experienced (Stanford Encyclopedia of Philosophy, 2008). In addition, the idea context for this study provides insights into how individuals build bridges between how they think and feel with how they act as much as it connects who they are with who they may become (van Manen, 2007).

On one hand, the study utilized direct examination by simply recording what occurred around a single organizing principle such as valuing diversity in the classroom. On the other hand, the investigator considered multiple ideologies such as developing civic competence and advancing multicultural education. Using a naturalistic, interpretive approach, the investigator prioritized explaining the phenomenon in terms of participants' meanings and perspectives. For example, the approach allows for teachers' personal presuppositions and interpretations of the concept, aka Dr. King's dream, and how their personal meanings of the concept intersect with its place in the contemporary elementary school classroom.

This approach gives conceptual space for examining whether it should be taught, when it should be taught, and how often it should be taught. Therefore, this qualitative study has the freedom to emerge with its own themes. Lastly, this conceptual framework was selected to develop the necessary structures to tell a story about the concept of Dr. King's dream and its relationship to 21st century schools and to teacher education with regards to the implications for how colleges of education prepare practicing teachers, provide professional development, and collaborate with schools.

Every learning environment takes into account knowledge of general and individual stages of child development and learning plus educational effectiveness. When teaching about the dream of Dr. Martin Luther King, Jr., teachers are guided by at least three plausible systems: the NCSS social studies standards, NCATE accreditation standards for valuing diversity, and Bank's transformative approach to multicultural education. The conceptual map (see Figure 1) offers a visual display expanding the social studies standards as the constructs grounding Dr. King's dream. The conceptual map also shows the integrated relationships among the concepts.

Dr. King's dream is at the core of the concept map. The tendrils represent preparation for democratic citizenry, a respect for diversity, as well as the incorporation of multiple perspectives for teaching and learning. This system of concepts frames the expectations for how teachers might honor this building block in the pillars of American history.

Methodology

Subsequent to the 40-year commemoration of Dr. King's death was an appropriate juncture in time to examine the status of Dr. King's dream in America's classrooms. This study was conducted using a qualitative research paradigm as it is useful for studying a limited number of participants. Qualitative research is also valuable for describing complex phenomena and for understanding and describing participants' personal experiences of the phenomenon in question related to Dr. King's dream. The qualitative approach allows for describing this phenomenon as situated and embedded in local contexts (Johnson & Onwuegbuzi, 2004).

In 2008, Americans commemorated the 40th anniversary of Dr. King's death and the 45th centenary since his *I Have a Dream* speech. During Dr. King's lifetime, the American Civil Rights Movement targeted ideals such as integration, justice, and equal access. The movement received notable mention for its victories in Little Rock, Arkansas, and in Memphis, Tennessee. In the 21st century, education is considered to be the

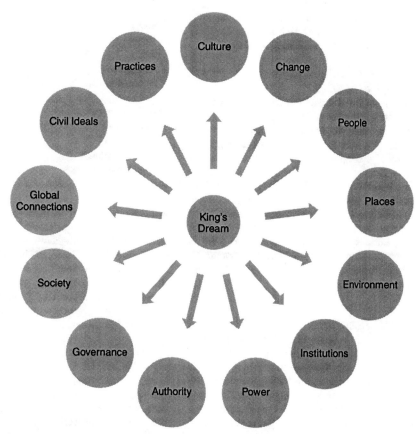

Figure 1   Conceptual Map Expanding the NCSS Themes

new civil right; therefore, the author focused the spotlight on a school in each of these cities to catch a glimpse of how teachers commemorate that moment in American history with regards to its significance and relationship to the life and times of current students.

Participating Cities

During the time of the study, the city of Little Rock proper was managed by a Caucasian mayor with an approximate population of 184,000, while the city of Memphis proper was governed by an African American mayor with an estimated population of 646,000 (Little Rock Community Profile, n.d.; Memphis Community Profile, n.d.). To revisit the Little Rock Nine situation, one can find the Little Rock Central High School Museum and Visitor's Center across the street from the continuously vibrant Little Rock Central High School as well as a memorial on the grounds of the state Capitol. Additionally, the street where the Capitol complex resides was renamed in honor of Dr. Martin Luther King, Jr. To memorialize the Memphis emergency, one can find the National Civil Rights Museum located in the, now defunct, hotel where Dr. King was slain. Each city hosts special events to celebrate the life of Dr. Martin Luther King, Jr., and across the United States the third Monday in January honors his life as the first national holiday that specifically honors the life of an African American.

Participating Schools

The participating schools and school districts in this study are located approximately 200 miles apart. At the time of the study, both school districts employed African American superintendents and both schools were led by African American principals. The majority of students at each school received free and/or reduced meals. Both schools were elementary schools serving students in grades PK-5. The Little Rock elementary school enrolled approximately 400 mostly Caucasian students while the Memphis elementary school enrolled approximately 1,000 mostly African American students. At the time of the study, the participating Little Rock elementary school was rated as "meets standards" according to the *No Child Left Behind Act* (NCLB), and the participating Memphis elementary school was rated as having a "good" NCLB standing.

Participating Teachers

The participating teachers included 18 teachers from the Little Rock elementary school and 32 teachers from the Memphis elementary school. The Little Rock teachers included 1 African American, 16 Caucasians, and 1 Native American. The only male teacher in the study was in Memphis with 22 African American teachers, 1 Asian teacher, and 9 Caucasian teachers. Credentials of the Little Rock teachers included mostly master's degrees averaging 20 years of experience whereas Memphis teachers held mostly graduate degrees (master's degrees and doctorates) with an average of 12 years of teaching experience. The majority of Little Rock teachers were over age 40

Table 1 Teacher Demographics

	Teachers (N=50)		
	Little Rock	Memphis	Totals
Gender			
Female	17	32	49
Male	1	0	1
Credentials			
Bachelors	6	12	18
Master's	4	10	14
Master's +	8	8	16
Doctorate	0	2	2
Age Range			
Under 30	3	3	6
31–40	3	14	17
41–50	4	5	9
51 +	8	10	18
Ethnicity			
African American	1	22	23
Asian	0	1	1
Caucasian	16	9	25
Native American	1	0	1
Home Residence			
Suburban	12	18	30
Rural	2	1	3
Unincorporated	1	1	2
Urban/City	3	12	15

while the majority of Memphis teachers were under age 40. The majority of teachers at both venues reported living in either urban or suburban neighborhoods. Teachers of language arts/literacy/literature, science, mathematics, social studies, music, and art participated from both schools. Other participants in the study included the counselor, speech pathologist/therapist and English Language Learning (ELL) teacher. All grade levels, Pre-K through 5th grade, were represented among the participants. Teacher demographics are displayed in Table 1.

Procedures

The investigator employed the three basic stages of research. She declared the research objective, collected the data, and analyzed and interpreted the data (Johnson & Onwuegbuzi, 2004). Before data were collected, written, site permission was granted in each case by the lead school administrator. Thereafter, surveys were placed in the U.S. mail to the school principal with a self-addressed envelope and necessary postage. Upon receipt, the administrator at each school placed the surveys in the faculty lounge with instructions for interested, volunteer teachers to complete and return to the envelope.

Teachers were provided an informed consent form notifying them of the potential benefits, that their participation was voluntary, and that the estimated time investment for completing the survey instrument was approximately 30 minutes. Teachers also were informed that they could refuse to participate, stop participation at anytime without penalty, or they could indicate their withdrawal by simply discontinuing their responses to the questions and returning the participation packet to the envelope or to the investigator. Teachers were further notified of confidentiality in that the data were not associated with their names and that their data would not be withdrawn from the study after it had been collected.

Instrumentation

The survey instrument was created by the investigator (see Appendix A). In order to determine a sufficiently valid and adequately reliable method of approaching the research questions, the investigator considered the types of information being pursued, uses of the information, individuals to be helped by receiving the information, the timeliness of the project, and the available resources (Krathwohl, 1993; Mathison, 1988; Patton, 1990). To those ends, this design was primarily selected for its potential to provide understanding and reasonable generalizability. As the chief interest of this study lay in exploring ways contemporary teachers honor the life of Dr. King, both qualitative and quantitative data were collected.

The survey questions were arranged with the intention of taking each participant through the same sequence and asking each participant the same questions using the same words. This method minimized variation in the questions posed thus affording data that are more systematic and thorough. The different kinds of inquiries helped to capture patterns and differences, attempting to understand the reasons for those differences and where they existed (Krathwohl, 1993; Mathison, 1988; Patton, 1990). The qualitative inquiries were particularly important in gaining insight into learning how teachers honored the life and legacy of Dr. King in the classroom, while the queries also aided in capturing the emotions of the participants on the subject.

The survey questions included what the MLK dream means to participants, the ways they celebrate the MLK holiday, the parts of the MLK dream they believe are important enough to integrate and model for students throughout the academic year, if the participants have taught lessons on the dream, the instructional approach(es) or practice(s) they used, and the ways that participants believe the MLK legacy should be preserved in school settings. The quantitative inquiries were represented in questions pertaining to culture, gender, age, years of teaching experience, subjects they teach, geographical residence, and degree of education.

Limitations

The investigator does not know the reasons that the 50 participating elementary school teachers were motivated to complete

the survey. Ultimately, 72 percent of the teachers from the Little Rock elementary school participated and 66 percent of the teachers from the Memphis elementary school participated. While the majority of teachers from each school participated, it is possible that only the teachers who were interested in the MLK legacy took the time to complete survey. Those teachers who chose not to complete the survey may or may not be sending a message. Neither interviews nor observations were conducted in the schools, methods that could have added to the depth, interplay, and interpretation of teacher practices. Because the data are contextualized and unique to the relatively few people included in the research study, the findings may not necessarily generalize to other people or other settings (Johnson & Onwuegbuzi, 2004).

Moreover, the principals at each location were not surveyed to denote their support or indifference about the study or its results. Contingent upon the liberties and/or reluctance of the participants, additional limitations may exist. The quantitative inquiries offered a number of predetermined response categories so that the experiences and perspectives of participants were measured in a standard fashion. Although the investigator used primarily a qualitative approach, the demographic data allowed comparison and descriptive measures as well as a generalizable set of succinctly presented findings.

Results

The data are based on the participants' own categories of meaning. In reporting the results of the study, the investigator used direct quotes and fragments of quotes in order to represent participants' opinions, approaches, and methods in their own terms while capturing the heart of their experiences in their own words. Participant perspectives yielded the emerging themes of equality, justice, fairness, peace, character, respect for, and celebration of cultures. The perspectives are presented in terms of their personal phenomenology, school practices, their phenomenology of practice, and their curricula ideals.

Teacher Phenomenology

Critical reflection has long been a staple of teacher education (Dewey, 1933) as a means for teachers to grapple with the historical, political, and cultural contexts of their work. Hence, this study asked teachers to describe what MLK's dream meant to them personally. The primary theme that teachers expressed related to equality. Teachers in Little Rock reported such sentiments as *it is a reinforcement of Christian beliefs that all people are of equal value and precious in God's sight;* that *all people can live and work together as equals; equal opportunity;* and that it represents *a society in which "color" plays no part.* Teachers in Memphis reported similar sentiments with statements such as *all people were created equal in the eyes of God;* the *end of segregation; equal access;* and that now *people can be judged by their character not their race.*

With respect to observing the MLK holiday in their personal or professional life, one group of teachers reported general activities whereas the other group of teachers reported highly specific events. In this study, 70 percent of the Little Rock participants reported having observed the MLK holiday with *church services* and non-specific *celebrations in his honor.* Other teachers reported observations *in college only.* Additionally, 80 percent of Memphis teachers reported observation of the MLK holiday with attendance at *parades, speeches, the Civil Rights Museum, prayer breakfast, MLK Annual Walk, Gandhi-King Conference,* and *rallies.* Other teachers reported taking time to reflect on his life or talking about how they can follow his example.

School Practices

As the principles of multicultural education call for an over-arching school structure that goes beyond curriculum and instruction (Banks, 2007), teachers were asked about ways that the MLK holiday is acknowledged at their schools. The teachers at one elementary school reported many more signs of recognition than the teachers at the other elementary school. Little Rock teachers reported that their school only acknowledges the MLK holiday in the *morning* via the *school news/announcements.* At this school, there are no school wide activities that address the life of MLK. Memphis teachers reported that their school acknowledges the MLK holiday by *reading the MLK dream over the intercom,* hosting an *assembly,* and by pointing it out in their *news/announcements.* The teachers also noted having *related music, displays of artwork, projects,* and examining his life through *Black history studies* that *extend throughout the year, not just in February.*

Phenomenology of Practice

In a sense, all phenomenology is pragmatic and lends itself to the practice of living (van Manen, 2007). Besides, praxis is the culmination and application of the knowledge, skills, and dispositions that define the substance of teaching (Ingram & Waters, 2007); therefore, teachers were asked if they had ever taught lessons on the MLK dream.

In this study, 80 percent of the teachers in the Little Rock elementary school reported affirmatively while 75 percent of the teachers in the Memphis elementary school reported affirmatively. Lessons from both groups of teachers can be primarily categorized as social studies, language arts, and art lessons. Miscellaneous activities also were reported. Little Rock teachers reported the following types of activities. In social studies, teachers led discussions on *MLK's contributions to society* and his *influence, equality, civil rights,* and the *historical* context of what Dr. King did. These teachers also reported *watching a history channel documentary,* watching a *video on united streaming,* and *visiting the MLK website using the data projector.* In language arts, teachers reviewed related *vocabulary words;* students wrote their own *I Have a Dream* papers, devised an *I Have a Dream* pledge, participated in various *writing and journaling* activities, and *read books about MLK.* In art classes, students *designed a medallion to wear all day; they made booklets, made a Dream Mobile* and other unnamed *art activities.* These miscellaneous activities included *visiting the Central*

High Museum, listening to the *I Have a Dream speech on tape,* and completing *diversity activity worksheets.*

The Memphis elementary school teachers reported other types of MLK activities. In social studies, teachers led *discussions on MLK's life as a child and his education* so that students could identify with him more readily as a child and student and not always as the adult hero. Students *wrote reports* and *watched films.* They also *studied a unit on MLK's life and legacy* that included the use of PowerPoint presentations, videos, and work sheets. *Students memorized parts of the dream that were important to them.* Further, one class *held a party to celebrate his birthday.* In language arts, students *made a booklet to celebrate the day, read related books,* and *read his autobiography.* In addition, students *recorded their own dreams then stood at the classroom podium and read their dreams to their classmates.* In art classes, students *participated in role play, drew their own dream; made a web of how to achieve their personal dreams, listened to his speech,* and *sang songs about Dr. King's life.* Miscellaneous activities included *visiting the Civil Rights Museum,* integrating *MLK's dream at the beginning of the academic year when students were generating their dreams and goals for the year,* and routinely holding *lessons on fairness* throughout the school year.

When teachers had taught lessons on the MLK dream, elementary school teachers in both Little Rock and Memphis reported that they designed their own lessons. Their schools did not provide related lessons in their designated curricula.

When asked about the educational settings where they learned multicultural approaches to instruction, teachers at both elementary schools reported learning about multicultural approaches to instruction from all five of the sources in the survey. They gained knowledge while enrolled in either their undergraduate or graduate programs or from professional development workshops offered by their schools.

Curricula Ideals

Curricula in multicultural education should interweave inclusiveness in ways that acknowledge and celebrate a multifocal, relational view of the human experience (Tetreault, 2007). To that end, teachers' opinions were sought concerning the parts of the MLK dream that are important enough to integrate and model for students throughout the academic year. Similar sentiments were expressed by each teacher in the categories of fairness, justice, equality, life success, peace, and character. The Little Rock elementary school teachers mentioned that *color should not influence discipline or learning;* that students are *free to be anything they want to be if they make good choices;* that *injustices happen and are wrong; being able to speak and write are important;* people should find *peaceful ways of solving problems and injustices;* that *character is about the person, not the color of skin;* that *trustworthiness and honesty count.* The Memphis elementary school teachers mentioned that people must *treat other people with dignity and worth;* that students must be encouraged to *follow their dreams* and *work hard so students can achieve.* The principles that were consistently mentioned were *fairness, justice,* and *equality.* Other regular comments supported the presence of *diversity in the curriculum,* the promotion of *non-violent/peaceful disagreement* and that *character is what matters.*

Teachers reported that the most ideal ways of preserving MLK's legacy/dream in a school setting included the significance and impact of MLK's life, justice, fairness, coming together, respect and celebration of cultures, peace, and character. The Little Rock teachers recommended the promotion of the *historical import* of the MLK legacy through the *discussion of diversity and what that looks like in schools today versus diversity before* the Civil Rights Movement. These teachers expressed their beliefs that there should be more *student based projects, presentations, posters,* etc., that capture the essence of MLK's impact. These teachers also shared that they want to remain cognizant of the fact that *all students have the same right to learn and be offered various teaching strategies in order to reach them all.* They promoted *working together, diversity, fairness, acceptance, patience, and celebrating cultures* plus *teaching conflict resolution and character to promote respect for all.*

The Memphis teachers recommended a more consistent means of effectively *presenting MLK's legacy* and *the study of the Civil Rights Movement* with *developmental appropriateness.* They also desired to routinely *teach children to have respect for all cultures and races* and to provide students with *opportunities to come together with different groups of people so that differences can be noticed but celebrated.* These teachers reported that they would appreciate *more school-wide observances and celebrations* so that their students could see *MLK's legacy as an everyday philosophy* modeled by all *teachers throughout the year* so that *some will not just focus on it in January and February only.* They also noted that they believe that *teaching the significance of character* and *encouraging students to dream* would be ideal as well.

Discussion

In examining the participating cities, schools, and teachers, similarities as well as differences were reported. Clearly, one city offers more MLK activities than the other city. The death of Dr. King in Memphis might explain the reasons that city has more related MLK activities and stimulates more involvement of its students and citizenry than the Little Rock school and community. Memphis may possibly have more activities than any other community besides Atlanta, where Dr. King lived during the height of the Civil Rights Movement. Likewise, the Memphis school, noticeably, may give more school wide attention to the MLK holiday and attempt to extend the MLK legacy more broadly.

The results of this study were uplifting and revealed a sense of agreement and forward thinking among the teachers who completed the survey from both locations. The findings are even more interesting considering that the participating teachers in the Little Rock elementary school are older and have many more years of teaching, on the average, than the more youthful teachers at the Memphis elementary school. What is consistent with conventional wisdom is that teachers are on the

front lines in classrooms every day, and their attitudes and aspirations can make a difference in what lessons are prepared and the ways in which they are led.

The ideals of equality, justice, fairness, peace, character, respect for, and celebration of cultures that emerged as themes from the participating teachers in both locations are noteworthy. The teachers' philosophies seem to be aligned with that of the current U.S. Secretary of Education, Arne Duncan, who asserts that education is a daily fight for social justice while it promotes opportunity and reduces inequality and that every child is entitled to a quality public education regardless of race, creed, or zip code (Duncan, 2009).

The participating teachers also demonstrated consistency with their ideals and serve as good role models for students when they attend community events that symbolize honor and respect for Dr. King's leadership. These teachers not only locate or design lessons that highlight the MLK dream, they also expressed strong beliefs that such principles are integrated and highlighted in instruction throughout the academic year employing pedagogy that is developmentally appropriate. When considering the ideal instruction of Dr. King's dream, teachers indicated use of many of the standards noted on the concept map. Some standards were used more often and in more depth than other standards, and a few standards such as environment, power, authority, governance, and global connections were not given much attention. This finding might speak to a need that colleges of education can fill.

Implications

The commentaries collected in this study represent a strident call to teacher educators that affirm NCATE obligations. Hence, colleges of education should customarily give teacher candidates opportunities and guidance in developing lessons about diverse populations as well as lessons that recount history from multiple perspectives. In order for teacher candidates and classroom teachers to gain the comfort, confidence, and competence they need to consistently demonstrate value for diversity, their education programs must routinely provide guidance in and practice with this topic that is compelling, meaningful, reflective, and related. It is valuable to know that, although the elementary schools in this study did not provide a curriculum for MLK activities, teachers were able to use what they learned about multicultural approaches from their respective colleges of education and their school districts' professional development opportunities. Perchance if candidates received more practice during their teacher preparation programs, more of them would attempt such lessons and they might be able to carry them out with even greater creativity, diplomacy, and teaching and learning effectiveness.

21st Century Colleges of Education

As America's public schools are increasingly more culturally diverse and aware of their diversity, colleges of education must rethink and reexamine their teacher education programs to ensure that they are able to prepare candidates for the populations that await them. For instance, colleges of education must ensure that their faculty are recalibrated to ensure that every instructor is up-to-date and prepared to integrate multicultural principles into their courses. Instructors must also hold students accountable for adopting multicultural practices and look for evidence of competency in assignments, field experiences, and internship appointments.

Basic multicultural principles and cultural understandings are important because instructional and curricular practices that employ a singular perspective are destined to disengage students (Irvine, 2003). More specifically, all teachers must teach with appreciation that communication of knowledge is conveyed through language and language is highly influenced by culture. Learning must be contextualized as opposed to decontextualized much like it is presented for the purposes of taking standardized achievement tests. When information is separated from students' realities rather than intertwined with their cultures, when instruction is misaligned with students' learning preferences, and when concepts and practices are void of everyday cultural experiences and students' ways of knowing and perceiving, then meaning is not constructed by the learner (Irvine, 2003). Without meaning, the relationships that connect new information with already stored information are splintered as is comprehension (Ormrod, 2009). Where there is no construction of knowledge, learners are merely consumers of knowledge absent ownership and equity.

Another critical consideration in multicultural education is that learning, for some cultures, is a social event, not necessarily an individual one (Irvine, 2003). Therefore, teachers must build in time for students to cooperate and collaborate; teachers must be prepared to indulge in repetition; teachers must initiate highly emotional engagement, lively discussions, stimulating instruction, controversy, creative analogies, symbolisms, and aphorisms (Irvine, 2003). Various assessments must be conducted over time that demonstrate verify competencies through traditional and unconventional means. Teachers must also generously extend encouraging gestures.

In essence, colleges of education should prepare candidates to take their place in the community as nation builders by empowering them to personalize and own the craft of teaching. Teacher education programs must combine critical theory with reflection and experiences that parlay theory into practice through practical and habitual application (Freire, 1970). This combination empowers teachers to become involved in the work of social transformation. According to Freire (1970), this is when teaching truly becomes praxis.

Conclusions

Although the sample of teachers surveyed in this study is small, the investigator believes that this study provides insight and implications for colleges of education that correspond to NCATE directives and relate to the optimal preparation of candidates for comfort, confidence and competence in 21st century classrooms. It is heartening, nonetheless, that such a beautiful American dream remains alive in 21st century classrooms through social studies, language arts, the arts, and through

interdisciplinary means. Even though teachers must remain faithful to mandatory frameworks and state academic standards, teachers are finding creative ways to bring historical context to elementary school students so that American ideals can be planted in their hearts and, thereby, extended into following generations. In terms of the status of the dream, it is promising.

References

Ayers, W., Kumashiro, K., Meiners, E., Quinn, T., & Stovall, D. (2010). *Teaching toward democracy: Educators as agents of change.* Boulder, CO: Paradigm Publishers.

Banks, J. (2007). Multicultural education: Characteristics and goals. In J. A. Banks & C. A. McGee Banks (Eds.), *Multicultural education: Issues and perspectives* (pp. 3–30). Hoboken, NJ: John Wiley & Sons.

Davis, B. (2009). *Tools for teaching.* San Francisco: John Wiley and Sons.

Dewey, J. (1933). *How we think: A restatement of the relation of reflective thinking to the educative process.* Boston, MA: Heath.

Duncan, A. (2009). *A call to teach: Secretary Arne Duncan's remarks at The Rotunda at the University of Virginia.* Retrieved from http://www.edgovblogs.org/duncan/2009/10/a-call-to-teach/

Freire, P. (1970). *The pedagogy of the oppressed.* New York: Seabury Press.

Gallavan, N. P. (2011). *Navigating cultural competence in grades K-5: A compass for teachers.* Thousand Oaks, CA: Corwin Press.

Gay, G. (2000). *Culturally responsive teaching: Theory, research, & practice.* New York: Teachers College Press.

Grant, C., & Sleeter, C. (2007). *Doing multicultural education for achievement and equity.* New York: Taylor and Francis Group.

Ingram, I., & Waters, T. (2007). A critical reflection model to teach diversity and social justice. *Journal of Praxis in Multicultural Education, 2*(1), 23–41.

Irvine, J. (2003). *Educating teachers for a diverse society: Seeing with the cultural eye.* New York: Teachers College Press.

Johnson, R. B., & Onwuegbuzi, A. J. (2004). Mixed methods research: A research paradigm whose time has come. *Educational Research, 33*(7), 14–26.

Krathwohl, D. (1993). Methods of educational and social science research. New York: Longman Publishing Group.

Ligon, J. (2005). Transforming schools into democratic sites. In A. Pearl & C. Pryor (Eds.), *Democratic practices in education: Implications for teacher education* (pp. 1–8). Lanham, MD: Rowman & Littlefield.

Little Rock Community Profile. (n.d.). Retrieved from http://www.epodunk.com/cgi-bin/genInfo.php?locIndex=11591

Mathison, S. (1988). Why triangulate? *Educational Researcher, 17*(2), 13–17.

Memphis Community Profile. (n.d.). Retrieved from http://www.epodunk.com/cgi-bin/genInfo.php?locIndex=1256

National Council for Accreditation of Teacher Education. (2008). *Professional standards for the accreditation of schools, colleges, and departments of education.* Washington, DC: Author.

National Council for the Social Studies. (2010). *National curriculum standards for the social studies: Executive summary.* Retrieved from http://www.socialstudies.org/standards/execsummary

Ormrod, J. (2009). *Educational psychology: Developing learners.* Upper Saddle River, NJ: Pearson Education, Inc.

Patton, M. (1990). *Qualitative evaluation and research methods.* Newberry Park: CA: Sage Publications.

Stanford Encyclopedia of Philosophy (2008). *Phenomenology.* Retrieved from http://plato.stanford.edu/entries/phenomenology

Tetreault, M. (2007). Classrooms for diversity: Rethinking curriculum and pedagogy. In J. A. Banks & C. A. McGee Banks (Eds.). *Multicultural education: Issues and perspectives* (pp. 159–181). Hoboken, NJ: John Wiley & Sons.

van Manen, M. (2007). Phenomenology of practice. *Phenomenology & Practice, 1*(1), 11–30.

Webster-Smith, A. (in press). *One night with a king.* Louisville, KY: Innovative Press.

Critical Thinking

1. What is the author's connection with Dr. Martin Luther King, Jr.?

2. How does this research reveal racial dynamics related to the reported outcomes?

3. What is the author/investigator seeking to learn in this research?

4. Why is this research important?

Create Central

www.mhhe.com/createcentral

Internet References

Martin Luther King, Jr., Center
http://www.thekingcenter.org/

Teach Martin Luther King, Jr.
http://www.wmich.edu/teachmlk/

Appendix A
Status of the Dream Survey

Check one response or fill-in-the-blank for items 1-11. Write a response for items 12a-12j.

1. Gender   ____ Female ____Male

2. Age   ____ Under 30   ____ 31-40   ____41-50   ____51+

3. Your culture   __African American __Latino __Caucasian __Asian __Native American

4. School district   _____

5. The community in which you live is most defined as __urban ___suburban __rural

6. Years of teaching experience_____

7. Your education: Bachelor's____   Master's ____   Master's+____ Doctorate____

8. Grade levels you teach this academic year_____

9. Subjects/academic disciplines you teach this academic year_____

10. Estimate the percentage of culturally diverse students you teach who identify as:

    __African American   __Latin Descent   __Caucasian   __Asian Descent   __Native American

11. Principal's Culture __African American __Latino __Caucasian __Asian __Native American

12. Please answer the following questions in the space given, on the back or on additional paper.

    a. Have you ever observed the Dr. Martin Luther King (MLK) holiday in your personal or professional life? If so, describe how.

    b. Do your students report ways in which they have observed the MLK holiday in their personal lives? If so, describe how.

    c. What does MLK's *dream* mean to you personally?

    d. What parts of the *MLK dream* are important enough to integrate and model for students throughout the academic year?

    e. Have you ever taught lessons on the dream of Dr. Martin Luther King? If so, give a brief example of the lesson.

    f. If you taught a lesson on the dream of Dr. Martin Luther King, was it part of your school's curriculum?   _____Yes _____ No

       OR did you design the lesson?   _____ Yes _____No

    g. In what educational settings have you learned multicultural approaches to instruction? Check all that apply.

       _____ Undergraduate _____ Master's_____ Master's+

       _____ Doctorate _____ Professional Development

    h. In addition to having a day away from school, are there acknowledgements of the MLK holiday at your school? If so, describe the acknowledgements.

    i. What do you think is an ideal way of preserving MLK's legacy/dream in a school setting?

    j. Are there MLK holiday activities in the community where you live? If so, give brief examples.

Article   Prepared by: Nancy P. Gallavan, *University of Central Arkansas*

Student Resistance to Schooling: Disconnections with Education in Rural Appalachia

KATIE A. HENDRICKSON

Learning Outcomes

After reading this article, you will be able to:

- Explain the inequalities in education that students in rural settings receive.

- Discuss student resistance stemming related to culture and cultural competence.

odern societies, particularly those functioning under oppressive circumstances, highly value revolutionaries, change makers, social agents, and critical thinkers. People who evaluate and question the status quo and critique aspects of society often benefit from their development of self-awareness and leadership skills (Giroux, 1983; Shor, 1992). These people function as social change agents who liberate themselves and others from oppressive situations, empowering underrepresented groups (Giroux, 1983). In such cases, they may be seen as highly resistant to current social norms, but in the long run, these people make a positive impact on the evolution of society.

In contrast, students who resist schooling are rarely considered to make a positive contribution to society. These students may feel disconnected from school and question the purpose of schooling, and they display their feelings through acts of resistance. However, teachers and school administrators often label these actions as misbehavior and administer disciplinary consequences to these students. As a result, resistant students often have negative school experiences that perpetuate the inequalities that are causing them to resist (Kohl, 1991; Willis, 1977). Future opportunities in life may be limited by a lack of academic credentials or being labeled as unwilling or unable to learn (Kohl, 1991). These students never experience the sense of freedom or control over their destinies that other resistant change agents in society may enjoy (Giroux, 1983; Shor, 1992; Sekayi, 2001).

Few studies about student resistance involve White students in rural areas; the majority concern ethnic and racial minority populations in urban areas. However, inequalities in socioeconomic status can lead to resistance in rural areas. Teachers generally come from middle class backgrounds, but students in rural areas frequently come from low-income families. This can result in a culture clash between students with close-knit families valuing place-based knowledge and teachers with a message of worldliness. Therefore, the purpose of this study was to contribute to reduce the gap in the student resistance literature by identifying and examining student resistant attitudes towards schooling in a rural school district.

Literature Review

Student resistance has been referred to as willful not-learning, school refusal, disengagement, alienation, apathy, noncompliance, attitude or defiance (Abowitz, 2000; Dickar, 2008; Gilmore, 1985; Kohl, 1991; McLaren, 1985). McLaren (1985) defines resistance as "oppositional student behavior . . . which contests the legitimacy, power, and significance of school culture in general and instruction in particular" (p. 85). Not all student misbehavior can be attributed to resistance, but often the behaviors are similar. Students may resist passively, such as sleeping in class, not doing class work, slouching in seats and rolling eyes; or actively, such as confronting the teacher, talking in class, causing disruptions, and asking questions at inappropriate times (Abowitz, 2000; Dickar, 2008; Giroux, 1983; Kohl, 1991; Olafson & Field, 2003; Walker & Sylwester, 1998).

Resistance theory suggests that resistant students are not intentional troublemakers; instead, student resistance is generally thought to occur as a reaction to social reproduction manifested in schools. According to reproduction theory, schools reproduce social norms by teaching specific types of knowledge and skills, preparing students for work within their social class (Giroux, 1983; Hebdige, 1979). Some students who are not content with the status quo of the school experience actively partake in resistant acts, either attempting to subvert the dominant culture of school or resisting an active part in the school experience.(Anyon, 1980; Giroux, 1983; Willis, 1977.) Working-class students reacting to oppression or culture clash may resist controlling aspects of the school process itself, such as the content of the curriculum or the teaching process (Aggleton, 1987).

However, since Willis's landmark 1977 study, very few studies have examined the phenomena of student resistance in rural, working-class areas. In fact, none of the resistance studies located for this review examined students in the Appalachian region or dynamics of resistance within current research on rural areas. Thus, following sections report research on students in rural areas that have potential links to resistance and reproduction theory.

Student and Teacher Rapport

A robust body of literature supports the correlation between student engagement in school and teacher rapport and respect. Students who fail to form meaningful relationships with teachers or develop a sense of school belonging are more likely to disengage with school (Burroughs, 2007; Good & Brophy, 1974; McFarland, 2001; Rueda, 2005, 2006).

These dynamics may be compounded by cultural differences in rural areas. Many teachers and school administrators in rural schools come from suburban or urban settings and middle class backgrounds and have difficulty understanding and relating to students (Purcell-Gates, 2002). These school employees lack awareness of local knowledge, values, economics, and social networks and do not have the histories and relationships with the community that the students possess (Corbett, 2007). Teachers may be less understanding of students with different cultural values if they are inconsistent with the values and norms familiar to the teacher (Sheets, 1996). In particular, linguistic patterns can cause discord within the classroom, particularly with regard to the linguistic rules for achieving power in the classroom (Delpit, 1995).

Further, teachers sometimes make assumptions about the students in rural schools, mistakenly attributing poverty to habits associated with poor people and blaming parents and families for living in poverty; some school employees in rural areas trivialize students' knowledge and culture with a "saving the poor" attitude toward education (Howley, Howley, Howley, & Howley, 2006). In contrast, Kohl (1991) engaged resistant students in classroom learning by enabling students to save face and encouraging students' questions and challenges.

Conflict of Opportunity

One source of tension for students in rural areas is the lack of economic opportunity coupled with family values of cohesiveness. Students in rural areas can highly value a sense of community and family relationships (Deaton, 2008; Herzog & Pittman, 1995). As a result, these students are more focused on the well-being of the family group than individual achievement or personal goals (Deaton, 2008). Rather than leaving for college, some students may be pressured to choose family cohesiveness and remain in the area (Corbett, 2007).

However, employment opportunities in rural areas have been decreasing with the decline of farming, mining, and fishing industries (Corbett, 2007). Thus, a higher proportion of working adults in rural areas are employed in working-class, low-paid jobs with little opportunity for advancement (Herzog & Pittman, 1995; Lucas, 1971), and people who attain higher education may educate themselves out of a job in the area (Corbett, 2007; Starcher, 2005). Students who do well in school and leave to obtain college degrees can have difficulty finding jobs

in the community and may move elsewhere to secure a higher income (Herzog & Pittman, 1995). Thus, "to resist schooling is therefore to resist mobility" and commit oneself to membership in the community (Corbett, 2007, p. 57).

Relevance of Education

Because jobs in the area do not require education, many students believe school education cannot help them in the future (Dehyle, 1995; Starcher, 2005). Further, many families in rural areas have not seen economic advancement as a result of schooling, so school is frequently not seen as a way to escape poverty or provide upward mobility (Corbett, 2007; Starcher, 2005). On the other hand, schools tend to promote the idea that good grades and graduation will lead to success and an improved socio-economic status (Fordham, 1996).

Often, the knowledge taught in school contradicts the working-class knowledge that is more valuable to the students' everyday lives (McFadden, 1995; Riley, 1996). Schools frequently portray a message of worldliness and broadening horizons, which tends to be inconsistent with place-based local values and local knowledge (Holt, 1995; Corbett, 2007). Willis (1977) found that groups of people have developed certain skills that are useful in their cultural circle, but are not helpful in developing other skills, including school achievement. For students whose family knowledge and experience conflicts with school ideology, school success means giving in to the dominant middle class culture and rejecting the family (Finn, 1999; Kipnis, 2001; Rueda, 2005). When forced with this choice, many students choose family success over traditional school values and disengage with school (Fordham, 1996; Munns & McFadden, 2000; Starcher, 2005).

Place-based education has the potential to bridge the gap between school content and local communities through locally relevant curricula, particularly in rural areas (Klein, Howley, & Howley, 2010). According to Smith (2002), place-based education "adopts local environments—social, cultural, economic, political, and natural—as the context for a significant share of students' educational experiences" (p. 30). This engages students in real problems related to community concerns and student interests, building a desire to learn. Place-based curricula also has the potential to help stimulate the local economy and revitalize the community (Doeden, 2001; Hynes, 2003). However, place-based curricula have not been widely used because their effectiveness relies upon their relation to the local place and culture and is not generalizable (Smith, 2002; Wither, 2001). While this topic is growing in the literature, research remains limited.

Methodology

Setting

The study was conducted at a small high school in Appalachian Ohio. The school, pseudonymous Pierce High School, is the only high school in the district. A vocational school is located on the school's campus so students do not leave to attend vocational courses. Further, some students from other high schools in the county come to Pierce for their vocational courses. Pierce High School is located in a low-income area; the median household income is $19,971 compared to the national average of $41,994 (US Census Bureau, 2000). No institutions of higher education are located in the county. According to the state report card, 36% of graduates had taken the ACT and the mean score was 19 (Ohio Department of Education, 2009).

Observational Data Collection

This study took a constructivist approach with a basic interpretive qualitative research design (Patton, 2002). Interpretive qualitative research, while borrowing from phenomenology in the sense that it attempts to capture and describe how people experience the world, does not claim to be free of bias (Patton, 2002). Nonparticipant observations were completed over eight weeks, with 67 class periods observed. Both junior and senior level general and college preparatory required courses were observed: notably, English, mathematics, and senior government. During the observations, copious anecdotal and reflective field notes described direct events in class and researcher impressions afterwards (Patton, 2002). Observational data was used to select students for interviews, develop interview questions, and refine the data analysis.

During observations, resistant students were identified for potential interviews via purposeful sampling (Patton, 2002). Resistance was operationally defined as open and outward displays of opposition to schooling, the school environment, and the behavioral and academic expectations of students. Resistant students were identified by the following typical behaviors: sleeping during class, not paying attention during class, defiant body language in class, not turning in assignments including homework and class work, not working on class work, distracting other students, challenging the teacher, causing disruptions in class, talking during class, skipping class, and making negative comments about the teacher or school.

In addition to consistent displays of resistance, interview subjects were also chosen based on poor grades (Ds or Fs in the subjects observed). Triangulation of sampling methods in this way enhanced the researcher's choice of the most resistant students (Patton, 2002). All students in each class were asked to fill out a form indicating interest in participating in an interview. Identified resistant students who indicated an interest in the interview were approached with consent forms. Those students who returned consent forms scheduled interviews during study hall periods.

Interview Data Collection and Analysis

Each interview lasted approximately 30 minutes. The interviews were semi-structured and open-ended to allow for probing of student responses (Patton, 2002). Students were asked general questions about school and future plans, as well as specific questions relating to individual student's behavior in class. General questions are listed in Table 1. The specific questions related directly to incidents observed in class, and differed for each student. Sample questions included "I noticed you sleep a lot during class. Why is that?" and "What happened before you were sent to the office the other day?" Because much of the literature on student resistance, and schooling in general, frequently reports teacher or parent perspectives, this study intended to privilege the students' voices. The importance of the student voice in research and decision-making has regained attention in recent years (Mitra, 2004).

The interviews were recorded and transcribed and then were coded by topic. Relevant observation data (for example, if it conflicted with or reinforced interview data) were included in the analysis as well. Including observation data in the analysis allowed for triangulation of data sources to confirm or disconfirm interview data (Patton, 2002). Coding followed grounded theory methods, allowing the themes to emerge inductively from the data (Charmaz, 2006). Specific codes regarding school resistance emerged, such as pleasing parents and no time for homework. These codes were examined for similarities and connections, and were then grouped into increasingly larger and broader categories. In general, the concept of resistance developed three angles, each of which influenced student resistance in a different way: parental influence, school factors, and student behavior. Thus, these three angles became the defining themes of the study: family values and expectations, quality and relevance of education, and misunderstandings between teachers and students. A second analysis of the raw data revealed further codes that had not been identified in the first analysis. See Table 2 for the organization of the categories into the themes.

Limitations

Some limitations may have affected the data. As this study was meant to privilege the student voice, only students were interviewed. Although interviews with parents, teachers, and other community members may have contributed to this discussion, for the purpose of this study they were not included. However, the lack of triangulation of interview sources leads to only one source of direct information–the students. The accuracy of the data may be limited by the honesty of the students interviewed. While I made every effort to portray myself as unaffiliated with the teachers or school, the students may have hesitated to give answers that would be unappealing to a school employee. Further, not all students approached for interviews returned the consent form, so some of the students who displayed the most resistance were not interviewed.

Findings

The analysis of the classroom observations and student interviews yielded three themes: family values and expectations, quality and relevance of education, and misunderstandings between teachers and students. These themes are described and illustrated in this section, first through an analysis of a single student's experience and second through descriptions as illustrated by the other participants. The case example provides a deep examination of a typical student's experience and the contradictions in his thinking. Although Cody recognized the conflict between his behavior and teacher expectations, he was not able to acknowledge the contradictions between his future plans and his current attitude toward coursework. The second

Table 1

Student names	Dan	Mark	Cody	Jody	Colton	Kelsey	Taylor
Male or female	Male	Male	Male	Female	Male	Female	Male
Year	Senior	Senior	Junior	Junior	Senior	Senior	Junior
Vocational program	Welding	Welding	A + (computers)	Agriculture	Work study	Cosmetology	Welding
Resistant behaviors observed	Sleeps in class, talks to friends, does not participate, take notes, or complete homework	Talks in class, interrupts teacher with questions and input, does not take notes or complete homework	Sleeps in class, does not take notes, class clown, argues with teacher	Talks to friends loudly in class, argues with teacher, defiant, tries to leave class	Sleeps in class, does not take notes or do homework, argues with teacher	Argue with teacher, does not take notes, talks loudly in class	Not in seat, talking in class, does not take notes, argues with teacher
Future college plans	Training	Training	Military or college	Classes near Pierce	Dreams of college, expects military	College in NYC	Training
Family relationships or influence	Going into father's business	Parents do not want him to move away, do not support future career	Family close	Family lives close, does not care what she does	Family close	Wants her to stay close, close but also fight	Going into father's business, close family
Perceived class behavior	Normal student, slacker	Pays attention, participates, does all hw	Class clown	Does not try, talks a lot	Sleeps a lot, enough to get by, jokester	Rude, obnoxious	Good grades
Plan to live in Pierce	Yes	Other familiar location	Yes	Yes	Yes	No	Yes
Parents encourage college	Yes	No	No	No	No	Yes	Some
Future career plans	Own mechanic shop	Racing business	Computer programming	Open daycare	Actor or storm chaser	Own art/ design business	Welding with father

part of each theme, the elaborated descriptions, reveal the ways in which other participants experience similar situations.

Participant Profiles

Seven students, five male and two female, were selected to be interviewed. Of the five males, three were juniors and two were seniors. Both females were juniors: one was repeating her junior year in order to begin the cosmetology vocational program.

Dan was a senior in the welding program. In English class, he sat in the back of the classroom and talked quietly to his friends during class discussions. He rarely participated, did not take notes, and did not complete his class work. The only time I observed him raise his hand to participate, the teacher never called on him, and he eventually put his hand down and turned back to his friends. In government, Dan again sat in the back of the classroom with his friends, and he was often reprimanded for talking or not paying attention during lectures. He did not talk back to the teachers, but made quiet comments to his friends afterwards.

Mark was a senior at another school in the county but was enrolled in the vocational welding program. Thus, he traveled to Pierce High School for English, government, and welding classes. At the time of the interview, he had just left the welding program due to a disagreement, and he was not clear about what he planned to do next. Mark was always fully engaged in class, frequently commenting, asking questions, and extending the lesson to other topics, but he never took notes or completed homework. His government teacher did not appreciate his frequent interruptions and often asked him to wait or be quiet, sometimes reprimanding him. When working on a group project in English one day, he wandered around the room talking to other groups and never participated with his group's work.

Cody was a junior in the A + computer vocational program. Due to being suspended for half of the previous year, he was also making up sophomore-level classes. Cody frequently slept in class, ignored the teacher, and neglected to take notes.

Table 2

General Interview Questions

On a scale of 1–10, how much do you like going to school? Why do you say that?

Can you tell me about a typical day in school? What do you like best about school? What do you like least about school?

On a scale of 1–10, how smart do you think you are? Why do you feel that way?

On a scale of 1–10, how well do you do in school? Why do you feel that way? Describe yourself as a student.

What do you do outside of school?

What are your plans for after graduation? What do your parents want you to do? Are you planning on attending college or a technical school? Are you planning on moving away from home or staying in the area?

Pick a class, either the one you like the most, or the least. What do you like/dislike about that class?

Do you ever not do something you are supposed to do in class? Can you give me an example? Why do you choose not to do something?

What are the teachers like in school?

What is the purpose of school? Does school have anything to do with your life right now? With your future?

Did you feel differently about school when you were in elementary and middle school? If yes, what changed?

What does your family think about your future plans?

He seemed angry and resentful about making up the coursework, complaining about it often. In math class, he frequently challenged the teacher loudly, interrupting the lesson and making rude remarks. In English, he made loud jokes for other students' enjoyment and often complained about the class work.

Jody was a junior enrolled in agriculture and horticulture courses, working towards a State Degree in agriculture. Jody was frequently sent to the principal's office for loud disruptive behavior in math class, and she usually complained and defiantly stomped out of the room. She frequently argued with the teacher, did not have her homework, and complained about being reprimanded for not having her homework completed. In English, she asked for hall passes multiple times each day, and preferred to read in the hallway.

Colton was a senior who was a year behind due to frequent mobility between school districts over the years. Colton often slept through class, responding sharply and aggressively to teachers who try to wake him. He never took notes or participated in math class, and he never had his homework completed. He responded negatively and disrespectfully to teacher requests. In English class, Colton joked about being far behind in the reading but he did not read during class.

Kelsey was repeating her junior year in order to take the courses in the cosmetology program and to make up some credits she had failed the previous year. She had transferred to Pierce High School that year in order to join the cosmetology program. Kelsey usually failed to complete her homework and often drew in her notebook instead of taking notes. She engaged in confrontations with teachers, challenging them and complaining loudly in class. A few times, she was sent to the principal's office for misbehavior.

Taylor was a junior enrolled in the vocational welding program, but before he started, he had been enrolled in college preparation courses. Taylor frequently walked around the classroom during lectures in math class, sometimes stopping at his friends' desks to talk. He rarely took notes or had his homework completed, and he was frequently absent from school. When teachers challenged his behavior, he responded sharply and disrespectfully.

Family Values and Expectations

The first theme involved a divergence between school values (e.g. grades, college) and home values (e.g. family, not moving away). Schools typically advocated college attendance, moving away from home, and gaining experience in the world. However, students reported that their families encouraged them to go into the family business, usually a vocational trade, and did not find college to be necessary. Although students at Pierce recognized the push for college attendance, they appeared to be more influenced by their parents and families.

Cody experienced the first theme as a tension between school and parental expectations. He wanted to please his parents, and so he attempted to follow school rules in order to avoid trouble with his parents. Much of his extended family lived in the area, and he enjoyed their physical and emotional closeness. He explained that "Pierce is where I was all my life" and that he wanted to return to the area. Cody said, "No one else in my house has been to college so far, so they're hopin' I'm the first." According to Cody, his parents were not familiar with the logistics of college, and were not actively encouraging college applications. He explained that he might study computers, but clarified that would be "if" he attended college. He said that he wanted to make a lot of money so he could take care of his parents.

This theme seen in Cody's story was found woven into other students' stories as well. The students reported valuing their parents' opinions and wanting to please them. Dan explained that his parents' opinions were important to him. He said, "I try to keep my parents happy." Students often reiterated their family's expectations for their futures. At one point in the interview, Taylor explained that he was not certain if he wanted to attend welding school, but he would because of his father: "My dad wants me to do what he does, but I always thought about going to college for so many years and becoming something where I can pretty much sit in an office with a nice, cool air conditioner and make more money, you know?" Taylor concluded that despite these reservations, he was planning to attend the one-year welding program after high school.

Because students' families were important to them, students seemed to be influenced by their family members' hopes for the students' future careers. According to students, their families discouraged them from moving away from the area, and most students expressed their desire to return to the community.

Mark's parents did not want him to go to college four hours away; they preferred that he stay nearby. Mark conceded, "I'd like to stay in this general area." Although Kelsey did not agree with her parents, she remarked on their desire for her to remain close to Pierce rather than move to New York. She said, "None of them really like it because it's so far away . . . they just want me to be somewhere safe, like the country."

Several students explained that their families did not know much about college or did not encourage college. Mark said that his parents never finished high school, and so they were "ignorant towards the fact of what's required for college" and they were not fond of the idea of his plans to go away to earn his two-year certificate. Colton explained that he wanted to go to college, but, "My parents think that I should drop out and get my GED and take the easy road." When elaborating on what her family thinks of college attendance, Jody said simply, "They don't mind it." The students also seemed undecided about which college to attend. Mark explained, "I don't feel the pressure to further my education," and Jody was not sure if she would take community college courses after graduation.

Students also reported that their families encouraged work that did not require a college degree, particularly if the occupation involved the family business. Most of these jobs were vocational careers that required only a year or two of technical training. Many students explained that they intended to study the same trade as their parents, or that they wanted to work at the family business. For example, Taylor said about welding school, "my dad went there, so he wants me to go. He supports me 100%." After obtaining his certificate, he planned to go to work with his father and uncle.

Quality and Relevance of Education

The second theme involved the students' reported feelings about the quality of the education received at the school. Students reported that the content of their courses did not relate to their lives beyond the direct application of skills learned in their vocational courses. While many students commented on the value of a diploma in obtaining a job, they did not seem to value the academic coursework represented by the diploma.

In relation to the second theme, Cody disliked his classes and felt that the required classes would not be helpful for his future life or career. He said that he did not take college preparatory classes, even though the guidance counselor recommended them, because he did not want the extra work. He admitted, "I just apply what's needed, enough to make me pass," only completing his homework when it would be graded. In some classes, Cody felt that "we don't learn nothing," so he did not pay attention or do the homework, even though he was failing those classes. He needed a diploma if he wanted to have a good job, so he said, "I just wanna get through; I wanna survive, get it done." Cody explained that he would rather spend his time in school doing "somethin' useful—to me, I mean—what I think would be useful." For example, he enjoyed his computer classes because he could do hands-on work repairing computers and providing technology support around the school.

Many students reported beliefs similar to Cody's, including the type of activities completed in classes. Unless the class involved hands-on work, the students did not enjoy the class and said that they did not "do anything" in that class. Jody explained, "most of the classes I have, we don't really do work in." On the other hand, students explained that hands-on classes like physics, welding, and gym helped them to learn. Dan explained, "In welding, we do hands-on stuff and it's not all bookwork," and he tried to do as many projects as possible. Colton said that he was better with hands-on classes like drama and gym that allowed him to display his learning physically, rather than classes that required memorization.

Similarly, several students explained that the content of their courses, with the exception of the vocational programs, did not relate to their lives. Kelsey said that teachers "think it's going to affect our lives, but it's really not. My classes that I'm taking right now, I really don't need to succeed in what I want to do in life." Some students said they had already learned everything they could from school; for example, Colton said that he already knew "enough to get me by in the future" and didn't understand how some courses would be helpful. On the other hand, both Dan and Kelsey clarified that their vocational courses related directly to their futures.

When describing the purpose of school, students provided characteristics of vocational or blue-collar careers, and explained that they learned more outside of school subjects. Taylor, Dan, and Colton said that the purpose of school is to prepare them to have a routine in the future, when they will need to wake up in the morning and go to their jobs every day. Likewise, several students explained that they learned just as much outside of school and through the social aspects of school. Colton stated that he learned more at work than at school. Mark said, "There's a lot of other things in life you can learn and apply than what a school has to offer," and Kelsey and Jody both reported learning more from social interactions than from class work.

Although the students described the uselessness of school and many of the classes, the students did understand the value of a high school diploma in achieving further training and education and obtaining a good job. Many students spoke about their impatience to complete school and receive their diplomas. Taylor explained the importance of a diploma when he said, "If you want a good job to support a family in a nice home and a nice car, you're gonna have to educate yourself, so you're gonna have to get a high school diploma." However, many students explained that they simply did not put in the effort needed to do well in school. Colton and Jody said they did the minimum amount of work necessary to pass the class or receive their diploma.

Misunderstandings Between Teachers and Students

The final theme related to discord between student behavior and teacher expectations. Students felt that their teachers failed to understand them or accommodate special student circumstances. Incongruence in the meaning of classroom behavior was evident; teachers viewed certain classroom behavior as disruptive, while students believed that this behavior was fun and entertaining for the teacher.

The third theme can be seen in Cody's suspension the previous year and his classroom behavior. He had been suspended from school for having a knife in his backpack, which he qualified as a misunderstanding. Cody worked on a farm and hunted on the weekends, and he had forgotten that a knife used for farm work was still in his backpack that Monday. Although the school rule prohibited weapons in school, Cody felt that he was treated unfairly because it was an accident. Further, Cody acknowledged that teachers did not appreciate his class clown behavior. He said, "I try to be funny, lighten stuff up a bit. Goof off. . .. It's just—I don't know what teachers see—if they see differently than what people my age see. It's like speaking two different languages, like what I'm saying to them, they mean something different to me." Although he disliked school and had a poor relationship with some teachers, he said, "I don't wanna come off as bad person to somebody." Cody acknowledged that the teachers viewed his actions as misbehavior, yet he did not express a desire to stop.

Students often expressed their feeling that some teachers misunderstood them or did not respect them. Colton explained that he did not pay attention in class because, "There's no point. Even if I did pay attention, she wouldn't care. She wouldn't notice. So there's no point in even trying." It was important for students to feel that the teacher cared about them. Dan explained that he had given up trying to participate in one class because the teacher favored a select group of students and only allowed this group to tackle interesting projects. Mark said that he tried to stay engaged in class, but "Every time I go to say something she'll cut me off. She wants us to ask her questions, but I'm like, you shut me out here." Similarly, Colton felt that some teachers did not care about the students, so he questioned, "Why should we take time out for them if they don't take time out for us?"

Sometimes the teachers failed to understand student issues or accommodate their special circumstances. For example, Taylor was reprimanded for standing near his friend's desk and talking after class had begun. When the teacher spoke to him about the incident after class, Taylor explained that his pregnant girlfriend had been in the hospital, and he was trying to get advice from his friend who was also a father. The teacher listened to his story but closed the conversation with the threat, "You're still getting written up—big time!" In another situation, Colton explained that he often did not have his homework finished because he went straight to work after school. He said, "They expect you to have it done, and it's not your fault, but it is your fault. It's kind of a lose-lose situation." In both examples, teachers did not appear to empathize with the multiple pressures that the students had in their lives, such as balancing high school with pregnancies or jobs.

Some students who were observed getting in trouble for their behavior in class said in the interviews that their classroom behavior was good, and they joked around in class to liven things up and make the teacher laugh. According to Colton, "I'm more of a jokester, to be truthful, but I mean no harm." Kelsey explained, "I don't ever really get in trouble. I'll say, "oh, you love me," and then she'll laugh. And then everything will be kind of better." Similarly, Taylor said,

"I'm pretty much a class clown, but I always know when it's time to stop, you know, start paying attention so I can learn. I make all my teachers laugh. I really don't get in a lot of trouble in class." However, these students were observed getting into trouble for their joking behavior in these classes. During the observations, the teachers did not appear to enjoy or appreciate the students' behavior, as they often wrote behavior reports for those students or sent them to the office.

Discussion

Through the findings, a common thread developed for these resistant students at Pierce High School. The general story for these students is as follows. First, the students described the importance of family cohesion and abiding their parents' wishes. Because families reportedly encouraged vocational work that enabled the students to stay in the area, the students often did not expect to attend college. Therefore, many students did not believe the school provided a quality education relevant to their lives. Only the vocational and hands-on courses were important to the students, and they applied just enough effort to earn their diplomas. Students described the failure of teachers to understand the multiple influences on students, and this misunderstanding resulted in negative consequences for the students. Thus, parents and families, teachers, and the students themselves all contributed to the dynamics of resistance.

In this case and according to student responses, parents contributed to student resistance through their tacit expectations for the students. The students highly valued their parents' opinions, as in Deaton (2008) and Herzog and Pittman (1995), wanting to please their parents and thereby internalizing the hopes and expectations of their parents. The parents, according to the students, valued family cohesiveness and wanted students to obtain jobs in the community. Because the majority of jobs in the area were low-paying and required low levels of education, students who obtained higher education may not be able to find jobs in the area. Therefore, ultimately neither family values nor potential career opportunities in the region encouraged student educational achievement.

The school system also perpetuated student resistance through the incompatibility of academic content and community life. Many students reported a belief that school subjects did not relate to their lives and would not help them in the future. Schools frequently promote cosmopolitan, worldly knowledge that is inconsistent with place-based knowledge and local connections, two strategies that might engage students in learning (Corbett, 2007). Thus, the students did not seem to buy into the process of school, and they neglected class work and homework. The disparity of home values and school values alienated students from school and possible higher education.

Ultimately, the students' misbehavior in class and resistance toward the education presented at the school may have been a reaction to these intersecting dynamics of parental influence and school values. At school, students were likely presented with ideas of college and worldliness, providing the students with dreams that they could aspire to—but these dreams starkly contrasted their parents' expectations. These students justified their resistant actions by blaming the teachers for not relating to them, much like the findings of Burroughs (2007). This may have been a result of students' attempts to save face and protect their culture by confronting teachers and disengaging with coursework, while lacking a critical understanding of these disparities.

Future Research

Because resistance and critical thinking are such important issues for students and schools, more research should examine these dynamics. First, rural areas are often overlooked in favor of studies in urban or suburban areas, but the complex dynamics in these areas and the number of students attending rural schools make them worthy of study. Second, more studies in the area of resistance and school change should give resistant students a voice. Schools serve all students, not just those who succeed easily, and the opinions of all students can be valuable. Finally, while this study was focused on the student perspective, future research should interview parents, teachers, and community members. Strategies that can turn resistance from a negative to a positive and that are already employed by teachers should be examined and replicated.

Implications

In sum, the data reveal multiple conflicting factors that may contribute to student resistance to school. Potential solutions to student resistance in rural schools could address some of these contradictions in student thinking, notably messages about college, the relevance of school, and outlets for critiquing their situation.

The first conflict for students was between the messages they received from home versus school regarding college and potential career options. Students often receive information about college at school, but they may have been receiving conflicting messages at home for years before they arrive at school. While parents' beliefs should not be trivialized, students can be shown that they do not have to choose between their families and a potential career. It is possible for students to obtain higher education and start a business in the area, or telecommute to businesses in more urban areas. Students who attend college and return to the community may be able to strengthen the viability of the community itself.

The second conflict experienced by these students related to the relevance or irrelevance of academic school subjects, decreasing their motivation to do the assigned work. While vocational courses have an explicit relation to careers, other "academic" courses do not. Teachers in rural areas can attempt to bridge the gap between school knowledge and place-based knowledge by connecting school content to "real life" and local content. Place-based learning presents educational activities that attempt to solve a community problem. In this way, students can be engaged in education-centered work that is good for the community and reinforces their family values.

Finally, students faced an inconsistency in their understanding of their own classroom behavior and resistance toward school. Teachers can open a dialogue with students to help them think through their critique of school and understand the reasons for their actions and beliefs about school. Then, students

can direct their energy into positive channels, vocalizing their concerns with school practices and advocating for change in their schools and communities. These opportunities would give students a role in changing their own behavior and developing positive solutions for school conflicts. Student resistance can therefore be an asset to rural schools and communities because it encourages a dialogue between students, community members, and schools.

Taken together, these three recommendations can allow students and teachers to begin a conversation about values that are beneficial in both school and home environments. By raising student consciousness about multiple options, students can experience growth and make informed decisions. Critical thinkers who have reconciled their conflicts with school and their communities will be prepared for a plethora of future opportunities.

Conclusion

The success of students in rural areas is vital to the success of the region, as these students will make up the community of the future. Resistant students in rural areas can be engaged in conversations and critical thinking about their resistance and the factors that prevent them from engaging with school. These students can then develop a voice for change, challenging the dichotomies of higher education and rural values. By voicing their concerns about intersections of school values, home values, and future opportunities, these students can become change agents for their communities. Ultimately, resistant students can be key to the evolution of rural communities.

References

Abowitz, K. K. (2000). A pragmatist revisioning of resistance theory. *American Educational Research Journal, 37*, 877–907.

Aggleton, P. (1987). *Rebels without a cause: Middle class youth and the transition from school to work*. New York: Falmer.

Anyon, J. (1980). Social class and the hidden curriculum of work. *Journal of Education, 162*(2), 67–92.

Burroughs, N. F. (2007). A reinvestigation of the relationship of teacher nonverbal immediacy and student compliance-resistance with learning. *Communication Education, 56*, 453–475.

Charmaz, K. (2006). *Constructing grounded theory: A practical guide through qualitative analysis*. Thousand Oaks, CA: Sage.

Corbett, M. (2007). *Learning to leave: The irony of schooling in a coastal community*. Halifax, Canada: Fernwood.

Deaton, M. J. (2008). *Academic success of Appalachian adolescents: The impact of parental authority and familism* (Master's thesis). Miami University, Oxford, OH.

Dehyle, D. (1995). Navajo youth and Anglo racism: Cultural integrity and resistance. *Harvard Educational Review, 65*, 403–445.

Delpit, L. (1995). *Other people's children: Cultural conflict in the classroom*. New York, NY: The New Press.

Dickar, M. (2008). *Corridor cultures: Mapping student resistance at an urban high school*. New York, NY: New York University Press.

Doeden, C. L. (2001). Community-based education and rural development. *Rural Funders Working Group Case Study No. 2*. Retrieved July 26, 2004 from www.nfg.org

Dunn, R. J. (2001). The rural education dichotomy: Disadvantaged systems and school strengths. Elmhurst, IL: North Central Regional Educational Lab.

Finn, P. J. (1999). *Literacy with an attitude: Educating working-class children in their own self interest.* Albany, NY: State University of New York Press.

Fordham, S. (1996). *Blacked out: Dilemmas of race, identity, and success at Capital High.* Chicago, IL: University of Chicago Press.

Gilmore, P. (1985). 'Gimme room': School resistance, attitude, and access to literacy. *Journal of Education, 167*(1), 111–128.

Giroux, H. A. (1983). Theories of reproduction and resistance in the new sociology of education: A critical analysis. *Harvard Educational Review, 53,* 257–293.

Good, T. L., & Brophy, J. E. (1974). *Teacher-student relationships: Causes and consequences.* New York, NY: Holt, Rinehart & Winston.

Hebdige, D. (1979). *Subculture, the meaning of style.* London, United Kingdom: Methuen.

Herzog, M. J., & Pittman, R. (1995). Home, family, and community: Ingredients in the rural education equation. *Phi Delta Kappan, 77*(2), 113–118.

Hobbs, D. (1994). Demographic trends in nonmetropolitan America. *Journal of Research in Rural Education, 10*(3), 149–160.

Holt, J. (1995). *How children fail* (revised ed.). Reading, MA: Perseus Books.

Howley, C. B., Howley, A. A., Howley, C. W., & Howley, M. D. (2006, April). *Saving the children of the poor in rural schools.* Paper presented at the meeting of the American Educational Research Association, San Francisco, CA.

Hynes, M. (2003). Revitalizing economies around Cobscook Bay. In *Engaged institutions: Impacting the lives of vulnerable youth through place-based learning* (pp. 9–21). Washington, DC: The Rural School and Community Trust.

Kipnis, A. (2001). Articulating school countercultures. *Anthropology & Education Quarterly, 32,* 472–492.

Klein, R., Howley, C. B., & Howley, A. A. (2010). Place-based practices in rural mathematics instruction: A select cross-case comparison study. In P. Brosnan, D. B. Erchick, & L. Flevares (Eds.), *Proceedings of the 32nd annual meeting of the North American Chapter of the International Group for the Psychology of Mathematics Education* (pp. 893–901). Columbus: Ohio State University. (online: http://pmena.org/2010/downloads/PME-NA%202010%20Proceedings%20Book.pdf)

Kohl, H. (1991). *I won't learn from you: The role of assent in learning.* Minneapolis, MN: Milkweed Editions.

Lucas, R. (1971). *Minetown, milltown, railtown: Life in Canadian communities of industry.* Toronto, Canada: University of Toronto Press.

McFadden, M. (1995). Resistance to schooling and educational outcomes: Questions of structure and agency. *British Journal of Sociology of Education, 16,* 293–308.

McFarland, D. A. (2001). Student resistance: How the formal and informal organizations of classrooms facilitate everyday forms of student defiance. *American Journal of Sociology, 107*(3), 612–678.

McLaren, P. L. (1985). The ritual dimensions of resistance: Clowning and symbolic inversion. *Journal of Education, 167*(2), 84–97.

Mitra, D. L. (2004). The significance of students: Can increasing "student voice" in schools lead to gains in youth development? *Teachers College Record, 106*(4), 651–688.

Munns, G., & McFadden, M. (2000). First chance, second chance, or last chance? Resistance and response to education. *British Journal of Sociology of Education, 21*(1), 59–75.

Ohio Department of Education (2009). Ohio Report Cards. Retrieved from http://www.ode.state.oh.us/.

Olafson, L., & Field, J. C. (2003). A moral revisioning of resistance. *The Educational Forum, 67*(2), 140–147.

Patton, M. Q. (2002). *Qualitative research and evaluation methods* (3rd ed.). Thousand Oaks, CA: Sage.

Purcell-Gates, V. (2002). "...As soon as she opened her mouth!": Issues of language, literacy, and power. In L. Delpit & J. K. Dowdy (Eds.), *The skin that we speak: Thoughts on language and culture in the classroom* (pp. 121–141). New York, NY: The New Press.

Riley, K. L. (1996). Education in the United States and the Rom. *The Educational Forum, 61,* 12–17.

Rueda, E. (2005, August). *Staying "good" kids and becoming "flunkies": Patterns of academic engagement in the transition from elementary to middle school among Mexican-origin students.* Paper presented at the annual American Sociological Association conference. Philadelphia, PA.

Rueda, E. (2006). *The meaning of resistance: Fluid and context-specific interpretations of student (dis)engagement in the transition to middle school.* Paper presented at the meeting of the American Sociological Association, Montreal, Canada.

Sekayi, D. N. R. (2001). Intellectual indignation: Getting at the roots of student resistance in an alternative high school program. *Education, 122,* 414–422.

Sheets, R. H. (1996). Urban classroom conflict: Student-teacher perception: Ethnic integrity, solidarity, and resistance. *Urban Review, 28*(2), 165–183.

Shor, I. (1992). *Empowering education: Critical teaching for social change.* Chicago, 1L: University of Chicago Press.

Smith, G. (2002). Going local. *Educational Leadership, 60*(1), 30–33.

Starcher, S. D. (2005). *The triracial experience in a poor Appalachian community: How social identity shapes the school lives of rural minorities* (Doctoral dissertation). Ohio University, Athens.

U.S. Census Bureau (2000). Retrieved from http://factfinder.census.gov/home/saff/main.html?_lang=en

Walker, H. M., & Sylwester, R. (1998). Reducing students' refusal and resistance. *Teaching Exceptional Children, 30*(6), 52–58.

Willis, P. E. (1977). *Learning to labor: How working class kids get working class jobs.* Westmead, United Kingdom: Saxon House.

Wither, S. (2001). *Local curriculum development: A case study.* Paper presented at the annual meeting of the American Educational Research Association, Seattle, WA. (ERIC Document Reproduction Service No. ED 456 022)

Critical Thinking

1. What are your assumptions about people from rural settings?

2. What are your experiences with people from rural settings?
3. What pedagogical strategies would be effective for getting to know your students with respect to their individual backgrounds and settings?
4. Why is it important for teachers to know their students individually and for all students to know one another?

Create Central

www.mhhe.com/createcentral

Internet References

EdWeek
www.edweek.org/ew/issues/rural-education/
National Economics and Social Rights Initiative
www.nesri.org/

KATIE A. HENDRICKSON is a master's student in education at Ohio University.

Article   Prepared by: Nancy P. Gallavan, *University of Central Arkansas*

Examining Second Language Literacy Development in an Urban Multi-Age Classroom

Sharon H. Ulanoff, Ambika Gopalakrishnan, Diane Brantley,
Susan Courtney and Richard Rogers

Learning Outcomes

After reading this article, you will be able to:

- Discover the application of ethnographic classroom research.
- Relate the findings to classroom instruction for all learners.

This paper describes a multi-year ethnographic study of literacy instruction for English language learners (ELLs) in a multi-age classroom in Los Angeles. This study was undertaken by three university professors and one of the two teachers of the multi-age classroom. Data collection began in July 2003 and initially focused on exploring the nature of literacy instruction in this classroom. Second-year data collection explored teacher and student discourse during classroom activities, focusing on teacher-student discourse and student-student discourse. This study is guided by the following question: *How does the multiage experience impact second language literacy learning for urban elementary school students in Los Angeles?*

This work is situated in a growing body of research that describes benefits and challenges for multi-age education (Anderson and Pavan, 1993; Chase and Doan, 1996; Guitierrez and Slavin, 1992; 1994; Lauer, 2000; Lloyd, 1999) and explores the implications for English literacy instruction for ELLs. Given the recent incarnation of the reading wars nationwide (Allington, 2002; Allington and Woodside-Jiron, 1999; Coles, 2000; Foorman, Fletcher, Francis, and Schatschneider, 2000; Garan, 2002) and a political move toward an English only ideology in the United States (see Crawford, 2000; García and Curry-Rodriguez, 2000; Ulanoff and Vega-Castaneda, 2003), it is important to look at ways to provide opportunities for social interaction that embed literacy instruction in context for those students learning to read and write in their second language L2.

It is also influenced by the literature that explores the ways in which teachers' and students' discourse patterns in classroom lessons and other interactions influence student learning (Cazden, 1988; Gutierrez, Rymes, and Larson, 1995). Within the framework of sociolinguistics and sociocognitive theory, it is argued that student learning is positively related to students' ". . . appropriation of social discourses" (Hicks, 1996, p. 105), which occurs as they participate in classroom interactions. Hicks (1996) suggests that "discourse is a central means through which new understandings are negotiated among participants" (p. 105). Gee (1996) further argues that students use language as a social tool to help them accomplish interactional tasks in order to internalize learning (p. 274). As students are scaffolded through the learning process by either teachers or more capable peers (Vygotsky, 1962) they are able to make meaning out of the interactions.

In addition to providing a variety of opportunities for teacher and student interactions, multi-age classrooms may have positive implications for English literacy learning and instruction for ELLs. Peer teaching and cross-age tutoring have been shown to be highly effective approaches for ELLs because they allow them to utilize language in a social and academic context thereby enhancing their overall language skills while maintaining a high degree of age-appropriate content area instruction (Johnson, 1988). They further allow for students to interact in multiple ways related to classroom discourse, specifically student and teacher talk.

Methodology

Data were collected at La Nieta School, an urban elementary school on a multi-track year-round calendar. La Nieta School has a student population of 96% Latinos, 3% African American and the rest a mix of other ethnicities. Seventy-nine percent of the students are labeled English language learners (ELLs) and 98% of the students at La Nieta receive free and reduced lunch. The neighborhood consists of both single-family homes and multiple family dwellings that were built decades ago. La Nieta School has an active relationship with a local university. There is also a Parent Center on campus. Many of the teachers at

La Nieta are bilingual and others hold certification that allows them to teach ELLs.

Data were collected by three researchers from a local university who served as non-participant observers in the classroom as well as by the two classroom teachers who acted as complete participants (Gold, 1958; Junker, 1960) for a period of three years beginning in July 2003 and ending in April 2006. Instruction was provided in English at all times, although Spanish was used as needed to clarify concepts or explain unknown vocabulary. Students generally enter the class in kindergarten and exit at the end of second grade. The classroom teachers had worked together in the multi-age classroom for nine years at the time the research study began.

At the beginning of the first year of study there were thirty-six students (29 English language learners and 7 English only learners) in the classroom community, 22 boys and 14 girls. There were twelve five-years olds, eight six-years olds and sixteen seven-years olds. Although the students were technically divided between the two teachers into separate class rosters, they functioned as one classroom with students moving fluidly between two connecting rooms to form the multi-age classroom. While the demographics of the class at the beginning of the second and third years of study were similar, there was a dramatic shift in the classroom population throughout the second and third years.

Beginning in July 2003, the classroom was observed once weekly by one or more of the researchers for a minimum of two hours to a maximum of the full day. Second year data collection included twice-monthly observations. Third year data collection consisted of sporadic observations to collect data to support data gathered during the first two years. Multiple data sources were collected to develop an in-depth understanding of the culture of the multi-age classroom. Ethnographic field notes, audio and video recordings, and student artifacts were collected (Emerson, Fretz, and Shaw, 1995) during each observation. Students were interviewed periodically as deemed necessary. The researchers met with the teachers formally and informally throughout the project, as a means of conducting member checks during the data collection and analysis phase of the study, allowing the researchers to clarify and/or modify any interpretations and conclusions they had drawn. The interview data served to enrich and triangulate the findings (Merriam, 1995).

The data were analyzed, categorized, compared, and contrasted using a methodology that seeks to "elicit meaning from the data" (LeCompte & Preissle, 1993, p. 235), rather than codifying and computing it, as well as the construction of categories or domains (Spradley, 1980). A domain analysis was used to sort the data into multiple categories, allowing a portrait to emerge that is reflective of the "big picture" of the literacy practices being utilized in the classroom (Frank, 1999).

Initial data collection focused on examining the construction of practice in the classroom. The second year of the study focused on the collection and analysis of the discourse taking place within the classroom between the student/s and teacher/s, the teacher and teacher and the student/s and other student/s. Using a meaning-based definition of discourse "as

a socially and culturally organized way of speaking through which particular functions are realized" (Schriffen, 1994, p. 32), allowed the researchers to move from a strict analysis of conversation to a view of discourse as socially-situated within a particular time, place and context adding richness to the data. While sociocultural theory (Jennings and Di, 1996; Rommetveit, 1974; Vygotsky, 1962; Wertsch, 1984) formed the foundation for the study, activity theory (Engestrom and Middleton, 1996; Leont'ev, 1978; Rogoff, 1990) provided a lens through which to view and understand the interactions and activities taking place within the learning situation.

Findings

Several overarching themes serve as the context for instruction in this multi-age classroom. First, Susan and Richard focus on allowing students to make meaning of school activities, learn and use literacy in meaningful ways, while connecting new learning to prior knowledge. By design they create spaces for L2 literacy development by creating a safe classroom environment where students are free to take risks with their learning and become valuable members of the classroom community. The following themes emerged that describe the structures in place that impact the creation of that community.

Community and Respect

Students in this multi-age classroom develop a sense of community and belonging from the first day they enter the classroom. There is an instructional focus on community and respect. Returning students are expected to be role models for newcomers. There is an equal level of respect for all community members, whether they are newcomers, teachers or returning students; everyone is important rather than no one is important. For example, during one lesson, Susan was listening to a student talk when Richard walked over to ask her a question. Susan looked at Richard and said, "Excuse me, but I am listening to Viviana (a pseudonym for one of the multiage students) now so I can't talk to you at this moment," indicating to students their equal status. This incident is only one example. Similar events take place throughout the school day. Furthermore, the class members consistently demonstrate respect and value for the diversity of languages, ethnicities and cultures in the classroom.

Communication

There is a high degree of communication between the two teachers; it is almost as if they function as one person. There are differences, for example, Susan is referred to by her first name and Richard is called Mr. Rogers, acknowledging each individual teacher's preferences and culture. Throughout the day, decisions are made by both teachers as to the direction they will take both procedurally and instructionally, with continual efforts to take both perspectives into account. It is always a discussion rather than a mandate. Moreover, parents are kept in the information loop. Not only do notes go home related to class activities, parents, teachers and students consistently communicate with one another.

Print-Rich Environment

The classroom provides the students with a print-rich environment in which all of the objects are labeled with English vocabulary. This environment emerges during the first few weeks of every school year school as the classroom community works to construct a literate environment. Student work is prominently displayed and changed throughout the school year. There is a library with several bookshelves and other book containers filled with both fiction and nonfiction texts in English at a variety of reading levels. There are charts and lists with important classroom information displayed throughout the room. All classroom print is in English, but as noted above, notes go home to parents in Spanish. . . .

High Expectations in a Safe Environment

Both teachers and students have high expectations for the quality of work students are expected to complete in class. These expectations include behaviors that students exhibit in class and on the playground. Everyone looks out for one another and there is no hesitation to step in and refocus a student as needed. It seems as if the students feel responsible for the group rather than just for themselves. These expectations are consistently communicated to students and parents. As part of these high expectations Susan and Richard create an atmosphere where students are called upon to actively engage in all classroom activities. Support is provided through the use of modeling, questioning and prompting as needed, and students are free to use their native language when they do not have the English skills to participate.

Integrated Curriculum

Music, literature, writing, and science are often integrated into weekly lessons. Both teachers spend time activating the students' background knowledge when introducing a new concept, unit or book. Beginning in kindergarten, reading and writing are presented across the curriculum with a focus on strategy instruction. This is interesting in light of the fact that teachers in this public school are required to follow the district's adopted scripted reading program that is heavily based on phonics and phonemic awareness instruction. Both teachers have adapted their use of the basal materials in order to present a thematic approach that embeds their instruction in context and supports the students. Rather than engage the students in decontexualized tasks throughout the day, the teachers emphasize metacognitive awareness and students are asked to verbalize the strategies they have or will use when reading, writing or approaching a specific task.

The Role of Teacher Talk

The teachers use language in ways that not only communicate, but also teach language and usage. Susan and Richard use targeted procedural and instructional talk aimed at both classroom management and instruction. They further work to "teach" students to use both procedural and instructional talk during classroom activities, through "self-talk," aimed at helping students internalize instructional and behavioral procedures. Teachers use a "questioning mode" to impel students to search for answers to instructional and procedural questions.

Throughout the day, both teachers use "teacher talk" in ways that both describe classroom procedures and also model those very procedures. Lessons consist of direct instruction but also allowed for independent activities on a daily basis. In addition to the direct instruction students engage in inquiry activities. The first few days of the school year are spent on group building and teaching appropriate classroom behaviors to the new students in class. Newcomers are paired with returning students in newcomer/role model pairs and returning students are expected to take on expert roles in acclimating the new students to the classroom culture.

Both teachers teach and use what they call self-talk with the students. This consists of specific phrases that help students know how to behave in the classroom. The teachers model the specific behaviors that they expect of students and then students create "posters" of these statements, which are then posted throughout the room. . . . Furthermore, teachers and students engage in choral self-talk chants at the beginning of the year to help the students learn the classroom procedures. At first they chant with prompting, but after a while students are asked to repeat the self-talk without prompts.

Susan and Richard are active participants in instruction, modeling behavior and "thinking aloud" as they engage in classroom activities. They both use questioning to get students to think about classroom activities and model vocabulary usage throughout instruction, posing critical questions and often responding with questions that hold students accountable for learning. It is through the use of questions that both Susan and Richard guide the students to take ownership for their learning as well as developing a sense of collaboration within the classroom community. This is evident during reading instruction when Susan reads aloud to the class. She consistently checks for understanding and then models the use of new vocabulary, embedding it in the context of the story being read. During lessons, Susan models the expectations she has for student behavior, including turn taking behavior during lessons and discussions. While students are expected to raise their hands when guest teachers and other visitors work with the whole class during lessons, Susan focuses on holding conversations with the class where students are free to participate without waiting for recognition. She often provides wait time allowing students to chime in when they have something to say. "Show me, don't tell me" is one of the mantras frequently heard in class by both students and teachers. The expert role models are quite adept at appropriately scaffolding the procedural information for the newcomers so that they are relatively indistinguishable by the end of the first month of school.

The Role of Student Talk

Despite the fact that all instruction in this class takes place in English, the second language of most of the students in this class, students use Spanish when they are working together, especially when they are giving instructions to other students, telling them what to do. While at first glance this appeared to be little more than translating to support one another and clarify instructions, upon further examination it appears that the students are operating within their comfort zone, using their first language for communication. It may also be used as a means of forming more personal relationships with other students in the class.

However, students consistently appropriated the self-talk used by Susan and Richard in the classroom and this self-talk was in English. What is interesting is that while this type of discourse was similar to that used by Susan and Richard, there were differences, demonstrating the students' ability to internalize and modify the self-talk to meet their communication needs. For example, one student, exasperated at another student who appeared to be critiquing his work, yelled, "I did it to the best of my ability, ok, huh?" This seems to mirror a question that Susan might have asked (Did you do it to the best of your ability?) but is slightly different. Students also appropriated teacher talk when they took on leadership roles in the classroom. It was not uncommon to hear [Ivonne as she leads the calendar] say, "We have about one minute left. . . ." or "Hey, raise your hand if you know" much as Susan or Richard might say to the class.

Conclusions

The present ethnographic research study documents the use of a multi-age K-1-2 classroom situation for educating and supporting ELLs within the public school system of California. The goal of the three-year study was to make visible those processes that allow ELLs to not only acquire English, but to excel within the educational system thus allowing them access to the same occupational and educational opportunities of their English only peers. During year one of the study, researchers collected data pertaining to the instructional practices in place within the classroom.

The findings indicated that the teachers spent time developing a classroom learning community that promoted respect for one another based on a high degree of communication between teachers and students, students and students, parents and teachers, and parents and students. At all times teachers and students maintained high academic and behavioral expectations for one another, generally holding each other accountable for fulfilling these standards. Additionally, instruction was provided in a safe, well-maintained print-rich environment through the use of a high interest, literature-rich integrated curriculum. Students were encouraged to take ownership of their learning, beginning within the first few weeks of entering kindergarten and increasing as they progressed into higher grade levels.

Over the course of the study Susan and Richard consistently engaged the students in the learning process through the use of higher-level questions, student-led lessons and activities, group-building strategies and genuine dialogue. In year two, the researchers explored the notion that students were appropriating and modifying "teacher self-talk" into conversations with their peers. It became apparent that the students had internalized much of the teacher self-talk modeled and reinforced over time because they were able to alter the language and use it within different academic situations. Through this process,

the students were able to create their own self-talk. This is an important finding as it shows that ELLs in the early stages of English language acquisition are able to understand and appropriate complex English language concepts through the use of scaffolded instruction by skilled teachers when it is reinforced across a period of 3 years.

These findings support the notion that students of diverse linguistic, economic and cultural backgrounds have opportunities to engage in "a continuum of teaching strategies that involves them in motivating, meaningful reading (and learning) experiences" (Au, 2002, p. 409). These experiences should take place within a safe learning environment with high academic expectations and a high degree of support from parents, teachers and students. The current study adds to the research literature by providing further support for the use of relevant instruction that promotes the active engagement of ELLs in academic dialogue within the classroom. Because students need time to acquire and internalize this language, the use of a multi-age classroom experience in the early stages of English language acquisition is suggested.

Implications

The debate over appropriate initial literacy instruction for ELLs in California is ongoing despite demonstrated success for properly implemented primary language programs (Krashen and Biber, 1988; Willig, 1985). Further arguments describe challenges to effective literacy instruction as a result of restrictions based on how and what is taught in reading (Moustafa and Land, 2002). Presently ELLs in California are being taught to read in English, most often through the use of scripted programs that do not always focus on the construction of meaning.

This study attempts to examine the impact of one multi-age experience on ELLs' literacy acquisition during their initial years of schooling in the hopes of describing ways to imbed literacy instruction within the classroom context. This study specifically explores the impact of student and teacher discourse on second language literacy learning. Advocates of multi-age education believe that the presence of older and younger children allows them to engage in meaningful literacy activities by encouraging collaboration and promoting a climate of "expected cooperation" (Katz, Evangelou, and Hartman, 1991, p. 10). It is during these exchanges that children learn to problem solve and negotiate alternative responses to the problems they encounter thereby scaffolding each other's learning experiences (Pontecorvo and Zuccthe classroom. It is during these interactions that literacy learning takes place. Multi-age classrooms encourage and promote collaborative learning experiences, and provide the context-rich environment needed to support ELLs as they acquire English.

References

Allington, R. L. (2002). *Big brother and the national reading curriculum: How ideology trumped evidence*. Portsmouth, NH: Heinemann.

Allington, D. and Woodside-Jiron, H. (1999). The politics of literacy teaching: How "research" shaped educational policy. *Educational researcher*, Vol. 28, No. 8, pp. 4–13.

Anderson, R. H. and Pavan, B. N. (1993). *Nongradedness: Helping it to happen.* Lancaster, PA: Technomic Publishing.

Au, K. (2002). Multicultural factors and the effective instruction of students of diverse backgrounds. In A.E. Farstrup & S.J. Samuels (Eds.), *What research has to say about reading instruction* (pp. 392–413). Newark, DE: International Reading Association.

Cazden. C. B. (1988). *Classroom discourse: The language of teaching and learning.* Portsmouth, NH: Heinemann.

Chase, P. (1994). Valuing. In P. Chase and J. Doan (Eds.). *Full circle: A new look at MULTI-AGE education.* Portsmouth, NH: Heinemann.

Chase, P. and Doan, J. (1994). *Full circle: A new look at MULTI-AGE education.* Portsmouth, NH: Heinemann.

Chase, P. and Doan, J. (1996). *Choosing to learn: Ownership and responsibility in a primary multi-age classroom.* Portsmouth, NH: Heinemann.

Coles, G. (2000). *Misreading reading: The bad science that hurts children.* Portsmouth, NH: Heinemann.

Crawford, J. (2000). *At war with diversity: US language policy in an age of anxiety.* Clevedon, UK: Multilingual Matters.

Doan, B. (1996). The option of choice. In P. Chase and J. Doan, (Eds.). *Choosing to learn: Ownership and responsibility in a primary multi-age classroom.* Portsmouth, NH: Heinemann.

Emerson, R., Fretz, R., and Shaw, L. (1995). *Writing ethnographic fieldnotes.* Chicago, IL: University of Chicago Press.

Engestrom, Y. and Middleton, D. (1996). *Cognition and communication at work.* New York, NY: Cambridge University Press.

Fitzgerald, J. (1995). English-as-a-second language instruction in the United States: A research review. *Journal of Reading Behavior, 27,* 115–132.

Foorman, B. R., Fletcher, J.M., Francis, D. J., and Schatschneider, C. S. (2000). Response Misrepresentation of research by other researchers. *Educational researcher,* Vol. 29, No. 6, pp. 27–37.

Frank, C. (1999). *Ethnographic eyes: A teacher's guide to classroom observation.* Portsmouth, NH: Heinemann.

Garan, E. M. (2002). *Resisting reading mandates: How to triumph with the truth.* Portsmouth, NH; Heinemann.

García, E. E. and Curry-Rodriguez, J. E. (2000). The education of limited English proficient students in California Schools: An assessment of the influence of Proposition 227 on selected districts and schools. *Bilingual Research Journal,* Vol. 24, Nos. 1 & 2., pp. 1–21.

Gee, J. P. (1996). Vygotsky and current debates in education: Some dilemmas as afterthoughts to *Discourse, learning and schooling.* In D. Hicks (Ed.). *Discourse, learning and schooling.* New York: Cambridge University Press.

Gold, R. (1958). Roles in sociological field observation. *Social Forces,* Vol. 36, pp. 217–223.

Guiterrez, R. and Slavin, R. E. (1992). Achievement effects of non-graded elementary schools: A best evidence synthesis. *Review of educational research,* Vol. 62, No. 4, pp. 333–376.

Hicks, D. (1996). Contextual inquiries: A discourse-oriented study of classroom learning. In D. Hicks (Ed.). *Discourse, learning and schooling.* New York: Cambridge University Press.

Jennings, C. and Di, X. (1996). Collaborative learning and thinking: The Vygotskian approach. In L. Dixon Krause (Ed.), *Vygotsky in the classroom: Mediated literacy instruction and assessment* (pp. 77–92). White Plains, NY: Longman.

Johnson, D. M. (1988). ESL children as teachers: A social view of second language. *Language arts,* February, 1988.

Junker, B. (1960). *Field work.* Chicago, IL: University of Chicago Press.

Katz, L., Evangelou, D., and Hartman, J. (1991). *The case for mixed-age grouping in early education.* Washington, D.C. : National Association for the Education of Young Children.

Krashen, S. and Biber, D. (1988). *On course: Bilingual education's success in California.* Sacramento, CA: CABE.

Lauer, P. A. (2000). *Instructional practices and implementation issues in multi-age classrooms.* Aurora, CO: Mid-continent research for education and learning.

LeCompte, M. and Preissle, J. (1993). *Ethnography and qualitative design in educational research.* San Diego, CA: Academic Press.

Leont'ev, A.N. (1978). *Activity, consciousness, personality.* Englewood Cliffs, NJ: Prentice Hall.

Lloyd, L. (1999). Multi-age classes and high ability students. *Review of educational research,* Vol. 69, No. 2, pp. 187–212.

Lodish, R. (1992). The pros and cons of mixed-age grouping. *Principal,* Vol. 7, No. 5, pp. 20–22.

Merriam, S. (1995). *Qualitative research and case study applications in education.* San Fransisco, CA: Jossey-Bass.

Miller, B. A. (1996). A basic understanding of multi-age grouping: Teacher readiness, planning, and parent involvement required for successful practice. *The school administrator,* Vol. 53, No. 1, pp. 12–17.

Moustafa, M. and Land, R. (2002). The reading achievement of economically-disadvantaged children in urban schools using Open Court vs. comparably disadvantaged children in urban schools using non-scripted programs. *2002 Yearbook of the Urban Learning, Teaching and Research Special Interest Group.* Los Angeles, CA: CSULA.

Ogbu, J.U. (1981). School ethnography: A multilevel approach. *Anthropology & Education Quarterly,* 12, 3–29.

Pontecorvo, C. and Zucchermaglio, C. (1990). A passage to literacy: Learning in a social context. In Y. Goodman (Ed.), *How children construct literacy: Piagetian perspectives* (pp. 59–98). Newark, DE: International Reading Association.

Rogoff, B. (1990). *Apprenticeship in thinking-cognitive development in social context.* San Francisco, CA: Jossey-Bass.

Rommetveit, R. (1974). *On message structure: A framework for the study of language and communication.* New York, NY: Wiley.

Schriffin, D. (1994). *Approaches to discourse.* Malden, MA: Blackwell Press.

Spradley, J. (1980). *Participant observation.* Orlando, FL: Harcourt, Brace and Jovanovich.

Ulanoff, S. H. and Vega-Castaneda, L. (2003). The sociopolitical context of bilingual instruction in 21st century California. *Proceedings of the annual meeting of the Hawaii International Conference on Education,* Honolulu, HI.

Valdes, G. (1998). The world outside and inside schools: Language and immigrant children. *Educational Researcher, 27,* 4–18.

Vygotsky, L. (1962). *Theory and language.* Cambridge, MA: MIT University Press.

Wertsch, J.V. (1984). *Culture, communication and cognition.* New York, NY: Cambridge University Press.

Willig, A.C. (1985). A meta-analysis of selected studies on the effectiveness of bilingual education. *Review of educational research,* Vol. 55, No. 3, pp. 269–317.

Critical Thinking

1. What are the three major themes of this study?
2. How can teachers improve the literacy development among their second language learners?
3. What techniques from this article are essential for teaching all young learners?
4. Why is risk-taking with vocabulary critical for all classrooms?

Create Central

www.mhhe.com/createcentral

Internet References

National Association for Bilingual Education (NABE)
www.nabe.org/

Teaching English Language Learners International Association
www.tesol.org/

SHARON H. ULANOFF, California State University, Los Angeles.
AMBIKA GOPALAKRISHNAN, California State University, Los Angeles.
DIANE BRANTLEY, California State University, San Bernardino.
SUSAN COURTNEY, Los Angeles Unified School District.
RICHARD ROGERS, Los Angeles Unified School District.

Article   Prepared by: Nancy P. Gallavan, *University of Central Arkansas*

Building the Movement to End Educational Inequity

Teach for America is working, Ms. Kopp argues. And studies show that TFA teachers do as well as or better than teachers with traditional certification.

WENDY KOPP

Learning Outcomes

After reading this article, you will be able to:

- Increase understanding of the Teach for America approach and philosophy.
- Explore issues related to the teaching, learning, and schooling for children of poverty.

Teach for America exists to address educational inequity—the stunning reality that in our nation, which aspires so admirably to be a land of equal opportunity, where one is born still largely determines one's educational outcomes. Despite plenty of evidence that children growing up in poverty can do well academically—when given the opportunities they deserve—the stark reality in our nation today is that the 13 million children growing up below the poverty line are already three grade levels behind children in high-income communities by the time they are 9 years old. Moreover, even the half of low-income children who do manage to graduate from high school are performing, on average, at the level of eighth-graders who live in affluent communities.

Why do we have this problem? We believe that the foremost reason is that children in low-income communities face extra challenges of poverty that other children don't face, including lack of adequate health care and housing and lack of access to high-quality preschool programs. The situation is compounded by the fact that the schools they attend were not designed to put children facing extra disadvantages on a level playing field with students in other areas. These circumstances persist because our national policies and practices, driven by our national priorities, have not been sufficient to tackle either the socioeconomic challenges or the inadequacies in our school systems.

At Teach for America, we know we can solve this problem because we see evidence in classrooms across the country that, when students growing up in poverty are given the opportunities they deserve, they excel. Knowing that we cannot expect every teacher to go above and beyond traditional expectations to the extent necessary to compensate for all the weaknesses of the system, however, we believe our best hope for a lasting solution is to build a massive force of leaders working from inside and outside education who have the conviction and insight that come from teaching successfully in low-income communities. We need such leadership working at every level of our school systems, working outside the system to address the socioeconomic factors that contribute so significantly to the problem, and working in policy and the sectors, such as journalism and business, that influence policy. In order to provide more students growing up in poverty today with excellent teachers and also to build this force of leaders, Teach for America recruits our nation's most promising future leaders, invests in the training and professional development necessary to ensure their success as teachers in our highest-poverty communities, and fosters their ongoing leadership as alumni.

The evidence indicates that our approach is working. Last year, more than 35,000 graduates of top universities competed for the opportunity to teach in urban and rural communities. Our incoming corps of 4,100 members achieved an average GPA of 3.6; 89% of them held at least one leadership position in a campus activity. Thirty percent of the corps members identify as people of color, and 32% are male. They come to this effort with a desire to reach the nation's most disadvantaged students, and based on the results of the most rigorous evaluation conducted to date, they are in fact teaching students who begin the year, on average, at the 14th percentile against the national norm.

The research actually does not show that our teachers have less impact than fully certified teachers, as Megan Hopkins seems to suggest. Multiple rigorous studies, such as the one she cites by Thomas Kane, Jonah Rockoff, and Douglas Staiger, have actually found that certification is a weak predictor of effectiveness and that Teach for America teachers do as well as or better than those from traditional preparation routes.

Moreover, the "small study" to which she refers was conducted by Mathematica Policy Research; the random-assignment methodology used in that study is widely considered the "gold standard" in research. This rigorous study found that students taught by Teach for America corps members made more progress in both reading and math than would typically be expected in a single year. In math, the impact of hiring a Teach for America teacher over another new teacher was the equivalent of reducing class size by eight students (as in the Tennessee class-size reduction experiment). The study found that Teach for America teachers produced gains in math that were not only larger than those of other beginning teachers but also larger than those of veteran and certified teachers.

The preponderance of evidence shows that corps members effect greater academic gains than other teachers in their schools. And while fewer than 10% of corps members report that they might have taught even if Teach for America hadn't been an option, more than 60% of our 17,000 alumni are working full-time in education. While they are still in their twenties and thirties, they are pioneering vital reforms, modeling excellence as teachers, serving as school principals and district administrators, and even getting appointed to superintendencies. They are making a tangible difference in communities across the country where we have been placing corps members for a decade or more. In our nation's capital, for example, Teach for America alumni serve as the schools' chancellor, deputy chancellor, 10% of school principals, one of two newly elected state board members, a policy advisor to the mayor, and the only national teacher of the year in the city's history. Other Teach for America alumni work from the social services and the legal profession to mitigate the pressures on schools in the first place, and still others work from corporations to marshal additional resources toward the effort.

In our program's 19-year history, we have engaged in ongoing research to continuously improve our program. In the process, we have given extensive thought to the suggestions made by Ms. Hopkins and have made decisions based on evidence of what is likely to maximize the impact of our model. For example, we have not moved to a three-year commitment because of evidence that doing so would significantly decrease the size, diversity, and quality of our corps, particularly in such key areas as math and science. We weigh this information against the reality that most of our corps members do, in fact, remain in education over the long term, despite the two-year commitment. We have also remained committed to enabling corps members to make first-year teacher salaries, knowing that asking them to work for a stipend or reduced salary would reduce the socioeconomic—and in turn racial and ethnic—diversity of the corps.

While we do remain committed to placing corps members in schools where they can reach our country's most underserved children, we have also made an unprecedented investment in their professional development. This is hard work, but by investing in measuring corps members' academic impact and in the continuous improvement of the training and professional development we provide, we aim to produce a corps of first- and second-year teachers who move their students forward significantly more than would typically be expected in a year.

It is also worth noting that principals in our partner schools give consistently high ratings to the preparation of our corps members. In a recent nationwide survey of principals with corps members in their schools, nearly all reported that corps members' training is at least as good as the training of other beginning teachers, and nearly two-thirds rate the training of corps members as better than that of other new teachers.

In very recent years, to increase the impact of our alumni, we have launched initiatives to support those who aim to pursue educational leadership through continued teaching, principalships, launching new social enterprises, policy and advocacy, and securing elected office. In some ways this development is responsive to Ms. Hopkins' suggestion that we offer incentives to entice members to remain in teaching, though, as outlined above, we continue to believe that it is important to foster the efforts of Teach for America alumni to effect change from other professions as well.

We laud the efforts of the local programs that Ms. Hopkins highlights. These programs show much promise for meeting the national need for qualified teachers. As we see evidence of their success, we look to such programs to help us identify good practices, and we incorporate those practices into our approach when applicable. Still, Teach for America is not beginning to meet the demand from districts and education reformers for our corps members and alumni, and this continuing demand fuels our commitment to grow even as we strengthen our program model and even as others experiment with new approaches to meeting the need for talent.

Finally, we are grateful to the university partners who work with us in pursuit of our mission. You can read about some of these partnerships elsewhere in this special section. We hope this conversation will open more opportunities for collaboration with others in the higher education community, and we appreciate Ms. Hopkins' willingness to bring this discussion to a broader audience.

Critical Thinking

1. What is Teach for America?
2. How are Teach for America teachers prepared for classrooms?
3. What is the emphasis for Teach for America teachers?
4. Why are alternative teacher preparation programs ideal for some schools and classrooms?

Create Central

www.mhhe.com/createcentral

Internet References

National Association for Children in Poverty
http://www.nccp.org/
Teach for America
http://www.teachforamerica.org/

Wendy Kopp is founder and chief executive officer of Teach for America, New York, NY.

From *Phi Delta Kappan*, June, 2008, pp. 734–736. Copyright © 2008 by Phi Delta Kappan. Reprinted by permission of Phi Delta Kappan and Wendy Kopp.

Unit 5

UNIT

Prepared by: Nancy P. Gallavan, *University of Central Arkansas*

Awareness of Teaching

Student success and satisfaction is contingent upon one single element in the classroom: the teacher. The teacher may possess an attentive awareness of others coupled with a well-honed awareness of self; likewise the teacher may be a graduate of a highly accredited teacher education program who passed all of the requisite exams. However, the teacher must be advanced in her or his awareness of teaching in order to make a difference in a student's learning and living.

Becoming attuned to one's own teaching practices and patterns is accomplished through honest reflection, natural assessment, authentic analyses, and holistic feedback. These four processes may be taught throughout teacher education courses and reinforced during clinical field experiences, but they are not mastered until the teacher has dedicated several years to their concepts, procedures, discoveries, and benefits. Teachers must possess self-motivation to enhance their own efficacy and increase their sense of agency to become reflective practitioners.

Honest reflection requires the teacher to identify criteria of importance and to think about one's proficiency with each criterion supported with specific and discernible evidence. Additionally the teacher must look at the criterion from multiple perspectives that fortify the clarity of the evidence. Honest reflection tends to illuminate the causes and effects related to many different situations related to the original reflection.

Natural assessment requires the teacher to measure progress with every day, usually events, using quantitative and qualitative data. Teachers should record numbers as well as text to describe the teaching before it begins, while the teaching occurs, and after the teaching has ended. The cycle of assessment collects preassessment, formative assessment, and summative assessment data to note change over time. Teachers must be well informed of their patterns.

Once criteria have been identified and data have been collected, authentic analyses begins. At this point, it may be more productive for the teacher to collaborate with a colleague, a cultural comrade. Like other people across all professions, teachers frequently see what they want to see and believe. The data may prove one set of practices, but the teacher may not want to acknowledge the patterns or may want to explain the patterns as stemming from a particular cause outside of the teacher's control. Authentic analyses may be difficult for teachers to conduct and prioritize without the cultural comrade.

Therefore, holistic feedback is essential. From the cultural comrade, teachers can be reassured of the practices and patterns they have incorporated into their professional repertoire that are positive and productive. And they can be guided and supported in understanding and revising the practices and patterns that may not be as positive and/or productive.

However, honest reflection, natural assessment, authentic analyses, and holistic feedback are accompanied by both insight and isolation. As dedicated teachers sharpen their awareness and improve both their strengths and weaknesses, frequently they discover that they have increased their isolation from their colleagues with whom they have considered themselves peers or equals. The teachers who commit themselves to enhancing their self-efficacy and fortifying their sense of agency with emphasis on cultural competence may find themselves enrolling in specialized university courses, taking professional development workshops, attending and/or presenting at professional conferences, traveling near and far, etc. that ultimately may redirect the teacher's journey to cultural competence along the road less traveled. In the quest to advance one's knowledge, skills, dispositions, and communications, teachers often discover that their isolation from current colleagues opens different pathways shared by new colleagues interested in the same theories, research, concepts, and practices. As teachers pursue cultural competence for themselves and their students, their own teaching becomes much more meaningful.

Article   Prepared by: Nancy P. Gallavan, *University of Central Arkansas*

Advancing Cultural Competence and Intercultural Consciousness through a Cross-Cultural Simulation with Teacher Candidates

NANCY P. GALLAVAN AND ANGELA WEBSTER-SMITH

Learning Outcomes

After reading this article, you will be able to:

- Learn about the experiences and benefits associated with Barnga, a cross-cultural simulation.

- Understand the discoveries and applications to society made by the candidates engaged in the simulation.

Teacher education programs accredited by the National Council for the Accreditation of Teacher Education are expected to incorporate curricula and guide instruction for teacher candidates to acquire meaningful knowledge and experiences with regard to diverse cultures and cultural characteristics (NCATE, 2008). Through their courses, particularly their multicultural education courses, candidates explore topics and issues focused on educational equity (Darling-Hammond, 2007) that impact teaching, learning, schooling, families, and society.

Using effective pedagogical strategies, teacher educators introduce and model the constructs of valuing diversity naturally, authentically, and holistically (Gallavan, 2007) so candidates can help all P-12 students learn and achieve.

Ideally, candidates are provided ample opportunities to apply new concepts, principles, and practices in their coursework and field experiences so they can better appreciate diversity within themselves, in classrooms, and across communities. Ultimately, candidates are expected to understand and demonstrate appropriate knowledge, skills, and dispositions for interacting with other people in many different contexts (Shulman, 1987). In essence, they are expected to be well-prepared, possessing the competence and confidence to demonstrate readiness (Gallavan, 2007) for their future teaching careers.

In order to afford teacher candidates in classroom assessment courses the opportunity to engage in unfiltered, authentic, and inclusive experiences, they participate in an intercultural simulation that cultivates their skills in connecting multicultural concepts with classroom practices. The simulation also advances their cultural competence (ATE, 2007) and intercultural consciousness (Karim, 2003) in an experiential context (Achenbach, & Arthur, 2002; Fowler, 1986). As Barnga, the simulation used in this study, distinctively fosters these objectives (Steinwachs, 1990; Thiagarajan, 1984), this study captures teacher candidates' thoughts, feelings and interactions as they occurred during this cross cultural simulation.

Conceptual Framework

The conceptual framework for this project stems from three primary sources. The first is the rarity that teacher candidates are taught the purposes, processes, and philosophies of reflecting in multiple contexts of education. Even though teacher educators routinely ask candidates to reflect on their practices, candidates are oftentimes missing the essential understanding, the necessary tools, and the refined techniques that ensure that reflection is principled, productive, and positive. To wit, they must receive guidance in analyzing and discerning their growth and development.

With that, Gallavan's Critical Components and Multiple Contexts of Self-Assessment Model (Gallavan & Webster-Smith, in press) guides teacher educators and candidates through the processes of reflecting thoughtfully, completely, and productively. The procedures provide the necessary scaffolding candidates need to examine both the strengths and the weaknesses of their principles and practices so they become more purposeful and positive in all contexts of teaching. Each of the three critical components of self assessment—reaction, response and reflection—is explored through multiple contexts of education that afford philosophical connections to teacher candidates' idealistic, realistic, pragmatic, and existential beliefs.

The second framework is important as it offers assumptions about human tendencies and inclinations associated with developing an intercultural consciousness (Karim, 2003) to include people are culturally encapsulated and ethnocentric in their world view; people feel cognitively, emotionally, and behaviorally challenged in unfamiliar situations and settings; people attempt to reduce cognitive dissonance; people prefer to avoid uncertainty and reduce anxiety; and people tend to behave in self-protective ways if they perceive threats to their psychosocial identity. Therefore, providing opportunities for candidates to connect their practical behaviors to their philosophical beliefs can prove to be enlightening.

The third framework is rooted in Achenbach and Arthur's (2002) cultural schema that represents three different dimensions of cultural awareness: self, other, and conditions. The perceptions associated with developing cultural schema are validation, evaluation, adjustment, negotiation, and incongruence. During experiential, intercultural learning situations the aforementioned sentiments are triggered. When students are unable to understand and reflect upon their own emotions and how they are represented in their behaviors, they are more challenged in interpreting the intended meaning of the overall experience. Hence, affording candidates reflective opportunities regarding culture is critical.

As teacher candidates build their funds of knowledge (Moll, Armanti, Neff, & Gonzalez, 1992) related to culturally responsive (Gay, 2000) and responsible content, pedagogy, and context, they should be developing cultural competence (ATE, 2007), raising their intercultural consciousness (Karim, 2003) and becoming reflective practitioners (Schön, 1987). One's cultural competence is developed by interacting with other people, like and unlike oneself, to increase one's comfort and understanding of people who are different in thoughts, beliefs, words, and actions.

Cultural competence (Gallavan, in press) is evident through interactions and through expressions individuals make about themselves as well as about and to other people individually and as members of various groups. Intercultural consciousness is more than comfort and understanding of cultural differences. Rather it requires intentional inquiry of others, patience, tolerance and flexibility in behaviors and thinking, along with the critical dimension of ethical and moral responsibility. Both cultural competency and intercultural consciousness promote local and global acumen.

Cultural competence and intercultural consciousness can be developed by providing safe opportunities for close proximity and positive interactions. In these environments, the propinquity effect manifests (Festinger, Schachter, & Back, 1950); that is, as individuals spend more time engaged in meaningful activities with new people unlike themselves, the more likely they will understand, accept, and become friends with the new people. Thus, harmonious outcomes (Dixon, 2006) and social cohesion (Friedman, 2004) occur between people and across groups building positive relationships and friendships between and among people who do not interact or converse regularly.

In classroom assessment courses, it is instructive to integrate a class activity that builds intercultural bridges. Such strategies help teacher candidates become more aware of potentially disparate and unfair assessment practices that may have an impact on the ability of diverse students to learn and develop in a psychologically safe, academic environment. Employing such an exercise might also help teachers gain a better understanding of the role their background plays in their teaching as well as cultivate skills in comparing and contrasting general curricular principles with culturally specific knowledge (Webster-Smith, 2008).

Purpose of the Study

The purpose of the study is to examine the three critical incidences (reactions, responses, and reflections) that teachers experience (Arthur, 2001) before, during, and after cross-cultural encounters. The benefit of using the simulation, Barnga is that it affords candidates perspective taking opportunities to question their beliefs about the certainty, source and structure of knowledge (Sleeter, 2009) as it allows them to grapple with multiple perspectives. Barnga also affords the instructor the expediency of closely observing teachers as they journey through the three critical incidences of self assessment and the ability to collect data in a controlled environment. As the authors have facilitated this simulation at least 30 times during the last 15 years with various groups of educators and are well-acquainted with the procedures and outcomes, their experience gave them a keen understanding of the potential power of the simulation to advance the conversation on diversity. In addition, the authors have researched and published findings on many topics and issues related to cultural competency.

The Research Questions

The classroom assessment course was selected so candidates would be exposed to similar cross-cultural experiences that contemporary P-12 students might encounter daily. Using Barnga, they would gain further understandings and representations of their beliefs as they relate to the impact of cross-cultural experiences on teaching, learning, and assessment.

Three research questions framed the study to examine candidates' cultural competency: (1) What are candidates' reactions when introduced to a new cross-cultural experience? (2) What are candidates' responses while involved in the cross-cultural experience? (3) What are candidates' reflections following the cross-cultural experience? Each research question in this study aligns with each of three critical incidences (reaction, response and reflection) associated with cross-cultural experiences.

Participants

Teacher candidates enrolled in three different sections of a classroom assessment course participated in this study. All 64 candidates had identified that they were aspiring to become middle level and high school teachers midway through their programs. Demographics of the participants showed that there were 46 females and 16 males. The racial distribution among the females included 7 African American, 2 Asian American, 31 Caucasian, and 3 Latino candidates. The racial distribution among the males included 5 African American, 0 Asian-American, 11 Caucasian, and 0 Latino candidates. The candidates ranged in age from 22 to 49 years.

Procedures

The professor facilitated Barnga early during the course to establish the importance of realizing the presence and power of possible preconceptions and prejudices that may influence a teacher's ability to assess students fairly. First, teacher candidates were guided through the simulation Barnga. Next the candidates participated in an interactive debriefing. Then a 10-item open-ended survey (which is embedded in the survey findings) was administered to collect feedback. Finally, a class conversation was held with each section of candidates following the data collections using the ten open-ended items as prompts allowing candidates to share their individual experiences and insights.

The mixed methodology combined non-experimental approaches during the simulation and debriefing. Narrative inquiry (Connelly & Clandinin, 1990) and naturalistic inquiry (Lincoln & Guba, 1985) data were collected during the survey. Category 1 Questions (1-5) probed initial reactions relating to preconceived notions expressed as candidates anticipated descriptions, rules and contexts of the upcoming cross-cultural interactions. Category 2 Questions (6-8) examined ongoing responses that candidates used to justify their behaviors and changes experienced during cross-cultural interactions. Category 3 Questions (9-10) investigated candidates' transformative processes after participating in the cross-cultural simulation and debriefing.

Survey Findings

Responses to Category 1 and Category 2 Questions (1-8) were analyzed and organized into groups based on a five-point range of emotions with the following descriptions: A-acceptance; B-curiosity; C-apprehension; D-irritation, and E-fury. These responses are aligned with foundations of the conceptual framework in terms of Achenbach and Arthur's (2002) perceptions associated with developing cultural schema and Karim's (2003) assumptions about human tendencies and inclinations. Each of these assumptions was perceived by study participants and revealed in the data. Category 3 Questions (9-10) were analyzed into a narrative summary. Whereas candidates' responses to every question fit into the prescribed categories, most of their responses were classified as expressing acceptance, curiosity, and apprehension. Sample responses are provided to authenticate the results.

Answering the "what" questions, the candidates' reactions (immediate, raw and nervous retorts offered without the benefit of deliberation and consideration) captured their immediate, emotional reactions about the simulation before it began.

Category 1 Questions: What were your feelings when . . .

1. you were assigned to a table without any choice?

A-acceptance	I trusted the teacher. I didn't care. We are all friends.
B-curiosity	It was a new adventure.
C-apprehension	We were not given a reason or explanation. I didn't have a choice.
D-irritation	Uneasy. I like sitting with my friends and choosing where I want to sit.
E-fury	I didn't want to move. I don't like change.

2. you were told to place all of your personal items to the side of the room?

A-acceptance	This classroom is a safe place.
B-curiosity	Now I began to wonder what we were going to do.
C-apprehension	What if there was going to be a quiz?
D-irritation	I wanted to keep my sweater, so I did. I felt uncomfortable and a little mad.
E-fury	I don't like being told what to do.

3. you learned the importance of the number on your table?

A-acceptance	Lucky! I landed at the top number.
B-curiosity	I wanted to know how I could move and move quickly.
C-apprehension	I thought the numbers were too competitive for our usual class activities.
D-irritation	Focusing on the card game was difficult since all I wanted to do was move up.
E-fury	I wanted to be at the best table. I kept moving to a lower number.

4. you were informed there would be no talking at any time or you would be told to leave the room?

A-acceptance	I figured we would have to be creative. This was just a game and I didn't care. Hooray, it would be a quiet time.
B-curiosity	I wondered what the reason was for this rule.
C-apprehension	I don't like to gesticulate and I don't read people well.
D-irritation	This rule frustrated me; I need to talk.
E-fury	This seemed extremely unfair. The facilitator was a dictator.

5. you read the directions and were told to put them back into the envelope?

A-acceptance	Fine; I play cards all the time. The rules seemed easy.
B-curiosity	This made the game more intriguing and exciting.
C-apprehension	It made me think something was going to be tricky. I read them much more closely than I usually read new information.
D-irritation	I was concerned that I could not remember them clearly.
E-fury	I wanted to keep the rules out to reread. This was too much pressure. I got worried.

While answering the "how" questions, the candidates' responses (perfunctory replies that occur with some attention and deliberation) captured their representations of their feelings and behaviors during the simulated cross-cultural interactions.

Category 2 Questions: How did you feel when . . .

6. you got to move to the table with the higher number after you had won a round at your table?

A-acceptance	Great! I won. I remembered the rules. Success!
B-curiosity	I don't play cards so I couldn't identify with the game.
C-apprehension	Moving into a new group made me nervous.
D-irritation	I didn't move; I didn't like it when new people came to my table.
E-fury	The new table seemed to have different rules that I didn't know. I wanted to ask questions, but we weren't allowed to talk.

7. you had to move to the table with the lower number after you had lost a round at your table?

A-acceptance	That's the way it happens. I lost the practice rounds so I expected to move down. This was just a game.
B-curiosity	I wondered about the rules at each table.
C-apprehension	I was fearful that I would continue moving down and never move up. Embarrassed.
D-irritation	Distressed!
E-fury	I didn't like being the lowest. Bummer! I felt like a loser. I was determined to move back up to a higher numbered table.

8. you discovered that the rules were different for different tables?

A-acceptance	The light bulb went off immediately! Enlightened! Thought provoking!
B-curiosity	I kept trying to think of a plan to overcome the differences so I could win. I thought it was funny thinking how the players behaved. It was amazing that I didn't figure this out sooner.
C-apprehension	I felt better knowing that it was the rules and not me. I wanted everyone to play by my rules and for my way to be respected.
D-irritation	I realized how competitive I am and I didn't like this discovery.
E-fury	I was frustrated. How can we play fairly if the rules are different?!? I just wanted to know THE rules.

Answering the "why" questions, the candidate's reflections (pensive interpretations that are punctuated with integrative connections) captured their understanding of the simulation's connections to prior lessons in diversity as well as to its larger purpose, meaning and significance to their role as 21st century educators.

Category 3 Questions: Why does this simulation . . .

9. apply to living?

This game is just like life: different rules for different people. You have to know the rules to play . . . and win. Sometimes it is hard to communicate. Every group has its own set of rules; other people interpret the rules the best they can. You have to adjust your way of thinking in order to be successful in other people's worlds. Life changes all the time; we must adjust or we'll be run over. We all must be able to move in and around all cultures with knowledge and comfort. We all need to be considerate of one another's differences and to be nice by playing by the same rules. We are a world that plays by different rules. We never know all of the rules or which rules are needed to win. The rules constantly change and are changed by the winners to ensure there is chaos and people can't win—to take away their power.

10. apply to teaching?

Teachers must explain the rules and keep them the same for everybody. Teachers should involve their students in establishing the rules. Teachers have to figure out how to communicate with every group of student and every student. Teachers cannot always have their own way in the school or the classroom. Students come from different backgrounds and need to understand their teachers and other students. The confusion and frustration experienced in this game is exactly what students experience every day. New teachers experience these too. Teachers must teach tolerance in every subject area. They must listen and connect with students. Teachers must model consideration, conservation, and cooperation with and among the students. All teachers should have this experience so they will remember the confusion of not knowing and wanting to be accepted and win.

Limitations of the Study

The simulation was facilitated by the course instructor. Candidates were well-acquainted with the instructor, and the instructor had established high levels of trust with the candidates during both formal and informal interactions. Survey responses occasionally referenced the candidates' sense of trust in their instructor. Further research will be conducted to examine feedback in environments where the candidates are not acquainted with the simulation facilitator.

Implications

The findings from this study imply that engaging in simulations with candidates opens their eyes about themselves, their outlooks toward and interactions with others, and their perspectives related to developing long-range goals and reasons for incorporating similar learning experiences in their own future classrooms. This is an important implication considering that most teachers are comfortable in schools and society, perceive that learning and achievement are available to everyone, and tend to deliver instruction from their own narrow viewpoints void of opportunities for students to exchange multiple perspectives (Ford, 2004).

Effective cross-cultural simulations result in four important outcomes for teachers and their students: self knowledge, acceptance of group conventions, multiple perspectives, and their passion or indifference toward equity and change (Delany-Barmann, & Minner, 1996; Pedersen, 2003). This study shows that as candidates progress through their coursework, especially their multicultural education courses, they benefit from

1. student-centered conversations extending honest investigations and analytical perceptions of all peoples and inequities in schools and societies—locally and globally (Marbley, et al., 2007); candidates can discuss the relationships between worldwide current events and the curricular content that they will be teaching.

2. controlled investigations of disenfranchised P-12 students and their families who do not feel valued, visible, or viable in today's classrooms; candidates can write questions probing connections between curricular content and specific populations.

3. frequent examinations of one's own personal values (Harry, 2008) that reveal growth and changes related to self knowledge, acceptance of group conventions, multiple perspectives, and passion or indifference toward equity and change; candidates can record their reflections in journals noting their personal changes

over time from multiple perspectives (Capella-Santana, 2003) as experienced by the propinquity effect and its importance when teaching their own students.

Conclusions

To develop cultural competency and intercultural consciousness, teacher candidates need opportunities to interact with people like and unlike themselves to experience the propinquity effect within a learning environment that allows for safe and supportive dissection and discussion of critical incidents. Simulations, such as Barnga, offer these benefits through experiential learning. Candidates engage in dynamic, interactive processes increasing their self knowledge, acceptance of group conventions, multiple perspectives and their passion or indifference toward equity and change by expressing and exchanging their reactions, responses, and reflections. Ultimately, the goal is for each candidate to experience a sense of cultural transformation (Banks & Banks, 2006) that becomes visible through the learners' successes, classroom support of students and colleagues, and their own professional satisfaction.

These three components of self-assessment capture the critical incidents (reaction, response, and reflection) of cultural competency and intercultural consciousness that teacher candidates should understand and demonstrate personally in preparation for their professional teaching careers. Then, as professional practicing teachers, they will be ready to guide their own P-12 learners with appropriate pedagogy to understand and demonstrate cultural competency and intercultural consciousness in their classrooms and communities.

References

Achenbach, K., & Arthur, N. (2002, Winter). Experimental learning: Bridging theory to practice in multicultural counseling. *Guidance and Counseling, 17*(2), 39–45.

Arthur, N. (2001). Using critical incidents to investigate cross-cultural transition. *International Journal of Intercultural Relations, 25,* 41–53.

Association of Teacher Educators. (2007). *Standards for teacher educators.* Retrieved from http://www.ate1.org/pubs/uploads/tchredstds0308.pdf

Babbie, E. R. (1990). *Survey research.* Belmont, CA: Wadsworth Publishing.

Banks, J. A., & Banks, C. A. M. (2006). *Multicultural education; Issues and perspectives* (6th ed.). Belmont, CA: Wadsworth Publishing.

Barrera, I., & Corso, R. M. (2002). Cultural competency as skilled dialogue. *Topics in Early Childhood Special Education, 22*(2), 103–113.

Capella-Santana, N. (2003, Jan/Feb). Voices of teacher candidates: Positive changes in multicultural attitudes and knowledge. *The Journal of Educational Research, 96*(3), 182–190.

Connelly, F. M., & Clandinin, D. J. (1990). Stories of experience and narrative inquiry. *Educational Researcher, 19*(5), 2–14.

Darling-Hammond, L. (2007). The flat earth and education: How America's commitment to equity will determine our future. *Educational Researcher, 36*(6), 318–334.

Delany-Barmann, G., & Minner, S. (1996, Summer). Cross-cultural workshops and simulations for teachers. *The Teacher Educator, 32*, 37–47.

Dixon, J. C. (2006, June). The ties that bind and those than don't: Toward reconciling group threat and contact theories of prejudice. *Social Forces, 84*(4), 2179–2204.

Festinger L., Schachter S., & Back, K. W. (1950). *Social pressures in informal groups: A study of human factors in housing.* New York: Harper.

Ford, M. (2004). Considering the standpoints of differently situated others: Teachers and arrogant perception. *Philosophy of Education Yearbook*, 337–345.

Fowler, S. M. (1986). Intercultural simulation games: Removing cultural blinders. *New Directions for Continuing Education, 30*, 71–81.

Friedkin, N. E. (2004). Social cohesion. *Annual Review of Sociology, 30*, 409–425.

Gallavan, N. P. (in press). *Navigating cultural competence.* Thousand Oaks, CA: Corwin Press.

Gallavan, N. P. (2007). Seven perceptions that influence novice teachers' efficacy and cultural competence. *Praxis: The Center for Multicultural Education, 2*(1), 6–22.

Gallavan, N. P., & Webster-Smith, (in press). Self-assessment: Analyzing reflectivity with candidates. In Association of Teacher Educators (Eds.) *The purposes, practices, and professionalism of teacher reflectivity: Insights for 21st century teachers and students.* Lanham, Maryland: Rowman & Littlefield.

Gay, G. (2000*). Culturally responsive teaching: Theory, research, & practice.* New York: Teachers College Press.

Harry, B. (2008, Spring). Collaboration with culturally and linguistically diverse families: Ideal versus reality. *Exceptional Children, 74*(3), 372–388.

Karim, A. (Sept/Oct 2003). A developmental progression model for intercultural consciousness: A leadership imperative. *Journal of Education for Business, 79*(1), 34–39.

Lincoln, Y. S., & Guba, E. G. (1985*). Naturalistic inquiry.* Beverly Hills, CA: Sage.

Marbley, A. F., Bonner, F. A., McKisick, S., Henfield, M. S., Watts, L. M., & Shin, Y-J. (2007). Interfacing cultural specific pedagogy with counseling: A proposed diversity training model for preparing preservice teachers for diverse learners. *Multicultural Education, 14*(3), 8–16.

Moll, L. C., Armanti, C., Neff, D., & Gonzalez, N. (1992). Funds of knowledge for teaching: Using a qualitative approach to connect homes and classrooms. *Theory into Practice, 31*(2), 132–141.

National Council for Accreditation of Teacher Education. (2008). *Professional standards for the accreditation of teacher preparation institutions.* Washington, DC: Author.

Pedersen, P. B. (2003). Multicultural training in schools as an expansion of the counselor's role. In P. B. Pedersen & J. C. Carey (Eds.), *Multicultural counseling in schools,* (pp. 190–210). Boston: Pearson Education.

Schön, D. A. (1987). Educating the reflective practitioner. Paper presented at the annual meeting of the American Educational Research Association. Washington, DC.

Shulman, L. S. (1987b). Knowledge and teaching: Foundations of the new reform. *Harvard Educational Review, 57*, 1-22.

Sleeter, C. (2009). Developing teacher epistemological sophistication about multicultural curriculum: A case study. *Action in Teacher Education, 31*, 1, 3–13.

Thiagarajan, S. (1984). BARNGA: *A flexim on cultural clashes.* Bloomington, IN: Instructional Alternatives.

Volkema, R., & Rivers, C. (2008, Jan/Feb). Negotiating on the Internet: Insights from a cross-cultural exercise. *Journal of Education for Business, 83*(3), 165–172.

Webster-Smith, A. (2008). Examining the role of diversity in school dynamics: An internship that helps to meet NCATE Standard 4. *International Journal of Educational Leadership Preparation.* http://cnx.org/content/m16317/latest/.

Webster-Smith, A. (2008). Roots and wings: A self examination of familial influences that ground diversity leadership and an assignment that lifts it. *International Journal of Educational Leadership Preparation.* http://cnx.org/content/m16315/1.1/.

Webster-Smith, A. (2008). Monitoring teacher knowledge, skills and dispositions for culturally responsive pedagogy: An internship experience that helps to meet NCATE Standard 4. *International Journal of Educational Leadership Preparation.* http://cnx.org/content/m16607/latest/.

Critical Thinking

1. What is Barnga?
2. How do the participants express their learning outcomes?
3. What are some of participants' discoveries related to their classrooms?
4. Why is cross-cultural simulation helpful for learning about people unlike yourself?

Create Central

www.mhhe.com/createcentral

Internet References

CARLA: Center for Advanced Learning on Language Acquisition
http://www.carla.umn.edu/culture/resources/exercises.html

Peace Corps: Cross-Cultural Simulations
http://wws.peacecorps.gov/wws/educators/lessonplans/section.cfm?sid=4

NANCY P. GALLAVAN, Ph.D, is a professor at the University of Central Arkansas in the Department of Teaching and Learning teaching performance-based assessment in the MAT program. An active member of Association of Teacher Education, the National Association of Multicultural Education, and the National Council for the Social Studies, Nancy has authored more than 100 publications. **ANGELA WEBSTER-SMITH**, Ph.D, is an assistant professor at the University of Central Arkansas in the Department of Leadership Studies teaching in the School Leadership Program working with public and open enrollment charter schools. Angela has taught in the United States and abroad; she is active in the National Council for Professors of Educational Administration.

Article

Prepared by: Nancy P. Gallavan, *University of Central Arkansas*

Re-centering Curriculum in the Urban Community: The Need for Participatory Democracy and Community-Based Curriculum

H. Prentice Baptiste and Emilie M. Camp

Learning Outcomes

After reading this article, you will be able to:

• Describe a democratic framework.

• Relate the impact of legislature during the terms of Presidents Johnson, Reagan, and G.W. Bush.

I've lost my home, my friends, and my school. I'm always on the verge of tears. But the worst part of it all is that the public officials—both elected and hired—who are supposed to be looking out for my education, have failed me even worse than the ones who abandoned me in the Superdome (Frazier, 2006, p. 32).

—María Hernandez, high school senior,
New Orleans, Louisiana.

Curriculum and Democracy: Economic Representation or Human Participation?

Curriculum development has been a point of contention in the United States for more than a century (Kliebard, 2004). The questions of *for whom* and *by whom* should curriculum be developed have been primary issues in the ongoing debate (Kliebard, 2004; Marshall, et al, 2000). Curriculum scholars have focused on a variety of issues specific to curriculum such as content, pedagogy, classroom management, vocational education, etc.

(Kliebard, 2004). In a more general sense, however, many curriculum workers have focused on democracy and its manifestations in education, and the role schools should play in fostering an ethic of democratic citizenship in students (Beyer, 1998; Dewey, 1916; Freire, 2003; Kliebard, 2004; Wood, 1998). However, mainstream conceptions of democracy often monopolize the discussion of the role of schools in the development of citizenship (Beyer, 1998; Wood, 1998). Wood (1998) describes the popular view of democracy as "protectionist" and "representative," asserting the current system of democracy fails to serve the interests of the citizenry by elevating elite political officials to the position of decision-maker, leaving the citizenry as mere spectators, powerless to effect change. Streck (2007) echoes this sentiment arguing, "citizens are just a mass of individuals who after being seduced to vote become invisible, excepting a small group who then become part of the circle of power" (p. 87). Thus, social change focused on social justice within this framework of democracy is difficult to achieve. Curriculum scholars lament over the infiltration of representative democracy into U.S. schools (Apple, 2004; Beyer, 1998; Wood, 1998). Suggested by the introductory quote by a New Orleans high school student, the uncritical acceptance of the "common sense" of representative democracy, has led to a U.S. education system that participates in the perpetuation of oppression of certain groups of people (Apple, 2004; Kumashiro, 2004). McLaren and Farahmandpur (2002) assert, "capitalist schooling participates in the production, distribution, and circulation of the knowledge and social skills necessary for reproducing the social division of labor, and hence, capitalist relations of exploitation" (p. 46). Consequently, schools function to reproduce the unjust economic and cultural stratification that benefits only a few privileged elites (Anyon, 1980; Apple, 2004). Additionally, protectionist democracy manifested in curriculum shapes the dispositions of students to become passive spectators and capitalist consumers rather than learning the importance of addressing other important social issues such as poverty, racial inequality, educational disparities, racism, etc. (Ladson-Billings, 2004; McLaren, 2006). Thus, education under this model serves the interests of capitalism rather than those of diverse student populations.

In contrast to a protectionist view of democracy which concentrates power in the hands of a few, participatory democracy extends power among all citizens and communities (Beyer, 1998; Rahman, 1994, 1991; Wood, 1998). Rahman (1994), in the spirit of a radical participatory democracy, distinguishes participatory from protectionist democracies by arguing for ". . .real *democracy,* not the democracy merely of periodic elections and the freedom to express words on what should be done, *but the freedom and opportunity of the people to take the initiative to do it themselves* [italics added] (p. 193). Conceived within curriculum development then, participatory democracy allows for citizen and community development of curriculum, placing the needs of the urban communities at the center, working simultaneously to solve local problems while instilling an understanding among students of their relationship to the larger national and global context (Spring, 2000).

Many scholars of curriculum and democracy (Beane & Apple, 1995; Freire, 2003; Spring, 2000; Wood, 1998) advocate for local needs and popular knowledge to drive curriculum development, instead of national economic interests. Proponents of radical participatory democracy subscribe to the belief that when community needs are met, individual needs are consequently met, pointing to the symbiotic relationship between the community and the individual (Rahman, 1994). Radical participatory democracy provides spaces for all people to use their voices and actions for the empowerment of the oppressed. The dialectical nature of participatory democracy leads to the mutually fulfilling work of community and the individual; each need naturally works to fulfill the needs of the other (Rahman, 1994). Haworth (2007) echoes this as he argues for a "democratizing" (p. 279) of public schools, asserting students and teachers are consequently transformed "through dialogical, reflective, and mutual action" (p. 279). Within this context then, curriculum can function to end the oppression of communities while simultaneously instilling an ethic of participatory democracy in students and community members.

The idea of community-driven curriculum, however, contrasts with current popular rhetoric on education. Is it possible for urban communities to develop curriculum focused on their own empowerment in the midst of an unprecedented federal interest and role in education with the passage of the No Child Left Behind Act? The authors in this article examine the struggle between grassroots curriculum development and national initiatives in education. As the former embraces participatory practices of democracy with the distribution of power among the people, the latter depends upon the concentration of power in the hands of elected representatives. Examples of urban community-driven curriculum are discussed in order to establish the abilities of urban communities to effect social change when power is taken by the people. Furthermore, the power of the highest elected representative in the U.S., the President, is examined within the context of educational policy, exploring the possibilities and/or constraints their power has had on

curriculum developed through participatory democratic community practices.

Re-Centering the Curriculum

Fregeau and Leier (2002) examine the implications of a graduate level education course, Teacher Envisioned Research and Reform Approach, or TERRA. The course, which focused on teachers' apprehension of the social injustices faced by the African American students they taught in rural Alabama, culminated in teacher proposals or implemented projects aimed at grassroots efforts to improve schooling for students experiencing social injustices. One particular project is highlighted by the authors. Working with parents as co-researchers, the graduate student/teacher learned that previously thought of student deficits were instead cultural differences between the students, families, and teachers. Working collaboratively, the school personnel and parents established a community center at the school, where at the time of publication, teachers and community members were actively collaborating on ways to improve the schooling experiences and education of the students. They were also dealing with hostilities within the community related to race and class. While early in its stages at the time of publication, this case reflects the potential to simultaneously address the needs of students and community in working to understand the needs and realities of all. Focusing on the realities of the students and community members reflects the potential benefits of working within a radical participatory democratic framework, as all voices are heard in the struggle to empower the community. As Spring contends, the use of thematic representations of lives can be powerful in reaching these understandings (2000, p. 106). Quite possibly, these representations could be utilized in the case of the aforementioned community center in order to develop curriculum related to student and community realities.

Two programs in California have experienced success in improving the education of Latino students as well as the lives of their parents (Delgado-Gaitan, 1993; Jasis & Ordóñez-Jasis, 2004/2005). Comité de Padres Latinos (Delgado-Gaitan, 1993) and La Familia Initiative (Jasis & Ordóñez-Jasis, 2004/2005) both are parent-initiated organizations, rooted in participatory democracy for electing leadership, and focused on mediating the cultural differences which were viewed by many teachers as deficits that interfered with student learning. Jasis and Ordóñez-Jasis use the word "convivencia" to describe the unique bonding that occurred between the parent-community in the San Francisco Bay area. "'Convivencia' refers to the flowing moments of collective creation and solidarity, the bonding that developed from a joint, emerging moral quest against the backdrop of experiential sharing" (p. 35). "Convivencia" is "the magic that took place when La Familia participants discovered together their power to change and improve their children's schooling" (p. 35).

While not explicitly stated as "convivencia" in the study on the Comité de Padres Latinos (COPLA) (Delgado-Gaitan, 1993), its essence is evident in the description of the community's experience. "They [COPLA members] confronted their enduring selves through continuity with their social history.

The Latino parents realized that they were whole and complete as they shared their life experiences with each other" (p. 408). The changes in school practices and willingness of the educators to collaborate with the communities to break down misconceptions of cultural differences echoes the belief of many that curriculum work should be focused on the interests and needs of humans as opposed to those of capitalistic institutions (Emery & Ohanian, 2004; Freire, 2003; Spring, 2000). Illustrated in the examples of the Comité de Padres Latinos and La Familia Initiative, curriculum can evolve into practices that aim for respecting and promoting the human rights of its citizens. In the case of these two organizations, that which initiated the community-driven curriculum reform was the parents' search for the "good life," which Spring (2000) believes is in part, the autonomy of each community to determine how they choose to participate in the wider world structures and economy.

While the previous examples demonstrate the collaboration of individual schools and communities, the following examples show what can be accomplished on a much larger scale. Gandin and Apple (2002) describe the Citizen School in Porto Alegre, Brazil. Based on radical participatory democracy, the long-term initiative (resulting from continued support of the Worker's Party) has led impoverished citizens "in an extensive pedagogic project involving their own empowerment" (p. 28). With the school system focused on liberating people from the oppressive conditions of rural poverty and the favelas (slums), it is managed by the people and students rather than by a centralized beauracratic power. Utilizing the students' personal histories as the foundation for curriculum, "official knowledge" is challenged and new, relevant epistemologies emerge. This approach to curriculum directly connects to Spring's calling for "thematic representations of life" (2000, p. 106). Gandin and Apple refer to it as "thematic complexes" (2002, p. 31). Regardless of its name, this approach is grounded in Freire's problem-posing pedagogy (2003) and reflects the importance of community engagement in recognizing one's oppression and acting to deconstruct oppressive structures.

The statistics Gandin and Apple (2002) present regarding decreased drop-out rates, increased enrollment, and increased numbers of schools, are staggering, highlighting Spring's contention that reaching for perfection may not lead to perfection, but can culminate in something close to it (2000). The Porto Alegre example shows the genuine possibilities in Spring's thinking. When schools are set up to place the human rights of its students and communities at the center of curriculum, enrollment can increase, drop-out rates can fall, and people are more inclined to radically participate in a democracy to uphold human rights.

Rossatto (2002) presents another Brazilian example: the social justice-focused school system of Sao Paulo. Begun during Paulo Freire's tenure as head secretary of education in Sao Paulo, the school system combines adult education with that of youth, placing Freire's problem-posing pedagogy (2003) at the center of curriculum. Like the Porto Alegre example, curriculum is defined around the lived experiences and oppression of the students and wider community. Through the collaborative workings of educators, students, parents, and community

members, citizens have gained a critical consciousness of their own realities, using their agency as democratic citizens to effect social change. Again, Spring's calling for education that leads to the "good life" is evident, for the citizens of Sao Paulo radically participate in the formation of a curriculum that centralizes their rights as human beings and leads to a better quality of life outside the schools.

In the aftermath of Hurricane Katrina, communities in the affected areas have struggled to rebuild, physically and emotionally (Frazier, 2006). New Orleans' schools have undergone tremendous hardships as students, teachers, and community members work to bring life back into surrounding neighborhoods. One successful curricular movement, Students at the Center (SAC), was established prior to the hurricane, and has been maintained since (Frazier, 2006). Although primarily conceived from within the school rather than the surrounding community, the centrality of the lived-experiences of students and the needs of their communities within the curriculum, demonstrates the possibilities of engaging students in challenging academic settings while concurrently making learning meaningful and relevant to each student. A SAC teacher relates this sentiment to student engagement:

> Ashanti [a SAC student] had no tolerance for assignments that appeared to her trivial or useless, like this test preparation material. However, she became one of the most dedicated and prolific memoir writers, continuing to work with me on hers even after school was out. . . . .(Frazier, 2006, p. 35).

The philosophy of SAC embraces the principles of radical participatory democracy, in part by listening to the survivors of the hurricane and its repercussions and using the stories as means for generating dialogue among students who then relate their own experiences of struggle through writing. "The voices of young people, of the poor and displaced, of those of us who work and live in New Orleans need to be at the center of dialogue about rebuilding the city" (Students at the Center After the Flood in New Orleans, n.d., p. 2). Student narratives, like that of María Hernandez, quoted at the beginning of the paper, reflect the need for this type of grassroots writing curriculum rather than the imposition of top-down policies. SAC clearly is a curricular movement rooted in the needs of the struggling community of New Orleans. With graduates of the program attending college, working as SAC staff, and beginning SAC initiatives in other cities to respond to the diaspora caused by the hurricane, SAC serves as a symbol of hope that community-driven curriculum is in fact empowering.

Given these curricular movements centered on community knowledge bases and experiences, common themes emerge. The communities identified an area or areas in need of improvement or change. Collaborating with institutional representatives (in this case, educators), the communities established their democratic authority, embedding participatory democracy within their work. Importantly, the educators understood themselves as facilitators and institutional resources rather than authoritative, vanguard experts. Above all, the communities' knowledge bases were central to each successful implementation.

As the above examples demonstrate, each community is unique, yet each example illustrates the commonalities of the various approaches to grassroots curriculum initiatives. Participatory democracy, use of institutional resources, and identification of problems to be addressed were all critical to the success of the highlighted examples. Therefore, are all critical to any such curricular transformation aimed for social justice.

Given these diverse examples of locally centered curriculum, it is evident that the public's investment and trust in their community to develop curriculum is vital to success. However, in an era of public misinformation regarding the quality of U.S. schools (Berliner & Biddle, 1995; Pinar, 2004), and the reliance on and acceptance of published numbers pertaining to standardized test performance by the general public speaks to the challenges of establishing community-based curricular initiatives. It also points to the tendency of the public to accept that for which elected representatives advocate regarding educational policies. The president of the United States has been one of those elected officials to which the public has looked for inciting educational change.

The U.S. Presidency and Education Policy

Three U.S. presidents have made their lasting marks on education, each in their own way, by holding three distinct philosophies on education and the federal government. President Johnson's passage of the Elementary and Secondary Education Act, President Reagan's lack of knowledge about the contents of the report *A Nation at Risk,* and the current President Bush's passage of the No Child Left Behind Act all highlight the tremendous power of the presidency in education affairs (Federal Education Programs, 1973; Guthrie & Springer, 2004; Lyndon Baines Johnson Library; Shaker & Heilman, 2004; Viteritti, 2004; Wong & Nicotera, 2004). How have these "events" in U.S. education policy history impacted the potential for democratic, grassroots development of curriculum?

President Lyndon B. Johnson: Advocate for Community Curriculum

"It means an educational system which does not simply equip the students to adjust to society, but which enables the student to challenge and to modify, and at times, reject, if necessary, the received wisdom of his elders" (Lyndon Baines Johnson Library). President Lyndon B. Johnson grew up in a poor rural community in Texas, and pursued a career in education (at least until entering politics) (Baptiste et al., 2007). While this quote is one of many from Johnson on education (Lyndon Baines Johnson Library), and it does not completely characterize his whole view of education, it does reflect his recognition of the need for continuous re-invention of American society; that America's democracy is not fixed, rather alive and fluid. He saw education as a means by which one learned to be a democratic participant, always in search of how to improve the system. Part of President Johnson's Great Society was a focus on education, particularly the education of the urban and rural

poor. Perhaps it was his own life experience living in poverty as a child that informed his Great Society (Baptiste, et al., 2007).

By passing the Elementary and Secondary Education Act (ESEA), Johnson sought to free children from poverty, allocating an unprecedented amount of money to school districts primarily in urban and rural communities (Baptiste et al., 2007; Viteritti, 2004). Johnson believed having equal educational opportunity was paramount to one's chances of being liberated from the oppression of poverty (Baptiste, et al., 2007; Federal Education Programs, 1973). Title I, the core component of ESEA, was flexible; funded directly to school districts, those in charge at the local/district level had discretion as to exactly how to use the money for improving the education of poor students (Federal Education Programs, 1973; Wong & Nicotera). Additionally, ESEA did not place requirements on Title I schools regarding curriculum, textbooks or personnel (Federal Education Programs, 1973), nor did it prescribe standardized testing to qualify for funding (Wong & Nicotera, 2004). In its original form, ESEA was quite simply an acknowledgement that urban and rural school children continued to be at a disadvantage educationally as a result of economic inequalities, and by providing additional resources, their chances of overcoming economic obstacles would greatly increase (Kozol, 1991; 2005).

Considering the framework of participatory democracy and its manifestations in curriculum, theoretically Johnson's ESEA allowed for the possibility of grassroots curriculum development. As ESEA, particularly Title I, was not prescriptive, it left the door open to opportunities for communities to conceive of curriculum that focused on how to liberate themselves from poverty. Johnson welcomed and wanted students to learn how to become active democratic citizens, to challenge the status quo, and become empowered participants/actors in the continuous shaping/re-shaping of American society.

> Most of all we need an education which will create an educated mind. This is a mind not simply a repository of information and skills, but a mind that is a source of creative skepticism, characterized by a willingness to challenge old convictions and to be challenged, a spaciousness of outlook, and convictions that are deeply held, but which new facts and new experiences can always modify (Lyndon Baines Johnson Library).

He saw schooling as the means for achieving this, as those who profess in the power of participatory democracy do as well (Beyer, 1998; Wood, 1998). Programs like those from California, Brazil, New Orleans, and Alabama, all in their distinctive identities, could have prospered under Johnson's initial passage of ESEA by utilizing the Title I resources in ways which directly benefited poor students and their communities; the decisions resting with the local communities rather than with the state or federal government.

Questions for further inquiry emerge; how did schools utilize Title I funds immediately following the passage of ESEA? Did the additional resources impact curriculum? Who made the decisions regarding how the resources were put to use? While it is beyond the scope of this article to answer these questions in depth, the fact that these questions are possible and to which the answers are potentially diverse, indicates the potential that existed under ESEA for communities to become active and authentic participants in the creation of empowering, democratic curriculum. President Johnson's respect for community autonomy and his understanding of the responsibility of the federal government to assist the communities without usurping their local control is quite evident in ESEA.

The Elementary and Secondary Education Act signified a significant expansion of the federal government's role in U.S. education (Baptiste, et al., 2007; Federal Education Programs, 1973). While the intent of Johnson seemed to leave educational authority with the local school districts, by the late 1970's, increased federal regulations over Title I funds and uses began to erode the local education agencies' authority over curriculum (Wong & Nicotera, 2004). The possibilities for grassroots developed curriculum, in theory, also eroded as a result of gradually shifting power.

Presidents Ronald Reagan and George W. Bush: Advocates for an Unworkable, "National Community Curriculum"

ESEA has remained in effect since its passage in 1965. However, it has evolved into something quite different than its original character with its renewal in 2001 as the No Child Left Behind Act (Federal Education Programs, 1973; Viteritti, 2004). The evolution of ESEA was marked with an immense shift of public perception of the U.S. education system during President Reagan's administration (Berliner & Biddle, 1995; Guthrie & Springer, 2004; Shaker & Heilman, 2004). The report *A Nation at Risk* (NAR) put out by the National Commission on Excellence in Education (COEE) in 1983 (Guthrie & Springer, 2004) would become the spark that caused a fire of public discontent with U.S. schools, as well as increased politicization of the entire educational system (Guthrie & Springer, 2004; Shaker & Heilman, 2004; Viteritti, 2004).

A Nation at Risk, relying on questionable data (Berliner & Biddle, 1995; Guthrie & Springer, 2004) reported that the U.S. educational system was "dysfunctional" (Guthrie & Springer, 2004, p. 8) and therefore largely responsible for the nation's economic misfortunes. The report supported the notion that schools were "threatening the nation's technological, military, and economic pre-eminence" (Guthrie & Springer, p. 8). "If an unfriendly foreign power had attempted to impose on America the mediocre educational performance that exists today, we might well have viewed it as an act of war" (National Commission on Excellence in Education, 1983). Written for the purpose of shocking the public (Viteritti, 2004), NAR was inherently political, although its politics did not reflect those of President Reagan. Despite Reagan's non-involvement in the report, the case can be made that he was the impetus for the massive public digestion of NAR.

President Reagan's ideas on the federal role in education differed significantly from those of Terrel Bell, his Secretary of Education (Guthrie & Springer, 2004). While Reagan sought to decrease the politicization of education, provide "vouchers and

tax subsidies" (Guthrie & Springer, 2004, p. 10) for students attending private schools, introduce prayer back into the classrooms, and ultimately dissolve the Department of Education, Secretary Bell created the COEE to publish a report in praise of America's public schools. With this, Bell hoped to gain support from the public and the president for the continuation of the Department of Education (Guthrie & Springer, 2004). However, the COEE instead produced the scathing report, citing a myriad of problems with U.S. schools, and fixing blame for much of the nation's problems on schools (Berliner & Biddle, 1995; Guthrie & Springer, 2004; National Commission on Excellence in Education, 1983). None of President Reagan's goals for education were included in NAR, but Reagan, who had not read the report, publicly praised the Commission for supporting vouchers, school prayer, and the termination of the Department of Education. This faux pas led to intense media attention on the report, bringing it to the forefront of the public's concern (Guthrie & Sprinter, 2004; Viteritti, 2004).

With much of the country suffering from the economic hardships that plagued the early 1980's, education became the scapegoat. A heightened politicization developed, with people increasingly looking to elected officials to "fix" the system (Guthrie & Springer, 2004). The dialogue surrounding education consequently became focused on how schools could best serve the national economic interests and global competitiveness (Berliner & Biddle, 1995; Guthrie & Springer, 2004; Wong & Nicotera, 2004). "They [the American public] even considered education more important than developing the best industrial system or the strongest military force, perhaps because they understood education *as the cornerstone of both* [italics added] (National Commission on Excellence in Education, 1973). Secretary Bell called for each state to develop higher standards for its schools, and placed political pressure on low-performing states by publicizing their "failures" (Berliner & Biddle, 1995; Viteritti, 2004). As the public watched, their trust in the current system declined, and they became inclined to support the institutionalization of standardized testing and accountability systems (Shaker & Heilman, 2004).

Although the calls to action of NAR did not immediately lead to reform, its "success" on shaping the public's perception of schools as being dysfunctional and culpable in the nation's declining global supremacy led to the common belief that the purpose of schooling should be economy-driven (Shaker & Heilman, 2004). NAR hovered over the national discourse on education during the presidencies of George H.W. Bush and Bill Clinton. Viteritti (2004) writes, "it is undeniable that NAR gave velocity to the standards movement" (p. 73). Both Bush and Clinton focused on forming a national agenda in education, attempting to place the country's global competitiveness at the forefront by enticing states to develop standards and subsequent measures of achievement (Viteritti, 2004). However, neither president would capitalize on NAR and its resulting public sentiment as successfully as President George W. Bush has with the No Child Left Behind Act.

"Here we have a Republican president engineering the most significant intrusion of federal power in the history of American education" (Viteritti, 2004, p. 80). The No Child Left Behind

Act, passed in 2001, is a massive extension of the federal government's role in education (Guthrie & Springer, 2004; Shaker & Heilman, 2004; Viteritti, 2004; Wong & Nicotera, 2004). Building on the foundation of NAR's calls for tougher standards and accountability, NCLB has transformed the rhetoric of NAR into national policy (Guthrie & Springer, 2004; Viteritti, 2004). NCLB, as a renewal of ESEA, is dramatically different from the 1965 version passed by President Johnson. While Johnson elected to allow local school districts decide how to best serve the educational needs of the poor with Title I money, President Bush, behind his rhetoric of advocating for educational equity, added restrictions to Title I schools.

Unlike Johnson, who believed curricular and instructional decisions were best left to the local communities/districts, President Bush has extended the reach of federal power into all schools receiving Title I money. While touting No Child Left Behind as allowing for more freedom and flexibility to local communities/school districts (U.S. Department of Education, n.d.b), President Bush has chosen to tightly regulate elements of curriculum in Title I schools. Despite the criticisms of many educators and curriculum scholars, NCLB requires Title I schools to implement phonics-based reading programs, claiming these programs are scientifically proven to work (U.S. Department of Education, n.d.a; Viteritti, 2004). Additionally, Title III now focuses specifically on the acquisition of English rather than on the development of bilingualism. Consequently, Title III funding no longer is contingent upon the implementation of proven to be effective bilingual education programs that support the development of two languages, but instead elects to only emphasize English acquisition (U.S. Department of Education, 2002).

The "centerpiece" (Viteritti, 2004, p. 77) of NCLB is the development and implementation of state standards and annual standardized tests. Each state, in order to receive federal funding, is required to establish "high standards" for content areas, specifically reading, science, and math. Little attention is given to the social studies, civics, physical education, or arts and humanities (Shaker & Heilman, 2004). Although the standards are developed by the individual states, they are evaluated by the National Assessment of Educational Progress (NAEP) (Viteritti, 2004). As each school receiving federal money must demonstrate "adequate yearly progress" (AYP) by the measurement of the NAEP, those who fail to meet AYP for two consecutive years can lose federal dollars, lose students to voucher programs, and lose control of the school to private management companies (Shaker & Heilman, 2004).

No Child Left Behind is the legacy of *A Nation at Risk*. It exploits the public mistrust of education that heightened after the publication of NAR, and links educational goals directly to economic goals and the global market, creating obstacles to locally-based curriculum. Grassroots, community-based curriculum development rooted in participatory democracy depends upon the active participation of the people. Unlike the 1965 version of ESEA, which kept the door open for this form of curriculum development, its renewed version, NCLB, likely inhibits the potential for such development. Requiring Title I schools to implement phonics-based reading programs ignores the professional judgment of teachers and local knowledge bases of the students to enrich literacy instruction.

In addition, the focus of Title III on English acquisition encourages states to implement English-only policies that can abolish proven effective bilingual education programs that embrace and celebrate local identities and biliteracy. "Citizens know intuitively what some of the best economists have shown in their research, that education is one of the chief engines of a society's *material* [italics added] well-being" (National Commission on Excellence in Education, 1983). The political, private, and economic influence and control over schools today (Emery & Ohanian, 2004) undercuts democratically created curriculum by focusing the goals of education on the expansion of capitalism rather than on the human needs of students (Freire, 2003). It is democratically created curriculum, though, that is necessary for the empowerment of oppressed communities (Beyer, 1998; Freire, 2003; Gandin & Apple, 2002; Rahman, 1994; Rossatto, 2002). NCLB, which directs financial *and* instructional policy towards "economic progress," silences the voices of those who are oppressed by the very nature of what the Bush administration (and others) consider as "economic progress." Spring (2000) posits that actions such as these are violations of the right of every human being to receive an education which encourages new ways of envisioning the nature of "economic progress." Participatory democracy within curriculum development implies curriculum for the people and by the people (Rahman, 1994). Since the publication of *A Nation at Risk*, however, the people of the United States have looked increasingly to elected officials to remedy the continued educational disparities between middle class whites, the poor and students of color (Guthrie & Springer, 2004). The dependency on elite representatives distracts citizens from their own responsibility to participate in the development of curriculum. The NCLB Act then, is fundamentally undemocratic. It potentially erases meaningful democratic considerations of curriculum with its manipulative language that plays on the "common sense" of many people (Shaker & Heilman, 2004). Scholars such as Apple (2004) and Kumashiro (2004) assert that our "common sense" must be challenged and scrutinized in order to uncover the hegemony that regulates mainstream ways of understanding the world.

How, then, do educators instill dispositions of problematizing "common sense" when NCLB exerts so much political and financial pressures on schools? How can the curriculum handed out by NCLB be taken back by the people when the "take back" goes against their "common sense?" We need a president, unlike Ronald Reagan or George W. Bush, who challenges the "common sense" approach to social policy; a president who is willing to concede some power and authority to the people so they may embrace the value and liberating potential of democratically derived curriculum.

Final Reflection: The need for Re-Centering the Curriculum

During the days just before and during Kentucky's state testing, walking through the halls in the school in which I taught*, I recall eerily silent halls and classrooms, stressed and frustrated

---

*The final reflection is based on the second author's experience in a public school

teachers, students lazily propping their heads up with hands smashed against cheeks, staring into space, and school-wide pep rallies cheering for students to get a good night's sleep, eat breakfast, and DO YOUR BEST ON THE TEST!!! The days were filled with constant reminders to students and teachers of the importance of the test, signifying the purpose for everyone's hard work throughout the year. The weary faces of students reflected the disconnect between state and federally-imposed regulations and the seemingly suppressed natural curiosity I have always admired in children.

A contrasting picture, however, emerges in memory during those two weeks of post-testing school days before the arrival of summer vacation. The school community, freed from thirty-eight weeks of testing constraints, transformed the environment into one where the elusive curiosity of the students surfaced. Walking through the halls during those days brought me the joy I have always cherished in my profession; students building contraptions for launching objects down the hall, armed with ordinary household objects, tape measures, and pencils and paper; students bringing worms for measuring to see who found the longest; teachers sitting on the front lawn with their students reading books or discussing ways students could help their neighborhood during the summer break; students wearing smiles. What will students remember when they leave school for the summer? The endless facts memorized for the state test, or discovering the contraption that cast the hackey-sack the farthest down the hall?

Students, teachers, parents, and community members *know* what meaningful curriculum looks like. All one needs to do is look at the faces of children as they work/learn/play at school. A United States president, with arguably the most power one single person has ever had, cannot *possibly* look at the faces of every child in America, cannot *possibly* know what is best for each child. Presidential policy regarding education must provide resources, but ultimately it must deliver those resources with the respect for individual and community autonomy, trusting in the power of empowered communities to uplift the nation from the crisis of its economic fixation and hegemony of representation.

References

Anyon, J. (1980). Social class and the hidden curriculum of work. *Journal of Education, 162*, 67–92.

Apple, M. (2004). *Ideology and curriculum*. RoutledgeFalmer. eBook.

Baptiste, H.P., Orvash-Kamenski, H. & Kamenski, C.J. (2007). Examining presidents Thomas Jefferson, Abraham Lincoln, and Lyndon B. Johnson. In H.P. Baptiste (Ed.), *The U.S. presidency and social justice: Implications for public education* (pp. 93–128). San Francisco: Caddo Gap Press.

Beane, J.A. & Apple, M.W. (1995). The case for democratic schools. In J.A. Beane & M.W. Apple (Eds.), *Democratic schools* (pp. 1–25). Alexandria, VA: ASCD.

Berliner, D.C. & Biddle, B.J. (1995). *The manufactured crisis: Myths, fraud, and the attack on America's public schools*. New York: Longman.

Beyer, L.E. (1998). Schooling for democracy: What kind? In L.E. Beyer & M.W. Apple (Eds.), *The curriculum: Problems, politics, and possibilities* (2nd ed., pp. 245–263). Albany: State University of New York Press.

Delgado-Gaitan, C. (1993). Researching change and changing the researcher. *Harvard Educational Review, 63*, 389–411.

Dewey, J. (1916). *Democracy and education*. New York: MacMillan.

Emery, K. & Ohanian, S. (2004). *Why is corporate America bashing our public schools?* Portsmouth: Heinemann.

Federal education programs, 1969–1972 legislative overview. (1973). *Congress and the nation, 1969–1973* (Vol. 3). Washington: CQ Press. Retrieved April 7, 2008 from CQ Electronic Library, CQ Public Affairs Collection https://catalog2.nmsu.edu:2273/cqpac/catn69-0008167387

Frazier, A. (2006). Narratives from Students at the Center. *High School Journal, 90*(2), 30–50.

Fregeau, L.A. & Leier, R.D. (2002). Praxis and teacher visions of socially just school reform. In J.J. Slater, S.M. Fain, & C.A. Rossatto (Eds.). *The Freirean legacy: Educating for social justice* (pp. 172–183). New York: Peter Lang.

Freire, P. (2003). *Pedagogy of the oppressed* (30th Anniversary ed.). New York: Continuum.

Gandin, L.A. & Apple, M.W. (2002). Can education challenge neo-liberalism? The Citizen School and the struggle for democracy in Porto Alegre, Brazil. *Social Justice 29*(4), 26–40.

Guthrie, J.W. & Springer, M.G. (2004). A Nation at Risk revisited: Did "wrong" reasoning result in "right" results? At what cost? *Peabody Journal of Education, 79*, 7–35.

Haworth, R. (2007). Why leadership is problematic: Resisting capitalist mimicry in the age of globalization and implications for public schools. In H.P. Baptiste (Ed.). *The U.S. presidency and social justice: Implications for public education* (pp. 267–281). San Francisco: Caddo Gap Press.

Jasis, P. & Ordóñez-Jasis, R. (2004/2005). Conviviencia to empowerment: Latino parent organizing at La Familia. *High School Journal, 88*(2), 32–42.

Kliebard, H. (2004). *The struggle for the American curriculum: 1893–1958* (3rd ed.). New York: RoutledgeFalmer.

Kozol, J. (1991). *Savage inequalities: Children in America's schools*. New York: Crown.

Kozol, J. (2005). *The shame of the nation: The restoration of apartheid schooling in America*. New York: Three Rivers Press.

Kumashiro, K.K. (2004). *Against common sense: Teaching and learning toward social justice*. New York: Routledge-Falmer.

Ladson-Billings, G. (2004). Culture versus citizenship: The challenge of racialized citizenship in the United States. In J.A. Banks (Ed.), *Diversity and citizenship education: A global perspective* (pp. 99–126). San Francisco: Jossey-Bass.

Lyndon Baines Johnson Library (n.d.). Remarks to the delegates to the White House conference on education, July 21, 1965. *LBJ for Kids! Quotations from Lyndon B. Johnson about Education*. Retrieved March 31, 2008 from www.lbjlib.utexas.edu/johnson/lbjforkids/edu_quotes.shtm

Marshall, J.D., Schubert, W.H., & Sears, J.T. (2000). *Turning points in curriculum: A contemporary American memoir*. Upper Saddle River, NJ: Merrill.

McLaren, P. (2006). Some reflections on critical pedagogy in the age of global empire. In C.A. Rossatto, R.L. Allen, & M. Pruyn (Eds.), *Reinventing critical pedagogy* (pp. 79–98). Lanham: Roman & Littlefield.

McLaren, P. & Farahmandpur, R. (2002). Freire, Marx, and the new imperialism: Toward a revolutionary praxis. In J.J. Slater, S.M. Fain, & C.A. Rossatto (Eds.), *The Freirean legacy: educating for social justice* (pp. 37–56). New York: Peter Lang.

National Commission on Excellence in Education (1983). *A nation at risk.* Retrieved April 16, 2008 from www.ed.gov/pubs/NatAtRisk/letter.html

Pinar, W.F. (2004). *What is curriculum theory?* Mahwah, NJ: Lawrence Erlbaum Associates Publishers.

Rahman, M.A. (1991). Glimpses of the "other Africa." In O. Fals-Borda & M.A. Rahman (Eds.), *Action and knowledge: Breaking the monopoly with participatory action research* (pp. 84–108). New York: The Apex Press.

Rahman, M.A. (1994). *People's self development: Perspectives on participatory action research; a journey through experience.* Dhaka, Bangladesh: The University Press Limited.

Rossatto, C.A. (2002). Critical pedagogy applied praxis: A Freirean interdisciplinary project and grassroot social movement. In J.J. Slater, S.M. Fain, & C.A. Rossatto (Eds.). *The Freirean legacy: Educating for social justice* (pp. 157–171). New York: Peter Lang.

Shaker, P. & Heilman, E.E. (2004). The new common sense of education: Advocacy research versus academic authority. *Teachers College Record, 106,* 1440–1470.

Spring, J. (2000). *The universal right to education: Justification, definition, and guidelines.* Mahwah, NJ: Lawrence Erlbaum.

Streck, D. (2007). The scale of participation: From municipal public budget to cities' conference. *International Journal of Action Research, 2,* 78–97.

Students at the Center After the Flood in New Orleans (n.d.). Retrieved April 1, 2008 from www.strom.clemson.edu/teams/literacy/sac/pubs/plans.pdf

U.S. Department of Education (n.d. a). Doing what works. Retrieved April 16, 2008 from www.ed.gov/nclb/methods/whatworks/edpicks.jhtml?src=In

U.S. Department of Education (n.d. b). Local control and flexibility. Retrieved April 16, 2008 from www.ed.gov/nclb/freedom/local/edpicks.jhtml?src=In

U.S. Department of Education (2002). No Child Left Behind. Retrieved April 16, 2008 from www.ed.gov/policy/elsec/leg/edpicks.jhtml?src=In

Viteritti, J.P. (2004). From excellence to equity: Observations on politics, history, and policy. *Peabody Journal of Education, 79,* 64–86.

Wong, K.K. & Nicotera, A.C. (2004). Educational quality and policy redesign: Reconsidering the *NAR* and federal Title I policy. *Peabody Journal of Education, 79,* 87–104.

Wood, G.H. (1998). Democracy and the curriculum. In L.E. Beyer & M.W. Apple (Eds.), *The Curriculum: Problems, politics, and possibilities* (pp. 177–198). Albany: State University of New York Press.

Critical Thinking

1. What was the legislative impact of President Lyndon B. Johnson?
2. What was the legislative impact of Ronald Reagan?
3. What was the legislative impact of George W. Bush?
4. What is a democratic framework?

Create Central

www.mhhe.com/createcentral

Internet References

UNESCO
http://unescostat.unesco.org
United States Government
www.firstgov.gov

H. Prentice Baptiste is Professor in the College of Education, New Mexico State University, Las Cruces. **Emilie Camp** is a doctoral student in the College of Education, New Mexico State University, Las Cruces. Baptiste@nmsu.edu, Emcamp@nmsu.edu.

Baptiste, H. Prentice; Camp, Emilie M. From *The National Journal of Urban Education & Practice,* vol. 11, 2008, pp. 312–323. Copyright © 2008 by the authors. Reprinted by permission.

Article   Prepared by: Nancy P. Gallavan, *University of Central Arkansas*

To Follow, Reject, or Flip the Script: Managing Instructional Tension in an Era of High-Stakes Accountability

JAMY STILLMAN AND LAUREN ANDERSON

Learning Outcomes

After reading this article, you will be able to:

- Discuss the tensions that exist between high-stakes accountability in schools with culturally competent pedagogy in teacher education programs.

- Propose one solution to this tension.

High-stakes accountability policies can and do influence language arts (LA) instruction (Achinstein & Ogawa, 2006; Coburn, 2001, 2005; Stillman, 2009, 2011). Recent accounts indicate that accountability pressures can lead educators to narrow the LA curriculum (Crosland & Gutiérrez, 2003; Valli & Buese, 2007), adopt reductive notions of what "counts" as reading (Pacheco, 2010a), abandon locally responsive curricula in favor of mandated, test-aligned LA programs (Mac-Gillivray, Ardell, Curwen, & Palma, 2004), and even engage in practices that oppose their professional understandings of and convictions about effective LA instruction (Dooley & Assaf, 2009; Valli & Chambliss, 2007). In tightly monitored "low-performing" schools, especially, research suggests that accountability policies can press teachers toward teacher-centered, skills-based LA instruction and away from student-centered approaches that balance skill instruction with the development of meaning-making competencies (Anagnostopoulos, 2003; McNeil, 2000).

As various scholars have noted, these trends are most prevalent, and arguably also most harmful, in schools serving youth from historically marginalized groups (Gándara, Rumberger, Maxwell-Jolly, & Callahan, 2003; Gutiérrez, 2006; McNeil & Valenzuela, 2001; Valenzuela, 2004). There, especially, they run the risk of exacerbating teachers' deficit ideologies (Pacheco, 2010b) and disadvantaging students by promoting fragmented, skills-based, and/or scripted instructional approaches that potentially increase the distance between their lived experiences, languages, and cultures and the LA curriculum (Brown & Ryoo, 2008; Gay, 2000; Gutiérrez, Baquedano-López, & Asato, 2000; Lee, 2007; Tharp & Gallimore, 1988).

For teacher educators, these risks raise critical questions: in particular, how can teacher education better prepare preservice teachers to design and deliver robust LA instruction—instruction that recognizes and builds upon students' cultural and linguistic resources (Gutiérrez, Baquedano-Lopez, & Asato, 2000) despite mandates to teach otherwise? In response, this article describes one preservice teacher's attempt to make a mandated reading program more responsive to the English Learners (ELs) in her second-grade student teaching placement. It then envisions how teacher educators might have better facilitated this preservice teacher's learning in relation to her teacher education program's vision of robust literacy instruction and in relation to contextual factors she encountered in the field.

Urgency and Authentic Purpose in Teacher Education

An emerging body of research describes skills and understandings teachers should have to teach responsively in the face of accountability-related pressures. These accounts detail teachers' efforts to integrate mandated programs' technical demands with instructional practices intended to serve ELs and other youth from historically marginalized groups (Cuban, 2008; Sleeter, 2005; Sleeter & Stillman, 2007). Some additionally consider teachers' explicitly political responses—for example, engaging in strategic negotiation with local administrators (Stillman, 2009, 2011) or resisting reforms on the basis of professional principles (Achinstein & Ogawa, 2006).

Still, we know relatively little about the roles that teacher educators play in facilitating learning among preservice teachers such that they emerge well-equipped to seize and create opportunities for responsive LA instruction. More specifically, we have little insight about whether and how teacher educators might ensure that student teaching placements—intended as spaces where preservice teachers begin *practicing* principled teaching—support preservice teachers in developing requisite knowledge about responsive LA instruction. Indeed, few studies capture evidence of the relationship between what teacher educators *do* with and for preservice teachers in the field and what preservice teachers subsequently *learn* about how to facilitate students' literacy learning (Brock, Moore, & Parks, 2007; Valencia, Martin, Place, & Grossman, 2009). This is the case despite evident awareness that accountability policies do indeed impact preservice teachers' opportunities to learn in K–12 placements (Anderson & Stillman, in press b; Lloyd, 2007; Margolis, 2006).

Study Context

The example of practice featured in this article was culled from data collected during a qualitative study of approximately 30 preservice teachers from two teacher education programs, both of which emphasize sociocultural perspectives on learning; press preservice teachers to explore issues related to educational equity, multiculturalism, language acquisition, and critical pedagogy; and situate student teaching placements in urban, high-needs schools. In the study, participants reflected on what they learned from student teaching and how student teaching experiences contributed to their successes and struggles as beginning teachers in similar contexts. Utilizing a grounded approach (Strauss & Corbin, 1990), we analyzed participant profiles, which were developed in consultation with participants' culminating master's projects, as well as transcripts of semi-structured, audio-taped interviews.

Similar to others who have documented pre-service teachers' experiences navigating between university-based and school-based teacher education (Grossman, Smagorinsky, & Valencia, 1999; Ritchie & Wilson, 1993; Smagorinsky, Cook, & Johnson, 2003), we found that participants struggled to reconcile discrepancies between the LA pedagogies advanced by their teacher education programs and those that prevailed in their "low-performing" placement schools. Most prominently, they struggled to make mandated content meaningful for and accessible to students, to determine which mandated program components to implement with fidelity and which to adapt or ignore, and to move beyond superficial "supplements" when attempting to make mandated programs more responsive to students. For example, participants often mentioned layering "realia" or "extra stories" on top of mandated programs in efforts to increase students' engagement and interest; their responses rarely revealed more sophisticated understandings of how to adapt or transform mandated curricula in order to facilitate more rigorous literacy learning (Anderson & Stillman, in press b).

Participants reflected on what they learned from student teaching and how student teaching experiences contributed to their successes and struggles as beginning teachers in similar contexts.

In light of these findings and so few examples detailing how teacher educators facilitate preservice teachers' learning about LA instruction in and for urban, high-needs schools, this article focuses on one recounted attempt by "Cristina," a student teacher in California, to make a mandated, phonics-based, English-only LA unit more responsive to the students in her placement. The article then uses this account as an opportunity to envision how teacher educators, like ourselves, might have more effectively facilitated Cristina's learning in light of both her teacher education program's espoused approach to literacy instruction and the contextual factors at play in her student teaching placement.

Teacher Education through the Lens of Cultural Historical Activity Theory

To guide our thinking, we draw on research that underscores the benefits of applying learning theory to the study of preservice teacher learning and the organization of teacher education. Smagorinsky et al. (2003) demonstrate how sociocultural learning theory can help teacher educators recognize the strengths and limitations of their programs—particularly in relation to field placements—and better anticipate and respond to preservice teachers' "twisting paths" of development (p. 1399). Similarly, others illustrate the affordances of social learning theory in supporting teacher educators to identify preservice teachers' zones of proximal development (Vygotsky, 1978) and to scaffold preservice teachers' learning in contextually sensitive ways (Johnson & Golombek, 2003; Zeichner, 2005).

Because we are most concerned with preservice teachers' learning in a particular kind of context, we frame our analysis using Cultural Historical Activity Theory (CHAT). Cole and Engeström (1997) explain that from a CHAT perspective, learning does not simply occur in one's head, but requires "additional cognitive resources . . . found in the sociocultural milieu" (p. 3). That is, learning takes place within consequential social, cultural, and historical contexts, where artifacts and rules mediate relations between subject and community, and participants negotiate the distribution of tasks, powers, and responsibilities. This collective, mediated, and contradiction-rife notion of learning—referred to as an "activity system"—provides an especially useful theoretical lens.

As we show in analyzing Cristina's account of her own practice, considering student teaching as an activity system can assist teacher educators and researchers to address the dynamism and complexity of preservice teachers' learning in and from student teaching. As a conceptual map, CHAT draws attention to the various people, norms, artifacts, and conditions that mediate preservice teachers' learning, and that of their students, in the field. Thus, it helps illuminate where, how, and why teacher educators might need to strategically *re*-mediate preservice teacher learning—that is, mediate preservice teachers' learning in ways that deliberately attend to the contextual factors that are themselves simultaneously (and consequentially) mediating preservice teachers' field-based learning. As the ensuing analysis indicates, such *re*-mediation may be necessary in order to ensure that preservice teachers learn to facilitate meaningful literacy learning among their students.

Learning and Struggling to Offer Responsive Literacy Instruction

As mentioned previously, Cristina was one of about 30 study participants, all of whom student taught in urban, high-needs public schools. Like others, Cristina recounted that student teaching had provided valuable opportunities to observe a more experienced teacher making use of a reading program that "going into [this district], you know you're going to have to teach." Like others, she also expressed concerns that the program—because of its fast pace, predetermined content and materials, English-only texts and vocabulary, and emphasis on teacher-centered, discrete skill instruction—was oftentimes inaccessible to her students. She additionally described watching her cooperating teacher implement some program components and "weed out" others, even as she wondered about his reasoning and what the program in its entirety would entail—information she believed would help her make instruction more responsive to students. Like others, she spoke of struggling with tensions between the "demands" of the job and the professional principles she aspired to enact.

> You're faced with all these demands, pacing, parents, teachers, . . . administration. You're pulled in many ways and you can't forget your goal, your program goals, your beliefs, what you want for the students. It's really hard to do all that together.

Concerning literacy instruction, Cristina juxtaposed administrators' expectations that she implement the mandated program with fidelity and her teacher education program's expectation—also her own—that she recognize students' "cultural wealth" and "use their knowledge to expand the curriculum."

Similar to others, Cristina described student teaching as a complex space that required a delicate balance of determination and deference regarding instruction, particularly in LA:

> It's not like I have the full command of the ship. You're kinda like in the back sort of saying, "Don't go here, go there!" But somebody else still calls the shots. . . . Now that doesn't mean that I have to submit to do whatever was in the [cooperating teacher's] classroom, but how can I marry my ways and the ways already set?

Thus, Cristina emerged from student teaching with a sense of agency and a commitment to finding common ground amidst competing demands. She emerged with some clarity about her teacher education program's goals and hopes concerning how she would take up those goals in her own literacy instruction—"not forgetting that these little bodies have so much they can offer, even in second grade and when you have assessments and pacing." Unfortunately, she emerged with less clarity about, "How do I make it work? . . . What's the first step?"

Despite uncertainties, Cristina's interview revealed several attempts to take "the first step" toward reconciling these tensions. Thus, while all participant interviews offered insight, Cristina's—and her response to one question in particular—stuck with us, cycling back into our consciousness and conversation over the following year. This response came when Cristina was asked to "describe a time in your student teaching where you were able to apply something that you had learned from your teacher education program." She described a mural strategy that was introduced in a university-based course and that she then implemented in her second-grade placement.

> It was during the [mandated reading program's] camouflage unit. . . . Since we were doing desert life and wildlife . . . I got three large pieces of butcher paper and cut it in half and said ok this side will be . . . a tropical rain forest [and] the other side was a desert. . . .

She then explicated the steps she took to engage students in constructing the mural and referenced evidence of their enthusiasm.

> I brought in groups, and I said ok on this side we're going to draw what you see in a tropical rain forest. . . . They started drawing trees and leaves. I had them sketch and then I had them trace. They loved it. . . . They'd be waiting for their turn. Then on the other side, we put the desert.

Next, Cristina recounted how students appropriated the mural as a space to communicate experiential and scientific knowledge, how she responded to students' revelations, and how the project culminated.

> On the second day, I started seeing them drawing crosses and rest in peace. I was like, rest in peace? I was really curious; why are they doing crosses and rest in peace? And at the same time, I was hearing in the news about immigration, how people were going through the desert, and they were dying and there was no water. . . . I started making sense of it and I asked them, "Why are you doing crosses here?" [I responded,] "Oh, for the people that are dying because they want to come over here." And I didn't want to stop it, but I didn't want to steer the direction and the focus of the mural. So I just let it be . . . and then they got really creative and started saying oh well a snake can be in both places. . . . So it was like they were really on their own and also culturally working together and all of that. . . . We [my cooperating teacher and I] talked about it very minutely.

When pressed for further detail about what preceded and followed this account, it became clear that Cristina's cooperating teacher had offered praise, but not constructive feedback or reflective coaching. Apart from the initial reference to the teacher education program course from which she drew the activity, Cristina mentioned no one who supported her to plan for, enact, or evaluate the instruction she provided or the learning she facilitated.

Factors Mediating Cristina's Student Teaching Experience

Conceiving of student teaching as an activity system helps illustrate contextual and cultural factors—and related discrepancies and tensions—mediating Cristina's learning in the field. In doing so, we identify Cristina as the learner or "subject" in Figure 2; we also identify student teaching's explicit general goal or "object" (drawn from the mission statement of Cristina's teacher education program) and more implicit literacy-specific goal or "object" (inferred by bringing this mission into conversation with Cristina's interview content): to enact robust LA instruction in ways that recognize and honor students' assets and interests, offer students multiple forms of participation, embed cultural relevance, encourage critical thinking, and reflect high academic and personal expectations.

Although Cristina's teacher education program aimed to prepare teachers to enact instructional approaches that aligned with the teacher education program's stated goal, this "object" was not necessarily shared by all "community" members in the activity system, nor readily enabled by established "rules"—whether advanced by the state (e.g., preservice teachers must practice teach for a certain number of hours), the school district (e.g., teachers must adhere to mandated programs and pacing plans), the teacher education program (e.g., student teachers must attempt to put teacher education program-espoused theories and pedagogies into practice), or permeating social interaction in the classroom (e.g., norms and routines for turn taking or collaborative grouping). For example, administrators who monitored classrooms at Cristina's placement school tended to be more concerned with teachers' fidelity to the mandated program, Open Court Reading, and ability to raise test scores, and less concerned with teachers activating students' prior knowledge, offering varied forms of participation, encouraging critical thinking, and/or enacting culturally responsive literacy instruction. Though Cristina's cooperating teacher offered space for Cristina to experiment with different approaches, he did not appear to know or understand the "object"—what Cristina's teacher education program expected her to learn—and/or did not view it as his responsibility to scaffold her learning in relation to that goal. These tensions were compounded by the fact that teacher education program faculty and school administrators did not always share similar ideas about how to treat students' prior knowledge, which did not necessarily reflect dominant notions of what primary grade learners tend to know and understand. Indeed, just addressing content raised by students could be seen as challenging more traditional notions of developmentally appropriate practice (Bredekamp & Copple, 1997).

This "common object problem" (Hakkarainen, 1999) was both a reflection of and reflected in multiple "artifacts"—including state standards, aligned standardized tests, and mandated curricula—and community members' differential uptake

of them. At the school level, pressure to teach the standards, raise test scores, and use with fidelity the mandated program impacted both what Cristina was expected to teach and what she observed on a daily basis. Although Cristina's cooperating teacher granted her some leeway to apply what she learned from her teacher education program, she was still required to use the mandated curriculum, which privileged externally determined content, whole-class and teacher-centered pedagogies, and discrete skill development. And because of the strict pacing calendar, Cristina explained she often found herself pressed to "cover" a lot of "official" material in a set amount of time. This left limited opportunity to uncover and build upon students' prior knowledge or native language capacities, engage them in critical thinking, or respond to needs as they emerged during instruction. In essence, Cristina's placement appeared oriented mostly toward the goal of implementing mandated programs with fidelity, rather than utilizing programs as tools to facilitate learning—tools that would necessarily be used differently contingent upon students' needs and variations in context and culture across communities, schools, and classrooms.

Another tension pertains to the "division of labor"—who does what, when, and how—during student teaching. That the feedback Cristina received on the mural included only vague encouragement from her cooperating teacher, with whom she "talked about it very minutely," has consequences for the depth and durability of her learning. It also raises questions about teacher education program resource constraints and allocations, and prompts consideration of how teacher education programs might better support cooperating teachers as teacher educators. While many teacher education programs continually grapple—and rightfully so—with that very issue, we opt to focus here instead on the role of university-based teacher educators—faculty and/or field supervisors—in helping re-mediate Cristina's learning so that she might emerge from student teaching better equipped to manage instructional tensions like those that prevailed in her placement (and in her own second-grade classroom the following year). We focus on these tensions because Cristina's account and prior research suggest they generate particularly acute challenges in urban, high-needs schools, and that preservice teachers and beginning teachers—despite some research suggesting otherwise (Lloyd, 2007)—struggle to reconcile these tensions (Barrett, 2009) without strategic guidance from more experienced others, who can help them envision both "what's principled" and "what's possible" (Crosland & Gutiérrez, 2003 cited in Anderson & Stillman, 2010, p. 237).

At the school level, pressure to teach the standards, raise test scores, and use with fidelity the mandated program impacted both what Cristina was expected to teach and what she observed on a daily basis.

With its emphasis on learning, an activity system lens serves as a reminder that teacher educators' ability to assist preservice teachers like Cristina rests on the clarity of teacher educators' goals for preservice teachers as learners and for student teaching as activity meant to facilitate that learning. Given literacy scholars' emphasis on the need for thoughtfully adaptive teachers (Duffy, 2005; Duffy & Hoffman, 1999), we maintain preservice teachers must develop capacities that enable them to generate sophisticated critiques of mandated curricula *as tools* (i.e., things that potentially facilitate and/or impede robust learning), rather than less nuanced but more common views of mandated curricula as either worthy or unworthy goals unto themselves (i.e., things to implement with fidelity or reject out-right). In turn, we emphasize the need for teacher educators, ourselves included, to support preservice teachers to make meaning of and with tools, including those they are required to use—that is, to assess the value of various tools, to determine where, when, and how tools (or their component pieces) might be of use in relation to robust literacy goals, and to discern how best to supplement, adapt, transform, and create tools in accordance with students' needs and features of the local context.

Envisioning *Re*-mediation

This subtle, but fundamental, shift from viewing (and dismissing) mandated curricula as *goals,* to critiquing and adapting or transforming curricula as tools takes on added importance given the employment vulnerability of beginning teachers (who face potential sanctions, including job loss, should they fail to demonstrate use of required tools) and the need to retain highly-qualified and committed teachers in urban, high-needs schools (NCTAF, 2003). In turn, it leads us to ask—again drawing on CHAT—what it *would* look like to *re*-mediate Cristina's learning in relation to the mandated reading program she was expected to teach, the mural she and her students generated, the local ecology at her placement site, and the notions of robust literacy instruction advanced by her teacher education program. This question is the one to which we now respond.

We would begin, for example, by encouraging Cristina to acknowledge the assets for learning already present in her instruction—namely students' mural contributions, which made transparent students' prior knowledge, learning preferences, information processing, and personal concerns and interests. This is important because it would allow us to acknowledge additional accomplishments: Cristina's courage, evident as she experimented in ways that converged with her teacher education program's goals and diverged from dominant modes of practice in her placement; her creation of an unscripted space for meaning making through joint productive activity (e.g., Rogoff, 1990); and her construction of an artifact (i.e., the mural) within which she could have situated meaningful, content-rich literacy instruction. In such conversation, it would likewise be important to press Cristina to identify and analyze the various and potentially conflicting literacy goals advanced by her teacher education program, the state's English Language Arts (ELA) standards, and the mandated reading program.

The development of an integrated social studies unit could serve as one forum for addressing these goals in concert. In addition to building upon Cristina's accomplishments, unit development would present an opportunity for Cristina to foster authentic literacy learning (Ogle & McMahon, 2003) and provide instruction that responds to students, state mandates, and local expectations. It would also allow teacher educators, like ourselves, to support Cristina to do the following:

- embed literacy learning in culturally relevant content (Au, 2001);

- balance opportunities to develop literacy skills (e.g., phonics; word study/analysis) with meaning-making and communicative capacities (e.g., comprehension, analysis) (Au, 2003; Pearson & Raphael, 1999);

- scaffold students' understandings and production of academic language in more specific ways (Brown & Ryoo, 2008; Lee, 2007); and

- provide unscripted spaces where students can make meaning on their own terms and draw more openly on their full linguistic toolkits (Gutiérrez et al., 2000; Souto-Manning, 2010).

Thus, we could take advantage of the mural as a concrete artifact around which to brainstorm ideas about what content such a unit might cover and what forms it might take (Souto-Manning & James, 2008). By starting from the mural, we could support Cristina to recognize the *occasion* she presented for learning and the knowledge that occasion revealed, while also pressing her to consider how she might leverage that knowledge in the service of more rigorous literacy goals. In that sense, creating an integrated unit could serve as a means for scaffolding Cristina's learning, starting from what she knows and can do, while also modeling for Cristina how to do the same for her students, starting from what she has learned about what *they* know and can do.

In the subsequent sections, we describe what this unit development might involve and what teacher educators might do to ensure that this occasion *for* preservice teacher learning and others like it are indeed generative *of* learning. Specifically, we describe how we might work with Cristina to embed in the integrated unit "robust" literacy practices—practices that "mediate . . . or assist learning in a variety of ways; utilize . . . [students'] social, cultural, and linguistic resources; regard diversity and difference as resources for learning; and define learning rather than teaching as the targeted goal" (Gutiérrez et al., 2000, p. 13). We then discuss how we might assist Cristina to develop a "most robust" version of the unit—an approximation of what's most principled, what's worth aiming for—then assist her through calibration exercises to consider what's possible and what forms this unit might take at different times and under different ecological conditions. This approach reflects our commitment to advancing educational equity in urban, high-needs schools, while also taking seriously the perspectives and vulnerabilities of our preservice teachers and beginning teachers and acknowledging the very real "dilemmas" they must manage in an era of accountability (Lampert, 1985).

> *Certainly, standards and prescribed curricula are not neutral, nor without flaw; like others, we look critically upon artifacts intended to standardize knowledge or practice.*

Anchoring with Content

Given students' contributions to the mural, we would press Cristina to identify what they appear to understand (e.g., "people dying"; "a snake can be in both places"; etc.) about the content in question (e.g., the desert) and explore potential connections between students' knowledge, the study of camouflage, and California's content standards. Certainly, standards and prescribed curricula are not neutral, nor without flaw; like others, we look critically upon artifacts intended to standardize knowledge or practice (Genishi & Dyson, 2009; Sleeter & Stillman, 2005). Therefore, we would suggest that neither standards nor prescribed curricula drive Cristina's instruction.

However, we do see power in using standards and prescribed curricula as mediating *tools* (not goals) and guides (not rules); thus, we would introduce them accordingly. Specifically, we would invite Cristina to bring them into conversation with teacher-education-program–espoused philosophies and pedagogies—identifying goal convergence and divergence, analyzing respective affordances and constraints, and considering how to take advantage of or create resonance across goals and tools. For example, we might discuss with Cristina the potential connections between students' mural contributions and specific standards, such as Social Science Standard 2.1: "students trace the history of their own families . . . and compare their own daily lives with those of their parents and other family members," or Standards 2.2 and 2.3, with their emphasis on "how the U.S. and other countries make laws, carry out laws, determine whether laws have been violated, and punish wrongdoers" and how "groups and nations interact with one another to try to resolve problems in such areas as trade, cultural contracts, treaties, etc." This kind of scaffolded analysis would support Cristina to develop an integrated unit of study (e.g., a unit on immigration) and to better articulate learning goals for students that would ideally reflect grade-level expectations, account for mandated curricula, and privilege students' prior knowledge.

Contextualizing Literacy Instruction

After working with Cristina to articulate subject matter goals, we would support her to explore possibilities for contextualized literacy instruction that could advance students' authentic literacy learning and the goals laid out in California's ELA standards and the mandated reading program, *Open Court Reading* (OCR). OCR suggests that second graders develop the following (E/LA standards-aligned) capacities, as they complete the *Look Again* ("camouflage") unit:

- learn to read;
- develop vocabulary related to conceptually challenging sections of text;
- use a variety of comprehension strategies and skills;
- read, speak, and write about camouflage-related topics; and
- learn about conducting book research (using expository text).

The ELA standards additionally encourage teachers to engage students in literary analysis. In light of Cristina's concerns that OCR was oftentimes inaccessible to her students, we would work with her to figure out how she might draw on her teacher-education-program–acquired knowledge to meet and extend, rather than reject altogether, OCR's recommendations. Likewise, we would explore possibilities for addressing OCR's emphasis on reading (over writing) and the program's tenuous links to subject matter. We might, for example, encourage Cristina to carve out time within the unit to engage students in authentic writing, using a structure such as Writers Workshop—one of the instructional strategies introduced to her by her teacher education program. These more discrete goals, at least in part, grow out of our concerns that overemphasis on decontextualized skill instruction in early grades can discourage, even impede, students' access to upper-grade literacy instruction, which generally relies on students already knowing how to write and read for meaningful purposes (Au, 2003).

Ideally, an integrated unit would support students to develop higher levels of literacy through exploration of meaningful content and to draw upon their literacy capacities as they deepen and expand their content understandings. For example, we might encourage Cristina to design learning experiences that would provide students with opportunities to research and document their families' or community members' immigration experiences. Here, we can imagine students collaboratively crafting and using interview protocols to capture key aspects of immigration experiences; in the process, they would have multiple, authentic opportunities to read (e.g., as they conduct interviews and share interviewees' stories), write (e.g., as they create protocols and document stories), and speak (e.g., as they conduct interviews and use text from interviews to engage in discussion) about locally relevant content. Students might additionally draw on what they learn from interviews to write narrative accounts of local immigrants' journeys (E/LA WS 2.1), thereby augmenting the OCR curriculum with meaningful writing instruction that captures voices from the community (Souto-Manning, 2009).

Ideally, an integrated unit would support students to develop higher levels of literacy through exploration of meaningful content and to draw upon their literacy capacities as they deepen and expand their content understandings.

We might also press Cristina to select various narrative texts that reflect diversity across immigrants' experiences and could be made available for multiple uses (e.g., Read-Aloud; Guided Reading; Shared Reading; Literature Study). Cristina might then be able to engage students in literary analysis (ELA RS 3.1; 3.3) and scaffold their development of the reading comprehension strategies (i.e., asking questions, making predictions, monitoring and clarifying, summarizing, and making connections) and word study skills (i.e., knowledge of phonics, dipthongs, prefixes and suffixes, and closed and open syllables) delineated in *Open Court Reading* and the standards (ELA RS 1.1; 1.2; 1.6; 2.2–2.5), while contextualizing in meaningful content.

As the unit facilitated deep understanding of immigration as a topic with human, historical, social, cultural, legal-political, and economic dimensions, we would encourage Cristina to leverage students' burgeoning knowledge to build academic vocabulary about now-familiar topics (e.g., discrimination, survival), which might then serve as the foundation for students' reading of expository texts. Time permitting, we can imagine how, with appropriate scaffolding, students might eventually produce expository essays comparing experiences of different immigrant groups in ways that draw on language and content previously developed through interviews and through reading related narrative and expository texts.

Re-mediating *Open Court Reading*

There are numerous ways that we might then support Cristina to draw connections between an immigration unit and OCR's *Look Again* content. Students' prior understandings and unit-based explorations of immigrants' journeys—particularly undocumented immigrants' journeys—would support students to construct culturally relevant understandings of human camouflage that could then be applied to the study of animal camouflage raised in OCR's reading selections. In fact, the OCR *Teacher's Edition* makes similar suggestions (e.g., have students "compare animal to human camouflage"), but fails to explain how teachers might do this or how such an exercise would work as more than a stand-alone activity.

In many ways, Cristina's mural project—though itself a stand-alone activity—had already done much to integrate some of the mandated program's discrete suggestions (e.g., activate relevant background knowledge, make a science connection, compare animal to human camouflage) in ways that could potentially build robust, interdisciplinary

understandings of camouflage. Indeed, the curriculum integration we describe would likely make students' interactions with OCR texts more meaningful and accessible (i.e., help students to understand the urgency associated with hiding for the purpose of survival)—features that are critical to students' literacy development.

We would additionally press Cristina to draw on literacy skills and strategies developed through the immigration unit. We can, for example, imagine supporting Cristina to consider how she might reinforce literary analysis as well as comprehension skills and strategies developed through the immigration unit as students read OCR texts about camouflage. She would likely also be well-positioned to help students make connections between their everyday language/knowledge (e.g., hiding), relevant experiential knowledge (e.g., a family member's military fatigues), and their academic language/ knowledge (e.g., camouflage) (Brown & Ryoo, 2008), thereby providing ELs with the scaffolding they might need to meet OCR's goal to "develop vocabulary related to conceptually challenging selections of text."

Cristina might also note possibilities for helping students understand the "elements authors use as they write expository prose" (a phrase used in the teachers' manual) by exploring connections between the features of their own expository writing about immigrants' experiences and those of OCR's expository texts. Finally, since students would have had some contextualized opportunities to strengthen word study skills, Cristina could draw explicitly on these experiences as students complete mandated OCR worksheets and tests aimed at assessing these capacities. In other words, Cristina might be able to leverage contextualized instruction (and its outcomes) to help students demonstrate knowledge on state-sanctioned artifacts (e.g., mandated program materials), since these often share properties (e.g., multiple choice questioning) with gate-keeping assessments.

If Cristina were supported to see the possibilities for facilitating deeper student learning in relation to the camouflage unit, we suspect this would support her to also see possibilities for deepening student learning across other mandated units. Indeed, Cristina voiced a strong critique (one we share) of OCR's fragmentation and lack of apparent or explicit resonance across units—Sharing Stories, Kindness, Look Again (aka, "The Camouflage Unit"), Fossils, Courage, and Our Country & Its People—all of which could be more meaningfully tied to the mural project (and the integrated unit it inspired) than they could be easily tied to one another in sequential order.

Nonetheless, we realize that developing and implementing such a unit while student teaching—particularly in a tightly monitored placement—might be untenable for various reasons. Still, the value of the curriculum development process holds if coupled with critical conversations that press pre-service teachers like Cristina to consider how one might have to adapt such a unit in order to "manage the dilemma" of privileging students' knowledge and principles of learning while maintaining employment and preparing historically marginalized students for the gatekeepers they are sure to face (Lampert, 1985).

Conclusion

Cristina's account suggests that she was able to generate a rich *occasion* for learning, but was less equipped to facilitate learning in relation to robust literacy goals. Consequently, what could have been dynamic formative assessment; fodder for further curriculum adaptation, integration, or creation; and/or the springboard for culturally relevant skill and concept development ultimately served as a standalone repository. Cristina's account also reveals insufficient *re*-mediation on the part of teacher educators charged to support her as a learner. By focusing on how we might have *re*-mediated her learning, we aim to take ownership of Cristina's instructional inadequacies in accordance with our view that those inadequacies are more a reflection of teacher education program structures, teacher educator practices, and local ecologies than they are attributable to the failures of individual preservice teachers—especially ones as committed and generous of spirit as we know Cristina to be.

Indeed, Cristina's struggle to reconcile her teacher education program learnings with the norms and practices she encountered in the field are not surprising, considering her position along the learning-to-teach continuum (Feiman-Nemser, 2001) and research suggesting that such struggles often ensue when preservice teachers navigate discrepancies between teacher education program expectations and student teaching realities (Anderson & Stillman, 2010, in press a; Smagorinsky, Cook, Jackson, Moore, & Fry, 2004; Smagorinsky, et al., 2003; Zeichner, 2005). Given the increasingly prevalent impact of high-stakes accountability on LA instruction, our own preservice teachers face new and potentially even wider discrepancies, especially when they student teach in high-needs schools, where manifestations of the policy context often stand in stark contrast to teacher-education-program–espoused theories and practices (Anderson & Stillman, 2010, in press a; Margolis, 2006; Valencia et al., 2009). Likewise, they stand to face these discrepancies in their future workplaces and to face them most acutely if they follow through on their commitments and our call for them to serve where they are most needed.

Given our claim of preparing highly qualified educators for such contexts, we feel an immense sense of urgency and an ethical responsibility to maximize preservice teachers' learning in light of and for such discrepancies. We realize this may require structural adjustments and resource allocations that address university-based teacher educators' limited direct access to preservice teachers' practice teaching. Indeed, we likely miss too many opportunities for meaningful (and perhaps even essential) *re*-mediation; likewise, we likely miss many opportunities to better understand placements' realities, thereby limiting our capacity to *re*-mediate preservice teachers' field- *and* course-based learning accordingly. Keeping in mind our difficulties in garnering resources to enable more frequent field visits, Cristina's account suggests the need for creative (and cost-effective) mechanisms (e.g., journals, multimedia portfolios, online forums) that enable student teachers to share more frequent detailed accounts with teacher education program faculty and/or to participate in innovative structures (e.g., paired student teaching) that allow for more frequent direct access.

But it is likely not just teacher education program mechanisms and structures that need adjustment; no doubt our practices do as well. That the most robust form of the integrated curriculum unit, as conceived above, might be impossible for a new teacher to implement within a tightly monitored school is precisely the point. Keeping that in mind, we must ask ourselves where, if not in teacher education, can we be certain our preservice teachers will develop the capacity to envision what's principled and the will and skill to work toward making possible approximations of that ideal practice in the context of their own classrooms? And where, if not in teacher education, can we be certain they will have access to conversations that intend to help them develop the political savvy necessary for balancing what is principled with what is permissible, possible, wise, and humane? Drawing again on CHAT, we argue for the critical importance of orienting preservice teachers toward principled "horizons"—"objects" offering direction, even if "never fully reached or conquered" (Engeström, 1999, p. 380). Such horizons, we believe, can anchor teachers as they manage tensions, potentially preventing them from getting lost in the "sea" of competing demands and pressures (Kauffman, Johnson, Kardos, Liu, & Peske, 2002).

References

Achinstein, B., & Ogawa, R. (2006). (In)fidelity: What the resistance of new teachers reveals about professional principles and prescriptive educational policies. *Harvard Educational Review, 76*, 30–63.

Anagnostopoulos, D. (2003). The new accountability, student failure, and teachers' work in urban high schools. *Educational Policy, 17*, 291–316.

Anderson, L., & Stillman, J. (in press a). Student teaching for a specialized knowledge base?: Opportunities to teach and learn in and for urban high-needs schools. *Journal of Teacher Education.*

Anderson, L., & Stillman, J. (in press b). Making learning the object: Using cultural, historical activity theory to analyze and organize preservice field placements in urban high-needs schools. *Teachers College Record.*

Anderson, L., & Stillman, J. (2010). Opportunities to teach and learn in urban, high-needs schools: Student teachers' experiences in urban placements. *Urban Education, 45*, 1–33.

Au, K. H. (2001). Culturally responsive instruction as a dimension of new literacies. *Reading Online, 5*(1). Available from http://www.readingonline.org/newliteracies.

Au, K. H. (2003). Balanced literacy instruction: Implications for students of diverse backgrounds. In J. Flood, D. Lapp, J. R. Squire, & J. M. Jensen (Eds.), *Handbook of research on teaching the English language arts* (2nd ed.) (pp. 955–966). Mahwah, NJ: Lawrence Erlbaum.

Barrett, B. D. (2009). No Child Left Behind and the assault on teachers' professional practices. *Teaching and Teacher Education, 25*, 1018–1025.

Bredekamp, S., & Copple, C. (1997). *Developmentally appropriate practice in early childhood programs* (rev. ed.). Washington, DC: National Association for the Education of Young Children.

Brock, C. H., Moore, D. K., & Parks, L. (2007). Exploring preservice teachers' literacy practices with children from diverse backgrounds: Implications for teacher educators. *Teaching and Teacher Education, 23,* 898–915.

Brown, B., & Ryoo, K. (2008). Teaching science as a language: A "content-first" approach to science teaching. *Journal of Research in Science Teaching, 45,* 525–664.

Coburn, C. E. (2001). Collective sensemaking about reading: How teachers mediated reading policy in their professional communities. *Educational Evaluation and Policy Analysis, 23,* 145–170.

Coburn, C. E. (2005). Shaping teacher sensemaking: School leaders and the enactment of reading policy. *Educational Policy, 19,* 476–509.

Cole, M., & Engeström, Y. (1997). A cultural-historical approach to distributed cognition. In G. Salomon (Ed.), *Distributed cognitions: Psychological and educational considerations* (pp. 1–46). New York: Cambridge University Press.

Crosland, K., & Gutiérrez, K. (2003). Standardizing teaching, standardizing teachers: Educational reform and the deprofessionalization of teachers in an English-only era. *Educators for Urban Minorities, 2*(2), 24–40.

Cuban, L. (2008). *Hugging the middle: How teachers teach in an era of testing and accountability.* New York: Teachers College Press.

Dooley, C. M., & Assaf, L. C. (2009). Contexts matter: Two teachers' language arts instruction in this high-stakes era. *Journal of Literacy Research, 41,* 354–391.

Duffy, G. G. (2005). Developing metacognitive teachers: Visioning and the expert's changing role in teacher education and professional development. In S. Israel, C. Block, K. Bauserman, & K. Kinnucan-Welch (Eds.), *Metacognition in literacy learning: Theory, assessment, instruction, and professional development* (pp. 299–314). Mahwah, NJ: Lawrence Erlbaum.

Duffy, G. G., & Hoffman, J. V. (1999). In pursuit of an illusion: The flawed search for a perfect method. *The Reading Teacher, 53,* 10–16.

Engeström, Y. (1999). Innovative learning in work teams: Analyzing cycles of knowledge creation in practice. In Y. Engeström, R. Miettinen, & R. L. Punamäki (Eds.), *Perspectives on activity theory* (pp. 377–404). New York: Cambridge University Press.

Feiman-Nemser, S. (2001). From preparation to practice: Designing a continuum to strengthen and sustain teaching. *Teachers College Record, 103,* 1013–1055.

Gándara, P., Rumberger, R., Maxwell-Jolly, J., & Callahan, R. (2003). English learners in California schools: Unequal resources, unequal outcomes. *Education Policy Analysis Archives, 11*(36). Available at http://www.usc.edu/dept/education/CMMR/FullText/ELLs_ in_California_Schools.pdf.

Gay, G. (2000). *Culturally responsive teaching.* New York: Teachers College Press.

Geneshi, C., & Dyson, A. H. (2009). *Children, language and literacy: Diverse learners in diverse times.* New York: Teachers College Press.

Grossman, P. L., Smagorinsky, P., & Valencia, S. (1999). Appropriating tools for teaching English: A theoretical framework for research on learning to teach. *American Journal of Education, 108,* 1–29.

Gutiérrez, K. (2006). White innocence: A framework and methodology for rethinking educational discourse. *International Journal of Learning, 12,* 1–11.

Gutiérrez, K., Baquedano-López, P., & Asato, J. (2000). English for the children: The new literacy of the old world order. *Bilingual Research Journal, 24,* 87–105.

Hakkarainen, P. (1999). Play and motivation. In Y. Engeström, R. Miettinen, & R. L. Punamäki (Eds.), *Perspectives on activity theory* (pp. 231–249). New York: Cambridge University Press.

Johnson, K. E., & Golombek, P. R. (2003). "Seeing" teacher learning. *TESOL Quarterly, 37,* 729–737.

Kauffman, D., Johnson, S. M., Kardos, S. M., Liu, E., & Peske, H. G. (2002). Lost at sea: New teachers' experiences with curriculum and assessment. *Teachers College Record, 104,* 273–300.

Lampert, M. (1985). How do teachers manage to teach?: Perspectives on problems in practice. *Harvard Education Review, 55,* 178–194.

Lee, C. (2007). *Culture, literacy and learning: Taking bloom in the midst of the whirlwind.* New York: Teachers College Press.

Lloyd, G. M. (2007). Strategic compromise: A student teacher's design of kindergarten mathematics instruction in a high-stakes testing climate. *Journal of Teacher Education, 58,* 328–347.

MacGillivray, L., Ardell, A. L., Curwen, M. S., & Palma, J. (2004). Colonized teachers: Examining the implementation of a scripted reading program. *Teaching Education, 15,* 131–144.

Margolis, J. (2006). New teachers, high-stakes diversity, and the performance-based conundrum. *The Urban Review, 38,* 27–44.

McNeil, L. (2000). *Contradictions of school reform.* New York: Routledge.

McNeil, L., & Valenzuela, A. (2001). The harmful impact of the TAAS system of testing in Texas: Beneath the accountability rhetoric. In M. Kornhaber & G. Orfield (Eds.), *Raising standards or raising barriers? Inequality and high-stakes testing in public education* (pp. 127–150). New York: The Century Foundation.

NCTAF. (2003). *No dream denied: A pledge to America's children.* Washington DC: National Commission on Teaching and America's Future. Retrieved from http://www.nctaf.org/documents/no-dream-denied_ summary_report.pdf.

Ogle, D. M., & McMahon, S. I. (2003). Curriculum integration to promote literate thinking: Dilemmas and possibilities. In J. Flood, D. Lapp, J. R. Squire, & J. M. Jensen (Eds.), *Handbook of research on teaching the English language arts* (2nd ed.) (pp. 1035–1051). Mahwah, NJ: Lawrence Erlbaum.

Pacheco, M. (2010a). English-language learners' reading achievement: Dialectical relationships between policy and practices in meaning-making opportunities. *Reading Research Quarterly, 45,* 292–317.

Pacheco, M. (2010b). Performativity in the bilingual classroom: The plight of English learners in the current reform context. *Anthropology & Education Quarterly, 41,* 75–93.

Pearson, P. D., & Raphael, T. E. (1999). Toward a more complex view of balance in the literacy curriculum. In W. D. Hammond & T. E. Raphael (Eds.), *Early literacy instruction for the new millennium* (pp. 1–21). Grand Rapids: Michigan Reading Association and Center for the Improvement for Early Reading Achievement.

Ritchie, J., & Wilson, D. E. (1993). Dual apprenticeships: Subverting and supporting critical teaching. *English Education, 25,* 67–83.

Rogoff, B. (1990). *Apprenticeship in thinking: Cognitive development in a social context.* New York: Oxford University Press.

Sleeter, C. E. (2005). *Un-standardizing curriculum: Multicultural teaching in standards-based classrooms.* New York: Teachers College Press.

Sleeter, C., & Stillman, J. (2005). Standardizing knowledge in a multicultural society. *Curriculum Inquiry. 35,* 27–46.

Sleeter, C., & Stillman, J. (2007). Navigating accountability pressures. In C. E. Sleeter (Ed.), *Facing accountability in* education: Democracy and equity at risk (pp. 13–29). New York: Teachers College Press.

Smagorinsky, P., Cook, L. S., Jackson, A. Y., Moore, C., & Fry, P. G. (2004). Tensions in learning to teach: Accommodation and the development of a teaching identity. *Journal of Teacher Education, 55*, 8–24.

Smagorinsky, P., Cook, L. S., & Johnson, T. S. (2003). The twisting path of concept development in learning to teach. *Teachers College Record, 105*, 1399–1436.

Souto-Manning, M. (2009). Negotiating culturally responsive pedagogy through multicultural children's literature: Towards critical democratic literacy practices in a first-grade classroom. *Journal of Early Childhood Literacy 9*, 50–74.

Souto-Manning, M. (2010). Teaching English learners: Building on cultural and linguistic strengths. *English Education, 42*, 248–262.

Souto-Manning, M., & James, N. (2008). A multi-arts approach to early literacy. *Journal of Research in Childhood Education, 23*, 82–95.

Stillman, J. (2009). "Taking back the standards": Equity-minded teachers' responses to accountability-related instructional constraints. *The New Educator, 5*, 135–160.

Stillman, J. (2011). Teacher learning in an era of high-stakes accountability: Productive tension and critical professional practice. *Teachers College Record, 113*, 133–180.

Strauss, A., & Corbin, J. (1990). *Basics of qualitative research: Grounded theory procedures and techniques.* Thousand Oaks, CA: Sage.

Tharp, R. G., & Gallimore, R. (1988). *Rousing minds to life: Teaching, learning, and schooling in social context.* New York: Cambridge University Press.

Valencia, S. W., Martin, S. D., Place, N. A., & Grossman, P. (2009). Complex interactions in student teaching. *Journal of Teacher Education, 60*, 304–322.

Valenzuela, A. (2004). *Leaving children behind: How "Texas-style" accountability fails Latino youth.* New York: State University of New York Press.

Valli, L., & Buese, D. (2007). The changing roles of teachers in an era of high-stakes accountability. *American Educational Research Journal, 44*, 519–558.

Valli, L., & Chambliss, M. (2007). Creating classroom cultures: One teacher, two lessons, and a high-stakes test. *Anthropology and Education Quarterly 38*, 57–75.

Vygotsky, L. (1978). *Mind in society.* Cambridge, MA: Harvard University Press.

Zeichner, K. (2005). Becoming a teacher educator: A personal perspective. *Teaching and Teacher Education, 21*, 117–124.

Critical Thinking

1. What is the tension between the states' high-stakes accountability and today's teacher preparation programs?
2. How can you adjust your curricular development to balance raising test scores and engage students in their own meaningful education?
3. How can you adjust your instructional strategies to support this balance?
4. How can you adjust your assessment techniques to account for this balance?

Create Central

www.mhhe.com/createcentral

Internet References

Resources for Multicultural Teaching and Learning
www1.umn.edu/ohr/teachlearn/resources/multicultural/resources/index.html

U.S. Department of Education
www.ed.gov/

JAMY STILLMAN is an assistant professor at the University of Southern California and can be reached at jstillma@usc.edu. **LAUREN ANDERSON** is an assistant professor at the University of Southern California and can be reached at lauren.anderson@usc.edu.

Stillman, Jamy;Anderson, Lauren. From *Language Arts*, vol. 89, no 1, September 2011, pp. 22–37. Copyright © 2011 by National Council of Teachers of English. Reprinted by permission.

Article   Prepared by: Nancy P. Gallavan, *University of Central Arkansas*

Reading the World: Supporting Teachers' Professional Development Using Community-Based Critical Literacy Practices

STACIA M. STRIBLING, ELIZABETH K. DEMULDER, AND MONIMALIKA DAY

Learning Outcomes

After reading this article, you will be able to:

- Delve into the power of critical reflection and analytical dialogue as professional development.

- Connect classroom learning with advocacy and action.

This paper shares the findings from a study that assessed the impact of a graduate level curriculum that engaged fifty-seven K-12 teachers in community-based critical literacy practices. The findings from the participants' written critical reflections following two community exploration activities showed that they gained enhanced awareness of social inequalities. In addition, some of the participants made connections between the observed community disparities and their civic responsibilities to work towards social justice.

> A high school teacher reflects: *"This year, our [community] walk was more geared toward hearing the voices of many people we never got a chance to talk to last year . . . my eyes were opened to things I never heard before. . . . It's amazing to think that if I hadn't taken the opportunity to do these walks, I would be totally oblivious of just how diverse my community is—different races, ethnicities—different socio-economic levels—different opinions on issues of race, gender, and right now immigration."*

This reflection is an example of what our graduate level students contemplate as they engage in critical explorations of their school communities. As teacher educators, we take seriously our role in pushing students to both "read the word" and "read the world" (Shor & Freire, 1987, p. 135) in order to explore the ways in which issues of diversity, such as the race, gender and immigration issues mentioned by this high school teacher, play out in their communities and consequently in their own classrooms. The purpose of this study, therefore, was to assess the impact of a graduate-level curriculum for K-12 teachers that engaged teachers in critical literacy practices in their school communities. The ultimate goal of the curriculum is to support teachers' professional development of dispositions and capacities that promote social justice and civic responsibility both in and through school practices. The study was designed to answer two research questions:

1. How do practicing teachers characterize the insights gained from the exploration of their school communities?
2. To what extent do teachers' exploration of their school community impact their awareness of issues of Social justice and civic responsibility?

Perspectives

The academic success of young children, especially those at risk due to their socio-economic, racial, or ethnic identification, is dependent on well-prepared teachers (Horm, 2003). As a result, much attention has been given to preparing classroom teachers who are knowledgeable in addressing diversity issues in their classrooms (Cochran-Smith, 1995; Noel, 1995; Villegas & Lucas, 2002). This effort is even more crucial when considering that the majority of the population that enters the teaching force is white, female, and middle-class (Zimpher, 1989), and as Ridgeway (2004) asserts, teach the way that they themselves have been taught.

Within the literature reviews organized to tease out potential "best practices" in preparing teachers to teach in culturally diverse settings (Grant, 1994; Sleeter, 2001; Zeichner, 1992), some common themes emerge related to instruction: 1) address teachers' dispositions, 2) build their pedagogical knowledge, and 3) offer them more experiences with diversity. We contend that these three instructional areas are not only essential for pre-service teachers, but are critical for the professional development of in-service teachers as well.

One way to address teachers' dispositions, build their pedagogical knowledge, and immerse them in experiences with diversity is through the practice of critical literacy. Critical literacy has only recently entered the discourse of education so there is no single definition for what it is and how it is enacted in classroom settings (see Janks, 2000; Ciardiello, 2004; Lewison, Flint, & Sluys, 2002 for example definitions). Perhaps the most powerful explanation of critical literacy is offered by Freire when he emphasized the power of not only reading the *word*, but reading the *world* (Shor & Freire, 1987, p. 135). He stressed the importance of critically examining the world in which we live and work in order to name existing inequities and begin to transform oppressive structures through the power of words (spoken, read, and written). The connection between literacy and liberation is at the core of critical literacy.

In our work with in-service teachers, we framed our curriculum around critical literacy using three different approaches highlighted in the literature: 1) critically examining texts for voice and perspective, 2) using texts as a vehicle through which one can examine larger social issues, and 3) using students' lives and experiences as the text and incorporating literacy practices. These three approaches are not mutually exclusive and, in fact, intersect in very natural and powerful ways.

Methods

A qualitative case study design (Creswell, 1998; Marshall & Rossman, 1999; Stake, 2000; Wolcott, 1994; Yin, 1994) was used as the framework for the study. The target population for the study was composed of 57 graduate students who were enrolled in a non-traditional, cohort-based master's program at a large university in a metropolitan area on the east coast from July 2006 through July 2007. The non-traditional structure of the program required that the teachers join in school-based teams of anywhere from two to six teachers. This professional development program, specifically designed for practicing teachers, focused on developing teachers' capacities to engage in critical pedagogy and critical literacy, school-based and community-based inquiry, collaboration, and continuous improvement. It offered an interdisciplinary curriculum that addressed central issues impacting educators, including language, culture, and moral professionalism.

Curricular Experiences

At the beginning of their graduate studies in the summer of 2006, teachers spent a day exploring their students' communities in their school-based teams. One year later, in the summer of 2007, teachers returned to these communities for further exploration and study. The first exploration was called "The Community Walk," and the second exploration was called "The New View Walk." The day after each "Walk," teachers created visual representations and shared their experiences in presentations and further discussion in class. In the year between The Community Walk and The New View Walk experiences, all

57 teachers enrolled in the same courses and attended class days together where they experienced a curriculum focused on issues of race, class, gender, special needs, and critical pedagogy, using Wink (2005), Howard (1999), Meier (2002), Harry, Kalyanpur and Day (2005), and Freire (1970/1998), among others, as texts. Over the course of the year, teachers also designed and conducted a series of four action research projects that repeatedly engaged them in the "name, reflect, act" process of critical pedagogy (Wink, 2005). These projects, conducted in the schools and school communities in which they completed both The Community Walk and The New View Walk, offered teachers opportunities to:

- Deepen their understanding of the critical issues introduced in class and texts,
- Strengthen their critical reflection and dialogue skills, and
- Take needed action in the context of their school communities and their classrooms.

The four projects in which the teachers engaged during the year were designed to gradually narrow the focus of inquiry from the larger community to the classroom. The first action research project required that they draw on both their experiences in the classroom and on The Community Walk in order to identify a topic to explore in more depth by gaining others' perspectives and challenging their own assumptions about the issue. This Community-School Connections project entailed developing an interview protocol, interviewing a community member who might provide an interesting perspective on the topic, coding the interview for themes related to the topic, and conducting a member check by sharing insights gained from the interview with the community member. From here, the teachers narrowed their focus and identified a moral issue/ dilemma they face in their school/classroom community. This second project, called the Moral Professionalism Classroom Project, entailed conducting observations in the school/ classroom setting that would provide insight into the moral dilemma. Teachers wrote up their field notes from these observations and coded them for emerging themes, writing a paper that synthesized their findings and new understandings of the dilemma. The third project, called the Case Study Project, narrowed in even further on an issue that was potentially influencing the learning of one of their students. Teachers conducted a case study where they took observational field notes of the particular student and conducted interviews with the student's family members to gain a better understanding of his/her learning processes. Teachers coded and triangulated the data for themes that helped them become more aware of the influence the issue they identified had on that particular student's learning. These initial three projects finally led up to a teacher research project conducted in the second half of the year where teachers posed questions about their practice, collected data, implemented strategies that addressed the questions, and collected and analyzed data to assess the effectiveness of the strategies. It was after the completion of these four projects in conjunction with reading texts and engaging in critical dialogue that the teachers returned to their school communities for The New View Walk.

Data Sources

In order to offer teachers opportunities for reflection on their learning experiences in the graduate program and to collect feedback to improve our own teaching practices, we collect teachers' written reflective responses after specific learning experiences and after every class day. These responses to particular prompts often offer a rich source of information about the ways teachers experience the curricular innovations, the challenges they face, and the insights they gain in the program that influence their attitudes and approaches to teaching. The data from this study come from the reflective feedback teachers wrote in the second summer after their New View Walk. A first set of questions focused on their New View Walk experience. The questions were:

1. In what ways was the "New View Walk" activity a learning experience for you?
2. What new insights did you gain from the "New View Walk" presentations/discussion?
3. What left you puzzled or concerned (e.g., assumptions that need to be examined more thoroughly)?

After teachers wrote these reflections, they were given the reflective feedback they wrote in response to the previous year's Community Walk experience and were then asked to consider the two "Walk" experiences together. The second set of questions included:

1. How did your experience last year compare with your experience this year?
2. What do you notice regarding the similarities and differences between the two experiences?

Our expectation was that the work throughout the year and the opportunity to return to the communities a second time might:

- Offer teachers new perspectives with which to view the community,
- Encourage teachers to examine and challenge their assumptions,
- Enhance teachers' understanding of the communities in which their students lived,
- Help teachers to envision ways that their new understanding might impact their teaching and their students' learning.

Data Analysis

Data analysis was conducted by three of the authors using the constant comparative method (Glaser & Strauss, 1967; Lincoln & Guba, 1985) to identify potentially meaningful themes in the data. The initial themes developed included the following: 1) exploration of school communities provided powerful learning experiences (**"eye-opening"**), 2) **connections** to the work teachers did throughout the year as they described inequities and injustices observed in the communities, 3) the **value** of gaining an in-depth knowledge of the communities in which their students live, 4) **greater comfort with and understanding** of the communities during the second walk, 5) **increased**

awareness of and openness to different perspectives, 6) more **critical self-reflection,** including questions and insights about their own privilege that challenge assumptions, 7) recognition of the **need for dialogue** about community issues, 8) **resolve** to make efforts that empower their students and the students' families, and 9) **unexamined assumptions and biases** that suggest that further work is needed. As we returned to the data to code for these nine themes, we found that many of them overlapped; in other words, something a teacher wrote could have been considered "eye-opening" but could also articulate the "value" of learning about the community. At this point, we decided to develop a concept map that would both collapse the codes as well as show the connections between the themes. Using the language of critical literacy, we developed the concept map shown in Figure 1.

Teachers had much to say regarding the differences between The Community Walk and The New View Walk, differences that indicated the experience of The New View Walk had been processed through the lens of the curriculum that we implemented during the intervening year. What resulted were two clear themes related to the processes and goals of a critical literacy curriculum. First, teachers indicated a greater capacity to "read the world;" they recognized inequities and injustices in the community and discussed these through the process of sharing insights, asking critical questions, and examining assumptions. Second, the experience of The New View Walk led some teachers to resolve to act. It is hypothesized that this action will only further enhance teachers' ability to read the world and continue in the name-reflect-act cycle.

Findings

The teachers reported tremendous excitement and learning from The Community Walk, so we were concerned that conducting The New View Walk would, to some extent, just be "more of the same" for them; in fact, The New View Walk proved to be a different experience for the teachers. Catherine described the difference in the following way, "It seems that the overall group is less 'in shock' this year about what they saw. Whereas before, they hadn't expected to find the struggles, they were now more questioning of what actions were being taken in the community." Furthermore Lindsey reported, "I think I broadened my view this time, in terms of looking at things from the perspective of people in the community." This shift from an "outsider" perspective to community perspectives was recognized by many of the teachers. Janna writes:

> It was interesting to hear that most presentations did not revolve around the physical aspects of communities as much as they did last year. Voices were the highlights of many presentations and how those voices are received in communities or valued/devalued and why.

This shift to community voices could be attributed to the fact that the experience of The New View Walk was processed through the lens of the curriculum in which the teachers engaged throughout the year since The Community Walk. A primary component of the curriculum focused on the often marginalized voices in the school community. This point was best articulated by Tammy:

> I just did not get it then! Oh my! Talk about being green. I suppose I needed more time to digest, assimilate, and really make sense of what I was learning that summer. Had I known then what I know now there would have been a more informed way that I could have presented that [first] walk. However, I REALLY needed to go through the entire year—go through and process all of my experiences, readings, research, reflection to appreciate my growth from then to now.

The feedback clearly indicates that the teachers benefited from multiple ventures into the community and that they had a different experience the second time. The following sections explore the major themes revealed in the data regarding the ways in which the teachers experienced this powerful second exploration of their school communities.

Capacity to "Read the World": Recognition of Inequities and Injustices in Communities

Teachers' feedback tended to illustrate a strong commitment to reading the world in which their students live. In conducting The New View Walk, many teachers were open to recognizing the inequalities that existed in their communities, and they articulated these inequities in three different ways: 1) by sharing insights about what they observed in the community, 2) by examining assumptions they held regarding the different groups of people living and working in the community, and 3) by asking critical questions about what they observed in the community.

Sharing insights. Several of the teachers shared insights they gained about the ways in which the members of the school community were not equally represented. As Dana stated,

> [We] noticed how much the community in which we teach is catering to an upper-middle/upper class white community. There are many people of different cultures living within [our school community], but they aren't represented when walking through the shops or looking for a place to eat.

Katrina shared her insights regarding the segregation that still exists in her school community: "I learned in the walk that even though our school and community are diverse, that the community is still segregated by race and by income."

For Crystal, the second community experience led to an insight that recognized one way that inequity becomes entrenched, making connections to the work of Freire that we had studied in class:

> I was offended by the fact that some want to pull the students of the illegal immigrants out of the school system. This reminded me of Freire and all of our talks about keeping the oppressed oppressed and feeling like they don't have the privilege of being educated.

In all of these examples, teachers shared their new insights about inequities gained through the experience of The New View Walk.

Examining assumptions. Teachers also examined the assumptions they had about their school communities and the people who lived there. As Rachel shared,

> This year I really thought about my own views and assumptions as I spent the day. Why was I surprised to see a lawyer with a Hispanic name or a student leader who was also a father? I feel that I am becoming aware of how I affect the world around me with my views.

Bonnie examined the assumption that she already "knew" the community in which her students lived. This assumption was challenged as she applied Freire's ideas to her observations and questioned her role in empowering non-dominant community members:

> We had been to the neighborhood before (last year's community walk) and I had some assumptions that I 'knew' this place; but when we went back I saw it in a different light. I knew the residents were poor and the trailers were small and (some) run down. But instead of just noticing the contrast between the "haves and have nots," I thought more about them in terms of being oppressed, and wondering what we can do to help them help themselves.

Bonnie learned to examine inequities in income through a critical lens rather than through a deficit lens.

Asking critical questions. Finally, teachers read the world by asking critical questions about what they observed in the communities, or in some cases what they did not observe. Mandy asks,

> Why don't our teenagers take advantage of social opportunities within the community? . . . Why doesn't our community have a larger percentage of minority families? . . . Growth is good, but who is motivating and monitoring that growth? . . . What can be done to help the transportation issues that prevent students and parents from being a bigger part of school/community events?

Janna posed critical questions related to the growing Hispanic population in her school community:

> As I sit back and think about our community, some has changed physically, but my perspective has undergone the most change. The way I view our community is more critically—why are the employees Hispanics and the customers primarily white? Why does the majority of the Hispanic culture live here vs. there? I certainly question things more than I did one year ago.

Whether teachers were sharing insights, examining assumptions, or asking critical questions, they were deeply engaged in critically reading the school community.

Resolve to Act

While critical literacy practices encourage participants to take a more critical look at their surroundings, the ultimate goal is for these participants to take action that impacts those surroundings in ways that lead toward equity and social justice. As Rachel said, "Now I want to find ways to be an agent for change—real change; not just a handout." Some teachers, including Mandy, resolved to learn more from community members:

The increased, friendly interaction with community members really ignited my interest in learning more. I've come to realize that time spent interacting in the community can really have a strong impact on my relationships with my students, parents, and fellow teachers.

Others, like Julia, expressed the desire to transform their classroom practice:

Gaining the knowledge of where they lived and what their lives were like felt powerful to me. It helped me realize that I wanted to change my classroom practices to meet the needs of all students.

Still others, such as Jackie, identified a particular issue that they needed to further explore:

I want to take a closer look at the disability lens because I've never really reflected on it before, and I think there is a lot for me to learn about in that community and with a new group of people.

A strong sub-theme emerged as teachers reflected on actions they planned to take due to their experience with The New View Walk. Many teachers were overwhelmed with the immigration issues playing out in their school communities and resolved to learn more. As Katrina wrote, "I need to examine more thoroughly the immigration problem facing [the] country. I hear about it on the news but the presentations that represented those areas made it real for me." As faculty, we made our own resolution to develop curricular experiences for the following year that specifically addressed the issue of immigration and its impact on the school communities. We believed that in order to help teachers become more critically literate, we needed to support them through all of the stages of critical pedagogy—naming, reflecting, *and* acting.

Conclusions

For the majority of our teachers, critical literacy practices had a strong impact on the ways in which they viewed their school communities. Teachers were more likely to recognize the inequalities and injustices present in their communities and articulated these inequalities through new insights, an examination of assumptions, and critical questions. We recognize, though, that becoming critically literate is a process. As a result, there were several responses from teachers that included unexamined assumptions and biases suggesting that further work is needed. For example, Anna wrote,

I noticed changes and the openness of the people on this walk. One area that had housed lower economic class people before now has people who take pride in their homes and their community.

While it is a positive step for her to recognize the pride of community members, Anna needs to further examine the assumption that low-income families usually do not "care" about their homes and communities. Nancy also continues to struggle with assumptions about what community members "know" about their worlds and what they value. She reflects,

I am still battling assumptions. Questions such as, "Is this all they know?" "Do they know to question these things?" keep bouncing around. It feels discriminatory to suggest "they don't know better." I assume everyone must want more in their lives than what many of these people have, but maybe that's wrong. What they value and what I value may be two different things and it doesn't mean one is right and the other is wrong.

It is important for Nancy to recognize that people's goals might be different from her own, but it becomes problematic to believe that people living in poverty are necessarily happy to be living that way. The assumptions and biases expressed by both Anna and Nancy are subtle and deeply embedded in the narrative of the dominant culture; it will take more time and a continued focus on critical literacy skills to fully deconstruct these ideas. The work has at least begun for these teachers.

This study is of utmost relevance and importance to teachers and teacher educators because it highlights the insights that teachers can gain from community-based experiences that serve to raise awareness and sensitivity to issues of difference and power that impact the lives of teachers and students. Exposing teachers to the Freirian process of "reading the world" on The Community Walk then "reading the word" by critically engaging with the graduate curriculum, followed by "re-reading the world" on The New View Walk allowed them to more deeply examine the context in which their students live and learn. The results of this process offer teacher educators a window into the range and complexities of teachers' attitudes and responses to curricula designed to support teachers' professional development toward critical pedagogy.

References

Ciardiello, A. V. (2004). Democracy's young heroes: An instructional model of critical literacy practices. *The Reading Teacher, 58*(2), 138–147.

Cochran-Smith, M. (1995). Color blindness and basket making are not the answers: Confronting the dilemmas of race, culture, and language diversity in teacher education. *American Educational Research Journal, 32,* 493–522.

Creswell, J. W. (1998). *Qualitative inquiry in research design: Choosing among five traditions.* Thousand Oaks: Sage Publications.

Freire, P. (1970/1998). *Pedagogy of the oppressed.* New York: Continuum Publishing.

Glaser, B. G., & Strauss, A. L. (1967). *The discovery of grounded theory.* Chicago, IL: Aldine.

Grant, C. A. (1994). Best practices in teacher preparation for urban schools: Lessons from the multicultural teacher education literature. *Action in Teacher Education, 16*(3), 1–18.

Harry, B., Kalyanpur, M., & Day, M. (2005). *Building cultural reciprocity with families: Case studies in special education.* Baltimore: Brookes Publishing.

Horm, D. M. (2003). Preparing early childhood educators to work in diverse urban settings. *Teachers College Record, 105,* 226–244.

Howard, G. (1999, 2nd edition). *We can't teach what we don't know: White teachers, multiracial schools.* New York: Teachers College Press.

Janks, H. (2000). Domination, access, diversity and design: A synthesis for critical literacy education. *Educational Review, 52*(2), 175–186.

Lewison, M., Flint, A. S., & Van Sluys, K. (2002). Taking on critical literacy: The journey of newcomers and novices. *Language Arts, 79*(5), 382–392.

Lincoln, Y., & Guba, E. (1985). *Naturalistic inquiry*. Beverly Hills, CA: Sage.

Marshall, C., & Rossman, G. B. (2006). *Designing qualitative research* (4th ed.). Thousand Oaks: Sage Publications.

Meier, D. (2002). *In schools we trust: Creating communities of learning in an era of testing and standardization*. Boston: Beacon Press.

Mueller, D. J. (1986). *Measuring social attitudes: A handbook for researchers and practitioners*. New York: Teachers College Press.

Noel, J. R. (1995). Multicultural teacher education: From awareness through emotions to action. *Journal of Teacher Education, 46*, 267–273.

Ridgeway, V. G. (2004). One teacher's journey. *Journal of Adolescent & Adult Literacy, 47*, 364–368.

Shor, I., & Freire, P. (1987). *A pedagogy for liberation: Dialogues on transforming education*. Westport, CT: Bergin & Garvey.

Sleeter, C. E. (2001). Preparing teachers for culturally diverse schools: Research and the overwhelming presence of whiteness. *Journal of Teacher Education, 52*, 94–106.

Stake, R. E. (2000). Case studies. In N. K. Denzin & Y. S. Lincoln (Eds.), *Handbook of qualitative research* (2nd ed.) (pp. 435–454). Thousand Oaks: Sage Publications.

Villegas, A. M., & Lucas, T. (2002). Preparing culturally responsive teachers: Rethinking the curriculum. *Journal of Teacher Education, 53*, 20–32.

Wink, J. (2005). *Critical pedagogy: Notes from the real world*. New York: Addison Wesley Longman.

Wolcott, H. F. (1994). Posturing in qualitative research. In M. D. LeCompte, W. L. Millroy, & J. Preissle (Eds.), *The handbook of qualitative research in education* (pp. 3–52). San Diego: Academic Press, Inc.

Yin, R. K. (1994). *Case study research: Design and methods* (2nd ed.) Thousand Oaks: Sage Publications.

Zeichner, K. M. (1992). *Educating teachers for cultural diversity* (NCRTL Special Report). East Lansing, MI: Michigan State University.

Zimpher, N. L. (1989). The RATE project: A profile of teacher education students. *Journal of Teacher Education*, 27–30.

Critical Thinking

1. What is the Community-School Connection Project and what are its benefits?

2. What is the Moral Professional Classroom Project and what are its benefits?

3. What is the Case Study Project and what are its benefits?

4. What is The New View Walk and what are its benefits?

Create Central

www.mhhe.com/createcentral

Internet References

Advocates for Youth

www.advocatesforyouth.org/policy-and-advocacy/cultural-advocacy

National Center for Family and Community Connections with Schools

www.sedl.org/connections/

STACIA STRIBLING is Instructional Faculty with the Initiatives in Educational Transformation (IET) Master's Program at George Mason University. Her research interests include early childhood education, critical literacy, teacher professional development, and multiculturalism. **ELIZABETH DEMULDER** is Associate Professor and Director of IET. Her research concerns interpersonal relationships in educational contexts, children's development and early education, and teacher professional development focusing on critical pedagogy and social justice issues. **MONIMALIKA DAY** is an Assistant Professor in the IET Program. Her research interests include cultural reciprocity, teacher professional development, and disability from a socio-cultural perspective focusing on families of children with special needs.

Stribling, Stacia M.; DeMulder, Elizabeth K.; Day, Monimalika. From *Journal of Praxis in Multicultural Education*, vol. 13, 2011, pp. 21–33. Copyright © 2011 by Journal of Praxis in Multicultural Education. Reprinted by permission.

Article   Prepared by: Nancy P. Gallavan, *University of Central Arkansas*

Colorblind to the Reality of Race in America

Ian F. Haney López

Learning Outcomes

After reading this article, you will be able to:

• Explain how the issue of colorblindness impacts schools.

• Understand why this issue is critical in today's society.

How will race as a social practice evolve in the United States over the next few decades? The American public, and indeed many scholars, increasingly believe that the country is leaving race and racism behind. Some credit Brown v. Board of Education, the revered 1954 U.S. Supreme Court decision pronouncing segregated schools unequal, and the broad civil-rights movement of which the decision was a part, with turning the nation away from segregation and toward equality. Others point to changing demographics, emphasizing the rising number of mixed-race marriages and the increasing Asian and Hispanic populations that are blurring the historic black-white divide.

My sense of our racial future differs. Not only do I fear that race will continue to fundamentally skew American society over the coming decades, but I worry that the belief in the diminished salience of race makes that more likely rather than less. I suspect that the laws supposedly protecting against racial discrimination are partly to blame, for they no longer contribute to racial justice but instead legitimate continued inequality. We find ourselves now in the midst of a racial era marked by what I term "colorblind white dominance," in which a public consensus committed to formal antiracism deters effective remediation of racial inequality, protecting the racial status quo while insulating new forms of racism and xenophobia.

The Jefferson County school district, in Kentucky, covers Louisville and surrounding suburbs. A target of decades of litigation to eradicate Jim Crow school segregation and its vestiges, the district has since 2001 voluntarily pursued efforts to maintain what is now one of the most integrated school systems in the country. But not everyone supports those efforts, especially when they involve taking race into consideration in pupil assignments. In 2004 a white lawyer named Teddy B. Gordon ran for a seat on the Jefferson County School Board, promising

to end endeavors to maintain integrated schools. He finished dead last, behind three other candidates. Indifferent to public repudiation, he is back—this time in the courtroom. Gordon's argument is seductively simple: Brown forbids all governmental uses of race, even if designed to achieve or maintain an integrated society.

He has already lost at the trial level and before an appellate court, as have two other sets of plaintiffs challenging similar integration-preserving efforts by school districts in Seattle and in Lynn, Mass. But Gordon and the conservative think tanks and advocacy groups that back him, including the self-styled Center for Equal Opportunity, are not without hope. To begin with, over the past three decades the courts have come ever closer to fully embracing a colorblind Constitution—colorblind in the sense of disfavoring all uses of race, irrespective of whether they are intended to perpetuate or ameliorate racial oppression. More immediately, last June the Supreme Court voted to review the Louisville and Seattle cases—Meredith v. Jefferson County Board of Education and Parents Involved in Community Schools v. Seattle School District.

Roger Clegg, president and general counsel of the Center for Equal Opportunity, is thrilled. As he gleefully noted in *The National Review,* there's an old saw that the court does not hear cases it plans to affirm. The Bush administration, too, supports Gordon and his efforts. The U.S. solicitor general recently submitted a friend-of-the-court brief urging the justices to prevent school districts across the country from paying attention to race.

At issue is a legally backed ideology of colorblindness that could have implications beyond schools—for higher education and the wider society. Yes, in a narrowly tailored decision three years ago, the Supreme Court allowed the University of Michigan to consider race as one factor in law-school admissions. But since then, conservative advocacy groups have used the threat of lawsuits to intimidate many institutions into halting race-based college financial-aid and orientation programs, as well as graduate stipends and fellowships, and those groups are now taking aim at faculty hiring procedures. This month Michigan voters will decide whether to amend the state constitution to ban racial and gender preferences wherever practiced.

And looming on the horizon are renewed efforts to enact legislation forbidding the federal and state governments from collecting statistics that track racial disparities, efforts that are themselves part of a broader campaign to expunge race from the national vocabulary.

Gordon predicts that if he prevails, Louisville schools will rapidly resegregate. He is sanguine about the prospect. "We're a diverse society, a multiethnic society, a colorblind society," he told *The New York Times*. "Race is history."

But the past is never really past, especially not when one talks about race and the law in the United States. We remain a racially stratified country, though for some that constitutes an argument for rather than against colorblindness. Given the long and sorry history of racial subordination, there is tremendous rhetorical appeal to Justice John Marshall Harlan's famous dissent in Plessy v. Ferguson, the 1896 case upholding segregated railway cars: "Our Constitution is color-blind, and neither knows nor tolerates classes among citizens."

Contemporary proponents of colorblindness almost invariably draw a straight line from that dissent to their own impassioned advocacy for being blind to race today. But in doing so, partisans excise Harlan's acknowledgment of white superiority in the very paragraph in which he extolled colorblindness: "The white race deems itself to be the dominant race in this country. And so it is, in prestige, in achievements, in education, in wealth and in power. So, I doubt not, it will continue to be for all time." That omission obscures a more significant elision: Harlan objected not to all governmental uses of race, but to those he thought would unduly oppress black people.

As viewed by Harlan and the court, the central question was where to place limits on government support for the separation of racial groups that were understood to be unequal by nature (hence Harlan's comfortable endorsement of white superiority). He and the majority agreed that the state could enforce racial separation in the "social" but not in the "civil" arenas; they differed on the contours of the spheres. Harlan believed that segregated train cars limited the capacity of black people to participate as full citizens in civic life, while the majority saw such segregation only as a regulation of social relations sanctioned by custom. The scope of the civil arena mattered so greatly precisely because state exclusions from public life threatened to once again reduce the recently emancipated to an inferior caste defined by law.

For the first half of the 20th century, colorblindness represented the radical and wholly unrealized aspiration of dismantling de jure racial subordination. Thus Thurgood Marshall, as counsel to the National Association for the Advancement of Colored People in the late 1940s and early 1950s, cited Harlan's celebration of colorblindness to argue that racial distinctions are "contrary to our Constitution and laws." But neither society nor the courts embraced colorblindness when doing so might have sped the demise of white supremacy. Even during the civil-rights era, colorblindness as a strategy for racial emancipation did not take hold. Congress and the courts dismantled Jim Crow segregation and proscribed egregious forms of private discrimination in a piecemeal manner, banning only the most noxious misuses of race, not any reference to race whatsoever.

In the wake of the civil-rights movement's limited but significant triumphs, the relationship between colorblindness and racial reform changed markedly. The greatest potency of colorblindness came to lie in preserving, rather than challenging, the racial status quo. When the end of explicit race-based subordination did not eradicate stubborn racial inequalities, progressives increasingly recognized the need for state and private actors to intervene along racial lines. Rather than call for colorblindness, they began to insist on the need for affirmative race-conscious remedies. In that new context, colorblindness appealed to those opposing racial integration. Enshrouded with the moral raiment of the civil-rights movement, colorblindness provided cover for opposition to racial reform.

Within a year of Brown, Southern school districts and courts had recognized that they could forestall integration by insisting that the Constitution allowed them to use only "race neutral" means to end segregation—school-choice plans that predictably produced virtually no integration whatsoever. In 1965 a federal court in South Carolina put it squarely: "The Constitution is color-blind; it should no more be violated to attempt integration than to preserve segregation."

Wielding the ideal of colorblindness as a sword, in the past three decades racial conservatives on the Supreme Court have increasingly refought the battles lost during the civil-rights era, cutting back on protections against racial discrimination as well as severely limiting race-conscious remedies. In several cases in the 1970s—including North Carolina State Board of Education v. Swann, upholding school-assignment plans, and Regents of the University of California v. Bakke—the court ruled that the need to redress the legacy of segregation made strict colorblindness impossible. But as the 1980s went on, in other cases—McCleskey v. Kemp, which upheld Georgia's death penalty despite uncontroverted statistical evidence that African-Americans convicted of murder were 22 times as likely to be sentenced to death if their victims were white rather than black, and City of Richmond v. Croson, which rejected a city affirmative-action program steering some construction dollars to minority-owned companies despite the fact that otherwise only two-thirds of 1 percent of city contracts went to minority companies in a city 50 percent African-American—the court presented race as a phenomenon called into existence just when someone employed a racial term. Discrimination existed only every time someone used racial language. Thus the court found no harm in Georgia's penal system, because no evidence surfaced of a specific bad actor muttering racial epithets, while it espied racism in Richmond's affirmative-action program because it set aside contracts for "minorities."

That approach ignores the continuing power of race as a society-altering category. The civil-rights movement changed the racial zeitgeist of the nation by rendering illegitimate all explicit invocations of white supremacy, a shift that surely marked an important step toward a more egalitarian society. But it did not bring into actual existence that ideal, as white people remain dominant across virtually every social, political, and economic domain. In 2003 the poverty rate was 24 percent among African-Americans, 23 percent among Latinos, and

8 percent among white people. That same year, an estimated 20 percent of African-Americans and 33 percent of Latinos had no health insurance, while 11 percent of white people were uninsured. Discrepancies in incarceration rates are particularly staggering, with African-American men vastly more likely to spend time in prison than white men are.

Or forget the numbers and recall for a moment the graphic parade of images from Hurricane Katrina. Or consider access to country clubs and gated communities, in-group preferences for jobs and housing, the moral certainty shared by many white folks regarding their civic belonging and fundamental goodness. Or, to tie back to Louisville, reflect on what you already know about the vast, racially correlated disparities in resources available to public (and still more to private) schools across the country. Racial dominance by white people continues as a central element of our society.

What may be changing, however, is how membership in the white group is defined. The term "white" has a far more complicated—and fluid—history in the United States than people commonly recognize. For most of our history, whiteness stood in contrast to the nonwhite identities imposed upon Africans, American Indians, Mexican peoples of the Southwest, and Asian immigrants, marking one pole in the racial hierarchy. Simultaneously, however, putative "racial" divisions separated Europeans, so that in the United States presumptions of gross racial inferiority were removed from Germans only in the 1840s through 1860s, the Irish in the 1850s through 1880s, and Eastern and Southern Europeans in the 1900s to 1920s. The melding of various European groups into the monolithic, undifferentiated "white" category we recognize today is a recent innovation, only fully consolidated in the mid-20th century. Now white identity may be expanding to include persons and groups with ancestors far beyond Europe.

Perhaps we should distinguish here among three sorts of white identity. Consider first persons who are "fully white," in the sense that, with all of the racially relevant facts about them widely known, they would generally be considered white by the community at large. (Obviously, racial identity is a matter not of biology but of social understandings, although those may give great weight to purportedly salient differences in morphology and ancestry.) In contrast to that group, there have long been those "passing as white"—people whose physical appearance allowed them to claim a white identity when social custom would have assigned them to a nonwhite group had their ancestry been widely known. Of people of Irish and Jewish descent in the United States, for example, one might say that while initially some were able to pass as white, now all are fully white.

Today a new group is emerging, perhaps best described as "honorary whites." Apartheid South Africa first formally crafted this identity: Seeking to engage in trade and commerce with nations cast as inferior by apartheid logic, particularly Japan, South Africa extended to individuals from such countries the status of honorary white people, allowing them to travel, reside, relax, and conduct business in South African venues that were otherwise strictly "whites only." Persons who pass as white hide racially relevant parts of their identity; honorary whites are

extended the status of whiteness despite the public recognition that, from a bioracial perspective, they are not fully white.

In the United States, honorary-white status seems increasingly to exist for certain people and groups. The quintessential example is certain Asian-Americans, particularly East Asians. Although Asians have long been racialized as nonwhite as a matter of law and social practice, the model-minority myth and professional success have combined to free some Asian-Americans from the most pernicious negative beliefs regarding their racial character. In part this trend represents a shift toward a socially based, as opposed to biologically based, definition of race. Individuals and communities with the highest levels of acculturation, achievement, and wealth increasingly find themselves functioning as white, at least as measured by professional integration, residential patterns, and intermarriage rates.

Latinos also have access to honorary-white identity, although their situation differs from that of Asian-Americans. Unlike the latter, and also unlike African-Americans, Latinos in the United States have long been on the cusp between white and nonwhite. Despite pervasive and often violent racial prejudice against Mexicans in the Southwest and Puerto Ricans and other Hispanic groups elsewhere, the most elite Latin Americans in the United States have historically been accepted as fully white. With no clear identity under the continental theory of race (which at its most basic identifies blacks as from Africa, whites from Europe, reds from the Americas, and yellows from Asia), and with a tremendous range of somatic features marking this heterogeneous population, there has long been relatively more room for the use of social rather than strictly biological factors in the imputation of race to particular Hispanic individuals and groups.

It seems likely that an increasing number of Latinos—those who have fair features, material wealth, and high social status, aided also by Anglo surnames—will both claim and be accorded a position in U.S. society as fully white. Simultaneously, many more—similarly situated in terms of material and status position, but perhaps with slightly darker features or a surname or accent suggesting Latin-American origins—will become honorary whites. Meanwhile, the majority of Latinos will continue to be relegated to nonwhite categories.

The continuing evolution in who counts as white is neither particularly startling nor especially felicitous. Not only have racial categories and ideologies always mutated, but race has long turned on questions of wealth, professional attainment, and social position. A developing scholarship now impressively demonstrates that even during and immediately after slavery, at a time when racial identity in the United States was presumably most rigidly fixed in terms of biological difference and descent, and even in the hyperformal legal setting of the courtroom, determinations of racial identity often took place on the basis of social indicia like the nature of one's employment or one's choice of sexual partners.

Nor will categories like black, brown, white, yellow, and red soon disappear. Buttressed by the continued belief in continental racial divisions, physical features those divisions supposedly connote will remain foundational to racial classification. The stain of African ancestry—so central to the elaboration of race in the United States—ensures a persistent special stigma for black people. Honorary-white status will be available only to the most exceptional—and the most light-skinned—African-Americans, and on terms far more restrictive than those on which whiteness will be extended to many Latinos and Asian-Americans.

Those many in our society who are darker, poorer, more identifiably foreign will continue to suffer the poverty, marginalization, immiseration, incarceration, and exclusion historically accorded to those whose skin and other features socially mark them as nonwhite. Even under a redefined white category, racial hierarchy will continue as the links are strengthened between nonwhite identity and social disadvantage on the one hand, and whiteness and privilege on the other. Under antebellum racial logic, those black people with the fairest features were sometimes described as "light, bright, and damn near white." If today we switch out "damn near" for "honorary" and fold in a few other minorities, how much has really changed?

In the face of continued racial hierarchy, it is crucial that we understand the colorblind ideology at issue in the school cases before the Supreme Court. "In the eyes of government, we are just one race here," Justice Antonin Scalia intoned in 1995. "It is American." That sentiment is stirring as an aspiration, but disheartening as a description of reality, and even more so as a prescription for racial policies. All persons of good will aspire to a society free from racial hierarchy. We should embrace colorblindness—in the sense of holding it up as an ideal. But however far the civil-rights struggle has moved us, we remain far from a racially egalitarian utopia.

In this context, the value of repudiating all governmental uses of race must depend on a demonstrated ability to remedy racial hierarchy. Colorblindness as a policy prescription merits neither fealty nor moral stature by virtue of the attractiveness of colorblindness as an ideal. In the hands of a Thurgood Marshall, who sought to end Jim Crow segregation and to foster an integrated society, colorblindness was a transformative, progressive practice. But when Teddy Gordon, Roger Clegg, the Bush administration, and the conservative justices on the Supreme Court call for banning governmental uses of race, they aim to end the efforts of local majorities to respond constructively to racial inequality. In so doing, they are making their version of colorblindness a reactionary doctrine.

Contemporary colorblindness is a set of understandings—buttressed by law and the courts, and reinforcing racial patterns of white dominance—that define how people comprehend, rationalize, and act on race. As applied, however much some people genuinely believe that the best way to get beyond racism is to get beyond race, colorblindness continues to retard racial progress. It does so for a simple reason: It focuses on the surface, on the bare fact of racial classification, rather than looking down into the nature of social practices. It gets racism and racial remediation exactly backward, and insulates new forms of race baiting.

White dominance continues with few open appeals to race. Consider the harms wrought by segregated schools today. Schools in predominantly white suburbs are far more likely to have adequate buildings, teachers, and books, while the schools serving mainly minority children are more commonly underfinanced, unsafe, and in a state of disrepair. Such harms acccumulate, encouraging white flight to avoid the expected deterioration in schools and the violence that is supposedly second nature to "them," only to precipitate the collapse in the tax base that in fact ensures a decline not only in schools but also in a range of social services. Such material differences in turn buttress seemingly common-sense ideas about disparate groups, so that we tend to see pristine schools and suburbs as a testament to white accomplishment and values. When violence does erupt, it is laid at the feet of alienated and troubled teenagers, not a dysfunctional culture. Yet we see the metal detectors guarding entrances to minority schoolhouses (harbingers of the prison bars to come) as evidence not of the social dynamics of exclusion and privilege, but of innate pathologies. No one need talk about the dynamics of privilege and exclusion. No one need cite white-supremacist arguments nor openly refer to race—race exists in the concrete of our gated communities and barrios, in government policies and programs, in cultural norms and beliefs, and in the way Americans lead their lives.

Colorblindness badly errs when it excuses racially correlated inequality in our society as unproblematic so long as no one uses a racial epithet. It also egregiously fails when it tars every explicit reference to race. To break the interlocking patterns of racial hierarchy, there is no other way but to focus on, talk about, and put into effect constructive policies explicitly engaged with race. To be sure, inequality in wealth is a major and increasing challenge for our society, but class is not a substitute for a racial analysis—though, likewise, racial oppression cannot be lessened without sustained attention to poverty. It's no accident that the poorest schools in the country warehouse minorities, while the richest serve whites; the national education crisis reflects deeply intertwined racial and class politics. One does not deny the imbrication of race and class by insisting on the importance of race-conscious remedies: The best strategies for social repair will give explicit attention to race as well as to other sources of inequality, and to their complex interrelationship.

The claim that race and racism exist only when specifically mentioned allows colorblindness to protect new racial politics from criticism. The mobilization of public fears along racial lines has continued over the past several decades under the guise of interlinked panics about criminals, welfare cheats, terrorists, and—most immediately in this political season—illegal immigrants. Attacks ostensibly targeting "culture" or "behavior" rather than "race" now define the diatribes of today's racial reactionaries. Samuel P. Huntington's jeremiad against Latino immigration in his book *Who Are We?: The Challenges to America's National Identity* rejects older forms of white supremacy, but it promotes the idea of a superior Anglo-Protestant culture. Patrick J. Buchanan defends his latest screed attacking "illegal immigrants," *State of Emergency: The Third World Invasion and Conquest of America,* against the charge of racism by insisting that he's indifferent to race but outraged by those with different cultures who violate our laws. My point is not simply that culture and behavior provide coded language for old prejudices, but that colorblindness excuses and insulates this recrudescence of xenophobia by insisting that only the explicit use of racial nomenclature counts as racism.

Contemporary colorblindness loudly proclaims its antiracist pretensions. To actually move toward a racially egalitarian society, however, requires that we forthrightly respond to racial inequality today. The alternative is the continuation of colorblind white dominance. As Justice Harry Blackmun enjoined in defending affirmative action in Bakke: "In order to get beyond racism, we must first take account of race. There is no other way."

Critical Thinking

1. What does the author mean by "colorblind to the reality of race"?
2. How does this issue impact schools?
3. What can you do in your classroom?
4. Why is this issue critical in today's society?

Create Central

www.mhhe.com/createcentral

Internet References

The Economist
www.economist.com/news/leaders/21583992-fifty-years-after-martin-luther-kings-speech-fixing-americas-racial-ills-requires-new

Race in America
www.race.pitt.edu/

IAN F. HANEY LÓPEZ is a professor at the Boalt Hall School of Law at the University of California at Berkeley. New York University Press has just issued a 10th-anniversary edition of his *White by Law: The Legal Construction of Race*, with a new chapter on colorblind white dominance.

As seen in the *Chronicle of Higher Education*, November 3, 2006, pp. B6–B9. Excerpted from WHITE BY LAW, 10th Anniversary edition (New York University Press, 2006). Copyright © 2006 by Ian F. Haney López. Reproduced with permission of the author.

Unit 6

UNIT

Prepared by: Nancy P. Gallavan, *University of Central Arkansas*

Awareness of Classrooms

Culturally competent teachers design, align, refine, and entwine cultural competence into their classrooms. These four steps spell the word DARE, as some teachers visualize the process as a challenge venture to transform an empty space into a living biosphere where students and teacher feel safe, welcome, excited, and rewarded. All four domains of learning and all five of the senses are maximized for learning that stimulates awareness of cultural competence; conducts informal assessments of students' reactions, responses, reciprocity, and reflections; features the four sources of efficacy; and reinforces a sense of agency.

Transforming a classroom from an empty space into a living biosphere begins with a design. No longer a classroom, the goal is for the environment to become a community, or perhaps a set of many different communities, unto itself. The community may be designated by grade level or content subject area; however, the intention is to construct a world that transports students into a group of individuals, both like and unlike themselves, to share a series of dynamic and diverse learning experiences.

The classroom design should address the physical space, the social desires, the effective security, and the academic expectations for both the students and the teacher across the immediate and the long range plans. A culturally competent community should include photographs of all people both represented in the classroom and from around the world. Opportunities for students to display their own productions and express their individual ideas should be allocated too. As teachers design their communities, they need to consider ways that the goals will be achieved and that students will transform throughout the school year. Maintaining the DARE, teachers may want to begin with only a few changes that increase in time. Ideally the design has an overall theme and purpose that guide the community's growth and development.

Designing a culturally competent community must align with the scope and sequence of the school, other classrooms, students, families, and neighborhood. Although the culturally competent community will be transformative, the DARE involves care, consideration, cooperation, and connections.

Article   Prepared by: Nancy P. Gallavan, *University of Central Arkansas*

As Diversity Grows, So Must We

Schools that experience rapid demographic shifts can meet the challenge by implementing five phases of professional development.

GARY R. HOWARD

Learning Outcomes

After reading this article, you will be able to:

• Become acquainted with the five phases of professional development and their usefulness throughout teaching careers.

• Examine applications of professional development in classrooms and schools.

M any school districts nationwide are experiencing rapid growth in the number of students of color, culturally and linguistically diverse students, and students from low-income families. From my work with education leaders in some of these diversity-enhanced school districts, I know they are places of vibrant opportunity—places that call us to meaningful and exciting work. In these "welcome-to-America" schools, the global community shows up in our classrooms every day, inviting us—even requiring us—to grow as we learn from and with our students and their families.

The Need for Growth

All is not well, however, in these rapidly transitioning schools. Some teachers, administrators, and parents view their schools' increasing diversity as a problem rather than an opportunity. For example, in a school district on the West Coast where the number of Latino students has quadrupled in the past 10 years, a teacher recently asked me, "Why are they sending these kids to our school?" In another district outside New York City—where the student population was once predominantly rich, white, and Jewish but is now about 90 percent low-income kids of color, mostly from the Caribbean and Latin America—a principal remarked in one workshop, "These kids don't value education, and their parents aren't helping either. They don't seem to care about their children's future." In a school district near Minneapolis with a rapidly increasing black population, a white parent remarked, "Students who are coming here now

don't have much respect for authority. That's why we have so many discipline problems."

Diversity-enhanced schools are places of vibrant opportunity—places that call us as educators to meaningful and exciting work.

Other educators and parents, although less negative, still feel uneasy about their schools' new demographics. In a high school outside Washington, D.C., where the Latino immigrant population is increasing rapidly, a teacher told me that he was disappointed in himself for not feeling comfortable engaging his students in a discussion of immigration issues, a hot topic in the community in spring 2006. "I knew the kids needed to talk, but I just couldn't go there." And a black teacher who taught French successfully for many years in predominantly white suburban schools told me recently, "When I first found myself teaching classes of mostly black kids, I went home frustrated every night because I knew I wasn't getting through to them, and they were giving me a hard time. It only started getting better when I finally figured out that I had to reexamine everything I was doing."

This teacher has it right. As educators in rapidly transitioning schools, we need to reexamine everything we're doing. Continuing with business as usual will mean failure or mediocrity for too many of our students, as the data related to racial, cultural, linguistic, and economic achievement gaps demonstrate (National Center for Education Statistics, 2005). Rapidly changing demographics demand that we engage in a vigorous, ongoing, and systemic process of professional development to prepare all educators in the school to function effectively in a highly diverse environment.

Many education leaders in diversity-enhanced schools are moving beyond blame and befuddlement and working to transform themselves and their schools to serve all their students well. From observing and collaborating with them, I have learned that this transformative work proceeds best in five phases: (1) building trust, (2) engaging personal culture,

(3) confronting issues of social dominance and social justice, (4) transforming instructional practices, and (5) engaging the entire school community

Phase 1: Building Trust

Ninety percent of U.S. public school teachers are white; most grew up and attended school in middle-class, English-speaking, predominantly white communities and received their teacher preparation in predominantly white colleges and universities (Gay, Dingus, Jackson, 2003). Thus, many white educators simply have not acquired the experiential and education background that would prepare them for the growing diversity of their students (Ladson-Billings, 2002; Vavrus, 2002).

The first priority in the trust phase is to acknowledge this challenge in a positive, inclusive, and honest way. School leaders should base initial discussions on the following assumptions:

- Inequities in diverse schools are not, for the most part, a function of intentional discrimination.
- Educators of *all* racial and cultural groups need to develop new competencies and pedagogies to successfully engage our changing populations.
- White teachers have their own cultural connections and unique personal narratives that are legitimate aspects of the overall mix of school diversity

School leaders should also model for their colleagues inclusive and nonjudgmental discussion, reflection, and engagement strategies that teachers can use to establish positive learning communities in their classrooms.

For example, school leaders in the Apple Valley Unified School District in Southern California, where racial, cultural, and linguistic diversity is rapidly increasing, have invested considerable time and resources in creating a climate of openness and trust. They recently implemented four days of intensive work with teams from each school, including principals, teacher leaders, union representatives, parents, clergy, business leaders, and community activists from the NAACP and other organizations.

One essential outcome in this initial phase of the conversation is to establish that racial, cultural, and economic differences are real—and that they make a difference in education outcomes. Said one Apple Valley participant, "I have become aware that the issue of race needs to be dealt with, not minimized." Said another, "I need to move beyond being color-blind." A second key outcome is to establish the need for a personal and professional journey toward greater awareness. As an Apple Valley educator noted, "There were a lot of different stories and viewpoints shared at this inservice, but the one thing we can agree on is that everyone needs to improve in certain areas." A third key outcome in the trust phase is to demonstrate that difficult topics can be discussed in an environment that is honest, safe, and productive. One Apple Valley teacher commented, "We were able to talk about all of the issues and not worry about being politically correct."

Through this work, Apple Valley educators and community leaders established a climate of constructive collaboration that can be directed toward addressing the district's new challenges.

From the perspective of the school superintendent, "This is a conversation our community is not used to having, so we had to build a positive climate before moving to the harder questions of action."

Phase 2: Engaging Personal Culture

Change has to start with educators before it can realistically begin to take place with students. The central aim of the second phase of the work is building educators' *cultural competence*—their ability to form authentic and effective relationships across differences.

Young people, particularly those from historically marginalized groups, have sensitive antennae for authenticity. I recently asked a group of racially and culturally diverse high school students to name the teachers in their school who really cared about them, respected them, and enjoyed getting to know them as people. Forty students pooling their answers could name only 10 teachers from a faculty of 120, which may be one reason this high school has a 50 percent dropout rate for students of color.

Aronson and Steele's (2005) work on stereotype threat demonstrates that intellectual performance, rather than being a fixed and constant quality, is quite fragile and can vary greatly depending on the social and interpersonal context of learning. In repeated studies, these researchers found that three factors have a major effect on students' motivation and performance: their feelings of belonging, their trust in the people around them, and their belief that teachers value their intellectual competence. This research suggests that the capacity of adults in the school to form trusting relationships with and supportive learning environments for their students can greatly influence achievement outcomes.

Leaders in the Metropolitan School District of Lawrence Township, outside Indianapolis, have taken this perspective seriously. Clear data showed gaps among ethnic groups in achievement, participation in higher-level courses, discipline referrals, and dropout rates. In response, district teachers and administrators engaged in a vigorous and ongoing process of self-examination and personal growth related to cultural competence.

Central-office and building administrators started with themselves. Along with selected teachers from each school, they engaged in a multiyear program of shared reading, reflective conversations, professional development activities, and joint planning to increase their own and their colleagues' levels of cultural competence. They studied and practiced Margaret Wheatley's (2002) principles of conversation, with particular emphasis on her admonitions to expect things to be messy and to be willing to be disturbed. They designed their own Socratic seminars using chapters from *We Can't Teach What We Don't Know* (Howard, 2006) and used the stages of personal identity development model from that book as a foundation for ongoing reflective conversations about their own journeys toward cultural competence.

As this work among leaders began to be applied in various school buildings, one principal observed, "We are talking about things that we were afraid to talk about before—like our own prejudices and the biases in some of our curriculum materials." In another school, educators' discussions led to a decision to move parent-teacher conferences out of the school building and into the apartment complexes where their black and Latino students live.

Phase 3: Confronting Social Dominance and Social Justice

When we look at school outcome data, the history of racism, classism, and exclusion in the United States stares us in the face. Systems of privilege and preference often create enclaves of exclusivity in schools, in which certain demographic groups are served well while others languish in failure or mediocrity. As diversity grows in rapidly transitioning school districts, demographic gaps become increasingly apparent.

Educators of *all* racial and cultural groups need to develop new competencies and pedagogies to successfully engage our changing populations.

In phase three, educators directly confront the current and historical inequities that affect education. The central purpose of this phase is to construct a compelling narrative of social justice that will inform, inspire, and sustain educators in their work, without falling into the rhetoric of shame and blame. School leaders and teachers engage in a lively conversation about race, class, gender, sexual orientation, immigration, and other dimensions of diversity and social dominance. David Koyama, principal of a diversity-enhanced elementary school outside Seattle, said, "One of my most important functions as a school leader is to transform political jargon like 'no child left behind' into a moral imperative that inspires teachers to work toward justice, not mere compliance."

Unraveling social dominance takes courage—the kind of courage shown by the central office and school leadership team in the Roseville Area School District outside the twin cities of Minneapolis and St. Paul. Roseville is in the midst of a rapid demographic shift. As we approached this phase of the work, I asked Roseville leaders to examine how issues of privilege, power, and dominance might be functioning in their schools to shape educators' assumptions and beliefs about students and create inequitable outcomes.

One of the workshop activities engaged participants in a forced-choice simulation requiring them to choose which aspects of their identity they would give up or deny for the sake of personal survival in a hostile environment. Choosing from such identities as race, ethnicity, language, religion, values, and vocation, many white educators were quick to give up race. Among the Roseville administrative team, which is 95 percent white, the one white principal who chose to keep his racial identity during the simulation said during the debriefing discussion,

"I seriously challenge my white colleagues who so easily gave up their race. I think if we are honest with ourselves, few would choose to lose the privilege and power that come with being white in the United States."

As an outgrowth of the authentic and sometimes contentious conversations that emerged from this and other activities, several core leaders and the superintendent identified a need to craft a strong Equity Vision statement for the district. The Equity Vision now headlines all opening-of-school events each year and is publicly displayed in district offices and schools. It reads,

> Roseville Area Schools is committed to ensuring an equitable and respectful educational experience for every student, family, and staff member, regardless of race, gender, sexual orientation, socioeconomic status, ability, home or first language, religion, national origin, or age.

As a result of the increased consciousness about issues of dominance and social justice, several schools have formed Equity Teams of teachers and students, and an Equity Parent Group has begun to meet. The district is looking seriously at how many students from dominant and subordinate groups are in its gifted and AP classes and is conscientiously working for more balance.

Like Roseville, other diversity-enhanced districts must establish clear public markers that unambiguously state, "This is who we are, this is what we believe, and this is what we will do." Any approach to school reform that does not honestly engage issues of power, privilege, and social dominance is naive, ungrounded in history, and unlikely to yield the deep changes needed to make schools more inclusive and equitable.

Phase 4: Transforming Instructional Practices

In this phase, schools assess and, where necessary, transform the way they carry out instruction to become more responsive to diversity. For teachers, this means examining pedagogy and curriculum, as well as expectations and interaction patterns with students. It means looking honestly at outcome data and creating new strategies designed to serve the students whom current instruction is not reaching. For school leaders, this often means facing the limits of their own knowledge and skills and becoming colearners with teachers to find ways to transform classroom practices.

In Loudoun County Public Schools, outside Washington, D.C., teachers and school leaders are taking this work seriously. One of the fastest-growing school systems in the United States, Loudoun County is experiencing rapid increases in racial, cultural, linguistic, and economic diversity on its eastern edge, closer to the city, while remaining more monocultural to the west. Six of Loudoun's most diverse schools have formed leadership teams to promote the following essential elements of culturally responsive teaching (CRT):

- Forming authentic and caring relationships with students.
- Using curriculum that honors each student's culture and life experience.

- Shifting instructional strategies to meet the diverse learning needs of students.
- Communicating respect for each student's intelligence.
- Holding consistent and high expectations for all learners. (Gay, 2000; Ladson-Billings, 1994; McKinley, 2005; Shade, Kelly, & Oberg, 1997)

CRT teams vary in size and membership but usually include principals, assistant principals, counselors, lead teachers, specialists, and, in some cases, parents. In addition to engaging deeply in the phases outlined above, these teams have begun to work with their broader school faculties to transform instruction. At Loudoun County's Sugarland Elementary, teacher members of the CRT team have designed student-based action research projects. They selected individual students from their most academically challenged demographic groups and then used the principles of CRT to plan new interventions to engage these students and track their progress.

As educators in rapidly transitioning schools, we need to reexamine everything we're doing.

In one action research project, a 5th grade teacher focused on a Latino student, an English language learner who "couldn't put two sentences together, let alone write the five-paragraph essay that is required to pass our 5th grade assessment." The teacher's first reaction was to ask, "How was this student allowed to slip by all these years without learning anything beyond 2nd grade writing skills?" When the teacher launched her CRT project, however, her perspective became more proactive. She realized that she couldn't just deliver the 5th grade curriculum—she had to meet this student where he was. She built a personal connection with the student, learned about his family culture and interests (a fascination with monkeys was a major access point), and used this relationship to reinforce his academic development. The student responded to her high expectations and passed his 5th grade writing assessment. And after missing its No Child Left Behind compliance goals in past years, Sugarland recently achieved adequate yearly progress for all subgroups in its highly diverse student population.

This phase requires a crucial paradigm shift, in which teachers and other school professionals stop blaming students and their families for gaps in academic achievement. Instead of pointing fingers, educators in Loudoun schools are placing their energies where they will have the most impact—in changing their *own* attitudes, beliefs, expectations, and practices. I frequently ask teachers and school leaders, "Of all the many factors that determine school success for our students, where can we as educators have the most influence?" After educators participate in the work outlined here, the answer is always, "Changing ourselves."

Phase 5: Engaging the Entire School Community

Changing demographics have profound implications for all levels and functions of the school system. To create welcoming and equitable learning environments for diverse students and their families, school leaders must engage the entire school community.

Leaders in the East Ramapo Central School District in New York State have committed themselves to just such a system-wide initiative. The school district, which lies across the Tappan Zee Bridge from New York City, has experienced a dramatic shift in student population in the past 15 years as low-income Haitian, Jamaican, Dominican, Latino, and black families from the city have moved into the community and middle-class white families have, unfortunately but predictably, fled to private schools or other less diverse districts.

In the midst of this demographic revolution, East Ramapo's broad-based diversity initiative has engaged all groups and constituencies in the school district community, not just teachers and administrators. For example, the district has provided workshops to help classified employees acknowledge their powerful role in setting a welcoming tone and creating an inclusive climate for students, parents, and colleagues in school offices, lunchrooms, hallways, and on the playground. For bus drivers, this work has meant gaining cultural competence skills for managing their immense safety responsibilities while communicating clearly and compassionately across many languages and cultures on their buses.

In one session that I led with school secretaries, we worked through their confusion and frustration related to all the diverse languages being spoken in the school offices and, in some cases, their feelings of anger and resentment about the demographic changes that had taken place in "their" schools. Asked what they learned from the session, participants commented, "I saw the frustration people can have, especially if they are from another country." "We all basically have the same feelings about family, pride in our culture, and the importance of getting along." "I learned from white people that they can also sometimes feel like a minority." In addition to these sessions, East Ramapo has created learning opportunities for school board members, parents, students, counselors, and special education classroom assistants. The district has convened regular community forums focusing on student achievement and creating conversations across many diverse cultures. White parents who have kept their children in the public schools because they see the value of diversity in their education have been significant participants in these conversations.

As a result of East Ramapo's efforts, the achievement gaps in test scores along ethnic and economic lines have significantly narrowed. In the six years since the district consciously began implementing the professional development model discussed here, the pass rate for black and Hispanic students combined on the New York State elementary language arts test increased from 43 percent in 2000 to 54 percent in 2006; on the math test, the pass rate increased from 40 percent to 61 percent. During that same period, the gap between black and Hispanic students (combined) and white and Asian students (combined) decreased by 6 percentage points in language arts and 23 percentage points in math. The achievement gap between low-income elementary students and the general population decreased by 10 points in language arts and 6 points in math—results that are particularly impressive, given that the proportion of economically disadvantaged students grew from 51 percent in 2000 to 72 percent in 2006.

A Journey toward Awareness

Professional development for creating inclusive, equitable, and excellent schools is a long-term process. The school districts described here are at various stages in the process. Everyone involved would agree that the work is messier and more complex than can be communicated in this brief overview. However, one central leadership commitment is clear in all of these rapidly transitioning districts: When diversity comes to town, we are all challenged to grow.

References

Aronson, J., & Steele, C. M. (2005). Stereotypes and the fragility of human competence, motivation, and self-concept. In C. Dweck & E. Elliot (Eds.), *Handbook of competence and motivation* (pp. 436–456). New York: Guilford.

Gay, G. (2000). *Culturally responsive teaching: Theory, research, and practice.* New York: Teachers College Press.

Gay, G., Dingus, J. E., & Jackson, C. W. (2003, July). *The presence and performance of teachers of color in the profession.* Unpublished report prepared for the National Collaborative on Diversity in the Teaching Force, Washington, DC.

Howard, G. (2006). *We can't teach what we don't know: White teachers in multiracial schools* (2nd ed.). New York: Teachers College Press.

Ladson-Billings, G. (1994). *The dreamkeepers: Successful teachers of African American students.* San Francisco: Jossey-Bass.

Ladson-Billings, G. (2002). *Crossing over to Canaan: The journey of new teachers in diverse classrooms.* San Francisco: Jossey-Bass.

McKinley, J. H. (2005, March). *Culturally responsive teaching and learning.* Paper presented at the Annual State Conference of the Washington Alliance of Black School Educators, Bellevue, WA.

National Center for Education Statistics. (2005). *The nation's report card.* Washington, DC: Author.

Shade, B. J., Kelly, C., & Oberg, M. (1997). *Creating culturally responsive classrooms.* Washington, DC: American Psychological Association.

Vavrus, M. (2002). *Transforming the multiculrural education of teachers: Theory, research and practice.* New York: Teachers College Press.

Wheatley, M. (2002). *Turning to one another: Simple conversations to restore hope to the future.* San Francisco: Barrett-Koehler.

Critical Thinking

1. Why is trust essential in professional development, classrooms, and school?

2. What are some ways to engage personal cultures that benefit learners and learning?

3. What is meant by social dominance and transformative instructional practices?

4. How are equity and excellent in classrooms dependent of valuing cultural diversity?

Create Central

www.mhhe.com/createcentral

Internet References

E3: Equity and Excellence in Education
http://e3ed.org/

National Education Association: Cultural Competence
http://www.nea.org/assets/docs/PB13_CulturalCompetence08.pdf

GARY R. HOWARD is Founder and President of the REACH Center for Multicultural Education in Seattle (www.reachctr.org); 206-634-2073; garyhoward@earthlink.net. He is the author of *We Can't Teach What We Don't Know: White Teachers, Multiracial Schools* (Teachers College Press, 2nd ed., 2006).

Article   Prepared by: Nancy P. Gallavan, *University of Central Arkansas*

"Some People Do Things Different From Us": Exploring Personal and Global Cultures in a First Grade Classroom

PAMELA JEWETT

Learning Outcomes

After reading this article, you will be able to:

- Explore cultural diversity through powerful children's literature.

- Relate the challenges encountered in the literature with learning and living from the perspectives of young learners.

"Some people do things different from us because of where they live and what they're used to. We don't eat tamales for Christmas but we have other stuff." I was sitting with a group of first graders who were in the midst of a conversation about Gary Soto's book, *Too Many Tamales* (1993). Peter's comment revealed his understanding that the characters in the book held cultural models (Gee, 1999) different from his about meals that people eat at Christmastime. This conversation was one of many in which the first grade children engaged as they discussed their personal cultural identities and the cultural identities of people whose lives were different from their own.

The children in this first grade classroom had been reading international children's literature as well as children's literature written in the United States in an effort to identify and then articulate aspects of their culture. I adhere to a view of culture as a system of "social value, cognitive, behavioral standards, worldviews, and beliefs used to give order and meaning to our lives as well as the lives of others" (Gay, 2000, p. 8). However when culture is studied in schools in this country, it too often focuses on surface elements of culture such as the food, dress, music, art, or celebrations of a group of people. Rarely do classroom explorations look at deep culture—what Nieto (2009) has called "the ever-changing values, traditions, social

and political relationships, and worldview created, shared, and transformed by a group of people bound together by a combination of factors that can include common history, geographic location, language, social class, and religion" (p. 136).

Breaking Down Borders with Children's Literature

Children's literature can broaden and enhance readers' views of themselves and others. Hazel Rochman (1993) argued that, "The best books break down borders. They surprise us—whether they are set close to home or abroad. They change our view of ourselves: they extend that phrase 'like me' to include what was foreign and strange" (p. 9). When we incorporate children's literature from abroad as well as from the United States into the literacy practices of a first grade class, the potential exists to widen the children's perspectives of the world and build insights about others. Additionally there exist openings to challenge cultural stereotypes and "the problem with stereotypes is not that they are untrue but that they are incomplete. They make one story become the whole story" (Adichie, 2009). In this article, I describe the experiences of a class of first-grade children who engaged with children's literature and crossed cultural as well as academic borders.

Learning about Cultural Identities with Children's Literature

Although we used multiple genres for learning about cultural identities (e.g. print and digital materials, photographs, videos, and music), children's literature that presented diverse cultural frames of reference served as our main resource. I chose both international children's literature and children's literature written in the United States that met this criterion. Given the limited number of international books published in the United States, I used a broad definition of international literature:

> Books written and published first in countries other than the United States (in English and translation), books written by immigrants to the United States about their home countries and published in the United States, books written by authors from countries other than the United States but originally published in the United States, and books written by American authors and published in the United States with settings in other countries. (Freeman & Lehman, 2000, p.10)

I did not use the term "multicultural literature" to describe the books I selected that were written in the United States about diverse cultural groups since definitions of multicultural literature can be problematic. One definition suggests that multicultural literature (multi + cultures) "should include as many cultures as possible with no distinction between the dominant and the dominated" (Cai, 2003, p. 271). A second perspective on multicultural literature centers on issues related to race and ethnicity. This stance has been criticized "as racial essentialism that excludes many cultures from the concept of multiculturalism" (Cai, 2003, p. 273), and it often places emphasis on developing social consciousness in European-American children toward the "other." Another view holds that all people are multicultural and that all literature is therefore multicultural. Cai (2003) argues, though, that multicultural literature is still a "much-needed separate category of literature, for its existence poses a challenge to the domination of all-white literature" (p. 273). To describe children's literature written in the United States about diverse cultural groups, I chose instead a definition that focuses on "ethnic and regional groups whose cultures historically have been less represented than European cultures" (Temple, Martinez, & Yokota, 2006, p. 91).

My hope was that in carefully selecting children's literature that illuminated diverse cultural frames of reference that the children would have the opportunity to reflect on the rich diversity of the people in the books. However, I was also concerned with the authenticity of the books I chose. Bishop (2003) defines authenticity as "the success with which a writer is able to reflect the cultural perspectives of the people about whom he or she is writing, and make readers from inside the group believe that the writer 'knows what's going on'" (p. 29). As I chose children's literature that represented diverse cultures in the United States and across the globe, I used criteria suggested by Temple, Martinez, and Yokota (2006) asking questions about the authenticity of perspectives, the multidimensionality of the portrayal of the culture, and the cultural details (e.g., if they were integrated and accurate). I relied on recommended book lists to locate children's literature about diverse cultures in the United States, for example lists such as those found in children's literature texts books that I use in my classes (e.g., Galda & Cullinan, 2009; Temple et al., 2011) and in professional journals such as the *Journal of Children's Literature* and *Language Arts* which review and recommend children's literature that represents diverse cultural perspectives. I used the same criteria

for the selection of international titles, and I also referred to journals such as *Bookbird,* and to booklists from organizations such as the International Board on Books for Youth, the United States Board on Books for Youth, and the International Reading Association Notable Books for a Global Society.

Cultural Models

Gee (1999) defined cultural models as theories we generate to help us make sense of the world and our experiences in it. They are rooted in our socially and culturally defined practices and describe what we believe about events and people in the world. All of us have large supplies of cultural models in our minds, pictures about our experiences in the world or with school or literature, and we treat these pictures as if they depict what is typical. Because they shape our judgments and beliefs, our cultural models are often our first thoughts or best guesses about what is expected or normal for a particular situation, and we rarely consciously articulate them. Like stereotypes, cultural models also condense our views of the world by helping us understand complex realities in order to focus on important elements and hide other ways of thinking. However unlike stereotypes, which have become pervasive and ritualized across cultural groups, our constructed cultural models are not static. As Keesing (1987) wrote, cultural models are "frameworks of interpretation," (p. 372) and as such they are fluid and dynamic, leaving room for choice and for alternative constructions.

Context of the Study

This study took place from fall semester 2009 through spring semester 2010 in a first-grade classroom with 21 students. Their teacher, Anne (all names are pseudonyms), was a third year teacher and a former student at the university where I am a faculty member. She had attended a graduate course I taught in which we studied the benefits and challenges of incorporating children's literature in elementary reading programs. Anne was struck by the possibilities inherent in introducing young children to diverse cultural perspectives, and she generously invited me to conduct this study in her classroom. I met with the children in their classroom 15 times in the fall and 12 times in the spring, and each meeting lasted between 45 minutes and one hour.

A Curricular Framework

I incorporated the first two elements of a curricular framework designed by Kathy Short (2008) for cultural studies: 1) studying personal cultural identities, and 2) engaging in cross-cultural explorations. The first part of the framework helps students identify and understand what matters in their own cultures before asking them to understand what matters in someone else's culture. In this stage, I wanted students to develop a general understanding of what culture is, and more importantly, I hoped they would come to understand that each of us has a culture that guides how we act and think in our everyday lives. To delve into these ideas, we relied on reading children's literature, talking about our reading, and responding through writing and art, as well as engaging in planned experiences to extend these concepts. For example, at one point in the fall, I sent cameras home with the children to take self-selected photographs of (what they determined to be) their culture. The students wrote about the photographs they took and brought these together to form a class book. They created personal cultural x-rays (Short, 2008) that looked at surface and deeper levels of their cultural identities. In the second part of the framework, students explored a global culture and identified points of view beyond their own. Making this cross-cultural journey involved using multiple media resources such as videos, CDs, and the Internet and engaging in classroom experiences such as readers' theatre, dance performances, and cultural x-rays about the global culture they studied. Most importantly, however, was the time we spent reading fiction and non-fiction picture books about a global culture, followed by dialogue among the readers.

Teaching as Cultural Inquiry

Instructional strategies have at their center the theoretical beliefs of the teacher who incorporates them; depending on the teacher, the same instructional strategy can look quite different. My beliefs focused on the importance of exploring the cultures of diverse groups of people. Therefore, as I worked with the first-grade children and their teacher, I tried to adopt the habits of mind that a teacher who is a cultural inquirer would embrace. To reach through surface levels and into deeper concepts of culture, I incorporated a stance toward instructional strategies that would allow us to explore the unique experiences of a group of people, their "beliefs, attitudes, values, worldviews, institutions, artifacts, processes, interactions, and ways of behaving" (Harris, 2003, p. 119). Although I chose books that represented diverse cultures, I also thought about the kinds of conversations I hoped to have with the children to explore cultural messages embedded within them. I asked questions such as, "What really matters about (this topic)?" and "What surprised you (or worried you) about (this topic)? Why?" As an example, the children wrote a class poem about the Cuban singer, Celia Cruz. To help them envision Celia's attitudes, the children sat together in small groups looking through the books we had read about her. I asked them to decide what Celia believed and valued. I asked them to think about what really mattered to Celia. They remembered how she valued her family, and how her family believed in the importance of school. They recalled how she loved music and the joy she expressed with the word *azucar*. Whatever the instructional strategy—whether drawing or journal writing or dialoguing about a book—I thought of the strategy as a way to slow down our thinking so that we could imagine the cultural beliefs and values of the people about whom we were learning.

The first grade classroom was a lively, active environment, and to help me make sense of what was going on in this context, I kept a research journal. I also collected student-created artifacts such as copies of writing and drawings from response journals, class poems, photographs taken by the children, vignettes written about their photographs, letters they wrote to me, videotapes of special class events, cultural x-rays they created, and the class book the children compiled. In addition, I audio-taped and transcribed the children's storytelling.

I decided upon storytelling as an approach because the children's stories would help me better understand their conceptions of culture (Davis, 2007). I prompted them in such a way that they responded in the third person, asking them to tell me a story about "A little girl/boy who wanted to know about her/his culture." This allowed the attention to be deflected away from them personally and toward a fictional, invented character. Since young children's responses are often susceptible to adults' cues (Weber, 1994), dialogue was shifted away from me and toward them. Daniel, a bright and imaginative student, was delighted to learn that the story did not have to be "true." He slipped in and out of third and first person as he told me the following story:

> Once upon a time, there was a little boy named Daniel who wanted to know his culture, and he was looking for a mom and dad to be his parents, and his parents taught him how to eat with chopsticks, knife, fork, and spoons, and he chose to eat with chopsticks. And so the parents had to get me some food with chopsticks, and they asked what kind of pet do I want, and I said, "a dog." Then, um, and then they taught me how to speak English and Spanish and they taught me how to read. So, um, and the end.

From the children's stories and other data sets, I learned some important lessons about the kinds of knowledge the children were constructing through their reading and discussions of children's literature. I found that the children relied on surface level aspects of culture to identify deeper levels of culture; they identified and made connections to aspects of a global culture very different from their own, and across their cultural journeys, they read extensively, intensively, and beyond expectations.

Students Relied on Surface Level Aspects of Culture to Identify Deeper Levels of Culture

Using Personal Cultural Models to Connect to the Cultural Models of Others

I began the fall semester by bringing children's literature that represented diverse cultural groups into the first-grade classroom. We read about children in our country and across the globe, and I purposely named aspects of culture the children noticed, and what they noticed was juxtaposed against their lived experiences, their cultural models. For example, they read *Carolina's Gift* (Diaz, 2002), a story of a girl in Peru who goes to the market to buy her grandmother a special birthday gift. The children talked about the way the characters dressed, their houses, and how Carolina celebrated her grandmother's birthday, all in relation to their own cultural models of dressing, homes, and celebrating birthdays. Heather identified a cultural model when she explained that "You need to buy a good present for your grandma, and the market looks different. It is outside, but Carolina found a good present." Heather was able to bring in her cultural model of gift-giving, and incorporate it into her school knowledge as she learned about another culture.

When we read *Whoever You Are* (Fox, 1997), the children were drawn to the illustration of students going to school in an outdoor classroom and using wooden panels to record their lessons—as opposed to their cultural models of school and the materials they use, e.g. paper and pencils within four walls. They were fascinated by how the Mexican American family in *Too Many Tamales* (Soto, 1993) ate tamales as a Christmas tradition which led to conversations about how their own families celebrated. They were surprised by the family in *How My Parents Learned to Eat* (Friedman, 1984) who used knives and forks as well as chopsticks. When I asked them to tell me what they thought about these diverse cultural ways of living, they told me repeatedly, "It is different but okay."

Kathy Short (2008) wrote that looking at culture "does not begin with the ability to consider other points of view but with the realization that you have a point of view" (p. 4), but young students (as well as many of their adult counterparts) find it difficult to articulate and recognize their own points of view, considering them to be the "norm." The students not only noticed the ways that children from other cultures lived their lives, but in doing so, they began to identify the cultural models that influenced their personal lives. In these examples, the children named their cultural models about holiday celebrations and gift-giving, and held them up to the light of the cultural models of other children. They were able to broaden their perspectives by identifying surface level aspects of another culture as it related (or did not relate) to their own experiences, and this was a necessary first step of looking at deeper levels of culture.

Bringing Together Surface and Deeper Levels

The children easily identified superficial aspects of book characters' cultures, aspects often referred to as the "Five Fs"—food, fashion, folklore, festivals, and famous people (Meyer & Rhoades, 2006). However, through extended discussions of the books we read, they began to make connections to deeper levels of culture. I would often forefront our discussions by asking what was really important about the experiences of the characters in the books. For example, I would ask what was really important about birthdays or grandmothers or family celebrations. This question served as means to help the children refocus and look beneath cultural surfaces. For instance, while the children noticed that the outside of homes looked quite different around the globe, I asked them to think about what was really important about homes. They wrote in their journals that the important parts of homes were the insides, referring to them in their journals as "safe places," "places to play with my friends," "places to eat," and "places where my family is." In another example, I asked them what was really important about schools, and they wrote "how you feel about your teacher" and "your friends," and "what you learn." At the opening of this article, I shared what Peter said about Christmastime meals. He explained, "Some people do things different from us because of where they live and what they're used to. We don't eat tamales for Christmas but we have other stuff." Here Peter noted that—at the surface level—the kinds of food families ate at Christmas might be different. However when I asked Peter what was really important about Christmas celebrations, he explained,

"It's important because my whole family is together . . . and we give presents to each other." This suggests how certain social practices and beliefs were valued, such as families being brought together to share in gift-giving.

While we used many strategies to work toward an understanding of both surface and deeper levels of the children's personal cultures, I found one strategy to be especially helpful, what Short (2008) refers to as a cultural x-ray, an outline of a person with a heart drawn inside. Surface aspects of culture, those that are visible, are listed around the periphery of the "person." The deeper, less-visible levels of culture such as the values and beliefs the characters held in their hearts are written on the inside of the x-ray. For example, the children remembered *My Name is Celia* (Brown, 2004) and *Oye, Celia* (Sciurba, 2007), two picture books about the Cuban singer, Celia Cruz. They also remembered a CD of her songs that they listened to throughout the year, commenting that even though they did not understand all of the words, they enjoyed her singing. In fact, Hannah wrote in her own words and spelling about this CD (one that her teacher played often during the day whenever the children asked for it), "The musick . . . was fantastick. I loved the music. I could just jump up and dance." Through our discussions of these books and Cruz's music, the children discovered (and were surprised to learn) that their classmates listened to multiple genres of music at home—from hip hop to hymns, from contemporary to country-western. The children said that the kind of music someone listens to should go on the outside of a person's cultural x-ray, but the way the music makes a person feel should go on the inside.

After much discussion and practicing using the characters of the books as our guides, the children created personal cultural x-rays thinking carefully about what shows on the outside of a person and what should be put on the inside. The children used descriptive language on the outside of their x-rays; for example, Courtney listed on the outside that she was a girl who spoke English, has blond hair, owns a dog, lives in a house, and eats with a fork, spoon, and knife. However, on the inside, the children's language was more affective, naming emotional attributes and beginning to articulate their frameworks of meaning. For example, Courtney wrote that she feels happy when she hears music and that she loves her family and dog.

Defining and Documenting Their Culture

I continued to name and asked the children to name aspects of culture from the books we read. After reading many children's books, followed by multiple conversations and experiences with writing, drawing, and listening, the first-graders generated a definition of culture: "What is important to me and my family and how we do things." With this definition in their minds, I wanted them to document what they had been learning about culture through photography, asking them to take photographs of what they perceived to be aspects of their culture and then writing about them. I informed their parents and provided the children with disposable cameras to take home.

With the help of family members, they came back with photographs of their families, homes, holiday celebrations, gift-giving events such as birthdays and Christmas, and family sports activities—elements that they had determined were reflections of their culture. They also noted that family pets played an important part in their culture. Because of our reading, the children knew that different cultures valued different kinds of pets, and in their writing, they talked about the role their pets played as extended members of their families. In this writing sample, accompanied by a photograph of his cat, Allan brought together concepts of pets and gift giving.

All of the children wrote descriptive vignettes about their photographs, and we incorporated them into a book that the children decided to call, "The Best Parts of my Culture."

Students Identified and Made Connections to a Global Culture Different from Their Own

The Best Laid Plans

In pre-planning the study with Anne, we decided that for the second part of the curricular framework, "making cross-cultural explorations," we would present the children with an overview of several cultures from around the world and have them choose one that engaged them. To that end, I created text sets of books about Afghanistan (Khan, 1988; Lofthouse, 2007; Pohl, 2008; Weber, 2006; Winter, 2009) and South Korea (Choi, 2001; Kwon, 2005; Liu, 2001; McMahon, 1993; Park & Park, 1998; Recorvits, 2003) with titles that I felt appropriate for first-grade students. The text sets included multiple genres including folklore and fictional picture books and non-fiction books that portray contemporary views of these countries, as well as links to internet materials. We also chose these two countries because there were no students in the class from either Afghanistan or South Korea who could be cast as the sole cultural representative.

However, the best-laid plans (teaching and otherwise) often go in unintended directions. Having been introduced to the picture book, *14 Cows for America* (Deedy, 2009) by a colleague, I wanted to share the engaging story and beautiful illustrations with the children. I brought the book to our next meeting and read it to the first-graders. They were fascinated by this true story of a group of Maasai people from Kenya who gave fourteen cows, animals that represent their well-being and livelihood, to the United States in the aftermath of the attacks on New York City on September 11, 2001. The children were touched by the generosity and compassion of the Maasai and wanted to know more about them. The decision about which global culture to study was made by the children's passionate interest in this story.

We supplemented our reading of *14 Cows for America* (Deedy, 2009) with other texts that I (quickly) located in libraries and on-line book stores about the Maasai people (Joose, 2005; Krebs & Cairns, 2004; Kroll, 1997), and although it was difficult to find books about contemporary Maasai culture, I was able to find a few that discussed both the traditional life of nomadic Maasai cattle herders as well as the lives of Maasai people who had moved to the city (Hetfield, 1996; Nicolotto, 2005) and were living more urban lives. I also found on-line photographs of Maasai to share with the children, for example a photograph of an

outdoor school that Maasai children near the Tanzanian border attended. It reminded the children of outdoor schools they had seen in Fox's (1997) book, and these representations of schools continued to challenge the first graders' conceptions of school and how children could learn in different kinds of classrooms. We found Kenya on a map and talked about how far away it was from our city and state, and I explained that Kenya was a country in the large continent of Africa.

This fact struck a note with one of the boys. With some degree of surprise, he worked his way through a new idea and told me, "They have skin like me. I'm African-American. They must be . . . African-Africans," and he mentioned this fact proudly to me on several occasions, finding a way to make a personal connection to the generous and compassionate Maasai.

After discussing the role of Maasai men as warriors charged with protecting their communities, I found videos from the internet of an *adumu*, a competitive jumping dance performed by the men of a village to show their strength and stamina as warriors. We discussed the underlying beliefs that supported this dance, and the children talked about how important it would be to protect the people and the cows from predatory animals about which we had read. Additionally, I was able to locate a Maasai music CD from the university's music library, one that the children used to accompany their interpretation of a Maasai jumping dance performed in the schoolyard outside their classroom.

Beyond reading, I extended the children's understanding of *14 Cows for America* (Deedy, 2009) with a readers' theater rendition of the story. In this strategy, the children took the parts of the characters and the narrator. Props and costumes were not used so that the focus was "on oral interpretation which allows stories to come to life" (Short, Harste, & Burke, 1995, p. 187). We began to prepare for the readers' theater with conversations about what makes a good gift. Mark said, "It makes people happy," and Carlos told me that "It is something that people like." However, when I asked the children if they had ever given away something of their own as a gift, the question was greeted with silence. We continued our conversation by imagining what it would be like to give away something about which they cared deeply, as the Maasai had done with their cows. As the children performed the readers' theater, I videotaped it. Hearing the language of the story aloud added a new dimension of meaning. Several of the "actors" adopted deeper voices and added gestures and movement to represent their characters. The children listened intently and carefully to the voices of their classmates. Dialogue during the practices and afterwards focused on the generosity of the Maasai.

As a culminating activity for the cultural exploration of the Maasai, we returned to the cultural x-rays that had helped the children define aspects of their personal cultural lives. Since the children were already familiar with this strategy, I believed it would serve as an engaging way for them to bring together what they had learned about themselves as cultural beings and what we had learned about the Maasai people. I created a poster-sized cultural x-ray and served as scribe. Small groups re-read and studied the illustrations of the books we had read.

On the outside of the x-ray, they asked me to write that clothing and jewelry were colorful and that some of the people decorated their skin with bright colors for celebrations. They added that the Maasai were tall and had dark hair and skin, and they sometimes used spears as weapons. They noted that boys and girls did not eat their meals together and that they spoke the Maa language. They asked me to include the facts that some were cattle herders who lived in the country and some lived in cities. They explained that mothers carried their babies in "back packs" and that they did not have to wear shoes if they lived in the country. They lived among African animals like lions. However, the children asked me to add items on the inside of the cultural x-ray, too, aspects of Maasai culture that were less visible. For instance, remembering the narrator of *14 Cows for America* (Deedy, 2009), a young man who was studying to be a doctor, they decided that the Maasai must value learning and studying. They also noted how the Maasai loved their children and cared for their cows. Because the cows were treated with such kindness, the children decided they must be happy, and pictures of contented cows proliferated.

In addition, because of their gift to the Americans, the children decided that the Maasai must also be compassionate and generous, words we learned along the way and that the children added to the "heart" of the Maasai cultural x-ray.

Across Their Cultural Journeys, Students Read Extensively, Intensively, and Beyond Expectations

Reading Extensively

Peterson and Eeds (1990/2007) wrote that children need to have opportunities to read both intensively and extensively. As we read across the semester, the children read intensively and often wanted to learn more about a particular point that puzzled or intrigued them from one of our books. For example, when we read *Carolina's Gift* (Diaz, 2002), students immediately noticed that the main character had a llama for a pet. They were enthralled by the idea of such a pet and they asked many, many questions—questions about what llamas ate, whether you could take them for a walk, how llamas are bathed, and where they sleep at night. I went to the library and found as many non-fiction children's books as were available that described llamas in detail as well as picture books that featured llamas as characters to help the children answer some of their many questions. In small groups, the children read the books and/or looked through the illustrations or photographs, talked together about what they were learning, and then reported on what they had learned to the class. These forays into self-directed, in-depth learning continued throughout the semesters as the children wanted to learn more about homes and schools around the world, too. When we read about pets, homes, or schools, I asked the children questions intended to help them get beyond surface level conceptions and explore deeper conceptions of culture related to them. I asked questions such as, "What surprised you or what made you wonder about pets/homes/schools in this book?" and followed up such questions with "Why?" For example, after reading books about homes, the children described how different homes

looked around the world. However, when I asked them what surprised them about the homes around the world, Ashley told me that "homes look different but they all hold families."

Reading Beyond Expectations

I did not know the reading abilities of any of the children except for what I intuited as we shared books with each other across the year, and because of this I had few pre-conceived ideas about the children's abilities. When it came time for them to choose parts for the readers' theatre, I allowed them to volunteer for any part. The children's excitement level was high as they practiced and prepared for this experience, knowing that everyone would have a part and that their performance would be videotaped. In a letter that Charles wrote me at the end of the semester, he described his experiences with the readers' theatre. In his own words and spelling, he explained, "I like when we did the readers theder. I loved my part. My part was narrader 2. The senses were long and the words were hard but I could still read them." Charles was proud of his performance, noting that he found the reading difficult, but he was able to persevere through challenging materials. He exceeded his own expectations. However, Sebastian not only exceeded his own expectations but surprised his teacher with his reading as well. He eagerly volunteered to be Narrator 1, the first speaker in the performance. He practiced his lines with the student teacher and with me, and when the time came for him to start reading, he read slowly, pronouncing each word carefully, placing emphasis on certain phrases to help convey meaning, and smiling throughout his performance. Afterwards, Sebastian came up to me and said, "I loved that," and later Anne told me that Sebastian struggled with the simplest reading materials and was not a strong reader. She could not believe how well he read his part. Sebastian's desire to be a part of this whole-class experience allowed him to exceed reading expectations—his and his teacher's.

Final Thoughts
Going Beyond Standards

I did not want to add to Anne's already busy teaching schedule as I conducted research in her classroom. Rather, I wanted to incorporate first-grade teaching requirements into my plans for the students whenever possible. For example, two Social Studies standards that first-grade children needed to meet included identifying personal identities and identifying the ways that people are alike and different in the United States and the world. These standards were naturally and authentically embedded in the cultural explorations. Additionally, first-grade reading standards require that students respond to reading with creative dramatics, writing, and visual arts. We were able to interweave these standards seamlessly into the cultural explorations by including readers' theatre, writing in response to reading and to the photographs they took, and incorporating the visual arts in the children's illustrated response journals. However, the interdisciplinary possibilities went beyond our careful beginning-of-the-year planning as the children also read extensively about self-identified topics of interest and read beyond their expectations while expanding their understanding of another global culture.

Bringing Things Together

Aspects of culture are learned as part of the natural processes of growing up in a family and community and from participating in schools and other social institutions. The curricular framework that engaged students in cultural explorations created a learning environment in which the children could learn by connecting to and building from their life experiences. The framework left open possibilities for bringing in students' community knowledge about their culture and disciplinary knowledge from the classroom, as well as building on students' interests and concerns. In searching for an understanding of their personal cultural identities, children were able to move between their home lives, the literature we read, digital resources, and their content-area learning. They made connections among many parts of their lives inside school and outside the classroom walls.

The teaching practices that Anne and I included also had fluid boundaries, creating overlapping disciplinary opportunities. Through this exploration, the students were able to authentically engage in language arts topics such as reading and writing, as well as performance activities such as readers' theatre and dance, and social studies topics such as learning about people from different parts of the world. Bernstein (1977) wrote that this kind of learning and teaching, what he referred to as "invisible pedagogy," creates classrooms in which "things must be put together" (p. 532), meaning that teachers' and students' home and school knowledge and content across disciplinary areas can be "put together," as opposed to being "kept apart" as happens in many traditional classrooms.

Possibilities and Potentials of Cultural Explorations

Children's experiences with literature have the potential to alter their views of the world. The study in which I engaged with the first graders was a step toward that goal. The books I chose and the instructional strategies I used to help the children unpack cultural messages embedded in the books was a beginning, not an ending. The children made strides toward understanding the difficult concept of culture; yet we—children and adults alike—never really "get there." These kinds of cultural explorations should be consistently embedded across grade levels and content areas so that students and their adult mentors have as a goal "moving toward" deeper understandings of and appreciation for the cultural beliefs and values of people in our communities and beyond.

References

Adichie, C. (2009, December 26). *The danger of the single story.* Retrieved from http://www.ted.com/talks/chimamanda_adichie_the_danger_of_a_single_story.html

Bernstein, B. (1977). Class and pedagogies: Visible and invisible. In J. Karabel & A. H. Halsey (Eds.), *Power and ideology in education* (pp. 511–534). New York, NY: Oxford University Press.

Bishop, R. S. (2003). Reframing the debate about cultural authenticity. In D. Fox & K. Short (Eds.), *Stories matter: The complexity of cultural authenticity in children's literature* (pp. 25–37). Urbana, IL: National Council of Teachers of English.

Cai, M. (2003). Multiple definitions of multicultural literature: Is the debate really just "Ivory tower" bickering? In D. Fox & K. Short (Eds.), *Stories matter: The complexity of cultural authenticity in children's literature* (pp. 269–283). Urbana, IL: National Council of Teachers of English.

Davis, P. (2007). Storytelling as democratic approach to data collection: Interviewing children about reading. *Educational Research. 49*(2) 169–84.

Freeman, E., & Lehman, B. (2000). *Global perspectives in children's literature.* Boston, MA: Allyn and Bacon.

Galda, L., & Cullinan, B. E. (2009). *Literature and the child* (7th ed.). Belmont, CA: Wadsworth Publishing Company.

Gay, G. (2000). *Culturally responsive teaching: Theory, research, and practice.* New York, NY: Teachers College Press.

Gee, J. (1999). *An introduction to discourse analysis: Theory and method.* London, England: Routledge.

Harris, V. J. (2003). The complexity of debates about multicultural literature and cultural authenticity. In D. Fox & K. Short (Eds.), *Stories matter: The complexity of cultural authenticity in children's literature* (pp. 116–134). Urbana, IL: National Council of Teachers of English.

Keesing, R. (1987). Models, "folk" and "cultural": Paradigms regained? In D. Holland & N. Quinn (Eds.), *Cultural models in language & thought* (pp. 369–393). Cambridge, England: Cambridge University Press.

Meyer, C., & Rhoades, E. (2006). Beyond food, festivals, folklore, and fashion. *Kappa Delta Pi, 42*(2), 82–87.

Nieto, S. (2009). *Language, culture, and teaching: Critical perspectives* (2nd ed.). New York, NY: Routledge.

Peterson, R., & Eeds, M. (1990/2007). *Grand conversations: Literature groups in action.* New York, NY: Scholastic.

Rochman, H. (1993). *Against borders: Promoting books for a multicultural world.* Chicago, IL: American Library Association.

Short, K. (2008). *Exploring a curriculum that is international.* Retrieved from http://wowlit.org/on-line-publications/stories/storiesi2/?page=5

Short, K., Harste, J., & Burke, C. (1995). *Creating classrooms for authors and inquirers* (2nd ed.). Portsmouth, NH: Heinemann.

Temple, C., Martinez, M., & Yokota, J. (2006). *Children's books in children's hands: An introduction to their literature* (3rd ed.). Boston, MA: Allyn and Bacon.

Children's Literature Cited

Brown, M. (2004). *My name is Celia: The life of Celia Cruz/Me llamo Celia: La vida de Celia Cruz.* (R. Lopez, Illus.). Flagstaff, AZ: La Luna Press.

Choi, Y. (2001). *The name jar.* New York, NY: Random House.

Deedy, C. A. (2009). *14 cows for America.* (T. Gonzalez, Illus.) Atlanta, GA: Peachtree Publishers.

Diaz, K. (2002). *Carolina's gift: A story of Peru* (G. Landolt, Illus.). Norwalk, CT: Soundprints.

Fox, M. (1997). *Whoever you are.* (L. Staub, Illus.). San Diego, CA: Harcourt.

Friedman, I. (1984). *How my parents learned to eat.* (A. Say, Illus.). Boston, MA: Houghton Mifflin.

Hetfield, J. (1996). *Maasai of East Africa.* New York, NY: PowerKids Press.

Joose, B. (2005). *Papa do you love me?* (B. Lavallee, Illus.). San Francisco, CA: Chronicle Books.

Khan, R. (1988). *The Roses in my carpet*. (R. Himler, Illus.). Markham, Ontario: Fitzhenry & Whiteside.

Krebs, L., & Cairns, J. (2004). *We all went on safari*. (J. Cairns, Illus.). Cambridge, MA: Barefoot Books.

Kroll, V. (1997). *Maasai and I*. (N. Carpenter, Illus.). New York, NY: Aladdin.

Kwon, Y. (2005). *My cat copies me*. La Jolla, CA: Kane Miller.

Liu, J. S. (2001). *Yellow umbrella*. La Jolla, CA: Kane Miller.

Lofthouse, L. (2007). *Ziba came on a boat*. (R. Ingpen, Illus.). La Jolla, CA: Kane Miller.

McMahon, P. (1993). *Chi-Hoon: A Korean girl*. (M.F. O'Brien, Illus.). Honesdale, PA: Boyds Mills Press.

Nicolotto, M. (2005). *Kuntai: A Maasai child*. Farmington Hills, MI: Blackbirch Press.

Park, F., & Park, G. (1998). *My freedom trip*. (D.R. Jenkins, Illus.). Honesdale, PA: Boyds Miller Press.

Pohl, K. (2008). *Looking at Afghanistan*. New York, NY: Gareth Stevens.

Recorvits, H. (2003). *My name is Yoon*. (G. Swiatkowska, Illus.). New York, NY: Farrar, Straus and Giroux.

Sciurba, K. (2007). *Oye, Celia: A song for Celia Cruz*. (E. Rodriguez, Illus.). New York, NY: Henry Holt.

Soto, G. (1993). *Too many tamales*. (E. Martinez, Illus.). New York, NY: Putnam & Grosset.

Weber, V. (2006). *I come from Afghanistan*. New York, NY: Weekly Reader Early Library.

Winter, J. (2009). *Nasreen's secret school*. New York, NY: Beach Lane Books.

Critical Thinking

1. How does children's literature open new worlds for readers?

2. How does children's literature help readers recognize shared problems?

3. How does children's literature present culturally diverse frames of references?

4. How does children's literature promote critical inquiry?

Create Central

www.mhhe.com/createcentral

Internet References

Jane Addams Peace Association
www.janeaddamspeace.org/jacba/

National Council for the Social Studies: Notable Tradebooks for Young People
www.socialstudies.org/resources/notable

PAMELA JEWETT is an associate professor in the College of Education at the University of South Carolina. She teaches children's literature, content area literacy, and reading methods courses in the Language and Literacy program. Her research focuses on children's and adolescent literature and critical literacy.

Jewett, Pamela. From *The Journal of Children's Literature*, vol. 9, Spring 2011, pp. 20–29. Copyright © 2011 by Children's Literature Assembly. Used with permission.

Article   Prepared by: Nancy P. Gallavan, *University of Central Arkansas*

Representations of Native Americans in Elementary School Social Studies: A Critical Look at Instructional Language

MICHELE R. MASON & GISELA ERNST-SLAVIT

Learning Outcomes

After reading this article, you will be able to:

- Understand ways to establish pluralistic perspectives and relate to the Other.

- Connect the goals of cultural competence found in university teacher preparation courses with clinical field placements.

Introduction

In a fourth grade classroom in the Pacific Northwest, a teacher and her students are reviewing one of the most infamous events in U.S. history: "The Trail of Tears," the forced resettlement of the Cherokee people from Georgia to Oklahoma—known by the Cherokee as "*nu na hi du na tlo hi lu i*" or the "Trail Where They Cried." After several teacher prompts, students cite the Indian Removal Act as the reason why the Cherokee were forced to move west of the Mississippi River. Seeking more information, Jeanette probes her students as she points to the Cherokee Nation's ancestral homeland in parts of North Carolina, Georgia, Tennessee, and Alabama:

> Jeanette: *And what was special about that land? There's tons of land. What was so unique about that? Joel.*

> Joel: *If you dug, like, deep enough, you could find, like, gold? Like a gold mine?*

> Jeanette: *[They] discovered gold.*

> Ashley: *Is that, like, the only reason why they [the Cherokee] had to move? Just because they [European-Americans] wanted to be rich?*

> Jeanette: *That was why.*

> Ashley: *Well, that's a dumb reason!*

> Students: *(laughing)*

> Jeanette: *I agree.*

Ashley's blunt comment evoked student laughter and the mild agreement of her teacher. The conversation continued with similar exchanges before students engaged in two culminating activities: (1) a written summary of The Trail of Tears and (2) a "pictograph expressing how the Cherokee felt."

During this 15-minute review one important learning objective was apparent: to have children empathize with the Cherokee Nation's point of view. This was certainly accomplished as demonstrated by Ashley's incredulous comment and by similar responses by her peers as discussed below. What was missing, however, was a space for children to critically analyze and problematize the basic cause of the displacement of the Cherokee. Jeanette, consciously or unconsciously, used questions inviting feelings of empathy for the *Other* but missed the opportunity to further explore historical reasons for unjust treatment, such as land theft.

The vignette above illustrates how Jeanette constructed—via language and representation—a way to interpret Western history, detached from a critical perspective. It is her speech that guides the discussion; her words and her silence frame and construct the "story" of The Trail of Tears. As Weedon (1987) explains,

> Language is the place where actual and possible forms of social organization and their likely social and political consequences are defined and contested. Yet it is also the place where our sense of ourselves, our subjectivity, is constructed. (p. 21)

The purpose of this article is to draw attention to the language used by fourth and fifth grade teachers during social studies instruction and to discuss the implications of how this language frames non-dominant groups, as in this case. Via the discussion of segments of instructional conversations, we point to the pervasive use of language that perpetuates stereotypes and biased representations of Native American history.

To frame the analysis, we discuss three different perspectives. First, we summarize the literature on *Otherness*, particularly, how the *Other* is constructed (1) through language, (2) in Western history, and (3) in classroom discourse. Second, we share information about the Critical Language Awareness movement rooted in the United Kingdom. This body of work is concerned with the relationship between language and social context, particularly educators' awareness of how ideology and power structures inherent in language play out during daily school routines.

In addition, we highlight the National Social Studies Standards' focus on helping students construct a pluralist perspective based on diversity. We argue that by carefully examining the talk that transpires in classroom discussions, we can have a window into how knowledge, identity, social positioning, and value systems are constructed by teachers and students. The paper ends with a list of specific suggestions for educators and teacher educators regarding language awareness, primary sources, and the importance of using balanced and comprehensive historical perspectives.

How the Other Is Constructed through Language

One way in which we use language to define and construct our world is in how *we* refer to people whom *we* perceive to be *different* from ourselves or the group with which *we* identify. Often we use a simple either-or dichotomy marked by the use of telltale pronouns like *we-they* or *us-them* (Eriksson & Aronsson, 2005). This positioning of identity and noticing of difference, or *otherness*, is well established (Davies & Harré, 1990; Gudykunst, 2004; Gutiérrez & Orellana, 2006; Rogoff, 2003; Sampson, 2008, 1993; Sollors, 1986; Ting-Toomey, 1993). As Yep (1998) comments on his own experience:

> For many Euro Americans, I am "a person of color." This view of marginality, of "otherness," is one of isolation, invisibility, alienation, and deprivation. Otherness *represents the undesirable, degraded, exiled, suppressed, deviant, disenfranchised, and incongruous elements of the "ideal order." (emphasis added; p. 83)*

Being labeled, treated, or talked about as *Other* is to be excluded from something. The *Other* can be as exotic as a Finn living in Peru, as fantastic as Paul Bunyan and Babe the Blue Ox, or as mundane as a comparison of physical attributes, choice of attire, or regional dialect. It is important to realize that in the United States, as well as in many other English-speaking parts of the world, power rests in the hands of the dominant group: White, middle-class, heterosexual, and usually male (McCarthy, 1996). Everyone else becomes the *Other*—and a more exotic *Other* the further they are perceived to be from the dominant norm.

Cultures and groups identify and use norms, or what groups consider to be *normal,* in order to construct, maintain, and differentiate their identity from other groups and/or to exclude outsiders or *Others*. Often such norms are so ingrained in a group, so taken for granted, that a group considers the norms to be obvious to any *normal* person (Verkuyten, 2001). In effect, it is as if the group's point of view is invisible to the group itself. The group believes its perspective is objective—a kind of "God's-eye view from Nowhere" (Sampson, 2008, 1993, p. 84)—and fails to recognize that its perspective is only one among many equally valid viewpoints.

How the Other Is Constructed in Western History

The construction of the *Other* can be traced back through the history of Western civilization. McGrane (1989) provides a compelling account beginning with the Renaissance and continuing through the twentieth century. In his book McGrane discusses how the *Other* was constructed and reconstructed as Western societal focus and identity shifted: from outside of Christianity—to outside of civilized or enlightened people—to living outside of time. As the reader will notice, this analysis is not new; other historians and anthropologists have arrived at similar conclusions (see, for example, Geertz, 1973; Greenblatt, 1991; Rogoff, 2003; Wolf, 1982).

How the Other is Constructed in Classroom Discourse

Recent studies by Eriksson and Aronsson (2005), Palfreyman (2005), and Yoon (2008) point to the insidious construction of difference or *otherness* in classrooms by teachers who seem unaware of how their language use contributes to such constructions. For example, in their study of booktalk sessions in a Swedish elementary school, Eriksson and Aronsson (2005) found that teachers implicitly or explicitly talked about "us Swedish children" when discussing books set in environments foreign to the students (p. 719). *Otherness,* in this case, was accomplished by foregrounding differences, setting up a series of contrasts between *us* and *them.*

Classroom discussions, particularly teacher talk, influence and shape the beliefs, ideas, values, and understandings of students. According to Cazden (1988), "[w]e have to consider how the words spoken in classrooms affect the outcomes of education: how observable classroom discourse affects the unobservable thought processes of each of the participants, and thereby the nature of what all students learn" (p. 99). In other words, children from traditionally underrepresented groups may feel very disconnected from a discussion of American history if they do not see a link to their own story. Adrienne Rich captures the overwhelming feeling of distress that narratives like this one have on students in a powerful quote: "When someone with the authority of a teacher, say, describes the world and you are not in it, there is a moment of psychic disequilibrium, as if you looked into a mirror and saw nothing" (Rich, 1986, p. 119).

By carefully examining the talk that transpires in classrooms, we can have a window into how knowledge, identity, social positioning, and value systems are constructed by teachers and students. These constructions, fortunately or unfortunately, can become powerful pillars upon which societal norms are built. Bourdieu (1977) makes clear his belief that schools actually reproduce societal norms, values, and conditions by inculcating in students the ideologies embraced by members of the dominant group—usually in charge of education. In today's society

> power is predominantly exercised through the generation of consent rather than through coercion, through ideology rather than through physical force, through the inculcation of self-disciplining practices rather than through the breaking of skulls . . . . It is an age in which the production and reproduction of the social order depend increasingly upon practices and processes of a broadly cultural nature. Part of this development is an enhanced role for language in the exercise of power: it is mainly in discourse that consent is achieved, ideologies are transmitted, and practices, meanings, values and identities are taught and learnt. (Fairclough, 1995, p. 219)

This vital role of language in issues of power, equity, and societal construction lead us to Critical Language Awareness, an approach that looks at teachers' language through a critical lens.

Critical Language Awareness

The Language Awareness (LA) movement has its roots in the United Kingdom beginning in the early 1980s (Andrews, 2007; Granville, 2003; Janks, 2000). In its most basic form, "[l]anguage awareness refers to the development . . . of an enhanced consciousness of and sensitivity to the forms and functions of language" (Carter, 2003, p. 64). Over the years two distinct foci have developed under the language awareness umbrella: Teacher Language Awareness (TLA) and Critical Language Awareness (CLA; for a partial review, see Svalberg, 2007). In this article, we will limit our discussion to Critical Language Awareness.

Critical Language Awareness is primarily concerned with the relationship between language and social context. Proponents believe that "language use is not neutral" (Carter, 2003, p. 64) and that the "nontransparent aspects" of language influence and are in turn influenced by: (1) representations and positioning of identity, (2) society, (3) politics, (4) relationships of power, and (5) ideologies constructed by and conveyed through language (Bolitho, et al., 2003; Carter, 2003; Clark, Fairclough, Ivanič, & Martin-Jones, 1991; Fairclough, 1992; Janks & Ivanič, 1992). This understanding of language has implications for teacher education and practice.

Teachers who embrace CLA: (1) acknowledge the implicit and explicit ideologies and power structures inherent in language, (2) understand that the use of such language, even unintentionally, can and does legitimate and reproduce social inequalities, and (3) strive to become agents of longterm change in society (Clark, Fairclough, Ivanič, & Martin-Jones, 1990). Teachers who demonstrate CLA are not only cognizant of the ideologies that shape language but are also aware of and exercise great care in their own use of language (Clark, et al., 1990). Consider the words of Lake (1990), a member of the Cherokee and Seneca tribes, to the teacher of his son, Wind-Wolf: "What you say and what you do in the classroom, what you teach and how you teach it, and what you don't say and don't teach will have significant effect on the potential success or failure of my child" (p. 53).

Critical Language Awareness is a melding of philosophy, ideology, knowledge, skill, and self-awareness in the critically conscious practice and sustained use of language in the every day routines of school—including the teaching of content area material (Clark, et al., 1990; Clark & Ivanič, 1999).

> . . . [G]iven that power relations work increasingly at an implicit level through language, and given that language practices are increasingly targets for intervention and control, a critical awareness of language is a prerequisite for effective citizenship, and a democratic entitlement. (emphasis added; Fairclough, 1995, p. 222)

Within this context, one of the most recognizable areas of education for citizenship and democracy is in the field of social studies.

National Social Studies Standards

Multicultural education goals and social studies standards in the U.S. try to address the need to mitigate and transform perceptions and constructions of *otherness* by educating students to be "'student-citizens,' young people who will soon assume the role of citizen" with global and pluralist perspectives (National Council for the Social Studies, n.d.-b, para. 25).

> Students should be helped to construct a pluralist perspective *based on diversity. This perspective involves respect for differences of opinion and preference; of race, religion, and gender; of class and ethnicity; and of culture in general. This construction should be based on the realization that differences exist among individuals and the conviction that this diversity can be positive and socially enriching. Students need to learn that the existence of cultural and philosophical differences are not 'problems' to be solved; rather, they are healthy and desirable qualities of democratic community life.* (National Council for the Social Studies, n.d.-b, para. 30)

If the "primary purpose of social studies is to help young people develop the ability to make informed and reasoned decisions for the public good as citizens of a culturally diverse, democratic society in an interdependent world" (National Council for the Social Studies, n.d.-a, para. 4), then we must provide students with diverse perspectives, resources, and opportunities to critically discuss the trajectory of different cultures and groups not as representatives of "dead and buried" cultures (e.g., as if Native Americans were extinct), or as unskilled laborers (e.g., "new" immigrants), or as undesirable settlers (e.g., the Chinese Exclusion Act). Students benefit from learning about different cultures and groups not merely as part of a chronological history of the United States through statistics and charts but as the stories of different groups of people—past and present—including conflicting accounts of their trajectories.

While in recent years textbooks and curricula have been deliberate in updating materials to avoid stereotyping and the construction of *otherness,* not all educators have been able to make that shift during classroom discussions (see Eriksson & Aronsson, 2005; Hollingworth, 2009; Palfreyman, 2005; Yoon, 2008). Using the combined lenses of the construction of the *Other,* Critical Language Awareness, and social studies goals, the following analysis seeks to address the following questions: What is the nature of the interaction in three upper elementary classrooms during discussions of Native Americans? How are teachers in these classrooms using language to refer to Native Americans during social studies instruction? What opportunities were given to students to critically explore the historical treatment of Native Americans?

Context of the Study

This work is part of a larger ethnographic (see Hornberger in Cumming, et al., 1994), sociolinguistic (Bloome & Clark, 2006; Erickson, 2006; Green & Wallat, 1981) and multi-site (Eisenhart, 2001) study that sought to unpack the different language *registers* (a variety of a language used for a specific purpose in a particular context) used by teachers during content-area instruction in fourth and fifth grade classrooms in southwest Washington (Ernst-Slavit, Mason, & Wenger, 2009).

Each participating classroom included at least five English language learners of varying levels of English proficiency. Participating teachers had at least five years of teaching experience, as well as advanced specialization in English as a Second Language (ESL) education, and were highly regarded by teachers and administrators. (See Table 2 for additional information about the teachers in this study. All participant and location names are pseudonyms.)

One or both authors observed content-area instruction over the course of one week. Each set of classroom observations ranged from 16–22 hours. Data collected included video and audio recordings, field notes, still photographs, teacher interviews, and pertinent written materials, such as handouts, worksheets, and student work.

For this article we focus on segments collected in one fifth grade and two fourth grade classrooms during social studies instruction. The topics centered on Native Americans:

(1) the formation of colonies in the *New World* and the relationship between colonists and the Native Americans; (2) the role of Sacagawea in the Lewis and Clark Expedition; and (3) the experience of the Cherokee Nation on the Trail of Tears.

Examples of the Other in Social Studies Classrooms

We ask the reader to consider the depictions of Native Americans as the *Other* constructed by 4th and 5th grade students and their teachers in the following segments. How are members of the non-dominant culture represented? How are students encouraged to think, feel, and talk about Native Americans? How is the impact of one group's actions on another discussed or avoided?

"Hostile Savages" Constructing the Other as Uncivilized But Potentially Useful Trading Partners

In the following segment, Kirsten is continuing a colonial era social studies unit, in which teams of student *colonists* would eventually apply for a *New World* colony charter from the King of England, represented by the male teacher in the adjoining classroom. Students, in four-to-five member teams, each have specific tasks to complete as explained in a teacher-created handout. In an attempt to make the project more authentic, all students were required to select and use an *English* name. Additionally, the text of the handout itself was printed in a cursive font, reminiscent of handwriting of a bygone day. Here, Kirsten is reading aloud from a section of the handout titled "Task One: Political Structure."

Segment 1

Kirsten: *There must be adequate protection for the inhabitants from attack by hostile savages, but you will also have to oversee friendly trade with the natives to ensure their proper treatment. We want the Indians to help us and not be our enemies. What will you do to make this happen? You will need to address that in your paper. Are you going to have Native Americans around you? If so, are they going to be friendly or not?*

Take a moment to count the number of different nouns used to refer to Native Americans (e.g., savages, Indians). Consider the connotations of the words selected and what the implications of those words suggest.

The use of "hostile savages" constructs Native Americans as dangerous, unpredictable, and uncivilized *Others.* The phrase "friendly trade with the natives" views the *Other* from a commercial or capitalistic perspective. Native Americans may have something needed (i.e., a useful commodity) or may want to trade for things they want. The use of the phrase "proper treatment" constructs the *Other* as a powerless child in need of protection. Finally, an unrealistic dichotomy is established by the words "friendly or not." Relationships between diverse groups of people and nations rarely distill down to such simplistic either-or dichotomies. Such depictions do not convey the reality that diverse peoples must consciously and diligently work to understand and value one another.

What may not be apparent in this colonial project is what has been excluded as a choice. Students only had the opportunity to approach this historical moment in the role of European colonizers. It was not an option for students to represent a tribe or sovereign nation of Native Americans. Once again, this absence represents a missed opportunity for students to fully explore more complicated historical events and in doing so, continue to develop complex understandings of social interaction between groups.

Finally, the teacher attempts to make the project authentic by recreating the conditions and language of the Colonial era. However, there was no evidence that the language used to describe Native Americans was problematized or that the perspectives and ideologies of the colonizers were critically explored, an observation particularly puzzling in a school with a Native American name.

"Do You Remember What a Slave Is?" Constructing Sacagawea as a Serviceable Other

During the week of observation in Keely's classroom, she and her students started a new unit on the Lewis and Clark Expedition. The excerpts below are part of a longer instructional conversation focusing on the status of Sacagawea as a slave, while at the same time highlighting the pivotal role she played in the survival of the Expedition. While drawing a previously traced image of Sacagawea, Keely introduced this important figure in U.S. history in an almost storylike manner.

Segment 2

Keely: *His wife served as a translator. Not only that, Sacajawea helped (beginning to trace over the light pencil already on the butcher paper—forming the garment worn by Sacajawea)—everyone find food and survive the winters. She showed them how they could capture food, how they could fish, and the berries they could eat—*

Joel: *She was very smart.*

Keely: *She was very smart. She played a very important role in the expedition.*

* * * *

Keely: *Sacagawea . . . was a Shoshone, Native American girl and she was taken from her family one day, um, during a raid by another tribe who were stealing their horses. So, at 16, actually she was 14 at the time, she was kidnapped by another tribe and taken. And she became a slave for that other tribe. Do you remember what a slave is?*

Students: *Yah.*

Keely: *Okay. What's a slave?*

Ashley: *Someone who, uh (many hands raised).*

Keely: *Uh, Max?*

Max: *Someone that, uh, um, works for another person and [xxx].*

Keely: *Yah. Um, were they usually treated really nicely?*

Students: *No.*

Keely: *No, not usually.*

Joe: *Sometimes they were though.*

Keely: *[xxx] times they were. So, at 14 she was taken and her job as a slave was to sew clothing for other Native American women in the tribe. That was her job. Well, when she got a little older, the chief of that tribe decided to sell her or trade her for goods to Charbonneau, the fur trader.*

* * * *

Keely: *She helped them locate food—roots along the way: special roots that they could use as medicine. William Clark served as the doctor on the trail, so William Clark and Sacajawea teamed up a lot, because she was able to show him roots and things that they could use as medication to treat people who got ill along the trail.*

* * * *

Keely: *So, one of the jobs, we know that she helped find food. She also served as a translator, because she could communicate with the Native Americans. She, uh, when she was doing her sewing for the other tribe, she was [xxx] beading [xxx] clothes, where they take the little beads and [xxx] looked really nice.*

After briefly mentioning Sacagawea's baby, Jean Baptiste or Pompe, the lesson continues with an extended description of the contributions and characteristics of another member of the expedition, Seaman, a Newfoundland dog. It was unfortunate that Sacagawea, the slave upon whom the expedition depended for food, medicine, seasonal survival skills, and communication skills, and Seaman, the dog, were presented as almost equally useful members of the Expedition.

In looking at the segment above we see a large list of ways in which Sacagawea was an asset to the Expedition. Taken together, they construct an image of Sacagawea as what Sampson (2008, 1993) refers to as a "serviceable" *Other*, an *Other* "constructed so as to be of service to the dominant groups' own needs, values, interests and points of view" (p. 4).

A brief discussion of Sacagawea's status as a slave also occurs. The teacher asks her students to recall what they know about slaves. Students respond with an incomplete and inaccurate depiction of a slave as someone who "works for another person" and who may or may not be treated well. Rather than clarifying or expanding upon this understanding, the teacher continues with the story of Sacagawea. The opportunity to hold a critical discussion of how a person was transformed into a commodity, to be purchased and sold, was lost. Additionally, as a slave woman used to service "the needs and desires . . . of men," Sacagawea was constructed as man's *Other*, "serviceable to man" (Sampson, 2008, 1993, p. 6).

"Would that be Illegal Today?" Constructing the Other as a Pitiable, Conquered People without Rights

The next segment occurs a few minutes following the opening vignette. Jeanette is reviewing the forced resettlement of the Cherokee people from the southeastern portion of the U.S. to the Louisiana Territory (the Trail of Tears).

Segment 3

Jeanette: *What were they [the Cherokee] promised when they moved west of the Mississippi?*

Diana: *It was land.*

Jeanette: *They were promised free land, weren't they? They were promised land. Give up your land here, and we're gunna give you some land over there. Okay Do you think they were very happy about that?*

Students: *No.*

Jeanette: *Give up your house here . . . give up your house here and everything you know here, because we said so.*

Arthur: *Huh No way (loud voice).*

Marisol: *[xxx] kind of mean.*

* * * *

Jeanette: *Jenny had a really good question and I don't think a lot of us heard it.*

Jenny: *Wouldn't it be, like, a crime, if, like, they [the European-Americans] made them [the Cherokee] move all the way over there and then they promised them a whole bunch of stuff that they never gave?*

Samantha: *Actually—yah.*

Adrian: *You should go to jail for it.*

Students: *(multiple overlapping comments, then hands beginning to raise.)*

Jeanette: *What do you think, Mark?*

Mark: *Would that be illegal today if they did that?*

Jeanette: *Well, I would like to think so . . . Unfortunately, governments do things, ours and others, do things that maybe people think are wrong or that maybe some people think are okay . . . and you have to look inside you when you're deciding what's right or what's wrong—what you would*

think. What do we think about this particular. . . .

Students: *Wrong. Cruel (loud voices).*

Jeanette: *I agree. Okay. Shhhh. What kinds of feelings do you think the Cherokee were having as they were making their thousand-mile trek on foot—because no cars—and they get to the end and there's nuthin'? I want to hear more than just "sad." I want more than one-word answers here. How do we think they felt?*

In the first section of the transcript, Jeanette encourages her students to consider the feelings of the Cherokee when they were forced to leave their home territories. Students respond by expressing their moral outrage at the treatment of the Cherokee in two ways. First, students respond emotionally—empathetically—as prompted by their teacher's request. Later, students begin to question the legality of the actions committed by the European-Americans and in that way go beyond just an affective response. By emphasizing and insisting upon an emotional response (i.e., pity) to the Cherokee's treatment, the opportunity to explore deeper, critical understandings of history, informed by diverse perspectives, was missed.

While expressing empathy is valuable in exploring and creating relationships between differing groups of people, by concentrating on the Cherokee's feelings, the teacher's repeated requests for an emotional response prevented a deeper discussion about the critical issues surrounding the Trail of Tears. In addition, by presenting the Cherokee as subject to the laws of the European-American leaders but without enforced rights under those same laws, the review of this event portrayed the Cherokee as a conquered people, as weak and pitiable *Others* (Eriksson & Aronsson, 2005).

This identity was reinforced by calling upon students to imagine how the Cherokee felt—to feel sorry for or pity them because of what happened to them. What happened and accountability for what happened were wholly disconnected from a recognizable, identifiable, concrete source (e.g., Andrew Jackson, United States). With hindsight, it is easy to claim the moral high ground and denounce the actions of our European-American ancestors while simultaneously constructing ourselves as "caring and empathizing" (Eriksson & Aronsson, p. 735).

Conclusions

By attempting to present the historical treatment of Native Americans as a story well-told, but without providing opportunities to critically analyze such treatment, educators may in fact be masking dominant ideologies and contributing to the reproduction of societal norms. In contrast to the stated goals of social studies standards, students are denied the opportunity to wrestle with the difficult topics that would develop their critical consciousness (Freire, 1970, 1993) and help them become ethical and moral beings in an interconnected world.

Instead, the classroom discussions we have presented explore history from a *safe* moral distance across time, obscuring the culpability of our European-American ancestors and the role each of us has in current social justice issues.

If U.S. educators are truly committed to nurturing a *"pluralist perspective* based on diversity" in students (National Council for the Social Studies, n.d.-b, para. 30), then contrary to the beliefs of some educators (Hollingworth, 2009), it is never too early to begin exploring complex and multifaceted issues with students (Morgan, 2009). As the transcript segments illustrated, we clearly have a lot of work ahead of us. Not even teachers with specialized linguistic and cultural preparation (i.e., English language learner coursework and certification) are immune to the implicit nature of ideologies cunningly entwined in the language of the classroom.

Suggestions for Practice
Analyzing Teacher Talk

As educators we can improve our teaching by analyzing our language via the use of video recordings. Video recordings can be done by simply placing a camcorder in a corner of the classroom. To avoid students getting distracted by the camcorder, start the camcorder before students enter the classroom and turn it off once students leave. We suggest having the camcorder in the classroom for a few days before the actual videotaping begins.

When viewing classroom videos, focus on different aspects of language use, such as:

1. How are whole-class discussions constructed (e.g., Are students challenged to think about, construct, defend, and revise their own ideas)?

2. What kinds of questions are asked (e.g., *display,* requiring a brief right-or-wrong answer; *open-ended,* which allow students to provide extended and personalized responses)?

3. Is sufficient wait-time provided for students' thinking after a question is raised? In our observations of classrooms, the average wait time after a question is between one and two seconds.

4. What kind of feedback is provided? For example, are we responding to students' questions with evaluative replies (e.g., "great," "right," "excellent," or "not really," "no, not quite," "almost"), which can limit student thinking instead of prompting students to support their answers logically (e.g., "Can you give us an example?" or "Why do you think that?") or request further clarification (e.g., "Tell me more." or "What do you mean by____?").

5. How are we referring to individuals, groups and cultures different than our own? Are we using words like *those* or *these* to refer to different groups? Are we *othering* groups by using the *us-them* dichotomy as in the Eriksson and Aronsson study (2005)?

There are many other aspects to observe when viewing tapes of our teaching such as, are we calling on boys and girls equally? Are we giving all our students a chance to speak? Are we encouraging students to ask questions? To lead the discussion? How are we bringing in different perspectives? (For additional information about discussions in content-area classrooms, see Flynn, 2009; Salinas, Fránquiz, & Guberman, 2006; Zwiers, 2008.)

Using Primary Sources

Primary sources include artifacts, authentic documents, photos, recordings, transcripts of interviews, or other sources of information created during or close to the event or time period studied. In today's electronic era, primary sources can be retrieved from digital collections, often containing substantial historical works. See for example, the Library of Congress (http://www.loc.gov/library/libarch-digital.html), university data centers such as the Labriola National American Indian Center at Arizona State University (http://lib.asu.edu/labriola), and Native American archives such as the Cherokee Nation (http://www.cherokee.org/Culture/History/TOT/Cat/Default.aspx).

It is important to realize that twentieth-century history can be studied using primary sources. As with topics such as immigration, World War II, and the Korean and Vietnamese Wars, Native American historical and current events can be explored via the knowledge and experiences of community or family members who lived through those times. Through exposure to and analysis of oral history interviews, video memoirs, and face-to-face interviews, students learn to ask meaningful questions, draw conclusions, and reflect on possible solutions and consequences. Primary sources allow history to come alive.

Using Contrapuntal Pedagogy

Contrapuntal pedagogy involves reading and accessing mainstream and non-mainstream texts (e.g., films, novels, poems, plays, newspaper reports) so that students have the opportunity to compare and contrast diverse perspectives, as well as realize how mainstream literature creates particular narratives of a society's history (Singh & Greenlaw, 1998). By using contrapuntal pedagogy teachers and students engage in inquiry and critique about how colonialism and imperialism have historically shaped and continue to shape mainstream knowledge about Native Americans.

This pedagogical practice creates space for the knowledge and perspectives of marginalized people to be present. It allows for diverse perspectives to be critiqued, compared, contrasted, and constructed in the classroom (DeJaeghere, 2009). One simple but effective example is the use of political cartoons, such as the two included with this article.

Providing Balanced and Comprehensive Historical Perspectives

Use timelines or graphic organizers to provide historical perspectives, to illustrate how cultures are born, evolve, and overlap in relation to other cultures in the same region or across the globe. This kind of comprehensive historical perspective will help students understand that life in the *Americas* did not begin when the first Europeans arrived but that there were a myriad of cultures already well established with rich and ancient histories (Good, 2009).

The story line in most school textbooks places Native Americans in the early history of colonial times, yet does not discuss their lives before Columbus. Most textbooks do not discuss where Native Americans lived, how their political structures worked, how they built their homes . . . nor how and what they hunted and gathered (Hawkins, 2002, p. 16).

In addition, timelines that extend from the past to the present day will assist students in debunking the notion that Native Americans are historical artifacts no longer present in our nation. It will also allow them to critically analyze the trajectory of different tribes in relation to issues and events (e.g., pilgrims, colonies, westward expansion, establishment of reservations, tribal sovereignty, hunting and fishing rights) and conflicts.

As Macedo stated so eloquently, "one cannot teach conflict as if, all of a sudden, it fell from the sky. The conflict must be anchored in those competing histories and ideologies that generate the conflict in the first place" (Freire, 1970, 1993, p. 24).

Critical Thinking

1. What is meant by the Other and Otherness?
2. What are the differences among contemporary context, historical context, and daily routines and references?
3. How is identity constructed in the classroom?
4. What is meant by social positioning?

Create Central

www.mhhe.com/createcentral

Internet References

Tribal Government Information
www.usa.gov/Government/Tribal.shtml
Voices from Gaps
http://voices.cla.umn.edu/teachingmaterial/identity.html

MICHELE R. MASON *is a doctoral student and Gisela Ernst-Slavit is a professor in the College of Education at Washington State University-Vancouver, Vancouver, Washington.*

Mason, Michele R.;Ernst-Slavit, Gisela. From *Multicultural Education*, vol. 7, Fall 2010, pp. 10–16. Copyright © 2010 by Caddo Gap Press. Reprinted by permission.

Article   Prepared by: Nancy P. Gallavan, *University of Central Arkansas*

A Case for Culturally Relevant Teaching in Science Education and Lessons Learned for Teacher Education

FELICIA MOORE MENSAH

Learning Outcomes

After reading this article, you will be able to.

- Explore culturally relevant teaching and learning as part of all content subject areas.

- Increase attentiveness for identifying culturally relevant teaching and learning in classrooms during P–12 clinical field placements.

The literature on multicultural teacher education emphasizes the preparation of teachers for diverse classrooms, with a great deal of the literature focusing on the preparation of White teachers for communities that have been traditionally underserved. In a literature review by Sleeter (2001), she discussed the effects of various pre-service teacher education strategies, ranging from recruiting and selecting students to program restructuring. She concluded that most of the research addresses teacher attitudes and the lack of knowledge that pre-service teachers have about multicultural teaching. She also acknowledged that research has not addressed how to populate the teaching profession with excellent multicultural and culturally responsive teachers.

To take this further, Furman (2008) conducted a review of the literature of multicultural teacher education (MTE) by examining previously published reviews and synthesized the field over the past two decades. Specifically, he "examined the ways in which the problem of MTE is established and understood, how these issues have been approached by various scholars, and the evolution and current state of the field" (p. 57). He noted specific contributions, limitations, and tensions faced by multicultural researchers and the field of MTE, and then discussed two major tensions within the field—the demographic tension: how best to prepare teacher candidates for increasingly diverse schools, and the effectiveness tension. The effectiveness tension is the one that connects to this current study.

Furman (2008) argued that the effectiveness tension for MTE lies in teacher education. He stated that "teacher education itself must be culturally responsive" (p. 69), yet in his examination of research reviews on teacher education programs, it was shown that this was not the case. Similarly, Villegas and Lucas (2002) argued that in order to move the field of teacher education, and equally, MTE, a vision of teaching and learning in a diverse society is needed. Furthermore, this vision should be used to systematically guide the infusion of multicultural issues throughout the pre-service curriculum. The next logical step is culturally relevant teaching (CRT). In other words, how might teacher education address the effectiveness tension? What is a framework of culturally relevant teaching that can be used as both a curriculum in the preparation of pre-service teachers and a strategy for teaching an increasingly diverse public school populace? Teacher education is one context to promote culturally relevant teaching practices with the hope that these kinds of practices would be implemented in classrooms. This current study argues for the teaching and learning of CRT principles in science teacher education as a means of preparing all teachers for diverse classrooms.

Ladson-Billings (1995a) explained that culturally relevant teaching rests on three criteria or propositions: "(a) students must experience academic success; (b) students must develop and/or maintain cultural competence; and (c) students must develop a critical consciousness through which they challenge the status quo of the current social order" (p. 160). In order for these propositions to be accomplished for student learning, we cannot assume that they will organically become the practices of teachers. In fact, teaching in culturally relevant and or multicultural ways requires a knowledge base about teaching for cultural diversity (Gay, 2002) as well as understanding the sociopolitical context of multicultural education (Nieto, 2004). Ladson-Billings (1995b) argued that "not only must teachers encourage academic success and cultural competence they must help students to recognize, understand, and critique current social inequities" (p. 479). Culturally relevant teaching practices give students the opportunity to learn in ways that are affirming, validating, and connected to their interests and backgrounds (Ladson-Billings, 1994). In order to have classrooms that are culturally relevant, we have to make stronger connections to the lives of students.

Therefore, in order to consider practices of culturally relevant teaching for urban school learners, a more foundational level is to promote culturally relevant teaching at the pre-service teacher level. This view encourages pre-service teachers to learn and implement these principles into practice. Ideally, if pre-service teachers understand CRT principles in teacher education, they can begin to transform theory into practice, and use these principles within the contexts of authentic classroom settings. The ultimate goal is to have these principles become an elemental part of their regular teaching practices as early career teachers and beyond.

Ladson-Billings in her initial interpretation of culturally relevant teaching did not focus on science. Content specific application of culturally relevant teaching seems to be the missing link in the research literature on CRT and teacher education. It has been shown that science is not a priority subject in elementary school programs (Spillane et al, 2001; Tate, 2001). This current study argues for the teaching and learning of CRT principles in science teacher education as a means of preparing all teachers and for the application of CRT in elementary science classrooms. The study in particular focuses on three elementary pre-service teachers' experiences in planning, teaching, and assessing a Pollution Unit in a 4th–5th grade science classroom and how they incorporate principles of culturally relevant science teaching. The study examines what the process was like for learning and enacting culturally relevant teaching in science for these three teachers, and how successful they were in promoting academic success, cultural competence, and critical consciousness for them as teacher learners in a science methods course and for urban students in an elementary science classroom. The research questions that guided this study were: What supports are needed in the preparation of pre-service teachers who focus on planning, teaching, and assessing science lessons and teaching in culturally relevant ways? What lessons are learned in preparing pre-service teachers to incorporate culturally relevant teaching in urban elementary science classrooms and their learning to become culturally relevant science teachers?

Description of Research Sites
University Methods Course
This article was written with data collected from an elementary science methods course at a large urban university located in New York City. Pre-service teachers (PSTs) were enrolled as graduate students seeking initial teacher certification, and the science methods course was one course within their teacher education program. The methods course lasted 16 weeks and focused on "science teaching through inquiry, multiculturalism, social justice, and the relevance of science to everyday life in the city and to urban school students" (Gunning & Mensah, 2010, p. 176). Out of the class of 14 pre-service teachers, three were asked to participate in this study: Niyah, Hope, and Estelle. (AU: names used in the study are pseudonyms.)

The three PSTs were of diverse racial/ethnic background and language. Niyah, Hope, and Estelle were interested in teaching the 4th grade. They had some teaching experiences or had worked with elementary students, yet they had no prior science teaching experiences. Because they did not have student teaching placements during the semester they were enrolled in the methods course, they were placed together in an East Harlem elementary school to conduct classroom observations (approximately 1–2 hours per week over the semester) and to support one another in planning, teaching, and assessing their science microteaching unit. As the instructor of the course, I observed them teaching their lessons. At the conclusion of the course, I invited them to participate in this study, which meant collection and analysis of their course assignments, observations and debriefings in the field, and interviews.

John David Elementary School
John David Elementary School (JDES) is a K–5 urban elementary school located in East Harlem, New York City. From the Department of Education school profile the student enrollment, at the time of this study, was 156 students (57% African American; 41% Latino/a; 3% Asian and other; 55% boys and 45% girls). The student body included 6% English Language Learners (ELL) and 26% special education students (http://schools.nyc.gov/accountability/tools/report/defaulthtm). The school was 60% eligible for Title I funding. JDES offered extracurricular programs that students attend during the school day, such as swimming, music and field trips.

In past years, the science program has been strained. For example, in 2004, the science teacher resigned. From that time, science was taught by substitute teachers who had no background in science teaching or teaching. I began working with the school more consistently and in greater capacity in spring 2005 and served as the science teacher for one semester on a voluntary basis. In 2006, they hired a science teacher, Miss Phoebe, who had no previous teaching experience and no content background in science. Since her appointment, I have been working with Miss Phoebe as the science specialist and assisting in developing the science program and her professional development as the K–5 science teacher. The school has been supportive in nurturing a university-school community partnership (Mensah, 2011). PSTs each semester complete observations, microteaching, and work with the students in the science classroom, and doctoral students have done research in the school. In addition, the regular classroom teachers at levels have allowed PSTs to make observations in their classrooms and to teach integrated science lessons as part of the PSTs' microteaching assignment.

Methods
Sources of Data
The study makes use of course artifacts from the elementary science methods course, such as the PSTs' pre-assessment interviews with elementary learners, microteaching papers, and lesson plans as the primary source. Individually, the PSTs

conducted pre-assessment interviews with one to two elementary students about the topic of pollution. They collaborated and used the interview data to plan culturally relevant lessons and assessments that would promote critical thinking around the topic of pollution. The format of the microteaching paper covered topics such as student misconceptions from conducting the pre-assessment, reflections on their microteaching, and professional growth as a science teacher. Other forms of data consisted of the PSTs' surveys (initial, to gather demographic data; and final, to gather comments about their learning and the course), and interviews (40–50 minutes, conducted at the end of the semester). The interview questions asked the PSTs about teaching in diverse classrooms, planning science, teaching science, future plans in teaching, and professional growth. Finally, a research journal was kept containing observations of the PSTs' microteaching at JDES, informal (debriefing) conversations after their microteaching lessons, and notes from the course.

Analysis of Data

The multiple data sources were coded using methods of constructivist grounded theory and comparative analysis for emergent themes (Charmaz, 2006; Strauss & Corbin, 1989). Using the microteaching papers as the primary data source, several codes and categories were generated from each of the three microteaching papers. These codes and categories were compared across the three papers individually and then across them collectively. Specific attention was given to culturally relevant connections on the topic of pollution. Categories were collapsed into larger themes, such as the planning process, teaching the lessons, assessing student learning, and reflecting on professional growth. These were also the major headings of their microteaching papers. The additional data sources were triangulated to corroborate evidence from the microteaching papers in order to shed light on themes generated from the study (Creswell, 2007). For example, the lesson plans that each of the three PSTs submitted—two lessons per teacher to create their Pollution Unit—were viewed and used to enhance descriptions from the microteaching papers and the classroom observations of their microteaching. The PSTs had to collect, assess, and discuss student learning from their individual lesson plans as part of their microteaching paper. The themes generated from the data analysis were enhanced through member checks and peer debriefing (Guba & Lincoln, 1989). The themes, after a brief description of the Pollution Unit, are given as emergent assertions in the preparation of teachers for culturally relevant science teaching.

Findings
Background of Lesson

The findings and discussion are written with a focus on pre-service teacher education and lessons learned from teaching in culturally relevant ways in an elementary science classroom and using CRT principles in science teacher education. Niyah, Hope, and Estelle taught a six-day Pollution Unit for one 4th–5th grade classroom. They took turns as the lead teacher for two days, with the other two acting as support in the classroom.

The "team teaching with co-role support" model (Estelle, Microteaching paper) served to be very beneficial for science teaching in the classroom and for supporting culturally relevant teaching throughout the Pollution Unit. For instance, informal conversations and classroom planning time during the course were valuable in helping Niyah, Hope, and Estelle to plan their lessons, to consider the appropriate content and assessments, and to enhance relevancy for teaching Pollution to urban 4th–5th graders.

The objectives of the Pollution Unit included

- students will learn about the different components that make up the air, and understand what air quality is;
- students will discover types of emissions that go into the atmosphere as a result of combustible byproducts from manufactured products (i.e., man-made objects including machines/industry, transportation vehicles and home products);
- students will understand the negative effects that these pollutants have on human beings, animals, plants, and environment; and
- students will know how they can help reduce air pollution in their own communities (Estelle & Hope, Unit Lesson Plans).

Emergent Assertions of Culturally Relevant Science Teaching

The findings and discussion of the study are written as assertions. The assertions, in italics, make use of CRT principles—quoted from Ladson-Billings (1995a)—within the context of science teacher education. The three large themes or assertions are supported by evidence generated from the data analysis (i.e., microteaching papers, lesson plans, researcher classroom observations, informal conversations, and interviews), and reveal the practices and considerations that the three PSTs used in planning, teaching, and assessing their Pollution Unit and implementing principles of CRT in science. The argument set forth in this study is that in order for students (i.e., students of diverse backgrounds, and the 4th–5th graders at JDES, in this case) to learn in culturally relevant ways, their teachers (i.e., in this case, the three PSTs) must learn and understand the principles of culturally relevant teaching in order to teach in this manner.

Assertion 1. *In order to teach in culturally relevant ways, PSTs must have collaborative support with diverse others in making connections and developing practices to teach science, such that they "experience academic success" (Ladson-Billings, 1995, p. 160), not only for themselves as teachers but also for their students.*

This first assertion pertains to how culturally relevant principles are enhanced in practice when learned with others, or within a community of learners (Wenger, 1998). Niyah, Hope, and Estelle spoke positively about their learning and development as teachers of science to enact culturally relevant teaching practices within their lesson plans. One of the most valuable practices for teaching in culturally relevant ways was group collaboration in which they supported each other in the planning and teaching process. Within the group collaborative process in the methods course, doing observations and their pre-assessments in the school, the PSTs were able to focus on the students and consider their needs during the planning of their unit. As an example, Niyah commented about collaborating and planning the Pollution Unit:

> Collaborating with my group members was also extremely valuable in my planning because we were able to brainstorm as a group what we thought would be best for these students. We had been observing this class [the 4th–5th grade] throughout the semester, so hearing about their observations [Estelle & Hope] was a valuable asset to my planning process. (Niyah, Microteaching paper)

During the planning process in the university classroom, the PSTs had several opportunities to work with each other and the researcher as the instructor of the course. The teachers at JDES were also helpful when the PSTs visited the school. Hope commented on the importance of group collaboration among "diverse individuals" during the planning process:

> Working with [Niyah and Estelle] and bouncing our group ideas with [Professor Mensah], our classmates and the classroom teachers and the science teacher at [JDES] gave me hope about how collaboration with diverse individuals can truly create a diverse curriculum. Having many points of view during the planning process was much better than the idea of having to face it on my own. (Hope, Microteaching paper)

The PSTs felt supported in teaching in culturally relevant ways and making learning about pollution engaging and fun for the students. Niyah felt that collaboration and support were needed in order to teach all students, and that "making science attainable for all students will certainly be a heavy task to accomplish, one that I surely cannot do on my own" (Interview). Niyah also wrote that "one of my needs as a science teacher is the support and guidance from my surrounding colleagues. It is only through this collaboration that a change in science education can be made" (Niyah, Microteaching paper). Both Hope and Niyah understood that collaboration with others was not only important for student learning and their academic success in learning science but also necessary for them to become successful teachers.

Assertion 2. In order to teach in culturally relevant ways, PSTs must use a language that allows them to elicit student roles that will empower students to want to do and learn science; this includes ways to engage students in the knowledge, language, and skills of science—formally (in school) and informally (at home)—and to make personal connections to science. The goals and content for teaching science must be educationally beneficial, such that PSTs "develop and/or maintain cultural competence" (Ladson-Billings, 1995a, p. 160) for the students they teach.

The second assertion addresses ways that students learn knowledge, language, and skills of science through real-world examples. The examples also connect to the lives of students. Therefore, teachers have to find ways of engaging students in relevant science learning that personally connects to them. For example, as the lead teacher for her 2-day lesson, Niyah conducted the Vaseline petroleum jelly experiment. In this experiment, used to represent "visible and invisible" particles in the air, students put Vaseline on index cards and placed them around the classroom to collect dust particles. While conducting her lesson, Niyah referred to the 4th–5th graders as "scientists." This language or reference to the work of scientists invited students to focus on their experiments and to take on the behavior and practices of scientists. The students became engaged in learning and doing science:

> One thing that I believe helped greatly was calling the students "scientists" and telling them that they will be doing a "special" air pollution experiment. This immediately caught their attention, and they were so excited to earn the role of a real scientist. They also displayed a great amount of thought and analysis in deciding where to put their samples of Vaseline, as well as hypothesizing what they believed they will see in the Vaseline the next day. (Niyah, Microteaching paper)

During the observations of the lesson, the researcher took pictures of students making observations of their index cards while conducting the Vaseline experiment. They used tools of science, such as magnifying glasses to analyze the samples they collected. The students were very excited about what they found and completed a data sheet to record their findings and ideas.

Ladson-Billings (1995a) described that teachers who promote cultural competence in the classroom find ways to bridge students' interests to school learning. Niyah, Hope, and Estelle "made a huge effort to figure out ways to make the Pollution Unit culturally relevant for their students" (Hope, Microteaching paper). Making the bridge between science and student interest was a challenge for the PSTs. For example, the researcher and the PSTs discussed during the course ways to make science relevant and connected to the lives of urban youth. We generated many ideas about how to promote science learning and content connections. We also discussed how to broaden our definition of what counts as science curriculum and what it means to teach real world examples in science (Researcher Journal). In teaching the Pollution Unit, these ideas became more concrete.

In lesson four, the PSTs asked students to think about how their Vaseline samples would have been similar or different if they placed them in their bedrooms, kitchens, and bathrooms at home versus the various placements in the classroom. Also during the extension exercise of this same lesson, the PSTs asked the students to think about ways that they, their families, and communities were impacted by the causes and effects of air pollution. As an activity in small groups, the elementary "scientists" were asked to brainstorm ideas on how they can decrease the amount of air pollution at home and in their community. Getting the students to talk about their learning and make connections to science at home, Niyah, Hope, and Estelle promoted science learning in culturally competent ways for their students. Being able to connect school science to self and community required a conscious effort to make scientific knowledge applicable and useful as well as personally relevant. Niyah, Hope, and Estelle planned for these ideas and provided multiple ways for 4th–5th graders to develop cultural competence in the context of science. They had to think purposefully about what knowledge, skills, and practices they wanted students to develop, while also taking into consideration diversity issues among their students. Hope wrote:

> [Niyah, Estelle] and I also made a strong effort to incorporate a variety of linguistic, artistic and analytic communication styles into the sequence in an effort to give all children a chance to explore the ideas and concepts of the sequence in many formats. Linguistically we included: verbal discussion (lessons one–five), silent reading (lessons one–four), out loud reading and listening comprehension (lesson four), and written responses—both text and graphic (lessons one–five). We enabled students to communicate ideas through the use of artistic expression including: observational drawing (lesson three), collage and imaginative drawing poster construction (lesson four), creative explanation (story telling) of group posters (lesson five). Finally, we asked students to use a range of methods for analyzing content material including: reading text (lesson four), observing concrete samples (lesson three), reading maps (lessons three and five). (Hope, Microteaching paper)

Finally, Hope stated, "I am so glad that [Niyah, Estelle] and I decided to incorporate such diverse teaching and learning styles" into the planning of the Pollution Unit.

Hope reflected however that she and her co-teachers "could have made the lessons even more culturally relevant" had they taken the class on a trip to the locations included on the community map, or have the whole class take the photographs together as a class assignment where students could draw out sources and effects of air pollution in the community through photography (Microteaching & Interview). These modifications to the Pollution Unit would have increased cultural competence in science, made the lessons more connected to the community and relevant to the lives of the students.

Assertion 3. In order to teach in culturally relevant ways, PSTs must also include their personal interests and reasons for teaching science content. The goals and content for the lesson must also be culturally and personally relevant and focus on real-world connections, such that PSTs "develop a critical consciousness through which they challenge the status quo of the current social order" (Ladson-Billings, 1995a, p. 160) for themselves and their students through science.

The third assertion promotes CRT that challenges the status quo and places the PSTs in positions to challenge and use their knowledge of science to improve their lives and their communities. Questioning the world around you and learning the content of science becomes personal. Estelle, for her 2-day lesson, focused on "environmental racism" where she wanted "to include a cultural/community perspective" (Microteaching paper) and question the effects of air pollution on students and

self. Specifically, Estelle wanted to make connections to pollution within the contexts of East Harlem, where most of the students of JDES lived, and the Bronx, where she lived with her two boys and mother. The idea to focus on "environmental racism" was generated from conversations with the JDES teachers who shared that many of the students in the school have asthma and often miss several days of school due to their asthma. Estelle's two young boys have asthma, and this personal relevance provoked her interest in planning, teaching, and assessing the Pollution Unit from a critical perspective. Estelle supported her reasoning for teaching the topic by stating her purpose and supporting it with research and statistics:

> I want to inform them about environmental racism without actually using those words because one microteaching lesson is not enough to explain the relevance of racism. Therefore my goal was to get students to ask why—Why their community is surrounded by major sources of air pollution, why they or someone they know have asthma, or other related health conditions resulting from air pollution. . . . According to one study, Bronx County has some of the highest rates of asthma in the United States [and] rates of death from asthma in the Bronx are about three times higher then the national average. Hospitalization rates are about five times higher in neighborhoods in the Bronx. It is estimated that 20% of the children have asthma. Within New York City the disparity in asthma hospitalization rates for asthma in Bronx county and East Harlem are 21 times higher than those of affluent parts of the city. (Estelle, Microteaching paper)

For lesson background, Estelle used the JDES neighborhood and the Bronx to make personally relevant connections to the topic of pollution As a lesson goal, she wanted students to become aware of the issue for their communities and show that the JDES neighborhood and the Bronx have "higher rates of air pollutants, which leads to allergies, which leads to higher asthma cases, which leads to higher asthma attacks" (Estelle, Microteaching paper). Estelle used several resource materials found from Internet searches, websites, and tips to save the environment. We discussed in class how to include information gathered from her research that could be understood by the elementary students. Estelle took digital pictures of the JDES neighborhood and created a poster of air pollution sources as a model for using real-world examples (Researcher Journal). She commented that the pictures "offered students a real connection to their communties" and the pictures were visual representations of community sources of air pollution that had an effect on the students' health (Researcher Journal). During her microteaching, Estelle asked students to use their own zip codes to map how close their homes were to major sources of air pollution (i.e., bus depots, waste treatment plants, waste transfer stations, MTA train yards), and student-groups used classroom computers to research asthma hospitalization rates in New York City. As an assessment of her lesson, Estelle noted that students' written responses "showed how they applied new concepts to their own life experiences" as they questioned the impact of air pollution on their health (Estelle, Microteaching paper).

From the process of planning, teaching, and assessing a culturally relevant science unit, and incorporating principles of CRT, Estelle "became more science literate about air pollution" because she had to research and evaluate her teaching (Researcher Journal). She shared that she wanted to be "confident in her instruction" as the science teacher. During the interview, Estelle talked about how much "time and effort" it took to conduct her research and to plan her lessons. It took her "an hour and twenty minutes" to teach her 2-day lesson as the lead teacher because she had "added the cultural perspective to the unit." The science teacher allowed this time and was patient in letting Estelle complete all that she had planned. The 4th–5th graders were given plenty of time to complete and present their final posters on what they had learned from the Pollution Unit. During the poster presentation in class, students demonstrated understanding of man-made causes of air pollution; negative affects of air pollution on humans, animals, plants, and the environment; and identified several components that make up the air and air quality.

Also assessing students' cultural competence at the end of the Pollution Unit, Niyah stated that as children living and growing up in the city the "real-world examples" that the students were able to make about the topic of pollution was exciting and personally meaningful for them:

> The topic of air pollution and air quality was something that the students could make a connection to. Living in New York City, they were able to give many of the real-world examples around them that showed them that air pollution is prevalent in their surroundings _____ I believe that this also made it more meaningful to them because air quality is something that affects us all. I literally saw the excitement in their eyes as they spoke about the types of air pollution they see every day. (Niyah, Microteaching paper)

Additionally, Niyah commented that the Pollution Unit was successful in allowing the students to take action about pollution in their lives: "They also learned, through the following lessons with [Hope and Estelle], that they could take actions to reduce pollution, which made it even more meaningful to them" (Niyah, Microteaching paper). Being able to encourage students to take action is part of challenging the status quo.

For the final microteaching paper, the PSTs had to reflect on their microteaching experience and offer a few examples of student learning. They were asked to construct a science teaching philosophy and write about changes they would make to their teaching and lesson plans based on their microteaching experience and teaching in culturally relevant ways and discuss their professional growth as teachers. The student assessments and philosophy statements, as well as informal conversations and interviews with the three PSTs, were useful in noting the lessons learned and making connections to CRT in pre-service teacher education and assessing their growth as teachers. Some examples were presented above, but more are provided in the following section.

Assessing Science Teaching

Niyah, Hope, and Estelle were reflective of their microteaching experience and what the 4th–5th graders learned from the Pollution Unit. Niyah, from assessing the whole process of planning,

teaching, and assessing student learning, commented in the interviews and debriefing sessions several things, such as the role of science and students' misconceptions. She replied that "science teaching should address the needs of diverse learners, and should incorporate the cultures of the students" and that "students need to learn science by making sense out of the world around them. This can best be achieved when they make the connection between science and their everyday lives." Furthermore, Niyah expressed that "implementing culturally relevant teaching was definitely challenging at times because to implement these successfully, teachers need to truly know their students and their backgrounds on an intimate level." Niyah was also honest in sharing her experiences in teaching students of diverse backgrounds. Although she had been around children from diverse backgrounds, being placed at JDES for the semester was her "first time acting as a head teacher to a whole group of diverse students." In learning to be a culturally relevant science teacher, Niyah made connections to her own learning as a student in the methods course:

> Through this experience, I came to gain a deeper understanding of the issues we have been discussing in class throughout the semester. I learned that acknowledging and validating the cultures of our students is crucial in making science meaningful to students. Part of this task is recognizing that as teachers, we are required to make critical decisions in the classroom.

In Hope's assessment of student learning from her lesson plans and microteaching experience, she commented extensively during the interview and debriefing sessions about the success and misunderstandings students had about science. As an example, she developed a graphic organizer for students to complete where they drew pictures, wrote observations, and made analyses of their observations from the science activities as part of her microteaching. She found the graphic organizers to be "a great success" for student learning, and noted that "after seeing students use them first hand, I realize how important visual methods of organization are to promoting diverse student learning." Hope also commented about what student learning looked like across the Pollution Unit. As a co-teacher, she assessed student learning through the poster presentations:

> All students responded to the major concepts of each question on the handout and I think it was because the questions were asked in a clear and visual format. Some students copied the exact phrasing from the written air pollution handout, but I noticed that during [Estelle's] lesson when students created posters and presented them that even though they copied phrasing, they still understood the major concepts at the conclusion of the lesson sequence. (Hope, Interview)

Similar to Niyah, Hope learned a great deal from the microteaching experience, particularly about classroom management. Working with the 4th–5th grade elementary students, she commented that good planning became the means for classroom management. From observing her microteaching on the second day of her lesson, Hope was calmer than day 1 where she directed the class in what to do. On day 2 she gave fewer directions and students were able to figure out what to do. She also allowed students to talk and share their ideas more on day 2 than day 1. She worked with the students by allowing them to express their learning through small and large group discussions. Hope realized "how important diverse teaching and learning styles are to implementing a successful lesson sequence." She commented:

> I learned how much students enjoy becoming scientists and using scientific processing skills and terminology. I watched them as they carried out experiments, observed and recorded data, analyzed and discussed results with each other and finally educated each other about air quality and air pollution. I learned that children are starving for meaningful scientific experiences and I am really glad that in between all the substitutes, classroom changes and testing preparation, [Niyah, Estelle] and I were able to teach them a carefully planned lesson sequence that connected scientific concepts to their everyday lives and promoted conceptual change in their thinking! (Hope, Microteaching)

Estelle also learned much from planning the Pollution Unit. Estelle chose several posters to conduct an evaluation of student learning and her teaching. She brought these posters to the university classroom and shared them with her teacher peers. Estelle commented that "students had developed an understanding of the major sources of air pollution" and that they were able to make connections to "the health effects associated with air pollution within their community" (Researcher Journal). Estelle wrote about one student in particular and assessed his learning:

> [Kevin] drew on his scientific concepts to explain how air pollution affects his community. His presentation and poster illustrated a community perspective. He conceptualized the correlation between air pollution and its affect on living organisms and the environment. He identified one of the sources of carbon monoxide as the [expressway running past his school]. He scientifically conceptualized that heavy traffic contributes to poor air quality and health hazards in his community. Overall, [Kevin] achieved community awareness, he identified a source of pollution, and the impact air pollution has on air quality, and what makes up the air. (Estelle, Microteaching paper)

From coding the microteaching papers of die three PSTs and using other data sources collected for this study, the principles of CRT are evident in the planning process, descriptions of their microteaching experiences, observations of classroom teaching, and reflections on student learning and professional growth. In the section that follows is a discussion of the findings of the study. The imputations and lessons learned in educating pre-service teachers about culturally relevant teaching in science and the implementation of this approach for teacher education in general are also provided.

Discussion and Implications

Educators argue for the use of culturally relevant pedagogy to address the learning needs of students in culturally diverse classrooms. Many employ Ladson-Billings' (1995a, 1995b)

three principles of culturally relevant teaching, which are: "(a) students must experience academic success; (b) students must develop and/or maintain cultural competence; and (c) students must develop a critical consciousness through which they challenge the status quo of the current social order" (p. 160). I argue that in order for students to learn in the ways that Ladson-Billings outlines, their teachers must learn them similarly so that they may teach in this manner. Therefore, CRT principles are introduced in an elementary science methods course with three pre-service teachers. I discuss Niyah, Hope, and Estelle's experiences in planning, teaching, and assessing a six-day Pollution Unit in a 4th–5th grade urban elementary science classroom in New York City. In this final section, the lessons learned as a teacher educator through the pre-service teachers' learning to implement principles of CRT in science education are discussed. The implications and limitations of the study pose additional ways that CRT can be used in teacher education and the eventual uptake of such practices in diverse, urban classrooms.

Science Teacher Education

Three assertions were introduced in this study that connect theoretically and practically with Ladson-Billings' (1995a, 1995b) principles of culturally relevant teaching for application in science teacher education. First, in order for pre-service teachers to teach in culturally relevant ways, they need support in the form of collaboration with diverse learners so that they have success in planning and teaching science in culturally relevant ways. Second, pre-service teachers need opportunities to adopt a language that elicits their roles as science teachers who are empowered to teach in culturally relevant ways, thereby engaging their students in the knowledge, language, and skills of science and empowering their students to be successful learners of science. Third, pre-service teachers are encouraged to find personal relevancy in the science content they are teaching as well as develop a critical awareness of how science can be used to deepen their understanding and application of science to empower and improve their lives and the lives of their students.

Generally, the findings of the study strongly suggest that collaboration and support, personal empowerment to teach, and personal relevance of the subject matter are important practices for teacher education to adopt in the preparation of teachers for diverse classrooms. These ideas connect to previous research such as the six salient characteristics that define culturally responsive teachers (Viliegas & Lucas, 2002) and Furman's (2008) demographic tension and effectiveness tension for multicultural teacher education. For science learning in particular, employing the principles of CRT in science teacher education opens opportunities for both teachers and students to move science as an elementary school subject and students traditionally marginalized from learning science to the forefront. This is particularly empowering when science teaching and learning happens within a diverse urban elementary school setting (Mensah, 2011). The three PSTs mentioned how important it is to their success in teaching the Pollution Unit to have the support of diverse others (i.e., their pre-service teacher peers, course instructor, and cooperating teachers at the school) to exchange ideas and to engage in conversations that focus on student diversity, student learning, and pedagogical and content connections. Therefore, safe and supportive learning environments, such as the elementary science methods course and the elementary school placement, are ideal for building pre-service teachers' efficacy to learn and teach in culturally relevant ways.

An additional component for teacher education in implementing CRT is through the microteaching experience—planning, teaching, and assessing a culturally relevant science unit for diverse learners. The microteaching experience increases teacher self-efficacy to teach science (Gunning & Mensah, 2011), and offers a collaborative context to learn and enact the principles of CRT in an authentic classroom setting with students of diverse backgrounds, learning styles, and interests. As teachers learning to teach diverse students, the PSTs interact directly with the students and teachers at JDES. These collaborative interactions are invaluable to the PSTs' growth and development as science teachers. The microteaching experience enables the PSTs to feel success in teaching science so that their students also experience success in learning science. The PSTs and their students learn about pollution in scientifically based ways, increasing their cultural competence about the topic and ability to bridge home and school connections. The PSTs address reasons for learning about pollution and focus on real-world examples so that the topic is engaging and motivating to students, as represented in students' science experiments, classroom discussions, and final poster presentations. The poster presentations underscore the students' academic success, cultural competence, and critical consciousness in learning the goals and objectives of the Pollution Unit. Moreover, the poster presentations solidify Niyah, Hope, and Estelle's success as culturally relevant science teachers and the use of CRT in science teacher education.

Lessons Learned

There are three lessons to share from conducting this study that may be helpful for teacher educators as they also consider curriculum and effective approaches in the preparation of teacher candidates for diverse classrooms. These lessons connect to the broad recommendations for the preparation of teachers for diverse classrooms (See Furman, 2008; Sleeter, 2001; Villegas & Lucas, 2002). First, it is vital that teacher educators develop strong collaborative partnerships between universities and urban schools. Both sites offer theoretical and pedagogical support (i.e., connect theory to practice) for teacher learning, student engagement, and enactment of CRT, particularly in teaching elementary science.

Second, planning, teaching, and assessing curriculum that is grounded in principles of CRT demands a lot of "time and effort" as Estelle's comments indicated, about planning and researching to include a cultural component in the curriculum. For PSTs who do not share common cultural knowledge and experiences similar to the students they will teach, additional support, suggestions, and resources will be beneficial in helping them to make relevant connections. As previously mentioned, spending time in diverse classroom settings, making observations, working with small groups of students, and discussing ways to meet the needs of diverse students, are suggested as essential

elements in a methods course. Moreover, pre-service teachers need ample time to plan, research, discuss, and teach culturally relevant curriculum throughout their teacher education preparation. This is especially required for topics that raise social consciousness and topics that are not traditionally addressed in the school curriculum. Niyah, Hope, and Estelle—as student observers who had not yet done student teaching—only touch the surface in talking about environmental racism in their Pollution Unit. However, within the one methods course, an early foundation to think about science curriculum through a social action/social justice or critical lens is introduced to Niyah, Hope, and Estelle. They are able to implement some initial understandings of what critical consciousness looks like and the possibilities it holds to engage students in science.

Finally, the last lesson addresses science as a priority subject in the elementary school program. Science in many elementary school settings is not a priority subject (Spillane et al., 2001; Tate, 2001). In many cases, the elementary school program is overtaken by disempowering policies and institutional barriers that inhibit real engagement in science teaching and learning (Carlone, Haun-Frank, & Kimmel, 2010; Mensah, 2010; Rodriguez, 2010). For PSTs to teach in culturally relevant ways in science classrooms, and for their students to learn science in a similar manner, then science in the elementary school must be given the time, resources, priority, and attention it deserves so that students experience academic success, develop and maintain cultural competence, and develop a critical consciousness through which they may challenge the status quo of the current social order. Teaching science in the elementary school is a challenge to the status quo.

Limitations and Conclusion

Although this study takes place in one section of a graduate level, elementary science methods course, with a small group of diverse PSTs, the findings suggest that fostering collaborations and partnerships, structuring classroom time to implement CRT in classrooms and in teacher education are valuable approaches in the preparation of all teachers for diverse classroom settings. In addition, the ideas explored in this article indicate that classrooms where this type of teaching is taking place requires that teachers experience learning in ways other than we expect them to teach. But, how will our teacher candidates teach in the ways we advocate if they have not experienced teaching and learning in these ways themselves? Villegas and Lucas (2002) commented that as teacher educators we should expect our PSTs "to demonstrate an initial ability to tailor their teaching to particular students within particular contexts, a central quality of culturally responsive teaching" (p. 30). Accordingly, pre-service teachers need sufficient opportunities to think, plan, teach, and assess their growth and development as culturally relevant teachers. In this study, science teacher education is suggested as one context. They realize that teaching for academic success, cultural competence, and critical consciousness is complex and requires collaboration and practice. As teacher educators, we serve as supporters and advocates for our pre-service teachers' ongoing professional development. In addition, we need thoughtful, well-planned teacher education curricula and activities that educate our pre-service teachers in learning what CRT is, and its potential usefulness not only in their classrooms but also for their education. Therefore, this study extends to readers the potential of culturally relevant science teaching within teacher education and its application in elementary science classrooms.

As a teacher educator, my hope is that my pre-service teachers carry models of teaching, foundational practices, and educative experiences from teacher education with them into their teaching careers, and build on their initial understandings of what it means to teach students of diverse backgrounds. However, they must experience this in positive, collaborative, and supportive teacher education programs, through courses and school-university partnerships that prepare them for increasingly diverse classroom settings. The contribution that this study offers is how and what it may look like in one elementary science teacher education methods course that is focused on the preparation of elementary science teachers for diverse, urban classrooms.

References

Carlone, H. B., Haun-Frank, J., & Kimmel, S. C. (2010). Tempered radicals: Elementary teachers' narratives of teaching science within and against prevailing meanings of schooling. *Cultural Studies of Science Education*, 5, 941–965.

Charmaz, K. (2006). *Constructing grounded theory: A practical guide through qualitative analysis*. Thousand Oaks, CA: Sage.

Creswell, J. W. (2007). *Qualitative inquiry and research design: Choosing among five approaches* (2nd ed.). Thousand Oaks, CA: Sage.

Department of Education. (2010). School profile data. Retrieved from http://schools.nyc.gov/Accountability/tools/report/default.htm

Furman, J. S. (2008). Tensions in multicultural teacher education research: Demographics and the need to demonstrate effectiveness. *Education and Urban Society*, 41, 55–79.

Gay, G. (2002). Preparing for culturally responsive teaching. *Journal of Teacher Education*, 53, 106–116.

Guba, E. G., & Lincoln, Y. S. (1989). *Fourth generation evaluation*. Newbury Park, CA: Sage.

Gunning, A. M., & Mensah, F. M. (2010). One pre-service elementary teacher's development of self-efficacy and confidence to teach science: A case study. *Journal of Science Teacher Education*, 22, 171–185.

Ladson-Billings, G. (1994). *The dreamkeepers: Successful teachers of African American children*. San Francisco: Jossey-Bass.

Ladson-Billings, G. (1995a). But that's just good teaching! The case for culturally relevant pedagogy. *Theory Into Practice*, 34, 159–165.

Ladson-Billings, G. (1995b). Toward a theory of culturally relevant pedagogy. *American Educational Research Journal*, 32, 465–491.

Mensah, F. M. (2010). Toward the mark of empowering policies in elementary school science programs and teacher professional development. *Cultural Studies of Science Education*, 5, 977–983.

Nieto, S. (2004). *Affirming diversity: The sociopolitical context of multicultural education* (4th ed.). Boston, MA: Allyn and Bacon.

Rodriguez, A. J. (2010). Exposing the impact of opp(reg)ressive policies on teacher development and on student learning. *Cultural Studies of Science Education*, 5, 923–940.

Sleeter, C. (2001). Preparing teachers for culturally diverse schools: Research and the overwhelming presence of Whiteness. *Journal of Teacher Education*, 52, 94–106.

Spillane, J. P., Diamond, J. B., Walker, L. J., Halverson, R., & Jita, L. (2001). Urban school leadership for elementary science instruction: Identifying and activating resources in an undervalued school subject. *Journal of Research in Science Teaching* 38, 918–940.

Strauss, A., & Corbin, J. (1998). *Basics of qualitative research: Techniques and procedures for developing grounded theory*. Thousand Oaks, CA: Sage.

Tate, W. (2001). Science education as a civil right: Urban schools and opportunity-to-learn considerations. *Journal of Research in Science Teaching*, 38, 1015–1028.

Villegas, A. M., & Lucas, T. (2002). Preparing culturally responsive teachers: Rethinking the curriculum. *Journal of Teacher Education*, 53, 20–32.

Wenger, E. (1998). *Communities of practice: Learning, meaning, and identity*. New York: Cambridge University Press.

Critical Thinking

1. What are the current strengths and weaknesses of multicultural teacher education on university campuses?

2. What are ways to improve multicultural teacher education on university campuses?

3. What are the current strengths and weaknesses of multicultural teacher education in P–12 clinical field placements?

4. What are ways to improve multicultural teacher education in P–12 clinical field placements?

Create Central

www.mhhe.com/createcentral

Internet References

Culturally Responsive Teaching Resources
www.culturallyresponsiveteachingresources.org

National Science Teachers Association
www.nsta.org

FELICIA MOORE MENSAH is an Associate Professor and Program Coordinator of Science Education at Teachers College, Columbia University. Her scholarly interests include urban and multicultural education, teacher education, teacher professional development, qualitative research methods, critical theory, and feminist poststructuralist theory.

Article   Prepared by: Nancy P. Gallavan, *University of Central Arkansas*

Multicultural Education in a K-12 Modern Language Department: Reconciling the Professional Development Experience

MARTHA BIGELOW, PAM WESELY, AND LORA OPSAHL

Learning Outcomes

After reading this article, you will be able to:

• Become familiar with the research and resources of James A. Banks, professor, University of Washington.

• Apply the methods of Understanding by Design developed by Grant Wiggins and Jay McTighe.

In this research, we explore the way a K-12 modern language department in a private school perceived a long-term professional development initiative to transform the curriculum of their entire school in ways that included a wider range of diverse perspectives, practices, and products. Our inquiry began as we considered how curricular transformation (Banks, 1995) occurs in a modern language department. When we went to the literature in the field of foreign language (FL) education, we found Michael Byram's words from some 20 years ago: "One of the contributions of FL teaching . . . is to introduce learners to and help them understand 'otherness.' Whether it be linguistic or cultural terms, learners are confronted with the language of other people, their culture, their way of thinking and dealing with the world" (1987, p. 26). Byram argued that "otherness" does not include only "foreigners" but also people born within our borders who are still perceived to be "othered." such as ethnic or racial minorities. Therefore, while most FL departments would be quick to claim multicultural education as a critical part of the everyday work they do, there are also challenges in incorporating a range of "foreign" perspectives, both global and local, within the overarching goal of producing students who are proficient in the FL.

This study is set within the context of a school-wide multicultural curriculum development initiative at a private preschool through 12th grade (P-12) school in the Midwest of the United States. We will refer to this school as "College School." All of the teachers at the school participated in professional development experiences that were designed to support them as they enhanced their existing curriculum to include more and varied multicultural perspectives or created entirely new curricula that would bring multicultural education into their classes in thoughtful and integrated ways. As an overlay to this initiative, College School teachers were also asked to conceptualize their new curriculum using a process of *backward design* set forth in Wiggins and McTighe's (1999, 2005) *Understanding by Design.*[1] This study focuses specifically on College School's FL teachers in the context of this initiative. The following discussion will compare two very different bodies of scholarly work focusing on culture—one centered on the integration of culture in FL teaching and the other set squarely in the realm of promoting social justice through transforming school culture in the United States.

Background

Research from the field of FL teaching shows that teachers have a wide range of existing beliefs and practices related to the role of culture or intercultural competence teaching in their FL classes (Klein, 2004; Sercu, 2005; Sisken, 2007). This research is supported by a survey conducted by the Social Science Education Consortium (1999) of 1,566 high school FL teachers which found that "no definition of culture is common among [FL] teachers" (p. 5). Nevertheless, the FL teaching profession in the U.S. clearly sees culture integration as a high priority and has included culture across a number of the standards for FL, known as the American Council on the Teaching of Foreign Language (ACTFL) Standards (National Standards in Foreign Language Education Project, 1999). Most notably, the second standard focusing on "Cultures" seeks to encourage students to "gain knowledge and understanding of other cultures." For this, the Standards use a practices-products-perspectives framework to conceptualize culture. The ACTFL Standards urge teachers to find and teach links between what a given culture does (practices, such as eating), what that culture creates (products, such as music) and what people of that culture believe or are concerned about (perspectives, such as status symbols). For example, in some families in Panama, New Year's Eve involves eating 12 grapes as midnight approaches, and counting the grape seeds. Once the clock reaches 12:00, people kiss friends and family and set off fireworks. After midnight, dinner is served and some people may go dancing to celebrate. These practices and products are tied to traditions from Spain, which in turn are grounded in religious beliefs and cultural values.

Other frameworks for considering the role of culture in FL teaching have been available to teachers and teacher educators for a long time (e.g., Byram & Zarate, 1997; Crawford-Lange & Lange, 1987; Kramsch, 1993; Seelye, 1997). Most current definitions of culture learning in the field of FL teaching tend to urge explorations beyond simple facts about people who speak some variety of a target language and to promote the understanding of culture through processes that engage students at multiple personal and intellectual levels. Paige, Jorstad, Siaya, Klein, and Colby (2003) offer this cogent description of the way in which learning about culture is often framed in FL education:

> [Culture learning] is the process of acquiring the culture-specific and culture-general knowledge, skills, and attitudes required for effective communication and interaction with individuals from other cultures. It is a dynamic, developmental, and ongoing process which engages the learner cognitively, behaviorally, and affectively (p. 177).

This definition is appealing to today's FL educators because it focuses on culture in terms of developing communicative competence (Canale & Swain, 1980; Hymes, 1971).

Nevertheless, facilitating this sort of learning is often challenging in a FL classroom because communicative activities carried out in the target language are often controlled by texts or teachers and informed by a limited amount of contextual/cultural information (Fischer, 1997). Other challenges to integrating culture into a FL classroom may occur because of teachers' limited or out-of-date experience with communities that speak the target language. Some teachers did not have the opportunity to examine approaches to integrating culture in their pre- or in-service teacher education experiences. The task of integrating products, practices, and perspectives, as the National Foreign Language Standards (1999) suggest, typically requires practice, dialogue, and exemplars (Schulz, 2007). Klein (2004) found that teachers tend to think about culture in terms of practices and products, not in terms of the meaning attached to the events of the world and the behavior of others. We concur with Sercu's plea that "language-and-culture learning has to be more complex and rich than the emphasis on communicative competence in FL education tends to suggest" (2005, p. 180). The present study will analyze these issues in the context of College School's multicultural curriculum initiative and explore how the language teachers felt as they participated in the school-wide reform effort.

Thus far, most readers will easily recognize these problems of practice related to the integration of culture into FL classes where the push is strongly toward proficiency goals. Teacher educators urge teachers to cultivate balance and nuance with regard to culture in FL curricula, be it to present a range of French speaking cultures to students (not just a monolithic Parisian culture), offer a range of images of Spanish speakers (not just of poor people), or expose students to a range of aspects of Chinese cultures (not just holidays, as traditionally celebrated). The field of FL teaching and learning has a long scholarly history of thinking about the integration of culture into classes across a range of levels and ages.

The scholarly literature used to discuss culture in the multicultural initiative at College School, however, was very different than what is typically used to frame culture in FL teaching. The readings offered to the teaching staff and the speakers invited to guide teacher learning were squarely set within the field of multicultural education, not the subject-specific literature such as that cited above. The initiative drew upon multicultural education scholars whose work is grounded in the U.S. public school context (e.g., Carl Grant & Christine Sleeter, 2003; James Banks, 1999). The multicultural education scholarship frames "culture" in terms of categories such as race, gender, social class, ethnicity, religion and sexual orientation. In other words, the discourse was about difference and was framed within U.S. American cultural systems of oppression. Teachers across all grades and disciplines were asked to consider how their curriculum could be more inclusive of a range of views, discover inherent bias in the existing curriculum, and examine injustice playing out in the local or school community. For this reason, the school leadership chose to use James Banks' work on multicultural education (Banks, 2005; Banks & McGee-Banks, 2003) to guide the initiative.

Curriculum transformation, according to Banks, aims to challenge mainstream curriculum that ignores the experiences, contributions, and perspectives of individuals from non-dominant groups in all subject areas. It aims to go beyond "celebrating" difference by the addition of a few heroes and holidays seen as valuable to minoritized groups. Rather, curricular transformation involves grappling with issues and concepts that are tightly bound to the subject matter and integrated in a way that is not perceived as superfluous. These transformations are meant to lead to social action and awareness as well as the full inclusion of students, families and staff from minoritized or non-dominant communities. Specifically crucial to curricular transformation are Banks. "Dimensions of Multicultural Education," namely, (a) content integration, (b) the knowledge construction process, (c) prejudice reduction, (d) an equity pedagogy, and (e) an empowering school culture and social structure (1999, p. 14).

Banks' work strongly emphasizes the need for teachers to move beyond the traditional, narrow view of multicultural education as just content integration, where teachers focus on using examples and content from a variety of cultures and groups to illustrate key aspects of their subject area. College Schools multicultural initiative, based on Banks' work, encouraged teachers to move into the knowledge construction process, where teachers first became aware of the implicit cultural assumptions, frames of reference, perspectives, and biases in their subject area, and then lead students to uncover them in the classroom. The dimensions of prejudice reduction, where teachers help students develop more positive attitudes toward racial and ethnic groups different from their own, and equity pedagogy, where teachers use techniques to reach students from diverse racial, ethnic, and social class groups, also influenced the development of the multicultural curriculum.

The following research question was formulated to allow for an examination of stories, observations, and documents related to the multicultural education initiative at the school:

> How do FL teachers experience a sustained professional development program designed to guide all teachers in their school community to integrate multicultural curriculum into their subject areas?

Methodology

The methodology used to understand the multicultural education professional development experience was a qualitative case study. The bounded unit of analysis was the FL department.

Setting

College School is a private school in a large metropolitan area. The school employs 150 teachers and enrolls approximately 1,100 students. Fifteen percent of the student body is from minoritized racial groups. The FL Department is well-known in the state for having strong K-12 programs in Chinese and Spanish. Students also have opportunities to begin a FL in middle and high school, including French at the time of the study. The strong FL program is a reason cited by some parents for sending their children to this school. It is important to note that as a private school, the majority of the students come from families considered wealthy. Given that, we recognize that "the more privileged the student, the more likely she or he is to have accepted socioeconomic stratification, educational tracking, and other hierarchies of race, class and gender privilege" (Martin, 1998, p. 46), making the multicultural initiative well-matched to this particular school setting.

An Outline of the Multicultural Curriculum Initiative

The three primary goals of the multicultural initiative were to teach students how to (a) take perspective, to develop skills to view the world from someone else's viewpoint; (b) function well in a diverse society; and (c) be effective change agents in our society. One of the important features of the multicultural curriculum initiative is the fact that it has spanned a long period of time and has offered teachers many ways to both learn about diverse perspectives and think about how to teach and assess the new or improved curriculum. Some of the ways teachers could engage with the theory and practice of multicultural education were through guest speakers, staff development workshops, intensive work with small groups of colleagues and larger units (Department, grade level), and feedback on assessment and lesson plans. Table 1 outlines the phases of the multicultural initiative through 2007.

In 2004–2005, the faculty were asked to develop multicultural lesson plans using a template developed by the department

Table 1　Phases of the Multicultural Initiative

Phase One: Self-Reflection

| 2000–2001 | • Cohort groups of teachers established |
| | • Faculty attend workshops to develop awareness of non-dominant cultures |

Phase Two: Studying the Other
Phase Three: Fundamentals of Multicultural Education

2001–2002	• Faculty listen to speakers about the American Indian experience
	• Introduction of Banks' Model of multicultural education
	• Invited speaker Christine Sleeter provides background about multicultural ed.

Phase Four: Multicultural curriculum

2002–2003	• Invited speaker James Banks addresses faculty about the background for the implementation of multicultural education
	• Introduction of Wiggins' *Understanding by Design*
	• P-12 departments begin to develop multicultural enduring understandings
2003–2004	• P-12 departments write multicultural learnings, defined as observable "chunks" that students must learn to develop, differentiated by gradeP-12 departments begin to identify evidence or assessments that would indicate that students understood the learning
2004–2005	• P-12 departments continue to refine the multicultural learnings that pertain to their enduring understanding
	• Faculty develop multicultural lesson plans based on the multicultural learnings that feature backwards design and formative and summative assessments
2005–2006	• Faculty are encouraged to refine, edit, and implement lesson plans
2006–2007	• Faculty are encouraged to refine, edit, and implement lesson plans
	• Faculty are asked to submit student work based on the lesson plans

heads, based on Wiggins and McTighe's *Understanding by Design* (1999). They created a performance task that would give evidence that the students achieved the identified learnings. This included assessment criteria for the performance task, formative assessment ideas, facets of learning, and a section on reflection and self-assessment.

There were additional ongoing facets to the initiative including summer readings for faculty on multicultural issues, faculty meetings in cohort groups to discuss readings and other topics, and consultant speakers from higher education to lead workshops to provide input to administrators and faculty members. The Headmaster of the school initiated and championed the effort. He was instrumental in forming a parents' group to discuss issues of diversity and chaired the school's Diversity Committee himself. It is also important to mention that teachers at this school were typically involved in a number of additional activities at the same time the multicultural curriculum work was unfolding (e.g., technology integration, reading in the content areas, curriculum mapping for accreditation). The professional climate at College School is one of invested, committed teachers who are given many responsibilities beyond their teaching assignments.

A Note on Author Roles

The three authors of this article had specific and distinct roles in this multicultural curriculum initiative. An explanation of their roles at the time of data collection and analysis can be useful in further contextualizing this study. Bigelow had worked closely with the school as an outside consultant for three years on the multicultural initiative. She had worked mainly with teachers who served as administrative leaders of the diversity committee and the curriculum committee, but later worked closely with department heads on the implementation of the curriculum and through joint observations of teachers in their departments. She also facilitated school-wide workshops about James Banks' dimensions of multicultural education (Banks, 1999) and creating and assessing performance tasks, as explained above. She observed numerous lessons across grades and content areas when teachers were implementing some part of their multicultural curriculum. Wesely had been a French teacher at the school for seven years, and she participated in the school workshops, discussions, summer reading, and other related activities from the beginning of the multicultural initiative. At the time of the study, she was a full-time graduate student and on leave from the school. Opsahl had a dual role as a FL teacher in the school (thus participating in all activities like Wesely) and as the head of the FL department at College School. In this second role, she was responsible for guiding her department in the creation and implementation of the new or revised multicultural curriculum. She was also responsible for monitoring the curricular shift and guaranteeing that students received a range of experiences with multicultural education as they progressed through their language classes.

The authors' professional experience with the multicultural initiative informs this study significantly. In effect, informal data were being collected well before the formal interviews began. Furthermore, data analysis occurred throughout the research via conversations and reflections of the authors (Rubin & Rubin, 2005), rather than at a specific stage of the study. This will be discussed more in the next section.

Participants

Participants in the study were six FL teachers. Four teachers were interviewed, and two participated via anonymous survey. Of the interview participants, two teach Chinese and are non-native English speakers (NNES), and the other two teach Spanish and are native English speakers (NES). These individuals were recruited via e-mail sent to the entire department from Opsahl, the head of the department. They were instructed to contact Wesely if they were interested in participating in interviews or to respond online to the anonymous survey. In keeping Wesely, a peer to the teachers in the study, in charge of communicating with participants, a strong attempt was made to reduce the coercive nature of the recruitment. Interview participants all signed consent statements, and they were informed that their identity would be kept confidential. With six participants, the final participation rate was 50% in the FL department of 12.[2]

Data Collection Procedures

Data from the six teacher participants were collected in one of two ways: via semi-structured interviews lasting approximately 45 minutes (4 participants) or anonymous online questionnaires with open-ended questions (2 participants). With some concessions to their difference in format, the interviews and surveys both had the objective of capturing the participants' personal narrative accounts of their experience with the multicultural initiative. Questions addressed their reaction to and assessment of the professional development opportunities and materials, the challenges and successes that they experienced in the course of the initiative, and the changes in how they viewed their own teaching practice, particularly relating to culture.

One important secondary data source was the professional development materials used during the initiative. These materials were collected by the three authors in the course of their participation in the initiative and consulted as needed during data analysis. Additionally, as mentioned above, the authors' personal experiences in the multicultural initiative served as an informal, foundational data source.

Data Analysis Procedures

The interviews, which were digitally recorded, were listened to at least twice by two of the researchers (Bigelow and Wesely), during which time all of the content (e.g., topics addressed, answers given, opinions offered, stories told) of each interview was noted in list form. The content lists from the interviews were coded topically in order to capture the range of information obtained in the interviews as well as the ways any steps were completed, themes in the interview data were noted through a process that was both inductive and deductive[3] (Miles & Huberman, 1994). The open-ended questions of the online questionnaires were similarly coded and considered for themes.

Finally, as participants in the process we brought our own views to the inquiry and used them to fuel discussion among ourselves and to understand the different experiences others had with the multicultural curriculum initiative. Our engagement with the multicultural curriculum effort at this school varied greatly among the three of us, but together we are able to offer a comprehensive account of what happened. As we engaged in this inquiry, we reminded ourselves that we too are products of schooling processes and "carry deep within us all manner of ideological baggage that . . . goes a long way to perpetuate the educational status quo" (Farber, 1995, p. 49).

Findings and Discussion

Of all the K-12 subjects taught in schools today, culture and FL teaching should go hand in hand. FL teachers are often seen as the ones who know about "culture" in a school. Isn't their mere presence in a school evidence that the curriculum is multicultural? Doesn't studying a FL guarantee students multicultural learning opportunities? What we have found and aim to demonstrate is that FL teachers may find it difficult to reconcile their notions of culture in the realm of Banks' multicultural education framework of transformative curriculum. Although multicultural education is a natural fit in most FL curricula, we will describe some of the hurdles FL teachers experienced in participating in the school-wide reform that seemed to cause ambivalence and disequilibrium as well as an increased awareness of how culture is dealt with in the curriculum.

Teacher Learning and Engagement

All of the teachers interviewed and surveyed had positive things to say about their professional development experiences at College School in the area of multicultural education. They specifically mentioned the following things as enjoyable or helpful:

- Watching and discussing movies with parents
- Discussing books with cohort groups
- Listening to speakers (e.g., Native American speaker)
- Learning about differences between people
- Learning to integrate culture

One teacher said, "I show them [students] that I respect different cultures. I used to just give the information. No discussion. Now I think those things are in my mind I integrate more." A similar experience was reported by another teacher when she said, "before I just did it and I didn't really think about it . . . but this time I'm really thinking about, if I do this, this, this, that's really gonna help them understand . . . or it would be more profound." Another teacher said that the most positive outcome of the experience was "Thinking more about culture in my teaching. Cultural understanding is big for their learning." This idea is mirrored by another teacher who said, "It makes me more aware of what I teach and how I teach it." The opportunity to focus on the thoughtful integration of multicultural learning and understanding seems to have helped teachers give this area of their teaching focused consideration, which led to changes in classroom practices.

These quotes suggest that language teachers, too, can benefit from learning opportunities related to multicultural education and reconcile the disciplinary differences between FL teaching and multicultural education. In fact, one teacher on the anonymous survey showed that he/she was engaging students in what Banks terms "knowledge construction." This teacher

said, "I now go more in depth in a unit of study, devote more time to perspectives, and wrestle with HOW to teach my students to understand that a lot of what they 'know' is filtered through someone's perspective." Interestingly, this teacher uses the word "perspectives," which is widely used in FL and multicultural education scholarship, but then focuses back on the students and the importance of understanding their own perspectives to better understand the perspectives of others.

These quotes suggest that the FL teachers at College School benefitted from professional development on the topic of multicultural education. On the other hand, some found it difficult to disentangle their current practice with what would be considered "multicultural" from the perspective of the professional development initiative. One teacher said that it was "frustrating, in that what we teach in a foreign language is pretty much multicultural in general. How do we differentiate what we are actually doing on a daily basis from something specifically multicultural?" This quote brings to the fore the debate that perhaps students do have a multicultural education experience by simply attending a French, Spanish, or Chinese class. We contend that, while this is possible, students can obtain much more multicultural learning from their language classes in addition to improved linguistic skills. The quote could also indicate that some teachers were further along in the process of understanding curriculum transformation than others. This latter possibility is reflected in this statement made by a teacher: "I had to put it in the format they wanted because it's something I've been doing for a long time." He saw the demands of the professional development as being purely administrative—that by reformatting his existing curriculum he had accomplished his task.

One teacher expressed a disjuncture between her world of teaching and what she saw as a very different way of being in professional development meetings. She said, "We're just so focused on doing our teaching, and so all of a sudden, you know, you're philosophizing about the reasons for all this . . . " This statement suggests a possible register or discourse difference that seemed to make the activities of teaching disconnected from the activities of developing multicultural curriculum. It is important to take note of this perceived disconnect and work to narrow the gap between "teaching" and "philosophizing" or "theory" and "practice." This rift is one that concerns us greatly. The whole point of the professional development opportunities was to transform teaching practices, but from some of the teachers' perspectives, the readings, lectures, and workshops often seemed quite distant from this aim. On the other hand, how can a school facilitate school-wide learning about complex issues that is grounded in research and theory while at the same time offer concrete assistance to teachers at many different stages in their careers with a range of formal teacher preparation?

The degree to which teachers in any school, in any professional development experience, engage and benefit from learning opportunities varies. It is our sense that the FL department, for the most part, willingly engaged and many teachers showed a great deal of interest in availing themselves of the conversations and readings intended to challenge them to make their curriculum more multicultural. But the degree to which some were willing or able to engage also may have been stymied by philosophical mismatches, perceived incongruities, mixed messages, and drawn-out discussion. This possibility is discussed next.

Department Goals and School Agenda

In the 2003–2004 academic year, the FL department at College School determined how they would focus their multicultural instruction. Together, they agreed that they wanted all of their FL students across all grades and levels to understand that "the study of language is a window into understanding the values and beliefs of a culture." This agreed-upon focus led to the multicultural learnings, which were drawn from the FL Standards (1999), as shown in Table 2.

Judging from the strong overlap with the FL standards, the learnings are mostly set within the FL field's conceptualization of culture. The last learning, however, offers an important point of departure. This learning, focusing on stereotypes, edges into the realm of multicultural education because it can directly challenge prejudice and bias. This particular learning is squarely focused on one of the primary goals of the multicultural curriculum initiative at College School: to teach students how to take perspective and to develop skills to view the world from someone else's viewpoint.

The teachers frequently expressed the feeling of not always knowing what was expected of them. There are a number of possible explanations, including teachers joining the process late, being on sabbatical, or missing key learning opportunities. Other issues expressed by the teachers dealt with the drawn-out nature of the professional development at College School, depicted in Table 1 (although research in teacher development would suggest that sustained professional development is best practice (Darling-Hammond & McLaughlin, 1995). One teacher said she felt, "frustration about how it's been presented. We've spent so much time going in circles, slowly, and I wonder, could it have gone quicker? Now I feel kind of beaten down

with it. It's been so long." Another teacher felt that the tasks they were asked to do were inconsistent. She said, "I would say there has been a lack of consistency about how the multicultural assessment plan should look. The messages have been mixed, unclear. That is frustrating to me."

One explanation for these feelings of frustration is that at some point[4] in the process the school leadership decided that the purpose of the multicultural curriculum initiative was to promote social justice by creating a curriculum that would afford College School students opportunities to connect the new curriculum to their own personal examination of bias and prejudice. The *critical* examination of difference and raising students' awareness of their own cultural frames and biases was not, however, the aim that was salient in many teachers' minds. Understandably, this shift from implicit to explicit focus on social justice seemed to cause disequilibrium among some teachers, including FL teachers. Their carefully honed learnings (Table 2) suddenly only partially overlapped with the expectations of school. It is our contention that this mismatch between their agreed-upon learnings and what the school decided would fall within multicultural education was at the root of some of the teachers' confusion and frustration. We believe that this may be one of the reasons some of the curriculum created for the multicultural initiative was met with some criticism. It would not, for example, be sufficient to offer new curriculum that presents culture in stereotypical, monolithic or static ways. If this were to happen, teachers would be asked to revise the curriculum in ways that show how it would ask students to reflect on their own ethnic traditions and how the cultural practices, products, or perspectives are informed by the past and influenced by the present. The dissonance between what "counts" as the integration of culture into language teaching and what "counts" within a multicultural education framework seemed to cause confusion for some teachers.

Table 2 Alignment of FL Department's Multicultural Learnings with the FL Standards

Multicultural Learnings	FL Standards
Students demonstrate an understanding of the relationship between the practices and perspectives of the culture studied.	Standard 2.1: Students demonstrate an understanding of the relationship between the practices and perspectives of the culture studied.
Students demonstrate an understanding of the relationship between the products and perspectives of the culture studied.	Standard 2.2: Students demonstrate an understanding of the relationship between the products and the perspectives of the culture studied.
Students acquire information and recognize the distinctive points of view that are only available through the FL and its culture.	Standard 3.2: Students acquire information and recognize the distinctive viewpoints that are only available through the FL and its cultures.
Students demonstrate an understanding of the nature of language through comparisons of the language studied with their own.	Standard 4.1: Students demonstrate an understanding of the nature of language through comparisons of the language studied with their own.
Students demonstrate an understanding of the concept of culture through comparison of the culture studied with their own.	Standard 4.2: Students demonstrate understanding of the concept of culture through comparisons of the cultures studied and their own.
Students identify and evaluate superficial stereotypes of the culture of the language being studied.	Not directly matched to the FL standards.

Native and Non-Native Speakers of English

The differences between the native English speaking instructors (NES) and the instructors who were native speakers of the target language but nonnative speakers of English (NNES) were marked in some of the data. On one level, many instructors struggled with issues of using new pedagogical terminology for writing lesson plans, which they sometimes termed *"jargon,"* in the initiative. One NNES respondent identified that terminology as a real hurdle for the other NNES teachers who were less proficient in English. This respondent stated that, even though many NNES instructors had been licensed in education in another country, they were *"very very hampered"* by the American *"educational jargon."* She appreciated the time that they were able to spend in a group where they all shared a common language (for instance, the French teachers all spoke in French together). That time in a small cooperative learning group, she stated, was really an opportunity to *"talk it out"* in the teachers' first language. Another NNES teacher also attributed difficulty with the initiative to his status as a non-native speaker of English, stating, "English is my second language. It is slow, and I need more thinking. This process is not very fun to me. It's kind of difficult."

There was also a disparity between NES and NNES instructors due to the difference in their connection to the culture that they were teaching. Several NNES teachers mentioned struggling with representing aspects of their own culture to NES students and faculty members. One NNES instructor described her own "evolution as an immigrant" as a process that had preceded the multicultural initiative at the school. In her early years as a teacher, she had a "defensive attitude" about teaching her culture, feeling that she was the "torchbearer." However, she soon realized that she needed to invite debate with her students in order to teach more effectively. She emphasized that this change occurred in her before the multicultural initiative began. Another NNES instructor mentioned a struggle with being a representative of a minority group on the staff as the multicultural initiative took place. He stated:

> On a personal level, I think that even between teachers, and within the teachers, the faculty, I think we still need to educate or let people have that kind of knowledge, to respect different races, different people. Because I'm a XXX minority in a group with people, . . . I think that the teachers are more sensitive or learn in these issues, and try to learn and understand others. This is great for me, it's easy to start or have a conversation, or talk a little about difference, or to go a little bit deeper in some issue that people want to know . . . Also even all this works, but still, some colleagues it's like they've already set up their minds and it's hard for them to change. But I hope that these things will make something change their mind.

This NNES teacher's statements echo that of several NES teachers relating to working in a community of teachers who have varying levels of acceptance of the multicultural initiative. However, for him, the acceptance or lack thereof is more personal, and more related to his own identity as a minority.

Conclusion

As teachers learned about multicultural curriculum, some experienced a competing view of what cultural content should be in their curricula. The experience served to complicate traditional FL perspectives on teaching culture, illustrating that teaching a FL from a multiculturalist perspective may be different than from a strict disciplinary perspective. For some, teaching culture through the lens of mainstream multicultural education added a new and critical element to how they thought about both cultural content and the instruction of teaching and assessing for deeper learnings and understandings. For others, this lens already existed. This fact reminds us that being a multiculturalist is not guaranteed among FL teachers and becoming a multiculturalist is not a linear process.

The most challenging hurdle teachers perceived was tracking the professional development experiences over so many years. While this sort of sustained and multifaceted professional development program is exactly what is touted as best practice in school-based reform, this is the part of the experience teachers often cited as most challenging. Furthermore, the process did not always seem to take into consideration the particular needs of nonnative English speakers who are an asset to the modern language department yet were often left feeling unsure about how to meet the expectations of the curriculum or diversity committee members.

This study has limitations, the most serious of which is the low participation rate of the teachers from the department. Only 6 of 12 agreed to participate in the study. Furthermore, we have interviews from only four because two decided to participate anonymously via an on-line survey. The study is also limited by the fact that our only data source from the participants was the teachers' interviews and/or surveys. Therefore it was not possible to triangulate data sources to verify findings. For example, had we obtained permission to analyze the participants' work, we may have found congruities or incongruities between what the teachers produced with what they expressed as challenges in their task to produce new curriculum. Had we observed them teach, we may have witnessed that teachers have more skill in teaching about multicultural issues than they do in expressing what they do to an outside audience using an unfamiliar format. The addition of these additional data sources would have made this analysis much more robust and rigorous.

This study suggests that there is still work to be done at College School on the multicultural curriculum. Curriculum work in general is never completed—there is always the need to adjust curricula according to changing times. However, it seems that when teachers engage in the much more challenging work of curriculum *transformation* that aims to integrate new and different perspectives, narratives, documents, images, and self-examinations into an already rigorous academic program, the process is an even greater negotiation of what is and what could be.

The process has been moving toward more departmental control over the multicultural education conversation. It will be very productive for department heads to devise content- and department-specific plans for talking about, reading about, and doing multicultural curriculum transformation. The FL department is well-poised to discuss, share, and debate how FL educators do multicultural education across languages and grade levels. College School took up the challenge of questioning their curricular status quo and most teachers came to the table willing to participate in the dialogue, to deliberate and negotiate. Although the learning needs of all of the teachers were not necessarily addressed all of the time, this step toward curricular transformation can serve as a model for ways other programs may begin the conversation about what multicultural education looks like in FL classrooms.

Notes

1. The work by Grant Wiggins and Jay McTighe is widely used in K-12 schools to engage teachers in thinking about their assessment practices and the links between assessment, curriculum, and instruction. The basic tenet of the approach is *backward design*, which first asks the teacher to define what are the most important "learnings" and "understandings" in their curriculum, consider what counts as evidence of understanding and finally teach for understanding and then create lessons to achieve this end.

2. The description of the participants is intentionally aggregated in order to preserve anonymity. This is also appropriate because the bounded unit of the case is the department, not the individual. We are aware that the terms "native" and "nonnative" may be needlessly dichotomizing, reflecting what Nayar (1994) has called the "implicational exclusivity of ownership" (p. 4). However, among our non U.S.-born participants who grew up speaking languages other than English and are bi- or multilingual, this socially-constructed label did have meaning for them in this particular setting.

3. Our inductive approach to qualitative data analysis involved systematic reading and coding of the transcripts for the purpose of finding themes in the data. A deductive approach was used later as we examined the related literature on the research topic and checked for whether we should add coding categories to our coding protocol.

4. We recall a meeting in 2003 when the entire faculty engaged in peer review of their plans. They were explicitly asked to check each others' ideas for the following: "Does the assessment plan explicitly address multicultural learning and understandings (e.g., biases, prejudice reduction, knowledge construction, multiple perspectives, cultural assumptions)?'

References

Banks, J. (1995). Multicultural education and curriculum transformation. *Journal of Negro Education, 64*(4), 390–400.

Banks, J. A. (1999). *An introduction to multicultural education* (2nd ed.). Needham Heights, MA: Allyn & Bacon.

Banks, J. A. (2005). *Cultural diversity and education: Foundations, curriculum, and teaching* (5th ed.). Boston: Allyn & Bacon.

Banks, J. A., & McGee-Banks, C. A. (Eds.). (2003). *Multicultural education: Issues and perspectives.* New York: John Wiley & Sons.

Byram, M. (1987). *Cultural studies in foreign language education.* Clevedon, UK: Multilingual Matters.

Byram, M., & Zarate, G. (1997). *The sociocultural and intercultural dimension of language learning and teaching.* Strasbourg, France: Council of Europe Publishing.

Canale, M., & Swain, M. (1980). Theoretical bases of communicative approaches to second language teaching and testing. *Applied Linguistics, 1*(1), 1–47.

Crawford-Lange, L. M., & Lange, D. L. (1987). Integrating language and culture: How to do it. *Theory into Practice, 26*(4), 258–266.

Darling-Hammond, L., & McLaughlin, M. W. (1995). Policies that support professional development in an era of reform. *Phi Delta Kappan, 76*(8), 597–604.

Farber, K. S. (1995). Teaching about diversity through reflectivity: Sites of uncertainty, risk and possibility. In R. J. Martin (Ed.) *Practicing what we teach: Confronting diversity in teacher education* (pp. 49–63). Albany, NY: State University of New York Press.

Fischer, R. (1997). Projects and other tools: Some strategic remarks on intercultural learner competence. In M. Byram & G. Zarate (Eds.), *The sociocultural and intercultural dimension of language learning and teaching* (pp. 73–82). Strasbourg, France: Council of Europe Publishing.

Grant, C. A., & Sleeter, C. E. (2003). *Turning on learning: Five approaches for multicultural teaching plans for race, class, gender, and disability.* New York: Wiley/Jossey-Bass Education.

Hymes, D. H. (1971). *On communicative competence.* Philadelphia: University of Pennsylvania Press.

Klein, F. (2004). *Culture in the foreign language classroom: Teachers' beliefs, opportunities and practice.* Unpublished doctoral dissertation, University of Minnesota, Minneapolis.

Kramsch, C. (1993). *Context and culture in language teaching.* Oxford: University Press.

Martin, R. J. (1998). Puzzles and paradigms: Connecting multicultural theory to practice. *Multicultural Education, 5*(4), 46–51.

Miles, M. B., & Huberman, A. M. (1994). *Qualitative data analysis* (2nd ed.). Thousand Oaks, CA: Sage.

National Standards in Foreign Language Education Project. (1999). *Standards for foreign language learning in the 21st century.* Lawrence, KS: Allen Press.

Nayar, P., B. (1994). Whose English is it? *TESL-EJ, 1*(1). [On-line]. Retrieved December 14, 2009 from www.kyoto-su.ac.jp/ information/tesl-ej/ej01/f.1.html

Paige, R. M., Jorstad, H. L., Siaya, L., Klein, F., & Colby, J. (2003). Culture learning in language education: A review of the literature. In D. L. Lange & R. M. Paige (Eds.), *Culture as the core: Perspectives on culture in second language learning* (pp. 173–236). Greenwich, CT: Information Age Publishing.

Rubin, H. J., & Rubin, I. S. (2005). *Qualitative interviewing: The art of hearing data* (2nd ed.). Thousand Oaks, CA: Sage Publications.

Schulz, R. A. (2007). The challenge of assessing cultural understanding in the context of foreign language instruction. *Foreign Language Annals, 40*(1), 9–26.

Seelye, H. N. (1997). The cultural mazeway: Six organizing goals. In P. R. Heusinkveld (Ed.), *Pathways to culture* (pp. 97–105). Yarmouth, ME: Intercultural Press.

Sercu, L. (2005). *Foreign language teachers and intercultural competence: An international investigation.* Clevedon, UK: Multilingual Matters.

Sisken, J. (2007). Call me "Madame": Re-presenting culture in the French language classroom. *Foreign Language Annals, 40*(1), 27–42.

Social Science Education Consortium. (1999). *Culture in the foreign language classroom: A survey of high school teachers' practices and needs - executive summary.* Boulder, CO: U.S. Department of Education.

Wiggins, G., & McTighe, J. (1999). *Understanding by design.* Alexandria, VA: Association for Supervision and Curriculum Development.

Wiggins, G., & McTighe, J. (2005). *Understanding by design* (2nd ed.). Alexandria, VA: Association for Supervision and Curriculum Development.

Critical Thinking

1. What is Banks' approach to curriculum transformation?
2. What is Wiggins and McTighe's backward design?
3. How do these two strategies help integrate culture and social justice?
4. What did the teachers learn from their professional development initiative?

Create Central

www.mhhe.com/createcentral

Internet References

James A. Banks, University of Washington
  http://faculty.washington.edu/jbanks/links.html

Understanding by Design
  www.ascd.org/research-a-topic/understanding-by-design-resources.aspx

Unit 7

UNIT

Prepared by: Nancy P. Gallavan, *University of Central Arkansas*

Awareness of Efficacy

Efficacy encompasses the belief in one's abilities to achieve a goal through the four domains of learning and five senses generating control of and responsibility for one's motivation, implementation, environment, and negotiations. Motivation addresses the question of why, offering the justification for our thoughts, beliefs, values, and assumptions based on external and internal stimuli. Implementation speaks to the question of how, providing the rationalization for the ways we conduct ourselves both when we are among other people and on our own as well as the ways we treat ourselves. Environment answers the questions of who, where, and when, establishing the contextualization of our existence and sense of place. Negotiations respond to the questions of what and what else, describing the current facilitation and exploring the potential possibilities for mediation, reconciliation, and balance.

An educator's sense of motivation, implementation, environment, and negotiations influence the selection of outcomes, the communications and setting associated with pursuing the outcome, and the conditions and compromises accepted along the way. Attuned to cultural competence, an educator would achieve greater efficacy by exploring the cultural characteristics of the learners in the classroom that would be more meaningful to them individually and as a group. By encouraging learners to share their backgrounds and beliefs with one another throughout the unit, activities can be added to the physical environment and educational climate to reflect learners' contributions to the classroom space, allowing learners to construct new concepts and conduct extended investigations to enrich the conversations.

These four words, *motivation, implementation, environment,* and *negotiations,* start with letters that spell the word *mien,* a word defined as demeanor and disposition. Teacher education programs and standards emphasize the understanding and demonstration of appropriate professional knowledge, skills, and dispositions. While teachers' knowledge and skills are well-defined and clearly stipulated in most teacher education programs, teachers' dispositions remain more elusive and undetermined. Enhancing educator efficacy is critical for the teacher's and students' abilities to achieve their goals.

Efficacy is gained from four primary sources: mastery experiences, vicarious experiences, verbal persuasion, and emotional state. Mastery experiences include experiences where the learner achieves success. When accompanied by satisfaction, this source of self-efficacy is the most robust. Motivation plays an extremely important role in mastery experiences. Learners must be encouraged and engaged honestly with activities and assignments connected to them personally.

Vicarious experiences involve experiences where the learner observes success and satisfaction in a peer. When the peer seems equally comparable, modeling self-efficacy is highly influential. Interactions between and among peers that are natural promote learners' beliefs supporting achievement. Verbal persuasion comprises experiences where the learner hears about success and satisfaction from a credible source partnered with persuasive and productive feedback. These messages stimulate students and foster their dedication to the endeavor. Environments with teachers, coaches, mentors, etc., who guide learners through tasks with authentic cognitive, affective, physical, and social support help advance self-efficacy.

Emotional state addresses experiences where the learner is mentored to maintain a successful outlook or satisfying attitude that energizes the individual and increases one's beliefs. Negotiations that capitalize upon one's strengths further increase one's strengths, especially when teachers work holistically to maximize productivity and minimize pressure.

For educators, efficacy requires doing what is right and good because it is right and good and doing it well. Teachers are responsible for motivating their students to engage in the learning and apply new concepts to their previous learning and future living by capturing their students' awareness. Through limitless instructional strategies, teachers implement learning experiences for their students to inquire, explore, hypothesize, discover, imagine, create, exchange, and reflect on new ideas in a variety of environments equipped with various tools. Throughout these processes, teachers are guiding their students through the negotiations associated with thorough resource acquisition and wise decision making. Ultimately, teachers want their students to experience success and satisfaction by increasing achievement. Through mastery, modeling, messages, and mentoring, teachers and students advance their cultural competence.

Article   Prepared by: Nancy P. Gallavan, *University of Central Arkansas*

"Everything That's Challenging in My School Makes Me a Better Teacher": Negotiating Tensions in Learning to Teach for Equity

ELIZABETH HOPE DORMAN

Learning Outcomes

After reading this article, you will be able to:

- Become acquainted with the concepts purposive activity in cultural contexts and identity construction.

- Apply the concepts and practices of purposive activity to teaching, learning, and schooling.

The achievement gap between White middle-class students and poor and working-class students of color has been well documented in the literature (Williams, 2003). Villegas and Lucas (2002) asserted that a significant factor in this achievement discrepancy is the cultural and linguistic gap between a teaching force that is overwhelmingly White, middle class, and monolingual and a public school student population that grows increasingly diverse each year (Cochran-Smith, Davis, & Fries, 2004; Hollins & Guzman, 2005; Zumwalt & Craig, 2005).

Although the majority of teachers—84 percent in 2011—are White females (Feistritzer, 2011), many teacher education programs are working to bridge this cultural divide between educators and their K-12 students. Programs are bolstering curriculum and field experiences to help preservice teachers develop culturally relevant, equity-oriented instructional approaches and dispositions that will help students make academic gains and achieve robust educational outcomes (Hollins & Guzman, 2005; Ladson-Billings, 1994). However, as Cochran-Smith (2004) noted, few empirical studies exist on the experiences of these "diversity-prepared" teachers once they are hired.

This paper responds to this call for further inquiry into the experiences of graduates of equity-focused teacher education programs. Its purpose is to present and analyze the experiences of Mia (pseudonym), a White, female, monolingual recent college graduate who earned her licensure in secondary social

studies through a graduate level urban teacher preparation program (UTEP; pseudonym) and then accepted a position at a large, traditional, diverse, urban middle school in the western United States. The school serves a predominantly Latino community and is "on watch" and being audited by the state because of historically low test scores. This research focuses on determining how negotiating tensions in the school context contributes to the identity development of a novice teacher with respect to culturally responsive, equity-oriented pedagogy. Specifically, I explore tensions within the curriculum and in interactions with colleagues.

Conceptual Framework

Two strands form the theoretical grounding for this paper: (1) the situated nature of purposive activity in cultural, historical contexts/activity settings and (2) identity construction from a sociocultural perspective. Development and learning cannot be separated from the activities and social contexts in which they take place. According to Mercer (1992), "All learning is situated, because any task or activity does not exist independently of the ways in which participants contextualize it" (p. 33). How people learn and develop, as well as the kinds of knowledge they develop, is intricately connected to the various activities and contexts in which the learning experience occurs. Thus, from this theoretical perspective, individuals and the contexts in which they operate are not viewed as separate constructs. The situated nature of development (Putnam & Borko, 1997, 2000) "suggests that the study of learning, especially in educational settings, must treat context and culture as part of what is being studied, not variables to be partialed out" (Mercer, 1992, p. 33). These theories are particularly relevant for studying how elements of the context in which Mia learns to teach have influenced her development and learning as a teacher for equity.

In addition, in sociocultural theory, identity construction is considered to be a form of human development that occurs by engaging in goal-oriented action within various social settings (Lave & Wenger, 1991; Smagorinsky, Cook, Moore, Jackson, & Fry, 2004). Similarly, Merseth, Sommer, and Dickstein (2008) remarked, "As teachers develop identity, context matters" (p. 90). Smagorinsky et al. (2004) observed that "one's identity is not simply the emergence of internal traits and dispositions but their development through engagement with others in cultural practice" (p. 21). Negotiating tensions, for example, those between the context and one's identity, can contribute to identity development (Smagorinsky et al., 2004).

Methodology

This study, which represents a piece of a larger research project, used qualitative, interpretive, case study methodology. Data sources included (1) field notes, audio files, and videotape transcripts from 12 hours of observation in Mia's classes during a 6-month period; (2) transcripts from 22 hours of semistructured interviews (16 with Mia and 6 with her support providers); and (3) artifacts, such as course assignments, lesson plans, student work, and school-issued documents.

Data analysis began during data collection and was iterative and recursive. The process was inspired by Spradley's (1980) domain, taxonomic, and componential analysis and LeCompte and Shensul's (1999) stages of (1) isolating specific items and working to label them accurately; (2) looking for and articulating patterns and structures; and (3) clarifying meaning by "linking together or finding consistent relationships among patterns, components, constituents, and structures" (p. 177). The validity and trustworthiness of the results were established through triangulation, adapting previously validated interview protocols (see Peressini, Borko, & Romagnano, 2004), member checking, and prolonged observation.

Participant and Setting

Like many who enter the teaching profession, Mia is a White, monolingual, English-speaking female. Mia grew up in the southern United States in a fairly sheltered environment "with a tight circle of friends who were all like me: None of our parents are divorced. We're all White. We all come from fairly middle class families. And we stuck together" (Personal communication, January 19, 2006). In her family, she was "taught to be a peacemaker in the sense of not causing controversy when there is no need to cause it."

During data collection, Mia was a first-year teacher at South Hill Middle School (pseudonym). The school's demographics reflect nationwide trends of increasing diversity. Of the school's almost 800 students, approximately 75% are from low-income families, nearly 70% are Latino (mostly of Mexican origin), about 27% are White, and small percentages are African American, Asian, American Indian, or of mixed heritage. More than half of the students learned something other than English as their first language. The demographics of Mia's classes are comparable to these statistics.

Findings: Mia's Case Story
Tensions in Curriculum

At South Hill Middle School, Mia has a fairly prescribed curriculum in terms of the topics that must be addressed in her sixth-grade social studies courses, as the school is "on watch" and being audited by the state due to its historically low test scores. However, she generally has some freedom in how she chooses to address the topics and which materials and resources she selects. Mia's approaches to various tensions that arise in the curriculum at South Hill illustrate important aspects of her evolving identity as a culturally responsive educator.

Mia was initially excited about the mandated unit on Mexican history because she thought she would be able to make it relevant and meaningful for her predominantly Latino students. However, the content turned out "to be not really culturally responsive." She lamented, "What they ended up learning about was some guy who lived 200 years ago who wound up reforming the Catholic Church. I mean *that's* not what they're interested in." The assigned textbook's portrayal of Mexican history contributed to the problem. The book's coverage of the topic was "not really inclusive; it's just about wars and men, and that just is not culturally responsive to me," Mia recounted. "I don't want the Mexican girls in my class to think, 'Where are we in this history? This is supposed to be our history and I don't see anybody like me'".

To balance out the textbook's "wars and men" perspective and generate more interest among her students, Mia developed a subsequent mini-unit on famous Latina women in the United States. Students had a chance to learn about women who had successfully followed career paths in which the students themselves were potentially interested (e.g., lawyer, author, singer, painter, civil rights activist) through research, writing, and a class presentation. Mia hoped that the Latina women they chose to research would serve as role models for her students.

Although Mia acknowledged that the famous Latinas project could have gone further in helping students develop conceptual understanding about the historical significance of the women's contributions, the project did at least introduce students to the role of women in the history of Latinos, thereby filling in the blanks of the textbook's portrayals to some extent. Mia's observation of the textbook's limited perspective and her subsequent adaptations illustrate an important aspect of culturally responsive pedagogy: identifying when the contributions or perspectives of certain groups are absent from the existing curriculum and adapting it to reflect a more inclusive approach.

Another aspect of culturally responsive teaching is to explicitly address issues of race, skin color, class, culture, gender, and so forth. Doing so is never straightforward or predictable, and the ensuing discussions are often emotional, political, and value laden. During the Mexican history unit, for example, Mia wanted her students to understand that "many Mexicans today are a blend of Spanish and indigenous cultures" because Mexico was "basically a Spanish colony for awhile." She had noticed that her many students of Mexican descent seemed to "have this sense of 'We're just Mexican and that's what we are'—like they've always been Mexican and nothing else."

Mia wanted to clear up potential misperceptions: "They need to understand that part of their culture comes from Spain, that there really is a mix of cultures in Mexico." To help them comprehend, she asked a few of the students, "Why is your skin color brown?" When they didn't offer much of a response, she told them, "It's because you're a mix of this darker Native American person and these light-skinned White people from Spain." She continued,

> And it was kind of shock to them that Spanish people are White people, too. They were like, "Really, they're White?" Yes, they're White. And then when Mexico originally became its own country, it was the White people, like Miguel Hidalgo who was born in Mexico, who were leading this movement. It was people of Spanish descent who no longer wanted to be a part of the Spanish crown . . . But, I didn't get that across.

When asked to reflect on why she thought she did not make her point understood, she acknowledged that she "felt uncomfortable . . . even talking about skin color." She questioned whether she should have asked the students to think about why their own skin color was brown, and she said the whole exchange "was very difficult." I asked her to say more about her discomfort:

Author: You said you feel uncomfortable talking about skin color. Is that just with your kids? Or do you feel like, just in terms of the identity of who you are, that makes you feel uncomfortable?

M: Yeah, I think in general I think it's something that I just am not totally comfortable with. Because like when I was growing up it was something that you don't point out. Does that make sense? Because if you do, then that makes you not accepting?

Author: Kind of like the mindset of not seeing differences? Like, "Oh, we're all just the same"? Kind of like that?

M: Right. Obviously there are differences, and I think it's okay to say that. Because I did. I did say that to my students. But it wasn't something that I was totally comfortable with, which is probably the biggest part of the reason why it was hard for me to teach it.

This passage illustrates one of the ways in which an aspect of Mia's identity—namely, how she was taught while growing up not to discuss people's skin color differences—shapes her approach to discussing this issue in the classroom. Addressing topics such as this one can be difficult and takes courage on the part of teachers, as reflected in Mia's comments.

These scenarios illustrate some of the effects of the mandated curriculum on Mia and ways that she responds to it. She attempts to make connections to students' background knowledge, culture, and interests so that they will be able to find more meaning in the content than they might otherwise. She said that these adaptations ultimately make her a better teacher. Thinking back on her first year at South Hill, she remarked that having to work within the constraints of the mandated curriculum "has really taught me a lot about culturally responsive teaching."

M: So I think that the curriculum challenges me to really understand what culturally responsive teaching is and to work really hard to become a culturally responsive teacher . . . It forces me to think of ways that I can be culturally responsive but still stay in line with the status quo—does that make sense?

Author: The status quo meaning the curriculum you're required to teach?

M: Right. And the way that it's normally taught, and having to fit in with that.

This passage alludes to an aspect of Mia's identity that is evident across many data sources—namely, the way she takes responsibility for ensuring that students get what they need to have effective learning experiences, no matter what constraints she faces within the context of South Hill Middle School. Her proactive approach to problem solving when faced with potential barriers contributes to her identity development. She is able to take many aspects of her school setting (such as prescribed curriculum) that could potentially constrain her equity-focused teaching and turn them into affordances.

Tensions in Interactions with School Colleagues

During one interview, Mia made the following comments, which characterize some of the tensions she experiences with her colleagues:

> Something else that I still need to learn how to do is— you need to know when to open your mouth with the rest of the staff and how to pick your battles. In my case, I need to be able to pick a battle to begin with because I normally just go along with the flow. But I'm recognizing that, if you just continue to go along with the flow, then that voice—that voice of social justice or cultural responsiveness or whatever—is not going to be heard. In my school, people are just not talking about the things that I think we should be talking about. And so I've been trying to coach myself on being more assertive.

Multiple data sources point to tensions in interactions between Mia and some of her colleagues at South Hill, mostly relating to viewpoints about diversity and equity. In fact, Mia succinctly stated, "I'm *about* something that other people in the building aren't."

Mia's responses to various tensions that arise illustrate other important aspects of her evolving identity as a culturally responsive educator. When asked about the extent to which the whole faculty had discussions about equity issues and the ways in which Mia perceived those interactions to mediate her conceptions of teaching for equity, her professional identity, and her practices, she responded,

> I just feel like it's a very missing piece. I think we talk about SIOP [an instructional protocol to assist English language learners] and how we need to be implementing SIOP, but it's always in a perspective of just "this is going to help our students be more successful on the tests," not that this is going to help our students maintain

their language or help support them in learning a new language, that kind of thing. We just don't ever talk about how the students' culture affects our school. We just really don't—unless it's in a negative way.

Mia expressed concern that at least some of her colleagues "have a superficial view of what culture is and how it should be recognized in the classroom" and that sometimes her colleagues' comments seem deficit oriented. She explained,

The team conversations about students' home life and cultural diversity always seem very negative to me. It was just very, like, well, "the parents aren't doing this for the kid and it's because they're—because they don't speak English, or because they're poor, or because they're working all the time"—or something like that. It wasn't really a lot about positive things that were going on in the home. Or about things that the kids were getting at home and bringing to school.

On the other hand, Mia took a step back to reflect on the context of the differences she perceives between her stance and that of some of her colleagues:

When I'm listening to other teachers I can see the difference in those viewpoints almost immediately when they start talking. And at moments I have to be very patient because I have to remember that, if I had not gone through this [UTEP] program, I would have thought the same way. I would be making the same comments.

When asked to reflect on how she thought all-faculty gatherings influenced her development as a teacher for equity, Mia remarked:

It makes me want to be more clear in who I am. And like what I'm trying to accomplish. It makes me want to speak up more. But it hasn't got to the point where I feel like totally brave enough to do that in that huge room full of people.

This disposition of learning to speak up in the face of biased, deficit-oriented comments is an aspect of Mia's identity that shows up frequently in the data. On the heels of these comments, she provided a specific example of a time during an all-faculty meeting when she tried on her emerging identity as someone who speaks up in the face of comments that have the potential to oppress others:

We were having a discussion one day about high expectations, and someone made a comment like . . . "Well, *some* people need to work at Wendy's, so it might as well be our students" or something like that. And my response was, "*We* are not the people who choose what roles people go into." And my comment was totally misunderstood. [People thought I meant] "we don't choose it; some cosmic force chooses it, and we just sort of go with it." What I meant was: we need to empower all our students so that *they* get to make the choice. But that wasn't heard and I felt guilty because I didn't continue to explain myself. And I felt kind of silly because I was like, this is not what I want to say.

These passages illustrate how Mia refines her identity by negotiating tensions that arise within her interactions with colleagues. Mia stated several times that the context of the UTEP—with its clear goal of developing in its participants both awareness of and strategies for ensuring equitable educational experiences for *all* students—influenced her concepts and helped her become more aware of equity and social justice issues. Now, when she encounters comments that she finds inappropriate based on her newly developing understandings, she does not feel right not saying something to interrupt the practice of using language that constitutes oppression to some degree. However, as seen in the passage just quoted, perhaps she has not yet developed the language with which to explain exactly why the remarks seem offensive to her. She is apparently much more aware about inequities in society than she was prior to her UTEP participation. However, she is still developing the concrete tools to describe the ways in which systemic factors in society advantage and disadvantage certain groups and to take social action toward reducing prejudice and inequity.

Discussion, Conclusions, and Implications

In this paper, I set out to explore how negotiating tensions in the school context contributes to the identity development of a novice teacher with respect to culturally responsive, equity-oriented pedagogy. Mia's case story presents various tensions that she experiences both within the school curriculum and with her colleagues.

One might think that these potential limitations of the school context would constrain Mia's overall experience of learning to teach for social justice. In some ways, they do serve to confine. However, these tensions forced Mia to engage in problem solving, a process which contributed to her identity development and her adoption of certain conceptions and practices of culturally responsive teaching. As sociocultural theory suggests, negotiating tensions can be productive (Smagorinsky et al., 2004). In Mia's situation, she had to negotiate tensions between her evolving identity and the context of her school. She pushed back on the potentially limiting aspects of South Hill Middle School and accommodated them in ways that were better suited to her identity. For example, she pushed back on her colleagues' practice of using deficit-oriented language about students of color and students from low-income backgrounds. Negotiating this tension mediated changes in her identity in terms of clarifying her own beliefs and learning to "find her voice" so she can speak out against bias and negative language. Because of Mia's disposition of taking responsibility and making the best of potentially difficult situations, she claims that these perceived limitations actually make her a more effective teacher. She even commented, "I think everything that's challenging in my school makes me a better teacher."

Mia's case story presents an example of the potential effects of equity-focused teacher education. Like many other White, middle-class women who enroll in teacher education programs, Mia entered with an open disposition, a willingness to accept and explore her potentially sheltered viewpoints, a naïveté about culture, and a curiosity to learn. The combination of her teacher education focused on issues of diversity, equity, and social justice in urban schools and the learning opportunities afforded her by encountering tensions in her curriculum and in interactions with colleagues helped Mia begin to shift her beliefs, attitudes, and practices about culturally responsive, equity-oriented pedagogy.

Perhaps this case story will provide ideas or inspiration for novice teachers who face some of the same challenges that Mia did, either in their school context or in their own identities as teachers. Perhaps this story will also inspire teacher educators to realize that their efforts in guiding candidates to learn to teach for social justice and equity do, indeed, make a difference. Such effects might not be immediately evident. As Darling-Hammond stated, "Learning to teach for social justice is a lifelong undertaking" (2002, p. 201). Indeed, Nieto concluded that "Becoming a multicultural teacher entails becoming a multicultural person" (cited in Zeichner & Hoeft, 1996, p. 529).

References

Cochran-Smith, M. (2004). *Walking the road: Race, diversity, and social justice in teacher education.* New York: Teachers College Press.

Cochran-Smith, M., Davis, D., & Fries, K. (2004). Multicultural teacher education: Research, practice, and policy. In J. Banks & C. A. M. Banks (Eds.), *Handbook of research on multicultural education* (pp. 931–975). San Francisco: Jossey-Bass.

Darling-Hammond, L. (2002). Educating a profession for equitable practice. In L. Darling-Hammond, J. French, & S. P. García-Lopez (Eds.), *Learning to teach for social justice* (pp. 201–212). New York: Teachers College Press.

Feistritzer, C. E. (2011). *Profile of teachers in the U.S. 2011.* Washington, DC: National Center for Education Information.

Hollins, E. R., & Guzman, M. T. (2005). Research on preparing teachers for diverse populations. In M. Cochran-Smith & K. M. Zeichner (Eds.), *Studying teacher education: The report of the AERA panel on research and teacher education* (pp. 477–548). Mahwah, NJ: Lawrence Erlbaum.

Ladson-Billings, G. (1994). *The dreamkeepers: Successful teachers of African American children.* San Francisco, CA: Jossey Bass.

Lave, J., & Wenger, E. (1991). *Situated learning: Legitimate peripheral participation.* New York: Cambridge University Press.

LeCompte, M., & Schensul, J. (1999). *Analyzing and interpreting ethnographic data.* Walnut Creek, CA: Alta Mira Press.

Mercer, N. (1992). Culture, context, and the construction of knowledge in the classroom. In P. Light & G. Butterworth (Eds.), *Context and cognition: Ways of learning and knowing* (pp. 28–46). Hillsdale, NJ: Lawrence Erlbaum Associates.

Merseth, K., Sommer, J., & Dickstein, S. (2008). Bridging worlds: Changes in personal and professional identities of preservice urban teachers. *Teacher Education Quarterly, 35*(3), 89–108.

Nieto, S., & Bode, P. (2012). *Affirming diversity: The sociopolitical context of multicultural education* (6th ed.). New York: Longman.

Peressini, D., Borko, H., & Romagnano, L. (2004). A conceptual framework for learning to teach secondary mathematics: A situative perspective. *Educational Studies in Mathematics, 56*(1), 67–96.

Putnam, R. T., & Borko, H. (1997). Teacher learning: Implications of the new view of cognition. In B. J. Bidle, T. L. Good, & I. F. Goodson (Eds.). *The international handbook of teachers and teaching* (pp. 1223–1296). Netherlands: Kluwer.

Putnam, R. T., & Borko, H. (2000). What do new views of knowledge and thinking have to say about research on teacher learning? *Educational Researcher, 29*(1), 4–15.

Smagorinsky, P., Cook, L. S., Moore, C., Jackson, A. Y., & Fry, P. G. (2004). Tensions in learning to teach: Accommodation and the development of a teaching identity. *Journal of Teacher Education, 55*(1), 8–24.

Spradley, J. P. (1980). *Participant observation.* Orlando, FL: Harcourt Brace Jovanovich.

Villegas, A. M., & Lucas, T. (2002). *Educating culturally responsive teachers: A coherent approach.* Albany, NY: State University of New York Press.

Williams, B. (2003). What else do we need to know and do? In B. Williams (Ed.), *Closing the achievement gap: A vision for changing beliefs and practices* (pp. 13–24). Alexandria, VA: ASCD.

Zeichner, K., & Hoeft, K. (1996). Teacher socialization for cultural diversity. In J. Sikula, T. J. Buttery, & E. Guyton (Eds.), *Handbook of research on teacher education* (pp. 525–547). New York: Macmillan.

Zumwalt, K., & Craig, E. (2005). Teachers' characteristics: Research on the demographic profile. In M. Cochran-Smith & K. M. Zeichner (Eds.), *Studying teacher education: The report of the AERA panel on research and teacher education* (pp. 157–260). Mahwah, NJ: Lawrence Erlbaum.

Critical Thinking

1. What is meant by the situated nature of purposive activity in cultural contexts?

2. What is construction of identity essential for teachers?

3. What are the tensions that teachers encounter?

4. How can teachers negotiate the tensions to promote culturally responsive, equity-oriented teaching, learning, and schooling?

Create Central

www.mhhe.com/createcentral

Internet References

Learning as Purposive Activity
www.learndev.org/dl/DenverJonassen.PDF

Situated Activity and Identity Formation
www.public.coe.edu/~lbarnett/445%20Readings/rt9.pdf

ELIZABETH HOPE DORMAN is an Assistant Professor of Education at Regis University.

Dorman, Elizabeth Hope. From *Journal of Urban Learning, Teaching, and Research*, vol. 8, 2012, pp. 83–92. Copyright © 2012 by Elizabeth Hope Dorman. Used with permission.

Article   Prepared by: Nancy P. Gallavan, *University of Central Arkansas*

Uncommon Teaching in Commonsense Times

A Case Study of a Critical Multicultural Educator & the Academic Success of Diverse Student Populations

EMILIE M. CAMP AND HEATHER A. OESTERREICH

Learning Outcomes

After reading this article, you will be able to:

• Differentiate uncommon teaching from commonsense practices.

• Describe ways that democracy can be featured in the classroom.

> *To me, it would not be easier for me as a human being to run off pre-made worksheets for my kids to do. It would be an assault on my senses and everything that's inside.*
>
> —*Rae*

Rae, a 5th grade teacher, challenges the commonsense approaches mandated in the era of *No Child Left Behind* (NCLB) that frequently require teachers to run-off pre-made worksheets of standardized curricula as a panacea to closing such educational woes as the gap in achievement between the White, middle-class students and the largely Latino population that she teaches. Her senses are assaulted by the thought of participating in a "homogenized" curriculum (Sleeter, 2005) which has resulted in pedagogies that fail to meet the diverse needs of students. She rejects the commonsense that "schools teach these things and students do these things" (Kumashiro, 2004, p. xxii) and demonstrates how quality educators problematize those ideas, or the "official knowledge" that is internalized as "commonsense" (Apple, 2004).

By repositioning *commonsense* with *uncommon* teaching, teachers like Rae challenge what it means for students to learn and teachers to teach by helping their students understand themselves in relation to others and their world (Allen, 2002, p. 110). Teachers who reject the commonsense of practices such

as pre-made worksheets, scripted lessons, standardized knowledge, and boxed curricula and programs are needed to challenge the dominant paradigm of the standards movement and actively advocate for a more critical, multicultural curriculum. Practicing uncommon teaching is not simply something that someone does, but rather is something someone is always becoming.

Exploring perspectives on how teachers like Rae become teachers who challenge commonsense with uncommon teaching offers insight about how to nurture, support, and sustain perspectives and possibilities for creating uncommon solutions to what have been situated as commonsense problems. When she brings herself to her uncommon teaching, we learn that while there are unique elements that exist in multicultural classrooms like and unlike Rae's (Marri, 2004), there is an interdependency of multiple complex aspects that create, support, and sustain teachers who engage in uncommon teaching. Understanding this interdependency informs teacher educators to create their programs with the integration of multiple, differing curricular offerings, pedagogical support, and educational life experiences.

Perspectives on Uncommon Teaching

Uncommon teaching offers the possibility of re-centering education on the students and away from the commonsense of scripted and restricted curricula to promote acquisition by students of a critical consciousness in order to become agents of change for social justice. Allen (2002), in his discussion of critical theory, describes consciousness as the "state of mind that acts upon an awareness of the circumstances of oppression" (p. 108). Apple (2004) argues for the responsibility of educators to problematize the "official knowledge" that teachers internalize as commonsense, even as they discuss how it defies all of what they have been taught and understand as good teaching.

By repositioning commonsense with uncommon teaching, teachers act with the intention of transforming reality and actively advocate for teaching that reaches out to rather than preaches to students (Sleeter, 2005). Teachers who resist curriculum driven by high-stakes testing and related policies anchor their practices of resistance in situating commonsense knowledge as uncommon and impossible, so that they are professionals who are empowered to invoke professional judgment in order to meet the diverse needs of their students (Achinstein & Ogawa, 2006).

Many researchers have taken an interest in the application and implementations of pedagogies that counter the oppressive, scripted curriculum derived from the standardization movement and situate teaching and learning against commonsense (Kumashiro, 2004) even as they name it critical, multicultural, antioppressive, and/or social justice pedagogies (Achinstein & Ogawa, 2006; Agee, 2004; Arce, 2004; Crawford, 2004; Marri, 2005). Case studies illustrate that teacher preparation programs do foster philosophies of resistance in pre-service teachers and this manifests in their initial teaching.

Yet, after beginning their teaching careers with dispositions to teach uncommonly in common environments, many teachers succumb to the pressures to conform to the standardized curriculum, internalize the commonsense of the prescribed curriculum, and even leave the field of teaching altogether (Achinstein & Ogawa, 2006; Agee, 2004; Crawford, 2004). Arce (2004) and Marri (2005) likewise utilize case study to focus on teachers who resist the imposed curriculum in order to employ uncommon and multicultural teaching to foster democratic empowerment within their students. While both studies offer hope that empowering multicultural education exists, neither significantly explore how teachers are able to maintain resistance to scripted, undemocratic, test-driven curriculum.

We have some understanding of how individuals develop a commitment to multiculturalism. Paccione (2000) discusses the stages of developing a commitment to multicultural education. Based on various life experiences of the participants, Paccione describes the four stages of developing a commitment to multicultural education in a linear fashion. Ford and Dillard (1996) outline four phases of "becoming multicultural" as a cyclical, lifelong process of becoming. In the face of dominant cultural ideologies and their influences on curriculum, teachers exhibit an ability to maintain multicultural pedagogies that create uncommon teaching in commonsense times (Wallace, 2006). However, there remains a need for understanding how commitment translates into shifting away from the current commonsense mentality of test-driven curriculum and pedagogy to uncommon teaching.

Additionally, what we understand of uncommon teaching in commonsense times tends to focus on solitary aspects such as the process of becoming multicultural (Ford & Dillard, 1996; Paccione, 2000), the struggle to persist in uncommon teaching (Wallace, 2006), characteristics of uncommon teaching in a classroom (Arce, 2004; Marri, 2005), or previous life experiences that potentially shaped individual teachers' commitments to uncommon teaching (Paccione, 2000). Although these studies contribute positively to the field of multicultural education

and how teachers create and maintain uncommon teaching against the commonsense of limiting curricula, more research is needed that explores the relationships between multiple complex factors to understand how teachers come to understand the commonsense of educational practices as uncommon and engage meaningful curriculum outside the bounds of test-driven curriculum.

Methodology

In an effort to explore the complexity of how teachers develop and sustain the ability to teach uncommonly in commonsense times, we conducted a life history case study of a fifth grade teacher at a local elementary school in the Southwest United States who has practiced and sustained uncommon teaching for four years (Wedgwood, 2005). Such a life history case study, with a focus on the participant's past and current life experiences, provides insight into the uniqueness of a teacher by revealing in-depth insight into life phenomenon that ". . . we would not otherwise have access to" (Merriam, 1998, p. 33).

We chose this particular teacher for this study based on her apparent commitment to uncommon teaching within a school culture that otherwise employs the commonsense of standardized, test-driven curriculum as its official policy. In our work as teacher educators, we find her to be "one of a kind" among her colleagues and even among the majority of teachers we have come to know in our professional careers.

Bogdan and Biklen (2007) discuss this approach to case studies in which researchers do not identify the 'type' of person they want to interview and look for appropriate examples, but rather they already know a person or persons who inspire a line of inquiry and decide to pursue it. An intrinsic interest on the part of the researchers is also a common reason for using the case study method (Merriam, 1998).

The Teacher

Rae is a White middle class woman who was raised by a religiously conservative family in an area of the Southwest which is home to Navajo Nation and therefore embedded in the diversities of race, class, gender, nationality, and spirituality. Although Rae valued diversity in her own life, surrounding herself with friends and experiences which enriched her understanding and appreciation for cultures other than her own, her schooling was driven by the commonsense curricula of Eurocentrism and standardization. Consequently, Rae struggled to find value in her schooling experiences.

She now teaches fifth grade in an elementary school in the Southwest where eighty-five percent of the students are Latino, twelve percent White, two percent Black, and one percent Asian. Located in a working class area of the city, Rae recognizes the struggles many of her students experience in relating to a curriculum which elevates middle class White culture and identity.

Rae exhibits an ability and a passion for providing rich contexts for learning beyond the boundaries of the standard curriculum, incorporating students' lived experiences and issues relating to social justice and democracy into the curriculum.

Her classroom consistently hums with activity. Rae's teaching exudes an organic quality as she shapes learning experiences around students' interests and experiences. Her tendency to recognize social injustices and her desire to combat such problems inform her own teaching, as she guides her students to understand their obligation to participate in democracy in order to fight injustice. Her life—past, present, and future—illuminates the complexity of becoming, committing, and persisting in uncommon teaching during commonsense times.

Methods

Combining observational and life history methods (Bogdan & Biklen, 2007; Merriam, 1998), we gathered data to illuminate Rea's life experiences that led to her commitment to multicultural education, the current "strategies" she uses to resist the scripted, test-driven curriculum, how her past and present allow her to maintain her empowering pedagogy, and what support, if any, she receives from colleagues and administration. We conducted two semi-structured interviews, two 40-minute formal observations of her classroom, and daily informal observations lasting from five to twenty minutes. Member checking was implemented to confirm findings (Hancock & Algozzine, 2006).

Becoming Uncommon

Basically I think every teacher teaches from who they are . . . I think every teacher brings themselves to their teaching in some form or fashion . . .

—Rae

As this quote highlights, during interviews and observations Rae reveals the complex interweaving of her life experiences, her sense of self, and her responsibility to uncommon teaching. As a result of this complexity, the following discussion and analysis of the data weaves her life experiences with observations and discussions of her teaching, because they are inseparable. Rae teaches who she is and demonstrates how her journey of becoming uncommon challenges the commonsense that uncommon teaching exists strictly as a result of life experiences prior to teaching (Paccione, 2000), or processes of development (Ford & Dillard, 1996; Paccione, 2000), or struggles that lead to eventual succumbing to commonsense practices (Achinstein & Ogawa, 2006; Crawford, 2004; Wallace, 2006). We highlight how her uncommon teaching emerges from the intertwining of her past and present life experiences and are further shaped and actualized by the structures and practices in teacher preparation and her social justice orientation.

Teacher Preparation: A Call to Action

Recent calls for transformation of teacher education programs have focused on stronger connections to schools, bringing together teacher education faculty, teacher candidates, K-12 students, and school teachers (Levine, 2006). On-site teacher preparation programs are touted for their ability to provide opportunities for their candidates to learn in real world situations and persist as professional teachers longer than their counterparts in programs without site-based education.

At the center of the call for more onsite teacher preparation programs is a focus on the inculcation of teachers into the commonsense professional practice of teachers. This focus ignores how on-site programs may actually provide the spaces to create and sustain teacher candidates' desire to practice uncommon teaching to challenge what exists in education to perpetuate inequities for K-12 students. Rea's participation in an on-site teacher preparation program demonstrates how this opportunity provided spaces for her continual development as an uncommon teacher in commonsense times.

Culture of Mediocrity

As a pre-service teacher, Rae participated in an on-site teacher preparation program during her final two semesters prior to student-teaching. Rae had the opportunity to become a daily participant in the culture of a public elementary school, spending a minimum of twelve hours each week working with students and a mentor teacher. When asked specifically about her on-site experience, Rae responded:

You know, I was [t]here for two semesters as an intern . . . and when I first arrived I left in tears probably sixty-five percent of the time . . . because of what I saw. And a lot of it had to do with the culture of the school, a culture of mediocrity, a culture of hierarchy that made no sense to me where the teacher was somehow above everything. And then we have a whole army of worksheet filler-outers. You know, and uh, it hurt me to be [t]here.

As Rea recalls the professional, intellectual, and emotional struggles created by her immersion in the school cultures, she specifically identified the limitations of teacher-centered pedagogy and unchallenging curriculum so common in schools with significant populations of students of low socio-economic status (Haberman, 1991). Rae became aware of the "hidden curriculum" which she terms a "culture of mediocrity, a culture of hierarchy" (Henderson & Gornik, 2007) of which she could not make sense. Her observation of the culture of mediocrity resonates with a "pedagogy of poverty. . .in which learners can 'succeed' without becoming either involved or thoughtful" (Haberman 1991, p. 291) and creates compliant hostages to a system that will continue to situate them as necessary tools in the social division of labor.

These cultures within the school assaulted her senses with her penchant for recognizing and addressing the injustices of "students trained as armies of worksheet filler-outers." However, Rae was not left without options as to how to counter these armies of students being enculturated into mediocrity. Recognized in literature of onsite teacher education programs (Levine, 2006), theory and practice must always be integrated for one to challenge the other. To simply drop students off without providing tools, techniques, and guided reflections on the practices within schools leaves our educational systems—both in PreK-12 and teacher education—unchallenged and subject to replication of existing power structures.

Inquiry as Conduit

The on-site university program also sought to support pre-service teachers in their development as teachers who could battle armies of worksheet filler-outers. Specifically, the program integrated required methods classes into a weekly seminar, stressing the pedagogical values of inquiry and constructivism. Teaching rooted in "constructivist best practices" (Zemelman, Daniels, & Hyde, 1993) allows students to use inquiry to construct meaning in order to make "personal connections between past experiences and the content they are studying" (Henderson & Gornik, 2007).

Students are viewed as active meaning-makers who engage in learning experiences which are personally meaningful (Henderson & Gornik, 2007). Rae recalled how this provided her with a conduit to connect her sense of critical consciousness and necessity to act in a world where injustice is inevitable.

> One of my most vivid memories of any part of my schooling is one day Dr. Garza taking out a box or a bag. . .and he just started pulling stuff out and putting it down. And some of the other interns were like (she makes a disinterested face), and I was just 'What is it?!' You know? And just those kinds of things that showed me that it's possible to spark enthusiasm and interest and curiosity without saying anything! Without saying 'you must learn this.' A new way of doing things.

The focus on inquiry at the on-site program became a tool that directed her implementation of the abstract principles of democracy, justice, and multiculturalism into comprehensible ideas for young students. Still today, Rae's students are consistently engaged in research and inquiry via various library resources, the Internet, literature, and guest speakers. However, their inquiry is embedded in concepts focused on democracy and justice. Rather than using inquiry simply for the sake of incorporating constructivism into her teaching, Rae elevates her teaching to a more purposeful and human level. Henderson and Gornik (2007) stress the value of making curricular decisions in the interest of democratic self and social understanding:

> All curriculum decisions are, at their heart, moral decisions. They touch the core of what it means to be human, to live in community with others, to find meaning and purpose, and to create a more just and peaceful world. (p. 12)

Rae's curriculum decisions reflect this human element of teaching, as she engages her students in inquiry with the intention of guiding them to an understanding of the complexity of the human experience.

Teaching as Social Action

Frequently, when teachers challenge the commonsense of practical and simple solutions with the complexity of social, cultural, political, and historical contexts of the lives of children, they situate their professional lives and exist in the necessity for action. This action occurs amidst short- and long-term visions of children's potential and capacity to succeed even when there seems to be little that exists in schools for their success (Knight, 2004).

Rae existed in this necessity of action by eventually securing a job in the same school after becoming certified, and has spent her first four years as a teacher in the school. Rather than viewing herself as a "savior" of suffering children, Rae, by her nature as a critical pedagogue, was drawn to the environment; it became an opportunity to bring the uncommon to a commonsense environment.

> When I was here as an intern, Dr. Garza was this little beacon of light. You know, the simplest light; just friendliness, acceptance, and caring. And that's what I saw was lacking in the classrooms I went into. And it was a jolt for me because the kind of person I am. I think I'm wired that way; I couldn't do this if I wasn't connected to each one of these kids, and invested in a part of who they were, and they're a part of who I am. And what I saw was shells of interactions but not meaningful ones. What I saw was an emptiness . . .

Rae responded to the jolt and the urgency to create spaces for students who have been socially constructed as less than, at-risk, deficient, and/or troublemakers to make connections to their schooling and enact change in their worlds. In the same way she situates her life relationships in the context of transformation, she entered her professional life without a disconnect between her students and herself, knowing that as long as one of us is oppressed, we are all oppressed (Lorde, 1994). She chose her teaching position not with a focus on her own comfort and ease, but on the necessity to live her life connected to those who had come before her and those who will come after (Knight, 2004).

> You know, I did my student teaching at Monarch Elementary and I loved it there. Um, it's closer to where I live and I felt more of a community connection there, but really I was like, I'm gonna try to go back [to the school where I interned] and have my own light, you know, light another candle over there!

As Rae's college professor, Dr. Garza, had been a light for her in the emptiness of the cultures of mediocrity and hierarchy, she wanted to return to not only be that for her students, but to cultivate a culture of inquiry for justice within the injustice she witnessed. Rae's *uncommon* philosophy on democracy and justice merged with the *uncommon* pedagogy supported by her university professors. Instead of forming an "army of worksheet filler-outers," Rae counters the commonsense of test-driven curriculum with her army of critical thinkers who seek to recognize injustice and work to end it through democratic participation and action.

Instead of forming an "army of worksheet filler-outers," Rae counters the commonsense of test-driven curriculum with her army of critical thinkers . . .

Social Justice: Experiences Manifest Action

[Students] need to be able to identify justice and injustice and I think that is a big part of who I am . . . You know, part of our role as teachers is to empower students to identify justice, injustice, and then what do we do about it.

Social justice saturates the classroom culture that Rae and her students have created. Social justice requires a "revolution of everyday life" which stems from our ability to read and transform the world in order to challenge and change inequities that exist (Ross & Vinson, 2006, p. 154). Interviews with Rae reveal her critical understanding of the world and that she views teaching as one way she can transform it.

From the time I was born, I knew how to identify justice, injustice . . . You know, there was injustice in my family . . . and people did not stand up for me! You know, that was, like, injustice! And at the same point, at the same time, you have people expressing rightness and righteousness, and this is the way to Heaven, and it didn't match for me.

Rae's experiences with injustice have led her to teach about injustice through justice. Her pedagogy often focuses on the identification of social injustices within a just, democratic, and empowering pedagogy; a pedagogy described within three areas: the negotiation of power, democracy, and multiculturalism. Rae uses all three to guide her students toward a critical consciousness of their world with the intention of fostering a sense of agency and democratic empowerment within them because all of these things have become integral to who she is based on her lived realities.

Negotiation of Power

Upon entering Rea's classroom, her negotiation of power with her students, the curricula, and her colleagues is almost immediately evident. When she tells the students it is time for reading, they choose some reading materials rather than gather in predefined reading groups labeled by a reading level. She chooses a book of her own, settles comfortably at a table and immerses herself in the literature. The students do the same, some quietly reading together, others alone. Occasionally, a student or two becomes off-task, and she then gently reminds them of their responsibility, and students return to reading, as does she. A teacher desk is no where to be found; all furniture seems to be for everyone, students and teacher alike.

The uncommon practice of the negotiation of power between Rae and her students is evident in the above description, particularly as it relates to the reciprocal relationship she has with them. Freire (2003) discusses this type of relationship, noting its pertinence to empowering students to think critically about their world as they develop their own agency. "The teacher is no longer merely the-one-who-teaches, but one who is himself taught in dialogue with the students, who in turn while being taught also teach" (p. 80). Interviews with Rae further divulge

the value she holds for relationships of this nature. When asked if she did in fact view her relationships with her students as reciprocal, she replied:

Oh yeah! It's me pulling up my chair to be a part of an audience while a student is teaching . . . I try to be a human being first, who is in this room with other human beings, and we're all trying to be better each day, and be bigger, and more than we were yesterday . . . It is relationships. It's relationships that make people change.

Power as Collegial and Policy Conflict

Rae not only negotiates power between herself and her students, but also with her administrators and colleagues. She expressed, quite emotionally, some of the encounters and conflicts she had with administrators and colleagues during her first year teaching.

My first year was like swimming with sharks . . . it was really a battle ground . . . I had colleagues who did everything they possibly could to sabotage me . . . I had, um, people insinuate that I wasn't teaching because kids were happy in my room . . . the administration at that point was different and several times, probably three or four times that year, I was asked to stop.

Despite the pressures to conform to prescribed curriculum, Rae stays grounded in her uncommon teaching and asserts her own power and defends her pedagogy with simple stubbornness at times, but also by actively pursuing current research and literature on education issues.

I have in my room "high-heeled" strategies posted. I use them. "Best teaching practices." I use them. You know, I do my research, it's not based in fluff and stuff like I just came up with it last night. I'm plugged into what I think is the future of education. So I do feel confident about what I'm doing, and even as a first year teacher, I was confident enough to say, "I will give that to my kids." I don't feel badly about it. I will not apologize for it.

Rae also refuses to allow common sense education and curriculum policies, such as the NCLB Act, to control her teaching. When asked about what she thought of the current state of public education, she replied:

Well, obviously No Child Left Behind is a huge, you know, that's what everybody's kind of talking about, but ultimately, to me, that doesn't matter! You know, I do care about it and I do follow it . . . but ultimately it's teachers in classrooms . . . I may teach kids a way to help them on the test because I want them to be successful on everything they do, but that's not what drives me in my classroom . . . it wouldn't matter what law was on the books really. I know what I'm going to do for my kids.

This overt resistance to the commonsense of prescribed curriculum is evidence of Rae's own critical consciousness and use of her own agency to assert herself as one who is empowered to make curricular decisions.

Democracy

The power to make decisions about curriculum does not simply rest in Rae's hands. Much of the power lies with her students. They make many decisions related to content, teaching, and problem-solving. Democracy then, also comes into play here. In this context, it is linked to the negotiation of power. Wood (1998) relates participatory democracy to power. Participatory democracy depends upon the "full participation" and "equal power on the part of the participants to determine the outcome of decisions" (p. 181). According to Wood, when students have voice and power over their own education, they are more likely to become active participants in a democratic society.

> Today we had a circle of kids sitting around, taking turns at the mike, reading a story out loud. Somebody went and got a footstool and propped their feet up, and in the back of my mind, I thought, because of my past experiences, I thought, 'That's not allowed!' But then, it's just, even a split second later, I thought, 'I want them to put their feet up and enjoy what they're reading. I want them to feel comfortable in this setting,' to say, 'Man, oh, I'm lovin' it!' You know? They're invested.

Uncommon teaching centers on the visibility and engagement of this democratic power. For example, while involved in a unit on the book *And Now Miguel*, students had options as to what activities they would take part in to demonstrate their internalization of the novel. Some students chose to create family trees, which were proudly displayed in the classroom. Students also participate in "buffet" activities periodically, having a choice over what to do.

For example, after an inclusive discussion of what students had read during their reading time, Rae announced it was time for "buffet" activities. She reminded students of their options; students dispersed to their chosen activities, quickly becoming engaged in their respective places. On another day, based on a discussion during earlier instruction, a chart on the board asked students to vote if they would be interested in participating in an intensive cursive writing workshop, to which many students had written their names under the "yes" or "no" column.

Rae wants her students to experience participatory democracy in her classroom so they will become invested in their education, developing political efficacy and use this as adults. By giving students choice over collectively developed activities, Rae invites students to make their own decisions, rather than allowing them to rely on others to make decisions on their behalf. This reflects the distinguishing factor between participatory and protectionist democracies; citizens in a participatory democracy have more power (Wood, 1998).

Within the negotiation of power, democracy is also visible when solving problems that surface in the classroom. Her statement about empowering students to identify justice and injustice is also relevant here. She concluded the statement with "and then what do we do about it." Rae not only wants her students to develop a critical consciousness, but uses democratic pedagogy to help foster an ability to problem-solve, to make right injustices.

For example, a conflict between two boys emerged. One of the boys complained to Rae, who responded, "You need to talk to him about it." The boys quickly and smoothly resolved the problem. Rae, when noticing problems, addresses them immediately, calling class meetings and encouraging students to work out problems as a class. In this way, the students have been socialized to respect one another and act as collaborative problem solvers. It is the active participation of the students in decision-making that speaks to the relationship between democracy and the negotiation of power in Rae's uncommon teaching.

Another aspect of her uncommon teaching exists in Rae's refusal to accept simple answers to complex problems. She talked about a student in a different class who used a racially derogatory term to describe himself in a poem. While many teachers would likely punish this student for using an offensive word, Rae reflects,

> . . . these things are so complex . . . the only way to negotiate that complexity is dialogue. You can't ignore it.

Dialogue is a critical component of democracy (Sleeter 2005), and by promoting dialogue among her students when solving problems, Rae demonstrates the importance of the complexity of problems students will encounter as adults, and the importance of considering various perspectives when making decisions to reflect collective interests.

Democracy as Speaking Out

> I remember all the things you have to write as a teacher to jump through this hoop and another, and I remember writing down that I will be willing to speak up if I think something is wrong. And, you know, I didn't know if that would please an employer or make an employer not want to hire me. I didn't care because that to me is part of a teacher's job. That's part of my job. To me, that's a qualification for teaching.

Using one's voice to make unjust situations more just is the responsibility of an active democratic citizen (Wood, 1998). Rae uses her voice through her multicultural pedagogy, speaking up to her colleagues and administrators regarding her beliefs on teaching and curriculum. When asked what she thought could be done to inspire other teachers to address issues of injustice in their classrooms she commented:

> I think modeling does a lot. I think when other teachers see, you know. When we had our posters out there of Cesar Chavez and Gandhi, I had a lot of adults comment. You know, so they noticed . . . putting it out there, being visible with it, invites a dialogue . . .

Rae's inclination to speak up comes from her past experiences seeing injustices and becoming outraged when people failed to speak out against them. Telling about her relationships with African Americans and Navajos, she describes her disillusionment at the poor treatment they were given.

> *And I didn't like that because I had people that I cared about . . . I never felt a hierarchy the way some people do . . . I never thought that was fair, I never thought it was right that people didn't speak up. And when I would speak up, people would look at me like, 'why are you talking?' And that's continued my whole life . . . You know, those issues, I've always spoken up.*

Integral to uncommon teaching, Rae believes that teaching is a platform from which to speak out against injustice. Rae views one's voice as vital to one's participation in democracy. The walls inside and outside her classroom are full of her and her students' voices, speaking out against injustice and announcing their opinions about various issues. A bulletin board with signs reading "Fight Against Injustice!" "Speak for Those Whose Voices Aren't Being Heard!" "Use Your Voices!" "Demand Justice!" was hung next to a prominent display of books about Martin Luther King Jr. and Coretta Scott King.

In the hall, students had created their own personal "*La Causa*" (The Cause) flags with themes such as cancer, violence, and animal abuse. Posters of Cesar Chavez, and Gandhi lined the walls outside her classroom for several weeks. Student posters on an economics project revealed the economic stratification between the United States and the Third World, offering opportunities for others to write their thoughts about it. On a "free speech" poster outside her classroom to celebrate Veterans Day, Rae had written that she liked our freedom to question government leaders and to demand change in policies we are unhappy with. Martin Luther King Jr., Cesar Chavez, and Gandhi, all figures she highlights in her teaching, serve as examples to her students of leaders who used their voices to demand social justice.

Beane and Apple (1995) relate this democratic pedagogy to social justice, claiming that democratic schools seek to "change the conditions that create" injustices (p. 11). Rather than teaching her students *about* democracy, Rae teaches them *through* democracy, providing them with opportunities to participate as citizens in dialogue with others to explore ways in which they can effect meaningful change in their classroom. This approach to teaching will likely foster participatory democratic values within her students, leading them to carry their participation to their adult lives (Wood, 1998).

Rather than teaching her students about democracy, Rae teaches them through democracy, providing them with opportunities to participate as citizens in dialogue . . .

Multiculturalism

A third theme in Rae's uncommon teaching focuses on the value for multiculturalism. Sleeter and McLaren (1995) define multicultural education as "a particular ethico-political attitude or ideological stance that one constructs in order to confront and engage the world critically and challenge power relations" (p. 7). Furthermore, Nieto (cited in Paccione, 2000) points to the development of multicultural teaching through the development of becoming a multicultural person. Life experiences that inform one about cultures different from one's own, make racism and bias apparent, and allow one to understand the world from various perspectives, all play vital roles in shaping an ethic of multiculturalism.

> *I've always been drawn to different kinds of people, and so growing up, I experienced social aspects of those relationships. For many years my best friend actually came from a family where her dad was Anglo and her mom was Navajo. So I experienced her cultural life with her mom's side of the family because we were best friends. And I was always very interested and really wanted to know more . . . When I had boyfriends of different races, um, I was aware of that. Family dynamics were very intense. African American boyfriend: big deal. Navajo boyfriend: big deal. And so, those issues were very close to me because I put myself in the center of them and probably did it on purpose.*

It is not simply Rae's exposure to people of diverse cultural backgrounds that fostered her multicultural disposition. She recognizes the injustices people close to her experienced, as described earlier, and the responsibility she felt, and still feels, to defend them. She does this through her teaching, by opening up spaces for her students to engage their world critically, identify injustices, and participate in the improvement of society.

Banks (1996) strongly asserts that multicultural education is much more than simply teaching *about* other cultures: it is also about respecting and valuing the "diverse funds of knowledge" all students bring to the classroom, connecting the curriculum to students' lives, identifying social inequities, and taking actions as democratic citizens to improve the quality of life for oppressed people. Rae's reflections on her own schooling point to her understanding of the importance of connecting the curriculum to students' lives and cultures.

> *I'm from northern New Mexico where there's a rich cultural heritage, and my teachers never tapped into that. You know, I never learned any Navajo words or about that culture, I never learned anything about the Hispanic culture, these people who I was sharing my friendships with or my life with. Or any other culturally significant anything.*

Rae discussed her disengagement in schooling as a result of being bored, unable to connect to the curriculum. She uses these personal experiences with schooling to inform her practice, ensuring that students have opportunities to make personal connections to the curriculum.

Right now we're reading And Now Miguel which is set outside of the Taos pueblo in northern New Mexico, and even that is so far removed you know, from here. These kids down here don't connect to northern New Mexico issues, places . . . it's been an eye opener for me, just understanding how culturally disconnected we are from even that area. I'm not, because I'm from that area; for these kids, they don't understand, the Spanishness up there is so different from the borderness . . . Miguel in this book is very interested in this family . . . it's the family and the generations, and some of my kids chose to do family trees. I mean . . . they do connect themselves and I want that to happen.

She also recalled,

. . . this unit we did on Cesar Chavez, I found out that I have students in my reading class whose families have been or still are field workers, and it's something that never would be addressed or taken into account . . . .

The overall environment of Rae's classroom reflects this desire to provide students with opportunities to make connections to their schooling. The freedom to make curriculum decisions based on personal interests has been discussed, but Rae even creates a physical environment that reflects her multicultural ethic. The reading center is full of hundreds of books, newspapers, and magazines, all representing a variety of cultures, languages, and genres.

Although Rae is not a bilingual teacher, she includes bilingual dictionaries and Spanish literature in her room, making connections to the Latino heritage of the majority of her students. The room is simply comfortable, inviting her students to enter as themselves with the promise that they will be able to remain themselves while in her classroom. This tenet of multicultural education serves as the catalyst to capture her students' interest, as they are gently propelled into her uncommon pedagogy of justice.

Implications for Education

Rae's story offers hope for the possibility that teachers can resist pressures to implement oppressive, prescribed curriculum. The unmistakable interdependency of life experiences, classroom experiences, research, and teaching practices demonstrates a strong responsibility in teacher education to adopt a multi-faceted approach to preparing teachers. Teacher education programs that provide authentic classroom experiences, unveil school cultures, and provide support for utilizing tools such as inquiry and constructivism as conduits for powerful learning experiences can offer schools uncommon teachers poised to release students from the binds of commonsense teaching.

Rae shows us that life experiences that expose one to social injustices can be instrumental in the formation of a critical multicultural approach to teaching. The profound influence of life experiences on Rae's teaching suggests that teacher education programs developed around providing multicultural

experiences for pre-service and in-service teachers may help foster a critical consciousness among educators. This can be the catalyst for asserting one's agency to transform social conditions.

While planned multicultural experiences may not be the equivalent of real-life experiences as Rae described, they nonetheless could serve as powerful elements in teacher preparation programs. Aspiring teachers who experience multiculturalism in ways that expose that social injustices are immersed in school cultures and who are presented with research and theory regarding the effectiveness of using inquiry as teaching tools may be awakened to a multicultural pedagogy aimed at teaching uncommonly in commonsense times.

References

Achinstein, B. & Ogawa, R.T. (2006). (In)Fidelity: What the resistance of new teachers reveals about professional principles and prescriptive educational policies [Electronic version]. *Harvard Educational Review, 76*(1). Retrieved September 6, 2008 from https:// catalogue2.nmsu.edu:3254/harvard06/2006/sp06/p06achin.htm

Agee, J. (2004). Negotiating a teaching identity: An African American teacher's struggle to teach in test-driven contexts. *Teachers College Record, 106*(4), 747–774.

Allen, R. L. (2002). Wake up Neo: White identity, hegemony, and consciousness in the Matrix. In J. J. Slater, S. M. Fain, & C. A. Rossatto (Eds.), *The Freirean legacy: Educating for social justice* (pp. 104–125). Lanham, MD: Roman & Littlefield.

Apple, M. (2004). *Ideology and curriculum.* New York: RoutledgeFalmer.eBook.

Arce, J. (2004). Latino bilingual teachers: The struggle to sustain an emancipatory pedagogy in public schools. *International Journal of Qualitative Studies in Education, 17*(2), 227–246.

Banks, J. A. (1996). Transformative knowledge, curriculum reform, and action. In J. A. Banks (Ed.), *Multicultural education, transformative knowledge, and action: Historical and contemporary perspectives* (pp. 335–348). New York: Teachers College Press.

Beane, J. A., & Apple, M. W. (1995). The case for democratic schools. In J. A. Beane & M. W. Apple (Eds.), *Democratic schools* (pp. 1–25). Alexandria, VA: Association for Supervision and Curriculum Development.

Bogdan, R., & Biklen, S. (2007). *Qualitative research in education: An introduction to theory and practice* (5th ed.). Boston: Pearson.

Crawford, P. A. (2004). "I follow the blue. . ." A primary teacher and the impact of packaged curricula. *Early Childhood Education Journal, 32*(3), 205–210.

Ford, T. L., & Dillard, C. B. (1996). Becoming multicultural: A recursive process of self and social construction. *Theory into Practice, 35,* 232–238.

Freire, P. (2003). *Pedagogy of the oppressed.* (30th anniversary ed.). New York: Continuum.

Hancock, D. R., & Algozzine, B. (2006). *Doing case study research: A practical guide for beginning researchers.* New York: Teachers College Press.

Henderson, J. G., & Gornik, R. (2007). *Transformative curriculum leadership* (3rd ed.). Upper Saddle River, NJ: Merrill Prentice Hall.

Knight, M. (2004). Sensing the urgency: Envisioning a Black Humanist vision of care in teacher education. *Race and Ethnicity in Education, 7(3), 211–227.*

Kumashiro, K. K. (2004). *Against common sense: Teaching and learning toward social justice:* New York: Routledge-Falmer.

Levine, A. (2006). *Educating school teachers.* Washington, DC: The Education School Project.

Lorde, A. (1984). *Sister outsider.* New York: Crossing Press.

Marri, A. R. (2005). Building a framework for classroom-based multicultural democratic education: Learning from three skilled teachers. *Teachers College Record, 107(5),* 1036–1059.

Merriam, S. B. (1998). *Qualitative research and case study applications in education.* San Francisco: Jossey-Bass.

Paccione, A. V. (2000). Developing a commitment to multicultural education. *Teachers College Record, 102(6),* 980–1005.

Ross, W. E., & Vinson, K. D. (2006). Social justice requires a revolution of everyday life. In C. A. Rossatto, R. L. Allen, & M. Pruyn (Eds.), *Reinventing critical pedagogy: Widening the circle of anti-oppressive education* (pp. 143–156). Lanham, MD: Roman & Littlefield.

Sleeter, C. E. (2005). *Un-standardizing curriculum: Multicultural teaching in the standards-based classroom.* New York: Teachers College Press.

Sleeter, C. E., & McLaren, P. L. (1995). Introduction: Exploring connections to build a critical multiculturalism. In C. E. Sleeter & P. L. McLaren (Eds.), *Multicultural education, critical pedagogy and the politics of difference* (pp. 5–32). New York: State University of New York Press.

Wallace, F. H. (2006). Under pressure: Controlling factors faced by classroom literacy teachers as they work through a professional development program. *Reading Horizons, 46(3),* 143–165.

Wedgwood, N. (2005). Just one of the boys? A life history case study of a male physical education teacher. *Gender and Education 17(2),* 189–201.

Wood, G. H. (1998). Democracy and the curriculum. In L. E. Beyer & M. W. Apple (Eds.), *The Curriculum: Problems, politics, and possibilities* (pp. 177–198). Albany, NY: State University of New York Press.

Zemelman, S., Daniels, H., & Hyde, A. (1993). *Best practice: New standards for teaching and learning in America's schools.* Portsmouth, NH: Heinemann.

Critical thinking

1. What is meant by commonsense practices and uncommon teaching?
2. How do democracy and demographic pedagogy feature in the classroom?
3. What is the value of multiculturalism?
4. What are the implications for education?

Create Central

www.mhhe.com/createcentral

Internet References

Infonation
www.un.org/Pubs/CyberSchoolBus/infonation/e_infonation.htm

Multicultural Education Internet Resource Guide
http://jan.ucc.nau.edu/~jar/Multi.html

EMILIE M. CAMP *is a doctoral candidate and Heather A. Oesterreich is an associate professor, both with the Department of Curriculum and Instruction of the College of Education at New Mexico State University, Las Cruces, New Mexico.*

Student Teaching Experience in Diverse Settings, White Racial Identity Development and Teacher Efficacy by D. S. Bloom and T. Peters

231

Article

Prepared by: Nancy P. Gallavan, *University of Central Arkansas*

Student Teaching Experience in Diverse Settings, White Racial Identity Development and Teacher Efficacy

DIANE S. BLOOM AND TERRI PETERS

Learning Outcomes

After reading this article, you will be able to:

- Detail White identity and its influence on teacher self-efficacy.

- Review how teacher bias can influence diverse student learning.

Introduction

A significant number of teachers in the United States continue to be from European-American and middle or upper-class backgrounds, whereas the student population has become increasingly diverse (Howard, 2010). The National Center for Education Statistics (NCES, 2011) reported that almost half of the United States student population in 2008–2009 was non-White. The racial/ethnic distribution of full-time teachers shifted slightly between 1999–2000 and 2007–08, with only a slight increase in teachers who were Hispanic, and no significant changes in teachers who were Black (NCES, 2011).

Over the past few decades, researchers have begun to explore and understand the role that race plays in the teaching and learning process. Although unintentional, many White teachers "participate in the reproduction of racial inequality" (Hyland, 2005, p. 429) when teaching students of color. A large body of research has been devoted to helping teachers understand multiculturalism or culturally relevant teaching (Au, 2009; Haviland, 2008; Jones, 2006; Solomon, Portelli, Daniel, & Campbell, 2005), and teacher education coursework on multiculturalism is common. However, less is known about how White future teachers construct their own White racial identity (WRI) or how WRI influences a teacher's efficacy for working with students of color. Past research (Buehler, Ruggles-Gere, Dallavis, & Shaw-Haviland, 2009; Howard, 2010; Ruggles-Gere, Buehler, Dallavis,

& Shaw-Haviland, 2009) indicates that educators who are White and middle class face obstacles as educators of children in diverse settings. Therefore, the purpose of our study was to examine how diversity of field placement affected student teachers' White racial identity development, as well as the relationship between White racial identity and teacher efficacy (TE).

Review of Literature

The programs and processes that are in place at American universities to educate and prepare teachers for their chosen profession have been at the forefront of the United States Department of Education's focus on teacher quality and the goal to improve performance of urban students of color (Ogbu, 2003). To achieve this goal, educators have enacted several strategies including school restructuring, changes in assessment requirements, raising standards and mandating improvement in teacher qualifications.

Urban Students of Color

Educational reform efforts have been created with the goal to reduce the achievement gap between suburban and urban students of color and their White peers (Howard, 2010; Kafer, 2001). These efforts, however, have not provided the mechanism for urban teachers to either improve the academic performance of students of color or the quality of their schools (Denbo & Moore, 2002; Kafer, 2001). A qualified teacher is significant for improving student achievement, yet qualification alone is insufficient for enacting change in student performance (McKeachie & Svinicki, 2006). Comer (2004) sees the role of the teacher as critically important; however, teachers must also be prepared to address the changing demographics of school communities and the academic and cultural needs of the diverse students they serve (Kyukendall, 2004; Rychly & Graves, 2012; Tomlinson, 2001).

Mckinley (2010) presents five core causes for the achievement gap between students of color and their White student peers; he suggests reducing that gap by focusing on a "culturally responsive teaching" environment. These types of environments provide a supporting framework for content mastery that is related to students' home cultures, aligns to learning with positive interpersonal interactions, and employs diligent assessment practices (McKinley, 2010). Teachers who demonstrate "culturally responsive pedagogy" are caring teachers who have high expectations for all students and also provide constructive feedback to students (Rychly & Graves, 2012). To become effective teachers of students of color, White teachers must reflect on their own world-views and continuously attempt to understand their students (Rychly & Graves, 2012).

Many public school districts across the nation that serve at-risk students contend that various strategies and interventions have not adequately addressed school failure for a large number of these students (Rychly & Graves, 2012; Welsh, 2010). For example, the standards movement articulated the need for all college-bound students to be fluent readers, writers, and mathematical thinkers; however the lack of clear standards for students not considered college-bound disproportionately hurt children of poverty, children of color, and children with disabilities, as teachers failed to identify them as college-bound students (Chenoweth, 2009).

Teacher Misconceptions about Diverse Students

Teachers must be prepared to address the changing demographics of school communities and the academic and cultural needs of the diverse students they serve (Kuykendall, 2004; Tomlinson, 2001). Teachers are often unaware of their biases and expectations of culturally diverse students, yet increased awareness of their unintentional behaviors and viewpoints can enhance student achievement (Rychly & Graves, 2012). Educators should be consciously aware of the impact of labels such as *culturally deprived, economically disadvantaged,* and *underprivileged* on the student's self-image and potential (Kuykendall, 2004).

A common and problematic misconception held by some teachers is that students from culturally diverse backgrounds, particularly Blacks and Hispanics, are less capable academically (Bryan & Atwater, 2002; Howard, 2010; Nieto, 2004). These misconceptions likely lead teachers to set lower academic goals and to rely more heavily on passive teaching methods (Science Education Research Center (SERC), 2009). Another misconception is that teachers should treat all students the same, regardless of class, gender, ethnicity, or race (Bryan & Atwater, 2002; Howard, 2010). This "color blind" approach leads to teaching methods that do not consider the disparate educational and cultural backgrounds in an urban classroom (Howard, 2010; The Coalition of Schools Educating Boys of Color (TCOSEBOC), 2010). The preexisting knowledge base may differ considerably among diverse students (Manzo, 2010; Marzano, Pickering, & Pollack, 2001; SERC, 2009).

Teacher Efficacy: Impact on Student Learning

Similar to the variability among the students they teach, teachers bring to their classrooms a world view about teaching and learning shaped through years of personal experience as learners within families, communities, and cultures. These teaching beliefs and practices shape the dynamics of student learning (Bryan & Atwater, 2002), because teachers' beliefs translate into classroom instructional practice (Kuykendall, 2004) and also influence student learning (Bryan & Atwater, 2002) and, in turn, teacher efficacy.

Teacher efficacy, an individual's belief that her or his teaching affects student learning (Raudenbush, Rowan, & Cheong, 1992; Woolfolk Hoy & Davis, 2006), has roots in seminal work by Bandura (1977, 1997). Bandura (1977, 1997) proposed that self-efficacy is a function of three interrelated factors: environmental, behavior, and internal personal factors (e.g., cognition, affective, biological). Individuals are thus products of the interaction between external influences, internal beliefs and current/past behavior. Self-efficacy impacts an individual's motivation, expectations, effort, emotions and persistence in situations of adversity; individuals with high efficacy will persevere when faced with challenging tasks (Maehr & Pintrich, 1997; Pajares, 1997).

Over a number of years, significant research has studied the impact of teacher efficacy on teacher quality and behavior. Research (Darling-Hammond, Chung, & Frelow, 2002) has demonstrated that a teacher's sense of preparedness is the strongest predictor of teaching efficacy (Darling-Hammond et al., 2002; Tschannen-Moran, Woolfolk Hoy, & Hoy, 1998), thus teacher efficacy is an important attribute to foster, because it can positively or negatively influence teacher behavior and, consequently, student learning and behavior.

Teacher efficacy is related to various positive classroom practices: (1) teachers' overall attitude toward teaching; (2) teachers' expectations of students; (3) willingness to persist with students who are struggling; (4) the ability to try various instructional techniques; and (5) student achievement (Gibson & Dembo, 1984; Soodak & Podell, 1997; Tschannen-Moran et al., 1998). Since teacher efficacy affects a teacher's ability to impact students in the classroom, a teacher's efficacy for working with students of color is paramount.

Many White teachers enter the profession without experience with diverse groups (Howard, 2010), and we questioned whether this lack of experience affects teacher efficacy and student outcomes. As noted by Siwatu (2011), preservice teachers felt better prepared to teach in suburban schools than urban schools. Siwatu (2011) also found that White teachers in suburban settings reported higher teacher efficacy for working with culturally and linguistically diverse students than when they are placed in urban settings. Conversely, other research found that student teachers placed in urban settings reported higher teacher efficacy at the end of the semester (Knoblauch & Woolfolk Hoy, 2008).

We argue that unless individuals critically examine the factors that influence the outcomes of students of color, including historical factors that have oppressed certain groups, they cannot begin to improve the gap between White students and those of color. However, teachers avoid discussions about race due to discomfort (Haviland, 2008) or a belief that race is no longer an issue in the United States (Howard, 2010). In addition, a recent longitudinal study found that preservice teachers maintained their beliefs about working in diverse settings throughout their teacher preparation program (Gau & Mager, 2011). White teachers must first examine their own beliefs and biases, as well as their students' perceptions of them as White teachers, before they can successfully work with students of color (Howard, 2010; Sleeter, 2001).

White Racial Identity

As teacher educators, we are committed to training preservice teachers to effectively work with all students. We struggle to understand how White preservice teachers navigate their urban field experiences. We also wonder if experiences in urban settings influence their understanding of their own background as well as their efficacy for working with students of color. The research on White racial identity provided a framework through which we began to understand the importance of White racial identity for promoting one's multicultural competence.

Helms' (1990) original theory of White racial identity (WRI) included six statuses, with higher levels representing more advanced understanding of one's Whiteness in the context of cross-cultural interactions. As empirical data were collected, however, Helms (2005) eliminated one of the statuses (immersion/emersion), yielding a model that consists of the following five statuses: (a) contact (unaware of the systemic presence of Whiteness, one's race, and the existence of racism); (b) disintegration (recognition of one's Whiteness, acknowledgement of racism, confusion and self-disorientation with respect to one's own Whiteness); (c) reintegration (idealization of being White, denigration of People of Color); (d) pseudo-independence (intellectual acceptance of one's race and racial privilege); and (e) autonomy (positive, antiracist White identity).

Higher levels of WRI represent more advanced understanding of one's Whiteness, and individuals at more advanced levels recognize injustices and are willing to take action to work for social justice (Helms, 2005). In contrast, individuals at lower level statuses (e.g., contact, disintegration) display an unawareness of White privilege and power or deny institutional racism. Moreover, certain statuses appear to predict racism (Pope-Davis & Ottavi, 1994).

Haviland (2008) articulated the "silencing power" of Whiteness in education and explored how the interactional styles of White people in White-dominated educational settings impede movement toward progressive, anti-racist education. Her data from a yearlong qualitative research study uncovered strategies that participants used to insulate themselves from implication in social inequality. Use of these strategies stymied attempts at transformative multicultural education and thus functioned to reproduce, rather than challenge, the status quo of educational

and social inequality (Haviland, 2008). Thus, Whites engage in "safe" dialogue and avoid discussions of race or racism, thereby perpetuating White privilege. Moreover, Whites who espouse "colorblindness" negate the impact of racism upon persons of color (Flores, Schwann, Dimas, Pasch, & deGroat, 2010), preventing the development of their own racial identities. Prior research also shows that Whites in instructional settings are often reluctant to share their feelings about race and racism due to fear of appearing racist (Chick, Karis, & Kernahan, 2009).

As indicated above, individuals avoid discussions of race and racism, and may adopt a "colorblind" approach to working with persons of color, behaviors that truncate their own WRI growth. Despite the frequent cultural mismatch between teachers and the students they serve, and the academic achievement gap between White students and those of color, a paucity of research has examined the influence of White teachers' White racial identity on their efficacy for working with students of color. Research demonstrates that teacher efficacy influences a teacher's ability to successfully work with all students (Tschannen-Moran et al., 1998), yet we found no empirical studies that examined the relationship between White student teachers' WRI and teacher efficacy.

Research Questions

We solely focused our study on White student teachers. Given the literature noted above, we desired to understand changes in these White preservice teachers' self-beliefs and perceptions about their abilities to impact students. We explored the inter-relationships among the diversity of student teaching placement, teacher efficacy, and teachers' WRI. Specifically, we examined whether: (1) there was a relationship between White racial identity statuses and teacher efficacy; (2) diversity of student teaching placement was related to White racial identity statuses and teacher efficacy; (3) those placed in more diverse settings showed changes in WRI; (4) those placed in non-diverse settings showed changes in WRI; and (5) diversity of placement affected changes in WRI development.

Method
Participants

We gathered information from participants enrolled in a teacher preparation program at a public university in the northeastern United States. Of 256 individuals who were enrolled in senior student teaching during the spring semester, 222 student teachers agreed to participate in the study. We were only interested in studying White student teachers for this study, so we only utilized data collected from individuals who self-identified as White. The final usable sample (completion of both pre and post measures) consisted of 146 White student teachers (91 females, 55 males), with an average age of 25.4 (range = 21 − 50). See Table 1 for demographic information for specific placements either categorized as high, low, or middle diverse school settings.

Table 1 Sample demographics for each type of school placement

Characteristic	Highly Diverse	Non-Diverse	Middle
	(n = 46)	(n = 70)	(n = 30)
Mean Age	24.84	25.89	25.34
Gender	16 M, 30 F	28 M, 42 F	11 M, 19 F
Licensure$_a$			
P-3	0	2.9	0
K-5	21.7	14.5	6.9
K-8	32.6	23.2	27.6
K-12	41.3	52.2	62.1
Other	4.4	7.2	3.4

Note. Middle = Student teachers who were placed in a school that was neither highly diverse nor non-diverse; non-specified were those who did not report a school.
a = expressed in percentages

Instruments

Teacher Sense of Efficacy Scale (TSES)

The TSES long form (Tschannen-Moran & Woolfolk-Hoy, 2001) consists of 24 nine-point likert items that ask respondents how much they believe they can influence student behavior (1 = not at all; 9 = a great deal) and consists of three subscales: (1) Instructional strategies; (2) student engagement; and (3) classroom management. Higher scores represent greater teacher efficacy. Past studies have shown high reliability of the TSES subscales, with alpha ranging from .87 to .91 (Tschannen-Moran & Woolfolk-Hoy, 2001). For our sample, we also conducted an inter-item reliability analysis of the three TSES subscales and found high reliability for each subscale, ranging from .88 to .92.

White Racial Consciousness Development Scale, Revised (WRCDS-R)

The WRCDS-R (Lee et al., 2007) is designed to measure White racial identity statuses that are aligned with Helms' (1990) theory of White racial identity development. The WRCDS-R consists of 40 five-point likert type items (1 = strongly disagree; 5 = strongly agree) that reflect four White racial identity statuses: (1) Contact reflects naïve thoughts and ignorance about racial differences; (2) Reintegration represents feelings of anger and resentment toward ethnic minorities, and individuals who score high on this subscale see persons of Color as inferior to Whites; (3) higher scores on Pseudo Independence signify an increasing awareness and understanding of the impact of White dominance and privilege on racist attitudes and behaviors; and (4) Autonomy scores represent a non-racist White identity with appreciation of racial differences and similarities.

The current version of the WRCDS-R is the result of Lee et al.'s (2007) multi-stage approach to revising the White Racial Consciousness Development Scale (Claney & Parker, 1989). After Lee et al. (2007) generated items, they conducted an exploratory factor analysis and subsequently eliminated several items and collapsed the disintegration items into the contact subscale. Next, Lee et al. (2007) performed a confirmatory factor analysis on the new 40-item WRCDS-R, using a sample of 168 White counselors and counselor educators (76% female, 24% male) who were recruited through several national databases (e.g., Counselor Education Supervision Network, American Family Therapy Association) in the United States. Results demonstrated satisfactory reliability, with Cronbach's alpha coefficients at .81 for contact, .86 for reintegration, .84 for pseudo-independence, and .71 for autonomy. We also conducted a reliability analysis of the WRCDS-R using our sample, and results showed high inter-item reliability with alpha =.82 for Contact, .84 for Reintegration, .77 for Pseudo Independence, and .81 for Autonomy.

Lee et al. (2007) also sought to establish scale validity, so they gathered data from 402 White undergraduates (31% male, 69% female) whom they recruited from campus classes and compared their scores to the counselor group noted above (n = 168). Findings indicated that the counselor group scored higher in the advanced statuses (pseudo-independence and autonomy) than undergraduate students, suggesting that the scale may be a valid instrument.

Diversity of Placement

On the demographic survey, participants were asked to record the name of their placement school, district, and city/town. From this information, the researchers used demographic information provided by the State to identify the percentage of White students in each school. For comparison purposes, placements were also coded into three categories: (1) highly diverse placements, schools where White students represented less than one-third of the student body; (2) non-diverse placements, schools where White students represented greater than two-thirds of the student body; and (3) average placements, schools that comprised the remainder of the placements (See Table 1).

Research Design

We utilized a causal-comparative design. Students who were placed in schools where the student population was predominantly White/Caucasian were compared to those who were placed in schools where the student population consisted primarily of students of color. The study examined how the diversity of placement affected White student teachers' WRI, as well as the relationship between WRI and TE.

Procedures

Prior to commencing our study, the research was approved by the university's Institutional Review Board and followed all requirements for ethical treatment of human subjects. At the beginning of the semester, researchers visited all class sections of student teaching seminars to obtain informed consent and distribute surveys. Students were informed about the study and its purposes, and those who wished to voluntarily participate completed the informed consent form, with the opportunity to ask questions before signing the form. The researcher collected the signed consent forms and then disseminated two likert surveys (TSES and WRCDS-R) and a demographic questionnaire. The researcher read the instructions, particularly indicating that only participants who self-identified as White/Caucasian were to fill out the WRCDS-R. Readings about the first year of teaching were included in the packet for those participants who either finished early or elected to not participate in the study. Upon completion of the student teaching experience at the end of the semester, White participants again completed the WRCDS-R and TSES, and students of color completed the TSES. We only used the data collected from student teachers who self-identified as White; all other data were securely stored but were not intended for use in our study.

Data Analysis

All data were entered into SPSS, and cases that were missing post-test data were eliminated. A Pearson product moment correlational analysis was used to examine the relationship between White racial identity statuses and teacher efficacy (research question 1), as well as the relationship between diversity of placement, White racial identity statuses, and teacher efficacy (research question 2). Paired sample t-tests were employed (research questions three and four) to investigate changes in White racial identity for individuals at specific sites (those placed in either highly diverse or non-diverse schools). For research question five, an analysis of covariance was conducted for each of the WRCDS-R sub-scales, using pretest scores on each sub-scale as the covariate to compare post test differences between student teachers placed in schools that served predominantly White students to those that primarily served Students of color.

Results

To address the first research question, a Pearson product moment correlational analysis examined the relationship between White racial identity statuses and teacher efficacy. The data indicated a significant negative correlation between scores on the contact subscale of the WRCDS-R and fcon all three subscales of the TSES (see Table 2). Contact is perceived to be a lower level of WRI development; therefore, as individuals reported greater naiveté or ignorance of racial differences (lower levels of WRI = higher scores on Contact), their beliefs about their ability to use effective instructional strategies, manage the classroom, and engage students decreased. The data also showed a significant negative correlation between scores on the Pseudo-Independence subscale of the WRCDS-R and scores on the Instructional Strategies subscale of the TSES. Pseudo-Independence represents greater awareness of the impact of White dominance and privilege on racist attitudes and behaviors; thus, as individuals reported greater awareness, their teacher efficacy regarding instructional strategies decreased.

Second, a correlational analysis was used to investigate the relationship between White racial identity statuses, diversity of field placements (measured by the percentage of White students in the school) and teacher efficacy. Results showed a significant

Table 2   Intercorrelations for subscale scores on the WRCDS-R and TSES

	N	SE	p	IS	p	CM	p
Contact	146	−.24*	.004	−.23*	.007	−.21*	.010
Reintegration	146	−.12	.153	−.08	.334	−.02	.843
Pseudo-Independence	146	−.16	.063	−.18*	.030	−.15	.070
Autonomy	146	.16	.054	.14	.078	.03	.669

Description: The four subscales of the White Racial Consciousness Development Scale-Revised (WRCDS-R) include Contact, Reintegration, Pseudo-Independence, and Autonomy; Contact and Reintegration are viewed as lower level statuses (Helms, 1990). The three subscales of the Teachers Sense of Efficacy Scale (TSES) include Student Engagement (SE), Instructional Strategies (IS), and Classroom Management (CM) (Tschannen-Moran et al. 1998).

*p < .05.

Table 3   Correlations between diversity of school[a] and subscales of the TSES

	N	r	Sig.
Student Engagement	146	.13	.11
Instructional Strategies	146	.17*	.04
Classroom Management	146	.21*	.01

Description: [a]Diversity of School is defined as the percentage of White students enrolled in the school.

*Correlation is significant (p < .05).

positive correlation between the diversity of the school and two subscales of the TSES: Instructional Strategies and Classroom Management (see Table 3). Thus, as the percentage of White students in the school increased, teacher efficacy regarding classroom management and instructional strategies increased. We found no significant correlation between subscale scores on the WRCDS-R and diversity of field placements.

To address research questions three and four, paired sample t-tests examined changes in the four subscales of the WRCDS-R for individuals placed in either highly diverse or non-diverse schools. The results indicated that neither group experienced significant changes on any of the WRCDS-R subscales (see Table 4).

Finally, an analysis of covariance was conducted for each of the four WRCDS-R subscales to compare post-test differences between those placed in predominantly White schools to those who were placed in more diverse settings. A separate ANCOVA was utilized for each of the four subscales, using the specific pre-test as the covariate. This provided a robust comparison, controlling for initial differences on the subscale pre-test. The results indicated no significant differences on any of the subscales (see Table 5).

Discussion

Schools of education across the United States are faced with the challenges of training teachers who are predominantly

Table 4 Changes in WRCDS-R for student teachers in either Highly Diverse (HD) or Non-Diverse (ND) schools

		Time 1		Time 2					95% CI	
		M	SD	M	SD	t	df	p	LL	UL
Contact										
	HD	14.02	5.58	14.70	5.45	1.05	43	.30	−1.98	.62
	ND	17.01	6.92	17.23	6.89	.37	68	.71	−1.39	.95
Reintegration										
	HD	39.05	8.06	38.95	9.01	.10	37	.92	−2.02	2.23
	ND	40.63	9.38	40.85	8.98	1.02	67	.31	−2.43	.79
Pseudo-Independence										
	HD	20.40	4.18	19.40	5.09	1.50	39	.14	−.35	2.35
	ND	18.88	4.02	18.10	5.00	1.44	66	.15	−.30	1.85
Autonomy										
	HD	32.36	7.53	32.05	7.52	.45	41	.65	−1.07	1.14
	ND	30.90	6.81	29.93	7.02	1.69	68	.10	−.17	2.16

Description: CI = confidence interval; LL = lower limit; UL = upper limit.

Table 5 Differences between student teachers placed in Highly Diverse (HD) or Non-Diverse (ND) schools on WRCDS-R subscores, controlling for pretest scores

WRCDS-R	Source	df	Mean Square	F	Sig
Contact					
	Intercept 1				
	Pre-test 1				
	School Type	1	10.02	.51	.48
	Error	110	19.62		
Reintegration					
	Intercept 1				
	Pre-test 1				
	School Type	1	5.65	.20	.66
	Error	101	18.63		
Pseudo-Independence					
	Intercept 1				
	Pre-test 1				
	School Type	1	9.47	.46	.50
	Error	101	10.43		
Autonomy					
	Intercept 1				
	Pre-test 1				
	School Type	1	28.82	1.34	.25
	Error	105	21.51		

Description: Pre-tests on the subscales served as covariates. School type consists of 2 levels: HD and ND.

Student Teaching Experience in Diverse Settings, White Racial Identity Development and Teacher Efficacy by D. S. Bloom and T. Peters

237

White to effectively work in schools with a large number of students of color. Unfortunately, many educators who prepare future teachers advocate a color-blind approach for working with students of color, despite ample research that supports the need for developing lessons based upon student background (Banks, 2007). Moreover, teachers who are specifically trained to work with culturally diverse students have greater levels of teacher efficacy to work with those students (Siwatu & Starker, 2010). Universities and colleges fall short in their attempts to address this, however, by providing either a single course or a single textbook chapter devoted to multiculturalism for the entire teacher preparation program. According to Banks (2007), having a formal curriculum and multicultural teaching materials are necessary, but not sufficient; materials are going to be highly ineffective by teachers who have naive, ignorant, and/or negative attitudes toward these diverse groups.

Surprisingly, the results of our study indicate that specific aspects of White racial identity, as well as diversity of field experiences, were related to student teachers' self efficacy. For example, as their awareness of the impact of White dominance and privilege on the establishment of inequities in society increased (score on Pseudo Independence), their teacher efficacy decreased. As White preservice teachers became more aware of the challenges facing students of color, perhaps they became more self-conscious and unsure of their ability to teach these students. Increased awareness and knowledge may lead to discomfort, which could also explain lower levels of teacher efficacy. Therefore, mere exposure without adequate training to work in diverse settings is insufficient to promote competence for teaching in diverse classrooms.

Our study presented findings at the culmination of 15 weeks of student teaching. We found that as the percentage of students of color enrolled in a school increased, preservice teachers reported lower levels of efficacy to implement both effective instructional strategies and classroom management techniques. We wondered if the strategies these teachers had learned and practiced in a prior setting were ineffective for working with more culturally diverse students. Alternatively, is it possible that teachers' perceptions of students of color correspond with lower expectations of their own abilities to work with these students?

Our research indicated that greater levels of ignorance about racial differences (Contact subscale of the WRCDS-R) also had deleterious effects on teacher efficacy, as indicated by its negative correlation with all three subscales of teacher efficacy. Thus, a color-blind approach apparently will not promote confidence for implementing pedagogical strategies with students of color. Individuals are often unaware of issues of race and racism due to the communities in which they live (Solomon et al., 2005), indicating that individuals need more cross-cultural contact to foster WRI development (Valli, 1995). Although contact may be a prerequisite for WRI development, our study did not find any differences in WRI development between student teachers who taught in either schools with a high or a low percentage of students of color. In addition, when investigating changes in WRI growth, neither group of student teachers (those placed in diverse or non-diverse settings) significantly changed over the course of the semester, suggesting that more than cross-cultural exposure is necessary to promote WRI growth.

Our study found that student teachers maintained their initial WRI beliefs and experienced lower levels of self-efficacy when teaching in diverse school settings where the dominant culture was different from their own. As noted by Pollock, Deckman, Mira, and Shalaby (2010), preservice teachers reported the need to come to terms with their own White privilege and guilt before they could develop specific classroom skills for working with students of color. Indeed, teacher educators should engage in conversations about race, racial identity, and race-related issues of privilege and power, topics that frequently are avoided in situations wherein participants are predominantly White (Pennington, 2007).

As noted by McKay (2010), critical pedagogy implies that educators must continuously question the dominant culture's perspective and consider alternative perspectives for working with diverse groups. Thus, open dialogue about educational practices and their impact on race are necessary to impact outcomes for students of color. Since the student population in public schools across the United States is becoming increasingly diverse, educators need to consider the inclusion of WRI in the training of future teachers.

Educators should consider reforms and strategies for change that not only embrace the teacher but also the students and their families (Banks, 2007). This approach will enable educators to better relate to and understand student behavior, thereby participating in "prejudice reduction." Banks expresses concern that children "come to school with many negative attitudes toward and misconceptions about different racial and ethnic groups" (Banks, 2007, p. 21) that influence cross-cultural interactions and academic success. Establishing positive images, role models, and sensitive multiethnic materials within a sequential curriculum may be one aspect that will foster student success. This approach can be addressed within teacher preparation programs. However, teacher training must move beyond the provision of multicultural materials and address the role of a teacher's race, as well as teachers' conceptions of classroom management, instructional strategies, and student engagement (Banks, 2001). Through dialogue with students and families from diverse backgrounds, teachers can reflect on their own beliefs, identify biases, and attempt to teach and manage a sensitive, efficient, effective classroom.

Conclusion

As perhaps the first empirical study to examine the relationship between White racial identity and teacher efficacy, and given the paucity of research on Whiteness in general, our study extends the current body of literature. Given the impact of teacher efficacy on student performance, understanding the relationship to White racial identity is imperative and warrants further study. Also, considering the demographics of the teaching force in the United States, cultural competence is paramount, and our study attempts to uncover the role of White racial identity in the development of teacher efficacy for working with students of color.

We found that student teachers who were placed in settings with larger numbers of students of color had lower levels of teacher efficacy. As noted by Wihak and Meral (2007), contact is a prerequisite for White racial identity development, but mere contact alone is insufficient for promoting positive White racial identity growth, as White individuals resist ideas of White privilege and power (LaDuke, 2009). Moreover, instructors who attempt to discuss these issues in multicultural courses report that students will attempt to change the subject or disengage from discussions of race (LaDuke, 2009).

We believe that schools of education must move beyond merely placing students in diverse classrooms. Instead, programs need to embed content about Whiteness throughout the curriculum and engage in dialogue about Whiteness issues, acknowledging and discussing personal bias and how biases influence teachers' misconceptions and assumptions about teaching and student learning. Addressing WRI in teacher training could increase White prospective teachers' awareness of their racial biases, the impact of these biases on their behavior, along with the unintended consequences of those behaviors (Castillo et al., 2006; Sue, et al., 2008). Educating White teachers regarding White racial identity, along with ample experiences in diverse settings, coupled with reflective discussions in accompanying seminars, may induce positive WRI development and, ultimately, positive classroom experiences for their students of color.

We acknowledge the limitations inherent in correlational research, but also recognize the implications of our study for future research. More controlled studies are warranted to investigate pre-post changes in WRI and teacher efficacy following training that focuses on cross-cultural communication and experience along with teachers' critical examination of their own beliefs and biases.

References

Au, W. (2009). Rethinking *multicultural education: Teaching for racial and cultural justice.* Milwaukee, WI: Rethinking Schools, Ltd.

Bandura, A. (1977). Self-efficacy: Toward a unifying theory of behavioral change. *Psychological Review, 84,* 191–215. http://dx.doi.org/10.1037/0033-295X.84.2.191

Bandura, A. (1997). *Self-efficacy: The exercise of control.* New York: Freeman.

Banks, J. A. (2001). Approaches to Multicultural Curriculum Reform. In J. A. Banks & C .A. M. Banks (Eds.), *Multicultural Education: Issues and Perspectives* (4th ed., pp.225–246). New York: John Wiley & Sons.

Banks, J. A. (Ed.). (2007). Multicultural education: Characteristics and goals. In J. & C. Banks (Ed.) *Multicultural Education* (6th ed., pp. 3–30). Hoboken, NJ: John Wiley & Sons.

Bryan, L., & Atwater, M. (2002). Teacher beliefs and cultural models. *Science Education, 86*(6), 821–839. http://dx.doi.org/10.1002/sce.10043

Buehler, J., Ruggles-Gere, A., Dallavis, C., & Shaw-Haviland, V. (2009). Normalizing the fraughtness: How emotion, race, and school context complicate cultural competence. *Journal of Teacher Education, 60*(4), 408–418. http://dx.doi.org/10.1177/0022487109339905

Castillo, L. G., Conoley, C. W., King, J., Rollins, D., Rivera, S., & Veve, M. (2006). Predictors of racial prejudice in White American counseling students. *Journal of Multicultural Counseling and Development, 34,* 15–26. http://dx.doi.org/10.1002/j.2161-1912.2006.tb00023.x

Chenoweth, K. (2009). *How it's being done: Urgent lessons from unexpected schools.* Cambridge, MA: Harvard Education Press.

Chick, N. Karis, T., & Kernahan, C. (2009). Learning from their own learning: How metacognitive and meta-affective reflections enhance learning in race-related courses. *International Journal for the Scholarship of Teaching and Learning, 3,* 1–28. Retrieved from http://academics.georgiasouthern.edu/ijsotl/v3n1.html

Claney, D., & Parker, W. M. (1989). Assessing White racial consciousness and perceived comfort with Black individuals: A preliminary study. *Journal of Counseling & Development, 67,* 449–451. http://dx.doi.org/10.1002/j.1556-6676.1989.tb02114.x

Comer, J. P. (2004). *Leave no child behind: Preparing today's youth for tomorrow's world.* London: Yale University Press.

Darling-Hammond, L., Chung, R., & Frelow, F. (2002). Variation in teacher preparation: How well do different pathways prepare teachers to teach? *Journal of Teacher Education, 53*(4), 286–302. http://dx.doi.org/10.1177/0022487102053004002

Denbo, S., L., & Jones, V. (2002). Foreword. In More Beaulieu (ed.), *Improving schools for African American students.* Springfield, IL: Charles C. Thomas.

Flores, E., Schwann, J. M., Dimas, J. M., Pasch, L. A., & de Groat, C. L. (2010). Perceived racial/ethnic discrimination, posttraumatic stress symptoms, and health risk behaviors among Mexican American adolescents. *Journal of Counseling Psychology, 57*(3), 264–273. http://dx.doi.org/10.1037/a0020026

Gao, W., & Mager, G. (2011). Enhancing preservice teachers' sense of efficacy and attitudes toward school diversity through preparation: A case of one U.S. inclusive teacher education program. *International Journal of Special Education, 26*(2), 92–107.

Gibson, S., & Dembo, M. (1984). Teacher efficacy: A construct validation. *Journal of Educational Psychology, 76*(4), 569–582. http://dx.doi.org/10.1037/0022-0663.76.4.569

Haviland, V. S. (2008). Things get glossed over: Rearticulating the silencing power of whiteness in education. *Journal of Teacher Education, 59*(40), 40–54. http://dx.doi.org/10.1177/0022487107310751

Helms, J. E. (Ed.). (1990). *Black and White racial identity: Theory, research, and practice.* Westport, CT: Greenwood Press.

Helms, J. E. (2005). Challenging some misuses of reliability coefficients as reflected in evaluation of the White Racial Identity Attitude Scale (WRIAS). In R. T. Carter (Ed.), *Handbook of racial-cultural psychology and counseling: Theory and research* (Vol. 1, pp. 360–390). New York, Wiley.

Howard, T. C. (2010). *Why race and culture matter in schools: Closing the achievement gap in America's classrooms.* New York, NY: Teachers College Press.

Hyland, N. E. (2005). Being a good teacher of Black students? White teachers and unintentional racism. *Curriculum Inquiry, 35*(4), 429–459. http://dx.doi.org/10.1111/j.1467-873X.2005.00336.x

Jones, J. M. (2006). *The psychology of multiculturalism in schools: A primer for practice, training, and research.* Bethesda, MD: National Association of School Psychologists.

Kafer, K. (2001). *A failing grade for s.1, the senate education committee bill.* Retrieved from http://www.heritage.org/Research/Education/BG1433.cfm.

Knoblauch, D., & Woolfolk Hoy, A. (2008). "Maybe I can teach those kids." The influence of contextual factors on student teachers' efficacy beliefs. *Teaching and Teacher Education, 24*(1), 166–179. http://dx.doi.org/10.1016/j.tate.2007.05.005

Kuykendall, C. (2004). *From rage to hope: Strategies for reclaiming black & hispanic students* (2nd ed.). Bloomington, IN: National Education Service.

LaDuke, A. (2009). Resistance and renegotiation: Preservice teachers interactions with and reactions to multicultural education course content. *Multicultural Education, 16*(3), 37–44.

Lee, S. M., Puig, A., Pasquarella-Daley, L., Denny, G., Rai, A. A., Dallape, A., & Parker, W. M. (2007). Revising the White racial consciousness development scale. *Measurement and Evaluation in Counseling and Development, 39*, 194–208.

Maehr, M., & Pintrich, P. R. (1997). *Advances in motivation and achievement.* Greenwich, CT: JAI Press.

Manzo, K. K. (2010). Spotlight on differentiated instruction: The personal approach. *Education Week Teacher Professional Development Sourcebook.* Retrieved from http://www.edweek. org/products/spotlight/05112020spotlighton Differentiated Instruction.pdf

Marzano, R., Pickering, D. J., & Pollack, J. E. (2001). *Classroom instruction that works: Research based strategies for increasing student achievement.* Alexandria, VA: ASCD.

McKay, C. L. (2010). Community education and critical race praxis: The power of voice. *Educational Foundations, Winter-Spring,* 25–38.

McKeachie, W. J., & Svinicki, M. (2006). *Teaching tips: strategies, research, and theory for college and university teachers.* Boston, MA: Houghton Mifflin Company.

McKinley, J. (2010). Raising Black students' achievement through culturally responsive teaching. Alexandria, VA: ASCD.

National Center for Education Statistics (2011). *The condition of education 2011.* Washington, DC: The United States Department of Education.

National School Board Foundation, (2002). *Leadership matters: transforming urban schools boards.* Retrieved from http://www.nsbf.org/report/index.html.

Nieto, S. (2004). *Affirming diversity: The sociopolitical context of multicultural education.* Boston, MA: person Allyn & Bacon.

Ogbu, J. V. (2003). *Black American students in an affluent suburb: A study of academic disengagement.* Mahway, NJ: Lawrence Erlbaum Associates, Inc.

Pajares, F. (1997). Current directions in self-efficacy research. In M. Maehr & P. R. Pintrich (Eds.), *Advances in motivation and achievement* (Vol. 10, pp. 1–49). Greenwich, CT: JAI Press.

Pennington, J. L. (2007). Silence in the classroom/whispers in the halls: Autoethnography as pedagogy in White pre-service teacher education. *Race Ethnicity and Education, 10*(1), 93–113. http://dx.doi.org/10.1080/13613320601100393

Pollock, M., Deckman, S., Mira, M., & Shalaby, C. (2010). "But what can I do?" Three necessary tensions in teaching teachers about race. *Journal of Teacher Education, 61*(3), 211–224. http://dx.doi.org/10.1177/0022487109354089

Pope-Davis, D. B., & Ottavi, T. M. (1994). Examining the association between self-reported multicultural counseling competencies and demographic and educational variables among counselors. *Journal of Counseling and Development, 72*, 651–654. http://dx.doi.org/10.1002/j.1556-6676.1994.tb01697.x

Raudenbush, S., Rowen, B., & Cheong, Y. (1992). Contextual effects on the self-perceived efficacy of high school teachers. *Sociology*

of Education, 65, 150–167. http://dx.doi.org/10.2307/ 2112680

Ruggles-Gere, A., Buehler, J., Dallavis, C., & Shaw-Haviland, V. (2009). A visibility project: Learning to see how preservice teachers take up culturally responsive pedagogy. *American Educational Research Journal, 46*(3), 816–852. http://dx.doi.org/ 10.3102/0002831209333182

Rychly, L., & Graves, E. (2012). Teacher characteristics for culturally responsive pedagogy. *Multicultural Perspectives, 14*(1), 44–49. http://dx.doi.org/10.1080/15210960.2012.646853

Science Education Resource Center (SERC). (2009). *How to engage and support urban students.* Retrieved from http://serc.carlton. edu/intrgeo/urban/how.html

Siwatu, K. O. (2011). Preservice teachers' sense of preparedness and self-efficacy to teach in America's urban and suburban schools: Does context matter? *Teaching and Teacher Education, 27,* 357–365. http://dx.doi.org/10.1016/j.tate.2010.09.004

Siwatu, K. O., & Starker, T. V. (2010). Predicting preservice teachers' self-efficacy to resolve a cultural conflict involving an African American student. *Multicultural Perspectives, 12*(1), 10–17. http://dx.doi.org/10.1080/15210961003641302

Sleeter, C. E. (2001). Preparing teachers for culturally diverse schools: Research and the overwhelming presence of Whiteness. *Journal of Teacher Education, 52*(2), 94–106. http://dx.doi. org/10.1177/0022487101052002002

Solomon, R. P., Portelli, J. P., Daniel, B. J., & Campbell, A. (2005). The discourse of denial: How white teacher candidates construct race, racism and "white privilege." *Race, Ethnicity and Education, 8*(2), 147–169.

Soodak, L., & Podell, D. (1996). Efficacy and experience: Perceptions of efficacy among preservice and practicing teachers. *Journal of Research and Development in Education, 30,* 214–221.

Sue, D. W., Nadal, K. L., Capodilupo, C. M., Lin, A. I., Rivera, D. P., & Torino, G. C. (2008). Racial Microaggressions against Black Americans: Implications for counseling. *Journal of Counseling and Development, 86*(3), 330–338. http://dx.doi. org/10.1002/j.1556-6678.2008.tb00517.x

Tomlinson, C. A. (2001). *How to differentiate instruction in mixed ability classrooms* (2nd ed.). Alexandria, VA: ASCD.

Tschannen-Moran, M., & Woolfok-Hoy, A. (2001). Teacher efficacy: capturing an elusive construct. *Teaching and Teacher Education, 17,* 783–805. http://dx.doi.org/10.1016/S0742-051X(01)00036-1

Tschannen-Moran, M., Hoy, A. W., & Hoy, W. K. (1998). Teacher efficacy: Its meaning and measure. *Review of Educational Research, 68,* 202–248.

The Coalition of Schools Educating Boys of Color (TCOSEBOC). (2010). *Standards and promises practices for schools educating boys of color: A self-assessment tool.* Metropolitan Center: New York. Retreived from http://www.successfulforblackboys.org/2/ post/2010/6/

Valli, L. (1995). The dilemma of race: Learning to be color blind and color conscious. *Journal of Teacher Education, 46*(2), 120–129. http://dx.doi.org/10.1177/0022487195046002006

Welsh, P. (2010, March 19). *At T.C. Williams High School, a "low achieving' label is a wakeup call.* Retrieved from http://www.washingtonpost.com/wpdyn/content/ article/2010/03/19/AR2010031901362_pf.html

Wihak, C., & Meral, N. (2007). Adaptations of professional ethics among counselors living and working in a remote Native Canadian community. *Journal of Multicultural Counselor*

Development, 35(3), 169–180. http://dx.doi.org/
10.1002/j.2161-1912.2007.tb00058.x

Woolfolk Hoy, A., & Davis, H. (2006). Teachers' sense of efficacy
and adolescent achievement. In F. Pajares & T. Urdan (Eds.),
Self efficacy beliefs of adolescents (pp. 117–137). Greenwich,
CT: Information Age Publishing.

Critical Thinking

1. What is meant by racial identity especially for White teacher candidates?
2. What is teacher self-efficacy in a sociocultural context?
3. What are teachers' beliefs and biases about diverse student learning?
4. How do sustained conversations about racial identity and self-efficacy benefit teacher candidates?

Create Central

www.mhhe.com/createcentral

Internet References

Education.com
www.education.com/reference/article/teacher-efficacy

Johns Hopkins School of Education
http://goo.gl/ksdPO

DIANE S. BLOOM College of Education, School of Curriculum and Teaching, Kean University, Toms River, USA

TERRI PETERS School of Education, Monmouth University, West Long Branch, USA

Article   Prepared by: Nancy P. Gallavan, *University of Central Arkansas*

"Oh, Those Loud Black Girls!": A Phenomenological Study of Black Girls Talking with an Attitude

No matter how backward and negative the mainstream view and image of Black people, I feel compelled to reshape the image and to explore our many positive angles because I love my own people. Perhaps this is because I have been blessed with spiritual African eyes at a time when most Africans have had their eyes poked out . . . . So, like most ghetto girls who haven't yet been turned into money-hungry, heartless bitches by a godless money centered world, I have a problem: I love hard. Maybe too hard. Or maybe it's too hard for a people without structure—structure in the sense of knowing what African womanhood is. What does it mean? What is it supposed to do to you and for you?
(Sistah Souljah, as cited in Richardson, 2003)

JACQUELINE B. KOONCE

Learning Outcomes

After reading this article, you will be able to:

- Understand TWA and its relationship to voice and choice.

- Explain the influence double-consciousness has on students.

Introduction

While I did not grow up in the ghetto like Sistah Souljah, the author of the above quote, I have come to love my people hard, and I aim to highlight their often unheard voices as they describe their experiences with teachers and their use of the speech practice, "Talking with an Attitude" (TWA; Troutman, 2010). As these girls navigate their school ecology, they are also exploring their identities as African American[1] females. Through the sharing of their lived experiences, I hope educators will walk away with more knowledge about the development of their multiple identities and of the TWA speech practice, which is part of the African womanhood Sistah Souljah mentions. But first, I want to share my journey by describing my experiences with the phenomenon.

First, as an African American adolescent, I attended public schools whose student populations were majority African American, and many of my female friends talked with an attitude. At the time, I did not understand talking with an attitude as a speech practice within the African American women's speech community (AAWSC; Troutman, 2010), but my recent studies have developed within me an interest in this language and literacy practice. Although other races, ethnic groups, and cultures may appropriate talking with an attitude, it has been recognized in the literature as part of the AAWSC and the Black Diaspora, so this study focused solely on African American girls because of its history within this community.

In the *Oxford English Dictionary Online* (2010), the word "attitude" has several meanings, including: fitness, adaptation, disposition, and posture, that is, an outlook on the world. When talking about attitude generally, among the White dominant culture, the meaning of attitude denotes these characteristics. For the AAWSC, talking with an attitude means so much more than an outlook. Troutman (2010) states:

*For many African Americans that self-identify as members of the AASC [African American Speech Community], attitude holds another layer of meaning, including to the extent that attitude becomes manifested overtly, through language and kinesics, by a speaker's ability to **talk** with an attitude, **walk** with an attitude, **act** with an attitude, **be** with an attitude. In many instances within the AASC, then,*

---

[1]Like Battle-Walters (2004), I will use the terms Black and African American interchangeably to include Black females who refer to themselves as Black and to provide a possible connection of this phenomenon to females of the Black Diaspora.

attitude actions are marked distinctly and can be read by other group members. These are actions that are learned socio-culturally in socially real contexts (emphasis in original; p. 107).

She goes on to state that those outside the AAWSC may look at TWA negatively, but to those inside the group, TWA can also be positive as noted by some of her participants quoted in the following text.

In Troutman's (2010) study of fifteen African American women ranging in age from 20-74, she noted that her participants defined TWA differently based on age. The older generation thought that attitude exuded confidence and self-esteem, while the younger generation thought that it meant having a chip on one's shoulder or talking back. I found the latter negative connotations to be true of some classmates in my early education, so that was how I defined TWA for many years until I went to college and graduate school. Now, I see TWA as an African American women's speech practice that is used to show confidence or resistance in oppressive situations.

As stated earlier, in my elementary grades, I had constant contact with girls who engaged in the practice of TWA, and my ideas on how TWA was operationalized were different. My thinking toward TWA continued to be negative because I saw what I perceived to be angry and threatening behaviors. My exposure to many girls who used this speech practice changed a little in high school when I entered honors and Advanced Placement classes, which many of them did not take.

As much as I hate to admit it, I was often intimidated by TWA and often did not respond adeptly. As a result, I hated this speech practice because I could not use it to stand up for myself, and consequently, as Morgan (2002) describes, I felt and looked like a fool. My lack of skillfulness with TWA was probably the case, in part, because of my family's child-rearing practices. For instance, my family taught me to restrain my tongue and avoid the semblance of conflict if at all possible. Even instances of using TWA to form camaraderie with classmates were frowned upon, so holding in my feelings may have created the inability to engage in TWA with my Black female classmates.

Another possible reason for my inability to engage in TWA may have been due to my socioeconomic status. My family was middle-class, and we lived in a Black suburban neighborhood, but I attended inner-city schools. Morris (2007) notes the tensions within Black communities because of social class, but specifically highlights the tensions among Black females. In his analysis of the relationships between teachers and their Black adolescent female students, Morris noted that Black female teachers often, but not in all cases, experienced friction over the expectation that these girls behave "ladylike" and avoid being loud or talking with an attitude (p. 506). He surmised this expectation had to do with the social class the Black female teachers acquired by virtue of their position. While Troutman believes TWA crosses social classes (personal communication, February 4, 2011), that was not my experience, and I think it should be studied further to parse out this possibility.

In college, these feelings dissipated as I attended a historically Black university. There were times when my friends talked with an attitude, but the practice was carried out differently. It was usually playful, and it created a connection between us.

The experiences of hearing African American females talk with an attitude continued when I entered the classroom as a student teacher in a redistricted suburban school with many students of color and English language learners from urban areas. My African American female mentor teacher and I once talked about our difficulties in reaching these girls, mainly because of their "attitudes." I remember her saying that out of the many years she had been teaching, she had noticed an increase in African American girls talking with an attitude. I wondered why these girls used this practice. Perhaps my mentor and I had a lack of understanding of the use of TWA among young Black girls (as opposed to older Black women) and, as a result, it may have been a deterrent to reaching them. Furthermore, we were also using many Eurocentric novels and texts. Because of our lack of understanding and our following school and district mandates to use several Eurocentric materials, we probably were not seen as allies and adults who truly cared about their well-being.

It was not until my graduate school studies that I began to understand the language and literacy practice of talking with an attitude and my Black "sistahs" who used it. I no longer loathed this practice, but began to appreciate it for both its seemingly positive and negative aspects. I now understand the self-esteem that comes with TWA that the older generation indexed, and I can appreciate its use as a form of resistance or as a way to make our voices heard.

At the end of my second year of doctoral studies, a former university professor asked if there was research or professional development available for teachers whose African American girls engaged in this practice, because the school district was suspending more girls for behavioral issues, which included TWA. Because of my own experiences, newfound knowledge, this professor's request, and my doctoral readings, I decided to undertake a study about TWA, as it relates to Black adolescent girls.

The research question for this study is the following: What is the nature of the experience for young Black girls who talk with an attitude with or around their teachers? I explored the phenomenon of talking with an attitude using the theoretical lens of Afrocentric feminist epistemology (Collins, 1990) and phenomenological methods (Van Manen, 1990). This theory and approach allowed me to get at the issues of voice for my participants. The study encompasses interviewing adolescent African American females about their experiences with their teachers when the students talk with an attitude. It was my goal to provide my participants with the opportunity to voice their lived experiences of talking with an attitude with their teachers without my judgment or criticism. I aimed to use their voices to provide an understanding of the nuances of their lifeworlds.

The issue of voice is important here because African American females, along with other historically-oppressed people, have been noted for having to face what W.E.B. Du Bois (1903/1994) calls a "double-consciousness." Du Bois states that the double-consciousness is "this sense of always looking at one's self through the eyes of others, of measuring one's soul by the tape of the world that looks on in amused contempt and pity" (p. 2). He continues, "One ever feels his two-ness,—an American, a Negro; two souls, two thoughts, two unreconciled strivings; two warring ideals in one dark body, whose dogged strength alone keeps it from being torn asunder" (p. 2). Here, Du Bois explicates the idea that African Americans have the burden of displaying two selves, one that is acceptable to dominant society and one that wants to be the true self. Both entities war within the African American. This conflict is reflected in the politics and realities of our day as well. For example, if one studies Arizona's ban on the teaching of ethnic studies, one might infer that this law aimed at increasing Americanism by banning curricula and instruction that officials believe re-segregate people (Downey, 2012). This tension creates a double consciousness for those who want to celebrate their culture. This example points to the reason why the voice of my participants is so important; they, even as young African Americans, may have a war raging within, as they have been privy to some racialized experiences with their teachers.

Double-consciousness does not stop there, however. Before Du Bois, Anna Julia Cooper introduced the concept of triple identity that outlines the difficulties of being Black, female, and an American. Carby's (1987) work explicates, "Cooper argued that women should not be confined to narrow ideologies of domesticity and sexual objectification in either White or Black spheres of influence..." (as cited in Giles, 2006, p. 631). This racialized experience is still part of the African American woman's experience. To explain, some African American women have stated that they had been sterilized against their wills throughout the 20th century (Volscho, 2007). This example points to the possibility of these women having the triple identity conflict because their color/race, gender, and Americanism all played a part in their sterilization. Most recently, the state of North Carolina acknowledged the plan of mass sterilization of poor minorities in the 20th century, but the North Carolina Senate refused to approve compensation that the House had approved for victims (Gann, Hutchison, & James, 2012). These examples point to the negotiation of multiple identities that African American women face.

These examples are not given to place judgment on the morality of these laws/issues of banning cultural studies and sterilization; rather, they point to the multiple identities that women of color have to face in current times. This contention of managing a triple identity remains in current society, so it may also be a part of the lifeworlds of my participants who are learning to navigate this reality in their schools.

In sum, many African American women take up having a triple identity, positively shown through our strength for navigating multiple identities in a racist and sexist society. Even Cooper (1892/1998) stated, "But to be a woman of the Negro race in America, and to be able to grasp the deep significance of the possibilities of the crisis, is to have a heritage, it seems to me, unique in the ages" (p. 117). Even now, we have many possibilities in our current crises, if not more, as Cooper mentioned of African American women in her time. However, it may still be burdensome for African American adolescent females who are on the cusp of learning to navigate these identities.

Conceptual Background

The literature on learning to navigate multiple identities provides a conceptual starting point for understanding why talking with an attitude is important for further study, especially for the school context. As part of the specific experiences of Black females, Troutman's (2010) participants explain what talking with an attitude means to them. First, however, Troutman explains that "*attitude* [is] a broad concept that can be displayed in language and/or kinesics" (p. 85, italics in original). She continues, "Its meanings and functions derive from social contexts and community norms" (p. 85). Troutman does not provide a definition of TWA because she uses the method phenomenology that involves putting co-researchers (referred to as participants for my study) in the subject position and allowing them, not the principal researcher, to co-define the term (D. Troutman, personal communication, February 4, 2011). Before presenting her co-researchers' definitions, however, Troutman provides the example below by Morgan (2002) to help the reader better understand the concept:

> *A verbal routine that I remember as a child resulted in my losing face when two of my very "best friends" were talking to each other. I innocently walked up to them, listened for a bit, and then offered my expert advice about their conversation . . . . [T]hey said to me: "This is an A and B conversation, so C your way out!" . . . . Fast forward to the new millennium, and what has happened to this kind of verbal death blow? It has becomes [sic] even more lethal. The eyes and head still roll, but the lips say something that requires insider youth membership. "Girlfriend" now says something like: "You just AAAAALLL UP in the Kool Aid!—And don't EEEVEN know the flavor!" or "Stop dippin' in my Kool Aid." (p. 41)*

Notice how Morgan calls this type of attitude a "verbal death blow" and "lethal" (p. 41). These adjectives describe a practice used negatively. To further support this point, Morgan goes on to say that her "sister overheard this and reported to everyone that [she] had no cool and had been made a fool" (p. 41). This is what I meant when I said that I felt foolish when faced with TWA as an adolescent. Although Troutman agrees that this example has negative implications for TWA, she adds that it also has attributes that are positive. She states that these "acts have been socially learned, transferred, and sanctioned by specific communities of practice" (p. 96). Although she believed this assertion to be the case, Troutman interviewed other Black women to get their perspectives. Nevertheless, in correspondence with Troutman, she stated that "Negative acts may have stood out most prominently from the Morgan example, yet it struck me that positive associations must have been and continue to be part of the TWA act; otherwise, it would not continue to be appropriated within and beyond the AASC" (personal communication, February 4, 2011). In other words, because TWA is still used within and beyond the AAWSC, it must be positive, as it has been maintained as a part of the cultural and ethnic community.

As stated earlier, Troutman's (2010) participants defined TWA in positive and negative ways. For example, one of them stated that it means "having a chip on your shoulder," or always being upset, and "flipping the finger," while another one said that it is an "inflection in voice; sass, talking back, but it's not disrespectful" (p. 99). Finally, another participant stated that it is "confidence; I see it as a positive. Some people say, 'Get rid of the 'tude.' When I first think of attitude, I think of it as positive" (p. 99). For instance, one of her participants stated, "models on a runway come out with attitude. [A] fashion director says, 'Give me some attitude'" (p. 99). Attitude to these women means exuding confidence, self-esteem, command-of-self, command-of-language, and being empowered.

When asked who talks with an attitude, some of the women stated that TWA is "associated with teens and betweens," "older and younger," "Black females usually," and "People who are self-assured, confident in status, in themselves, in their community, their work, [and] their roles" (Troutman, 2010, p. 100). They added, "Teachers may [TWA]; ministers may; leaders do it; males in their own way; females in their own way" (p. 100). All of these definitions demonstrate the polyvocal nature of the term. In addition, one of Troutman's co-researchers stated that for older African American women, TWA means confidence, but it was often looked at negatively by their younger counterparts. As it will be seen later, my participants also conceived TWA as a negative act. However, talking with an attitude on the part of young people could very much mean more than just having a chip on one's shoulder—as it is sometimes interpreted by teachers—but could also be used as an act of resistance on the part of Black adolescent girls (Fordham, 1993; Morris, 2007).

Possible Reasons Behind Adolescents' Use of TWA

Black girls talking with an attitude is not new. Grace Evans (1980), a former secondary teacher in Inner London comprehensive schools, "had a political background which included a commitment to feminism and the exploration of race as a personal and political reality," which informed her work (p. 183). As a former teacher of social studies, English, English as a Second Language, and special needs students, she heard her White colleagues exclaim, "Oh, those loud Black girls!" in the lounge of an inner-city secondary comprehensive London school (p. 183). Evans adds that this exclamation was often "followed by the slamming of a pile of folders on to a table and the speaker collapsing into a chair or storming off to get a cup of coffee" (p. 183). Evans continues her narrative with the statement below:

> The words were usually uttered in response to a confrontation in which the teacher's sense of authority had been threatened by an attitude of defiance on the part of a group of Black girls...they patrolled this territory with much skill, sending out a distinct message of being in and for themselves. (p. 183, emphasis added)

These teachers were not necessarily remarking on the volume of the girls' speech (see Mitchell-Kernan (1972) on loud-talking); instead, they were incensed at the girls' attitudes of defiance. These teachers were frustrated because they felt that their authority was undermined by skillful speakers who knew how to speak their mind and rebel against what they perceived as unfair uses of the teachers' authority. Again, this use of TWA is positive, in that the girls used it to maintain their cultural integrity.

Evans (1980) also argues that these girls, like their Black male counterparts, are not represented in the curriculum, in school exhibits, or in books. This was also generally the case in the school district where I taught. In fact, this "hidden curriculum," as Evans termed it, suggested that Black students were destined to work the jobs of those low on the social hierarchy of the school. In her school, the majority of the teachers were White, and many of the cooks, cleaners, and additional employees were Black women. Evans (1980) states, "Looking at the subject hierarchy of the secondary school, it is a small intellectual leap to make from identifying the subjects with the least status—home economics, needlework, child development—to observing that it is in these spheres of work that Black women are to be found in the outside world [of school]" (p. 187). These females had few role models of Black women from the higher social hierarchy from which to glean information that would help them climb this ladder without negating their language and literacies. In fact, Evans states that a "good" education often comes at the cost of one's Black cultural identity.

Finally, the author points out the challenges that these girls face by being Black and female. She notes that the experience of marginalization is different for Black and White women; for Black women have been castigated as "the mammy, the Aunt Jemima figure, the masculinised beast of burden and the sexually licentious, exotic nightclub singer/dancer/prostitute" (p. 188). These images, often found in the media, are difficult to erase when attempting to replace them with positive ones, such as the person who is excelling in the arts or sports. Even putting forth an image of a Black female as *only* able to succeed in arts and sports is somewhat marginalizing her. Images of women in business, education, finance, and politics present careers to which young Black adolescent girls should be exposed, in addition to arts and sports. A lack of access to positive images of Black women is a challenge that Black girls struggle with as they begin to develop their identities (Evans, 1980). Images of Black women who have been able to operate successfully in the dominant society are missing, and so are the ways in which they navigated TWA in their climbs up the social ladder. This lack of positive images is problematic because teachers of Black girls' may also lack these positive images, which may affect how they interact with them.

Similar to Evans' chapter, Morris' (2007) article outlines the educational obstacles and perceptions that Black girls face, but in an American public neighborhood middle school. Unlike Evans, Morris noted that Black female teachers, as well as White teachers, disciplined Black girls for talking with an attitude. His examples show that teachers who share the same race and gender can also carry out oppressive practices. In his findings Morris noted, for example, that Black female teachers presumed that each of their Black female students lacked "interactional skills" because of her family's socioeconomic status (p. 504). Female-headed households in these socioeconomic groups were presumed inadequate to pass on values that the dominant society esteems. However, Morris made sure not to demonize these teachers, because their intentions seemed to be caring. They did not want their Black female students to be marginalized by the racist and sexist society that they knew awaited them. Although my participants noted the racialized nature of their experiences when talking with an attitude, it is important to note that teachers who share the same race may engage in oppressive practices as a result of several factors including class, as noted by Morris.

As a result of his research, Morris noticed three themes that are relevant to the present study. The first theme was perceived challenges to authority, and it was noted because teachers often chastised girls for subverting their authority in classrooms. After one teacher scolded one of her Black female students for being assertive by asking questions, the girl put her head down on the desk and was disengaged for the rest of the class.

Another theme that coincides with my research is perceived loudness. Loudness here not only represents the volume of the girls' speech, but attitude as well. One of the teachers told Morris: "The boys here are always quiet and the girls are real loud. Girls are loud at this age, they have *attitude*. They won't want to do something, or think something is stupid, and move their heads back and forth and click at me" (emphasis added, p. 505). While this teacher was speaking of girls in general, the author notes that her description of clicking and head movement is stereotypical Black female behavior. This perception of Black girls as loud often resulted in discipline from many teachers.

The third theme is related to an African American male teacher in Morris' study, who described Black girls specifically as loud and confrontational. However, he added, "...[T]hey've learned to be combative because they don't have the system behind them. They've learned this to survive" (p. 506). Morris states this teacher's statement reflects scholarly research. My participants used their loudness or TWA in the same way.

TWA as a Form of Resistance

Several authors have discussed some aspects of language and literacy practices such as TWA among African American women and the women's struggles in American society. One such author, Gwendolyn D. Pough (2004), speaks of some practices as "bringing wreck," a means of resistance. Specifically, she states, "Bringing wreck, as the term is used here, is a rhetorical act that has close ties to various other speech acts that are often linked to Black womanhood: talking back, going off, turning it out, having a niggerbitchfit, or being a diva" (p. 78). I would dare to say that if Troutman (2010) had written about TWA at the time this article was written, the term might have been included in that list. In fact, Pough cites Troutman, stating that Black women use their speech acts as a form of resistance. She references Troutman when she states, "Black women have had to develop and pass on to future generations of Black women a form of verbal and nonverbal expression that combines politeness with assertiveness" (Pough, p. 78). Pough

is indexing here Troutman's 2001 analysis of the Anita Hill/ Clarence Thomas investigation, in which she analyzed Anita Hill's assertive style throughout the questioning. Anita Hill's assertiveness was used as an act of resistance, just as TWA is used in some situations.

Helping Black Adolescent Females Negotiate their Triple Identity

Similar to Pough's discussion on the struggles of Black women, Battle-Walters (2004) talks about Black women's challenges with being Black and female in her published research study, *Sheila's Shop: Working-Class African American Women Talk about Life, Love, Race, and Hair.* Battle-Walters, who studied the impact of race on a group of Black women in a hair salon, discusses the realities of being discriminated against for being Black and a woman, reinforcing Philomena Essed's (as cited in Battle-Walters, 2004) concept of gendered racism. To begin this discussion on gendered racism, Battle-Walters begins by asking her participants what it is like to be a Black woman in America today. The responses particularly resonated with one of her participants: "It's hard!" (p. 31). This client was alluding to the idea that it is hard for Black women to be successful because they find resistance from supervisors and institutions.

This concept of the gendered racism is similar to the previous discussion on Du Bois' (1903/1994) concept of double-consciousness and Cooper's (1892/1998) notion of the triple identity. Black women have felt compelled to navigate multiple identities as a result of not only wanting to express themselves to the world, but also to gain access to the culture of power, or the economic and social power associated with the White or dominant society (Delpit, 1995). As previously stated, Black adolescent girls also feel the effects of the triple identity. Elaine Richardson (2003) makes comments on the conflicts African American girls' face in regard to their language and literacies. She states:

> For many African American girls...[t]here has been a conflict, between our mothers and others, about what language is and does for us. This conflict is so prevalent that many Black females at some time or another internalize it: Should we respect our language and ways of knowing as little girls, or in our homes as we develop into women? Or should we gradually have our minds (our mother wits) erased with each passing year of formal schooling? (p. 76)

This quote speaks to the need of helping Black adolescent girls in the development of their identities by respecting their ways of knowing and educating teachers about their literacies. Providing this information to teachers will help them to understand and to educate Black adolescent females, so that their cultural expressions are validated while they are simultaneously taught how to access the culture of power (Delpit, 1995; Richardson, 2003). This knowledge will help all teachers, regardless of race. However, in this study, three White teachers may have needed this information to avoid the racialized incidents with the two participants. Knowledge about Black girls' literacies, and how these girls may use them as a defense mechanism, may have curbed the conflicts between the girls and their teachers. This concept of understanding TWA as an avenue that Black girls use outside cultural contexts to defend themselves is a point illuminated through the lens of Afrocentric feminist epistemology and phenomenology.

Theoretical and Methodological Traditions

Afrocentric feminist epistemology, a tradition best explicated in the work of Patricia Hill Collins, came about because Black women wanted to have the ability to combine both Afrocentric *and* feminist standpoints (Collins, 1990). She lists four dimensions to Afrocentric feminist epistemology: (a) concrete experience as a criterion of meaning; (b) the use of dialogue in assessing knowledge claims; (c) the ethic of caring; and (d) the ethic of personal accountability. Concrete experience as a criterion of meaning indicates that Black women place greater value on wisdom gained through experience than on knowledge of a concept (Collins, 1990; Ladson-Billings, 1994). The Black adolescent females in this study were treated as experts having wisdom because of their lived experiences with the phenomenon. During interviews with these adolescents, I purposed to place value on their accounts in order to honor the wisdom they brought to the phenomenon. Placing value on their experiences is critical because while I had exposure to TWA, I had never used it with teachers, so their wisdom served as enlightenment for me as a researcher and educator.

I also employed Collins' use of dialogue in assessing knowledge claims by talking "with" and not "to" the participants in order to dialogue with them instead of treating them as objects. Therefore, we dialogued as subject to subject. To elaborate on this tenet, Collins (1990) states, "For Black women new knowledge claims are rarely worked out in isolation from other individuals and are usually developed through dialogues with other members of a community" (p. 212). Therefore, my participants and I worked through their knowledge claims by delving deeper into their stories through clarifying questions in order to come to a better understanding of their experiences.

Furthermore, in using the ethic of care, I encouraged them to tell their stories because I wanted them to walk away feeling the value placed upon their lived experiences. Care was also established through the solidarity gained by our interactions during their activities at the Boys and Girls Club. The girls' own ethic of care was demonstrated when they talked about their experiences witnessing classmates being verbally attacked by teachers. Through my research, they wanted other teachers to understand that everyone has feelings, and one may not know a student's life experiences.

Finally, I incorporated the ethic of personal accountability that involves an individual taking full responsibility for her knowledge claims and the researcher's evaluation of an individual's character, values, and ethics. Through my participant observation of the girls during their Boys and Girls Club

activities and probing to ensure they indeed had these experiences, I held the girls accountable for their knowledge claims. In turn, they held me accountable, while I clarified their responses, for getting their stories right.

Along with Afrocentric feminist epistemology as a theoretical framework, I also used the method of phenomenology to get at essential meanings from my participants' lived experience accounts. In phenomenology, participants' experiences are reduced to a description of universal essences (Creswell, 2007). An essence refers to the "nature of an experience" (Van Manen, 1990, p. 10). Phenomenological research, according to Van Manen, is at its core the human scientific study of essences. My research question gets to the essence of the experience under study. Again, it is, "What is the nature of the experience for young Black girls who talk with an attitude with or around their teachers?" This question gets at the meaning of the lived experience instead of just the facts of the experience (Van Manen, 1990). For example, in my research, I identified the phenomenon of African American adolescent girls talking with an attitude with or around their teachers, and collected data from five girls who might have experienced the phenomenon. Two were chosen because of their experience with the phenomenon, and after the interviews, I developed a description of the essences, or nature of the experience, for both participants. Also in the study of lived experiences, it is only possible to understand the experience through reflection, or after it has taken place, because it is impossible to reflect upon the experience as one is living it (Van Manen, 1990). This statement means that phenomenological research is also the explication of phenomena as they presented themselves to consciousness. Therefore, in this research study, I attempted to provide an environment in which the participants were in a natural attitude so that they could provide the concrete, detailed account of their experiences (Van Manen, 1990).

Van Manen (1990) states that "[it] does not offer us the possibility of effective theory with which we can now explain and/or control the world, but rather it offers us the possibility of plausible insights that bring us in more direct contact with the world" (p. 9). He means here that we attempt to grasp the world pre-reflectively and immediately. This line of thought is similar to twentieth-century German philosopher Heidegger (1927/1962/2006), in that for him phenomenology values lived experiences, precisely because the subject's experiences are "ready-to-hand" (p. 98). In other words, the experience is action-oriented. The subject is being by doing. In this research study, I was interested in my participants' ready-to-hand experiences. However, when I analyzed the research, I took on the position of "presence-at-hand" (p. 101). This phrase simply means that I stepped back and examined or observed the phenomenon in order to discover what is happening. For instance, after I read the interview transcripts, I concentrated on meanings as they were presented, in order to illuminate them and provide an analysis of themes as they appeared in the transcripts.

Another aspect of phenomenological research is that it is the description of the experiential meanings we live as we live them. In other words, phenomenology values meaning over statistical relationships among variables, frequency of behaviors or statements, and so on. Van Manen (1990) also states that phenomenology differs from "other disciplines in that it does not aim to explicate meanings specific to particular cultures (ethnography), to certain social groups (sociology), to historical periods (history), to mental types (psychology), or to an individual's personal life history (biography)" (p. 11). Instead, phenomenology seeks to give meaning to our everyday experiences in this lifeworld (Van Manen, 1990). Thus, I also strive to give meaning to the African American adolescent girls' experiences. Therefore, my purpose in this research is not to develop cultural meanings based on a certain social group but to come to more universally shared meanings that may be relevant to those outside of the group[2].

Studying the human science of phenomena is also a part of phenomenological research. Phenomenology is scientific in that it is the systematic, explicit, self-critical, and intersubjective study of our lived experience. Phenomenology is a human science because it studies the meaning of the "lived *human* world" (p. 11, italics in original). In studying the human world, phenomenological research is also the attentive practice of thoughtfulness toward our subjects.

As I interviewed my participants and analyzed their experiences, I purposed to practice thoughtfulness and care, going back to Afrocentric feminist epistemology.

Phenomenological research is also a poetizing activity. Like a poet, phenomenologists speak the world rather than speaking about it. The phenomenological researcher will use language not to give the latest information, summarize, or conclude, but to try to elucidate the goings-on in the world. As we speak the world, it helps us improve it by giving voice to participants' experiences and making meaning out of them. This research empowers participants and enlightens readers to a phenomenon they may not have considered but to which they can in some way relate.

Orbe, Drummond, and Camara (2002) discuss how Afrocentric feminist epistemology aligns well with phenomenology, and are therefore both important models for my own work. First, both frameworks treat participants "as experts of their life experiences" (p. 125). These personal experiences are considered as solid evidence in research (Collins, 1990; Orbe et al., 2002). Like Afrocentric feminist epistemology, phenomenology also asserts that personal expressiveness and emotion are important to knowledge, theory, and research. Next, both traditions "focus on the power of dialogue in creating knowledge" (p. 125). All in all, "Phenomenological inquiry creates a discursive space where African American women can give voice to the circumstances that are central to the ways in which they experience life" (p. 125). Providing a space to voice experiences was my goal in this study: to use the voices of African American adolescent girls to explain their experiences with teachers when they enacted TWA. Afrocentric

feminist epistemology and phenomenology enabled me to get at the core of their lived experiences in order to understand the phenomenon of teacher engagement with these speech practices.

Data-Gathering Methods and Analysis Procedures
Sample and Participant Selection

I gathered data through two interviews with each of the two participants: one in-depth interview with a follow-up interview. These interviews were with two African American girls over a one- month period. I interviewed several girls, but only two of them, who participated in a Boys and Girls Club in a Midwestern city, met the criteria for the study. To request their participation, I distributed a flyer to inform the girls and their families of the research. The Teen Director also allowed me to have a meeting with all of the African American adolescent girls in the program to describe my study. In addition to providing this information, I participated in their games and other activities to become less of a stranger to them. Olivia and Stephanie (the assigned pseudonyms for the participants) were chosen because of their experiences with the phenomenon and their willingness to participate in the study. They coincidently belonged to the same middle school, so this fact probably played a part in the similarity of their experiences. As suggested above, they were not chosen based upon the fact that they attended the same school; their willingness to discuss their experiences with TWA was the reason that they were selected.

Research Procedures

In my interviews with these girls, I aimed to get the full story of what it was like to talk with an attitude with their teachers by attempting to create an environment conducive for a natural attitude or relaxed state. This attempt was made by asking the girls to tell me about their day, what they did, and if they enjoyed themselves that day. I also asked them to tell me about themselves, including their hobbies, their favorite parts about school, and what they liked most about the Boys and Girls Club. During the main part of the interviews where I tried to ask questions more pointedly about the phenomenon, I used reduction, the process of withholding one's prior knowledge, in order to try and see their experiences freshly. In other words, I withheld my knowledge and experience with TWA in order to listen and understand their experiences as if the concept was new to me. However, in analyzing the data, I followed Van Manen's (1990) method of using my prior experiences with the phenomenon to inform my interpretation of it. I found this method helpful in understanding the girls' feelings about their teachers' behaviors.

I audiotaped the interviews, and after these sessions, I transcribed the interviews verbatim and reread them several times, looking for significant statements to arrive at essential meanings which Van Manen describes as the selective approach. While this method helped me gain greater insight into the girls' lived experiences, I did struggle with making meaning

---

[2]Although TWA is located more in the AAWSC, it has possible applications beyond this group as well. For example, others reading this article may remember an experience of friction with teachers and identify with it. This example is part of what phenomenology is all about. It notes the importance of the phenomenon to the individual or specialized group, but some aspect of the experience could have universally-shared meanings.

out of them. Because of this struggle, I solicited the help of a colleague well-versed in phenomenology to help me arrive at themes from the data. His probing and insight helped me to think more deeply about the themes within the text and how the meanings could be universally shared.

To arrive at the themes, I had to determine the usefulness of those themes brainstormed by questioning whether they got at the meaning of the experience of these African American adolescent girls (Van Manen, 1990). The themes that were ultimately chosen seemed to get at the core of the "notion" we were trying to understand while also understanding that "no thematic formulation can completely unlock the deep meaning, the full mystery, the enigmatic aspects of the experiential meaning of a notion" (p. 88). Therefore, as the researcher, I did my best to get at the core of the experience, but also understood that my analysis might not completely get at the full mystery of the phenomenon. Van Manen (1990) captures developing a theme perfectly when he states: "As such, a so-called thematic phrase does not do justice to the fullness of the life of a phenomenon. A thematic phrase only serves to point at, to allude to, or to hint at, an aspect of the phenomenon" (p. 92).

Again, to isolate thematic statements, I used the selective/highlighting approach, which requires looking for any phrases that stand out. Therefore, I looked for sentences or part-sentences that seemed to be thematic of the experience of talking with an attitude with or around teachers (Van Manen, 1990).

Next, I attempted to transform these sentences linguistically to develop a theme that pointed to the experience, followed by the description that Van Manen (1990) calls "phenomenologically sensitive paragraphs," or the poetizing activity referred to earlier. Like my descriptions, I also attempted to word my themes in ways that got at the nature of the lived experience, but also used poetic language. In this research, for example, I developed the theme, "My Cup Overflows—Talking with an Attitude as a Defense Mechanism," as a result of one of the participants' following statements: "And, then I'll try to tell them and stuff and sometimes they may want to get an attitude and stuff, *but I try to hold it in as much as possibly like as long as I can. Sometimes, I do.*" This theme gets at the nature of the experience, but does so with language befitting phenomenology because it transcends "everyday talking and acting in that it is always arrived at in a reflective mood" (Van Manen, 1990, p. 97).

Furthermore, Van Manen explains that phenomenology seeks to develop a story that explains themes while remaining true to the experience. Developing these paragraphs required a "creative, hermeneutic process" (p. 96). To write the story, I reread the selective statements in the interviews several times trying to determine the meaning behind them. I wrote down one-word phrases to begin my process of developing the themes, eventually created phrases, and consulted my aforementioned colleague for his input. I followed this process in the development of the themes' accompanying descriptions shared in the next section.

Results

The following themes represent my participants' lived experiences. I went through the process of meaning making out of their interactions with teachers as they talked with an attitude. In other words, I stayed close to the girls' experiences as they were lived and avoided any attempt at a description of objective reality (what "really happened").

In this research, I had expected that the participants would initiate TWA and that, as a result, their teachers would not understand, thereby resulting in conflict between the two persons. I made this assessment as a result of my observations and Kochman's (1981) work that explains that miscommunication often happens between Whites and Blacks. Instead, I found that in the world of the girls' experience, teachers started and/or escalated tense situations with the girls, making them feel like they had to talk with an attitude in order to defend themselves or to resist what they perceived to be disrespectful behavior (attacks on their cultural being).

My themes are organized in a temporal sequence—reflecting the temporal nature of lived experience. The participants' life-worlds reflected

1. their sense of being constantly exposed to a hostile school environment, which resulted in:
2. their feelings of confusion;
3. their feelings of disrespect;
4. their compulsions to talk with an attitude.

This temporal process will be described here in the form of themes.

Theme one: Living in a hostile school ecology

A constant throughout the girls' narratives is their feelings of living in a hostile ecology at their school. This perceived climate is not only a hindrance to their learning, but it also makes the girls feel uneasy and unhappy with their school. Through their words, it is evident that the girls expect school to be a safe place not only physically, but also psychologically and emotionally. Instead, they witness and receive teachers' frustrations, so the reality of the situation does not measure up to their reasonable expectations.

In her first account, Olivia described her hostile school ecology. She stated:

Um. There's this one teacher. He's my, um, Western Hemisphere teacher. I think he was racist, but he proved not to be because he treated White kids the same way. But, um, he would like whenever you would ask him a question or try to talk to him, he'd be standing right next to you and pretend like he don't hear you or whatever. He just be staring and stuff and – I don't know you just have to wait on his terms for everything. He'll be like, "Okay, I heard you," and stuff, and we'll be like, "well what are you waiting for?" I mean, like he – and he don't be doing nothing. And, he'll be like, "well wait until I get done doing what I'm doing." We be like, "So, what exactly are you doing?" and stuff. And, he just, I don't know. Nobody really likes him. And then his grading doesn't add up because when we get our progress reports, like if you had a certain grade, but all your papers at the percentages and stuff supposed to add up, so yeah my mom got on me a lot about him, but I would try to explain to her. But that might have been the class I got a bad grade in for an overall grade or whatever. And I was mad. Yeah.

In this narrative, Olivia and other students appealed to their teacher to answer their questions. Instead, they perceived him as ignoring them and only answering once he had had enough of their persistent questioning ("he'd be standing right next to you and pretend like he don't hear you"). The behavior was so offensive to Olivia that she thought that he was racist at first, which demonstrates the hostility she sensed in her school environment. This excerpt also shows how much power she attributed to the teacher and how she distrusted him ("And then his grading doesn't add up . . . but all your papers at the percentages and stuff supposed to add up . . .") She also found little relief that "he treated [the] White kids the same way." Olivia's experience is one where her teachers did not care; indeed, if anything, she found them to be going out of their way to mock and ignore them, and to hurt them by unfairly changing their grades.

Another part of the dialogue that is worth noting is her use of the word "um." Olivia seemed hesitant to share her story about her Western Hemisphere teacher ("He's my, *um*, Western Hemisphere teacher—But, *um*, he would like whenever you would ask him a question – he'd be standing right next to you and pretend like he don't hear you or whatever.") Her hesitation to share might point to a possible fear of reporting what was really happening in her school environment. As she continued to share her story, she became less hesitant demonstrating that she was more comfortable with me and in the "natural attitude," a term phenomenologist Max van Manen (1990) uses to denote this comfort in telling the whole story.

Olivia's second narrative about this same teacher also demonstrated the hostile ecology created among students. She stated that although this teacher never got an attitude directly with her, she had witnessed him getting one with another student. She recalled:

Yes. Ah, he disrespected this boy's mom. He, dang, he had got smart with the boy and then they just kept going back and forth or whatever. And, then he said something about the boy's mom and then everybody was like [gasps]. He was sort of calling her a h-o-e, but I forgot how in the terms he used it. He's like "Well, your mom blah blah blah blah blah-" something. I forgot exactly what he said, but we was like, "Oh my gosh." And we tried to protest the teacher so many times and stuff, and

the security guards they knew how he was, and they would try to tell the principal, and the principal just I don't know—He was White and she was White, so—The security guards were Black, and most of the class was Black. There was like three or four White students, but yeah, so. . . .

Olivia experiences school as a place where White people oppressed Black people. Her voice, along with other Black students and Black adults, did not matter. Her lived experience leaves one to question how she can go about learning in school with these thoughts of perceived injustice at the back of her mind.

Stephanie, another participant, also provided a narrative that described the school as a hostile place. She said about a teacher, "Like she's known for yelling. Like she's always yelling at someone or like getting mad. Like moving you or touching you. Sometimes, she can get annoying like a little kid." Notice that in Stephanie's description, she notes yelling and most notably, touching ("like moving you or touching you"), as a boundary that has been crossed. This boundary took away her feeling of safety. It is as if Stephanie, in order to get through the day, must set up a boundary around herself. When hostile teachers violate this space, feelings of strong annoyance are a result. She saw her teacher's behavior as childlike instead of demonstrating the caring adult figure she expects in this position.

When I asked Stephanie what the teacher did on one of the days that she chose to say something back to her, she said, "I kept on talking like, and she'll say, 'Go in the hallway.' I'll ask her why, and she'll be like, 'Don't argue with me.' She'll just take your stuff, and go out there. And, then sometimes, some, like – this one kid she put her hands on."

These experiences show how school can be perceived as a dangerous place. Olivia and Stephanie did not feel safe in an environment where they believed the very people who were supposed to care for them did not respect their human rights. Instead, she was left to use whatever tools she had to defend herself and survive in this environment. One of these tools was TWA, but before she used this cultural practice in this institutionalized context, she first went through this process of noting this hostile, dangerous ecology to a state of confusion. Why are people who are supposed to care for her carrying out these incidents?

Theme two: Confusion as a Result of Unmet Expectations

In American society, teachers are expected to care, or in other words, have interest and concern, for students. As alluded to earlier, the girls felt no different, and told stories of teachers blatantly disrespecting them by unjustifiably yelling at them and using sarcasm to make them feel stupid. In the stories the girls told, these teachers seemed to expect the worst from their students and were on the offensive all the time. Their lenses colored what they saw in situations, and these teachers behaved like loose cannons by blowing up and yelling at the girls and other students.

The girls were confused as a result of their unmet expectations, and they wondered why their teachers were mean, sarcastic, and angry. These students believed that they did not provoke their teachers' anger, so they were bewildered by it. They seemed to have the following questions: What would make a teacher so angry with students? Were they burned out? Did bureaucracy frustrate them? Had they been stepped one too many times by previous students and administrators? If so, these girls were not able to feel sympathy for their teachers.

Stephanie's remarks cited earlier also show confusion ("I kept on talking like, and she'll say, 'Go in the hallway.' I'll ask her *why*, and she'll be like, 'Don't argue with me.' She'll just take your stuff, and go out there"). Stephanie was unsure of why her teacher wanted her to go into the hallway. The teacher's anger seemed unnecessary, so confusion set in. Stephanie also noted that she sometimes forgot who she was talking to when using TWA with teachers. She stated, "Yeah, I got angry with some teachers—[S]he'll yell like get really loud with me. I be like, '*Okay, you don't have to get loud with me.*' I just like forget who I'm talking to sometimes. Like, I'm talking with a friend or something, and I've crossed the line." Stephanie recognized that she was talking to a teacher, an adult figure, only after she used TWA (see italics), which shows that she is confused by her teacher's behavior because she perceived it to be childlike.

Olivia gave one example of a time when she was confused: "It wasn't an argument, it was just like he got smart and like I left it alone. Sometimes, I do try to say something back because he try to make a lot of people feel so stupid and I be like "*Why you got to be like that? It doesn't take all that?*" I mean, eh [exasperation] I don't know. He try to make you feel stupid and be sarcastic and stuff." Later, as she recounted her thinking about the incidents, Olivia wondered, "Why are you [the teacher] acting like this? But he acts like that all the time." Clearly, Olivia was taken aback by her teacher's stupefying actions. In addition to her confusion, she talked with an attitude to her teacher during one of his sarcastic moments (see italics). Her account also shows that she shut down when her teacher used sarcasm ("...it was just like he got smart and like I left it alone."). Overall, Olivia felt powerless, and her questioning the teacher in TWA was the only way to regain that power. These feelings of confusion and powerlessness led to an awareness of the disrespect they felt as a result of their teachers' behaviors.

Theme three: *Living in an Environment of Disrespect*

After the girls went through the process of bewilderment as a result of their teachers' behaviors, the feelings of disrespect set in. They felt as if they were not being respected as young students, and their teachers' behaviors were unacceptable. Being yelled at without reason violated the ethic of care that they expected to receive, and it angered them. Furthermore, the girls also expressed frustration with the consistency of their teachers' actions. Olivia told me, "I just got tired of it all that time, and I would never do anything for him to act like that." Olivia learned to expect this behavior, but it did not take away her or Stephanie's frustration with experiencing the teachers' same disrespectful, angry behavior day in and day out.

Olivia stated as she recounted incidents of disrespect from the teachers, "Yeah, and I was about to ask my question. Before I got to do that, he was like 'Well, of course you have a question. That's why you raised you hand. Duh.'" This incident really seemed to bother her because she mentioned it twice in the interview. When she first mentioned this incident, she stated, "He'll *always* be sarcastic with you and stuff...he get on my nerves." Olivia recalled the frequency of the teacher's sarcasm that she interpreted as a put down. It also took a toll on her as evidenced by the statement that it "get[s] on my nerves."

Olivia later commented on a teacher yelling at her. She gave the supposition, "I may have been like, '*Well you don't have to yell at me or whatever.*'— I'd just tell him, you don't have to yell at me." One can hear her sheer frustration and hurt over this teacher's disrespect through yelling. Notice too, Olivia's use of TWA (in italics) when her teacher yelled at her. She used it to stand up for herself against her teacher. Olivia wanted the teacher to behave as a caring and respectful individual.

Olivia continued her account, "...[C]ause I remember he had said something, and he was just yelling at me like I was stupid. And, he actually called the students stupid before. He's like, 'YOU GUYS ARE SO STUPID!' or whatever—We didn't even do anything—I was like, '*You don't have to yell at me.*'" Again, Olivia used TWA (see italics) to defend herself because of behavior that offended her. She continued, "'Cause I don't like being yelled at. I really don't...you got to consider people's feelings because you don't know what they've been through or whatever." In this quote, Olivia used TWA with the teacher to assert herself.

In this same vein, Stephanie, as cited earlier, got so incensed that she forgot that she was talking to an adult who is supposed to, in her opinion, be treated with respect ("I be like, '*Okay, you don't have to get loud with me.*' I just like forget who I'm talking to sometimes. Like, I'm talking with a friend or something, and I've crossed the line."). However, when teachers crossed her boundary and showed disrespect, she forgot this principle and talked to them with an attitude.

Theme four: *My Cup Overflows – Talking with an Attitude as a Defense Mechanism*

The teachers' disrespectful behaviors of yelling and using of negative sarcasm resulted in the use of TWA that the girls knew well. However, in this instance, they used it not in play, nor as an expression of confidence, or self-esteem as noted by many older members of the AAWSC, nor as a way to shame the receiver into a spirit of camaraderie as understood by those within that community. Instead, they used it (see italicized dialogue for instances of TWA) in an institutional context to defend themselves and to regain power. Olivia explained that sometimes her teachers' negative behavior caused her cup to overflow. She stated:

> No. I try to be civilized as I can possibly be, but sometimes it's just the way they want to act toward you or if it's about a grade, I'll go up and confront them and I'll be like, "Excuse me, um, I think you

might have made a mistake." And, then I'll try to tell them and stuff and sometimes they may want to get an attitude and stuff, but I try to hold it in as much as possibly like as long as I can. Sometimes, I do.

In this instance, Olivia remembered trying to hold in her feelings and refrain from using the TWA speech practice with teachers, but as she stated, she could hold it in for only so long, so she sometimes talked with an attitude.

Olivia also shared a story of when one of her teachers yelled at her and she became withdrawn from the classroom conversation. She remembered: "I think it was just like 'UH, OLIVIA! [says in an exasperating way]' He just kept going on and on. He wasn't like, 'I wasn't yelling at you' like I expected him to say. He just kept going on and on and on about what he was talking about. *I was like why are you yelling at – I was listening, but I wasn't listening.* He was standing in front of me or whatever, and I was just like whatever and stuff, so, 'cause he yelled at me then. Um. Yeah." When this teacher yelled at Olivia, she shut down, which probably disengaged her from learning concepts that day.

Stephanie also gave examples of when her cup overflowed. As mentioned before, she stated, "*I just like forget who I'm talking to sometimes.* Like, I'm talking with a friend or something, and I've crossed the line." In this quote, Stephanie talked about forgetting to whom she is talking sometimes, which is an indication that she had had enough of the teachers' disrespectful behavior. Later, Stephanie noted that her teachers also "cross[ed] the line with [the students] too much" resulting in her use of TWA as a form of resistance.

Yet, by using this practice (which is already outside many of their teachers' cultural context), it was used as a mark against them, as is seen in the stories of these girls. They are seen as "those loud Black girls," or girls with attitude as defined by those outside of the speech community.

Consequently, the girls used TWA as a way to resist perceived oppression by their teachers. Of course, their teachers also may have viewpoints about their use of TWA, but that would go beyond the scope of this study. The purpose of this study is to hear the lived experiences of these girls and to gather meaning from it.

Concluding Thoughts

To reiterate, when I started this research, I anticipated that these girls' teachers would not understand them when they used TWA, and as a result, conflict would exist between the two. While this reasoning may still be the case, I found that their teachers, according to the girls' accounts, started the verbal duels in class. This finding was not what I anticipated, but I believe it is important to study further in order to help Black girls and teachers develop more positive relationships with each other so that learning can take place.

This research is unique in that it captures reality in a way that helps us all live more tactfully. It also gives a voice to a demographic that is often missing in the literature and lends

itself to an understanding of the perspectives of Black female adolescents. This understanding is the first step a teacher needs in order to communicate effectively with these girls who have made it clear that they feel extremely misunderstood and mistreated. The individual interviews were also strong because the girls were less distracted and could therefore focus on their own experiences instead of mimicking their peers. Although there is not much research on this topic, I am hopeful that other researchers will take it up so that Black families and educators will be better educated about ways teachers and Black girls can interact in ways that create an environment conducive for learning. I am also confident that there are already many teachers and administrators who are committed to the well-being of Black girls and are working toward helping them achieve their academic and career goals.

However, as a phenomenological study with two participants, this research is not designed to give ready-made solutions to this complex problem of teacher-student relationships when Black girls talk with an attitude. However, it puts forth the voices or lived experiences of girls who may not have had the opportunity to share their experiences otherwise. Unfortunately, the girls described a school ecology where there seemed to be no opportunities for the legitimate expression of their own voices. TWA seems to be their only opportunity to use voice, and then, it was used as a defense mechanism. Using the phenomenological method gave the participants the opportunity to use voice in a way that affirmed them because of the value I placed upon their accounts. All in all, much can be learned from their voices as we evaluate our teaching and develop appropriate relationships with our marginalized students.

This study is important to me, not only because of its implications for educators, but also because of its impact on me as a Black female educator. I hope this research impacts others like me and of other races to pay attention to Black girls and take the time to talk with them and knowledgeable others who can help facilitate appropriate classroom practice.

As mentioned earlier, phenomenology seeks to give meaning to our everyday experiences in this lifeworld, and does not attend to certain social groups, cultures, and so on, so the meanings gathered from the study are not exclusive to African American adolescent girls. The lessons can be applied to all genders and races. For example, many students, regardless of race or gender, have been victims of disrespect by teachers. The great thing about phenomenology is that it notes the importance of the phenomenon to the individual or specialized group, but some aspects of the experience could have universally-shared meanings. This point implies that there is something for everyone to learn from this research. Another important lesson is for teachers to reflect and make sure they are teaching empathically. Ensuring empathic pedagogy may not only reduce teaching problems, but also foster an understanding about how all students experience school.

Albeit, for this cultural group, we must recognize that navigating when and how to talk with an attitude may be challenging for African American adolescent girls. These particular students may lack mainstream society's cultural and social capital, which they could use to make their voices heard and resist hegemonic practices in public school classrooms. These girls are in a position in which they have access to this speech practice and appropriate it in ways different from its cultural import because they feel disempowered. The solution lies in the voices of these girls, and educators should listen to them in order to evaluate the stance with which they take them. When teachers step back and reflect upon their practices, perhaps things could improve for both parties.

References

Attitude. (2010). In *Oxford English Dictionary Online* (2nd ed.). Retrieved from http://www.oed.com.proxy2.cl.msu.edu/view/Entry/12876?redirectedFrom=attitude#

Battle-Walters, K. (2004). *Sheila's shop: Working-class African American women talk about life, love, race, and hair.* Lanham, MD: Rowman & Littlefield.

Collins, P. H. (1990). Toward an Afrocentric feminist epistemology. In P.H. Collins (Ed.), *Black feminist thought* (pp. 201–220). Boston, MA: Unwin Hyman.

Cooper, A.J. (1892/1998). The status of woman in America. In C. Lemert & E. Bhan (Eds.), *The voice of Anna Julia Cooper: Including a voice from the South and other important essays, papers, and letters* (pp. 109–117). Lanham, MD: Rowman & Littlefield.

Creswell, J.W. (2007). *Qualitative inquiry and research design: Choosing among five approaches* (2nd ed.). Thousand Oaks, CA: Sage.

Delpit, L. (1995). *Other people's children: Cultural conflict in the classroom.* New York, NY: The New Press.

Du Bois, W.E.B. (1903/1994). *The souls of Black folk.* New York, NY: Dover.

Evans, G. (1980). Those loud Black girls. In D. Spender & E. Sarah (Eds.), *Learning to lose: Sexism and education* (pp. 183–190). London, England: The Women's Press.

Fordham, S. (1993). "Those loud Black girls": (Black) women, silence, and gender "passing" in the academy. *Anthropology and Education Quarterly, 24*(1), 3–32.

Gann, C., Hutchison, C., & James, S. (2012, June 22). North Carolina Senate denies funds for sterilization victims. *ABC Good Morning America.* Retrieved from http://abcnews.go.com/Health/WomensHealth/north-carolina-senate-blocks-compensation-sterilization-victims-eugenics/story?id=16628515#.UDqliUQYIb1

Giles, M. (2006). Special focus: Dr. Anna Julia Cooper, 1858-1964: Teacher, scholar, and timeless womanist. *The Journal of Negro Education, 75*(4), 621–634.

Heidegger, M. (1927/1962/2006). *Being and time.* J. Macquarrie & E. Robinson (Trans.). Malden, MA: Blackwell.

Kochman, T. (1981). *Black and White styles in conflict.* Chicago, IL: The University of Chicago Press.

Ladson-Billings, G. (1994). *The dreamkeepers: Successful teachers of African American children.* San Francisco, CA: Jossey-Bass.

Downey, M. (2012, January 30). Arizona bans teaching courses that breed resentment of a race or class of people or advocate ethnic solidarity [Web log post]. *The Atlanta Journal-Constitution.* Retrieved from http://blogs.ajc.com/get-schooled-blog/2012/01/30/arizona-bans-teaching-courses-that-breed-resentment-of-a-race-or-class-of-people-or-advocate-ethnic-solidarity/

Mitchell-Kernan, C. (1972). Signifying, loud-talking and marking. In T. Kochman (Ed.), *Rappin' and stylin' out: Communication in urban Black America* (pp. 315–335). Urbana: University of Illinois Press.

Morgan, M. (2002). *Language, discourse and power in African American culture.* Cambridge, UK: Cambridge University Press.

Morris, E. W. (2007). "Ladies" or "loudies"?: Perceptions and experiences of Black girls in classrooms. *Youth & Society, 38*(4), 490–515.

Orbe, M., Drummond, D., & Camara, S. (2002). Phenomenology and Black feminist thought: Exploring African American women's everyday encounters as points of contention. In M. Houston & O. Davis (Eds.), *Centering ourselves: African American feminist and womanist studies of discourse* (pp. 123–143). Cresskill, NJ: Hampton Press.

Pough, G.D. (2004). *Check it while I wreck it: Black womanhood, hip hop culture, and the public sphere.* Boston, MA: Northeastern University Press.

Richardson, E. (2003). *African American literacies.* New York, NY: Routledge.

T Volscho. (2007, September 22). Sterilization and women of color [Web log post]. *Racism Review.* Retrieved from http://www.racismreview.com/blog/2007/09/22/sterilization-and-women-of-color/

Troutman, D. (2001). African American women: Talking that talk. In S. Lanehart (Ed.), *Sociocultural and historical contexts of African American English* (pp. 211–237). Amsterdam: Benjamins.

Troutman, D. (2010). Attitude and its situatedness in linguistic politeness. *Poznan Studies in Contemporary Linguistics, 46*(1), 85–109.

Van Manen, M. (1990). *Researching lived experience: Human science for an action sensitive pedagogy.* London, England: The University of Western Ontario.

Critical Thinking

1. What is TWA, what are the causes of TWA, and what are the effects of TWA?
2. What is double-consciousness and how does it impact students?
3. How can teachers cope with TWA and double-consciousness?
4. How can teachers give voice to students from underrepresented populations?

Create Central

www.mhhe.com/createcentral

Internet References

National Association for Multicultural Education (NAME)
www.nameorg.org

National Black Child Development Institute
www.nbedi.org

JACQUELINE B. KOONCE is a doctoral student in Curriculum, Instruction, and Teacher Education at Michigan State University.

Koonce, J. B. (2012). Journal of Language and Literacy Education [Online], 8(2), 26–46. Available at http://jolle.coe.uga.edu/wp-content/uploads/2012/06/Loud-Black-Girls.pdf

Developing Collective Classroom Efficacy: The Teacher's Role as Community Organizer by LeAnn G. Putney and Suzanne H. Broughton

253

Article

Prepared by: Nancy P. Gallavan, *University of Central Arkansas*

Developing Collective Classroom Efficacy: The Teacher's Role as Community Organizer

LeAnn G. Putney and Suzanne H. Broughton

Learning Outcomes

After reading this article, you will be able to:

- Understand the meaning and sources of self-efficacy.
- Explore the research of Vygotsky.

Scenario of a fifth-grade classroom:

As a university researcher who became the resident classroom ethnographer in Ms. Falls's fifth-grade classroom, I entered the classroom on a day in mid-October with a visiting faculty candidate who was interested in seeing the classroom in action. The students were in reading groups, pouring over their assigned novels. After introducing the visitor to Ms. Falls, we went to sit in the back of the room, just to observe.

We were approached by Bethany who offered to introduce us to the class, and who asked Ms. Falls if it was ok to tell the visitor about their reading response activities. Ms. Falls agreed, and the students began to talk about the various kinds of reading response formats. What was common to all of these students was that they had to become the characters and perform the ideas from the novels they were reading. As they were trying to explain, Beto exclaimed, "This is too hard to explain, we need to just do it!" Bethany agreed and called for "Fishbowl" with the group reading *Pedro's Journal.*

Immediately the group sprang into action, moving chairs to the center of the room. Beto assigned students to sit in close as they were the "evaluators" of the performance. Ms. Falls reminded the others that they were to get ready to ask "probing questions." Jaz said, "You know, the kind of questions that make us say 'why' something happened." As the students continued into their performance, I caught the look from our visitor that indicated

something special was happening here. On our way out of the school, she asked, "How did that group of kids get to be so independent that they could just take control of their learning in that way?"

The question posed by the visitor to this classroom creates an interesting area of inquiry related to classroom instruction and learning. As part of an ongoing ethnographic study with this classroom teacher, we noted that in each of the four years studied the participants constructed a community in which student responsibility appeared to be central to the learning environment. At the same time, this was not the first person visiting the classroom who expressed admiration for the way the "class runs itself."

In sifting through the research journals of the resident classroom ethnographer, we read such comments anecdotally from other visitors she had taken into the classroom, from other classroom teachers at the same school, from the principal of the school, from substitute teachers who left notes to the teacher, and in interviews with preservice teachers. The bigger questions for us as researchers at that moment became, how did this sense of collective responsibility develop over time, and how was it promoted through participation in classroom activities? Was the sense of responsibility and belonging also related in any way to collective efficacy?

The central tenets of collective efficacy relate to how well group members respond and relate to one another as they work toward common goals. They also relate to the resilience of a group and the willingness of group members to continue to work through difficult situations (Goddard, Hoy, & Hoy, 2004). Knowing these central tenets led us to question whether collective efficacy could be examined through a sociocultural lens, which focuses on the learning and development of individuals through their participation in a cultural collective. Could using a Vygotskian (1986) approach provide a means to demonstrate how teachers and students establish a cohesive sense of responsibility toward their learning and toward each other that result in performance capability?

Our intention is to examine collective classroom efficacy as a construct that is socially constructed and that develops over time between members in a classroom context. To do so we needed to combine the initial construct of student self-efficacy and collective efficacy from Bandura's (1997) work with a perspective that allows us to examine collective functioning from its genesis to its realization, which Vygotsky provides. It is as if we were shining two spotlights from different angles onto the same stage to better illuminate what the classroom participants are playing out through their dialogic interactions.

Sociocultural Theory

A Vygotskian perspective allows us to understand learning and development of the individual as part of a collective. One goal of a sociocultural approach is to make visible relationships between human mental functioning and the cultural, institutional, and historical situations in which this functioning occurs (Wertsch, del Rio, & Alvarez, 1995). Hence, the individual is as much part of the collective as the collective is made up of individuals.

Vygotsky's representation of development presumes "two dimensions of development: one that resides in the individual and the other in the collectivity" (Souza-Lima, 1995, pp. 447–448). Thus, development is not linear, nor is it totally predictable. Learning and development are in a reflexive relationship that is recursive, transformational, and primarily socially enacted. In other words, it involves a transformation of people and the world as they know it through productive activity. In this sense, knowing means to purposefully change the world and oneself, whereas knowledge is the practice of change rather than merely a discrete body of facts, concepts, or rules that can be transferred from one situation to another (Vygotsky, 1978, 1986).

Neo-Vygotskian scholars have examined the notion of distributed cognition to suggest that "human thinking is not reducible to individual properties or traits. Instead, it is always mediated and distributed among persons, artifacts, activities, and settings" (Moll, 2000, p. 265). Along with the construct of distributed cognition, the work of Lave and Wenger (1991) examined how learners in a community of practice shared in the learning process. From their framework of legitimate peripheral participation, learning occurs as newcomers participate in various peripheral roles alongside more experienced or competent members in community practice. In their work together, the less experienced members gradually become able to fully participate in such contexts. As related by Mercer (2000), sociocultural psychologists have primarily examined the shared thinking of adults and children to determine its influence on individual children's development. He suggests that "we should also try to explain children's development as *interthinkers*" by examining how experienced community members act as "discourse guides" as they guide novices into "ways of using language for thinking collectively" (Mercer, 2000, p. 170).

In his construct of the zone of proximal development, Vygotsky (1978) theorized that participants working together to solve a problem are able to accomplish collaboratively what they would not yet be able to do on their own. It is through their dialogic work that classroom participants provide opportunity for students to reformulate problems and possible solutions in their own words. What began as a collective work has the potential to be transformed as students actively internalize the common language and knowledge of the collective. In other words, students who are working together on a shared text in an inquiry-based situation have the opportunity to construct knowledge that has potential for becoming both collective knowledge as well as individual knowledge (Edwards & Mercer, 1987; John-Steiner & Meehan, 2000; Mercer, 2000; Putney, Green, Dixon, Duran, & Yeager, 2000). This pedagogical stance offers opportunities for education to be an avenue for creating a classroom culture in which all students can contribute to the collective knowledge and development (Bruner, 1986). Likewise, this pedagogical stance offers opportunities for a classroom culture in which students can develop self- and collective efficacy. As suggested by Wheatley (2005), researchers can more closely examine this process through direct observation and dialogic interpretation as opposed to self-report surveys.

Self- and Collective Efficacy

Researchers have studied at length the influence of self-efficacy on academic achievement (Bandura, 1993; Goddard, Hoy, & Woolfolk Hoy, 2000; Schunk, 1990), including math and reading achievement (Pajares, 2001; Pajares & Valiante, 2006). In addition, efficacy researchers have focused on the efficacious beliefs of a group and how those beliefs affect performance (cf. Goddard & Goddard, 2001; Tschannen-Moran, Woolfolk Hoy, & Hoy, 1998). Much of this research at the collective level has investigated teacher beliefs for schoolwide student achievement.

However, as noted by Wheatley (2005), several gaps exist in the literature on teacher and collective efficacy. One area that has not yet been closely examined, but is of importance to the present study, is the view that efficacy is a continuous variable, developing over time, rather than a dichotomous, all-or-nothing variable. Another gap is the focus on how to use the efficacy literature in a way that enhances teacher education and the subsequent impact on classroom pedagogy. Also missing from the efficacy research is the opportunity for more democratic teaching practices to be understood. Wheatley (2005) asserted,

> As it is currently operationalized, collective teacher efficacy measures do not clearly assess the co-construction of teaching and learning. Thus, while many "democratic" approaches to education portray some social distribution of agency in teaching, neither teacher efficacy nor collective teacher efficacy measures explicitly assess such agency. (p. 754)

By focusing on how the teacher helps students develop a sense of collective responsibility and belief in their accomplishments, we may begin to help fill one gap in the literature on how collective classroom efficacy can be developed and enhanced through collective action on the part of the classroom members.

In what follows we briefly describe some of the seminal work on self-efficacy in academic settings as well as the more contemporary research on teacher and collective efficacy at the school level. What has been less well defined is the construct of collective efficacy at the micro level of the classroom, which we are calling collective classroom efficacy. The purpose of this study is to begin to explore collective classroom efficacy and how it can be developed and facilitated by the classroom participants. By examining discursive classroom interactions, we will make visible how teachers' instructional practice can promote collective classroom efficacy.

Self-Efficacy

Self-efficacy, as conceptualized by Bandura (1997), is a belief in one's capabilities to organize and accomplish a given task. Students possessing high levels of perceived self-efficacy are more likely to persevere through challenging activities, demonstrate resilience to adversity, have high aspirations, and believe they can accomplish a task (Bandura, 1993; Schunk, 1995). Thus, self-efficacy is task specific and is based in part on past experience. In addition, self-efficacy is linked closely to initial task engagement, persistence, analytical thinking, and successful performance (Bandura, 1993; Pajares, 1996). Compared with less efficacious students, those higher in self-efficacy are more likely to select challenging tasks, expend more effort, and persist when encountering difficulties (Bandura, 1997; Pajares, 1996).

Schunk (2003) cautions that self-efficacy is one of multiple factors influencing academic achievement. When students lack the requisite skills and knowledge, high self-efficacy will not necessarily result in academic achievement. In addition, motivation researchers have found that students who view ability as being changeable with effort and who focus on learning goals rather than on proving their ability to others do not rely on confidence (Dweck, 2000). In other words, students with low efficacy beliefs who also believe that ability can be changed with effort are often just as persistent as those with more confidence (Dweck & Leggett, 1988).

Sources of Self-Efficacy

Bandura (1997) illustrated four sources of self-efficacy: enactive mastery experience, vicarious experience, verbal persuasion, and psychological and affective states. First, enactive mastery experiences are those that provide the most authentic evidence of individual success that then build the belief in personal efficacy. Mastery does not presume that all experiences are immediately successful. Rather, facing some difficulties, enactive mastery experiences can result in resilience with opportunities to learn how to exercise better control over events by encouraging perseverance.

As a second source, vicarious experiences (Bandura, 1997) are those in which individuals may rely on modeling from more proficient others to improve their own capabilities. Although individuals attempt to maintain a sense of efficacy during a struggle with difficulties, it may be easier to do so if others use the third source, verbal persuasion, to encourage the individual to continue in the task. Through verbal persuasion, individuals

may try harder to succeed if the positive appraisal is realistic and they believe that they will be able to produce positive effects through their efforts.

The fourth source of self-efficacy, physiological and affective states, recognizes that people can actually produce a negative performance through their stress reactions to a situation (Bandura, 1997). For example, if students can be persuaded to control emotional reactions through mastery experiences that demonstrate their capabilities, they will be less likely to feel vulnerable in a testing situation. These four sources relate to self-efficacy on an individual basis; however, researchers have expanded their investigations of self-efficacy to examine efficacy as a group construct. In what follows we unfold the definition of collective efficacy as it has been identified currently by researchers.

Collective Efficacy

The construct of self-efficacy has expanded to include individual teacher efficacy and collective efficacy, which focuses on "the performance capability of a social system as a whole" (Bandura, 1997, p. 469). Similar to self-efficacy, collective efficacy relates to the goals of a group and how well members of the group work together toward those goals (Goddard et al., 2004). Collective efficacy also has been associated with the group's resilience and willingness to persist in difficult situations (Goddard, 2002; Goddard & Goddard, 2001; Tschannen-Moran et al., 1998; Woolfolk & Hoy, 1990).

Since collective efficacy has been translated at a school level to individual teachers' judgments concerning the faculty's ability to plan effectively and implement lessons that result in positive student achievement (Goddard, 2001), we now refer to this construct as teacher collective efficacy beliefs. The emphasis of that research has been to identify characteristics and resulting relationships of teachers and schools with high levels of collective efficacy. Although these studies examined teachers' beliefs about their ability to have a positive impact on student academic achievement at a schoolwide level, the measures did not examine whether teachers worked together in a synergistic effort to accomplish that goal (Wheatley, 2005). An additional gap in the teacher collective efficacy beliefs literature is that these studies did not include an examination of the synergistic relationship of teachers and students in classrooms. In general, these sources of self-efficacy relate to the individual and the individual's responses in particular situations according to Bandura's perspective.

Analogous to this rich body of research on teacher collective efficacy beliefs at the macro or school level is the potential of examining how individuals at the micro or classroom level operate both personally and collectively in terms of these sources of self-efficacy. As asserted by Bandura (1993) in studying Vygotsky (1962), "Children's intellectual development cannot be isolated from the social relations within which it is embedded and from its interpersonal effects. It must be analyzed from a social perspective" (p. 120). Therefore, in this research we explore the genesis of collective classroom efficacy through dialogic activities among classroom participants in their social setting.

Teacher as Guide and Community Organizer

To understand the synergistic relationship among teachers and students as it relates to collective classroom efficacy, we need to make visible the role of the teacher in setting expectations for classroom interactions. Vygotsky advocated for the role of the teacher to be one of instructional guide in a classroom in which the teacher and students are active with one another through the curriculum (Vygotsky, 1997). In a similar fashion, Goddard and Goddard (2001) described the role of highly efficacious teachers as one of helping students arrive at appropriate answers without giving them the answer directly. In addition, highly efficacious teachers utilize activities that foster positive affect while promoting high expectations for achievement (Ashton & Webb, 1986). Bandura (1997) noted the role of community organizer in terms of collective efficacy, stating,

> The role of a community organizer is not to solve people's problems for them but to help develop their capabilities to operate as a continuing potent force for bettering their lives and upholding their sense of self-worth and dignity. The organizer serves as the community enabler rather than as the implementer of action plans. (p. 501)

The initial task of community organizer is to select and develop local leaders to unite the collective for a common cause. In the case of democratic classrooms, students serve as local leaders, and the common cause is overall academic achievement and responsibility for self and others. The collective establishes a social community that shapes its efforts to achieve its common academic and personal goals. One primary task of the classroom community organizer is to construct a self-directing collective that unifies, enables, and motivates its participants to recognize that many of their academic issues are shared issues that can be alleviated primarily by working together. Also important is the ability of the classroom community organizer to establish a learning environment where warm interpersonal relationships are constructed throughout the academic and social activities (Ashton & Webb, 1986). Our goal is to illustrate ways in which the classroom teacher becomes classroom community organizer, especially as relating to the development of collective classroom efficacy.

Research Questions

In this article, our purpose is to examine collective classroom efficacy during the classroom collaborative activities and through the interactional discourse, with the teacher in the role of community organizer. As indicated by Moll (2000) normative research often does not capture all of the diversity of life. Indeed, Vygotsky (1986) argued,

> Psychology cannot limit itself to direct evidence. . . . Psychological inquiry is investigation, and like the criminal investigator, the psychologist must take into account indirect evidence and circumstantial clues—which in practice means that works of art, philosophical arguments and anthropological data are no less important for psychology than direct evidence. (pp. xv–xvi)

Furthermore, Gumperz (2003) argued that survey research attempts to measure objectively constructs such as self- and collective efficacy. However, survey research produces self-report data and does not allow for understanding the dynamic and interactive classroom context surrounding those individuals. In examining classroom key events, we make visible what participants place in the public sphere through their talk and actions. When examined through focused ethnographic inquiry, across events and over time, we begin to build "replicable information on relevant beliefs and values" (Gumperz, 2003, p. 215). These interactions among classroom participants have the potential to make visible a classroom version of collective efficacy as a construct associated with how classroom members view themselves within their classroom collective and in relation to their learning and development with one another.

Our research question to unfold the social construction of collective classroom efficacy was, in what ways can collective classroom efficacy be evidenced through an ethnographic inquiry of interactional discourse? More specifically, how does collective classroom efficacy develop with the teacher as classroom community organizer and students as local leaders?

Method

Participants and Setting

The data for this exploration were culled from an extensive ethnographic data set from one teacher's fifth-grade classroom over four years. The orienting approach of interactional ethnography was selected to frame the study and to make visible the constructed patterns of beliefs and practices over the length of the academic year (Castanheira, Crawford, Green, & Dixon, 2000; Putney et al., 2000). Interactional ethnography also contains a component of sociolinguistic and critical discourse analysis, which makes it possible to examine how these beliefs and practices were constructed in particular moments by members.

The first author was the resident university ethnographer during those four years. The classroom in which this study took place was in an elementary (K-5) public school in partnership with, and located at, an urban university in the southwestern United States. At the time of the data collection, the school was conducted as a year-round school, meaning that the school calendar started the fourth week of August and ran until the second week of August of the next year. Students and teachers were assigned to one of five calendar-based tracks (time periods) that were scheduled to run with periodic three-week breaks scheduled throughout the year.

Of the school's nearly 900 students, 85% were participating in the free and/or reduced lunch program. The official transience rate was 65%, with a school population of 50% Hispanic, 29% Anglo-American, 14% African American, 6% Asian, 1% Native American, 15% special education, and 46% limited English proficient. The particular classroom selected also reflected these

Table 1   Domain Analysis: X Is What Teacher Holds Constant in the Classroom Setting

Classroom management	Class election of executive council
Personal accountability	Constructing a class constitution
	Constructing norms
	Authentic class jobs
	Team and individual responsibilities
	Work ethic rubric
	Role models for the school
	Really getting to know each other
	Goal setting and extending
	Bottomliners—respect, responsibility, caring, collaboration
Teacher role	Guide
	Leader
	Facilitator
	Initiator
Student role	Problem solving
	Asking probing questions
	Clarifying for each other
	Supporting ideas with evidence
	Negotiating meaning
	Valuing and supporting each other
	Responsibly governing

demographics. The teacher in this classroom, Ms. Falls, had more than 10 years of experience in urban elementary classroom settings and was well known by her colleagues as a teacher who incorporated inclusive practices with excellent classroom management techniques.

Data Analysis

The classroom events in the four year data set had been videotaped on a regular basis: daily for the first three weeks of the school year then at least twice monthly thereafter. At the teacher's request, additional videotaping, interviewing, and data sessions took place to capture particular classroom activities. Anecdotal evidence across the four years suggested that this classroom teacher was consistently successful in fostering a strong sense of interdependence among students as an avenue in building a democratic classroom. For example, we encountered comments about how well the "class ran itself" from classroom visitors, other classroom teachers at the same school, the principal, and substitute teachers who left notes to the classroom teacher and in interviews with preservice teachers.

In examining the entire data set, we looked for evidence beyond the anecdotal data that could theoretically illustrate the construct of interest to us, collective classroom efficacy. After selecting the data set from Year 4 as a telling case, or one that makes visible a theoretical construct (Mitchell, 1984), we

further examined that data set for examples that illustrated different elements of collective classroom efficacy. We selected the classroom as the unit of analysis because from a Vygotskian perspective, development takes place both as an individual as well as collective process. In addition, we were examining interactions among teacher and students that added to the knowledge base of both individuals and the collective unit as suggested by Edwards and Mercer (1987).

We examined field notes, interview transcripts, and video data to construct the telling case of developing collective classroom efficacy. We relied on various formats of triangulation. In one aspect of triangulation, the data analysis consisted of utilizing both primary and secondary researchers (Putney & Broughton, 2007). The first author as classroom ethnographer could bring forward the context of the classroom because of her past experience of researching with the classroom teacher. The secondary researcher brought forward her expertise as a former classroom teacher as well as her researcher lens in examining data that she did not collect but with which she became highly familiar. Bringing together these distinct yet complementary angles of vision allowed us to validate the findings and co-construct the telling case through our dialogic interactions about the data.

A second aspect of triangulation involved juxtaposing different forms of data from the data set. For example, we purposefully selected an interview with the teacher that revealed her teaching philosophy. We then chose a segment of classroom interaction from the first days of school involving the teacher and students discussing the construction of the classroom norms that reflected her democratic teaching philosophy. To examine more closely the democratic interdependence among classroom participants, we chose a particular activity, Visible and Invisible Walls, as a series of discursive events in one related content area of social studies. This multileveled analysis demonstrates the format of instruction, the teacher role and expectations, and participant interactions as a form of triangulation.

The field notes and transcripts were coded for evidence of the co-construction of collective classroom efficacy through both interpersonal and academic events. Juxtaposing the social skill building against the academic knowledge building within key classroom events becomes what we are calling dialogic triangulation. This micro analysis makes visible the potential for co-construction of the interdependence and shared academic knowledge among classroom participants.

The ethnographic data across four years with this classroom teacher indicate that she held certain classroom values constant as cornerstones of her curriculum and classroom management. At the same time the particular content changed each year as students jointly constructed knowledge together in the classroom. The domain analysis (Table 1) illustrates the values related to classroom management, personal accountability, teacher role, and student role that the teacher held in common across the four years.

As part of her role as community organizer, the teacher gradually shifted the classroom management over time from teacher-driven to a student-led governance system in which they jointly constructed their norms for living and working together. Although the community each year began to solidify by the third week of school, they continually reviewed their norms and assessed their behavior and their academic work on a regular basis using a "work ethic rubric" scale from zero to four (Putney, 2007). By keeping these classroom values constant, the teacher maintained a classroom style that supported a strong community identity through personal and academic accountability.

Although the value of student governance stayed relatively constant across the four years, what changed year by year was the curricular focus of the major classroom project. These projects consisted of conducting classroom businesses in Years 1 and 2, with a shift in focus to an interest apprenticeship program in Year 3 in which students worked with local community mentors to improve their artistic skills. The focus in Year 4, illustrated in this article, was Visible and Invisible Walls: Examining Tolerance, to examine the use of walls throughout history to oppress people. Across the four years, even though the curricular focus changed, what did not change was the teacher's insistence that students work together responsibly to construct their learning.

We selected Year 4 because of the richness of the data set in relation to the construct of classroom collective efficacy. We surveyed data across the year and initially constructed domains of activity that related to the following themes: developing classroom community, establishing norms, teacher role, student role, life skills (respect, responsibility, caring, and collaboration), types of learning activities, and developing tolerance. From the initial domains, we further analyzed the data to see what the elements within the domains had in common. The common elements formed into subsets that we placed into tree diagrams or taxonomies, in particular one related to participant roles that subsumed both domains of teacher and student roles.

As we examined the teacher role in more detail, we began to notice a trend supporting Bandura's notion of the role of community organizer as part of collective classroom efficacy. These roles included developing self-improvement capabilities, upholding sense of self-worth and dignity, serving as the community facilitator, constructing a self-directing collective, promoting unity, and motivating interdependence in solving shared issues. Although Bandura initiated the construct of community organizer in a more global sense, we could see the application of such at the classroom level. In the results section, we illustrate how the teacher in the classroom was enacting the characteristics of community organizer while promoting individual and collective learning and development (Putney et al., 2000; Vygotsky, 1986). We further examined the synergistic effort among classroom participants in co-constructing an interdependent classroom community.

Results

We examined the role of teacher as community organizer because this role is central to fostering a sense of collective among the individual members of the group (Bandura, 1997). Data from an interview with the teacher about her teaching philosophy illustrated her role as a classroom community organizer. As detailed by Bandura, a community organizer is one who does not seek to solve people's problems. What the community organizer does is to foster capabilities of the members by promoting self-worth and dignity. The community organizer must also foster local leaders who can unite the collective for a common cause. In the case of Ms. Falls, we quickly recognized her take-up of the role of community organizer, as will be made visible in the following excerpt from her interview:

> This is my definition, based on what I do. My classroom is one that develops, nurtures, and extends the social and academic potentials and interests of all members within the class. It is a place that encourages autonomy, respect, and accountability through active participation with our diverse environment. [My classroom] values what one thinks, cares how one feels, and supports student learning experiences. . . . Let the children develop the life skills authentically. Respect is giving it, expecting it, not about writing a poem. You can write a poem, yes, but live it! The ones I really insist they have from day one are *respect, responsibility, cooperation,* and *caring.*

This excerpt reveals the primary emphasis on social and academic success of the individuals within the classroom as well as for the collective in general, which is a central tenet of the construct of collective classroom efficacy. In addition, this construct consists of a goal orientation, which Ms. Falls facilitates among the students in the collective by encouraging autonomy, building respect, and expecting accountability at both the individual and collective levels. The way in which she claims to promote achievement of these goals is by having students actively participating in authentic activities that foster life skills. This is brought forward in her statement that respect is not just talked about and enacted but actually lived throughout their school experience. Expectations are that students will live this within her classroom as well as in other academic and social contexts. Ms. Falls's claims and expectations that emanate from her philosophy are evidenced throughout the following analytic segments.

Norms and Work Ethic Rubric

From a prior ethnographic study of this classroom (Putney, 2007), we recognize that Ms. Falls commonly established a social structure in which students made responsible choices about how they would work to become productive classroom citizens. Through the norms and work ethic rubric, she established a social framework or set of practices that required students to demonstrate responsibility toward self and others while becoming academically proficient.

Following her own philosophy and as the classroom community organizer, Ms. Falls co-constructed classroom norms with her students beginning the first day of the school year. As she stated to students at the onset of the norm construction activity, "We don't have rules, boys and girls, we have norms. Norms are ways that people live and work together. These become our guidelines for how we will act in this classroom community" (Field notes, Day 2 of school). When she began the discussion about what the norms might be, she reminded students of her "bottomliners" of respect, responsibility, caring, and collaboration. They constructed norms related to listening with respect; being responsible, organized, and persevering; and respecting opinions of others and believing that you can do whatever you need to do if you follow through (Putney, 2007).

The norms constructed by the students in this case highlighted the notion of continuing to work toward their goals by emphasizing "persevere at all times" to Norm 2 that related to being responsible and organized from the previous year. Recall that a central tenet of efficacy is one's belief in the ability to attain a goal, no matter how challenging. By emphasizing the notion of perseverance, the students were establishing the foundation for developing academic efficacy through their everyday work together. Although the norms were individually directed, they also became collectively oriented as students used them to encourage one another to respect everyone's opinions and to carry on when the work was difficult. The following excerpts make visible how the teacher continued in her role of community organizer to foster a sense of collective efficacy among the individual members of the group.

Self-Worth, Unity, and Interdependence

"Take an intelligent risk . . . we should learn and stretch ourselves. Is that what I hear you saying?" (Ms. Falls, field notes, Day 2 of class). Ms. Falls consistently encouraged her students to take academic risks as a central feature of building collective efficacy in this classroom. In her role of classroom community organizer, Ms. Falls set the expectation that students would take an intelligent risk when participating in learning activities. At the same time, she held the expectation that students would contribute to the knowledge base by helping each other solve common issues.

The first example is one that we deemed typical of the type of interactions that took place in this classroom over the year. A common classroom practice was for students to review their norms each morning to monitor their progress in constructively working together. A new student, Jordan, had just transferred in to the school. In this excerpt the discourse reveals a common practice of students inviting each other to take a risk and participate in the learning activity with the more knowledgeable other offering assistance. The excerpt begins with the Mayor, Jaz, calling on a new student, Jordan, to explain one of the norms that they review in class each morning.

In leading the discussion, Jaz encouraged Jordan to take a risk and make sense of one of the norms (Table 2, Lines 105–108) and then offered assistance from a more experienced other in the class if he could not provide an answer (110–111). Once Jordan offered an explanation (112–113), David acknowledged Jordan's response (114) and offered additional information for the class (115–117). From a Vygotskian perspective, this is an example of intersubjectivity as classroom members offered explanations for the benefit of all in the collective to take up and use individually in making meaning from the text under discussion.

In the beginning days of constructing this classroom culture, this type of incident would have been initiated by the teacher in her role as classroom community organizer. By the time that this example occurred (six weeks into the first semester), the students were enacting the expectations established collectively during the first days of school. When the new student, Jordan, struggled to answer a question, Jaz encouraged him to ask for "a lifesaver." To be a lifesaver, you would first have to be actively listening so that you could offer a potential answer to the relevant question put before the class. As a lifesaver, it was expected that you would not say that a person was wrong because that would stop them from learning. Instead, students (as in the case of David above) were expected to build on what the other person said so that their answer added to the discussion while taking nothing away from the other students.

Table 2   Taking a Risk

Actor	Line	Dialogue	Vygotskian construct
Jaz	105	Jordan	Personalizing the learning; invoking historicity in reviewing the norms each day; connecting learning day to day
	106	can you please explain norm number two	
	107	don't say can't	
	108	you can do it if you put your mind to it	
Jordan	109	[hesitates before attempting an answer]	New student maybe has not yet internalized completely
Jaz	110	you can ask for a lifesaver Jordan	More knowledgeable other may assist if needed
	111	but first try it on your own	
Jordan	112	if you say you can do it	Offers explanation to the extent he has made sense of the idea
	113	you can	
David	114	adding to what Jordan just said	Offers additional information to be considered; puts ideas in the intersubjective space for all to access if they choose
	115	if you say you can't do something	
	116	then you send a message to your mind	
	117	that stops you from learning	

The concept of lifesaver utilizes three of the features of community organizers. It serves the purpose of upholding students' sense of self-worth and dignity while also promoting unity and motivating interdependence in solving shared issues (Bandura, 1997). What is evident in this interchange among Jaz, Jordan, and David is that the students have embraced the concept of lifesaver and used it themselves in their discussions. They acknowledged that a newer student might not have a complete understanding of the question posed; however, they encouraged him to take an intelligent risk while still offering the option to request assistance (lifesaver) from another student. In addition, David extended the answer given by Jordan, thus he upheld the others' sense of trust while working interdependently in solving shared issues. The discourse suggests that taking intelligent risks and striving to establish and maintain trust during classroom activities contribute to the development of collective classroom efficacy.

The developmental aspect of collective classroom efficacy is made visible by following the concept of lifesaver throughout the academic year as a tracer unit (Putney et al., 2000). In the following excerpt, we further illustrate how the concept of lifesaver actually occurred during a classroom academic discussion (in the 10th week of school) surrounding a topic that had been introduced the day prior. In this example, a question was posed to the students related to a new word, *perpetrator.* The teacher posed the question, and when the answers given were acknowledged as approaching the appropriate answer, a female student (Tanya) suggested that a lifesaver was perhaps in order (Table 3).

As in the previous example, we recognize that the students have accepted the concept of lifesaver as being an appropriate way to answer a question when someone is searching for the meaning of the question. In this excerpt, the student, Tanisha, acknowledged that Matthew's answer is approaching the meaning of the word, perpetrator (Line 233). Ms. Falls encouraged Matthew (234–236) to continue his line of thinking by rephrasing the question (237–239). When he hesitated to answer, Tanya offered the possibility of using a lifesaver (240). The teacher acknowledged the request for a lifesaver and sought someone to take on the role (241). When Adriana raised her hand, Tanya called on her to offer an answer (242), with the teacher offering encouragement (246).

Table 3 Calling for a Lifesaver in Week 10

Actor	Line	Dialogue	Research comments
Ms. Falls	225	What's a perpetrator?	Teacher linking back to prior day's discussion
Jamal	226	Is that a traitor?	Jamal attempts although absent day prior
Ms. Falls	227	Not quite, not quite	Teacher signaling need for another response, nods toward Matthew
	228	A perpetrator	
Matthew	229	What I think a perpetrator is	Matthew uses terms from prior day's discussion but not quite the correct answer, tries to self-correct, still not quite the right answer
	230	is a person who crosses the	
	231	uh his own boundary	
	232	his or her own boundary	
Tanisha	233	Almost	Tanisha encouraging Matthew
Ms. Falls	234	Almost	Teacher reiterates encouraging response of Tanisha and adds to it
	235	you're real close	
	236	you're real close	
Ms. Falls	237	What other boundary do they cross	Teacher reiterates the question with a hint about the other boundary
	238	the perpetrator?	
	239	There's another boundary they cross	
Tanya	240	Lifesaver	Tanya suggests that student can ask for help from another student
Ms. Falls	241	Who wants to be a lifesaver?	Teacher calling for student to help
Tanya	242	Adriana	Adriana and others with hands raised
Adriana	243	A perpetrator is somebody who	Adriana responds with her definition using the prior day's terms
	244	will cross their own boundary	
	245	plus another person's boundary	
Ms. Falls	246	Right, great	Teacher verifying response

The interchange between Adriana and Tanya illustrates how the teacher as community organizer motivated interdependence among students as they solved the shared problem of understanding the concept of perpetrator. From a Vygotskian perspective, this happens in the zone of proximal development when a more experienced other provides hints or suggestions or prompts to assist in the learning. In this case, the students were taking on the role rather than relying completely on the teacher to initiate such a form of scaffolding. This handing over of the role of more knowledgeable other by the teacher was part of her classroom management plan that stems from her value system.

In addition, this example suggests that the teacher helped students maintain their sense of dignity and self-worth as they took risks, asked for a lifesaver, and then shared their ideas about this new vocabulary word. As community facilitator, the teacher kept the discussion student centered rather than teacher directed to encourage students to work together to solve the common issue. As the school year progressed, students were more willing to take intelligent risks and to ask for or offer lifesavers to help the individual and the collective reach their academic goals.

Self-Improving and Self-Directing Collective

In the following excerpt we look at additional roles of the teacher as community organizer: developing self-improvement capabilities, constructing a self-directing collective, while continuing to promote unity and motivate interdependence. In addition we examine the tracer unit of lifesaver as a telling case of development of collective classroom efficacy. The classroom activity, Visible and Invisible Walls, was initiated by the teacher to have students investigate the meaning of tolerance by examining the acts of intolerance represented by the walls. Several walls were discussed in class and chosen by the students for in-depth research projects to be presented by the citizens in February, Week 25 of the school year. Examples of the physical walls that were to be studied through use of the Internet over the course of the next month were the Berlin Wall, the Great Wall of China, and the Vietnam Memorial in D.C. The invisible walls were examples of discrimination such as the Aboriginal Wall and the Nelson Mandela Wall (see, e.g., Talking Walls Software).

For the Visible and Invisible Walls project, students were assigned to small groups and chose which particular wall they intended to study. Over the course of several weeks, they used nonfiction texts, almanacs, the Talking Walls Software, and Internet resources to construct a poster or PowerPoint presentation. Their presentation was to contain information about the wall they researched as well as the process they used to conduct the research. On the day of presentations, Ms. Falls set expectations for participation of all students during the activity. Ms. Falls had asked for students in the audience to be "critical friends." In her words, she asked them to "listen with a critical ear, not a criticizing ear, a researcher's ear." After each presentation Ms. Falls asked the other students to offer feedback in the form of helpful critique.

One group finished their presentation, answering questions about the topic from fellow students as well as the teacher. When the next group proceeded with their presentation on the Aboriginal Wall, it quickly became apparent that they were not as well prepared with their topic knowledge. With each advancing point in their presentation, questions from fellow students went unanswered by the group members.

The teacher asked for constructive feedback from the class members who had been listening to the presentation. Given that one of the common teaching practices in this classroom was to ask "probing questions, ones that make you answer why," it was not surprising that a female student, Anna, suggested, "You should have known Ms. Falls was going to ask questions. You should have spent more time studying your notes and looking over your presentations, and you should have worked together so that everyone knew what was being talked about." Other students offered productive critiques of the group's knowledge base. For example, Tomas stated, "You needed to understand the meanings of the words you presented." Shaylon offered, "You should have helped each other with pronunciation. When one of you didn't know how to say a word, another should have helped." Another female student, Cristina, offered, "Why don't you do another presentation, so go home and study over track break."

The discussion then moved to reflection on the part of the group members who made the Aboriginal Walls presentation. As with each presentation, the students rated themselves on a rubric of zero to four, with zero meaning that they interfered with someone's learning and a four meaning that they worked together collaboratively to improve their learning. The group rated themselves a one, meaning that they were working individually with not much comprehension. One student observer gave them credit for making an attempt and suggested that a two was more appropriate; however, Barbara stated that she respected their decision to give themselves a one and praised them for not attempting to rate themselves a three. The class settled on a one and one half effort grade but suggested that the group be allowed to present again after their upcoming break from school to improve their score.

Ms. Falls restated, "You did show some effort, but you have lots of work to do, don't you? You had suggestions from the community . . ." The Aboriginal Walls group members responded, "We need to work together and help each other," "We should help each other with the words," and "We should study over track break." In this example, the role of the classroom community organizer was to help students develop self-improvement capabilities by refocusing their efforts to improve their understanding of their particular topic and how it related to the larger focus on tolerance.

What is interesting is that the students themselves offered specific and productive input and encouraged the group to work together and try again to improve on their presentation so that all could be successful. This encouragement illustrates the development of the concept of lifesaver as well as the development of collective classroom efficacy. During the initial days of school, lifesaver took the form of taking intelligent risk and being offered help from another. Further into the school year, the use of lifesaver developed into explicitly requesting assistance from others. Toward the end of the school year, students commonly used lifesaver implicitly as part of their interactional discourse during classroom activities.

This collaborative effort suggests that students were likely to be focused on the academic success of the entire class since they strongly encouraged their peers to achieve the academic goal of the collective. As explained previously, a central tenet of Ms. Falls's teaching philosophy was to construct a self-directed classroom collective. Ms. Falls initiated this goal by positioning students as audience members to be critical friends and offer constructive feedback to one another.

The feedback from the other class members provides further evidence of the developing self-directed classroom collective. For example, the classmates in the audience suggested to the small group members that they should have been better prepared to present their work and to work together over school break so that they could present again on return to school. This suggestion gave the group an opportunity to improve on their presentation and also to improve their grade for the project. Ms. Falls supported the audience members in encouraging the small group to work on their project during school break. She, in turn, supported the small group by taking up the audience suggestion of giving them a second opportunity. She reminded them that they still have work to do and that they can be successful if they follow the suggestions given.

Discussion and Implications

Bandura's (1997) construct of collective efficacy was initialized at a global community level. As shown in our review of the literature, researchers narrowed the field to examine collective efficacy at the schoolwide level. Our intention is to extend the literature by further narrowing the field in examining collective efficacy at the classroom level by placing classroom in the center of the construct. In applying the construct in this way, the classroom teacher takes on Bandura's community organizer role, thus facilitating classroom interdependence as an avenue for developing collective classroom efficacy.

In this article, we bring forward the notion of collective classroom efficacy as a social construct that can be developed over time as opposed to being viewed as a dichotomous variable. From a Vygotskian (1986) perspective, development is not a phased phenomenon but rather a dynamic and reciprocal process in which individuals utilize thoughts and ideas placed into the intersubjective space through interactive classroom activities, thus making personal sense through interactions with others. Through her role as community organizer, the teacher paved the way for the social and academic interplay among students of various skill levels. Over time their interactions resulted in a shared sense of efficacy across the different learning activities.

Our purpose in examining this telling case of one elementary classroom is to provide an understanding of how collective classroom efficacy evolves over time through classroom interaction and how classroom teachers may act as community organizers in actuating the developing collective classroom efficacy. From this perspective, collective classroom efficacy,

much like classroom literacy, "is not a generic process or state of being but a continual expansion of practices, a continual dynamic development" (Putney, 1996, p. 130). A further goal was to provide a perspective that teachers and researchers can use to examine the local and historical practices that shape collective classroom efficacy.

Through the data analysis, in particular the dialogic triangulation of social skill building and academic knowledge building, we illustrated how the construct of collective classroom efficacy can be co-constructed as a reciprocal process. The sense of collective classroom efficacy that we illustrated went beyond the social aspect of belonging to a group because the sense of belonging was also related to academic goals. The teacher actively encouraged students to take intelligent risks as they worked to achieve their academic and interpersonal goals, which has been established as a cornerstone of self-efficacy (Bandura, 1997). She further fostered capabilities of the members by promoting self-worth and dignity through the use of the classroom norms. As local leaders, students took on the role of uniting the collective for a common cause of encouraging autonomy, respect, and academic accountability. This synergistic unification of academic and social accountability mirrors the synergy of teacher efficacy and student efficacy that can lead to collective classroom efficacy.

In a society steeped in the individual race to the top with proof of ability testing, the notion of collective classroom efficacy exemplifies the need for more research examining a community-oriented notion of efficacy. The existing literature on teacher efficacy and self-efficacy, and even collective efficacy, is individually oriented (Wheatley, 2005). However, it is possible that research on efficacy can involve a more inclusive approach to determine how classroom participants view themselves in relation to others in developing collective classroom efficacy. The examination of teacher as efficacious community organizer via the characteristics offered by Bandura (1997) led us to theorize the unification of teacher and student self-efficacy in dialogic reciprocal relationship as the foundation of collective classroom efficacy. More research is warranted to establish this relationship definitively and to examine the influence of collective classroom efficacy on student achievement.

A limitation of this study was that it involved data collected from one elementary classroom. As such, it could be inferred that collective classroom efficacy was the result of the work of an exemplary teacher and cannot be generalized to other classrooms. However, as we worked through the data and saw an ever-increasing example of how this teacher took up the role that Bandura (1997) recognized as community organizer, we could not help but consider that these data could be reminiscent of other classrooms as well. This suggests that further research needs to be conducted for cases from other classroom settings, grade levels, and types of schools to investigate further the role of teachers and students in constructing collective classroom efficacy.

As Renshaw (2007) argued, in a commentary related to similar types of studies, this format of addressing teachers and practitioners in this way invites them "to draw upon their own recollections of similar voices and experiences" (p. 244). In addition, he noted that such studies "are designed to persuade teachers that it is possible to transform any classroom into a relational learning community" (p. 244). In a similar vein, we add to this commentary that this study of Ms. Falls's classroom is designed to illustrate what it takes for classroom teachers to transform their classrooms into ones that develop a sense of collective classroom efficacy.

The implications of this study indicate that, as Bandura (1997) suggested for schoolwide collective efficacy, the role of community organizer becomes a critical aspect for development of collective classroom efficacy as well. In conjunction with Bandura's perspective, Vygotsky's (1978, 1986) view of individual and collective development provided the lens for us to illustrate how classroom members can develop a sense of collective classroom efficacy. They do so as they work together to construct common knowledge in the intersubjective public classroom space and to set and achieve academic goals. Based on the findings of this investigation, some ways in which teachers can serve as community organizers in pursuit of collective classroom efficacy include encouraging informed risk taking by (a) creating a sense of belonging, (b) setting and working toward personal and academic goal attainment, (c) taking responsibility for self and others' learning, and (d) believing in individual and collective capabilities.

References

Ashton, P. T., & Webb, R. B. (1986). *Making a difference: Teacher's sense of efficacy and student achievement.* New York, NY: Longman.

Bandura, A. (1993). Perceived self-efficacy in cognitive development and functioning. *Educational Psychologist, 28,* 117–148.

Bandura, A. (1997). *Self-efficacy: The exercise of control.* New York, NY: W.H. Freeman & Co.

Bruner, J. (1986). *Actual minds, possible worlds.* Cambridge, MA: Harvard University Press.

Castanheira, M. L., Crawford, T., Green, J., & Dixon, C. (2000). Interactional ethnography: An approach to studying the social construction of literate practices. *Linguistics and Education, 11*(4), 295–420.

Dweck, C. S. (2000). *Self-theories: Their role in motivation, personality, and development.* Philadelphia, PA: Taylor & Francis.

Dweck, C. S., & Leggett, E. L. (1988). A social-cognitive approach to motivation and personality. *Psychological Review, 95,* 256–273.

Edwards, D., & Mercer, N. (1987). *Common knowledge: The development of understanding in the classroom.* Cambridge, MA: Routledge.

Goddard, R. D. (2001). Collective efficacy: A neglected construct in the study of schools and student achievement. *Journal of Educational Psychology, 93*(3), 467–476.

Goddard, R. D. (2002). A theoretical and empirical analysis of the measurement of collective efficacy: The development of a short form. *Educational and Psychological Measurement, 62*(1), 97–110.

Goddard, R. D., & Goddard, Y. L. (2001). A multilevel analysis of the relationship between teacher and collective efficacy in urban schools. *Teaching and Teacher Education, 17,* 807–818.

Goddard, R. D., Hoy, W. K., & Hoy, A. W. (2004). Collective efficacy beliefs: Theoretical developments, empirical evidence, and future directions. *Educational Researcher, 33*(3), 3–13.

Goddard, R. D., Hoy, W. K., & Woolfolk Hoy, A. (2000). Collective efficacy: Its meaning, measure, and impact on student achievement. *American Educational Research Journal, 37,* 479–508.

Gumperz, J. J. (2003). Interactional sociolinguistics: A personal perspective. In D. T. D. Schiffrin & H. E. Hamilton (Eds.), *The handbook of discourse analysis* (pp. 215–228). Malden, MA: Blackwell.

John-Steiner, V. P., & Meehan, T. M. (2000). Creativity and collaboration in knowledge construction. In C. D. Lee & P. Smagorinsky (Eds.), *Vygotskian perspectives on literacy research. Constructing meaning through collaborative inquiry* (pp. 31–50). New York, NY: Cambridge University Press.

Lave, J., & Wenger, E. (1991). *Situated learning: Legitimate peripheral participation.* Cambridge, UK: Cambridge University Press.

Mercer, N. (2000). *Words and minds: How we use language to think together.* London, UK: Routledge.

Mitchell, J. C. (1984). Case studies. In R. F. Ellen (Ed.), *Ethnographic research: A guide to general conduct* (pp. 237–241). San Diego, CA: Academic Press.

Moll, L. (2000). Inspired by Vygotsky: Ethnographic experiments in education. In C. D. Lee & P. Smagorinsky (Eds.), *Vygotskian perspectives on literacy research: Constructing meaning through collaborative inquiry* (pp. 256–268). New York, NY: Cambridge University Press.

Pajares, F. (1996). Self efficacy beliefs in academic settings. *Review of Educational Research, 66,* 543–578.

Pajares, F. (2001). Toward a positive psychology of academic motivation. *Journal of Educational Research, 95,* 27–35.

Pajares, F., & Valiante, G. (2006). Self efficacy beliefs and motivation in writing development. In C. A. MacArthur, S. Graham, & J. Fitzgerald (Eds.), *Handbook of writing research* (pp. 158–170). New York, NY: Guildford.

Putney, L. G. (1996). You are it: Meaning making as a collective and historical process. *Australian Journal of Language and Literacy, 19,* 129–143.

Putney, L. G. (2007). Discursive practices as cultural resources: Formulating identities for individual and collective in an inclusive classroom setting. *International Journal of Educational Research, 46,* 129–140.

Putney, L. G., & Broughton, S. H. (2007, April). *Exploring collective efficacy opportunities available through juxtaposition of primary and secondary data analysis.* Paper presented at the American Educational Research Association annual conference, Chicago, IL.

Putney, L. G., Green, J. L., Dixon, C. N., Duran, R., & Yeager, B. (2000). Consequential progressions: Exploring collective-individual development in a bilingual classroom. In C. D. Lee & P. Smagorinsky (Eds.), *Vygotskian perspectives on literacy research: Constructing meaning through collaborative inquiry* (pp. 86–126). New York, NY: Cambridge University Press.

Renshaw, P. D. (2007). A commentary on the chronotopes of different "cultures of learning": Transforming classrooms from trading-places into relational-places of learning. *International Journal of Educational Research, 46,* 240–245.

Schunk, D. H. (1990). Goal setting and self efficacy during self-regulated learning. *Educational Psychologist, 25,* 71–86.

Schunk, D. H. (1995). Self-efficacy and education and instruction. In J. E. Maddux (Ed.), *Self-efficacy, adaptation, and adjustment: Theory, research, and application* (pp. 281–303). New York, NY: Plenum.

Schunk, D. H. (2003). Self efficacy for reading and writing: Influence of modeling, goal setting, and self-evaluation. *Reading & Writing Quarterly, 19,* 159–172.

Souza L. E. (1995). Culture revisited: Vygotsky's ideas in Brazil. *Anthropology and Education Quarterly, 26*(4), 443–457.

Talking Walls Software Series [Computer software]. Redmond, WA: Edmark.

Tschannen-Moran, M., Woolfolk Hoy, A., & Hoy, W. K. (1998). Teacher efficacy: Its meaning and measure. *Review of Educational Research, 68,* 202–248.

Vygotsky, L. S. (1978). *Mind in society: The development of higher psychological processes.* Cambridge, MA: Harvard University Press.

Vygotsky, L. S. (1986). *Thought and language.* Cambridge, MA: MIT Press.

Vygotsky, L. S. (1997). *Educational psychology* (R. Silverman, Trans.). Boca Raton, FL: St. Lucie Press.

Wertsch, J. V., del Rio, P., & Alvarez, A. (1995). Socio-cultural studies: History, action, and mediation. In J. V. Wertsch, P. del Rio, & A. Alvarez (Eds.), *Socio-cultural studies of mind* (pp. 1–36). Cambridge, UK: Cambridge University Press.

Wheatley, K. F. (2005). The case of reconceptualizing teacher efficacy research. *Teaching and Teacher Education, 21,* 747–766.

Woolfolk, A. E., & Hoy, W. K. (1990). Prospective teachers' sense of efficacy and beliefs about control. *Journal of Educational Psychology, 82,* 81–91.

Critical Thinking

1. What do conversations contribute to classroom communities?

2. How does the teacher serve as organizer?

3. What techniques can the teacher use?

4. Why are promoting and participating important in shared efficacy?

Create Central

www.mhhe.com/createcentral

Internet References

Social Learning Theory; Bandura and Self-Efficacy

http://psychology.about.com/od/developmentalpsychology/a/sociallearning.htm

Vygotskian Approach

www.toolsofthemind.org/philosophy/vygotskian-approach/

LeAnn G. Putney coauthored *A Vision of Vygotsky,* a book relating Vygotskian theories to pedagogy for teachers. Her ethnographic research of diverse classroom activity has been published in *Journal of Classroom Interaction, International Journal of Educational Research,* and *TESOL Journal,* among others. **Suzanne H. Broughton** researches emotion's influence on conceptual, attitude, and belief change. Her investigations of refutational text interventions for conceptual change are published in the *Journal of Educational Research.* She also researches development of collective classroom efficacy through classroom community practices.

Funding—The author(s) received no financial support for the research and/or authorship of this article.

Declaration of Conflicting Interests—The author(s) declared no potential conflicts of interests with respect to the authorship and/or publication of this article.

Unit 8

UNIT

Prepared by: Nancy P. Gallavan, *University of Central Arkansas*

Awareness of Agency

Education resembles the arts, business, government, sports, and many other aspects of life in that individuals can be passive spectators who tend to watch from the side and/or perform tasks reluctantly and perfunctorily, or individuals can be dynamic participants who tend to launch themselves eagerly and creatively into the center of action demonstrating control and responsibility. Spectators must be led to new situations where they offer few constructive suggestions and rarely volunteer to assist, much less lead. Items of concern, especially items requiring thoughtfulness, teamwork, and change, must be brought to the attention of spectators; then they must be provided detailed instructions for completing their portion of the task and realizing the value of the processes and outcomes for themselves and other people.

Conversely, participants frequently initiate and organize themselves as new situations arise, establishing viable avenues to engage in leadership, creative thinking, problem solving, and decision making that benefits everyone equitably. Participants may anticipate tangential items of concern as current items of concern are being scrutinized. Participants reflect upon the processes and outcomes throughout the engagement and readily apply their discoveries to other parts of their lives.

Far too many educators are spectators; they "walk" through their jobs each day giving the minimal amount of time and energy to each task other than maintaining the "wall" they have built between themselves and their students, classrooms, and schools. Whether these educators have always believed that passivity holds the key to teaching or embodies the best approach for them to survive challenging situations, spectator teachers have not acquired an awareness of agency.

Agency, in education, describes an individual's sense of ownership, internalization, responsibility, and control for oneself and all other persons for whom the individual is accountable. Delving into a topic or issue, making personal and professional connections, applying major concepts extending from the topic or issue to new situations, and advocating support and transformation are associated with agency.

Thus, awareness of agency in the context of cultural competence is essential for all educators. Given that cultural competence includes curricular content, instructional strategies, assessment techniques, and management procedures, ownership, internalization, control, and responsibility must be exercised with all students and at all times. As students become culturally competent, they must be guided by teachers with a sense of agency who provide the students with information, access, opportunities, and equipment to know, go, do, and respect themselves, other people, society, and institutionalized systems.

To advance awareness of agency, students must be offered information, access, opportunities, and equipment related to voice, choice, ownership, change, and advocacy. Voice enables one person to formulate and express a purposeful thought in a respectful and equitable environment as another person listens carefully and provides a meaningful response. Finding one's voice advances one's ability to think clearly, speak articulately, and interact responsibly. Voice allows for the natural development of self.

Choice allows a person to pursue the right and authority of selecting an outcome, from among several options, in ways that are honored within the context of everyone who is impacted by the selection. Exercising choice empowers one's competence and confidence in the acts of powerful thinking, problem solving, decision making, and critical reflecting for oneself and for other people. Choice encourages honest interactions with others.

Ownership gives a person sole possession and authentic accountability of one's thoughts, words, actions, and interactions expressed internally and externally with both individuals and groups. Taking and receiving ownership entail attending to all aspects of the structure, function, directions, and rigor within the system and frequently transferring these constructs authentically to other contexts.

Change extends from minor adjustments to major modifications in oneself, between individuals, and within systems, conducted with integrity. Change may include an alteration in social order, social progress, or even social evolution. In any instance, change empowers meaningful transformation within self, others, and society.

Awareness of agency through voice, choice, ownership, and change provides individuals with the courage for advocacy. Educators must become appropriate role models sharing their messages, demonstrating their methods, and guiding through mentorship to equip all students to become advocates of cultural competence.

Article   Prepared by: Nancy P. Gallavan, *University of Central Arkansas*

Community Partnerships: Working Across Institutions to Support Parent Advocacy and Education

JENNIFER MCCORMICK AND SARA M. OZUNA

Learning Outcomes

After reading this article, you will be able to:

- Understand the presence, power, and importance of parents and families to support their children's learning.

- Recognize the importance of communication between homes and schools in ways that are useful for both groups.

Decades of research have shown that parent involvement positively affects student achievement (Epstein et al, 2002, Quezada, 2003). Further research confirms that when parents know the role schools need them to play and feel they can effectively play that role, they are more likely to become involved in their children's education (Hoover-Dempsey, 2005) The impetus for this study was to provide information to families, school staff and community organizations that would help them set academic goals for students in grades 6 through 12. More specifically, it was a collaborative effort between representatives from a university and a community based organization to develop parent advocate, education standards (6-12th grade). To write the standards, we reviewed parent engagement literature and the workshop objectives of a community organization; then we asked parents, teachers and principals what they thought parents should know and do to effectively support their child's academic success.

Conceptual Framework

There has been a range of research pointing to a positive correlation between parent involvement and student achievement (Epstein, 1991; Hoover-Dempsey, 2005; NMSA, 2000; Valdez, 1996; Vaden-Kiernan, 2005). This correlation initiated the research that led us to develop parent advocate education standards. As our project progressed, however, we increasingly relied on scholarship that outlined the socioeconomic

challenges working, immigrant parents face in order to frame both our research and the standards themselves.

Scholars documenting parent involvement have highlighted the social networks that working-class, immigrant parents activate in order to exchange resources (Bolivar & Chrispeels, 2011; Jackson & Cooper, 1989; Moll, 1992). Through ethnographic analysis, Luis Moll identified the cultural wealth in Latino communities, conceptualizing it as "funds of knowledge." His work became an impetus for educators willing to acknowledge the biases often found when teachers and principals work with low-income parents. Those biases include the assumption that working-class parents' homes are void of the culturally significant resources that educators claim contribute to a well-rounded learning experience. Moll's critique of "accepted perceptions of working-class families as somehow disorganized socially and deficient intellectually" ultimately served as a lens through which we viewed our own language (1992, p.3).

Moreover, when discussing the difference between what parents know about the school system and what teachers and principals want them to know, the authors examined the factors that often lead to knowledge gaps for working-class, immigrant parents. Smith (2008) states, "the true differences are created by possession or absence of information about college and substantial experience with college" (2008, p. 3). He implies that experience enhances one's understanding of crucial information. Based on this perspective, the authors questioned how to distribute critical information to parents who had little experience with the American public school system, college course requirements and collegiate scholarships. Ultimately, our revision of the parent advocate education standards came from a belief that the action needed to implement these standards would be "based on a model in which parents help other parents to create individual action plans to address parent complaints that are sensitive to cultural contexts" (Carter, 2007, p. 6).

A sociocultural perspective helped us create a document that was both informative and responsive to the needs of the parents for whom it was intended. Sociocultural theorizing emerged from the work of L. S. Vygotsky (1978), who argued that learning did not occur in isolation within an individual, but rather took place in socially mediated contexts. Sociocultural theory focused our attention on the beliefs and practices of working-class, immigrant communities. Specifically, it enabled us to identify how information traveled through social networks and the necessity of activating those networks in schools and communities where finances are low. Moreover, a sociocultural perspective reinforced a belief that parent advocate education standards are best created through negotiation and co-interpretation.

Methods
Participants
Thirty-five parent participants [6 fathers and 29 mothers] came from working class neighborhoods in a large urban area. Most were first generation immigrants from Mexico; nearly all were Latino. Their backgrounds varied with respect to immigration status, years of education and years spent in the United States. Parent focus groups were conducted in Spanish.

All ten of the principal and teacher participants taught in schools that served a working-class, and predominately Latino population. According to one middle school teacher, 20 to 30 percent of the parents who have children in the school "recently crossed the border," and a majority work for a well-known clothing manufacturer or other factories in the area surrounding the school. All teacher and principal participants had been working in their respective schools for five years or more.

Data Collection
Our method for this study was to conduct focus groups with samples that were comprised of parents, teachers and principals. The focus group sample data ranged anywhere from ten to twenty participants.

Drawing from the work completed by local high schools and community based organizations on the development of standards and guidelines for parents, we created advocate education standards that fell into seven categories:

Understand Your Child's Academic Status
Know How the School System Works
Choose and Evaluate Schools
Support College and Career Pathways
Know About Adolescent Social, Emotional and Physical Health Issues
Access an Academic Environment at Home & in the Community
Be Your Child's Educational Advocate

Once standards were created, the authors ran focus groups and subsequently relied on qualitative analysis to evaluate the discussion that emerged from open-ended questions.

After translating the standards into Spanish, we sought feedback from parents, teachers and principals on what parents need to know and do in order to support adolescents in schools.

The feedback was obtained from four focus groups convened in distinct locations: a high school, a middle school, a reading clinic and a community based organization. We began each focus group with the following open-ended questions:

What do you think parents need to know to help their secondary children be successful in school?
What do you think parents need to do to help their secondary children be successful in school?

The open-ended questions led to a discussion that enabled us to document information that was not included in our list of standards. This data came directly from participants before we distributed the standards. Consequently, it was never influenced by information provided through a pre-conceived document.

We then distributed standards we had devised and told principals and teachers to read them and make notes. After they read, we asked the following questions.

Which standards do you have questions about?
Which standards within the groups are most important?
What is missing?

After distributing the standards, we elicited a discussion around what information was missing and how language use affected understanding.

We varied the parent protocol to accommodate parents who were not literate in their first language. With each focus group, we asked if parents preferred us to read the standards to them, or if they preferred to read the standards individually. All of the parent groups decided they wanted us to read the standards. By reading them, the document became an oral/aural one—enabling both researchers and parents to experience it collectively. Hearing the language of the original standards influenced our analysis of the standards, specifically the use of language in each category.

Data Analysis
Given that the goal of the research was to elicit information from distinct groups, we reviewed each session after it occurred to capture fresh impressions. These review sessions were recorded and transcribed. Each focus group session was transcribed. Two researchers then developed analytical notes that captured the common themes that emerged within and across the four distinct focus groups: two parent groups, one teacher group and one principal group. We began analysis by highlighting comments that appeared repeatedly. We noted all comments that triggered strong responses, either in agreement or disagreement, and we noted comments that yielded additional comments from other participants.

Recursive reading of the data led to a reevaluation of the term standard. The process of translating group discussions and the repeated analysis of the document exposed how the language that is often used to communicate between teachers, administrators and parents can be problematic. In addition to the critical feedback we received from parents, reading the standards to parents, and hearing the document, affected our conception of it. Reading forced us to hear the language repeatedly which made us aware of the actual tone that syntax established. For example, the following "standard" erased the economic reality that working class and working poor families face and left no room for parents to discuss their concerns: "Parents need to know that financial aid is available for most students attending college...money is not an obstacle." The declarative statement—money is not an obstacle—left no room for parents to express a fear of debt or a fear of losing their homes. The finality of the statement denied parents the opportunity to seek and interpret information that would be useful to them.

The oral/aural rendering of the document drove home the necessity of interaction. Consequently, the term *standard* came to be viewed as a guideline rather than a set of norms upon which parents would be assessed and ultimately judged. We argue that this conception of the term *standard* will enable the document we created to "live and breathe" within a number of diverse parent networks that exist in one of the largest, immigrant cities of the United States. The term *guideline* lends itself to flexibility, discussion and active exchange.

Results
Critical Information

Findings can be distinguished according to two categories: 1. What parents need to know and 2. How that information might be best conveyed. An analysis of the responses to open-ended questions across parent, principal, and teacher focus groups revealed that parents need to distinguish between college preparation coursework and general education requirements. The following interaction exemplifies the kinds of questions parents asked us and each other during focus groups:

> Parent 3: This one [points to a standard] that says if your child has completed Algebra and Pre-Algebra, what does this one mean?
> Parent 4: Is this the same as the California High School Exit Exam (CAHSEE[1])?

Principals validated our analysis by strongly stressing the need for information that distinguishes general education requirements from the college access sequence. All stakeholders [parents, teachers and principals] pointed to the need to be familiar with the college course sequence, but each focused on distinct aspects of the sequence. Principals noted the importance of providing information about extracurricular activities. "And extracurricular activities, that isn't the end all to itself, it's what the kids learn being in those extracurricular activities; discipline, persistence, sticking with something for four years, friendships, team work, initiative that the kids learn, and that's what colleges are looking for when they're asking for those things." Another principal suggested "a podcast or a video or something that you could just download or access on a website and then have the assessments or descriptions of the assessments and do it all there" to be used as an online interactive tool at schools.

[1] *The CAHSEE tests students English and math skills. Students begin taking the test as sophomores and can retake it five times by the end of their senior year. The class of 2006 was the first required to pass the exam for graduation.*

The third point that generated a general consensus related to the need to know how the system works, specifically, information on how the school hierarchy is structured. Our data showed that parents did not always understand how the school hierarchy functioned, which impeded communication. For example, many could not identify the channels of communication that impacted decisions regarding student achievement. This resulted in parents' inability to access those channels needed, which in some cases caused missed opportunities.

Discussion

Findings point to the ways effective communication might occur. Principals mentioned the need for active versus passive language that would indicate what parents should do to support the academic achievement of their children. Teachers noted that an interactive tool should accompany the standards. Principals also noted that an interactive tool was necessary, and recommended that it should be located at the school site where resources and parent liaisons were readily available. One principal has instituted a partnership program that entailed parents touring the school with a template that they fill-out while observing interactions in classrooms and school corridors. After the observations are completed, parents are invited to discuss what they saw with the principal. Another principal suggested "a podcast or a video or something that you could just download or access on a website and then have the assessments or descriptions of the assessments and do it all there" to be used as an online interactive tool at schools.

Parents, on the other hand, focused on how communication should occur. They were specifically critical of the way standards were framed in the category entitled "Create an Academic Environment at Home." One standard in the category stated, "parents need to nurture a family that highly respects literacy." Several described the ways that literacy existed. The criticism led to an assessment of the entire category, as we began to consider whether the phrasing of a standard conveyed a unilateral directive or a guideline for assertive action. Parents openly questioned a standard in the category labeled "Support the College Pathway," which indicated money was not an obstacle. Many wondered how they would pay back loans while maintaining a home.

The beliefs of each group of participants and the collective reading of a written document reminded us of the need for authentic communication. Language that indicates what parents should do must be conceived in a context that acknowledges what they can do and already do on an ongoing basis. Ultimately, our analysis revealed that educators and community based organization staff should assess how language reinforces relationships between educators (teachers, principals and CBO staff) and parents. That assessment requires interpersonal interaction and a continuous evaluation of how information is received. The principal who encourages parents to visit classrooms and then invites them to discuss what they see demonstrated one way to access parent interpretations of the school environment. We developed a document that should be used to initiate discussion and elicit questions regarding what parents should know and do to support their children's learning. Similar to an invitation to talk about what parents see in classrooms, the document stands as an open invitation to raise questions regarding critical information on how parents can help their children be successful.

Conclusion

Extant research documents the fact that parent involvement is linked to student achievement (Delgado-Gaitan & Trueba, 1991; Henderson & Mapp, 2002). However, there has been less discussion around how to communicate critical information to parents. Parent standards that validate the knowledge, sensibilities and needs of multiple stakeholders remove the barriers that prevent effective communication and move educators toward a practical application of scholarship. This research yielded an important tool that can be used in both parent education curriculum development and in school staff professional development programs.

Finally, the model for the research, cross-institutional collaboration, lends itself to the development and maintenance of an interactive network that supports parents. This work has been disseminated through numerous partnerships [university credential programs, public schools, and community based organizations] to enhance parent involvement and student achievement.

References

Bolivar, J. & Chrispeels, J. Enhancing parent leadership though building social and intellectual capital. American Educational Research Journal, (48), 1 p. 4–38.

Carter, J. H. (2007). The challenge of parent engagement in urban small schools reform. Online Yearbook of Urban Learning, Teaching, and Research, 46–55. Retrieved from EBSCOhost.

Delgado-Gaitan, C & Trueba, H. (1991). Crossing cultural borders: Education for immigrant families in America. London, UK: Falmer.

Epstein, J.L. (1991). Effects on student achievement of teacher practices of parent involvement. Advances in Reading/Language Research, 5, 261–276.

Henderson, A.T. & Mapp, K.L. (2002). A new wave of evidence: The impact of school, family and community on school achievement. Austin, Texas: National Center for Family and Community Connections with Schools, Southwest Educational Development Laboratory.

Hoover-Dempsey, K. V., Walker, J. M. T., Sandler, H. M., Whetsel, D., Green, C. L., Wilkins, A. S., & Closson, K. E. (2005). Why do parents become involved? Research findings and implications. Elementary School Journal, 106(2); 105–130.

Jackson, B & Cooper, B. (1989). Parent choices and empowerment: New roles for parents. Urban Education, (24)3, p. 263–286.

Moll, L. C. et al. (1992). Funds of knowledge for teaching: Using a qualitative approach to connect homes and classrooms. Theory into Practice, 31(1), 132–41. Retrieved from EBSCOhost.

NMSA. (2000). NMSA Research Summary #18: Parent involvement and student achievement at the middle level. NMSA. Westerville: National Middle School Association.

Smith, M. J. (2008). Four steps to a paradigm shift: Employing critical perspectives to improve outreach to low-SES African-American and Latino students and their parents. Journal of College Admission, (201), 17–23. Retrieved from EBSCOhost

Vaden-Kiernan, N. (2005). Parents' reports of school practices to provide information to familiies: 1996 to 2003. National Center for Education Statistics & National Household Education Surveys Program.

Valdez, G. (1996). Con respeto: Bridging the distances between culturally diverse families and schools. New York: Teachers College Press.

Vygotsky, L. (1978). Interaction between leaning and development. From: Mind in Society. (P. 79–91). Cambridge, MA: Harvard University Press.

Critical Thinking

1. What information do parents need to know from teachers and principals?
2. What are effective ways preferred by parents that teachers and principals should share information with them?
3. What would you want to know about the hierarchy of the school and system?
4. What are ways to improve school community partnerships?

Create Central

www.mhhe.com/createcentral

Internet References

FINE: Family Involvement Network of Educators

http://www.hfrp.org/family-involvement/fine-family-involvement-network-of-educators/member-insights/how-can-we-prepare-teachers-to-work-with-culturally-diverse-students-and-their-families-what-skills-should-educators-develop-to-do-this-successfully

National Center for Family and Community Connections with Schools

http://www.sedl.org/connections/

JENNIFER McCORMICK is a Demonstration Teacher at UCLA Lab School. SARA M. OZUNA is a Qualitative Researcher at UCLA.

McCormick. Jennifer; Ozuna. Sara M. From *Online Yearbook of Urban Learning, Teaching and Research.* vol. 7. 2012. pp. 26–32. Copyright © 2012 by the author's. Reprinted by permission.

Using Multicultural Children's Literature about Criminal Justice Issues: Fostering Aesthetic Reading Responses by Mary Ellen Oslick

271

Article

Prepared by: Nancy P. Gallavan, *University of Central Arkansas*

Using Multicultural Children's Literature about Criminal Justice Issues: Fostering Aesthetic Reading Responses

MARY ELLEN OSLICK

Learning Outcomes

After reading this article, you will be able to:

• Discover the benefits of culturally rich children's literature for content and comprehension.

• Learn to select literature for specific purposes and outcomes.

Introduction

Banks (1992) wrote that education within a pluralistic society such as the US should validate and educate students about their home and community cultures, while also freeing students from their cultural boundaries. Focusing on just what students enter the classroom with, the understandings they bring from home, is not enough for education within a democratic society. Educators need to prepare students "to participate in civic action to make society more equitable and just" (p. 32). The challenge is for educators, administrators, and policymakers to transform curriculum. This transformation comes in the form of multicultural education, which is designed to reduce race, class, and gender divisions (Banks, 1992; Banks, 1998; Banks, Cookson, Gay, Hawley, Irvine, & Nieto, 2001; Banks, 2003; Copenhaver-Johnson, 2007; Ladson-Billings, 1994; Ladson-Billings, 1995; Moll, Amanti, Neff, & Gonzalez, 1992; Nieto, 2003).

Nieto (2003) defined multicultural education as "an anti-racist education that is firmly related to student learning and permeates all areas of schooling" (p. 7). This means that learning about cultures does not have to be limited to certain holidays or one month of the year. Furthermore, the Multicultural Education Consensus Panel (2001) published twelve essential principles that describe ways to improve educational policies and practices related to diversity. These principles came from both research and practice and were organized into five themes: teacher learning; student learning; intergroup relations; school governance; and assessment. All of these areas are important in order to address the needs of all learners and to promote a multicultural approach that affects all aspects of school.

In the research about multicultural education, Ladson-Billings (1994) found five influential areas for students: teachers' beliefs about students, curriculum content and materials, instructional approaches, educational settings, and teacher education (p. 22). As a researcher, I am most concerned with the significance of curriculum content and materials on diverse student populations. Specifically, I wanted to examine multicultural children's literature and readers' responses to it. Sims Bishop (1982) quoted African-American author, James Baldwin, who said, "Literature is indispensable to the world.... The world changes according to the way people see it, and if you alter, even by a millimeter, the way a person looks at reality, then you change it" (p. 1). To help students see their worlds differently and to expand those views beyond their own backyards, educators must expose them to quality multicultural children's literature. Doing this helps accomplish the goals of multicultural education.

Multicultural Children's Literature

Several features of multicultural children's literature contribute to its purposes in the classroom. One is that children's literature can be viewed as ethnography (Botelho & Rudman, 2009). That is, by reading a book about a particular culture, the reader should come away with accurate knowledge of the beliefs, attitudes, and important characteristics of that culture. This can be done by an author who is from that particular culture or by an author who has researched that culture (Short & Fox, 2004).

Another way to view multicultural children's literature is by the three metaphors: mirrors, windows, and doors (Botelho & Rudman, 2009; Sims Bishop, 1990). First, literature needs to be a mirror, so that children can see themselves in books. This act helps to validate the experiences of a child: yes, there are others in the world like me and I am not the only person ever to go through this experience. On a broader note, children also need to see their families and their communities reflected in a book to achieve feelings of affirmation. Sims Bishop (1990) wrote that, "Literature transforms human experience and reflects it back to us, and in that reflection we can see our own lives and experiences as part of the larger human experience. Reading, then, becomes a means of self-affirmation…" (p. ix). Multicultural children's literature also serves the purpose of being a window for children. After feeling that their experiences are affirmed, children need to learn about other experiences. The key here is for children to have familiarity with a variety of cultures. Literature can help make this happen especially when classrooms, schools, or communities are homogeneous. Rice (2005) wrote about her experiences of introducing multicultural children's literature to small groups of White students from similar socioeconomic groups (mid-to-high middle class). Those students struggled to relate to stories with universal themes when the cultures of the main characters (Mexican-American) were different from their own. Rice labeled this as "aesthetic restriction" and described it as an immediate, but unconscious rejection of a text (p. 344). Students must be exposed to multicultural children's literature to combat aesthetic restriction.

The last metaphor Botelho and Rudman use is children's literature as a door. While reading about their culture and then reading about other cultures are both important acts, they are not enough for multicultural education and the pedagogy of social justice. Children also need to use books as a door. James Gee (1996) wrote that, "It is the job of the teacher to allow students to grow beyond both the cultural models of their home cultures and those of mainstream and school culture" (p. 89). This requires that children be allowed and encouraged to pose critical questions about what they read, including an examination of issues such as class, race, and gender. This is not always an easy task for educators. King (1991) wrote about her experiences with preservice teachers and their uncritical identities. She explained that these students, by not being critical of what was happening around them, were practicing dysconscious racism, which is "a form of racism that tacitly accepts dominant White norms and privileges" (p. 135). From looking at literature, educators and children can move to looking at situations in the real world.

Criminal Justice Issues in Multicultural Children's Literature

Although many students have experiences with the criminal justice system (both in the school and community setting), there are few books that address these issues. Within this microcosm of multicultural children's literature, though, several themes have emerged. For example, there are children's books about civil disobedience, political prisoners, the witness protection program, and child characters whose parents are prison guards or executioners. There are also stories about hate crimes, child detectives who consult with the police, and teenage lawyers, as well as books in which young readers get to render their own verdicts in fictional and historical court cases. Throughout this broad range of relevant works, however, the most recurrent topics in children's books about the criminal justice system remain incarcerated parents and other relatives, historical novels about prisons, juvenile crime, and criminal trials.

Book Selection Process

I used scholarly journal articles (e.g., Damico & Riddle, 2004; D'Angelo & Dixey, 2001; Lewison, Leland, & Harste, 2000; Leland, Harste, Ociepka, Lewison, & Vasquez, 1999; O'Neil, 2010; Pierce, 2006; Pohan, 2000; and Tyson, 1999), as well as online sources like the Database of Award-Winning Children's Literature (www.dawcl.com) and Children's Literature Comprehensive Database (www.clcd.com) to find texts. I also turned to a children's literature email listserv for appropriate suggestions. Then, I used the model established by Botelho and Rudman (2009) of using a historical, sociopolitical, and narrative lens to problematize these texts. The combination of these factors helped me to read "knee-deep" (Jewett, 2007), which means I moved beyond my personal responses to the books and include critical responses. Accepting the messages of an author or illustrator without questioning can be seen as taking away the power of a reader and the community of readers (Botelho & Rudman, 2009).

This article will focus on four texts that tackle complex issues of the criminal justice system; two where the protagonist has an incarcerated parent and two books that deal with youth violence. Scholars have a variety of names for books like these: "brave and diverse" literature (Ballentine & Hill, 2000); "critical literature" (Houser, 1999); and "risky stories" (Simon & Armitage-Simon, 1995). Lewison, Leland, and Harste (2000) called them social issues children's literature and developed several criteria for identifying them: (1) they do not make differences invisible, but rather explore how differences in culture, language, history, class, gender and race make a difference; (2) they enrich our understanding of history and life by giving voice to those who have traditionally been silenced or marginalized—we call them 'the indignant ones'; (3) they make visible the social systems that attempt to maintain economic inequities; (4) they show how people can begin to take action on important social issues; (5) they explore dominant systems of meaning that operate in our society to position people and groups of people; and (6) they help us question why certain groups are positioned as 'others' (p. 10). The books I chose met at least one of the criteria.

Book Descriptions
Incarcerated Parents

The books about incarcerated family members address many issues. When the incarcerated family member is a parent, the issue of where does the child live now arises. Historically, men have been identified as the incarcerated parent, but proportionally, more women are now going to prison (Sabol, Couture, & Harrison, 2007). When a father is in jail, the children usually live with their mother. When a mother is incarcerated, though, children are more likely to go live with another relative who is not their parent. These caregivers are often not prepared to care for a child in need and experience stress because of the situation (Clopton & East, 2008).

Another issue of children with incarcerated parents is visitation. Many children do not have face-to-face contact with their parent while they are in prison for different reasons. One reason is that an incarcerated parent is dependent on the current caregivers to make a visit happen (Clopton & East, 2008). For a variety of reasons, the current caregiver might not want the child to visit his/her parent in prison. Another cause for not visiting is the cost. Almost half of the parents incarcerated in Federal prisons live more than 500 miles from their last residence (Mumola, 2000). In situations like these, there are costs of travel, food, and lodging that go along with visitation. Both of these issues were addressed in the picture books, *Nine Candles* (Testa, 1996) and *Visiting Day* (Woodson, 2002).

Nine Candles

Nine Candles by Maria Testa (1996) portrays a son's sadness before, during, and after visiting his mother in prison on his seventh birthday. Raymond knows that his mother stole money from the cashier with her job as a waitress, but he still wishes it were his ninth birthday when Mama has promised to be home with his dad and him. Although he already knows the answer, he still begs for her to come home and asks when she will finally be home with him.

Details of prison life, such as the fences, uniformed people with guns or dogs, and the experience of walking through a metal detector all add to this sensitive story. Testa shows the boy's sadness and his anger (at the system, not at his mother, which isn't entirely realistic), as well as his youthful resilience in the face of family trauma. The colorful, cheerful paintings of this family are done in strong, bold strokes. This book has been described as, "a thought-provoking picture book that shows the cost and consequences of crime" (Blair, 1996). In her author's note, Testa wrote that, "Raymond's story is not unusual." She further provides some statistics regarding incarcerated parents, mothers in particular, and offers some advice for children with an incarcerated parent and children who know other children in that situation.

Visiting Day

In the same vein, Jacqueline Woodson's *Visiting Day* (2002) is about a young girl getting ready to visit her father in prison. At first, both text and artwork keep the destination a mystery, focusing instead on the excitement of the upcoming reunion. Wordless spreads depict Grandma fixing the narrator's hair and the pair climbing aboard the bus. Meanwhile, the girl imagines her father making his own preparations. Ransome portrays a handsome man in khaki shirt and slacks; a calendar on the wall marks the days to his daughter's visit, hanging next to her artwork accented with red hearts. Ultimately, "the bus pulls up in front of a big old building where, as Grandma puts it, Daddy

is doing a little time" (unpaged). Ransome shows barbed-wire atop high walls and a guard tower in stern relief against a perfect blue sky.

Told completely from a child's perspective, the narrative makes no judgment about what Daddy did or why he is incarcerated. There is also no mention of the girl's mother. A shared feeling of hope and family togetherness, however, pervades each spread, from Grandma cooking fried chicken in the morning for the bus ride, to the little girl sitting down with crayons when she gets home to make her father more pictures. Woodson provided her rationale for writing the book on her webpage (www.jacquelinewoodson.com/pb.shtml): "Because once a month when I was a little girl, I would go upstate and visit my favorite uncle. I remember those days well and wanted to write about them. This book isn't completely autobiographical but there is a lot of me in it."

I used a questioning strategy suggested by Jewett (2007) to support my exploration of these two texts: Whose Voices. For each story, I asked: whose voices are being heard; and whose voices are not heard (and what might they say). The voices heard in these stories were from the children of incarcerated parents. This gives children a unique perspective into this common situation. Another frequent voice heard was that of the incarcerated parent. When the parents spoke in the stories, they all communicated remorse for their crimes, a desire to be with their children, and a resolve to change their ways. These values seem to be consistent with mainstream culture.

When the caregiver was the other parent, his voice was heard. He tried to explain what the crime committed was and why Raymond's mother had to be in prison. Additionally, he communicated through actions and words that the incarceration was a hardship for the family. Raymond's father apologizes to his son because he cannot afford to get him many presents for his birthday. Going from two incomes to one is a burden for the family.

The voices that are not heard in the stories are those of the other family members as caregivers. The reader does not know how the grandmother feels about taking care of her granddaughter or how Raymond's father feels about the choices his wife made that resulted in a prison sentence. There is also a parent missing from a *Visiting Day* because only *Nine Candles* has both parents in the story. Where is the little girl's mom in *Visiting Day*? Why isn't she mentioned? Does she know that her child is being cared for by another relative?

Juvenile Violence

A major theme within the topic of juvenile violence is gangs. Gang violence has received much attention in recent years, even though estimates from law enforcement suggest that no more than youth ages 10–17 are gang members (Snyder & Sickmund, 2006). In a 2005 survey of students ages 12 to 18, however, 37% of African Americans reported that gangs were present at their schools versus only 17% of white students (Dinkes, Cataldi, & Lin-Kelly, 2007). Kunjufu (2007) offered several reasons why African-American males are especially tempted to join gangs: money; power; identity; protection; fun; intimidation; shock; romance; family involvement; low self-esteem; and academic problems. The books I chose to help discuss issues of youth violence within the framework of gangs touch on many of these reasons for gang membership.

Your Move

Eve Bunting, in a noticeably different approach from some of her other books, collaborates with Ransome on *Your Move* (1998), a gripping picture book told through the first-person narrative of a boy who nearly joins a gang. One evening, while their mother works at her waitressing job, 10-year-old James takes his six-year-old brother, Isaac, along to meet up with the K-Bones, a gang to which James wants to belong. As part of his initiation, James must spray-paint the K-Bones name over the name of a rival gang, the Snakes, on a freeway sign. After James completes his initiation task, he learns that the gang also steals for fun, and starts to have doubts about joining. Then they run into the Snakes gang, who fire a gun at the boys. Although no one gets hurt, James rethinks his association with the K-Bones and ultimately turns down membership in the gang.

Ransome's oil paintings convey the tension and looming danger of the boys' misadventure. His illustrations effectively put readers in James's shoes. The text, simple and direct, lets the message come through without being preachy. However, it may not be realistic for the gang leader to give up on his recruits and for the kids to be able to resist the temptations offered by gang membership. Damico and Riddle (2004) echo this critique in their analysis of classroom discussions about *Your Move*.

Yummy

In 1994, an incident of Southside Chicago gang-related violence captured national headlines. Eleven-year-old Robert "Yummy" Sandifer shot and killed his 14-year-old neighbor Shavon Dean. The graphic novel, *Yummy* (2010), is Neri's retelling of the events based on public records as well as personal and media accounts from the period. Neri recounts Yummy's three days on the run from police (and, eventually, his own gang) through the eyes of Roger, a fictional classmate of Yummy's. Roger grapples with the unanswerable questions behind Yummy's situation, with the why's and how's of a failed system, a crime-riddled neighborhood, and a neglected community. Yummy, so named because of his love of sweets, was the child of parents who were continually in prison. While living legally under the care of a grandmother who was overburdened with the custody of numerous grandchildren, Yummy sought out the closest thing he could find to a family: BDN or Black Disciples Nation. In the aftermath and turmoil of Shavon's tragic death, he went into hiding with assistance from the BDN. Eventually the gang turned on him and arranged for his execution.

Neri frames the story with this central question: Was Yummy a cold-blooded killer or a victim of his environment? In one of the final panels, Roger states, "I don't know which was worse, the way Yummy lived or the way he died" (p. 94). Realistic black-and-white art further intensifies the story's emotion. A significant portion of the panels feature close-up faces which offers readers an immediacy as well as emotional connection to this tragic story. Like Roger, in the end readers are left with troubling questions and, perhaps, one powerful answer: that

they can choose to do everything in their power to ensure that no one shares Yummy's terrible fate. In his author's note, Neri addresses the ambiguity of the story:

> So, was Yummy a cold-blooded killer or a victim? The answer is not black-and-white. Yummy was both a bully and a victim—he deserves both our anger and our understanding . . . . If you can find a way to make the choice of life, then other decisions may be easier. Choose wisely. (p. 95)

In both of these stories, the voices of youth are emphasized, while other voices (e.g., parents, caregivers, and teachers) are silenced for the most part. These stories also focus on the voices of their male characters. The protagonists, James and Yummy, are caught between being young and relatively innocent and taking on the responsibilities of gang membership. While James refuses the invitation, Yummy whole-heartedly embraces it. The readers are privy to both their concerns and their approvals of youth violence within gangs.

Parents, caregivers, and teachers may have things to say to James and Yummy, but their voices are silenced in these books. By doing this, both authors seem to draw focus on how alone and independent their protagonists are. In *Your Move*, James' father has left the family and his mother works at night to provide for the two boys. Only towards the end does James realize the significance of his possible membership in the K-Bones: his younger brother, Isaac, follows his every move and would surely want to join as well. James sees that he is not alone because his move would inspire a move by Isaac. Yummy's grandmother is his main caregiver, but her role is minimal throughout the story. Yummy turns to Monster, the leader of the Black Disciples, a father-figure, although the results prove to be deadly for him.

Using Multicultural Children's Literature about Criminal Justice Issues

In the fall of 2010, I conducted a research study to examine the responses Black boys had regarding children's literature that addresses criminal justice issues. I wanted to see how students connected to diverse characters' experiences with the criminal justice system. How did these stories reflect their personal or family's experiences with punishment at school and also in the community? This examination helped illuminate local reactions to punishment and to the criminal justice system in the U.S. Specifically, I asked the research question: How do Black boys respond to multicultural children's literature addressing criminal justice issues? To better understand their responses, I asked two other questions to guide my inquiry: a) What do Black boys' responses say about their personal connections to the stories? and b) What do Black boys' responses say about their perceptions of society, specifically their understandings of how justice works in their lives and their communities?

Conducted during their Extended Day Education Program (EDEP), four African-American boys read and discussed the previously examined multicultural children's literature texts that addressed criminal justice issues. Combining social issues, children's literature, and critical literacy practices with the experiences of these African American boys produced important conversations. Their responses were interpreted through the method of critical discourse analysis. This stance illuminated and interrogated the ways that power and knowledge were reproduced, consumed, and transformed through the dynamic interplay of micro and macro interactions and human agency (Fairclough, 1995; Rogers & Mosley, 2006).

Rosenblatt's (1978) transactional theory of reader response guided me to examine the responses of my four participants. She argued that the transactions between the reader and a text formed lived-through experiences, invoking a sense of a reading as the creation of a dynamic, alternative reality—one that requires a performance of producing the poem that results (Rogers, 1999). Furthermore, Probst (2002) explained that Rosenblatt's transactional, "theory suggests that each reader comes to the text with a unique history, a unique set of circumstances and abilities and inclinations, and has to take that into account as s/he shapes an understanding of the text and his/her reading of it" (p. 31). My participants brought with them specific social, political, and cultural factors that then influenced their interactions with the stories we read together and discussed. These personal interpretations are both valid and desirable (Rosenblatt, 1978). Rosenblatt (2002) also suggested that stances, or perspectives when reading, are aspects of an individual's consciousness. Furthermore, McLaughlin and DeVoogd (2004) wrote that, "When reading from a critical stance, readers use their background knowledge to understand relationships between their ideas and the ideas presented by the authors of the text" (pp. 57–58).

I organized and examined the responses of my participants through the lens of the transactional theory of reader response and Critical Discourse Analysis (CDA). I developed broad analytic categories that allow me to talk about the form of the interactions while paying attention to the relationships between language and social structure (Chouliaraki & Fairclough, 1999; Rogers, 2004). Then, I selected powerful examples that represented "cruces" or tension spots (Fairclough, 1995). I examined these instances more closely to create critical vignettes. A critical vignette is a summative statement including the larger context and a CDA on the event (Rogers, 2003).

Findings

I analyzed the data by using Glaser and Strauss's constant comparison method, as described by Guba and Lincoln (1994) to identify categories. To start, I used categories of their reader response stances intuitively and continued as I coded the statements within the literature circle discussions. Then, I continuously compared key words with others in the same category and other categories, which reflected any insights and connections (personal and otherwise) to the literature. Using Fairclough's (2004) orders of discourse, I analyzed each utterance for its genre (ways of interacting), discourse (ways of representing), and style (ways of being). The annotation of genre, discourse, or style has been abbreviated as G, D, or S.

I treated Discourse within a CDA framework differently than how linguists, socio-linguists, or conversation analysts

would normally treat it. CDA researchers treat Discourses as always being socially, politically, racially, and economically loaded (Rogers, 2004). Gee (1996) made a distinction between "d"iscourse and "D"iscourse. Little "d" refers to the grammar of what is being said. "D"iscourse refers to the ways of representing, believing, valuing, and participating with "d"iscourse. Discourse also includes the identities and meanings that go along with ways of speaking. Gee's (1999) analytic procedures contain a set of connection-building activities that aim to help the analyst with describing, interpreting, and explaining the relationships between "d"iscourse and "D"iscourse. The activities allow the analyst to construct meaning from discourse patterns and include: semiotic building, world building, activity building, socioculturally situated identity building, political building, and connection building. Gee provided questions to ask for each task. For example, under the task, semiotic building, Gee asked, "What signs systems are relevant (and irrelevant) in the situation?" Therefore, I used CDA to analyze both what is said (in the text) and what is left out (missing) (Rogers, 2004).

Throughout this process, I also kept in mind the 'cool poses' that each of the participants enacted. Tatum (2005) wrote about the Black male's response to turmoil of enacting a cool pose where they can exude power and toughness while coping with conflict and anxiety. My experiences with the boys in both the literature circle settings and the informal settings reinforced this idea. While not all of the boys portrayed the same 'cool pose,' each one had a persona that he presented to the rest of society. In the next sections, I examine the responses of Alex, Connor, JJ, and Trishawn in accordance to their 'cool poses' and to the themes of aesthetic and critical reading response stances by using CDA.

Aesthetic Reading

Cai (2008) described the three central modes of aesthetic reading responses: perception, association, and affection. When responding in the perception mode, the reader pays attention to things in the text that are intriguing, significant, and/or shocking. In the association mode, the reader makes connections to aspects of the story including characters, plot, and setting. Finally, in the affection mode, the reader responds by sharing emotions regarding what happens in the story. The aesthetic responses of Alex, Connor, JJ, and Trishawn are organized and examined according to these three central modes.

Real Life Experiences with the Criminal Justice System

Harvey and Goudvis (2007) wrote that, "Readers naturally make connections between books and their own lives" (p. 92). Some connections, however, can be superficial and not lead to a deeper understanding of a text. While those connections in common (e.g., sharing a name with a character) may be important to engagement, they can be distracting, whereas other connections can truly help the reader transact with the text. In our literature discussions and interviews, I found the personal connections JJ, Trishawn, Alex, and Connor made to the criminal justice system to be beneficial in their understandings of our shared texts, multicultural children's literature that addressed criminal justice issues.

Table 1 provides a concise representation of JJ, Alex, and Trishawn's personal experiences with the criminal justice system, in regards to police, courts, and corrections.

Most personal connections had to do with the corrections part of the criminal justice system, which is consistent with real-world statistics. In 1999, approximately 1.5 million minor children in America had a parent in prison (Mumola, 2000). That works out to be equivalent to one child in fifty who are in this situation. More than half of those children were under the age of ten. Additionally, I was surprised that both Trishawn and JJ had experiences with courts. JJ, especially, shared a detailed and lengthy description of attending a court hearing regarding the custody of his mother's friend's children (Literature discussion, 11-16-10). Alex was the only participant who shared a personal connection to cops, although Trishawn and JJ might also have had experiences with cops based on their other answers, but chose not to share.

One participant is noticeably absent from this table: Connor. He claimed not to have any experience with the criminal justice system (no relatives in prison), but he did have extensive knowledge of the system of justice and discipline that was enforced at the school because of his membership in safety patrol. He was concerned with rules and proper procedures to be carried out by both adults and other students in EDEP and during our literature circle discussions. I believe these experiences helped him connect emotionally to the books we read, especially *Your Move*.

Case Studies

Having presented an overview of the personal connections the participants had to the criminal justice system, I now want to examine in greater detail two of those experiences: JJ sharing that his father is in prison and Alex sharing that his two male cousins are in prison. I was not actively seeking boys who had incarcerated family members. JJ and Alex, along with their parents, agreed to participate in the study and share their personal connections with me and the other members of the literature discussions.

JJ

JJ positioned himself in EDEP and in our literature circle discussions as being a moderate version of an outlaw. He seemed to be torn between following in the footsteps of his older brother, who was best friends with Alex, and being more of an enforcer. For example, he was often influenced by his brother and Alex to go against the behavior expectations set by the EDEP program director and other employees (e.g., playing tag). On the other hand, JJ was good friends with Trishawn and they both bragged to me that they were on the honor roll and had special seating assignments at lunch because of their high A. R. point totals. His 'cool pose' was further complicated by what he shared with me and Trishawn during our literature discussion of *Nine Candles*.

He should be getting out in like a month: Towards the end of *Nine Candles*, I asked both boys if they had ever been to a prison to visit someone. Trishawn replied right away that his uncle was a prison guard and that he had spent the day with him at work. JJ was quiet during this exchange.

> **212 MEO:** {*to JJ*} Have you ever been {to a prison}?
> **213 JJ:** Let me say, {*pause*} my dad is in prison
> **214 MEO:** He is?
> **215 T:** What'd he do?
> **216 JJ:** I really don't know what he did (Literature discussion, 11-16-10)

JJ starts off dramatically with the phrase, "let me say" (S, line 213). With this hook, he grabs our attention and takes control of the conversation. He also pauses here for almost three seconds; he might have been debating whether to share this information or he could have been mimicking a style of pausing before revealing bad news. When he discloses that his "dad is in prison," Trishawn immediately asks, "What'd he do?" (G, line 215). There are several ways to look at Trishawn's question. First, the bluntness with which he delivers it could be the result of his familiarity with JJ; they are good friends at school and have the same third-grade teacher. Secondly, the bluntness could be caused by the familiarity Trishawn has with other friends or people in his community who have incarcerated family members. Or perhaps Trishawn's style while asking this question was due to his immaturity in handling delicate

Table 1   Overview of Personal Connections

Participant	Police	Courts	Corrections
JJ		Attended a custody court hearing	Grandfather's friend in prison for "doing cocaine" "My dad is in prison"
Trishawn		"My step-sister's dad is a judge"	Lives close to "huge juvie" "My uncle works at a prison" "My dad went to jail for a night"
Alex	"My grandpa's a police, used to be"		2 cousins in prison

Compiled from literature discussions and interviews

Using Multicultural Children's Literature about Criminal Justice Issues: Fostering Aesthetic Reading Responses by Mary Ellen Oslick

277

situations, such as asking your friend about his father in prison. Regardless of his question's intent, JJ bows his head down at this point (S) and replies in a quieter voice (S) that he does not have an answer to why he father is in prison (G, line 216).

JJ then goes on to explain that he only knows a little bit of what happened from the perspective of his aunt. He contradicts himself during the retelling, first stating that his father was picked up by the cops at his place of work and then saying that the cops found him hiding at his aunt's workplace. This might be the first time JJ has had to tell this story and that could be why there are so many inconsistencies. There is also the possibility that other adults in his life (e.g., his mom or his aunt) might not be giving him all of the details and JJ has had to piece together a story for himself.

> **227 MEO:** Oh okay. So do you ever go visit your dad? In prison?
> **228 JJ:** Well, I went to visit him when he was in jail, but I haven't visited him yet but he
> **229** said this church went over and saw him
> **230 MEO:** Oh yeah?
> **231 JJ:** And like talked to him about his business and then the church um called my
> **232** grandma and said we're allowed to write notes and stuff and then they said he was
> **233** going to send birthday presents, I mean, uh, Christmas presents
> **234 MEO:** Well, that's nice, but he won't be home for Christmas?
> **235 JJ:** I really don't know {*smiles & laughs*}. He should be getting out in like a month
> **236 MEO:** Oh okay (Literature discussion, 11-16-10)

JJ makes the distinction here that he did visit his father in jail, but has not been to visit him in prison (S, line 228). In our other conversations about jails and prisons, he could have used this knowledge to determine one of their differences, but he does not seem to reference this. When I asked during member checking why he had not visited his father in prison, JJ told me that his dad was far away (2-3-11). Unfortunately, JJ was in a situation faced by many other children. One reason they do not have face-to-face contact with their parent while they are in prison is that an incarcerated parent is dependent on the current caregivers to make a visit happen (Clopton & East, 2008). Another cause for not visiting is the cost. Almost half of the parents incarcerated in Federal prisons live more than 500 miles from their last residence (Mumola, 2000). In situations like these, there are costs of travel, food, and lodging that go along with visitation.

Although he was not able to see his father, JJ was involved in some kind of dialogue about him because of the church that was working with him and their communication with JJ's grandmother (Lines 231–233). JJ seemed excited to "write notes and stuff" (S) and he expected to receive Christmas presents from his father. The only hint of insecurity and vulnerability came at the end of the conversation. JJ gives a half smile and nervous laugh when he responds to me that he's not sure if his dad will be home for Christmas (S, line 235). He further conveys

his uncertainties with the comment, "he should be getting out in know like a month" (S). If JJ does not what his father has done, he probably does not know the timeline for his release. As of member checking in February 2011, JJ's father was still in prison (2-3-11).

Trishawn remains quiet after asking the initial question of "what'd he do?" He shows that he is listening attentively by nonverbal cues: leaning towards JJ as he is speaking and intermittently nodding his head (S). Trishawn lets JJ take control of the conversation by giving up his verbal turns and by letting me ask questions that keep JJ talking. This display of compassion might be unusual for third-grade boys, but I was pleasantly surprised by how Trishawn handled himself here.

Alex

Alex positioned himself as an outlaw to the EDEP and our discussions. Alex was seen as a rebel or nonconformist when it came to the established norms. He was also a leader, taking control of situations in the EDEP (e.g., playing football) and in our discussions (e.g., leading turn-taking). During one of our informal conversations, he expressed some bafflement as to why he had not been selected as part of the school's safety patrol (Researcher's notes 12-7-10). Alex told me that, "all you had to do was write an essay," but he did not seem to understand how much his 'cool pose' and its repercussions had already affected his reputation at school and his chance of joining. Other teachers assumed from his pose that he would not set a good example for other students as a member of the safety patrol. Just as with JJ, his family experiences further confused how he positioned himself at EDEP and in our discussions.

I don't know if they trying to shoot someone or they just shot: During our discussion of *Visiting Day,* I ask both Connor and Alex if they had ever been to a jail or prison to visit someone. Connor replies quickly with a "no" (G, line 111), while Alex waits but then answers with hesitation (S, line 113).

> **110 MEO:** Have you guys ever been to a jail or prison?
> **111 CO:** No
> **112 MEO:** Never been to a prison?
> **113 A:** Uh, I have
> **114 MEO:** Yeah? Who did you go visit?
> **115 A:** {*long pause*} Nobody, I, my cousins are in jail
> **116 MEO:** Oh really?
> **117 A:** One of them gonna get out soon
> **118 CO:** Why?
> **119 A:** They were being bad
> **120 CO:** Why?
> **121 A:** They got in trouble
> **122 CO:** HOW?
> **123 A:** One of 'em had a gun, that's how and one of them was doing something else in
> **124** Georgia
> **125 MEO:** But they're gonna get out soon?
> **126 A:** One of 'em is, the other one has to stay in about three more years
> **127 MEO:** Oh, okay
> **128 CO:** The one that was living in Georgia?

129 A: I think he's coming out, I don't know. One of 'em's coming out

130 MEO: Were they, were they in prison close by or were they far away?

131 A: One of them was in Georgia and one of them was in um G {*nearby college town*}

(Literature discussion, 11-16-10)

Alex pauses for a long time (9 seconds) and I almost let him off the hook by saying that he does not have to share if he does not want to. Then it seems like he might change his mind about sharing, as well, because he starts off by saying, "nobody" (G, line 115). Alex finally ends his statement by revealing that his cousins are in jail, which is another example of how the participants interchanged the two terms. Alex makes it apparent from other conversations (including this one) that he knows the difference between the two places, but he uses the term, jail, for prison here.

Alex does continue that one of his cousins will be getting out "soon" (S, line 117), which is even more vague than JJ's assertion that his dad will be "getting out in like a month." Connor has been sitting next to me this whole time with his eyes wide open (S), watching and listening to Alex. He asks a simple, but deliberate question: "Why?" (G, line 118). Alex seems to understand that Connor was not asking why the cousin was going to get out of prison soon, but rather, why the cousins were in prison in the first place. In response to Connor, he repeats another vague phrase, "they were being bad" (S, line 119). The tone of Alex's voice is very steady and authoritative; he seems to want to placate Connor and then move on with the conversation (S).

Connor has shown throughout our discussions, though, that when he really wants to know something, he does not back down from asking questions. This instance is another example of the tenacity Connor exhibits as part of his 'cool pose.' He asks, "why?" (G, line 120) again focusing on why the cousins were in trouble and not really asking Alex why his cousins "were being bad." At this time, Connor's voice is starting to rise in volume; he seems to become frustrated that Alex is not answering him in a forthright manner (S). This added dramatic effect gives Alex a lot of power in the conversation; he knows that he has information that Connor wants and he seems to enjoy watching Connor get so exasperated.

Alex gives another hazy answer of, "they got in trouble" (S, line 121) before Connor counters with an explosive, "HOW?" (S, line 122). Connor's outburst was followed by a more detailed response from Alex. And yet, Alex does not have all of the particulars for why his cousins are in prison, similar to JJ's situation. He knows "guns" (line 123) were involved for one cousin and just knows the setting, "Georgia" (line 124) for the cousin's crime. This lack of information on Alex's part could have made it important for him to be perceived as an authority in the conversation with Connor. He was able to carry out an illusion of knowledge (and, therefore, power) with Connor by responding repeatedly with unclear answers to Connor's questions.

Alex clarifies that only one cousin will be getting out soon while "the other one has to stay in about three more years" (S, line 126). Still, his clarification is marked with uncertainties (e.g., "about"). Connor presses for more information and asks if the cousin in Georgia is the one who had three more years of time

left in prison (G, line 128). Alex answers with a cognitive statement (S), but then says, "I don't know" (S, line 129); he ends his answer by repeating with resignation that, "one of 'em's coming out" (S). Alex does have an answer to my question that one cousin is in Georgia and the other is in a nearby town, although he pauses briefly before revealing the name of the closer town (S, line 131). He also uses the past tense, "was," when referring to where they are currently incarcerated (D). When asked during member checking, Alex could not remember why he said, "was" and quickly changed the subject to something else (2-3-11). Using the past tense could have been an attempt to distance himself from his cousins. Even though Alex felt compelled to share this story, it is interesting that he does not use either cousin's name and does not offer any personal information about them. He is connected to them as a cousin, but he also shows that he is distanced from them (perhaps because of another adult's influence). Our conversation continues in a different vein when Alex shares that his grandfather is a retired police officer and we eventually make our way back to discussing *Visiting Day*.

Two months later during our literature discussion about *Yummy*, Alex volunteered more information about his incarcerated cousins, without any provocation from me or Connor.

378 A: My cousin already been in jail for ten years

379 MEO: Ouch

380 A: Two of 'em

381 MEO: Yeah

382 A: One's coming out this year

383 MEO: Yeah, you told me about that. Is he the one in Georgia?

384 A: I don't know which one but

385 CO: Why are they in jail?

386 MEO: Remember we talked about this?

387 A: BANG BANG

388 MEO: They had guns and they got in trouble for being out with guns, right?

389 A: And they shot one

390 MEO: They shot someone?

391 A: No, they just shot

392 MEO: Shot the guns? Okay

393 A: I don't know if they trying to shoot someone or they just shot

394 MEO: Just shot the gun?

395 A: I don't know if they trying to shoot anybody or nothing

(Literature discussion, 1-14-11)

Alex had just asked me how many years Yummy could face in prison for killing Shavon and then proceeded to say that his cousin has already been in jail for ten years (G, line 378). Knowing the timeline, it is more understandable that Alex would not know all of the details of his cousin's crime or that he would have a relationship with him at all. If Alex is correct that his cousin has been in prison for ten years, then he went away before Alex was even born.

Connor joins the conversation with a question that mimics his curiosity from our *Visiting Day* literature discussion: "Why are they in jail?" (line 385). By doing this, it is apparent that knowing what crimes have been committed is extremely important to Connor. Alex dramatizes his response and also provides humor by saying, "BANG! BANG!" and using his hands as two pistols (S, line 387). Alex seems to be more comfortable sharing this information a second time around; his manner could also be the result of getting to know both Connor and I more intimately after two months of talking together.

Alex continues by saying that "they got in trouble for being out with guns" (G, line 388). Alex offers more information at this point which is new to our discussion of his cousins. However, this information, like before, is cloudy; Alex makes a statement (line 389) but then has to backtrack when I start asking for more clarification (line 390). At the end of this exchange, we learn that Alex's cousins got in trouble for not only having guns, but also firing them. This revelation is more consistent with Alex's assertion that they had already been in prison for ten years. What Alex does not know (and neither do Connor or I) is what the target was for his cousins' bullets. Alex uses the pronouns, "someone," "anybody," and "nothing" (S, lines 393 & 395) as the intended marks in his explanation for his cousins' shooting, which leads us to believe that his cousins could have been shooting at inanimate objects or real people.

This personal connection for Alex of his cousins in prison was powerful enough for him to share during two different literature discussions. I was especially impressed that he made the connection himself when talking about how long Yummy might be incarcerated for and then spoke about that connection. Because we discussed *Yummy* late in the study, I have to wonder if practicing those conversations and responding to texts aesthetically aided in his thoughtfulness and confidence.

I was impressed that both JJ and Alex shared their personal connections about incarcerated relatives with me. In the spring of 2011, while supervising preservice teachers in their school, I experienced something that I believe makes this research so important. A Kindergarten student walked into class late and when asked about his tardiness, he very simply began to relay that his mother has been arrested that morning. His teacher immediately stopped him mid-sentence and told him (and the class) that such conversations were not appropriate for her classroom. She silenced him in that instance and set the precedent for the entire class population that matters of criminal justice (in this case, an incarcerated parent) were not to be discussed. JJ and Alex may have had similar experiences in their classrooms of a teacher silencing them outright. More likely, though, very subtle cues were used to make it known to JJ and Alex (and others) that such discussions had no place in their classrooms. Our literature circles were important opportunities for those conversations to happen.

Concluding Thoughts

The inauguration of federal initiatives, such as No Child Left Behind, have left many clouded with what teachers, districts, and states must teach and/or not teach and the requirement of using specific instructional materials (Ladson-Billings, 1994). This furthers complicates the inclusion of multicultural children's literature addressing social issues, such as the criminal justice system. Many districts in large states have adopted a one-size-fits-all curriculum in reading instruction, irrespective of the economic, social, cultural and academic diversity present among the population. A recent survey of Florida teachers (Zeig, 2007) found that teachers' reported practices are intimately aligned with the current political mandates. Even if teachers were willing to incorporate taboo books into their classrooms, a mandated curriculum from the district or state may be stopping them. The consequences of such mandates can be severe. Copenhaver-Johnson (2007) wrote that, "Curriculum and procedures imposed on teachers and children with "empirical precision" (Kozol, 2005, p. 50) often result in ethnocentric practices that fail to account for the understandings students bring to school (Delpit, 2003) and the ways that children respond to those one-size-fits-all practices" (p. 44).

Youth violence, gangs, and incarcerated parents could all be considered taboo subjects because they deal so closely with students' lives. The literacy knowledge and personal connections that Alex, Connor, Trishawn, and JJ shared with me about the criminal justice system are not being read about to them in the classroom. Therefore, there is a disconnection between what they value as part of their home/community literacy and the school's literacy. Many researchers and educators have written about situations where this disconnect was an impetus for failure in the school system (Banks, 1992; Banks, et al., 2001; Banks, 2003; Delpit, 1995; Edelsky, 1999; Ladson-Billings, 1994; Ladson-Billings, 1995; Luke, 2003; McDaniel, 2004; Paley, 2000; Sims Bishop, 1982; Zambo & Brozo, 2009). If there were more opportunities to connect school with what was happening in students' lives, perhaps such failures could be avoided. I believe that sharing social issues children's literature that addresses criminal justice matters has the power to transform a classroom. It can support children who have experienced similar circumstances while helping others understand their classmates. It can unite students and teachers in engaging in critical and sophisticated conversations about their communities and justice in our country. Finally, it can build a bridge between what students learn about at home and what they learn about in school.

References

Ballentine, D., & Hill, L. (2000). Teaching Beyond Once Upon a Time. *Language Arts, 78,* 11–20.

Banks, J. A. (1992). Multicultural Education: For Freedom's Sake. *Educational Leadership,* 32–36.

Banks, J. A. (1998). The Lives and Values of Researchers: Implications for Educating Citizens in a Multicultural Society. *Educational Researcher, 27* (7), 4–17.

Banks, J. A., Cookson, P., Gay, G., Hawley, W. D., Irvine, J. J., Nieto, S., et al. (2001). Diversity Within Unity: Essential Principles for Teaching and Learning in a Multicultural Society. *Phi Delta Kappan,* 196–203.

Banks, J. A. (2003). Teaching Literacy for Social Justice and Global Citizenship. *Language Arts, 81* (1), 18–19.

Blair, J. M. (1996). Nine Candles Review. *School Library Journal*

Botelho, M. J., & Rudman, M. K. (2009). *Critical Multicultural Analysis of Children's Literature: Mirrors, Windows, and Doors.* New York: Routledge: Taylor & Francis Group.

Cai, M. (2008). Transactional Theory and the Study of Multicultural Literature. *Language Arts, 85* (3), 212–220.

Chouliaraki, I., & Fairclough, N. (1999). *Discourse in Late Modernity: Rethinking Critical Discourse Analysis.* Edinburgh, Scotland: Edinburgh University Press.

Clopton, K. L., & East, K. K. (2008). "Are there other kids like me?" Children with a parent in prison. *Early Childhood Education* (36), 195–198.

Copenhaver-Johnson, J. (2007). Rolling Back Advances in Multicultural Education: No Child Left Behind and "Highly Qualified Teachers". *Multicultural Perspectives, 9*(4), 40–47.

Copenhaver-Johnson, J., Bowman, J. T., & Johnson, A. C. (2007). Santa Stories: Children's Inquiry about Race during Picturebook Read-Alouds. *Language Arts, 84*(3), 234–243.

Damico, J., & Riddle, R. L. (2004). From Answers to Questions: A Beginning Teacher Learns to Teach for Social Justice. *Language Arts, 82*(1), 36–46.

D'Angelo, A. M., & Dixey, B. P. (2001). Using Multicultural Resources for Teachers to Combat Racial Prejudice in the Classroom. *Early Childhood Education Journal, 29* (2), 83–87.

Delpit, L. (1995). *Other People's Children.* New York: The New Press.

Dinkes, R., Cataldi, E. F., & Lin-Kelly, W. (2007). *Indicators of School Crime and Safety.* Washington, DC.: U.S. Department of Justice.

Edelsky, C. (1999). Introduction. In C. Edelsky (Ed.), *Making Justice Our Project: Teachers working towards critical whole language pactice.* Urbana, IL: National Council of Teachers of English.

Fairclough, N. (1995). *Critical Discourse Analysis: The Critical Study of Language.* New York: Longman.

Gee, J. P. (1996). *Social linguistics and literacies: Ideologies in discourses* (2nd ed.). London: Falmer.

Gee, J. P. (2004). Discourse Analysis: What Makes it Critical? In R. Rogers (Ed.), *An Introduction to Critical Discourse Analysis in Education* (pp. 19–50). Mahwah, NJ: Lawrence Erlbaum Associates Publishers.

Guba, E. G., & Lincoln, Y. S. (1994). *Fourth Generation Evaluation.* London: Sage.

Harvey, S., & Goudvis, A. (2007). *Strategies that Work* (second ed.). Portland: Stenhouse Publishers.

Houser, N. O. (1999). Critical Literature for the Social Studies: Challenges and Opportunities for the Elementary Classroom. *Social Education, 63* (4), 212–215.

Jewett, P. (2007). Reading Knee-Deep. *Reading Psychology, 28,* 149–162.

King, J. E. (1991). Dysconscious Racism: Ideology, Identity, and the Miseducation of Teachers. *The Journal of Negro Education, 60*(2), 133–146.

Kozol, J. (2005). Still Separate, Still Unequal: America's Educational Apartheid. *Harper's Magazine, 311* (1864), 41–54.

Kunjufu, J. (2007). *Raising Black Boys.* Chicago: African American Images.

Ladson-Billings, G. (1994). What We Can Learn from Multicultural Education Research. *Educational Leadership,* 22–26.

Ladson-Billings, G. (1995). Bad That's Just Good Teaching! The Case for Culturally Relevant Pedagogy. *Theory into Practice, 34* (3), 159–165.

Leland, C., Harste, J., Ociepka, A., Lewison, M., & Vasquez, V. (1999). Talking about Books: Exploring Critical Literacy: You Can Hear a Pin Drop. *Language Arts, 77*(1), 70–77.

Lewison, M., Leland, C., & Harste, J. (2000). 'Not in My Classroom!' The Case for Using Multi-View Social Issues Books with Children. *The Australian Journal of Language and Literacy, 23* (1), 8–20.

Luke, A., & Elkins, J. (2002). Towards a critical, worldly literacy. *Journal of Adolescent & Adult Literacy, 45* (8), 668–673.

McDaniel, C. (2004). Critical Literacy: A Questioning Stance and the Possiblity for Change. *The Reading Teacher, 57* (5), 472–481.

McLaughlin, M., & DeVoogd, G. (2004). Critical Literacy as Comprehension: Expanding Reader Response. *Journal of Adolescent & Adult Literacy, 48* (1), 52–62.

Mumola, C. J. (2000). *Incarcerated parents and their children.* Retrieved June 12, 2009, from U.S. Depatment of Justice: www.ojb.usdoj.gov/bjs/pub/pdf/iptc.pd

Nieto, S. (2003). Profoundly Multicultural Questions. *Educational Leadership,* 6–10.

O'Neil, K. (2010). Once Upon Today: Teaching for Social Justice with Postmodern Picturebooks. *Children's Literature in Education, 41,* 40–51.

Paley, V. (2000). *White Teacher* (second ed.). Cambridge, MA: Harvard University Press.

Pierce, K. M. (2006). Recognizing and Resisting Change: A Teacher's Professional Journey. *Language Arts, 83* (5), 427–436.

Pohan, C. (2000). Practical Ideas for Teaching Children about Prejudice, Discrimination, and Social Justice through Literature and a Standards-Based Curriculum. *Multicultural Perspectives, 2* (1), 24–28.

Probst, R. (2002). Response to "Reader Response in Perspective". *Journal of Children's Literature, 28* (1).

Rice, P. S. (2005). It "Ain't" Always So: Sixth Graders' Interpretations of Hispanic-American Stories with Universal Themes. *Children's Literature in Education, 36* (4), 343–362.

Rogers, R. (2003). *A Critical Discourse Analysis of Family Literacy Practices.* Mahwah, NJ: Lawrence Erlbaum Associates, Publishers.

Rogers, R. (2004). An Introduction to Critical Discourse Analysis in Education. In R. Rogers (Ed.), *An Introduction to Critical Discourse Analysis in Education* (pp. 1–18). Mahwah, NJ: Lawrence Erlbaum Associates, Publushers.

Rogers, R. (2004). Setting an Agenda for Critical Discourse Analysis in Education. In R. Rogers (Ed.), *An Introduction to Critical Discourse Analysis in Education* (pp. 237–254). Mahwah, NJ: Lawrence Erlbaum Associates, Publishers.

Rogers, R., & Mosley, M. (2006). Racial Literacy on a Second-Grade Classroom: Critical Race Theory, Whiteness Studies, and Literacy Research. *Reading Research Quarterly, 41* (4), 462–495.

Rogers, T. (1999). Literary Theory and Children's Literature: Interpreting Ourselves and Our Worlds. *Theory into Practice, 38* (3), 138–146.

Rosenblatt, L. M. (1938/1995). *Literature as Exploration.* New York: MLA.

Rosenblatt, L. M. (1978). *The reader, the text, the poem.* Carbondale, IL: Southern Illinois University.

Sabol, W. J., & West, H. C. (2010). *Bureau of Justice Statistics.* Retrieved March 16, 2011, from Office of Justice Programs: http://bjs.ojp.usdoj.gov/index.cfm?ty=pbdetail&iid=2232

Short, K. G., & Fox, D. L. (2004). The Complexity of Cultural Authenticity in Children's Literature: A Critical Review. In J. Worthy, B. Maloch, J. V. Hoffman, D. L. Schallert, & C.

Using Multicultural Children's Literature about Criminal Justice Issues: Fostering Aesthetic Reading Responses by Mary Ellen Oslick

281

M. Fairbanks (Eds.), *53rd Yearbook of the National Reading Conference* (pp. 373–383). Oak Creek, Wisconsin: National Reading Conference, Inc.

Simon, R., & Armitage-Simon, W. (1995). Teaching Risky Stories: Remembering Mass Destruction through Children's Literature. *English Quarterly, 28* (1), 27–31.

Sims Bishop, R. (1982). *Shadow and Substance.* Urbana, IL.: National Council of Teachers of English.

Sims Bishop, R. (1990). Mirrors, Windows, and Sliding Glass Doors. *Perspectives, 1* (3).

Snyder, H., & Sickmund, M. (2006). *Juvenile Offenders and Victims: 2006 National Report.* Office of Juvenile Justice and Delinquency Prevention. Washington, D.C.: U.S. Department of Justice.

Tatum, A. (2005). *Teaching Reading to Black Adolescent Males: Closing the Achievement Gap.* Portland, ME: Stenhouse Publishers.

Tyson, C. A. (1999). "Shut my mouth wide open": Realistic fiction and social action. *Theory into Practice, 38* (3), 155–159.

Zambo, D., & Brozo, W. G. (2009). *Bright beginnings for boys: Engaging young boys in active literacy.* Barksdale, Delaware: International Reading Association.

Critical Thinking

1. How do students' experiences with literature depend on the students' cultures?
2. How do teachers' proficiencies to guide students influence the students' connections to the literature?
3. Why are some genres of children's literature considered taboo in the classroom?
4. Why is it important to be aware of students' cultures to provide them with specific selections of children's literature?

Create Central

www.mhhe.com/createcentral

Internet References

The Coretta Scott King Book Awards
www.ala.org/emiert/cskbookawards

Scholastic Award Winning Children's Books
www.scholastic.com/teachers/article/teach-award-winning-childrens-books

Article   Prepared by: Nancy P. Gallavan, *University of Central Arkansas*

Taking Multicultural Education to the Next Level: An Introduction to Differentiated-Multicultural Instruction

Sidonia J. Alenuma-Nimoh

Learning Outcomes

After reading this article, you will be able to:

- Describe the effectiveness of differentiated multicultural instruction.
- Relate differentiated multicultural instruction to knowledge construction, content integration, and prejudice reduction.

Although there has been a great deal of research on multicultural instruction and on differentiated instruction in isolation, there is hardly any research on the possibility of blending them and taking multicultural education to the next level. Blending these two instructional approaches would result in a superior instructional strategy, i.e. differentiated-multicultural instruction. Multicultural instruction and differentiated instruction are similar in many ways. They are both set on the premise that good teaching caters to the needs of ALL students by ensuring that all students reach their full potential. This article illustrates how combining individual components of differentiated instruction and multicultural instruction can be helpful in meeting the needs of exceptional learners and students from diverse backgrounds in the general education curriculum. This article would demonstrate to readers the ways in which effective teaching must ensure that ALL students are learning by combining the relevant components of differentiated instruction and multicultural instruction.

As Ralph Waldo rightly puts it, methods are important but principles are just as important and without principles, we are tied to our methods and are not able to be flexible enough to adapt them to our specific needs in different situations. This article is about developing methods of instruction that are grounded in a set of principles. The focus of this article is on taking multicultural education to the next level and broadening its focus by exploring its full potential vis-à-vis other another instructional approach that shares the same agenda. This article would foster hope among teachers and scholars (and their students) of multicultural education by offering them the possibilities of teaching ALL students through *differentiated-multicultural instruction,* the result of the blend. This article reworks intersections between multicultural education and a related instructional approach and thus reframes the debates on multicultural education. The proposed resultant approach from blending two unique instructional approaches, i.e. multicultural instruction and differentiated instruction would be a superior approach that would foster hope among scholars and teachers who are interested in helping ALL students attain their full potential in the American education system. Thus, multicultural education would be viewed from a broader and more innovative perspective.

The article begins with a discussion of the premises of each of the instructional approaches, i.e. multicultural instruction and differentiated instruction, by giving a gist of the meaning of each of the inclusive pedagogy and their key elements and their classroom implications. This is then followed with a comparison of the two and how their key elements can be combined. The blend of the two, differentiated-multicultural instruction is discussed at length with examples of classroom implications.

The Basic Premises of Differentiated Instruction (DI) and Multicultural Instruction (MCI)

The basic premise of differentiated instruction is to systematically plan curriculum and instruction that meets the needs of academically diverse learners by honoring each student's learning needs and maximizing each student's learning capacity (Tomlinson, 1999; Tomlinson & Eidson, 2003). Differentiation is a philosophical perspective, it is a way of thinking about teaching and learning, and it is a set of principles. Learning to differentiate instruction will require rethinking one's classroom practice and results from an ongoing process of trial, reflection, reflection and adjustment in the classroom itself. Most teachers who remain in a classroom for longer than a day do pay attention to student variation and respond to it in some way—especially with students who threaten order in the classroom. However, very few teachers proactively plan instruction to consistently address student differences in readiness, interest, and learning profile. Although differentiation is an instructional approach, effective differentiated instruction is inseparable from a positive learning environment, high-quality curriculum, assessment to inform teacher decision-making, and flexible classroom management. To the extent that any one of those elements is weak, the others are also diminished. (Tomlison & Imbeau, 2010).

Comparatively, multicultural instruction is an educational strategy in which students' cultural backgrounds are used to develop effective classroom instruction and school environments. It is designed to support and extend the concepts of culture, diversity, equality, social justice, and democracy in the formal school setting. The equality and social justice aspects of multicultural instruction lend it readily compatible with differentiated instruction by way of being inclusive. To elaborate, multicultural instruction is grounded in a philosophical perspective on teaching, namely, multicultural education. Sonia Nieto (2012) defines multicultural education as ". . . a process of comprehensive school reform and basic education for all students. It challenges and rejects racism and other forms of discrimination in schools and society and accepts and affirms the pluralism (ethnic, racial, linguistic, religious, economic, and gender, among others) that students, their communities, and teachers represent. Multicultural education permeates the curriculum and instructional strategies used in schools, as well as the interactions among teachers, students, and parents and the very way that schools conceptualize teaching and learning" (p. 42).

Thus, multicultural instruction and differentiated instruction share a lot in common. Exploring the relationship between differentiated instruction and multicultural instruction, examining their interrelationship and blending the relevant components of each would result in superior instructional method, *differentiated-multicultural instruction,* that takes multicultural education to the next level and ensures student learning. This presentation therefore, ties well with the conference theme by demonstrating how two inclusive teaching strategies that affirm the intersecting nature of social difference can blend together to ensure student learning, offering a source of hope for all dedicated multicultural advocates and practitioners.

A Gist of Multicultural Instruction (MCI) and its Basic Key Elements

Multicultural Instruction (MCI) is grounded in a philosophical perspective on teaching, namely, Multicultural Education (MCE). According to James Banks (2008), the key elements of

multicultural instruction include: Content Integration, Knowledge Construction Process, Equity Pedagogy, Prejudice Reduction, An Empowering School Culture and Social Structure.

What does MCI look like in the Classroom?

This section discusses the key elements of MCI and their implications for classroom practice, beginning with Content Integration. Content Integration entails the use of a variety of examples to illustrate key concepts and principles. For example, the use of biographies of women and persons of color who are mathematicians, use of primary documents about the history of non-Anglo-European, reading and creating multicultural literature as well as including images of many kinds of families in the curriculum.

As far as the second element, the Knowledge Construction Process, is concerned, MCI requires the teacher to examine the degree to which minority authors are included in the curriculum. It also requires the teacher to include multiple perspectives of both dominant and non-dominant ones in describing historical conflict as well as examining labels applied to people with disabilities from their perspective. Other ways of practicing multicultural instruction include, validating the importance of languages other than English, discussing the differences between Western and non-Western views on science, and interviewing community elders about their immigration experiences.

The third key element of MCI is equity pedagogy. This requires the teacher to modify teaching to accommodate for the needs of diverse (all social differences) students. In order to do this, the teacher needs to know the cultural backgrounds of hers or his students and incorporate them into classroom instruction and procedures. It is also important to use cooperative learning or group experiences with students who learn best collaboratively. Additionally, by placing them in pairs, students are encouraged to engage in question and answer exchanges that enhances student learning.

Prejudice reduction is the fourth key element. This element or component of MCI focuses on the characteristics of students' racial attitudes and how teaching methods and materials can modify these racial attitudes. One way of this is by using heterogeneous groups (students of all social difference categories) in cooperative learning groups. There is research that confirms that having a positive or healthy racial identity of oneself has a positive impact on one's racial attitude (Tatum, 2003). It is therefore, crucial to assist students in developing positive racial identities through activities such as having students trace their cultural and family heritage using family trees. Teaching with emphasis on prejudice reduction also entails teaching the concept of race as a social and not biological construct, studying various religions in the context of a winter holiday season or historical event.

The fifth and final key element of MCI is empowering School Culture & Social Structure. This entails including students in determining class rules or allowing them choice of assignment, including students with disabilities or all students who try out for a performance, working to reduce the numbers of African Americans and Hispanics who are inappropriately placed in special education programs, working with families to provide mentoring and tutoring programs and involving families in school decision making bodies.

A Gist of Differentiated Instruction (DI) and its Basic Key Elements

Differentiation is a philosophical perspective, it is a way of thinking about teaching and learning, it is a set of principles. Learning to differentiate instruction will require rethinking one's classroom practice and results from an ongoing process of trial, reflection, reflection and adjustment in the classroom itself. Most teachers who remain in a classroom for longer than a day do pay attention to student variation and respond to it in some way—especially with students who threaten order in the classroom. However, very few teachers proactively plan instruction to consistently address student differences in readiness, interest, and learning profile. Although differentiation is an instructional approach, effective differentiated instruction is inseparable from a positive learning environment, high-quality curriculum, assessment to inform teacher decision-making, and flexible classroom management. To the extent that any one of those elements is weak, the others are also diminished. (Tomlison, C. A., & Imbeau, M. B. 2010).

What does DI look like in the Classroom?

This section of the paper discusses the classroom implications of DI, beginning with Content. Content is about what is taught and how access to information and ideas is given. It requires emphasis on students' access to key content by utilizing different tactics that would facilitate this rather than change the content itself. For example, tactics such as independent reading, partner reading, text on tape, text with images, small group instruction would facilitate and enhance fulfillment of this key element or component of DI.

Process, the second key element, has to do with how students come to understand and "own" the knowledge, skills, and understanding of the material or curriculum. Process in DI can be attained and maximized by varying the pacing of student work. In order to do this, the teacher may use cooperative grouping strategies; for example, think-pair-share and jigsaw. It also requires developing activities that seek multiple perspectives, highlighting critical passages in a text and using tiered assignments.

Product, the third key element of DI is about the student's demonstration of what s/he has come to know, understand and be able to do. To ensure that this happens, the teacher, in differentiating instruction, needs to provide bookmarked Internet sites at different levels of complexity for resources, develop

rubrics for success based on grade-level expectations and individual learning needs, teach students how to use a wide range of product formats such as presentation software.

The fourth key element of DI is Affect. It is about how students link thought and feeling in the classroom. A teacher that practices differentiated instruction would model respect for students, help them examine multiple perspectives on important issues and consistently ensure equity participation of every student.

Finally and closely related to Affect is Learning Environment. This component deals with classroom function and feeling. To enhance learning environment, the teacher needs to rearrange furniture to allow for individual, small-group and whole group work, ensure the availability of supplies and materials (e.g. paint, paper, pencil) as well as establish appropriate procedures for working at various places in the room for various tasks.

The Blend: An Introduction to Differentiated-Multicultural Instruction and its Classroom Implications

MCI and DI overlap considerably. Their various elements and contributions can further enrich curricular and pedagogical options, while widening the scope to the school and society levels. It is important to plan instruction that takes into consideration the important aspects of MCI as well as DI. The strategies and materials needed by students with special needs are often helpful to others in the class and thus, would lead to the possibility of *teaching them ALL*.

In order to be able to teach ALL students, teachers need to adopt a holistic format in their pedagogy and one way of doing so is to comprehend analyses of the differences and commonalities of MCI and DI. As indicated in the previous chapter, MCI and DI overlap considerably. However, MCI is more extensive with its emphasis on moving beyond the classroom to a school wide and society level and emphasis on cultural competence. Both are inclusive and require the teacher to take an extra effort by taking into account the comprehensive nature of elements of teaching and learning and their implications for classroom instruction.

The *Content* element of DI may be integrated with other elements of MCI; i.e. *Content integration, Knowledge construction* and *Prejudice reduction*. The classroom implications of this mixture include the use of specific techniques. Here is what a teacher who wishes to use D-MCI in their classroom can do:

1. Introduce key terms and concepts; provide guided notes; unit study guide.
2. Make use of primary documents.
3. Use of a variety of non-dominant perspectives (Latino, Black, Native American, women, GLBT).

4. Bring in guest speakers to cover areas that s/he might be less knowledgeable in.
5. Utilize interactive and assistive technology that takes advantage of the digital generations' ability to be technology savvy.

This list is of course not all-inclusive but sets that stage for further explorations.

The *Process* element of DI can be blended with various elements or components of MCI such as *Equity pedagogy,* and *Prejudice reduction.* This process can be further enhanced by the use of technology and result in D-MCI. This mixture can manifest itself in the classroom in various ways. Here is how this will look in the classroom setting:

1. The teacher will make use of cooperatively structured groups
2. Peer tutoring
3. Groups will be allowed to choose different aspects or perspectives for mini projects and become experts
4. The teacher will also allow groups to each research different data bases
5. Students in such a class where D-MCI is used will fulfill various roles at different times
6. A D-MCI teacher uses call and respond discussions, humor, pep talks
7. Such a teacher will use democratic discussions on issues of prejudice
8. Another important aspect of teaching with a D-MCI perspective is the use of colleagues with or without similar expertise as consultants. Teachers of D-MCI will therefore engage in co-teaching and working with other individuals in settings such as classroom and labs, to ensure that every student in the class learns.

The Product Component of DI may be combined the following elements of MCI:

A third way in which DI components, elements or characteristics may be merged to result in D-MCI is by adding these two MCI characteristics, *Knowledge construction* and *Content integration,* to the *Product* aspect of DI. The classroom implications for this merger may become materialized in these various ways:

1. The use of study guide that is produced by the class
2. Varying activity structure by using different graphic organizers such as timelines, charts, thinking maps, etc.
3. This aspect of D-MCI may also manifest itself in the form of providing students with a variety of options for completing their activities, exercises and assignments, e.g. encouraging students to make use of options such as written formats, illustrations, performances, oral presentations, etc.
4. Use of thematic essay tests is another good idea
5. In this instance, advanced learners may be encouraged to engage in independent study projects
6. It is also advised that teachers who want to explore D-MCI instruction should relate what is being learned to current issues

The final elements, *Affect* and *Learning environment* of DI may be merged or incorporated into another element of MCI; i.e. *Empowering school culture* and further enhanced with the use of technology, resulting in D-MCI. In the classroom, this aspect of D-MCI will manifest itself in the form of:

1. Using classroom posters that display writings and drawings created by students, arrangement of furniture and classroom décor manipulation in various ways.
2. Using computer labs for research
3. Using classroom posters displayed including writings and drawings created by students
4. Encouraging the formation and membership of school groups such as diversity clubs, LGBT, student associations
5. Encouraging the recruitment and retention of school board, administrators, teachers of color and other minority groups.

Conclusion

Multicultural instruction and differentiated instruction are well researched and popularized among educators at all levels. Most of the research and publications on these two inclusive instructional approaches have focused on one in isolation of the other. Yet a close examination of both reveals how closely interrelated and intertwined/compatible they are as they share several commonalities. For educators to make progress in their quest for the most appropriate instructional approach for teaching ALL students, they need to make a special effort to build on and merge the plethora of approaches to result in best practices rather than the binary, comparatively narrow approaches with specific as opposed to comprehensive focus. This paper is only a most attempt at doing just that. It is proposed that blending multicultural and differentiated instructional approaches would result in a superior instructional strategy, i.e. *differentiated-multicultural instruction.* In this article, the author discusses how multicultural instruction and differentiated instruction are similar in many ways because they are both set on the premise that good teaching caters to the needs of ALL students by ensuring that all students reach their full potential. The article takes a step further to illustrate how combining individual components of differentiated instruction and multicultural instruction can be helpful in meeting the needs of exceptional learners and students from diverse backgrounds in the general education curriculum. The article then demonstrates the ways in which effective teaching must ensure that ALL students are learning by combining the relevant components of differentiated instruction and multicultural instruction. Practical suggestions of how differentiated and multicultural instruction as well as the newly instructional approach, differentiated-multicultural instruction is provided throughout the article. With the introduction of differentiated-multicultural instruction, it is hoped that the researchers with expertise in specific instructional approaches will begin to pay more attention to the benefits of finding commonalities among inclusive instructions and merging or incorporating them to arrive at superior best practices that serve the learning needs of

ALL students. Flexibility rather than prescription and provision of step-by-step rules will serve educators better in their quest for best practices. To conclude therefore, I would like to repeat this quote: *Another set of methods . . . if we only learn methods, we are tied to those methods, but if we learn principles, we can develop our own methods . . . ~* Ralph Waldo Emerson (culled from Tomlinson & Imbeau, 2010)

References

Banks, J. A. (2010). Multicultural Education: Characteristics and Goals. In J. A. Banks & C. A. M. Banks, (Eds.). *Multicultural Education: Issues and Perspectives* (7th ed). NJ: John Wiley & Sons, Inc.

Banks, J. A. (2008) ***introduction to multicultural education.

Garderen, D. & Whittaker, C. (2006). Planning Differentiated Multicultural Instruction for Secondary Inclusive Classrooms. In *Teaching Exceptional Children.* 38 no. 3, pp. 12–20.

Nieto, S. (2012). *Affirming diversity: The sociopolitical context of multicultural education.* New York: Longman.

Taylor, L. S. & Whittaker, C. R. (2009). *Bridging Multiple Worlds: Case Studies of Diverse Educational Communities.* Boston, MA: Allyn & Bacon.

Tomlinson, C. A., & Imbeau, M. B. (2010). *Leading and managing a differentiated classroom.* Alexandria, VA: Association for Supervision and Curriculum Development.

Tomlinson, C. A., & Eidson C. C. (2003). *Differentiation in practice: A resource guide for differentiating curriculum.* Alexandria, VA: Association for Supervision and Curriculum Development.

Tomlinson, C. A. (1999). *The differentiated classroom: Responding to the needs of all learners.* Alexandria, VA: Association for Supervision and Curriculum Development.

Critical Thinking

1. What is differentiated instruction?
2. What is multiculturalism?
3. What is differentiated multicultural instruction?
4. Why is differentiated multicultural instruction effective?

Create Central

www.mhhe.com/createcentral

Internet References

State of the World's Children
www.unicef.org/apublic
The World Bank
http://web.worldbank.org

SIDONIA ALENUMA-NIMOH is an Assistant Professor at Gustavus Adolphus College.

Alenuma-Nimoh, Sidonia J. From *The Journal of Multiculturalism in Education.* vol.8. October 2012. pp. 1–17. Copyright © 2012 by West Texas A&M University. Reprinted by permission.

Article   Prepared by: Nancy P. Gallavan, *University of Central Arkansas*

Sustaining Ourselves under Stressful Times: Strategies to Assist Multicultural Educators

PENELOPE WONG AND ANITA E. FERNÁNDEZ

Learning Outcomes

After reading this article, you will be able to:

- Comprehend the reasons for and manifestations of resistance among teacher candidates to multicultural education.

- Explore the ways and reasons professors of multicultural education redirect the resistance.

Resistance that educators face in teaching multicultural education courses, particularly from preservice teachers, is well documented (Carpenter, 2000; Cochran-Smith 2004; Cruz-Janzen & Taylor, 2004; Horton & Scott, 2004; McGowan, 2000, O'Donnell, 1998; Valerio, 2001). Much of the literature around resistance tends to focus on strategies that multicultural educators can employ in overcoming preservice teacher resistance (Young & Tran, 2001).

However, preservice teacher resistance is not the only kind of resistance to multicultural education. Less well documented is the resistance to multicultural education from fellow educators who sometimes exhibit the same kinds of resistance as preservice teachers (Ahlkvist, Spitzform, Jones, & Reynolds, 2005; Ghosh & Tarrow, 1993). While there is little literature concerning teacher/faculty resistance to multicultural education, even more sparse is any literature concerned with *the effects* of such resistance on multicultural educators.

The small body of literature in this area, more often than not, has focused on multicultural educators of color and the resistance they face in teaching such topics and the strategies they used to counter such resistance (Boutte, 1999; McGowan, 1996, 2000; Valverde, 2003). Rarely has there been any discussion on how multicultural educators cope and sustain themselves in the face of continual resistance. In fact, there is virtually no literature on *how* multicultural educators address these effects and the *strategies* they employ to sustain themselves on a daily basis.

The purpose of this article is address this void in the field by providing a theoretical framework of the ways in which multicultural educators might address such resistance so as to preserve themselves and keep from suffering some of the negative effects of continual resistance, such as despair, hopelessness, and burnout.

Rationale/Motivation behind the Creation of the Framework

The development of this framework occurred over a period of three years when the authors, two women of color teaching in a predominantly White rural northern California teacher preparation program, were hired to address multiculturalism and diversity, which was lacking in the program. We soon came to the realization that a number of stakeholders, not only students but also fellow faculty and administrators, thought that the *idea* of multiculturalism and multicultural education was more appealing than the actual practice of it.

This discomfort from various stakeholders manifested itself in the forms of passive resistance on one hand (e.g., not wanting to address or engage on multicultural education topics at all) to outright hostility on the other (e.g., denouncing various multicultural education concepts). As a result of these reactions, we were forced to develop strategies to help us continue to be effective and healthy educators.

As we struggled to figure out strategies and any means to handle the effects of such resistance (i.e., frustration, anger, sadness, etc.) we began to systematically identify dimensions of our personal and professional lives that were impacted by the resistance we encountered. Specifically, we identified five aspects of our lives that we felt were most directly impacted by resistance to our work. They were the intellectual, emotional, physical, ethical, and spiritual dimensions of ourselves.

Methodology and Overview of the Framework of Sustainment

The development of the framework evolved as we encountered various incidents of resistance and collected data in the form of personal journal entries, notes from conversations and meetings, minutes from meetings, and other documents. It was only after months of reflection that the framework assumed its present form. During the first year, there was no framework because we realized that we were individually addressing each instance of resistance as a unique event seemingly unrelated to any other events of resistance. It was only over time were we able to detect patterns.

For example, fairly early on (in the first year) it was clear that one of the most pervasive and immediate types of resistance we encountered was in the intellectual realm when the credibility of the content we were teaching was questioned. Once we recognized this pattern, we came up with systematic ways to address this intellectual challenge.

Another area in which the resistance was extremely challenging was the emotional arena. While we could intellectually rationalize the resistance we encountered toward the various multicultural issues, such as sexual orientation, it was much more difficult to deal with the *feelings* of anger, hurt, and frustration associated with addressing these issues. The emotional energy expended on handling conflicts in the classroom, hostility, and passive resistance was at times almost overwhelming, and we had to come up with concrete psychological strategies to ensure we did not lose hope and simply give up in despair.

Another area of our lives that was showing signs of stress during this time was our physical health. We both realized early on that being constantly challenged intellectually and emotionally did take a physical toll on our health. In short, we were more vulnerable to being sick, suffering from fatigue and lacking vitality precisely because our positive energy was being diverted to addressing the intellectual and emotional resistance we encountered. When we realized what was happening, we came up with some very specific and personal strategies to make sure that we maintained our physical health, so we could continue working.

While it was incredibly helpful to specifically identify the kinds of resistance (i.e., intellectual, emotional, and physical) we encountered so we could address each type of resistance with specific strategies, sometimes we still felt we needed something more. It was at these moments we turned to the spiritual dimension of our lives. This dimension provided a rather unique lens through which to examine our experiences. For one of the authors, the spiritual dimension was the most significant and critical one in enabling her to affirm *why* she continued to be engaged in such demanding work.

Finally, we considered the ethical dimensions of our work. Unlike the other above-mentioned dimensions, we found the ethical dimensions of who we are as educators raised more questions than provided answers. However, it was the process of deliberating the ethical aspects of the various incidents of resistance we experienced that helped reaffirm our work and purpose.

In providing this brief overview of the framework we want to stress a few points. First, these dimensions are perhaps best visually seen as interconnected rings, much like the symbolic Olympic rings. Or, as some people recommended, as slices of a pie. Others saw the dimensions as separate boxes all leading to one bigger box of overall health. The point is that the framework can take any form, but what matters is that it works for the individual who is using it.

Second, these dimensions are not necessarily equal in significance or presence to one another. In other words, for one of the authors, the spiritual dimension was the most prominent dimension in her overall health for awhile, and for the other author it was the physical dimension. The point is that these dimensions are somewhat fluid. At different times, different dimensions will offer the answers sought at just the right time and will be prominent in one's exploration of how to address and overcome resistance. At other times, other dimensions will be foregrounded. To this end, even though the dimensions will be individually discussed in a linear fashion, we are in no way implying that there is a hierarchy of importance.

Finally, by using ourselves as models, we provide a case example to concretely illustrate how a particular incidence of resistance seemed to speak to a specific dimension of our health; then we discuss how we addressed the resistance using strategies and resources that enabled us to directly draw on this dimension and work through the resistance. This framework is based on the unique experiences of two multicultural educators and is offered as a strategy to current educators and future educators alike to help them proactively think about how they will handle resistance they potentially or are currently encountering.

Expressions of Resistance

While the purpose of this article is not to discuss resistance per se, it is necessary to briefly identify the common types of resistance that have been discussed among multicultural educators because sometimes one type of resistance falls in the province of one of the dimensions we discuss and thus requires a specific set of strategies to be addressed.

Dittmar (1999) and Tatum (1994) have documented facing resistance and outright hostility when addressing multicultural issues in teacher education. Griffin (1997) divides resistance into four types: anger, immobilization, distancing, and conversion. While anger tends to be the kind of resistance that is most uncomfortable for educators, all four of these types of resistance contribute to the overall feelings of stress and disequilibrium which we attempt to provide strategies for preventing.

The Intellectual Dimension

The situation: Having completed her doctoral work in anti-racist, multicultural education, one of the authors accepted a position at an institution seeking a faculty member with expertise in the area of multicultural education. She accepted the position expecting to continue the work she had been doing over the last several years. Once her new role of teacher educator began, it became quite clear that not only were many of the students she worked with completely skeptical of and resistant to multicultural education, but also most faculty and administers as well. This assistant professor was faced with the reality that her new colleagues were much more prone to "talking the talk" than "walking the talk" and she found herself constantly having to explain, defend, and justify multicultural teacher education to a variety of stakeholders.

This scenario was not all that unusual as multicultural educators around the country face similar challenges when trying to teach about issues that challenge students' preconceived notions of diversity. The surprising element was the resistance on the part of faculty and administration to understanding the need for students to engage in addressing difficult and challenging multicultural topics. As students complained, some faculty members started to question the need for such a course. In essence the very existence of multicultural education was being questioned.

Naturally, in an attempt to defend the validity of multicultural education as a body of knowledge and justify the need for future teachers to study it, she employed an intellectual response. She realized it was important to speak the language of the context—in this case the academy. Students, faculty, and administration would only ever be convinced of the legitimacy of multicultural education if it could be presented in terms they knew: theory, statistics, current literature, and research results.

With regard to the above mentioned scenario, the author realized that the intellectual dimension was the most tangible way to sustain herself as a multicultural educator. Thus, the strategies she employed in this realm were to strengthen her theoretical framework by remaining current in the literature and learning ways to use this intellectual information in such a form that was not threatening or radical to her colleagues or students.

More specifically, when confronted with resistance, she would reach into her intellectual side to ask the question *what does the literature say about this?* By doing so, she found that her ideas were affirmed because she could use state law, current research, and testimonies as intellectual rationalizations for the topics being addressed.

A second intellectual response to the situation above was to find allies who shared the same intellectual philosophy concerning multicultural education and diversity. In this case, it was the authors of this article supporting one another. Without the support of a colleague to discuss multicultural issues, and the resistance that comes with those issues, there is a danger of being worn down and overwhelmed by the resistance.

Intellectual allies were another source of critical information that could be used in countering the resistance. They can play the role of "devil's advocate," or in this case "resister to multicultural education," and provide sound counsel on how to handle various situations. Just as importantly, intellectual allies were those individuals who were willing to publicly support multicultural education and faculty who taught such courses.

All of these elements of the intellectual dimension of sustaining ourselves were deeply interconnected with the emotional dimensions as well. As our intellect supported us in *what* kind of work we did (i.e., the content), our emotions often determined how we did the work (i.e., the teaching approaches and strategies).

The Emotional Dimension

The situation: After viewing the film Color of Fear a class of pre-service teachers were asked to write down their immediate reactions on an index card. As the instructor read through the cards she came across one that said, "If White culture is the dominant culture, then it is meant to be that way, for it has been for centuries. If non-White people have a problem with that get off your butts and do something about it. Change the system, SHOW ME YOU ARE BETTER THAN ME!" Although not completely surprised by this comment, this incident, combined with recent local hate crimes and a lack of support for multicultural education in her college, put this instructor in an emotionally drained state.

We defined the emotional dimension of the framework as the feelings or the affective responses we had to the work we did as multicultural educators. The emotional output that one engaged in during the course of teaching a multicultural education course was unlike that of many other disciplines. As we heard about the daily injustices that not only occured in larger society but also in schools, it is easy to feel emotionally taxed.

However, this situation, combined with the resistance from our students and colleagues to either not acknowledge and/or not be willing to address such issues made a difficult situation even more challenging and we often feel "burned out" or completely emotionally exhausted.

One of the ways we have attempted to sustain ourselves emotionally was to recognize when we were reacting emotionally versus when we were reacting intellectually. We noticed that when students made comments, such as the one above, our immediate reactions were emotional ones (i.e., anger, frustration, etc.). The author in this scenario engaged in a strategy that focused on reacting with empathy rather than anger or disgust at such beliefs. Bell Hooks referred to this as engaged Buddhism. In other words, the work of multicultural educators is built on loving kindness and it is this loving kindness that can prevail in times of deep emotional crisis.

A second strategy was to train oneself to never react immediately to something that triggered a negative reaction. We found that participating in a cool-down period enabled us to respond to faculty and student comments in a purposeful and controlled manner and prevented further escalation of an already emotionally trying situation. By spending some time thinking about why the resistance occurred, we could be more rational and less emotional when actually responding to an individual.

Finally, it was crucial for our emotional well-being to celebrate the small victories rather than becoming overwhelmed by the big picture or the constant state of inequity around the world and in many schools. When a student reached an epiphany about diverse perspectives or an administrator seemed to better understand why it is we feel so strongly about the work we do, such was a small victory to be applauded and it raised our spirits immeasurably.

The Physical Dimension

The situation: Four young males of large stature were becoming increasingly volatile during a conversation about gay and lesbian issues in education. As the discussion proceeded, *they became physically agitated: They were red in the face, postured defensively, raised their voices, and gestured aggressively. At the height of the outburst, one of the males yells, "What do those fags expect parading around the Castro [the location of an annual gay pride parade in San Francisco]?" The instructor immediately addressed the language that was used but was cut off and interrupted by the other three males. At this point she noticed that her heart was racing, she was breathing heavily, perspiring, and physically distancing herself from them.*

We define the physical dimension as the "bodily" realm of the work we do as multicultural educators. For the the purposes of this article, we define "bodily" as literally our physicality. In this situation, the author was caught off guard by the violent reactions of the students, precisely because they were expressions of physical resistance rather than the more traditional emotional and intellectual forms of resistance we were accustomed to experiencing. This was not a situation one would expect in a classroom setting, particularly in a university. An immediate strategy the author employed in this "fight or flight" situation was to defuse the tension by switching topics.

While changing the topic achieved the immediate effect of defusing a potentially volatile physically violent reaction, it was clear the issue could not end on this note. In the days before the next class meeting the instructor agonized over her next course of action and felt physically ill (i.e., stomach cramps) at the thought of having to face the same students in class. She had trouble sleeping and suffered physical signs of stress.

In reflecting on the class, the instructor wondered if any of the students themselves were also suffering physical signs of stress due to disruptive nature of the previous class meeting. So the instructor began the subsequent class by asking students to respond in writing to the situation that had taken place the week before. In reading the responses, it became clear that many of the students, mostly the females, felt physically intimidated to come to class.

To handle such situations, we developed a set of strategies to address the physical nature of this aspect of our work. When facilitating tense classroom situations, we made a point of explicitly monitoring and being aware of our own and our students' physical reactions to the situation.

For example, we monitored our breathing (i.e., took a few deep breaths), monitored our facial expressions, and spoke in a calm and quiet voice. However, we also held on to the role of teacher-leader by staying on our feet and moving about the room when necessary. With respect to our students, we became much more adept at reading body language and taking short breaks if students exhibited signs of physical stress.

Finally, at the beginning of new classes, we discussed with students this scenario and how it was (1) inappropriate behavior, (2) what they should do if they feel themselves being physically stressed out, and (3) that to some degree such physical stress will likely happen in reaction to some topics discussed over the course of the semester.

Along with these in-class strategies, we also recognized the importance of stress-reducing practices to maintain our own physical health in order to avoid illness. For example,

both of us began practicing yoga, which conferred a number of benefits, such as stress-reduction, breathing techniques, and an overall sense of well being. Additionally, one of the authors engaged in more physically active and intensive activities, such as horseback riding.

Multicultural educators must engage in some physical activity that provides an outlet for the intensity and stress they experience. Although the physical dimension of teaching was not commonly considered, we found that it had a great impact on our overall well-being as well as our teaching both in and out of the classroom.

The Spiritual Dimension

The situation: After several years of teaching the department's multicultural education course, one of the authors noticed a gradual but definite change in attitude among preservice teachers. There was clearly less tolerance for diversity, let alone acceptance, and more and more students were emboldened to immediately denounce the concept of multicultural education from the beginning, whereas several years earlier, students were just questioning its legitimacy. Perhaps most disturbing, the usual responses to such challenges were failing. Intellectual responses grounded in statistical, empirical, and other data were ignored by unwilling intellects. Affective approaches highlighting personal stories of individuals who had experienced a life different from the status quo fell on deaf ears. Even ethical explorations that asked students to examine for themselves current injustices (let alone past injustices) could not penetrate their hearts. It was at this point that one of the authors realized she was on the brink of despair and turned to the spiritual dimension of her life to look for answers that could address this professional crisis.

The spiritual dimension was perhaps the most elusive and difficult to articulate of all the dimensions of the framework we have discussed so far. To begin with, the "spiritual" aspect of education is a topic infrequently discussed (Noddings, 1992). While a universal definition of the spiritual dimension of teaching would be impossible to articulate, Parker Palmer, who has written extensively on this subject, offers a definition of spirituality in the context of teaching which is helpful. He defines spirituality as "the eternal human yearning to be connected with something larger than our own egos" (Palmer, 2003, p. 377). It is this definition that we use as a departure point for exploration of the spirtitual dimension of teaching.

In addition to being difficult to define, it is also difficult to articulate exactly how the spiritual dimension of education functioned in the lives of educators because this was often a very personal endeavor. Some strategies that worked for one of the authors in exploring this aspect of her professional life included three main activities: (1) meditation, (2) journaling, and (3) identifying role models and mentors (not necessarily in education) who drew on their spirituality to sustain them.

In terms of meditation, the author explored this activity by learning as much as possible about it (i.e., reading and instruction) and incorporating it into her daily life. In terms of journaling, the author wrote daily to engage in consistent and deeper self-reflection about her experiences. It provided a safe place to explore any ideas. Finally, the author sought role models and mentors who engaged their spiritual side as a source of inspiration and instruction for the work they did. For example, she read about ordinary individuals who engaged in activist causes, such as antiracist work, and learned how spirituality sustained them (Thompson, 2001).

For one of the authors, the above mentioned strategies were extremely beneficial precisely because strategies in the other dimensions were failing her. By utilizing non-educational sources of guidance, such as spiritual texts (Tolle, 2005), Buddhist and Taoist works, and other alternative information sources, she was able to view her work as a multicultural educator in unique, non-traditional, non-academic ways that helped her reaffirm her commitment to multicultural education.

The Ethical Dimension

The situation: A student was seeking admission into a teacher preparation program. The candidate was not atypical from many of her peers: She was from a small town and had little experience working and interacting with individuals culturally different from herself (i.e., racially, religiously, linguistically, politically, etc.). She was not a particularly strong student academically but expressed a sincere desire to be a teacher. Over the course of the semester in a multicultural education course, the student's comments during class discussions, in various papers, and in journal reflections revealed some disturbing features: racism and homophobia. When the candidate was asked to examine the beliefs and values that undergirded these apparent tendencies, she became a bit withdrawn and shut down in class. In effect, she refused to examine her belief system and its possible impact on the children she would be teaching. The faculty denied her admission to the program, using the same criteria used for all other candidates. However, due to parental pressure, the denial of admission reached the highest administrative levels of the University, who overturned the faculty's decision despite protests from some of the faculty.

Of all the scenarios discussed thus far, the above-mentioned one was perhaps the most challenging to us as multicultural educators because the action that should have been taken seemed so clearly unequivocal—the student should not have been admitted. However, as the vignette clearly illustrated, not all the parties who had the power to take action were in agreement.

In this very complex situation there are two salient ethical dilemmas. When, if at all, is it ethical to deny a candidate admission to a teacher preparation program based on his/her dispositions? How do multicultural educators maintain their ethical integrity (i.e., commitment to social equity and justice) in the face of institutional pressure asking them to do otherwise? We will not discuss the first dilemma (though it is extremely significant) because it is beyond the scope of this article and because it does not directly pertain to the issue of sustainment of multicultural educators.

So, what strategies might multicultural educators/faculty who find themselves in a similar situation do to maintain their own sense of ethical integrity under seemingly impossible circumstances? Our first strategy was to garner all the professional and institutional codes of ethics we could find that demonstrated that there are credible professional bodies that do consider the ethical dispositions of future teachers to be a critical criterion for admission.

In our case, we had the National Education Association and American Federation of Teachers' "Codes of Ethics." We also had the California Standards of Teacher Practice and our own Department's mission statement concerning democratic education. In short, there was no lack of ethical codes of conduct to support our decision not to admit the candidate in this regard.

We quickly learned that ethical codes or frameworks were just that. They were not binding documents; they were not legal mandates. In essence, they held no weight. They were regarded as "helpful guides" but if necessary could be ignored when they interfered with a desired administrative decision.

What we realized in hindsight was that ethical codes, and even our own Department's mission, meant nothing if the faculty as a group was not clear about the values they held regarding critical multicultural issues. The faculty initially voted to not admit the candidate; it only took some external pressure for individual faculty members to cave and submit to the administration's overturning of the decision. While some faculty stuck to their original vote, others were willing to compromise and/or abandon ethical principles under duress.

It was in hindsight that we realized there should have been ongoing and sustained discussion about cases such as this one, where faculty were given the time and space as a group to converse and clarify the multicultural and social justice values they believed future teachers should possess. Additionally, use of a systematic ethical framework to shape discussions (Strike & Soltis, 1998) would have also helped individual faculty members clarify their positions on various issues and allow the faculty as a group to reach consensus, not mere agreement of the majority, on key issues.

It was unlikely in this particular case that even if the faculty had been unequivocal, clear, and strong in their reasons for non-admission, that the outcome would have been different. The administrative pressure at the highest institutional levels was just too strong. At the very least, however, the case would have generated much needed discussion and possible future action to prevent another similar event from occurring.

So, what are multicultural educators to do when they want to "walk the talk" and maintain their ethical commitment to social justice and equity but in the end are forced to compromise such principles due to political and legal power? There seemed to be only two viable choices: Accept the decision and continue to do the work we were doing, or resign. We both chose to resign from the institution. One of us resigned immediately and the second one a year later.

Many may have viewed this situation as "giving up." Others pointed out that if change agents keep leaving then change will never occur. But as we have hopefully and convincingly demonstrated throughout this article, multicultural educators must also be very protective about sustaining themselves. In this particular context, sustainment meant knowing that we had done all that was professionally possible to maintain our ethical integrity in terms of multicultural issues. Our ethical response as multicultural educators was to recognize the point at which we had effected as much change as possible at that particular institution at that particular time.

Most important, when we realized it would be impossible to maintain any sort of individual ethical integrity concerning our beliefs about multicultural education and social justice, we realized we had to separate ourselves from that particular institution. In hindsight we both felt we made the correct decision because it reinforced our commitment and beliefs in multicultural education and allowed us to sustain ourselves not only ethically but also in the other dimensions we have described in this article, and thereby continue our work elsewhere.

Conclusion

As stated earlier, this framework can take many forms and include different dimensions, depending on the individual. In presenting this framework at a recent National Association for Multicultural Education annual conference, one participant recommended that we consider the "political" dimension in future research. The framework suggested here is the one that fit our individual needs at the time and should be altered as necessary.

While some of the dimensions for either of us might have taken on different levels of significance at different times, we both felt that these five dimensions were at work at some level for both of us and strategies of how to take care of each of these dimensions of our teaching lives were necessary to achieving balance and thus overall "good health" in dealing with the resistance we encountered.

References

Ahlkvist, J., Spitzform, P. Jones, E., & Reynolds, M. (2005). Making race matter on campus. In N. Peters-Davis & J. Shultz (Eds.), *Challenges of multicultural education: Teaching and taking diversity courses*. Boulder, CO: Paradigm Publishers.

Boutte, G. (1999). Higher education. In G. Boutte (Ed.), *Multicultural education raising consciousness* (pp. 199–227). Menlo Park, CA: Wadsworth.

Carpenter, A. (April 2000). An ethnographic study of preservice teacher resistance to multiculturalism: Implications for teaching. Paper presented at the annual meeting of the American Educational Research Association, New Orleans, LA.

Cochran-Smith, M. (2004). *Walking the road: Race, diversity, and social justice in teacher education*. New York: Teachers College Press.

Cruz-Janzen, M., & Taylor, M., (2004). Hitting the ground running: Why introductory teacher education courses should deal with multiculturalism. *Multicultural Education, 12*(1), 16–23.

Dittmar, L. (1999). Conflict and resistance in the multicultural classroom. In J.Q. Adams & J.R. Welsch (Eds.), *Cultural diversity: Curriculum, classroom, & climate*. Macomb, IL: Western Illinois University.

Ghosh, R., & Tarrow, N. (1993). Multiculturalism and teacher educators: Views from Canada and the USA. *Comparative Education, 29*(1), 81–92.

Griffin, P. (1997). Facilitating social justice education courses. In M. Adams, L. A Bell, & P. Griffin (Eds.), *Teaching for diversity and social justice. A sourcebook*. New York: Routledge.

Horton, J., & Scott, D. (2004). White students' voices in multicultural teacher education preparation. *Multicultural Education 11*(4).

McGowan, J. (1996). African American faculty challenges in the classroom at predominately White colleges and universities. Paper presented at Kansas Regents Diversity Conference, October, University of Kansas, Lawrence, KS.

McGowan, J. (2000). Multicultural teaching: African-American faculty classroom teaching experiences in predominantly White colleges and universities. *Multicultural Education, 8*(2), 19–22.

Noddings, N. (1992). *The challenge to care in schools: An alternative approach to education*. Teachers College Press: New York.

O'Donnell, J. (1998). Engaging students' recognition of racial identity. In R.C. Chavez, & J. O'Donnell, (Eds.), *Speaking the unpleasant: The politics of (non) engagement in the multicultural education terrain* (pp. 56–68). Albany: State University of New York Press.

Palmer, P. (2003). Teaching with heart and soul: Reflections on spirituality in teacher education. *Journal of Teacher Education, 54*(5), 376–385.

Strike, K., & Soltis, J. (1998). *The ethics of teaching*. New York: Teachers College Press.

Tatum, B. D. (1994). Teaching White students about racism: The search for White allies and the restoration of hope. *Teachers College Record, 95*(4), 462–476.

Thompson, B. (2001). *A promise and a way of life: White anti-racist activism*. Minneapolis, MN: University of Minnesota Press.

Tolle, E. (2005). *A new earth: Awakening to your life's purpose*. New York: Penguin.

Valerio, N.L. (2001). Creating safety to address controversial issues: Strategies for the classroom. *Multicultural Education, 8*(3), 24–28.

Valverde, L. (2003). *Leaders of color in higher education: Unrecognized triumphs in harsh institutions*. Walnut Creek, CA: Rowman & Littlefield.

Young, & Tran, (2001). What do you do when your students say "I don't believe in multicultural education"? *Multicultural Perspectives 3*(3), 9–14.

Critical Thinking

1. How do teacher candidates exhibit resistance to multicultural education?

2. Why do they resist?

3. How can professors of multicultural education redirect the resistance?

4. Why is it important to sustain professors of multicultural education?

Create Central

www.mhhe.com/createcentral

Internet Reference

FINE: Family Involvement Network of Educators
www.hfrp.org/family-involvement/fine-family-involvement-network-of-educators/member-insights/how-can-we-prepare-teachers-to-work-with-culturally-diverse-students-and-their-families-what-skills-should-educators-develop-to-do-this-successfully

Helping Faculty Teach Diverse Students and Diverse Topics Effectively
"http://newscenter.sdsu.edu/diversity/files/00327-Helping_%20Faculty_%20 Teach_%20Diverse_%20Students.pdf" http://newscenter.sdsu.edu/diversity/ files/00327-Helping_ Faculty_ Teach_ Diverse_ Students.pdf

PENELOPE WONG is a professor in the Department of Education at Centre College, Danville, Kentucky, and **ANITA E. FERNÁNDEZ** is a professor in the Department of Education at Prescott College, Prescott, Arizona.

From *Multicultural Education*, Spring, 2008, pp. 10–14. Copyright © 2008 by Caddo Gap Press. Reprinted by permission.

Article   Prepared by: Nancy P. Gallavan, *University of Central Arkansas*

Realizing Students' Every Day Realities: Community Analysis as a Model for Social Justice

You can't guide your students to overcome challenges of social injustice if you cannot relate material to the lives of your students outside of the classroom. And in my opinion, the most important reason for a teacher to understand the challenges facing their students outside the classroom is so that the teacher can become motivated to promote social justice in their own daily life as well as within their classroom and to not be naïve to the problems that truly exist in our society. —Darren, pre-service teacher

JEANETTE HAYNES WRITER AND H. PRENTICE BAPTISTE

Learning Outcomes

After reading this article, you will be able to:

- Examine the purposes and benefits of learning communities.

- Delve into inequities and inequalities in teaching, learning, and schooling.

This article examines the implications and effect of the Community Analysis (CA) Project assignment that we utilize in the Multicultural Education (MCE) course[1] at New Mexico State University, located in Las Cruces, New Mexico. The CA enables pre-service teachers to critically examine, through a social justice lens, the manifestations and intersectionalities of race, class, gender, sexual orientation, language, ability, and religion in PreK-12 students' communities, which may be rejected and ignored, or embraced, serving to connect students' lives to learning contexts and opportunities in their schools. The CA compels pre-service teachers to analyze systemic inequities and inequalities in communities which impact the everyday lives of students. They discover organic knowledge possessed by students and families to bridge students' knowledge and the knowledge promoted within the school curriculum. Pre-service teachers also contemplate how their privileged or disadvantaged identity statuses intersect with their future students' privileged or disadvantaged statuses, or impact how they read communities.

The ultimate goal of the CA, through this reflective practice, is to prepare pre-service teachers to provide equitable and just learning environments for all students.

With the examination and discussion of the CA, we offer educational professionals knowledge and information that can assist them in the implementation of multicultural education from a critical analysis perspective. We maintain that MCE must be formulated within a social justice framework, which purposefully transcends the "heroes and holidays," or what we refer to as the "food, fun, festivals, and foolishness" approach. It is only from multicultural education practice anchored to a social justice theoretical framework that we establish and maintain equitable and just learning environments.

The Conceptualization and Facilitation of the Course— Situating Our Teaching Context

Our teaching context is in Las Cruces, New Mexico. We are located at the south end of the state, approximately forty-two miles from the Texas border and approximately an hour's drive from Juarez, Mexico and the Mexico/US border. We are in the "borderlands" in terms of political boundaries, as well as in metaphorical, social, and cultural borderlands in regard to how various identities (race, citizenship, sexual orientation, religion, etc.) often times intersect in a confrontive manner. Our pre-service teacher population is typically one-half white and one-half Mexican American/Hispanic, the latter being divided into those who have immigrated to the area recently, either in their own or their parents' lifetimes, and those whose families have lived in the US for generations. We have a richness to draw from in linguistic ability and experience. Undergraduate courses host a higher percentage of women; the presence of men tends to increase in graduate courses. In terms of socio-economic class, white pre-service teachers typically occupy the middle class status; those who are Mexican American/Hispanic come from a mix of middle-class and working-class backgrounds.

Jeanette has been a faculty member in the Department of Curriculum and Instruction since fall of 1996; her primary teaching responsibility is the undergraduate and graduate MCE courses. Prentice has been with the department since 1997; previous to his teaching responsibility of the MCE course, he served as College of Education Dean for two years. Prentice began using the CA with his undergraduate and graduate courses in the 1980's during his tenure at the University of Houston. The community analysis module emerged from an activity called the Princeton Game. It was first modified by James Anderson for a course and further modified by Prentice at the University of Houston and Kansas State University before Prentice introduced it at New Mexico State University. He shared the assignment with Jeanette and she has been using the assignment for approximately five years. Previously, Jeanette had employed the community service option for her pre-service teachers, using the CA first in the graduate MCE course.[2] However, she extended the CA to all of her MCE courses because of the deep understandings obtained from the assignment.

Theoretical Underpinnings

Although a significant amount of literature has been developed in the field of MCE (Banks & Banks, 2001; Baptiste, 1986; Bennett, 2001; Boyer & Baptiste, 1996; May, 1999; Nieto & Bode, 2008; Sleeter & Grant, 1987), scholars have not settled on a specific definition. For our purposes, we utilize the following definition:

> Multicultural Education is a comprehensive philosophical reform of the school environment essentially focused on the principles of equity, success, and social justice for all students. . . . Social justice in schools is accomplished by the process of judicious pedagogy as its cornerstone and focuses on unabridged knowledge, reflection, and social action as the foundation for social change. (Baptiste, 1995, as cited in Boyer & Baptiste, 1996, p. 5)

May (1999) contends the MCE movement "promised much and delivered little" (p. 1). Recently, Jeanette visited a kindergarten teacher at a local elementary school. Within the conversation the teacher remarked that a fellow teacher planned to have the children "dress up like Indians and pilgrims for Thanksgiving." We know that the "heroes and holidays" form of MCE is happening in public schools, so we strategically work to move pre-service teachers from the "celebrating diversity" frame of reference to one of social justice.

Bell (1997) describes social justice as "both a process and a goal" (p. 3). Social justice interrogates the manifestations of power and the dynamics of oppression, such as in individuals' and groups' access to resources and the experiences those individuals and groups have due to their status that either advantage or disadvantage them. From this interrogation, a plan of action

is developed to transform systems of oppression. Along with social justice, critical pedagogy is a vital aspect of our work in the MCE courses because it involves the teaching of critical analysis. As expressed by Oakes and Lipton (2007), critical pedagogy "links knowledge of diversity and inequality with actions that can make the culture more socially just" (p. 100).

The CA is a critical pedagogical tool to transform the awareness and consciousness of our pre-service teachers to recognize oppressions and to strategize circumventions for those oppressions. The CA encompasses these ideas by moving social justice from "words on a page" into a tangible, hands-on learning opportunity.

Constructing the Course Syllabus and Assignments

The background, goals and vision of the MCE course establishes that:

> Students from a variety of language, cultural, class, gender, and exceptionality backgrounds attend school everyday and interact with each other in academic, social and personal ways. Besides academic learning, the school environment fosters socio-cultural learning—be it positive or negative, implicit, or explicit. The teacher's role can maximize or minimize the positive or negative multicultural learning that unfolds. This role develops through the teacher's personal knowledge, awareness, sensitivity, and critique of diversity and pluralism in a democratic context. The teacher is encouraged to create a sense of self that will promote a nurturing respect for self and others in order to genuinely promote equal and accessible education (EDUC 315 Syllabus).

In the first class meeting, Jeanette clarifies that this is not a "how to do MCE" course, it is a conceptual, research-based course where pre-service students develop awareness, skills, and abilities to intellectualize what MCE is and what social justice looks like. She explains that after reading the course texts and other readings, struggling with the concepts, and conducting their CA, pre-service teachers will be able to read communities and the educational terrain to be effective in various teaching locations and situations.

Banks (1994) and Vavrus (2002) maintain that teacher education programs should facilitate pre-service teachers' understanding of their cultural heritages before expecting them to understand those of their students. Other scholars (Artiles & McClafferty, 1998; Haynes Writer, 2002a; Mahlios & Maxson, 1995; Stachowski & Frey, 2003) articulate the value of surveys, inventories, and other methods of assessment of pre-service teachers' conceptualizations, beliefs, and attitudes in teacher education programs and teacher development. Jeanette does this by having the pre-service teachers conduct an analysis of their socialization employing Harro's (2000) "Cycle of Socialization." Pre-service teachers work though their seven core identities (race, class, gender, sexual orientation, language, ability, and religion/spiritual orientation) to identify their dominant or subordinate identities and identify how their identities intersect with each other. Haynes Writer (2002a) asserts,

"After 'inventorying' one's own conceptualizations, attitudes, and beliefs, a student must then find her or his own courage for critical transformation as a critical multicultural teacher, to change what is incorrect and inequitable" (p. 13).

Utilizing Harro's Cycle of Socialization, each pre-service teacher presents her or his identities and socialization process to the class; Jeanette presents her Social Identity Project to the pre-service teachers first to serve as both a model for the presentation and as reciprocal disclosure of her socialization. As the pre-service teachers present, they bring in knowledge that all can access; they provide counterstories to the oppressions found in the dominating society; and they confront assumptions they had of colleagues. The assignment assists pre-service teachers to become aware of and name their subordinate statuses, as well as their privileged statuses that may "blind them" to the realities of students, families, and communities that are situated in subordinated identities or contexts. At the end of the semester, pre-service teachers write an "Epilogue" to discuss how their colleagues' presentations added to their knowledge base or how the CA transformed their understandings of community as they position themselves as critical educators; most students write about the impact of the CA.

Community Analysis Project Assignment

Too often a school and its staff constitute an island, which is physically within, but culturally and epistemologically removed from the surrounding community. The need is for direct experiences to give pre-service teachers knowledge and understanding of the problems and the strengths of the people in the kind of community in which she or he may teach. The CA develops in the pre-service teachers a critical lens as they examine communities in ways they have not before.

Each individual selects a school site, but is instructed not to go into the school; the pre-service teacher is to learn about the community around the school, not the school itself. The CA purposefully de-centers the authority of the school, while centering the authority of the community. The everyday realities of the students who go to the school are examined, as is the organic knowledge they bring to the school context. The pre-service teachers have to imagine themselves as future teachers at their particular school, asking these questions: How are the core identities manifested in the community? What are their intersections? How is power played out? What are the issues in the community that serve as obstacles for the students? What are the strengths and resources of the community? How will I bridge school curriculum with the organic knowledge that students bring to school? The CA is an overarching, culminating project that encompasses several assignments.

Activities within the CA Project Assignment

Pre-service teachers construct a Descriptive Map of their selected school community, including the names of the specific areas, villages, streets, or roads in the community; they may use the school district's boundaries or construct a purposeful boundary of their own. Using a color and number code to fill in the map, the following are designated: schools; federal/public community service agencies; religious/spiritual or political organizations; substandard housing; places where children and teenagers play or gather; places where the unemployed gather; major industries/businesses; and condemned buildings or areas.

Pre-service teachers also complete two Observation Logs regarding the presence or absence of two core identities that Jeanette selects; the logs coincide with the readings at that point in the semester. The logs are developed as ethnographic observations with accompanying personal reactions/questions, grounded with course readings and readings outside of class. Pre-service teachers are instructed to use this formula to examine the remaining core identities as a means to generate analyses and references for the Critical Analysis Paper. In addition, pre-service teachers collect various kinds of data concerning their community to complete the 20 question Questionnaire. The questionnaire focuses pre-service teachers' attention to such issues as quality and availability of food and housing, social issues, physical infrastructure viability, and perspectives of residents regarding the community.

The Critical Analysis Paper is developed based on the critical intellectual synthesis of information from community observations, interviews with residents and community service personnel, course readings, research articles, statistical data, and the information gathered for the questionnaire. The following questions are addressed: (1) What have you learned about the manifestations of race/ethnicity, socio-economic class, gender, sexual orientation, language, ability, and religion in the community?; (2) How are power and oppression connected to these identities displayed or played out in the community?; and (3) How will you circumvent the seven oppressions (racism or ethnocentrism, linguicism, classism, sexism, heterosexism, ableism, and religism) to address critical issues in the community through your work with students in the classroom and their caregivers?

The pre-service teachers share their new understandings with colleagues during the Community Analysis Reports. Each prepares a Power Point presentation and, taking turns in small groups of 3 to 4, discusses their communities with their "critical colleagues." As critical colleagues, the pre-service teachers listen, ask questions, provide feedback in comparison to what they have seen in their communities, and ground the conversation to the Oakes and Lipton (2007) text and other course readings.

Several times during the semester progress checks are conducted in class, as scaffolding mechanisms, to see where pre-service teachers are in their CA. They have the opportunity to dialog with one another on what they are discovering, what difficulties they are having, and what resources they are tapping. In their research, pre-service teachers consult print and on-line research journals; governmental, community, and organization websites; US Census data; and talk to individuals in the community. The project is designed to expand pre-service teachers' resourcefulness in locating community information and resources.

The Pre-Service Teachers

Whereas, Jeanette has utilized the CA for a number of years, in Spring 2008 she collected papers from her undergraduate MCE course for the purpose of this article. Of the twenty-two pre-service teachers, sixteen described themselves as Hispanic, Mexican or Mexican American and six as White or Caucasian; fourteen were female and eight were male. Self-describing one's socioeconomic status, the class was comprised of a mix of socioeconomic classes, the majority claiming middle-class status with a few claiming working-class status. Of the twenty-two pre-service teachers, eighteen signed consent forms for the gathering of CA documents. Of these, seven Critical Analysis Papers and Epilogues were first selected for their completeness and depth; three were then analyzed further for discussion in this article.

After spending twelve weeks in their selected communities talking to students, parents/guardians, community members and personnel from community businesses, agencies and public services, frequenting various websites, and researching the scholarly literature to complete their Questionnaire, as well as constructing their Descriptive Maps, and completing Observation Logs, the pre-service teachers wrote their Critical Analysis Paper. This paper brings all the information together in a cumulative, intellectually-grounded, meaning-making paper. This is the opportunity, as Jeanette tells them, to "show what you know."

In the subsequent pages readers follow three students, Darren, Teresa, and Carlos, as they progress through their Critical Analysis Paper and Epilogue. Here, readers are introduced to the pre-service teachers and witness the transformation of their critical knowledge base, awareness of their dominant or subordinate identity statuses, and movement towards a social justice perspective.

Darren is a mono-lingual English-speaking, heterosexual, able-bodied white male in his early 20s, who was raised in a community that is a border town to the Navajo reservation. He described himself as middle-class, and came from a family that was economically sound and educated. His father is a veterinarian and he and his siblings were all expected and able to attend college. During his time in K-12 schools, he had Navajo classmates and related a story of being beat up because he was "a white boy." He also described himself as a person of strong Christian faith and at the beginning of the course inquired why evolution, which he did not support, was privileged over intelligent design. This was an issue of struggle within his trajectory of becoming a high school science teacher.

Teresa is a bilingual, able-bodied, middle-class, heterosexual Mexican American female in her early 20s. She is of the Catholic faith and was raised and went to school in the El Paso area. Teresa focused her examination on the community of Sierra Vista, located approximately twenty-five miles south of Las Cruces. Teresa stressed that the CA made her realize that teaching was not "a simple profession." As she studied her community, she found that interviews were important because of the sense of the community she gained from talking with residents, "The way the community members looked at the world is how their children, my students, were going to look at it as well." Teresa revealed that her point of challenge—and

opportunity for transformation—revolved around the issues of homosexuality and heterosexism. She admitted that, "In order for me to try and confront homophobia in my classroom, . . . I had to really push my beliefs aside and take into consideration the discrimination against innocent individuals."

Carlos is a heterosexual, able-bodied Mexican male in his early 20s who is fluent in Spanish and English. He lives in Fairfield, which is a short drive north of Las Cruces. Instead of examining the immediate community surrounding one of the four schools in Fairfield, Carlos choose to study the entire community. Fairfield is a small, rural farming community. The backbreaking labor within the lucrative agricultural business in Fairfield comes from fieldworkers, many who are migrant laborers from Mexico, thus US citizenship and anti-immigrant sentiments play out in complex ways. Carlos was born in Mexico and has his US residency documents. He is a participant in the College Assistance Migrant Program at NMSU, which provides financial and educational support to students from migrant and seasonal farm working families. He described himself as being from a lower socioeconomic class; Carlos's mother works in the fields, as does he during the summer. Carlos was very quiet in class and rarely spoke in large group discussions. Jeanette sometimes wondered how and if he was making sense of the course content—was he engaged? His Critical Analysis Paper answered that question with a resounding "yes!" Carlos researched the community and deconstructed it along the seven core identities deeply and critically. As he analyzed the community, Carlos confronted some of his own oppressions—both what has been waged upon him and what he has participated in. He desires to become a bilingual teacher; he found that his linguistic skills benefited him in the CA Project, "Throughout my analysis I was able to make observations that a person that only spoke one language would either miss or not notice."

Question 1: Manifestations of the Seven Core Identities in the Community

Within the Critical Analysis Paper, the first question the pre-service teachers addressed was: What have you learned about the manifestations of race/ethnicity, socio-economic class, gender, sexual orientation, language, ability, and religion in the community? To discuss this question, we concentrate on specific identities, those with which the pre-service teachers personally struggled or those which stood out to them.

Becoming conscious of his strong Christian identity through the Social Identity Project, an identity he named as dominant for himself, Darren explored how religion manifested within the Las Cruces community around Sun View Elementary, specifically in the form of Christian religious organizations. Connecting course readings[3] and our class discussions to what he was observing in the community, Darren recognized how discrimination could be formulated due to historical biases and recent events.

Within the city of Las Cruces there are over 180 religious organizations or churches. Of at least thirty-six religious institutions within one mile of the community, the majority of them are Catholic, Protestant, or other Christian-based churches. . . . The fact that the majority of churches in the Sun View community are either Catholic or Protestant may indicate that the discrimination against other religious views could be common. Following the attacks of September 11, 2001, a steep increase in discrimination against Muslim people has occurred on a national level. Those events have most likely created similar feelings for some people living in the Sun View community.

He connected this to how religious groups outside of the Christian mainstream may be targeted, including students from those religions.

Because young children are so easily influenced by parents, friends, the media, etc., many students have already developed negative stereotypes of people of certain religious groups or of non-religious people. This may lead to discrimination among these young people in schools based on religion by other students or even by faculty. . . .

Like Darren, Teresa also identified her religious identity, Catholic, as a dominant identity. Viewing discrimination as a moral and ethical issue, she challenged her beliefs to assess the homosexual presence, or rather, absence, in her community.

There were no gay/lesbian groups or clubs that were easily detected. Fliers in stores and in restaurants had pictures of heterosexual couples. In asking around the community about homosexuality I did not get very many responses because some people did not wish to talk about it. The ones who did answer said that it was not common in Sierra Vista to see a gay or lesbian couple. Usually you see them at the gas station fueling up because they are just passers-by.

For Carlos, particular identities became very clear in Fairfield. Homes in the community illustrated a stark stratification based on the intersections between race, class, and citizenship or "arrival" in the US. Looking at various sections of the community, Carlos found a few "mansions" and "miniature mansions"; these were homes of Anglos who "owned or were related to people who owned the biggest money-making businesses in Fairfield." The areas where the poor lived reminded Carlos of what he had studied regarding the Hoovervilles from the Great Depression, homes that featured "doors made out of street signs," that were "literally falling apart," and apartments made of adobe that "seemed to have been built by the Spaniards themselves on their first conquistas." Whereas, the wealth and upper-class status in Fairfield was possessed by Caucasians, Carlos remarked that, "[M]ost of the middle-class . . . was Mexican American, while most of the lower-class was mostly of full Mexican descent. The middle-class seemed to be mostly second and third Mexican American generations."

Question 2: Examining How Power and Oppression are Displayed in the Community

The second question in the Critical Analysis Paper was: How are power and oppression connected to these diversities displayed or played out in the community? Carlos specifically examined race; he studied US Census data to establish the racial demographics of his community, which showed that Hispanics were numerically dominant. Carlos discovered that power did not, however, follow the numbers once socio-economics intersected with race in the power dynamic.

Many may assume that the town is run by the Hispanic population because if you enter any business the managerial positions are all occupied by Hispanics. But after further investigation it slowly starts to become apparent that all of the businesses are managed by Hispanics but in reality they are owned by Anglos.

Driving around the community, Carlos found that most of the store signs and business advertisements were in English, however, the majority of the employees in the stores and businesses conducted business in Spanish. There was one exception:

In the hardware store everyone only spoke English. The employees understood Spanish but they never spoke it. . . . I started to make the connection at the hardware store where the majority of customers were Caucasian; a few Hispanics would trickle in but it seemed that they were just in and out. . . . [I]t seemed that the whites almost used it as a clubhouse.

To critically analyze the intersections of race, class, and language, Carlos drew upon the course readings. He specifically cited Tatum's (2000) words that others are the mirror in which we often see ourselves, and Harro's (2000) Cycle of Socialization as to how Hispanic community members were collectively socialized to acquiesce to the Anglos' English. Carlos stated,

[Tatum] kept making sense in my head because the reason I believe everything was in English was for adaptation purposes. The subordinate group in Fairfield is the Hispanic community and the dominant group is the Caucasian community. In this town the dominant group's population is more than doubled by the subordinate population, yet the language is adapted for the group whose population is smaller. . . . The Hispanics have gotten [so] used to always accommodating the whites that everything they do is to make life easier for the dominant group.

Teresa interrogated the power dynamic of heterosexism[4] in Sierra Vista; she affirmed that,

Heterosexuality is dominant in Sierra Vista. The fact that some residents refused to talk about homosexuality is evidence that it is subordinate. . . . There are no support groups for adults or for children who are homosexual in Sierra Vista. Who are young gay and lesbian children going to run to if they have a problem? A child that is living in fear to come out is not healthy.

As she investigated her community to examine the power of heterosexuals, Teresa connected the absence of homosexuals as an issue of power and a position of invisibility, which may have the potential to place gay and lesbian individuals or students at risk in that community.

Question 3: Developing Strategies as Teachers to Circumvent Oppressions

The third question in the Critical Analysis Paper was: How will you circumvent the seven oppressions to address critical issues in the community through your work with students in the classroom and their caregivers? The three pre-service teachers had transformed themselves from being individuals unaware of their identities to "teachers-in process"; they were intellectually strategizing disruptions of discriminatory actions and discourses in their classrooms.

Darren transformed from being a young man who defended his privileged Christian identity, maintaining at the beginning of the course the need to present intelligent design on the same footing as or in place of evolution,[5] to a future educator who situated himself as being attentive to all of his students' religious orientations.

> One of the things that I will undoubtedly encounter in my science classroom will be the origin of life. I hope to explore various religious and non-religious views with my students that pertain to the origin of life, and to engage students in expressing their opinions about this. Religion is something that I do not believe should be "taught" in any way in the classroom; however, I want to encourage my students to express their beliefs while being respectful and open-minded in learning about the beliefs of other people. I feel that my experiences with various religions and the information that I have learned from this project and in this class have prepared me to create an environment that is conducive to helping students develop respect for and diminish negative stereotypes of various religions.

Carlos situated himself as a social justice teacher by connecting to the everyday realities of his students. He would have them become active and see themselves as change agents.

> As an educator I will address these problems [that he found in his community] . . . I will strive to open the eyes of my students and help them see that the answer to their problems is right in front of them. I will not only promote equality but equity as well. . . . Oppression will always exist and I don't intend of abolishing it but I do intend on creating a socially just atmosphere in my classroom, home, and school.

Carlos began envisioning himself as a transformative educator, one whose work does not stay in the classroom but moves out into the community in an effort to create alliances and motivation for change.

> Always with great hope that my work will spill over to the community and create a bridge not only with myself and the school but with everyone in the community creating an interlaced network that fights for the same objectives with the same motives in mind.

"As a social justice educator I need to fight homophobia in my classroom because children are [placed] at risk." Teresa wrote extensively about what steps she would take to address homosexuality and homophobia in her classroom, from obtaining permission to show the film "It's Elementary: Talking about gay issues in school" (Cohen & Chasnoff, 1996), to putting up pictures in her classroom which portray families in various forms, to drawing upon suggestions from the book, Queering Elementary Education (Letts & Sears, 1999). She would also dialogue with her students regarding what homosexuality is because,

> I know that someday they will come across this word. I want to teach them before they are given a negative definition. . . . I also want my students to be aware of homophobia and the negative effects it has on individuals. I will certainly be open for any child who has a problem about coming out or just needs someone to talk to. I will make sure that bullying does not go unpunished, especially when it has to do with homophobia.

New Realizations and Understandings of Social Justice

James B. Boyer asserts that "The absence of instructional vision results in the absence of social and academic justice" (Boyer & Baptiste, 1996, p. 177). Darren, Teresa, and Carlos, through the CA, developed a new vision of their responsibility and possibility as teachers, moving them toward social and academic justice as they garnered new realizations and understandings about social justice.

Darren spoke of his transformation as a journey, "As a white, future educator, I have been on a journey to understand racism and white-privilege so that I am better prepared, as a strong believer and promoter of multicultural education, to challenge these problems in our schools." In his Epilogue, Darren wrote this regarding social justice:

> I learned from this project, and this class as a whole, the various factors that shape our identity, the fact that so much of who we are is not decided by us, and the importance of being an agent of change for social justice and equity. As teachers we are in the position to change the world by affecting the students that we come in contact with every day. This is a power that should not be wasted or abused. Teachers who are not in touch with the students in the classroom and are not aware of the struggles, disadvantages, and problems that students face in the community and home life will not be as able to integrate their curriculum into the real-life, situational type of education that students need to be able to confront and overcome the issues of social justice in their lives.

Carlos reflected on the impact of the CA as a catalyst to examine his home community through a social justice lens, revealing things he had not been aware of before, and facilitating realizations about himself:

> [T]here was so much I never took the time to notice in my own home town. . . . This community analysis paper was an eye-opening experience to say the least. I have

learned so much about myself and I have grown as an educator. I feel now that I am equipped with new tools to become a great educator. Learning about one's self may be hard sometimes because accepting the bad sides can be difficult, but this course has taught us social justice is not to be shown to other people, but to ourselves as well.

Teresa felt empowered to tackle oppressions as a teacher:

Observing the seven core identities in Sierra Vista has raised my awareness of what it really means to be a teacher. The observations really helped me open my eyes to things I never took the time to care about. I hope to take with me the knowledge I gained from this project and from my multicultural class when I enter the teaching field. One day I will confront these issues and I will have the tools to battle them.

Conclusion

In regard to our own praxis as critical multicultural educators, our work constantly reminds us of what we must do in MCE to advance the movement toward "'MCE as social justice,' to rid ourselves, our educational institutions, and ultimately the larger society from the 'food, fun, festivals, and foolishness' form of MCE" (Haynes Writer, 2008), to shift us into Baptiste's (1994) Typology of Multiculturalism, Level III, for social justice and social action. We must provide opportunities for our pre-service teachers to operationalize MCE concepts, not merely recall terminology from course texts, as a means to assist them in synthesizing theory and practice. As Teresa realized, "A book could not teach the students about their community and the injustices in it, but a teacher who has done her [or his] research could."

Assignments such as the CA facilitates the recognition of the core identities in lived contexts, enabling pre-service teachers to recognize the manifestations of power and oppression in the everyday, so those oppressions become part of the curricular content and social justice becomes a pedagogical imperative. The pre-service teachers addressed the metaphorical, social, and cultural borderlands that our location sustains, prompting the pre-service teachers' identification and understanding of the educational marginalization that often happens to diverse, less powerful students and communities.

In summary, this article examined the implications and effect of the CA Project assignment on pre-service teachers, providing them opportunity to critically examine the manifestations and intersectionalities of race, class, gender, sexual orientation, language, ability, and religion/spiritual orientation in PreK-12 students' communities. They identified organic knowledge from the communities, enabling them to envision and strategize curricular and pedagogical connections to students' lives. The CA required pre-service teachers to analyze systemic inequities in communities which impact the everyday lives of students, compelling them to intellectually analyze how their privileged or disadvantaged identity statuses impact how they read communities or will intersect with their students' privileged or disadvantaged identities. Because the CA is situated within a social justice framework, and functions as a critical pedagogical tool, it works to end or greatly challenge the educational marginalization that so many students experience. This engages the pre-service teachers with MCE teaching conceptualizations and strategies that purposefully transcend the "food, fun, and festivals" approach as a means to establish and maintain equitable and socially just learning environments for all students.

Notes

1. All pre-service and in-service teachers must pass the MCE course to seek admission to NMSU's teacher education program. The MCE course is offered at both the undergraduate and graduate level. Whereas, the courses are similar in MCE content and emphasis on social justice, the courses differ in the texts utilized. Assignments may differ as well due to the professors or graduate assistants teaching the various course sections; up to seven sections are offered per semester at the undergraduate level and two at the graduate level.

2. Prentice uses the CA with graduate students, but they work in teams. For the purpose of this article, we examine the use of the CA at the undergraduate-level as an individual assignment.

3. Readings addressed the influence of media bias on the social constructions of the Muslim community (Haynes Writer, 2002b), and a teacher's pedagogical choices in working with a Muslim student (Karp, 2001).

4. Pre-service teachers completed the "Writing for Change" exercise which provided a definition of "compulsory heterosexism," and had them provide various examples of compulsory heterosexism and place themselves in scenarios. We also saw a portion of the film "It's Elementary: Talking about gay issues in school" (Cohen & Chasnoff, 1996).

5. With Darren's comment in class, Jeanette problematized the issue of presenting only "two sides of the story," the Biblical genesis story and the theory of evolution, by discussing that the over 575 federally recognized tribal nations in the US have their own "genesis" or origin stories. Thus, it was no longer a matter of two privileged sides, but hundreds of "sides."

References

Artiles, A. J., & McClafferty, K. (1998). Learning to teach culturally diverse learners: Charting change in preservice teachers' thinking about effective teaching. *The Elementary School Journal, 98*(3), 189–220.

Banks, J. A. (1994). *Multiethnic education:* Theory and practice. Boston, MA: Allyn and Bacon.

Banks, J. A., & Banks, C. A. M. (Eds.). (2001). *Multicultural education: Issues & perspectives* (4th ed.). New York: John Wiley & Sons, Inc.

Baptiste, H. P. (1986). Multicultural education and urban schools from a sociohistorical perspective: Internalizing multiculturalism. *Journal of Educational Equity and Leadership, 6*(4), 295–312.

Baptiste, H. P. (1994). A comprehensive multicultural teacher education program: An idea whose time has come. In M. M. Atwater, K. Radzik-Marsh, & M. E. Strutchens (Eds.), *Multicultural education: Inclusion of all.* Athens, GA: University of Georgia Press.

Bell, L. A. (1997). Theoretical foundations for social justice education. In M. Adams, L. A. Bell, & P. Griffin (Eds.), *Teaching for diversity and social justice: A sourcebook* (pp. 1–15). New York: Routledge.

Bennett, C. (2001). Genres of research in multicultural education. *Review of Educational Research, 71*(2), 171–217.

Boyer, J. B., & Baptiste, Jr., H. P. (1996). *Transforming the curriculum for multicultural understandings: A practitioner's handbook.* San Francisco, CA: Caddo Gap Press.

Cohen, H. (Producer), & Chasnoff, D. (Director). (1996). *It's elementary: Talking about gay issues in school* [Film]. San Francisco, CA: Women's Educational Media.

Harro, B. (2000). The cycle of socialization. In M. Adams, W. J. Blumenfeld, R. Castañeda, H. W. Hackman, M. L. Peters, & X. Zúñiga (Eds.), *Readings for diversity and social justice: An anthology on racism, anti-Semitism, sexism, heterosexism, ableism, and classism* (pp. 15–21). New York: Routledge.

Haynes Writer, J. (2002a). No matter how bitter, horrible, or controversial: Exploring the value of a Native American education course in a teacher education program. *Action in Teacher Education, 24*(2), 9–21.

Haynes Writer, J. (2002b, Fall). Terrorism in Native America: Interrogating the Past, Examining the Present, Constructing a Liberatory Future. *Anthropology and Education Quarterly, 33*(3), 1–14.

Haynes Writer, J. (2008). Unmasking, exposing, and confronting: Critical race theory, tribal critical race theory and multicultural education. *International Journal of Multicultural Education, 10*(2), 1–15.

Karp, S. (2001). Arranged marriages, rearranged ideas. In B. Bigalow, B. Harvey, S. Karp, & L. Miller (Eds.), *Rethinking our classrooms, volume 2: Teaching for equity and social justice* (pp. 188–193). Milwaukee, WI: Rethinking Schools, Ltd.

Letts, W. J., IV, & Sears, J. T. (1999). *Queering elementary education: Advancing the dialogue about sexualities and schooling (curriculum, cultures, and (homo)sexualities).* Lanham, MD: Rowman & Littlefield Publishers, Inc.

Mahlios, M., & Maxson, M. (1995). Capturing preservice teachers' beliefs about schooling, life, and childhood. *Journal of Teacher Education, 46*(3), 192–199.

May, S. (Ed.). (1999). *Critical multiculturalism: Rethinking multicultural and anti-racist education.* Philadelphia, PA: Falmer Press.

Nieto, S., & Bode, P. (2008). *Affirming diversity: The sociopolitical context of multicultural education* (5th ed.). Boston, MA: Allyn and Bacon.

Oakes, J., & Lipton, M. (2007). *Teaching to change the world* (3rd ed.). Boston, MA: McGraw-Hill College.

Sleeter, C. E., & Grant, C. A. (1987). An analysis of multicultural education in the United States. *Harvard Educational Review, 57*(4), 421–444.

Stachowski, L. L., & Frey, C. J. (2003). Lessons learned in Navajoland: Student teachers reflect on professional and cultural learning in reservation schools and communities. *Action in Teacher Education, 25*(3), 38–47.

Tatum, B. D. (2000). The complexity of identity: "Who am I?" In M. Adams, W. J. Blumenfeld, R. Castañeda, H. W. Hackman, M. L. Peters, & X. Zúñiga (Eds.), *Readings for diversity and social justice: An anthology on racism, anti-Semitism, sexism, heterosexism, ableism, and classism* (pp. 9–14). New York: Routledge.

Vavrus, M. (2002, October). *Connecting teacher identity formation to culturally responsive teaching.* Paper presented at the National Association of Multicultural Education in Washington, DC.

Critical Thinking

1. What are learning communities?

2. How does the Community Analysis (CA) Project combat inequities?

3. What steps are taken to bridge families and studies with the curriculum, instruction, and assessments?

4. Why is leveling privilege and power key to equity in education?

Create Central

www.mhhe.com/createcentral

Internet References

Association of Supervision and Curriculum Development (ASCD): Professional Learning Communities

www.ascd.org/publications/educational-leadership/may04/vol61/num08/What-Is-a-Professional-Learning-Community%C2%A2.aspx

Teacher Learning Communities

www.ncte.org/library/NCTEFiles/Resources/Journals/CC/0202-nov2010/CC0202Policy.pdf

JEANETTE HAYNES WRITER is an associate professor in the Department of Curriculum and Instruction at New Mexico State University in Las Cruces, New Mexico. Her areas of specialization include critical multicultural teacher education, social justice and equity; Critical Race Theory and Tribal Critical Race Theory, and Indigenous education. She also serves as the department's coordinator of the multicultural education specialty. **H. PRENTICE BAPTISTE** is a professor in the Department of Curriculum and Instruction at New Mexico State University in Las Cruces, New Mexico. His areas of specialization include multicultural and science education. His research interests include the process of multiculturalizing educational entities and culturally diversifying science and mathematics instruction. His most recent research interest is an analysis of U.S. presidential domestic policies and actions through a multicultural lens. (*We would like to thank the students in Jeanette's Spring 2008, EDUC 315 course for providing us permission to use their papers for this article, especially, Carlos, Darren, and Teresa. The development of this article enabled us to think more deeply about our teaching.*)